PATHWAYS TO LITERACY

PROCESS TRANSACTIONS

PATHWAYS TO LITERACY
PROCESS TRANSACTIONS

SECOND EDITION

Michael Sampson
East Texas State University

Mary Beth Sampson
East Texas State University

Roach Van Allen
Professor Emeritus, The University of Arizona

HARCOURT BRACE COLLEGE PUBLISHERS

Fort Worth Philadelphia San Diego New York Orlando Austin San Antonio
Toronto Montreal London Sydney Tokyo

Publisher: Ted Buchholz
Senior Acquisitions Editor: Jo-Anne Weaver
Senior Project Editor: Angela Williams
Senior Production Manager: Kenneth A. Dunaway
Art Director: Garry Harman

Cover Image: Steven Kellogg

Requests for permission to make copies of any part of the work should be mailed to: Permissions Department, Harcourt Brace & Company, 6277 Sea Harbor Drive, Orlando, Florida 32887–6777.

Special acknowledgments of copyright ownership and of permission to reproduce works (or excerpts thereof) included in this edition begin on page 557 and constitute an extension of this page.

Address for Editorial Correspondence
Harcourt Brace College Publishers
301 Commerce Street, Suite 3700
Fort Worth, TX 76102

Address for Orders
Harcourt Brace and Company
6277 Sea Harbor Drive
Orlando, FL 32887
1–800–782–4479, or 1–800–433–0001 (in Florida)

ISBN: 0–15–501316–5

Library of Congress Catalogue Number: 94–76459

Printed in the United States of America

4 5 6 7 8 9 0 1 2 3 032 9 8 7 6 5 4 3 2 1

To the teachers featured in the classroom vignettes of this book.
Thanks for sharing your classrooms with us!

The Pathway Begins

Travelers in the ancient Roman Empire didn't have much to read as they trudged down the dusty pathways that led from city to city. However, they did have one literacy encounter to look forward to. Whenever two or more pathways intersected, signs were posted that told of important information the Romans wanted known. You can imagine a weary traveler nearing an intersection and hurrying to receive the news of the day.

Our word *trivia* comes from the Greek word that described these intersections and their literacy messages. This book, too, is an intersection of pathways and ideas. It's a place where teachers, and teachers to be, can come together and share together. But an important distinction exists: What we share is not trivia, but vital because the things we learn can be life changing, for our students as well as ourselves.

And share we will. We'll tell you about the Literacy Transaction Model that this text is built upon, and we'll begin every pathway in every chapter from that theoretical model. We'll share classrooms across America with you—more than 200 classrooms are featured in our Classroom Vignettes feature. We'll use these vignettes to show you how theory is put into practice.

The language arts are interwoven. It is impossible to discuss listening apart from speaking, to discuss reading apart from writing. Yet, for the purpose of organization, we have arranged this text into chapter formats that focus on individual aspects of the language arts. Chapter 7, for example, focuses on writing, but includes all aspects of the language arts—drama, reading, art, listening, singing, and so on.

We started writing the second edition of this text two years ago. We thought we could simply update the book with new information, but the human mind and spirit is not content with taking the easy road. Instead, we've rewritten the entire book. We'll mention seven new features we know you'll love.

First, we added more literature throughout the book. You'll encounter more than 500 children's books. And you'll hear from the master of children's books himself—Bill Martin Jr, who wrote Chapter 14, Pathways to Children's Literature. In that chapter Bill shares his favorite books and ways of using them with children.

Second, we added a brand-new chapter on thematic units. We asked two fine educators to construct the chapter for us: Geoff and Cherry Ward from Queensland, Australia. The Wards discuss thematic teaching and leave you with a model that will help you write more interactive units yourself.

Third, we did a total rewrite on our writing section. You'll find more on writer's workshops, mini-lessons, and conferencing with writers than we included in the first edition. You'll also find hundreds of new examples of children's writings and stories.

Fourth, we've included a new chapter on comprehension strategies. After rewriting the reading process chapter, we just had to share some exciting new ways of involving children with text.

Fifth, we decided to do what business is doing with the Total Quality Management (TQM) movement. We asked elementary students what they thought of schools and teachers. Seventeen seventh graders rate their elementary school education and give teachers tips on how they can be better teachers. This feature, called Kids' Corner, is included in every chapter. Be sure and read each one!

Sixth, we decided poetry is so important that you deserve at least one poem per chapter. So we asked Brod Bagert, America's hottest children's poet, to write seventeen poems for you. And write he did! Brod composed a poem for each chapter that interacts with the topic of the chapter. You'll love this new feature, which we term The Poet Ponders.

Seventh, and best of all, we interviewed 17 great children's authors just for this edition of *Pathways to Literacy*. You'll be able to read the comments, in a feature we call The Book Makers, of such great writers and illustrators as Eric Carle, Tomie dePaola, Jerry Spinelli, and Steven Kellogg.

We've added a new subtitle, Process Transactions, because those two words truly describe the text. We believe literacy learning results from the transaction between children's self-expression and children's impressions from the world that surrounds them. And we believe the skills, or conventions of literacy, are learned in the process of these authentic literacy transactions.

Our appreciation is extended to our constructive and insightful reviewers of both the first and second editions: Dan Darigan, West Chester University; Connie Bridge, University of Kentucky; Wendy Kasten, University of South Florida; David Yaden, University of Houston; Linda Grambrell, University of Maryland; Jane White, East Texas State University; Harry Hawn, Oakland University; Mary Beth Seaborg, Baltimore County Schools; Marty Harrison, Memphis State University; Ellen Jampole, SUNY Cortland; Elletta Kennison, Seattle Pacific University; and Karen McCain, University of Alaska, Anchorage.

But most of all we wish to think Tommy Thomason of Texas Christian University, who knows this book more than any of us because he's answered hundreds of our questions, proofed copies, and offered excellent suggestions on how to make the text more reader friendly. Appreciation is also extended to two others who have put in long hours helping us move ideas from our minds to computer images and finally to the copy you see before you: our hard-working colleagues Bob Nottingham and Shelby Crawford.

Steven Kellogg, dear friend and noted children's book illustrator, graciously provided the cover and part-opening art for the text. We are, of course, grateful for his beautiful illustrations that enhance the design of the book.

Our gratitude is extended to Harcourt Brace and the finest acquisitions and project editors in college publishing—Jo-Anne Weaver and Angela Williams. And to the rest of the Harcourt team—Ken Dunaway, Laura Lashley, Garry Harman, and Pam Hatley—thanks for making this second edition better and more beautiful than the first!

But most of all, we thank the children and teachers who have been fellow learners with us as we have traveled down pathways of learning and discovery.

ABOUT THE AUTHORS

 **Michael Sampson** is one of the country's most sought after literacy consultants. After completing his Ph.D. at the University of Arizona, he quickly established himself as one of the nation's top authorities in the field of literature-based, meaning-centered instruction. He has written more than 50 articles and authored 5 books. Michael's material for children includes thematic units and two children's books: *The Football That Won the Superbowl* and *Star of the Circus*. Sampson teaches at East Texas State University where he serves as director of programs in language arts and reading.

 **Mary Beth Sampson** is an assistant professor of elementary education at East Texas State University, where she co-directs a regional, field-based teacher education program. An outstanding researcher, she was honored by the International Reading Association for writing one of the top ten dissertations of 1992. The author of numerous professional articles, Mary Beth presents keynote addresses and workshops to teachers throughout the United States. She has a special talent for translating theory into practice and for helping learners make connections.

 **Roach Van Allen** has worked as a classroom teacher, school administrator, and university researcher and professor. Throughout his career, Van has devoted much time and energy to the promotion of literacy through a language-experience and child-centered approach. Professor emeritus at The University of Arizona, he has been recognized and honored by the International Reading Association as a recipient of their Lifetime Achievement Award. Van's bibliography of publications includes more than 300 entries, with numerous books, professional articles, and instructional materials for children. His predictable storybook, *I Love Ladybugs,* is a favorite of children throughout the United States.

CONTENTS

PATHWAYS TO LITERACY

PROCESS TRANSACTIONS

FOUNDATIONS
OF LITERACY

▶1 PATHWAYS TO MEANINGFUL INSTRUCTION

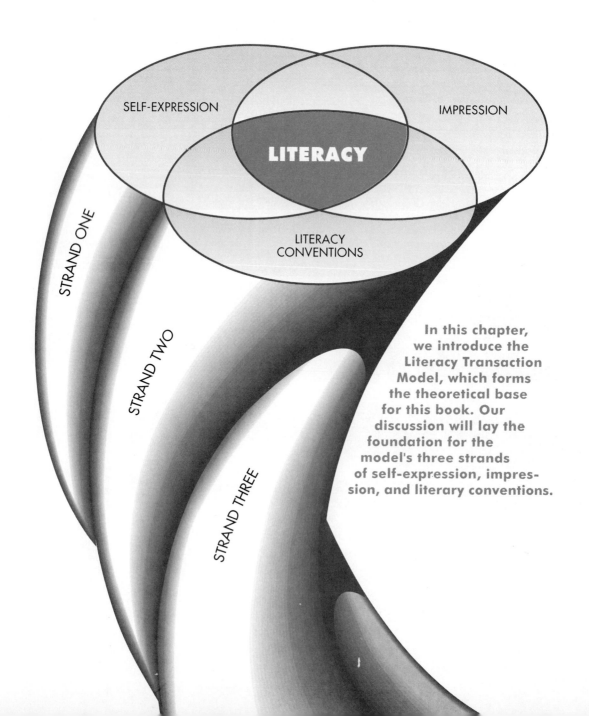

SELF-EXPRESSION

IMPRESSION

LITERACY

LITERACY CONVENTIONS

STRAND ONE

STRAND TWO

STRAND THREE

In this chapter, we introduce the Literacy Transaction Model, which forms the theoretical base for this book. Our discussion will lay the foundation for the model's three strands of self-expression, impression, and literary conventions.

CHAPTER OUTLINE

PATHWAYS TO PONDER

▶ **WHAT IS A MEANING-CENTERED CLASSROOM?**

▶ **WHICH OF THE THEORIES OF LANGUAGE ACQUISITION IS MOST IN LINE WITH YOUR BELIEFS ABOUT HOW CHILDREN LEARN?**

▶ **WHY IS IT IMPORTANT FOR TEACHERS TO ILLUSTRATE THE INTERACTIVE NATURE OF THE LANGUAGE ARTS?**

▶ **WHAT HAPPENS WHEN COMMUNICATION EXPERIENCES ARE FRAGMENTED?**

▶ **HOW CAN TEACHERS ILLUSTRATE AND DEMONSTRATE THE RELATIONSHIPS AMONG SPEECH, WRITING, AND READING?**

WHAT IS A MEANING-CENTERED CLASSROOM?

Together we begin an exciting exploration of literacy. In the pages ahead you'll encounter language-arts activities that involve children both cognitively and affectively. You'll see examples of children's work. You'll meet many classroom teachers and their students through the classroom vignettes featured in each chapter.

You'll discover that literacy is synonymous with learning and that learning is synonymous with thinking. And you'll discover many pathways through which students may become empowered through language and literacy.

What is language? We define language as communication. In this broad sense, language is not restricted to oral forms. Rather, language is a Picasso painting, it's a Beethoven composition, it's a figure skater's performance at the Winter Olympics. Yes, language may be "seen" in children's writing or heard in children's voices, but let us always remember that language encompasses much more.

Language is rooted in experiences. The more students know about the world that surrounds them, the more articulate they will be in communicating their ideas about that world. Thus our goal is to build language through experiences. Experiences with books, experiences with art, experiences with drama, experiences through sharing together—all of these experiences build the language foundations of the student.

How do we build language skills? We must remember the skills of language reside in the arena of communication. Children best learn language through interacting with the ideas of others. Thus a school environment that fosters language growth is one in which children are active in sharing their personal ideas and active in considering the ideas of others—their classmates, their teachers, the authors and artists they meet through books.

THE POET ▶
PONDERS

CHILDREN, BOOKS AND SUNSHINE

When I have to study facts
It makes my life a bore,
And memorizing great big words
Is such an awful chore.
But with interesting stories and
*   colorful art*
My brain gets very very smart
And learning feels like play,
Good books can make the sun shine,
Even on a rainy day.

Copyright Brod Bagert 1994
All Rights Reserved

THEORIES OF LANGUAGE ACQUISITION

So where do we begin as we plan for language-arts instruction in a meaning-centered classroom? We start with one question: "How do children learn language?" The answer will determine how teachers structure the learning environment and what types of instruction they provide students.

Many explanations of how children learn language have been proposed. These major language-acquisition theories stand in sharp contrast to one another. One position holds that language learning is an innate ability; another views language learning as an imitation of adult speech. A third position holds that language learning is a process of human interaction and that teachers must stress the child's own active role in experiencing and acquiring language. (Figure 1.1 contrasts the differences in these language-learning theories.) A meaning-centered classroom, as elaborated in this text, relies heavily on the

LANGUAGE-ACQUISITION THEORIES ◄ FIGURE 1.1

BEHAVIORAL VIEW: Stresses the rewarding of certain behaviors through stimulus-response bonds. The student's personal production of language is of no consequence in behavioristic model.

ENVIRONMENT > > > LEARNER

NATIVISTIC VIEW: Language is innate and the learner is central. Learning is related to the assimilation of internal knowledge. Fails to explain how we get from the child's innate knowledge to overt performance.

ENVIRONMENT < < < LEARNER

COGNITIVE FIELD VIEW: Stresses the process of an interaction between learners and their environment. Language is embedded and shaped by the social-cultural environment in which it is generated. Meanings result as children interact with environments.

PERSONAL MEANINGS

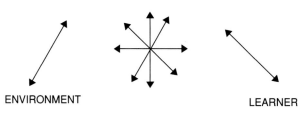

ENVIRONMENT   LEARNER

interactive/communicative explanation, which is known as a *cognitive field theory*.

BEHAVIORISM

Behaviorism holds that knowledge is discovered by observing the world and that facts or statements are only true when they correspond with what has been observed. Skinner (1957) views thinking as an internalized product of speaking and listening. Thus language and thought originate in the environment. Infants, then, are believed to learn all things from their environment. Consequently, learning would be shaped by positive reinforcement of desired behaviors and negative reinforcement of undesirable behaviors (Wardhaugh, 1971). The relationship between a stimulus and a response is the core of behaviorism.

Bloomfield (1933), an early supporter of behaviorism, saw children as passive vessels who only reacted to outside stimuli. He viewed language learning as a process of imitating sounds, words, and phrases that was rewarded by needs fulfillment and praise. The behaviorists who followed Bloomfield examined language patterns in order to identify the components of language. They used rewards to encourage children to demonstrate these components in their speech and actions. The adult role was seen as modeling words and phrases that children would imitate.

Skinner believed the adult would provide reinforcements to children as their approximations to the model became clearer. These responses would become habitual as they were "conditioned." For example, a 10-month-old infant's babbling sounds might resemble "dada." The father's excited response would then "shape" the vocalization to resemble and mean "daddy."

The learning of words can be explained through behaviorist theory. However, the analysis and synthesis of sound–symbol relationships do not equal meaning. Language always involves an active interpreter or it is not language. The difference, according to Labov (1982), "between a parrot and human saying, 'I'll meet you downtown,' is that the human is likely to show up."

In addition, Pflaum (1986) questions the theory's application when it comes to the acquisition of sentences. Children often produce sentences that they have never heard before as they apply rules and make hypotheses. Ferreiro and Teberosky (1982) argue that "neither imitation nor selective reinforcement, the key elements of associationistic [behavioristic] learning theory, can account for children's learning of syntax" (p. 11).

Thus the process of learning to communicate is much more complicated than what the behaviorists claim. They fail to recognize what children bring to the learning environment, and they also lose sight of the child as a hypothesis tester. In truth, through this hypothesis testing, children develop their own rules for analyzing language and form abstract understandings about language that they apply on a daily basis.

NATIVISM

The move to a more cognitive perspective on language and its acquisition was led by Noam Chomsky (1965). He described language as being present in some potential form at birth, and stated that language develops innately as children interact with their environments. This nativistic perspective declares that children learn language when they encounter it and have a need to understand and communicate with others.

Chomsky describes this inductive process through the analogy of an imaginary "device" that children have within them. This language-acquisition device (LAD) receives information from the environment in the form of language. The language is analyzed and rules generated. These rules are then applied as expression takes place through language communication. The LAD continues to operate as a generating rule system for language as children pass through the levels of maturation. Thus children are able to organize incoming characteristics of language, including rules, grammar, categories, and other linguistic structures. This internal learning is viewed as developing in a natural manner.

Carol Chomsky elaborates by stating that although children cannot be taught language in a formal sense, they can acquire it naturally "in the course of maturing and developing in an environment where [they] are adequately exposed to it" (Chomsky, 1980, p. 228). Consequently, nativism leads to a "hands-off" view of teaching in language-arts classrooms. Advocates point out that children will best learn the important communication skills through the practice of reading and writing and not through isolated studies of skills (Smith, 1985).

However, wise teachers can structure learning environments in a manner that ensures children will encounter the language arts in a natural and creative way. Pure nativistic theory fails, however, to take advantage of the

◀ Children learning together.

opportunity schools have for creating the "teachable moments" that serve as demonstrations to students of how language and literacy work in communication. Cognitive field theory, which follows, offers perhaps the best model for advancing a natural but structured curriculum.

COGNITIVE FIELD

Cognitive field theory recognizes that learning is a process that evolves as children, through interactive relationships, develop new insights and re-model old ones within a psychological environment or field. In this view, it is believed children acquire knowledge about language as they test hypotheses and restructure their thinking according to new things learned (Canady, 1977).

Cognitive field theorists refuse to see parts as distinct from whole processes. The outmoded atomistic perspective of listening, speaking, reading, and writing is replaced with a holistic perspective. In this perspective, meaning exists neither in the environment nor in the learner. Instead, it is the result of the learner's interacting with the environment, and the product or meaning created is greater than the sum of the two parts. Language is viewed as open and changing as learners build personal meanings for words and concepts. Words are viewed as being cognitive "placeholders" that have multiple meanings. One child's specific meaning for "fish" might be somewhat different from another's. However, both children share a common meaning for the word because they are members of the same interpretive community.

The research of Harste, Woodward, and Burke (1984b) confirms that children acquire the interpretive rules of language use through "social interaction at very early ages" (p. 56). As children interact through language, they test insights that enable them to construct their own rules of meaning and the grammar of language. The learning is at the subconscious level—they probably would be unable to articulate the internal rules that their language mastery demonstrates. As an adult user of our language, you probably are in the same position. You may use "school" grammar but might not be able to voice the rules you somehow use as you build words into phrases and sentences. Garth Boomer (1984) puts it succinctly: "We know more than we can tell" (p. 576).

Cognitive field theory and nativist theory are similar in many respects. Both hold that individuals are born with the potential to learn language (Page & Pinnell, 1979). The key difference lies in implications for instruction. Nativists support a "hands-off" position. Cognitivists support teaching/learning environments that accelerate the constructive nature of language learning in students. Together, these language-acquisition theories are intertwined into a meaning-centered curriculum that is elaborated in this text (see Figure 1.1).

As a teacher you must fine-tune your beliefs about children and how they learn. Theory is crucial because it determines classroom practice. Clarifying your position does not involve learning names of theories or memorizing information from texts. Instead, you need to ask yourself questions about how you think children learn and how students acquire language. Perhaps these theoretical positions will serve as reference points as you examine our assumptions that children are active, purpose-seeking learners.

THE LITERACY TRANSACTION MODEL

Our instruction of children should be influenced by our knowledge of how children learn. Good teachers do more than just present information to students. They invite children's participation by introducing material in an exciting, enticing manner. Unfortunately, schools have often been places where students enter with great excitement but depart with great boredom. The reason? Students spend 12 or 13 years in school, answering questions they didn't ask. The research we have reviewed thus far suggests that learning best occurs when teachers approach students with a more transactive instructional stance.

Schools in the past have focused on the receptive domain, asking children to "learn" material and information the teachers and texts have presented. We must go beyond the receptive! True, children do benefit greatly when they read great children's books. They learn by listening to others and by studying the world that surrounds them. However, learning is enhanced when children's personal ideas are valued—when they are allowed to share their own ideas and understandings with others in the school setting.

Our theoretical model, which we call the *Literacy Transaction Model,* is based on the theory that learning occurs in the transaction between impression—children's *receptive* activities—and self-expression—children's *expressive* activities. Our view is that skills, or conventions of literacy, are developed within this transaction of impression and self-expression.

We have developed a model (Figure 1.2) that pictures the transaction and serves as the theoretical model of this text. We use this model throughout the text to tie the language arts together. In order to visualize this model, think of the strands of a rope, and how much stronger a rope is when the strands

CURRICULUM MODEL FOR A MEANING-CENTERED PERSPECTIVE ◀ FIGURE 1.2

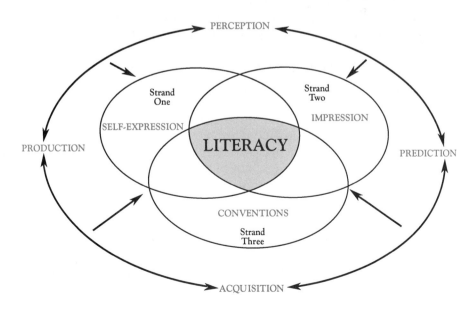

are woven together. The three strands of our rope, or model, are self-expression, impression, and conventions.

▶ **Strand 1** emphasizes acquiring literacy through *self-expression* activities and experiences.

▶ **Strand 2** emphasizes *impression,* the influence of the language and ideas of others on literacy development.

▶ **Strand 3** emphasizes the exploration of those characteristics or *conventions* of language structure that help a person to be literate.

The model does not suggest that teachers should "teach" these strands in isolation. Instead, it pictures learning as an interaction among these literacy areas. The instructional focus is not on the three strands, but on their overlap. Thus literacy lessons are integrated so carefully that the three circles merge into one. Skills are not presented in isolation, but in the context of their function.

STRAND 1: SELF-EXPRESSION

Strand 1 emphasizes the natural ways of self-expression—talking, painting, singing, dancing, acting, and writing. All students are unique and have their own language style. The school should preserve this uniqueness while helping students discover alternative forms of expression.

Meaning-centered teachers recognize that fluency and flexibility in language help pupils make adjustments to life and value their own ideas and feelings. These teachers help students understand and appreciate classmates who are culturally different. Language values relate to all effective teaching/learning situations. Some of these values are described next.

1. **Creative language experiences provide for individual differences.** Students think and reason differently. They have varying abilities, interests, drives, and talents. Students work best when their tasks are appropriate to their age and abilities and when these tasks are flexible enough to permit individual ways of thinking and working.

2. **Creative language experiences develop imagination.** All young people are endowed with the power of imagination. This resource is available in every classroom at no extra cost. Education sometimes diminishes the power of imagination, however, as other facets of personality are developed. Teachers who implement Strand 1 of the Literacy Transaction Model are careful not to limit their students' imaginations.

3. **Creative language experiences build self-confidence.** Students must search their own storehouses of experiences and use their own skill, knowledge, and language to solve speech and writing problems. Students need to set personal standards rather than use uniform standards that foster classroom competition.

4. **Creative language experiences provide for emotional expression.** Schools should emphasize ideas and experiences that have

emotional importance to children. When students involve their emotions in their subject—whether oral or written—others will respond to their output. Masterpieces in writing, art, and music are usually expressions of basic emotions that evoke human responses.

5. **Creative language experiences develop the aesthetic sense.** Students who have been free to express themselves through writing or art can appreciate the written and artistic expression of others. The quality of that expression is not so important. What is important is that students have experience in communicating ideas in various forms.

6. **Creative language experiences deepen appreciation of other people's writing.** Students should have the opportunity to appreciate the work of others in the classroom. A student who has struggled to communicate ideas—orally or in writing—is appreciative of other students who have expressed their ideas in beautiful or diverse ways. Creative language experiences bring balance to educational activities.

7. **Traditional school curricula are convergent in nature.** However, students need a balanced classroom experience, one that takes their creative powers into account while they learn the fundamental skills of handwriting, spelling, reading, and the conventions of usage. Meaning-centered programs provide many such opportunities for divergent thinking. This freedom to create personal communications is a

---

JOSE ARUEGO

◀ **THE BOOK MAKERS**

1. Which book of yours has given you the greatest pleasure?

Leo the Late Bloomer. It was 24 years ago and I was just starting out as an illustrator and I didn't know a lot of what I do now. I just did it by instinct. I guess I was more of a free spirit then.

2. Which book has surprised you most in terms of its public reception?

Gregory the Terrible Eater. I had no idea how popular it would become because of its emphasis on junk food vs. healthy food.

3. What would you like people to remember about your work?

The books I write and the books I choose to illustrate are humorous. The drawings are fun and I want people to get a good feeling when they read them.

4. What impact do you hope your work will have on children?

Children tend to copy my drawings. Teachers tell me kids find a favorite character in a favorite book and they copy that character. My characters are simple to draw and the children enjoy getting into the artwork themselves by drawing.

José Aruego has delighted readers for years with his lively characterizations of animals. His work includes *Leo the Late Bloomer, Whose Mouse Are You?, Where Are You Going Little Mouse, Come Out and Play Little Mouse, Another Mouse to Feed,* and *We Hide, You Seek.*

Writing is an ▶
excellent
pathway for
children's
self-expression.

welcome change from the kinds of learning that require students to ar-rive at the same solution.

Strand 1 skills are developed in meaning-centered programs as students share their thoughts and ideas with others.

STRAND 2: IMPRESSION

Strand 2 of the Literacy Transaction Model emphasizes the influences of the language and ideas of others on the student's personal language and ideas. The focus is on how others use language. Teachers expose students to many forms of communication, helping them choose to change and improve their own language creatively. Six traits characterize the classroom emphasizing Strand 2 activities:

1. Students acquire new ways of saying things by repeating ways in which authors write stories and poems.

2. Teachers provide opportunities for art, creative writing, and drama to help students interpret ideas they gained from listening and reading.

3. Students develop organizational abilities—like those required for com-prehending reading—in learning situations that do not require reading and writing abilities, such as painting pictures, constructing, sculpting, and making collages.

4. Students write, expressing their personal ideas through personal lan-guage and in predetermined poetry and predictable story patterns.

5. Students compare personal ideas with those of other people who have communicated on the same topic.

6. Teachers encourage questions, which are more important than answers in stimulating students to search many sources for information.

A meaning-centered curriculum helps students build confidence for communicating in ways that reflect the influence of authors and artists who communicate in beautiful and effective ways. Students grow in confidence as they see how other language users communicate.

STRAND 3: CONVENTIONS: HOW LANGUAGE WORKS IN LITERACY

Strand 3 of the Literacy Transaction Model emphasizes that skills, or the conventions of literacy, are learned in the process of reading and writing. It is different from other literacy programs in that students' own stories and poems are used—along with those from other printed sources—to show the relations of personal language to printed language. Six important points underlie Strand 3:

1. The words students use most frequently in speech and writing are the same ones that are most used in the writings of other people (both students and adults). These words tend to be words that are meaningless in themselves. Many of them are nonphonetic (e.g., *the, are,* etc.). These words *must* be learned in context—attempts at phonetic analysis only produce nonsense.

2. Students need to develop an awareness of high-frequency words to facilitate independent reading.

3. Students examine the relation between the sounds of speech and the use of the alphabet to represent those sounds. Understanding of these graphophonic relations occurs as students encounter them over and over again in the language. Practice for mastery is provided by the emphasis on writing—rather than reading—in a meaning-centered classroom.

4. Students acquire language through listening and talking with others, through new experiences, and through the application of new vocabulary to old experiences.

5. Language grows as students learn the names of things, words of movement, and words of description.

6. Listening to and repeating well-written materials extend students' understandings of the many ways that authors express their ideas and feelings.

Strand 3 emphasizes the study of the specifics of language that contribute to literacy. These specifics have been identified over many years of research and study. They are elaborated and extended throughout this text.

IMPLEMENTATION OF THE LITERACY TRANSACTION MODEL

Implementation of the Literacy Transaction Model can make literacy learning joyous and successful. The growth is not the result of teaching literacy skills directly in the conventional sense. Rather, it is the result of the interaction of language learnings within the three strands of the Literacy Transaction Model. Illustrated in Figure 1.2, this model suggests that at any point at which the learnings overlap, the result is literacy. The truly literate person relates the strands of the Literacy Transaction Model so completely that the three strands merge into one. In this model, literacy is holistic. It is always greater than the sum of its parts.

The instructional objective is one of planning and implementing programs that include some emphasis from each strand daily. Three major ideas interlock in the model:

1. Each day, students communicate in many ways and through many means. They use personal ideas and personal language.

2. Each day, students are influenced by the language and ideas of many people through what they see and hear. In the process, their personal language becomes more and more like the language they are encountering.

3. Each day, students explore those components of language that have most to do with achieving literacy. In the process of communicating, they learn how an alphabetic system of notation works for them as well as for others.

As indicated in the model shown in Figure 1.2, instructional programs are generated in the outer parts of the model. They feature four major classes of activities:

acquisition

perception

prediction

production

These four classes of activities are presented in many formats and instructional experiences. Figure 1.3 pictures the Literacy Transaction Model for a meaning-centered approach as it is being implemented in the classroom. Note that the Strand 3 experiences on the outer edge of the model facilitate the interaction between self-expression (Strand 1) and impression (Strand 2). Successful implementation of these meaning-centered experiences will accelerate the overlap of the strands and thus contribute to the goal of attaining literacy. We present and discuss these literacy-centered strategies throughout the text.

LANGUAGE FOR LITERACY: A TRANSACTIVE MODEL ◀ FIGURE 1.3

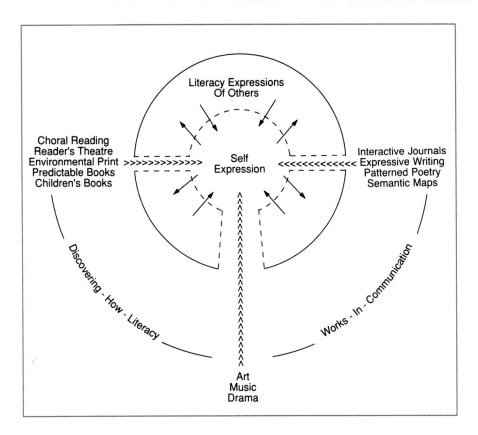

ACQUISITION

How do students acquire new language in school? Through transactions with literacy. These transactions include activities that involve singing, chanting, reading, listening to reading, interacting with computer programs, listening to stories and poems, acting out stories and poems, and choral reading.

Teachers give priority to acquisition of vocabularies of nouns, verbs, adjectives, and adverbs. Teachers also help students:

▶ hear language in new and meaningful contexts;

▶ say things with new words and new language patterns that become permanent through use;

▶ write with an ever-increasing repertoire of personal language resources; and

▶ sing songs to celebrate language that has rhyme, rhythm, and repetition.

PERCEPTION

In a meaning-centered approach, students learn basic skills in the process of communication, not through emphasizing these skills in isolation. A major difference between meaning-centered and conventional programs is that in meaning-based programs the teacher trusts the student's own language to illustrate the characteristics of the language of literature.

Literacy conventions are developed as students communicate. Much of the direct instruction occurs as students edit the works they have written. Skills are reinforced and extended as students read the written works of others. Both the personal language of the student and the language of others illustrate the basic rules and skills of language. Students come to think along with an author and to use their predictive abilities, meaning clues, and visual clues to satisfy their need to communicate with an author.

PREDICTION

Selections for listening and reading in a meaning-centered classroom include exposure to materials with repeating patterns and dependable lines. These selections permit students to predict and repeat words, phrases, and whole stanzas without seeing the print. They learn to anticipate language and language patterns that repeat frequently in stories.

Poetry with repeating lines and patterns is important in a meaning-centered approach. This visual impact of patterns in printed material is helpful in encouraging or releasing students to try to read new materials. They can observe that only a few words are different as they read. Much of the print is repeated. In poetry, the patterns of rhyming words usually give some clue to new words at the end of lines.

Reading in chorus is useful in establishing the phonological structure of predictable stories and poems. Once the sound pattern has been established, the words that follow can be predicted with a high degree of certainty. Shy readers lose their hesitation when their voice unites with 30 other voices.

Singing songs and doing chants that repeat language patterns afford children an opportunity to try out new ways of saying things that are atypical of personal language. This practice enables students to recognize those patterns in print and to predict the flow of language. Prediction skills are crucial to the reading process. Our goal is for students to incorporate a predicting attitude toward all literacy transactions.

PRODUCTION

In a process classroom, children create products in the process of self-expression activities. These products include, but are not limited to, individual books, class books, dramatic productions, musical productions, and art displays.

One highlight of the instructional program should be the use of student-authored materials as a cornerstone of the language environment. Such student-authored books reflect familiar vocabulary and current interests. Because the content and language are known to the student authors, these

Misty Hodges Name
13 years Age
Go to movies, listen to music Interests
Swim, read R. L. Stine Books
Ride in Rodeos, talk on phone

What do you like most about school? I like to read a lot in School & I also love to do Math! I guess I would have to say I like athletics the best because it is hard work and the coach's are very fun to be with.

What's your favorite subject? Why?
My favorite subject is Math. The reason for it is I am good in Math, so it makes it easy. It is also a great subject that needs to be taught & learned very well.

What's your favorite book? Why do you like it?
My favorite book is The Dare by R. L. Stine. A few reasons I like it is it is a very suspensful book and in a way romantic. It also pertains to my life.

What advice do you have for teachers?
The advice I have for teachers is to teach it from their mouth and not just reading out of the book. I also think teachers should NOT give homework on Wednesday or Friday. The reason is Wednesday is a church day and Friday is suppost to be a time for fun with friends and family, but if they plan of having a test on Thursday or Monday they should tell the students to study.

authors can become teachers as they share their books with others. When original manuscripts are read aloud by their authors, the emphasis can be placed on effective interpretation through reading rather than on recognition skills.

Imagination is encouraged in the process of producing literacy materials. Experiences are expressed through art, media, acting, and talking. Some of the experiences are recorded through independent writing and then reproduced through reading. Students gain a firm grasp of the notion that their ideas, expressed with words, can be written. What is written becomes reading.

As students mature enough to compare and contrast, they realize several things:

► The words they use to write about a topic are much the same as those used by others.

► The sounds they make when they talk are recorded by writing, using an alphabet that is the same for everybody.

► What other people write about comes from real experiences or from imagination.

► Characters must be described so listeners and readers can form mental images even though they have never seen them.

► The settings of stories must be described so listeners and readers can form mental images even though they may have never been there.

Editing of manuscripts to be used in the reading curriculum is a significant part of the production process. Students learn the fine points of reading by editing their writing, just as they learn the fine points of writing by reading well-written materials.

LINGUISTIC DIVERSITY AND THE LANGUAGE-ARTS PROGRAM

Linguist Michael Halliday said, "A child doesn't need to know any linguistics in order to use language to learn; but a teacher needs to know some linguistics if she or he wants to understand how the process takes place—or what is going wrong when it doesn't" (Halliday, 1980, p. 11). Thus classroom teachers implementing the basic philosophy of a meaning-centered curriculum learn to function as linguists during the process of instruction. They become students of human speech and learn to listen to variations in pronunciation and speech patterns. They manifest positive attitudes toward differences in speech. This method is in sharp contrast with the traditional approach, which tends to try to eliminate differences.

A prime responsibility of the teacher is to illustrate and demonstrate continually the relations among speech and writing and reading. A central focus exists:

► Speech is the language.

► Writing is an imperfect representation of that speech.

► Reading is a transaction among the reader, the text, and the situational context.

This central focus results in changed attitudes toward students and language. Students with limited language development are valued as class members. Those whose first language is not English can illustrate differences and can provide a learning environment for contrasting and comparing different ways of saying the same thing.

LINGUISTIC PRINCIPLES FOR TEACHERS

Teacher practices are influenced by several linguistic principles in meaning-centered programs:

1. **Language is a creative activity of each person.** Each person's language differs from that of every other person in the world. The teacher must value that language and help students understand how oral language relates to written language. Teachers with a communication-centered attitude provide a learning environment with repeated opportunities for contrasting and comparing the personal language of one person to the language of another.

2. **Language patterns are well established by the time a child is 5 or 6 years old.** Even though their grammar and pronunciation can be nonstandard, students use a variety of sentence patterns when they start school.

3. **Language habits, once learned, change slowly.** Students do not change their oral language patterns as a result of lessons. Lessons merely expose students to alternatives. If any significant change is made, it will be made as a result of *choice*. Teachers with communication-centered attitudes work to provide intelligent choices for language change.

4. **The writing system, or code of English, is alphabetic and has certain inadequacies.** The symbols we use to write the words we use when we talk do not have specific sounds. Human beings make the sounds of words and sentences, and each person has to develop understandings of how these sounds can be represented.

   Phonics is a language study that is flexible in the use of an alphabet to record human speech. It is not a study of a system that is the same for everybody. When dictating and writing, students experience phonics in a functional setting, especially if they are writing at the same time they are beginning to read.

5. **Language is changing continuously. It has a history.** Both meanings and pronunciations of words change. Students in process-centered curricula get excited about language changes and are interested in adding new words to the English language. They learn how to make up new words, say them, write them, and then test the writing to see if another person who has not heard the word can reproduce it by reading the printed form.

6. **Language varies with the age, socioeconomic group, and geographic region of the speaker. This is dialect.** The use of a standard alphabet and standard spellings of words has not erased the dialects that are widespread in our country. Dialects persist because there is not a one-to-one correspondence between the sounds of speech and the sounds represented by the symbols of the alphabet. Meaning-centered programs value this linguistic diversity and consider dialects as reflections of the diversity and beauty of language.

7. **The concept of correctness is replaced by a concept of alternatives in pronunciation, word choice, phrasing, and construction.** When teachers view literacy—the ability to read and write—as an extension of personal language, they are not concerned with uniformity of self-expression. In the same sense that they value the variety of ideas reflected by students in their paintings, teachers value the variety of ways that students say and write things.

Errors in grammar are modified through environments that provide opportunities to hear how others express ideas. Meaning-centered curricula provide opportunities to participate in unison and choral language experiences that permit students to try out new ways of saying things—with confidence they will not be singled out for corrections. Each person, in effect, develops a wardrobe of languages—one suitable for home, one for school, and one for the peer group.

SUMMARY

In process-centered curricula, teachers recognize that the language students bring to the school is uniquely their own. This personal speech is a reflection of the vernacular the children have heard used in their homes and communities.

Consequently, teachers who endorse a meaning-centered approach to literacy strive to let their students know this personal speech is worthy and welcome as they accept, respect, and build on their literacy communications.

The teacher should be careful to provide some emphasis each day from the Literacy Transaction Model presented in this chapter. In doing so, the teacher will assure that every student has opportunities for self-expression through Strand 1 activities. The students' personal language will be influenced through Strand 2 activities. Literacy skills will emerge from Strand 3 as students encounter the wonder and beauty of language through holistic activities.

►2 PATHWAYS TO LITERACY BEGINNINGS

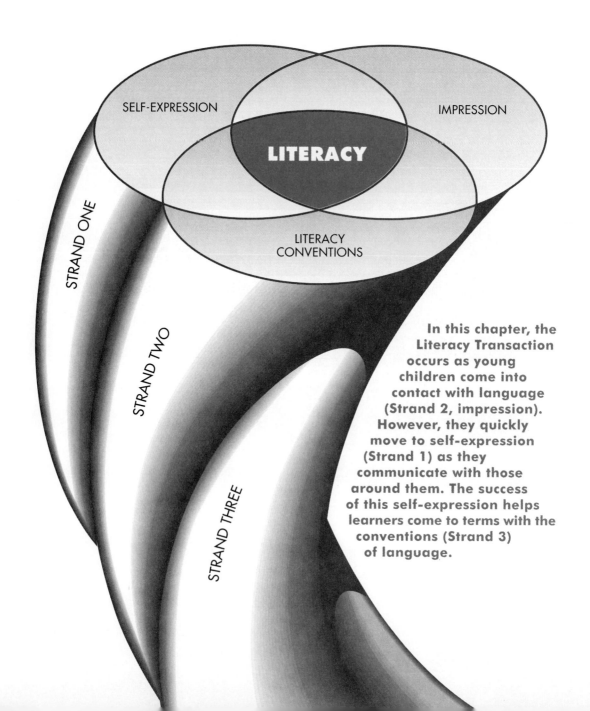

SELF-EXPRESSION

IMPRESSION

LITERACY

LITERACY
CONVENTIONS

STRAND ONE

STRAND TWO

STRAND THREE

In this chapter, the Literacy Transaction occurs as young children come into contact with language (Strand 2, impression). However, they quickly move to self-expression (Strand 1) as they communicate with those around them. The success of this self-expression helps learners come to terms with the conventions (Strand 3) of language.

CHAPTER OUTLINE

. . . .

READING: THE BEGINNINGS

    HOW CHILDREN BECOME AWARE OF PRINT

    NATURAL READERS

. . . .

WRITING: THE BEGINNINGS

    DISTINCTIVE FEATURES OF BEGINNING WRITING

. . . .

LITERACY LEARNING IN SCHOOL SETTINGS

. . . .

EXPERIENCES: THE FOUNDATIONS OF LITERACY

    RESPONDING TO THE NATURAL ENVIRONMENT

    RESPONDING TO SENSORY IMPRESSIONS

. . . .

SUMMARY

. . . .

PATHWAYS TO READING LIFE EXPERIENCES

. . . .

PATHWAYS TO PONDER

. . . .

▶ **WHAT IMPACT DOES THE EXPOSURE OF CHILDREN TO PRINT IN THEIR ENVIRONMENTS HAVE ON THEIR READINESS FOR LITERACY INSTRUCTION?**

. . . .

▶ **WHAT IS THE RELATIONSHIP BETWEEN THE BEGINNINGS OF READING AND THE BEGINNINGS OF WRITING?**

. . . .

▶ **WHAT PRINCIPLES FROM NATURAL LITERACY LEARNING SHOULD BE INCORPORATED INTO THE SCHOOL CURRICULUM?**

. . . .

▶ **HOW ARE LIFE EXPERIENCES THE "FOUNDATIONS OF THINKING"?**

. . . .

▶ **HOW MAY LIFE EXPERIENCES IMPACT LITERACY INSTRUCTION?**

. . . .

From the first moments of life, infants hear language. Imagine what it must be like being born into our language-rich world, being bombarded with the sounds of an environment rich with language stimuli. And the language is directed at you as you are immediately immersed in the river of language interaction that flows around you. As you seek to make meaning of the world around you, family members play a vital role as language models and suppliers of language during this period of language acquisition and discovery.

Within days the infant's role quickly changes from that of a listener to one of a participant as he or she begins to communicate with family members. A miracle of learning soon occurs. An infant's learning of language is fast and sure—virtually every child achieves near mastery of his or her language by age 6 (Read, 1980).

This mastery is also evident outside the literacy-dominated culture of the United States. For example, Pflaum (1986) reports that children in nonliterate Papua, New Guinea, acquire substantial communication skills at an early age.

Language learning is more complicated than it might appear. Language is more than words, language is more than sentences. Children come to know that the same word has many different meanings and that context influences meaning. Thus the need to communicate leads children to refine their language through experimentation. For example, 3-year-old Jonathan was asked to bring the "tape" during a Christmas package-wrapping session. His mother had just played his favorite music on the stereo. So he responded by bringing the cassette tape. Fortunately, children quickly learn the "tricks" of language depending on the context of the situation. They discover language is not a constant, but a variable.

As children move through the preschool years, they begin to gain control of language as they are exposed to the communication of others. This internalization of language is then expressed through oral sharing. The process of input—through the communication of others—and output—in the form of self-expression—may be seen as preschoolers "scribble" messages and develop as writers.

READING: THE BEGINNINGS

HOW CHILDREN BECOME AWARE OF PRINT

We have already discussed how children learn language by comparing and contrasting three views of language acquisition. We saw that children learn language because of their need to communicate with significant others and that the process of learning language is a natural product of these transactions. The same holds true of reading and writing.

One of the greatest mistakes we have made through the years has occurred in kindergarten and first-grade classrooms through our efforts to get children "ready" to learn to read. In reality, children become readers much earlier than this as they become aware of print in situational contexts. However, many reading programs fail to build on children's early experiences with print as they "teach" reading and reading "skills" in isolation from the student's language base and knowledge of print.

Research has indicated that children become aware of print at a very early age as they interact with the world about them (Clay, 1975; Doake, 1988; Teale, 1986a). This first exposure occurs as children encounter print "embedded" in their environments (Goodman, 1980; Wells, 1986). Harste, Burke, and Woodward (1982) concluded that children begin their literacy learning process by observing this embedded print and constructing schemata concerning its meaning in context.

Daily activities of young children reinforce their concept of what print is and its value to the significant adults in their lives. When young children go to the store they are bombarded with printed visual stimuli displaying products they have seen advertised on television. They quickly learn to recognize the printed symbols that signal their favorite restaurants, stores, and landmarks. They learn that certain signs on highways and public buildings control the actions of people. Children assimilate this information and begin to make generalizations concerning print. They realize that print carries a message. Generalizations occur as children quickly learn that generic terms may be substituted for specific trade names. For instance, children may call both Colgate and Crest "toothpaste," but when asked how they know that information they will point to the printed word (Goodman, 1980).

Children's print awareness is not limited to learning from situational contexts. Children's knowledge of print is also enhanced as they are exposed to print in books, newspapers, magazines, letters, and other printed matter (Goodman, 1980; Jaggar & Smith-Burke, 1985; McGee & Richgels, 1990). These early experiences with books and other printed material directly influence the print awareness of the child (Holdaway, 1979, 1986). Thus the more children are read to and the more they see others reading and writing, the more importance print will have in their lives. Environmental print and written discourse both make children aware that print conveys meaning. They also prompt children's awareness of other linguistic constraints that govern their particular language. One of the mainstays of many "reading readiness" programs has been the teaching of print directionality through exercises in the classroom. However, the concept of directionality of print is a linguistic one that develops at a young age. In addition, as we survey environmental print, we discover it is often presented vertically and does not always move from left to right. The adaptability of children is apparent because they assimilate this information and recognize it to be the exception rather than the norm (Goodman, 1980). Once again, we find that children know more about language and print than they are usually given credit for.

In addition, children develop the concept that print occurs in groupings of letters that represent verbal responses. The length of the print becomes equated with the length of the utterance (Goodman, 1980). Four-year-old Chrissy received a letter offering her the opportunity to "win" a new car by visiting a real estate development. When her mother finished reading the letter without including the postscript at the bottom of the page, Chrissy corrected her by saying, "But there's more here, Mom!"

FIGURE 2.1 ▶ **WRITING SAMPLES FROM 4-YEAR-OLD CHILDREN**

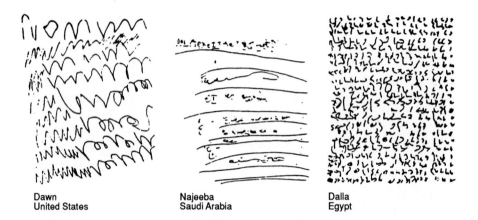

Dawn
United States

Najeeba
Saudi Arabia

Dalla
Egypt

Other generalizations that children develop include knowledge of the form of their particular written language. Harste, Burke, and Woodward's (1982) work with 4-year-olds attending an Indiana preschool illustrates this. When children at the school from three different countries were instructed "Write everything you can write," the results were revealing, as indicated in Figure 2.1. In discussing these scribbles, the researchers stated:

> In contrast to the other sample, Dawn's scribbles look undeniably English. When Najeeba finished her writing, she said, "Here, but you can't read it because it is in Arabic." Najeeba then went on to point out that in Arabic one uses "a lot more dots" than in English. Dalia is an Israeli child whose writing bears the predictable look of Hebrew.

(Harste, Burke, & Woodward, 1982, p. 107)

Thus, when asked to write, young children will make markings that reflect the print of their cultures. This is an indication that the psycholinguistic processes of reading and writing are sociologically rooted (Harste, Burke, & Woodward, 1984a).

THE POET ▶
PONDERS

TRAINING WHEELS

This is my bookshelf, and these are my books,
I know each one by heart.
I just look at the pictures and wait for my Dad
To give me a little start.

Some day I'll read all by myself
With confidence and speed,
But for now, these pretty picture books
Are everything I need.

Copyright Brod Bagert 1993
All Rights Reserved

Maria Flores is a first-grade teacher who values the knowledge and experiences that children bring with them to her classroom. Her perspective is that of a cognitive field advocate: she believes the teacher's job is to set up situations where children can use their knowledge about language and print as they learn more about literacy. Maria allows children to discover how much they know about reading and language through the use of environmental print. She uses cereal boxes, soft drink containers, and fast-food restaurant sacks as a natural link to literacy during the first few weeks of class. She asks the students to bring in words to include on a bulletin board labeled "Words We Can Read."

Children's insights about environmental print provide Maria with valuable clues concerning their knowledge about literacy. She knows her analysis of the student's response to environmental print provides a much richer picture of the child's "readiness" for a given activity than information provided by conventional reading readiness tests. She uses this informal assessment as she plans the instruction a given child will receive and the learning environments she will establish in her classroom.

NATURAL READERS

Children who become readers without direct instruction before entering school typically come from homes where literacy is a part of daily life and routines. Studies have shown that in such homes adults modeled interaction with all types of reading materials (Heath, 1983b; Morrow, 1992; Teale, 1986a, 1986b). Print was utilized in meaningful and frequent situations. The children were read to regularly, and discussions of the books occurred during and after the reading. Writing materials were present, and children saw adults writing frequently for real-life communicative needs and were included in this communication. In addition, the children had easy access to paper and pencil and their communicative efforts were recognized and praised.

From Teale's observations and reviews of research, he offers several suggestions to create home environments that foster literacy development:

▶ Provide a wide variety of reading and writing materials that are readily available to the child; in addition to children's books, include magazines, various types of writing instruments (pens, markers, pencils, crayons, chalk), and paper.

▶ Have parents (and other family members such as siblings and grandparents) who themselves engage in a variety of reading and writing activities model for the child the activities and the pleasure and satisfaction found in these experiences.

▶ Read to the child on a regular basis.

▶ Encourage the child's reading and writing activities, both in interaction with the parent and as independent activities by the child.

Children discover ▶
that they can
read many words
from their
environment.

▶ Have responsive parents answer the child's questions about language, books, reading, and writing (Teale, 1986a, p. 23).

Literacy should not be pushed on preschoolers. Reading and writing should be enjoyable and natural. Contrived "instruction" can destroy the joy of literacy and rob children of a love of reading. However, it is to a child's advantage to be a reader when beginning school. Taylor (1986) states that it's the early experiences children have with literacy in the home that enable them to overcome the "impossible ambiguity of the decontextualized reading exercises" of first-grade classrooms. Therefore, teachers should encourage parents to share books with children and to promote their natural literacy inquiries.

WRITING: THE BEGINNINGS

At very young ages, children begin to experiment with writing. They represent meaning through scribbles (Harste, Woodward, & Burke, 1984b; Vygotsky, 1978) and demonstrate their growing awareness of the functions of print through these written communications. The first scribbles produced by a toddler may seem meaningless to an adult, but they represent the child's experimentation with the concept that written marks convey meaning in a permanent and concrete way. In a massive study of children's early literacy encounters, Harste, Woodward, and Burke (1984b) discovered that "all" children "wrote" with the "intent to mean."

Children also realize at an early age that the marks which convey meaning have certain unique characteristics. Remember Dawn, Najeeba, and Dalia's uninterrupted writing samples shown in Figure 2.1? They demonstrate that the cultural form of print is internalized at an early age without formal instruction (Harste, Burke, & Woodward, l982).

Some educators believe that if children were left to their own devices, writing would precede reading (Chomsky, 1971). Others claim that reading is the first accomplishment. A more current perspective is that both reading and writing are developmental; hence they are learned simultaneously through children's explorations with environmental print and scribbles. In cases where reading precedes writing, the development is likely a reflection of parents' and teachers' emphasis on reading and the lack of opportunities for young children to write. It is difficult to determine how this emphasis affects the natural development of reading and writing.

Recent studies have further explored the interactive development of reading and writing as children's concepts concerning print are developed. The case studies of Baghban (l984), Bissex (1980), Kamler (1984), and Rhodes (1979), and the observational research of Heath (1983a), Schickedanz and Sullivan (1984), Taylor (1983), and Teale (1986b) illustrate the concurrent development of literacy awareness in reading and writing. Wells, in an important longitudinal study (1986), determined that children's early communications were always directed toward communicating meaning, and that children expect others to have this same meaning-oriented stance.

Such research has reinforced the concept that a child's perception of the world includes a strong realization that print is a vital, valuable, and useful part of the environment. Children strive to make sense of print and to find ways of making it a tool of communication. Our goal should be to provide opportunities in the curriculum for children to continue their discovery, in school settings, of how print functions in communication.

DISTINCTIVE FEATURES OF BEGINNING WRITING

When investigating the representation of written language, children move from scribbling to making marks that begin to look like writing. During this developmental process children often rely on concrete representations to facilitate the transfer of meaning to the written page. This reliance is illustrated in research studies (Ferreiro & Teberosky, l982; Morrow, 1992). Figure 2.2 illustrates this principle. Four-year-old Joshua wrote a note to his father. He wanted to say "I love you" five times. He represented this oral language with symbols very effectively, as shown in his "letter" (Figure 2.2). This literacy experience illustrates the interplay that children are constantly involved in as they strive to make sense of the relation between print and the concept or concepts it represents.

In the process of developing ways to communicate messages through print, children often incorporate art experiences into their writing. This inclusion of art reinforces the concept that concrete representation is a part of the process of manipulating writing in a way which makes it meaningful and useful to the child. Figure 2.3 shows what happened when Jonathan (age 4 years 1 month) signed his name on a thank you note to a friend; he wrote it with the comment, "Now she will know it is me."

FIGURE 2.2 ▶   **A 4-YEAR-OLD WRITES "I LOVE YOU" FIVE TIMES**

Children's scribbles are not random; they usually represent meaning the child is recording on paper. Figure 2.4 shows the story Eric (age 3 years 5 months) wrote for his father as a Christmas present; it was given with the instructions that "I'll read this to you when you are ready." Eric had internalized that print, even the scribbled variety, conveys a message.

Clearly, children are interested in "writing" from an early age and, if given the opportunity, will explore ways to convey messages in print.

FIGURE 2.3 ▶   **"SIGNATURE" OF A YOUNG CHILD**

WRITING SAMPLE FROM A 3-YEAR-OLD ◀ FIGURE 2.4

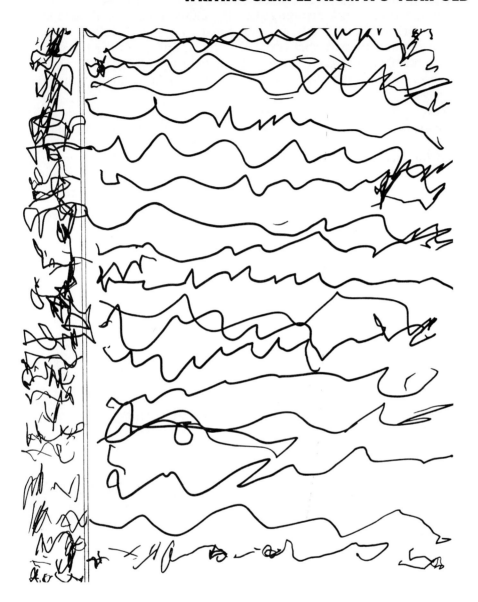

LITERACY LEARNING IN SCHOOL SETTINGS

In the school curriculum, students learn best what they want to learn. The teacher's task, then, is to work in ways that create in each student the desire to know and the desire to act on knowledge. Teaching with this orientation is the art of improving students' sensitivity to their human and physical environment so they can see more, hear more, feel more—discover the extraordinary in the ordinary—and then communicate their thoughts with clarity, enthusiasm, versatility, and exactness.

Most students do not learn something before they have developed an interest in it through personal experience. Some degree of meaning must be present before new meanings can be added, especially those meanings that are technical or come from printed materials. We, therefore, take advantage of natural curiosity that is present and operating all the time. Teachers must remember that each student has a natural language—divergent as it may be—and that new language learnings must be related to that natural language.

Because of the wide range of natural language abilities expressed in an assortment of dialects, it is impossible to propose a standard program for the development of basic literacy at any grade level. Rather, it is the responsibility of the teacher to be familiar with the wide range of classroom possibilities. No matter what skills and abilities are emphasized or what experiences are introduced, teachers should help each student to develop competence in several areas:

▶ Communicate effectively with others in many ways.

▶ Succeed in those tasks involving speaking and writing in daily living.

▶ Compare and contrast personal ideas and language with those of others.

THE BOOK ▶
MAKERS

KEITH BAKER

1. Which book of yours has given you the greatest pleasure?

Who Is the Beast? More people identify with the tiger than with any character I have created. The tiger was able to make peace with all those who were afraid of him.

2. Which book has surprised you most in terms of its public reception?

The Dove's Letter. More people than I ever imagined tuned into its message of love and hope—and that includes a lot more boys than you might first imagine. I thought it would be seen largely as a folktale, but its message has adapted well to the needs of a '90s audience.

3. What would you like people to remember about your work?

I want people to say that my work made them stop and think, that it moved in them an emotional response.

4. What impact do you hope your work will have on children?

I want my work to help people see one small part of the world in a different way from the ways they have viewed it before.

In each of Keith Baker's books, the reader will find clues and secrets hidden among the rich textures and lush colors of his illustrations. His works include *The Dove's Letter, Who Is the Beast?, The Magic Fan, Big Fat Hen, Hide and Snake,* and *Elephants Aloft.*

▶ Add pleasure to life through such activities as reading, writing, storytelling, choral speaking, pantomime, singing, dancing, and painting.

The best classroom environments for literacy learning in school settings are the ones modeled after principles of natural learning. Holdaway (1986), in studying how children learn before schooling, established the principles of sharing and doing as being critical in school literacy programs.

Sharing involves the teacher displaying the desired skills (reading, writing, and publishing) to the children. Holdaway writes that observing the skilled behavior in the teacher, with "absorbing curiosity and desire," leads the learner into participation.

TEACHER ROLES

1. Demonstrating authentic skill—sharing personally loved literature and engaging in reactions to it.
2. Inducing and rewarding participation.
3. Sharing skill—reading and writing with the children—showing how it's done (Holdaway, 1986, p. 67).

PUPIL ROLES

1. Observing and emulating—enjoying teacher's literacy.
2. Engaging in response to test with teacher and peers.
3. Participating as a skill user.
4. Identifying personally with the skill (Holdaway, 1986, p. 67).

These activities usually take the form of reading and writing to and with the students. Teachers choose from a rich range of literature the books that both they and the children deeply enjoy. Using enlarged print enhances the communal impact of the literature and provides the opportunity for participation without threat of embarrassment. The teacher also writes and "publishes" for and with the children. Song, chant, dance, and mime contribute to the wholeness and vigor of the experiences.

Doing involves "hands-on" experience. Students have the desire to master the skill or act, and want to practice it in realistic ways. The practice is usually chosen, controlled, and paced by the learner.

The confidence that results from this role playing, and the feeling of belonging in a print culture, result in a desire to perform. Such natural performance takes two forms: (1) attempts to use the skill in "real" or purposeful ways to the limit of current competence—or beyond; and (2) attempts to share, to gain approval, to "show off"—especially to the model or bonded people being emulated (Holdaway, 1986, p. 67).

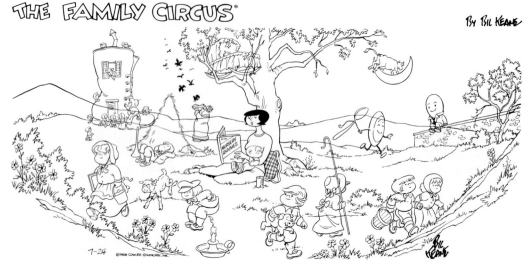

Reprinted with special permission of Cowles Syndicate, Inc.

TEACHER ROLES

1. Providing support, encouragement, and suggestions.
2. Acting as an appreciative audience.
3. Observing, recording, and responding to individual need ("diagnosing").
4. Managing the environment.

PUPIL ROLES

1. Role playing as reader, writer, meaning maker, publisher, and so on (includes word processing).
2. Accepting self-regulation as reader and as writer—self-correcting.
3. Exploring meanings through related arts.
4. Learning skills through instruction and practice.
5. Reading and writing for friendly audiences—teacher, peer(s), or class (includes drama, mime, puppetry, book illustration, murals, etc.) (Holdaway, 1986, p. 67).

EXPERIENCES: THE FOUNDATIONS OF LITERACY

The experiences a child has in life form the child. What we experience creates the base for interpretations and extension of our own ideas and the ideas of others.

Piagetian theory is based on life experiences as the very foundation of thinking (Piaget, 1959). This theory says that spontaneous curiosity can be deadened or hindered in certain environments in which children grow—at home and especially at school. The theory, in addition, holds that spontaneous curiosity must be nourished if children are to reach an operational level of thinking when involved in the school curriculum. In *Piaget for Teachers*, Hans G. Furth (1970) summarizes much of what Piaget has to say on this topic:

> Assuming that many children who come to school are intellectually impoverished but still have enough internal motivation to grow intellectually—as is shown by the fact that their intellects will continue to grow with or without school—what, in effect, is the school offering the child? This is the message that he [or she] gets: "Forget your intellect for a while, come and learn to read and write; in five to seven years' time, if you are successful, your reading will catch up with the capacity of your intellect, which you are developing in spite of what we offer you." Mark well these twin conditions: learn reading and forget your intellect. These things go hand in hand. . . .
>
> (Furth, 1970, p. 4)

Some clarification of the dilemma suggested by Furth is available for teachers through a definition of primary reading abilities as the term is used at the Claremont College Reading Conference (Spencer, 1970).

Spencer explains that letters and words are maps for ideas but not ideas in themselves. These symbols must be linked to meanings that have origins in direct experiences. These concrete experiences must precede or accompany the reading of symbols. Spencer terms this environmental reading *primary reading*, and states that it is foundational to successful *secondary reading*, or the reading of printed materials.

> We must provide for and make use of primary reading both as a way of behavior and as a source of meaning and of judgments of significance. Word symbols are impotent to supply these. Consequently, a program for reading development which is concerned only with skills of word recognition and the analysis of word patterns is inadequate.
>
> (Spencer, 1970, p. 16)

Children feel a sense of accomplishment in being able to "read" in their environment and from their experiences. They come to understand through repeated emphasis that most of their life experiences require the reading of primary sources and that some of them require the reading of secondary sources—the reading of printed materials (Spencer, 1970).

Primary sources are among the nonalphabetic reading that children encounter normally and naturally. These sources include numerals in many forms and in many places, such as clocks, dials, and price tags. They include the reading of maps and graphs and also the reading of meaning into photographs and paintings.

All children need to experience primary reading as a part of school programs, but it is essential that children who are slow to read the language represented by alphabetic symbols have repeated opportunities to do so. The reading must be a recognized part of the school program. It must be

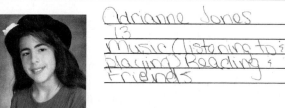

Name *Adrianne Jones*

Age *13*

Interests *Music (listening to & playing) Reading & Friends*

What do you like most about school? That's really a hard question since I like everything! I suppose I mainly like to learn & be with friends, though.

What's your favorite subject? Why? I don't have a favorite subject, I like them all. Math, because it's so exact. Reading & writing, because I enjoy them so much. Soc. St. because it's a lot of fun to learn about history & so far, I've been very lucky to have exclent teachers.

Science, because I love to work "hand & science is the only place where I really get to do that.

What's your favorite book? Why do you like it? I have a lot of favorite books, but right now I'm reading Rebecca. It's very good & I like it because, first, it's writen well & it's just a terrific book!

What advice do you have for teachers? Be more exciting! Really, you don't learn unless you remember. I don't remember unless I have fun learning. Do creative things after all you only get one chance for an education and so you, the teacher, make it a fun, memorable one.

important enough in day-to-day operations for children to feel a sense of reading achievement when they participate in the activities. Teachers must feel that primary reading sources are major sources for language acquisition. They must experience over and over the fact that language grown from primary sources is useful in lessons and activities requiring the reproduction of language represented by the alphabet. It is folly to pretend to study science and social studies with students who have not had experiences verbalizing their personal responses to their natural environment, to their sensory impressions, to numerals and numbers, and to some of the graphic aids that are helpful to them in solving problems.

RESPONDING TO THE NATURAL ENVIRONMENT

All children who enter school have had experiences reading signals in their natural environment. Some of them follow.

WEATHER:
Is it hot or cold?
Is it wet or dry?
Is it windy or calm?

PLANTS:
Are they large or small?
Are they green or brown?
Are they for shade or for food?

ANIMALS:
Do they have fur or feathers?
Are they domestic or wild?
Do they hop, run, or fly?
Do they communicate with people?

WATER:
Is it running or still?
Is it dirty or clean?
Is it liquid or frozen?

AIR:
Is it clear or polluted?
Is it moving or still?
Is it warm or cold?

EARTH:
Is it wet or dry?
Is it rocky or sandy?
Is it farmed or forested?

Most experiences in life have a relationship to the reading process. They give meaning to reading. These experiences increase interest in reading and create a need to read printed materials. However, students in most schools have been made to feel that reading is simply a subject to be studied, not a dynamic process that brings pleasure and meaning to life.

A young scientist ▷
studies animal
life.

Students are usually willing to do the things necessary to learn the skills associated with reading and do not complain they are being denied primary reading experiences. In contrast, in a meaning-centered curriculum, reading is focused on the experiences students encounter in nature and in their environment.

Students who view their world and respond to it through language or writing must be able to read nature's signals and must possess the necessary vocabularies to translate their experiences into communication units that share their feelings with others.

Students encounter references to nature in literary selections so frequently that a knowledge of nature from experience is required for a high level of comprehension. Fortunately, the things of nature are available to all. Travel may be required for extended experiences, but the most basic experiences are local to all and need only to be recognized as a major source for language acquisition.

RESPONDING TO SENSORY IMPRESSIONS

Sensory impressions provide information from experience that we use to recall and apply meaning when we read. Basic to the whole idea of a meaning-centered approach is the notion that reading is accelerated by the continuous experience of communicating in many ways what we see, hear, touch, taste, and smell. Sound–symbol relations are strengthened by verbalizing sensory impressions apart from the printed symbols used to record those impressions.

SIGHT

Color, size, and shape are among the impressions gained through sight. There is an unlimited variety of sensory impressions, which are critical to

Dee Finley uses weather as a continuing topic to expand vocabulary and increase interest in reading. Frequently, as she reads aloud, she asks the children to listen for the first weather word the author uses. Through this emphasis she leads the children to generalize that words which tell about the weather are used frequently by authors. From this experience the children collect weather words for the Writing Center and use them to improve their own writing.

She translates the interest in weather into reading by asking children as they report on the day's weather to tell about the weather in other places. They listen to television and radio reports, use weather maps from the newspapers, and watch for news articles that relate directly to weather. Many children with limited interest in reading enjoy reading newspaper accounts and watching television coverage of weather.

Stephanie Reed uses the sky as a continuing emphasis in art. She invites children to observe the sky day after day and to try to portray it in its many colors and moods: blue with white, fleecy clouds; dark with rain clouds; lightning flashing from a huge cloud; and a rainbow bending across the sky.

She asks them to remember the sky at times when they are not at school: sunrise with a pink glow; sunset with many different colors; a full moon in a night sky; and a black sky with sparkling light from the stars.

The children make captions for their sky pictures. These include appropriate words of color, size, mood, and movement. They read nature's signals as they increase their vocabularies in meaningful ways.

Jesus Olivares projects filmstrips with no captions to increase the use of the vocabulary of the senses. He shows the filmstrip once with no comment. During the second showing, children talk in groups of two or more about what they see and feel in connection with each frame. Jesus encourages them to extend their imaginations to possible sounds and smells. They talk about the texture of things they see. They talk about the taste of things. If there are characters in the filmstrip, children follow up with a group story or individual stories that include every frame. The emphasis on sensory response usually results in talking and writing that includes sense words.

communication in the arts and sciences. Thousands of words have been generated in order to make fine distinctions and to record accurate observations about them. Most of us make these verbal distinctions hundreds of times each day, yet some children come to school with little oral vocabulary in these areas of description. Nonalphabetic reading *must* precede relating the sounds of words to the alphabetic recording of those words.

CLASSROOM VIGNETTE

Maria Hernandez has a collection of photographs and paintings on the same or similar subjects. She includes animals, people, houses, mountains, trees, automobiles, and landscapes. Some are very realistic. Others are abstract or give only a faint impression of realism. Some are full color, and others are black and white. Some may be answers to questions in the mind of the viewer; some may seem to ask questions of the viewer.

The pictures are used to stimulate discussion about how each of us views the world in unique ways. According to the way we see things, we respond with words that tell the color, size, shape, and relation of objects or ideas. In order to communicate impressions, many sense words are required. Maria listens and records words used by the children. The lists go into the Writing/Publishing Center for use during creative writing and into the Game Center as resources for making word games that give practice in sight recognition and spelling.

Color, size, and shape concepts are fruitful in developing figurative language because many of the words and ideas are so common that new and uncommon ideas can be initiated through comparisons. Some of these ideas are illustrated by:

as green as new grass

cardinal red

small as a tiny ant

an X-shaped design

pointed like a pyramid

Jeannie Seaberg provides practice in the concept of size by helping children to arrange objects according to size—books, rocks, blocks, and other objects. Children choose one set of objects and then arrange them from the smallest to the largest. As they talk, they gain practice in seeing the size of things in relation to the size of others. Some of her arrangements call for the use of words such as *small, large, short, tall, long, wide,* and *narrow.*

SOUND

Reading of print is a natural result of understanding the relation of the sound of language (talking and listening) to the alphabetic recording of the sounds (writing). Prior to and during the reading of print, children need opportunities to expand and refine their awareness of sound and to talk of the sensory impressions that are derived from sounds.

SMELL

Sensory impressions relating to smell are not as critical in building language meaning for reading as are some of the others, but they are a part of life experiences and include a vocabulary that is repeated over and over.

The vocabulary of smell is available in many places and for all children. Flowers and food have odors that may be familiar to many children, but the children may not have words to communicate what they smell.

CLASSROOM VIGNETTE

Megan Mercer is an ESL teacher who has the fortune of teaching in a classroom where five different languages are spoken. Her children make tremendous gains in the acquisition of the English language because she provides many opportunities for them to use and play with language in nonthreatening ways. Opportunities include the following:

1. Singing songs in unison to give children confidence in saying words they have never said before.

2. Imitating sounds of machines, animals, and people doing things.

3. Telling and reading stories with voice changes to represent different characters and moods that children can then imitate by responding to the model.

4. Listening for rhyming words in rhymes and poems and repeating them.

5. Playing rhythm instruments and talking about the sounds they make, such as *scraping, harsh, high, low, clear, jingling, clinking,* and *muffled.*

6. Listening for the sounds in the environment and naming them as the class takes listening walks.

CLASSROOM VIGNETTE

Gina Guccini includes a vocabulary of smell words in her efforts to introduce children in her second grade to the vocabularies of sensory experiences. She does several things to provide real experiences with smell:

1. Making a collection of spice cards by brushing glue on cards and sprinkling some spice on them so children can pass the cards around and talk about the odors.

2. Preparing foods, such as applesauce, chile con carne, and gingerbread with spice in them so children can taste things with and without the spice.

3. Making available toilet articles, such as toothpaste, cold cream, soap, cologne, perfume, shaving cream, and after-shave lotion for children to smell and name the odors.

4. Dramatizing different smell words with facial expressions.

5. Cooking things such as popcorn that change odor in the process of cooking so children can smell them before and after cooking.

TASTE

Sensory impressions from tasting experiences occur daily, but they do not assure the acquisition of a vocabulary of words of taste that might be encountered in reading. These words can be acquired through classroom activities.

CLASSROOM VIGNETTE

Meredith Klesius has a Cooking Center in her classroom. It is an integral part of the language development program. Although she teaches some social skills as a result of the cooking activities, her major purposes are centered around language growth. Language of all the senses is inherent in cooking and eating, but the language of taste is seldom experienced for instructional purposes apart from Cooking Center activities. Meredith works to develop vocabulary in several ways:

1. Maintaining a sweet-and-sour chart on which children list words to describe the sweetness or sourness of foods they taste.

2. Tasting the same foods before and after cooking to compare and contrast tastes.

3. Tasting the same food, such as apples, in many forms—raw, and as applesauce, apple juice, apple jelly, and apple vinegar.

4. Having taste talks after school lunches to gather new words for the list of taste words for the Writing/Publishing Center or Word Wall—for example, *delicious, pleasant, yummy, tart,* and *bitter.*

5. Listening for words that tell about taste during the reading of stories and poems.

CLASSROOM VIGNETTE

Terry Hargrove helps children relate the vocabulary of how things feel to everyday life. As they experience the sense of touch and exchange words to describe it, she gathers the words for future use.

1. They touch things in the classroom—metal, wood, plaster, glass, crayons, erasers, paper—and talk about how they feel.

2. They go outside to feel things—bark, bricks, grass, soil, rocks, wire, water, mud—and say words to tell about their sense of touch.

3. They collect fabrics of different textures and mount samples for touching in the Discovery Center.

4. They make collages out of items that have interesting and unusual textures.

5. They collect words for the section of the Word Wall devoted to touch words— *scratchy, prickly, slippery, chilly, bumpy, hard, soft, gooey, waxy.* These words become a valuable resource for Terry's young authors and appear frequently in their journals and stories.

TOUCH

Our fingers can tell us as much about our surroundings as our eyes do. There is magic in the sense of touch that can release vocabulary useful in responding to sensory impressions throughout life. Vocabulary relating to the sense of touch is found throughout literature to the extent a person lacking that vocabulary is at a disadvantage in responding to the meanings intended by authors.

SUMMARY

A miracle occurs during the early years of life as children begin to make sense of the world about them. They respond to the love and language of others from birth. They learn language because they have a need to communicate with others.

Writing and reading rapidly become important to children as they seek to extend their knowledge and influence. Meaning-centered teachers are aware of how children learn before they come to school and incorporate these principles of early learning into the classroom.

Literacy instruction should be centered on the life experiences the children have had and on present experiences that can be used to facilitate literacy growth. The classroom teachers featured in this chapter are good examples of caring, enlightened teachers who demonstrate holistic and natural literacy instruction in their interactions with students. Their classrooms are pictures of the internalization of language arts.

PATHWAYS TO READING LIFE EXPERIENCES

The students read nature's signals and interpret meanings from:

- ► weather
- ► plants
- ► animals
- ► water
- ► air
- ► earth

They read sensory impressions and have vocabulary to interpret personal meanings from impressions from:

- ► sight (color, size, shape)
- ► sound
- ► smell
- ► taste
- ► touch

CHAPTER
▶3

PATHWAYS TO THE LANGUAGE-ARTS PROGRAM

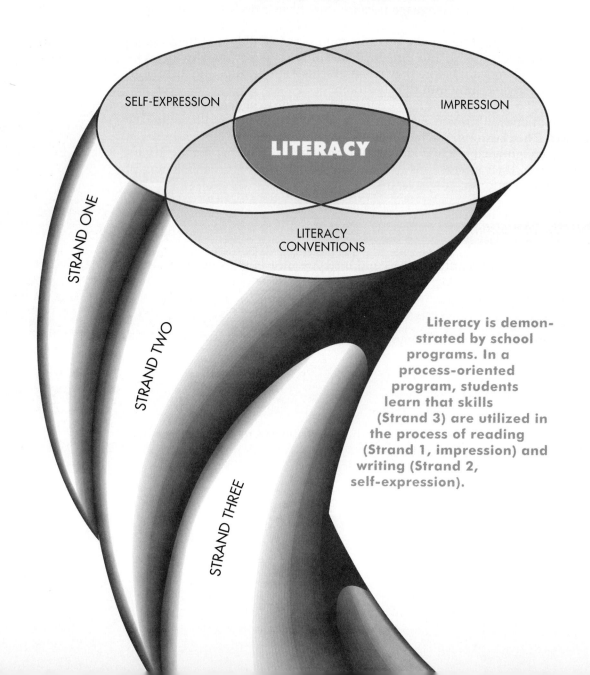

SELF-EXPRESSION

IMPRESSION

LITERACY

LITERACY CONVENTIONS

STRAND ONE

STRAND TWO

STRAND THREE

Literacy is demonstrated by school programs. In a process-oriented program, students learn that skills (Strand 3) are utilized in the process of reading (Strand 1, impression) and writing (Strand 2, self-expression).

CHAPTER OUTLINE

PATHWAYS TO PONDER

....

▶ **WHY IS IT IMPORTANT FOR CLASSROOMS TO FEATURE VARIANT TEACHER-STUDENT INTERACTION PATTERNS?**
....

▶ **WHY IS IT IMPERATIVE THAT PARENTS UNDERSTAND THE PROCESS-CENTERED PROGRAM?**
....

▶ **HOW CAN PROFESSIONAL ORGANIZATIONS HELP SUPPORT YOUR TEACHING?**
....

These are exciting times for American teachers. The educational reforms of the 1990s are leading to schools that are free to implement the types of programs the professional teachers at each campus deem best. Thus we see many different management schemes being implemented, such as the multiage classroom. In this chapter, we look at instructional planning and organization. We examine Tom Wrightman's Oregon classroom and Randy Methven's New York classroom. We look at different patterns of grouping—whole class, small groups, and teacher as resource. We consider the benefits of the multiage classroom. We examine ways we can better inform parents about our programs. The chapter closes with this question: What are the pillars of the language-arts program? Of all the things teachers do in the name of language arts, which ones really matter? Hold on tight—we are off to an exciting examination of the process classroom.

Process-centered classrooms of today optimize opportunities for students to communicate. Through classroom organization, we can increase each child's possibilities for communicating. The possibilities are countless: listening to others speak and reading the "talk" of others; appreciating the authorship of others; painting and understanding both the ideas and feelings of others who have painted; and reading both orally and silently to interpret the ideas and feelings of authors.

The goals of the meaning-centered approach can best be achieved by using various methods and materials (1) to help each child experience communication in a variety of situations, (2) to relate the communicated ideas of others to personal experiences, and (3) to study the aspects of communication that produce refinement.

Highly structured programs can stifle true growth because they devalue the personal language of the learner in favor of language from outside sources. It is important, therefore, that anyone who uses a meaning-based approach understand some of the fundamental requirements of planning and organization, although no one can tell another *exactly* how to develop a meaning-centered curriculum.

Each teacher must come to grips in a personal way with several classroom elements:

► the basic philosophy
► the literacy transaction model
► the classroom organization
► the use of many types of materials

A classroom that promotes communication balances like a mobile in constant motion. For every emphasis on creative self-expression, there is a balance of refining specific skills that enhance communication. For every product of the individuals in the classroom, there is an influence from outside sources that reflects excellence.

WHAT DOES A PROCESS CLASSROOM LOOK LIKE?

Students' communication skills are developed through numerous activities, experiences, and strategies. To increase the chances of success for more students, every teacher must know and use many ways of involving children in the language arts. One tool is the *instructional schedule,* which provides time for the teacher and students to explore and learn together.

Let's look at the classroom of Tom Wrightman, a third-grade teacher in Bend, Oregon. Figure 3.1 depicts his daily schedule.

CLASSROOM VIGNETTE

Tom Wrightman believes the most important function of the teacher is to establish a sense of community in the classroom. Therefore, Tom sets his classroom up in such a way that children are constantly interacting. As you see in Figure 3.1, he starts the day with music. Language arts is the total morning focus. From singing together, children move on to poetry. They write in free form modes as well as patterned poetry modes like we discuss in Chapter 7. Tom's language core, which begins at 9:15, incorporates a potpourri of whole-language strategies. Children work on individual activities, read silently, listen to tapes in the listening center, and meet in small focus groups. After recess, children continue the language core. Monday and Tuesday are devoted to literature patterns (see Chapter 7) and class books that support the current thematic unit (see Chapter 15). Wednesday's encounter is with literature (see Chapter 14); Thursday and Friday are devoted to writer's workshop (see Chapter 8). At the end of the day, children record what they've learned into their learning logs; they then finish the day by reading chapter books.

Math is a special focus in Tom's classroom. Children solve problems with manipulatives and examine multiple solutions as math is presented as a natural attribute of life. Children's books are used to present math concepts and patterns as Tom brings math and language arts together.

Throughout the day, science, health, and social studies content is integrated into the language core. Tom believes children learn content through meaningful holistic activities. His students demonstrate that they learn language-arts skills the same way.

Tom is a successful teacher because of the trust he has in the abilities of his children. He simply creates an environment where literature, art, music, math, and storytelling are daily pathways that carry children to literacy and learning.

FIGURE 3.1 ▶ **A THIRD-GRADE CLASSROOM**

SAMPLE DAILY SCHEDULE

8:00–8:45	**ARRIVAL (Morning Business, Personal Projects)** *The goal is personal contact during this time.* *Soft music is playing during this time.*
8:45–9:00	**SINGING and PLAYING WITH POETRY**
9:00–9:15	**SHARING STORIES (Daily News)** *READING BOOKS—Author Studies, Theme-related (SSR)*
9:15–10:15	**LANGUAGE CORE** *Individual Literacy Activities, Math Words,* *Assigned Readings, Listening Center, Independent* *SSR, Focus Groups: small/large-phonics in context*
10:15–10:30	**RECESS**
10:30–11:15	**LANGUAGE CORE continued** *Monday and Tuesday—Literature Patterns, Class Books* *related to theme of study during this time.* *Wednesday—Literature-related activities* *Thursday and Friday—Writing Workshop*
11:15–12:00	**LUNCH/RECESS**
12:00–12:45	**MATH** *12:00–12:15 Problem of the day (soft music)* *12:15–12:45 Small/Whole Group activities*
12:45–1:15	**MUSIC/P.E.**
1:15–2:15	**SCIENCE/HEALTH/SOCIAL STUDIES CORE**
2:15–2:30	**RECESS**
2:30–2:45	**LEARNING LOG (soft music)** *Summary of the day's events for LEARNING LOG*
2:45–3:00	**CHAPTER BOOKS (children come to rug when finished)**
3:00–3:15	**CLOSING BUSINESS and SINGING**

It should be noted that Science, Health, and Social Studies are also integrated topics throughout the Language Core in the morning.

Now we move to the classroom of Randy Methven, a first-grade teacher in Long Island, New York. We look at the physical arrangement of his room (Figure 3.2); but, most importantly, we examine his philosophy of teaching and learning.

PHYSICAL ARRANGEMENT OF A FIRST-GRADE CLASSROOM ◀ FIGURE 3.2

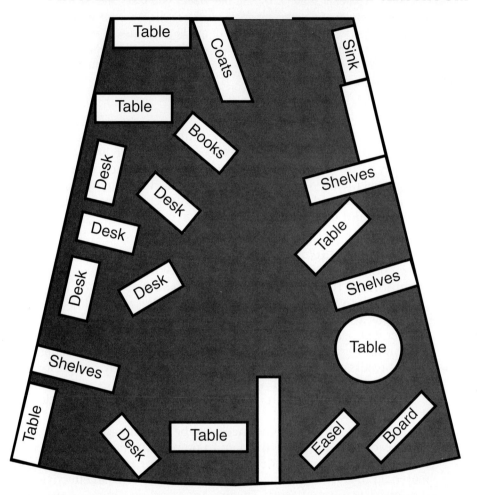

Continued

CLASSROOM VIGNETTE

Visiting Randy Methven's classroom is like visiting Disney World—the environment is permeated with joy and excitement. One of the first things you notice is the openness—not merely in the physical arrangement, but in the spirits of the children. The next thing you notice is print—poems and stories are everywhere—dangling from the ceiling, on posters, even on the windows. You can read about how Randy invites children's interactions with print in Chapter 14. Last spring, Bill Martin Jr visited Randy's room, and was so impressed with the print-rich classroom that he features Randy in our children's literature chapter (Chapter 14).

Randy believes that child-centered classrooms require space for children to work collaboratively. Thus he has arranged his room with groupings of desks and tables that allow for group work (see Figure 3.2). He has also rearranged time blocks because he believes teachers need to look at the day as a whole rather than as small segments of time. During the week, you'll see Randy interacting with his students in the following modes and strategies: (1) reading together; (2) shared book experience; (3) sustained silent reading; (4) guided reading; (5) individualized reading; (6) language experience; (7) children's writing; (8) content area literacy; (9) evaluation; and (10) sharing. We tell you about these strategies throughout this book.

Now that we've looked at these two classrooms, let's think about your room. What kind of environment can you construct? We believe that what you create has to fit your personality and ways of interacting. The components and arrangements you choose are up to you. However, in our studies of classrooms, we've noticed that the most successful classes include the following components and practices:

1. **Read to the class every day.** Reading to students is basic reading instruction. They must have an opportunity to hear the way hundreds of authors say things. The ability to listen to other people's language is prerequisite to any level of silent reading.

   Various arrangements can be made for oral reading. Frequently the teacher will read to the total class. Students must view the teacher as a *reader* if they are to profit from reading instruction by that teacher. Skills in oral reading should be illustrated over and over by the person who is sharing those skills with students.

   Other arrangements can be made. The teacher can invite older children from the intermediate grades to specialize in oral reading to younger ones. These students need not be the highest achievers, however. Teachers can work with them to prepare the reading before meeting with the younger students. Some reluctant readers of sixth-grade material profit from reading simple stories and poems in effective ways. Readers' Theater and Story Theater are excellent activities that highlight both reading and listening abilities. For examples of Readers' Theater scripts, see Appendix H.

2. **Guide the students in reading or reciting in unison.** Students love to join voices through choral reading, responsive reading, unison reading, and singing.

   Choral reading is essential for the development of confidence in oral reading. Students need coaching in voice modulation, pause, emphasis, stress, and pronunciation. These abilities can be illustrated and practiced in choral reading situations without embarrassing individuals.

   Big books are especially good for use with younger children. The enlarged type and illustrations make it possible for an entire class to see the book, just as a single child sitting in a parent's lap sees a regular-size book. Group or responsive reading of big books builds confidence.

Unison reading prior to individual oral reading assures children that they can say the words. It also builds a background of meaning impossible to acquire from poor oral reading.

Singing songs provides an opportunity to build rhythm into reading. Chants also have rhythm helpful in reading and can be learned in unison reading and reciting.

3. **Discuss topics of interest with students.** Deepening sensitivity to people and events is an ongoing goal of a meaning-centered approach. Students must be encouraged to talk about the things they observe, hear, and read about. They must hear words they have never heard before if they are to extend reading vocabularies. Students cannot reconstruct printed words they have never heard. How can they hear an increasing number of words without discussion on topics of interest? How can they be expected to comprehend through silent reading something they cannot understand through discussion?

   Helping students see the relation between discussion and silent reading are times in which students are invited to add their thinking to topics, interact with the thinking of others, argue, change points of view with new information, prove points with facts, and seek other information to substantiate positions. Through activities like the Author's Chair (Chapter 6), students come to view an author as an absent person who has something of interest or importance to say. They develop interest in trying to carry on a discussion with a person who is present only through print. As in a live discussion, the reader will agree and disagree, like and dislike, be happy and sad, accept and reject, expand and abandon. To ask most students to develop these sensitive, personal skills *only* through silent reading and follow-up activities is to relegate many to failure.

4. **Tell stories based on real and imaginary experiences.** Telling a story calls for important reading skills. It requires an understanding of sequencing of events, portraying character, establishing setting, and organizing plot. A child who has mastered these abilities will probably have less comprehension difficulty in silent reading than one who has not had a chance to explore these abilities in informal ways.

   When a meaning-centered approach is used, there must be time and opportunity for oral composition of stories in addition to the sharing of events and the discussion of topics of interest. A teacher or a child might tell a story and let other students act it out in pantomime. One child might tell the beginning of a story and let several children give personal endings.

   A tape recorder may be used to record stories; occasionally one of them might be transcribed and published as a book for the library.

5. **Read with individual students each day.** Reading with individuals and small groups is a continuing opportunity for the teacher to demonstrate ability and interest as a participating reader rather than as a monitor of students' reading. During individual conferences the

teacher can arrange to read a sentence, a paragraph, or a page alternately with the student. This interaction between the two and performance by the one is reflected in greater achievement and more interest in improvement. The experience can result in meaningful follow-up activities for the student.

Students who write and publish books should be honored by having the teacher read the book with the author. Prior to a scheduled reading to the whole class by the author, the teacher can demonstrate effective presentation strategy that may or may not be imitated by the author when reading.

6. **Value art as an expression of feelings and ideas.** In a meaning-centered approach, art expression is essential at all levels. Young students paint so they can have reading experiences. Painting is a part of reading. This concept is in contrast with classroom organizations in which students are permitted to paint if they finish their work and have been quiet. Painting breeds thinking. The germ of an idea that emerges at an easel or with other art material can be expanded through talk, can be written once it is said, and can be read once it is written. Art expression materials are as essential in intermediate grades as in primary grades. Students need to feel they can express their ideas in many ways and with many media. Many student authors illustrate their writing. Some team up in an author-illustrator combination. They continue to view art expression as a way of saying things to others, and they come to see the relation between different types of writing and different types of art.

Abstract paintings might be compared with nonrhyming poetry. In both instances the producers invite the viewer or listener to bring personal thinking and experiences to the work, to add to it, and to interpret it. They leave room for self in their work. This concept is an essential skill in the interpretation and reflection of reading done silently. It is doubtful the skill will ever mature through silent reading alone.

7. **Promote publishing projects.** An essential ingredient of a meaning-centered approach is a continuing program of publishing the work of students, who can form a publishing company for the purpose of producing newspapers, magazines, and books. In addition to the jobs of authors and illustrators, they assume responsibilities for editing, proofreading, making layouts, binding, and distributing the products. Some classes have been very successful in projects of writing and illustrating books for young students to read (see Chapter 8).

Students should have frequent opportunities to read their own writings to the entire class, to small groups within the class, and to other groups in the school. The child who is reading personal writing is using material that is easy to read because he or she wrote it. Nothing is new in the content. Thus attention in oral reading can be devoted to clarity of expression, effectiveness of presentation, interpretation, punctuation, and other necessary details that make listening to oral reading a pleasure.

Motivation for improving language form and usage comes as students' writing is read by others. Pride in published works stimulates young authors to seek language forms that will be understood by others. They are also influenced by what they read and what others read to them.

As students express their own ideas, they may become interested in finding out, through reading, what other people think and say about topics of interest to them. Wide reading, in turn, can stimulate individual authorship.

Teachers must remind themselves continually that *the way a child feels about herself or himself and reading is more important than any method or material.* To be an author and to understand processes of publishing builds strong links between a child and the authors he or she will come to know and respect.

8. **Use multisensory materials.** Language skills are extended and ideas are refined as students listen to tapes and records. Hearing a variety of people talking and reading can help students develop an ear for varied speech patterns.

Filmstrips without words printed on them can be used over and over as guides for students' language development. The teacher shows the filmstrip, shows it again a frame at a time, and lets students make the commentary on what they see in the pictures. Several versions are made, and then one of them is taped to use with the filmstrip. The accompanying recording, if there is one with the filmstrip, is played only after the students have invested much of their own thinking and oral language in making a commentary.

INTERACTING WITH YOUR STUDENTS

COOPERATIVE LEARNING

Teachers in process classrooms recognize that children learn best when they learn together. Learning together is the essence of a movement that is sweeping American education—cooperative learning. Cooperative learning is defined as "the instructional use of small groups so that students work together to maximize their own and each other's learning" (Johnson, Johnson, & Holubec, 1993, p. 6). One key word in that definition is *maximize,* for research has shown that as students collaborate with each other they improve in content knowledge (Slavin, 1987), and experience increased productivity, self-esteem, and intrapersonal skills (Johnson, Johnson, & Holubec, 1993). As students have the opportunity to work with other students to achieve a goal, their learning is enhanced as they share understanding and knowledge (Vygotsky, 1978).

Note another component of the definition of cooperative learning: "Students work together to maximize *their own* and *each other's* learning." Therefore, this definition of cooperative learning is based on the principle that "when you win, I win" or that "we are all in this together." When this mode

Melanie Sudderth — Name

13 — Age

I like nature. Plants — Interests
and Animals, mostly

What do you like most about school? I like the learning experience
the most, because I like to learn new things everyday.
I have the chance that some people don't have.

What's your favorite subject? Why?

I love Science, because I get to learn about the
parts of plants and animal. I also like learning about
the human body, I learn about what happens
to your body if you have a disease. I just like
Science.

What's your favorite book? Why do you like it?

I think my favorite book is Anne Frank, The Diary
of a Young Girl. I like because, when you read it, you
can picture what it was really like. In some way,
you can see what they were going through and
what Anne Franks family and friends had to go throug

What advice do you have for teachers?

My advice is never give up and never stop trying
because someone needs you, you can make
a difference in a childs life.

of learning is operating in a classroom, all children have the opportunity to utilize their strengths and be "winners." This is in contrast to the competitive principle of "I win, you lose" that is found in many traditional classrooms where some children are classified as "high achievers" or "winners" and others as "low achievers" or "losers" (McDanial, 1984).

With this definition in mind, we can see that cooperative learning can be useful in a variety of ways in the process classroom. Cooperative groups can be used in writing, peer editing, implementation of comprehension strategies, researching and reporting, thematic studies—in actuality, any activity where active participation, sharing of ideas, and risk taking are desired.

IMPLEMENTATION OF COOPERATIVE LEARNING

Cooperative groups can vary in size; however, a general rule of thumb is "the smaller, the better" (Johnson, Johnson, & Holubec, 1993). Typically, groups range from two to five based on how old the students are, how much familiarity the students have with cooperative group work, and how many students are needed for the particular assignment (Lindgren, 1986). When planning for cooperative groups, it is important to consider the goal or goals of the group, the task or tasks the group is to complete, the relationships or interdependence between the group members, and the roles or responsibilities of the members within the group (Vacca & Vacca, 1993).

Let's examine some of the considerations just listed and their importance in the implementation of various cooperative learning groupings. The goal of the group must be made clear. Let's look at the cooperative learning activity of jigsaw, which requires each child to become an "expert" in his or her assigned area and then teach the information to the rest of the group (Aronson, 1978; Hotchkiss, 1990). Jigsaw groups are comprised of three to six members, depending on the number of subtopics or themes in a reading selection, topic, or study. Each group member is assigned or chooses one of the subtopics to become an "expert" in. After the group members have had time to read the material, decide on the important areas, and plan how they will "teach" the material to their peers, each member takes a turn in teaching "his or her part of the puzzle" to the other group members. In order for this strategy to be effective, the children must understand that the goal of the group is not only for each group member to learn the information he or she is presenting, but also to learn the information presented by the other group members. In order for the group to succeed, all members must succeed.

The students must understand the steps in the cooperative learning structure. For instance, an activity such as Think-Pair-Share (Kagan, 1990) involves two students who first silently think about their own responses to a question or issue and secondly share their ideas with each other and discuss the reasons behind them. Formulate-Share-Listen-Create (Johnson, Johnson, & Bartlett, 1990) is a comparable structure that can involve more children. Here are the steps: (1) Silently think about your own response to a question or issue; (2) Take turns sharing and listening to responses of group members; and (3) Work together as a team to formulate a new response that can be shared with the class. Although these may seem like simple procedures, their effectiveness is diminished if students do not follow the procedures of engaging in individual thought time first and then moving into sharing. Therefore, it is helpful if the teacher models the steps of any cooperative learning procedure with a small group before the entire class tries it. As the children become accustomed to noting the steps to the procedure and then adhering to the format, their experiences in cooperative learning will be enhanced.

As we mentioned earlier, the interdependent relationship of the group is critical. The members of the group must understand that the philosophy of the group must be "you win, I win" or "we are all in this together." The teacher may observe the groups to determine if they are engaging in the project or procedure as a group. Individual team building activities, such as deciding on a group name and exploring interests to determine commonalities, can be conducted. In addition, the group should realize that both individual and group accountability are important.

For instance, when students are involved in a group investigation (Sharan & Hertz-Lazarowitz, 1980; Sharan & Sharan, 1990), the complexity of the structure requires each group member to contribute to the group. The steps of a group investigation are as follows: (1) Identify the major topic of study;

through brainstorming and group discussion identify subtopics; identify re-search/investigation groups for the subtopics; (2) Research/investigation groups meet and determine job responsibilities for group meetings; decide what parts of the subtopic they plan to investigate; decide how and who will research the various parts (in pairs, individually, etc.); determine deadlines; report decisions to teacher; (3) Investigate the topic, which includes daily meetings to determine progress and revise assignments; (4) Organize to pre-pare for final report includes meeting with the teacher to determine the best way to present the findings to the class; plan individual's contributions to the final presentation; devise the final report; (5) Present the final report to the class and solicit reactions from the class; (6) Self-evaluation and group evaluation are conducted by the group members; individual research report, group research report, individual presentation role, and group presentation are evaluated by the teacher.

As you can see, success of this cooperative learning structure depends on the participation and commitment of all group members. If one member of the group is not participating or progressing, problem-solving strategies must be used to draw the person into the interaction of the group. Perhaps this is one of the most important components of cooperative learning; children have the opportunity to develop intrapersonal skills as well as content skills.

One step that seems to aid in all members participating in the group is to be sure the roles and responsibilities of all group members are defined and to determine that each group member has a responsibility. Here is a list of sample roles and responsibilities:

Reader: reads instructions and materials to group.

Recorder: writes down important information generated by the group.

Summarizer: verbally organizes the important information generated by the group so the Recorder can write it down.

Materials Handler: collects and distributes all needed materials for group work.

Timekeeper: monitors the time and keeps the group on task.

Reporter: presents group's information to whole group (if desired, this is a role/responsibility that can be shared by all members of the group).

Praiser: supplies support and confirmation to group members so they are encouraged and continue to participate.

Interactive Listener: restates or rephrases what has been said.

Spy/Explorer: searches for new and additional information from other groups.

Inspector: makes sure everyone in the group understands the concept and what is going on in the group.

Please note this is a sample list. Roles can be combined—such as Reader and Materials Handler—or deleted—such as the Spy/Explorer. Roles should be based on the needs of the group and the particular assignment. However, as we noted before, it is very important that each group member have a role or

Pre-K teacher Paula Witt effectively uses cooperative learning with her 4- and 5-year-olds. When introducing a unit on dinosaurs, she distributes models of dinosaur bones to the children and tells the students they are going to have an opportunity to Think-Pair-Share. The students have engaged in the activity before, so they join in with joy as Paula begins by saying, "You have a chance to be a detective. Look at the bone you have. Think about the dinosaur that had a bone like this. What does this bone tell you about the dinosaur? Can you tell if it moved quickly or slowly? How? Can you tell how big it was? How? Can you tell what type of food the dinosaur ate? How? What other information does this bone give you? How did you figure it out? Which dinosaur do you think it was, and why?

"You will have four minutes to think and five minutes to share. Each person has one minute to share observations and then you can discuss. The person who has the smallest dinosaur bone will share first." While Paula sets a timer for four minutes, the children take their bone samples and move quickly to their mats on the floor and sit back to back for their "think" time. When the timer buzzes, the children turn around and face each other, and the child with the smallest dinosaur bone begins to share the information gleaned from the examination. When the timer buzzes, the other child begins to share. When the timer buzzes again, the children begin to discuss their bone samples, contrast and compare, and make new discoveries. At the conclusion of the sharing time, the children have the opportunity to share with the large group. Children volunteer and share many observations because they have already "tried out" their ideas with a peer in a small, nonthreatening group situation.

Charles Jones uses marathon writing to bring closure to a unit on weather with his fourth graders. Children number off to form groups of four. Charles hands each group a different shape of cloud with its name written on it, such as cumulus or cirrus. Charles then instructs the children to think about all they have learned about that particular type of cloud, such as how it is formed, what type of weather usually occurs when they see that cloud, if it is a common or uncommon cloud and why, why it has that name, and any other information they can think of. The children are given one minute for "think" time and then are told to get out a sheet of paper. Each child starts writing about his or her group's cloud. Then "time" is called and the paper is passed clockwise to the next person in the group. Students are given a short period of time to read what has been written, and then they write again, but this time they try to continue the train of thought started by the first writer so the paper will be coherent. Charles calls time again, and the process is repeated until the fourth and last writer has the paper before the paper returns to its originator. Students are instructed to read the paper and bring it to closure during this writing period. When "time" is called to stop the writing, students return the papers to the original writers. They then share the papers and decide which one they would like to share with the class. Charles finds that this part of the procedure is extremely valuable as children compare and contrast ideas and the presentation of those ideas. He often gives the group an opportunity to revise a paper and include "the best" from all of the selections. As children refine their writing about the subject, their content knowledge is increased.

JERRY SPINELLI

1. Which book of yours has given you the greatest pleasure?

Space Station Second Grade. To some extent it was autobiographical, and it took me back to my own junior high experience. I can remember laughing out loud as I wrote. I had written four other books that nobody wanted, and I was pleasantly surprised both that somebody wanted to publish it and that it was received so warmly by readers.

2. Which book has surprised you most in terms of its public reception?

Maniac Magee. I wrote it first for myself. It was my first book not in first person, not written in a kid's voice. I thought it might appeal more to big people than to little people because of the sentence structure and the vocabulary. But I underestimated the children. All kinds of children, of all ages, have told me how much they loved it.

3. What would you like people to remember about your work?

I want people to feel like they have gotten in touch with themselves and with others through reading my books.

4. What impact do you hope your work will have on children?

I have envisioned a different impact for each book. They were written first as stories, but second as lessons. But overall, I hope my books promote a general understanding and sympathy with all kinds of people.

The voice rings true, the incidents are genuine, and the fun never stops in Jerry Spinelli's novels, which include *Maniac Magee,* the *Bathwater Gang Series,* and the *School Daze series.*

responsibility. The most effective way to ensure a member feels important and maintains interest in the group is for that member to have a well-defined role to fulfill.

These vignettes illustrate cooperative learning in action. We believe the keys to the success of the current whole-language movement reside in two factors: (1) Teachers are teaching with children's literature, and (2) Cooperative learning permeates the entire social and organizational structure of the classroom. Throughout this text you'll see examples of children working together and learning together in small groups. Cooperative learning theory is the driving force behind our desire to have children work together in groups. But the reward goes beyond the immediate success of cooperative learning classrooms. The most exciting aspect of cooperative learning is that children are acquiring valuable skills they'll use the rest of their lives—the ability to work with others.

HETEROGENEOUS OR HOMOGENEOUS GROUPING?

One of the worst mistakes made by literacy programs in the past was grouping students by ability. Such a school practice—one that usually made reading achievement the *measure of success* in the early grades—highlighted lack of success and usually destroyed the child's self-image as a reader rather than improving his or her reading skills. Instead of homogeneous grouping, we recommend flexible grouping. Flexible groupings emphasize students' success and accepts the fact that every child is different and has different strengths and knowledge levels in different areas. Groups should constantly be changing as activities change—in membership, in size, in focus.

Learning situations must be organized in ways that permit children to view themselves and others as worthy and successful. They must experience working alone, working with other students of similar ability, and working with those whose abilities are significantly different from theirs. They must have repeated opportunities to interact with groups and with the total class. Heterogeneous grouping arrangements are vital to this end. The multiage classroom, which we now discuss, is perhaps the best means of ensuring this diversity in groups.

WHAT ABOUT MULTIAGE CLASSROOMS?

Multiage instruction, or classrooms comprised of children of varying age levels, is not a new concept. Rather, the one-room schools that existed through the middle part of this century were the original multiage classrooms. The one-room school has not returned, but its best feature—multiage groupings—is back. Throughout the United States, school districts are grouping children across age ranges (Kasten & Clarke, 1993). Why are they doing so? There are numerous benefits; let's consider four:

1. **The multiage classroom is more reflective of society.** Only in schools do we divide people up according to age. In neighborhoods, children don't play together according to what age they are. Rather, they join together because of proximity or interests. Throughout life, humans have to communicate and get along with diverse ages. Why not practice this skill in school?

2. **The multiage classroom is more developmentally appropriate.** It's impossible to narrow a sequence of skills that children are expected to attain to one grade level. The philosophy of the multiage classroom is that children will come to primary school, stay three or four years, then move on to intermediate school. The mad rush to cover the curriculum of the grade is avoided. Parents don't have to answer the tough question "Should our child repeat first grade?" Instead, there's time to develop, time to explore, time to learn.

3. **The multiage classroom is like a family.** As we discuss throughout this text, children make more progress when they are in friendly, nonthreatening environments. Children become comfortable with their room, their teacher, and their classmates in the multiage classroom. They form deep friendships and really feel "at home" at school.

4. **The multiage classroom allows teachers and children to stay together for three to four years.** Traditional schools lose so much time starting the school year, getting acquainted, ending the school year. Multiage classrooms avoid these starts and stops; hence

momentum is not lost and learning can continue. Teachers have a better overall view of the children because they can know them better, and they can track their progress over a longer period of time.

PROGRAM PLANNING

Program planning for a meaning-centered approach is enhanced by a few basic guidelines:

1. Select activities from all three strands (Chapter 1) for each planning period. Plans may be on a daily, weekly, or other time basis. Over a month or six weeks, plan to extend learnings through different strand activities. Details of the three strands are found throughout this book; they include explanations, examples, and pathways to literacy development.

2. Plan for flexible groupings to meet the needs of students in the total class setting, in small groups, and for individual exploration. Every day there should be opportunities for students to participate in a total group activity and to spend time on individual interests. Most of the small group activities emerge to meet special needs felt by students or identified through teacher-pupil conferences. The same activity, such as a computer simulation, might be used for the total group one day and then be available in a learning center for individuals and small groups over several days.

3. Activate learning centers that best serve the language concepts being emphasized. Five or six learning centers usually serve the needs of a class, but more can be activated if their purposes serve the goals of the instructional program. Some centers such as those involving art, reading, and writing are used most of the time, but materials in them need to be changed to keep them fresh and meaningful.

4. Select evaluation procedures appropriate to the objectives of the instructional program. Informal checklists can be created. Evaluation devices already in place, such as anecdotal records, work samples, and student self-evaluations may be used. Personal conferences can be used to evaluate progress for many of the objectives. (See Chapter 11.)

The program planning chart (Figure 3.3) illustrates a way of recording decisions for a program. It can be duplicated as it is or enlarged to include other items. A collection of plans for a year's work becomes a valuable professional resource that can be shared with other teachers. It also serves as evidence of program development in any study of accountability.

PARENTS AND THE LANGUAGE-ARTS PROGRAM

Communication between parent and teacher is always important. However, in a meaning-centered curriculum this importance is magnified. The role of

PROGRAM PLANNING CHART ◄ FIGURE 3.3

Name_____ Class_____ Dates _____ to _____

Theme or language emphasis:_____

Activities from the Three Strands	Classroom Organization*			Notes	Evaluation ‡			
	TC	SG	I		1	2	3	4
SELF-EXPRESSION								
IMPRESSION								
CONVENTIONS								
OTHER ACTIVITIES								

* TC - Total Class
SG - Small Group
I - Individuals

‡ 1. Anecdotal Records
2. Checklists
3. Work Samples
4. Student Self-Evaluation

Program Planning Chart

the parent as an active participant in the child's learning is greatly enhanced when parents are made aware of the goals of the program and are provided with suggestions concerning ways in which to aid their children in meeting those goals.

Many teachers have found it useful to have parents come to school early in the school year. During this visit, parents may meet the teacher and other parents and receive an overview of the language-arts program. This overview is especially important in a program that allows children to explore language and writing. Differences between a child's edited and unedited work may be explained and the importance of encouraging the child's exploration of language and writing stressed. Through these discussions, teachers can convey important information to the parents about the need for educational support in the home. For example, parents will come to understand that the child will be hesitant to read and write at home if the parent assumes the role of a critic rather than that of an encourager (Erickson, 1989).

CLASSROOM VIGNETTE

CLASSROOM VIGNETTE

Cherry Ward is a primary teacher in Queensland, Australia. Her classroom is the perfect example of a process-oriented classroom. She teaches through thematic units (she's the co-author of our chapter on thematic units in this text) and believes the key to the success of a program lies in good communication.

In addition, Cherry frequently sends letters to parents in which she shares what their children are learning and how they may help their children at home. Here's a copy of the letter she sent to parents to explain the grading system:

Dear Parents,

This folder will be used for the whole year. Inside the cover is a record sheet to show you what the homework is, and to remind me of what I sent home. Please use it for two-way communication whenever necessary. For example, you might want to tell me that your child loved reading a book to or with you and that you would like to have it sent home again. Or you might want to tell me of a problem of some kind. Don't feel that you must write a comment every night.

Please return the folder with contents each day. Don't keep the book (or other activity) at home as we may need it in class the next day. Please initial and date the sheet each night. This lets me know that the book (or other) was used and I will change it. I often prepare the folders at lunchtime when the children are not around for me to ask whether the homework was done. Your initials save me lots of time.

Homework on Tuesdays will be sharing a library book with you. Children will need a cloth library bag for taking their book home. The library book can be kept home for one week, so it can be read several times.

On Wednesdays, children will bring home diaries to share with you. To foster the idea of writing for communication, I write a comment or ask a question each week. Encourage your child to respond in writing too. Remember that young children are just beginning the long but exciting road to writing and can't be expected to write with 100% accuracy! "Words under construction" is a good way of thinking of spelling in early writing. I would love you to write a further comment on the diary page. On Tuesday mornings, you might like to discuss what they might write about in their diary that day.

Children will also bring home books to read. They will work at different levels. Some children may already be reading independently. Many of the younger ones will have memorised the text and may seem to you to be "not really reading". This is a very important and natural

Continued

Letters to parents help parents understand your program and the work children do in your classroom. It's good to tell parents face to face about your classroom, but it's even better to put it into writing in the form of a letter.

Parent conferences throughout the year keep the lines of communication open between the parent and teacher. Conferences should be a sharing of stage. In this case, you can ask your child to show you the word that says ". . .", or cover a word and ask what it starts with, or ends with, or talk about other letters in words, words that start the same way, etc. If your child is tired or unwilling to read, or if a book seems too long, take turns reading a page each, or have your child point as you read, or follow along as you point. The important thing is that you enjoy your time together. If it is not fun, stop. Don't be concerned if your child brings home a book two or more times. Favourite books are great for developing readers. And don't be concerned if a book is "not hard enough". Children enjoy a range of books and some of those that they enjoy are at a difficulty level lower than that at which they are capable of working. At school, children are engaging with a range of books from caption books and highly predictable books to complex informational materials. Please come along and talk with me any time you are concerned about home reading. We want our children to be joyfully literate.

At times a homework sheet will be sent home. I would like you to help your child with the activities shown on these. I do not expect that children will do them alone. One of the purposes of these sheets is to give you a glimpse of what is going on at school.

On the back of the folder is some more sharing work. Some children have poems to share and possibly memorise; a song to have fun with; and the days of the week to read, recite and later write. And there are some numbers you can have fun with. You may help your child find the number pattern, chant them, say the ones that come in between, or even halve them. Other children have the alphabet written out in the school's handwriting style. There are lots of games you can play with this sheet. It is helpful if your child gets to know the letters and associates them with the words written. Cover a word up and ask what it starts with, sing the alphabet song together as your child points, ask for other words that start with a given letter, etc. Use the proper names for the letters. This should not be a drill, but a short time of fun. Even if the contents of the folder have fallen out by the port rack there is still some homework on the back that you can do together and enjoy!

The first couple of years of school are exciting as we watch the development of our young learners. I look forward to a happy and productive year's partnership with you as we work together with your child to make this year the best it can possibly be.

Kind regards,
Cherry Ward

information between parent and teacher concerning the child's home and school progress. Such meetings provide a valuable opportunity to discuss the "at home" versus the "at school" child. Many times the child who the teacher deals with at school is different from the child the parent sees at home. It is important for the parent to be aware of this difference, and it is vital the

THE POEM ON MY PILLOW

I felt very small
And the house was dark
But those cookies kept calling from
  the kitchen
So I tiptoed downstairs
And peeked around the corner
To made sure there were no
  monsters.

Then I saw my dad,
Alone at the kitchen table
With an open book
And a pencil and paper.
He wrote very carefully,
Then he stopped and listened . . .
And he smiled.

This morning I found this poem on
  my pillow

*To the Little Boy Who Hides
I listen for your breath while you
sleep.
I follow your footsteps across the
floor above me.
I hear the creak of wooden steps as
you tiptoe down,
And I feel your fear of darkness.
Oh little son,
You need not hide from the night,
Speak out!
Your courage will make light.*

When I read the poem I thought:
My gosh . . . he heard me!
Was he angry?
Did he think I had been bad?
Then I noticed how he signed the
  poem:

*To my Son . . . with love . . from
Dad.*

teacher know as much as possible about the child at home (Routman, 1988; Seaborg, 1994).

In addition, a class newsletter is a useful communication tool. The teacher of primary grade children may want to develop a newsletter that gives a brief synopsis of the week's events and a preview of "coming attractions." A grade 3 example is provided in Figure 3.4; a grade 6 example is found in Figure 3.5.

A suggestion for an at-home activity that would correlate with the instructional activities of the class is usually welcome. For instance, a teacher might explain that the ability to match things is an important readiness skill. A parent could aid a child in developing this skill by allowing the child to participate in household activities such as matching socks when folding laundry, arranging groceries that are alike on a shelf, stacking plates and saucers that match, or sorting silverware. The teacher could include suggestions for simple matching games, such as saving labels from groceries that are frequently used and stacking them or matching them with items on the grocery storage shelf in the home. The child could also go on a grocery shopping trip with the parent and match the labels to items on the grocery shelf.

A THIRD-GRADE NEWSLETTER ◀ **FIGURE 3.4**

MR. B'S GRADE 3 NEWS
VOLUME 1, ISSUE #6   MAY/JUNE 1988
SPECIAL SCIENCE FAIR ISSUE

MOTHER'S DAY ♥MESSAGES♥

Hills are pretty
And sweet
And you are sweet,
Just like them
And you remind me
Of a beautiful city.

I LOVE YOU
YOU LOVE ME
WE LOVE EACH OTHER
WE DO, TOO!
I LOVE YOU,
YOU KNOW THAT.
DO YOU LOVE ME?
TELL ME THAT.

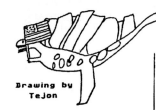

Drawing by
TeJon

FLAGOSAUR by Kai & TeJon
Once upon a time
There was a Flagosaur.
It was a weird, woolly,
And wonderful Dinosaur.
And it had
Eleventy-four
Red, white, and blue
Wings to soar.
And it always sang
The Star-Spangled
Banner-saur.
Flagosaur
Went to a store
And bought lots of pots
With polka-dots.
Then he got
Lots of shots
For his spots
Which turned out to be
Dino-pox.

FIELD DAY EVENTS

CHUTE DOGIN' By Damon
    I liked it when the cowboys were wrestling the steers and they couldn't throw the steers down on the ground. They didn't get a time or a ribbon, but I liked to watch them.

Drawing by Chad

PIG CHASE By Kathleen
My brother Christopher caught a tail of a pig. The pig pulled and pulled and jerked and Christopher pulled and pulled. But when the pig jerked, Christopher let go. When he came back, we made up that if he did get a pig, he would give it to our Mom for Mother's Day.

TRACTOR RIDE By Olaina
    My brother rode on a tractor and got first place. But he gave the ribbon to the people that had the tractors. He rode in the parade and got another ribbon. It was white and fourth place.

WHAT'S INSIDE

The teacher of intermediate and middle grades may also want to incorporate students' work into the newsletter. This gives students a practical opportunity to utilize their writing and editing skills and guarantees parental interest in the newsletter.

Students can work alone, in pairs, or in groups to write stories concerning activities in the classroom. Book reviews are appropriate. Some students may

FIGURE 3.5 ▶ **PAGE ONE OF A JUNIOR HIGH NEWSLETTER**

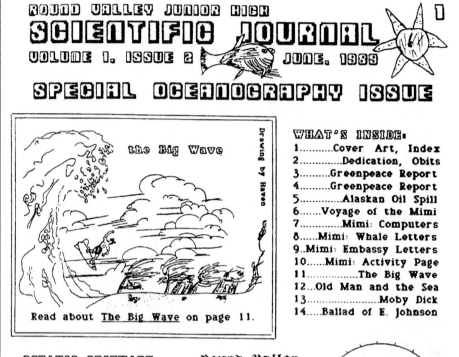

ROUND VALLEY JUNIOR HIGH
SCIENTIFIC JOURNAL
VOLUME 1, ISSUE 2   JUNE, 1989
SPECIAL OCEANOGRAPHY ISSUE

The Big Wave

Drawing by Haven

Read about The Big Wave on page 11.

OCEANIC OBITUARY
MR. SEA OTTER
by Shane, Rustin, & Jason

Mr. Sea Otter died because of an oil spill in Prince William Sound. He was 62 years old and liked to fish and catch clams. He is survived by a wife and two kids and many grandchildren. His burial will be at 3:00 tomorrow at Prince William Sound Memorial Cemetery.

(More "Ocean Obits" on page 2)

Round Valley
Junior High
P.O. Box 276
Covelo, Calif.
95428

Drawing by Beau

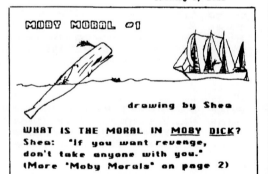

MOBY MORAL #1

drawing by Shea

WHAT IS THE MORAL IN MOBY DICK?
Shea: "If you want revenge, don't take anyone with you."
(More "Moby Morals" on page 2)

want to contribute short stories or samples of their art. Other ways to maintain contact with parents include telephone calls and notes sent home to parents. The teacher should be sure these communications do not always convey negative information. Parents enjoy hearing from teachers when good things happen.

Teachers should be aware that, in addition to the formal feedback the school provides, parents are constantly receiving information concerning the literacy program from their children. Students' attitudes toward reading, writing, and other language activities provide one of the most powerful messages the parent receives. Homework and the attitude toward homework convey vivid messages concerning the language-arts program. If parents constantly see an uninterested and discouraged child with numerous ditto sheets that involve fill-in-the-blank activities or with numerous definitions to look up, a distinct message is conveyed about the instructional program. However, if the child is involved in assignments that require creative thought and the use of verbal, reading, and writing skills, the parents receive a different message. For example, a child might have the assignment to interview his or her parents concerning the television or radio programs the parents enjoyed as children. The completion of this assignment would require using language-arts skills in the context of an enjoyable activity and would make a positive statement about the program.

A classroom in which parents are welcome to visit enhances communication. Although the parents' work or the rules of the school means that teachers may have to plan these visits in advance, the key is that parents know they are welcome in the classroom. Many teachers involve parents in assisting with instructional activities or learning centers. In a learning environment extra help is always welcome.

NATIONAL COUNCIL OF TEACHERS OF ENGLISH LANGUAGE-ARTS GUIDELINES

One more valuable resource merits mention. The National Council of Teachers of English (NCTE), in an effort to improve elementary language-arts programs, has compiled a set of assumptions, aims, and recommendations for teachers to consider as they strive to improve curriculum. These guidelines are included in Figure 3.6 to stimulate thoughts and ideas for teachers who seek to integrate the entire curriculum with language-arts activities.

PILLARS OF THE LANGUAGE-ARTS PROGRAM

The Information Age is upon us. With this explosion of information and technology, the world of today will be obsolete tomorrow. As we move to process instruction and as we learn more about how children learn, we must decide how our classroom time will be used as we drop many past practices and add new ones. Because decisions are being made so hurriedly, we'll close this chapter with pillars that will support your literacy program regardless of what happens in the Information Age. Technology will change, but human nature and human learning principles will not. Certain pillars will support learners. These pillars can be trusted for anchoring plans and procedures.

Here's what we know about children and how they learn. We provide six statements about literacy learning and their corresponding pillars.

FIGURE 3.6 ▶ **NCTE ASSUMPTIONS, AIMS, AND RECOMMENDATIONS FOR LANGUAGE-ARTS PROGRAMS**

ASSUMPTIONS

1. The language arts (reading, writing, speaking, and listening) are inextricably related to thinking.
2. Reading, writing, speaking, and listening are social and interactive.
3. Learning is a process of actively constructing meaning from experience, including encounters with many kinds of print and nonprint texts.
4. Others—parents, teachers, and peers—help learners construct meanings by serving as supportive models, providing frames and materials for inquiry, helping create and modify hypotheses, and confirming the worth of the venture.
5. All students possess a rich fund of prior knowledge, based on unique linguistic, cultural, socioeconomic, and experiential backgrounds.
6. Acknowledging and appreciating diversity is necessary to a democratic society.

AIMS

1. To empower students
   — as lifelong learners whose command of language is exemplary and who gain pleasure and fulfillment from reading, writing, speaking, and listening.
   — as active inquirers, experimenters, and problem solvers who are able to use the arts of language as a means of gaining insight into and reflecting upon their own and others' lives.
   — as productive citizens who use language to take charge of their own lives and to communicate effectively with others.
   — as theorizers about their own language and learning, able to read, write, and reflect on texts from multiple perspectives.
2. To empower teachers
   — as active learners who serve as coaches, mentors, and collaborative creators of learning experiences rather than as dispensers of information.

   — as decision makers in every aspect of schooling.
3. To integrate the arts of reading, writing, speaking, and listening throughout the curriculum.

RECOMMENDATIONS

The child and learning are at the center of any discussion of what English studies should be or how English should be taught. At the most general level, elementary schools aim to help children develop into competent, knowledgeable, and self-confident language users. Such children *learn about* language; they *learn how* to listen, speak, read, and write; and they *learn why* language and literacy are central to their lives.

The following recommendations for curriculum and for classroom practices and materials guide teachers, administrators, teacher educators, policy makers, and others who strive to build exemplary elementary school language arts programs.

Curriculum

1. Base the curriculum on sound research in child growth and development, psychology of language and literacy, language and literacy acquisition, as well as work in learning theory and the teaching of language and literacy.
2. Emphasize both content and process in the curriculum. The language arts curriculum is concerned both with what students need to know and with what they are able to do. Process is taught in a holistic way, stressing skills as part of an overall process, not in isolation or as ends in themselves. In a similar fashion, the content of the language arts curriculum does not focus on particular facts, lists of literary works or characters, rote definitions of literary terms, or isolated language or literacy facts. Rather, content gives meaning to language arts instruction by providing an idea-oriented curriculum.
3. Link listening, speaking, reading, and writing in the curriculum and make them a focus of every subject area.

4. Recognize that commercially published materials provide only suggestions and should not become the curriculum.
5. Design assessment so that teaching and testing are brought together in ways that help teachers teach.
6. Develop curriculum within school communities of teachers and students.

Classroom Practices and Materials

1. Strive to create a community of readers, writers, and learners in the classroom.
2. Make literature the center of the curriculum. Literature serves as a springboard for reading, writing, speaking, and listening.
3. Build voluntary reading habits among students by providing opportunities and motivation for reading various kinds of extended texts (e.g., novels, informational books, biographies, magazine and newspaper articles) in class and for continuing such reading at home.
4. Create a library in every classroom. The classroom library promotes positive reading habits and attitudes, and it complements the role of the school library and public library in building literacy.
5. Teach writing from what is known as the process approach. Help students build strategies for planning their writing, for composing, for revising, and for editing and proofreading.
6. Promote writing by providing opportunities for students to write for a wide variety of purposes and audiences and by making available a wide variety of writing materials and media.
7. Include in the classroom materials that promote language and literacy use through drama, art, and multisensory activities. Examples of such materials are props and scripts; a variety of artifacts, animals, and plants; and various tools, models, and collections.
8. Use textual and other materials that reflect the characteristics and diversity of society. In this way all children can connect with the world of literacy.
9. Use time in flexible and fluid ways that enable students to engage in a variety of language and literacy activities for real purposes. Especially important are extended blocks of time that allow the teacher to weave the various aspects of the curriculum into a rich fabric.
10. Use flexible grouping patterns that enable whole-group, small-group and one-to-one work. Create student groupings that enable interactions among all members of the class for various purposes and in a variety of settings.
11. Recognize in planning activities and in selecting materials that the student is ultimately a constructor of his or her own knowledge and skill. To construct language and literacy knowledge and skill, students should have many opportunities to observe a variety of uses of language and literacy; to interact with the teacher, other adults, and peers in language and literacy activities; and to engage in reading, writing, speaking, and listening on their own.

The English Coalition Conference

Assumptions, Aims, and Recommendations of the Elementary Strand

Compiled by William H. Teale, Julie M. Jensen, and Janie Hydrick on behalf of the English Coalition Conference/Elementary Strand: Carol S. Avery, Rosalinda B. Barrera, Rudine Sims Bishop, Fredrick Burton, Donna Carrara, Mary M. Kitagawa, Mary M. Krogness, John C. Maxwell, Vera Milz, Diane T. Orchard, Faith Z. Schullstrom, and Susan Stires.

NCTE National Council of Teachers of English
1111 Kenyon Road, Urbana, Illinois 61801

1. **The single most influential factor that contributes to success in beginning literacy—writing and reading—is the level of language the learner brings to the tasks involved.**

   This fact about language and learning was the only point of widespread agreement to result from an international conference on language acquisition and early reading (Allen, 1985). Linguists, psycholinguists, psychologists, and educators from 22 countries from around the world agreed the most important educational variable for success in literacy activities was the extent to which teachers based instruction on the personal language of their students. This development can be influenced by computer technology, but literacy development remains an interactive process between children and caring adults in the home and school.

   PILLAR: Keep an interactive learning environment available for students so their personal language can grow strong enough to communicate some of what they learn as knowledge becomes more and more accessible. Don't depend on technology to do this.

2. **Understanding doesn't necessarily result from knowing how to read. The process requires interaction of personal meanings with those inherent in the text.**

   The text alone does not hold the meanings. Literacy researchers have conducted extensive research to examine comprehension in the reading process. The data from this research reinforces what is already known: It is impossible to teach just the "how" of reading. Reading, therefore, cannot be taught by system and technology alone. Computers and word processors can serve learners in a multitude of ways to refine and expand literacy skills, but they cannot do the job without personal involvement.

   PILLAR: Learners must be involved in the process of thinking *with* authors. To do this effectively, they must have opportunities to expand their base of experiences with all types of computer technology and electronic media, including television and video. They must be released from the idea of "correct answers only" to appreciate that, as readers, they have the responsibility to agree, disagree, accept, reject, and modify the ideas gained from reading. Then they must be allowed to record and refine their own thinking through the writing process.

3. **Direct instruction in "how to read and write" as the primary mode is of limited, if any, value. The development of reading and writing ability is more an art form than an assembly-line process.**

   To be effective in our efforts to improve literacy in general, and reading and writing specifically, teachers must function as artists as well as scientists. The "how" of gaining literacy in our society is a very personal matter. Although each learner is ultimately alone in crossing threshold after threshold, the teacher will help unravel the mystery of becoming literate.

PILLAR: Teaching is the art of raising the learner's levels of sensitivity to both classroom and outside environments. Can the learner see more, feel more, say more, imagine, extend, extrapolate, synthesize, analyze, and generalize? Can the learner do these things with increasing depth of perception that can be communicated in ever-maturing and more effective language? The First Grade Reading Studies resulted in one basic conclusion: The *teacher* makes the difference with the use of any method or any material (Bond & Dykstra, 1967). This fact will remain true in the Information Age of education.

4. **We know that exact replication of text as the major goal of instruction is questionable.**

Meanings and influences derived from reading are not required to be an exact replication of the text, for it is a waste of teacher time and energy to overstress such literalness. Instead, retelling in one's personal language and with one's personal knowledge is essential.

PILLAR: Teachers must use a variety of meaning-centered methods and a great array of books and materials to meet the personal requirements of learners. The teacher, administrator, school board member, or parent who tries to impose "one best" method or computer program on all learners is out of step with the Information Age in education. The complexity of developing literacy in our society requires variety.

5. **Literacy must permeate the environments of our students.**

Classrooms must be full of many sources of literacy encounters: books by professional authors and student authors, magazines, pamphlets, and computer software. Reading and writing activities must be integrated into every period of the school day, not just during reading and language-arts periods. Can we expect students to become literate if we focus on literacy during just the language-arts period in school? The answer, of course, is no. Literacy activities and responses must permeate the day. Students should be engaged in reading and writing as a part of all content studies. These interactions should be frequent and should take many forms—magazines, novels, brochures, technical materials. Rote study of skills denies students an opportunity to engage in the actual process of reading. Gambrell (1986), for example, reports that students spend only minutes per day doing actual reading in school.

Literacy should permeate the home environment of students, too. Teachers must communicate to parents the vital nature of the role model parents play as readers and writers. As we've discussed, schools can help by sharing information about literacy with parents and by involving children in active library programs. Parents are especially valuable when they agree to spend time with their children talking about the books and stories they are currently reading.

PILLAR: Any literacy program that depends on a rote learning process lacks meaning to the learners. Meaning requires multiple approaches and literacy interactions. Technology can support and extend some of the approaches, but they cannot supplant human interaction, which is necessary for language to grow and become useful.

6. **We know that learning situations must be designed so each student will be challenged as a person to acquire the skills and knowledge necessary for performing literately.**

   Personal discipline in any learning experience is a mark of growth toward self-direction and maturity. It is in this area that computer support may have its greatest value. Immediate feedback is possible at the personal level. Resources that formerly had to be sought out in books are now available with the press of a button. The ease of text editing on the computer helps students understand the editing process better.

   PILLAR: Independent, creative self-expression is a major goal in effective literacy programs. A real danger in the use of worksheets in our schools is that students will gain their major satisfactions from giving an endless round of *someone else's answers* to questions they did not ask. What would be better training for successful living in an authoritarian society? To preserve freedom in every aspect of life, our children must be able to ask questions, seek solutions, and communicate what they know and believe in effective and accurate ways. This pillar has no place for authoritarian-oriented procedures. It is one that is centered, first of all, in the valuing and use of each student's language. Effective writing accompanies meaningful reading as students mature toward creative self-expression. In the Information Age, each student should be able to communicate personal ideas as a free person at the same time as assimilating others' language and concepts.

While other pillars for literacy development exist in the Information Age, several of the more important ones have been reviewed which will assure effective programs that

- ▶ are based on the learner's language and experiences;
- ▶ reflect goals of a society that values creativity and divergent thinking;
- ▶ include learning experiences that generate productive thinking, allow freedom of expression, stimulate individuality, value ingenuity, and satisfy curiosity;
- ▶ promote personal satisfaction in acquiring ever-maturing and more complex skills and knowledge.

SUMMARY

Literacy programs must be built on the language strengths that students bring to the classroom. Teachers are the key to good programs. They must value the language of students, possess an understanding of how oral and written communications evolve, and view language learning as an integrated process.

Teachers must operate as professionals, balancing state or district requirements with student needs, capitalizing on students' interests, and using their professional judgment wisely as they seek to integrate all of these needs into the curriculum. Such teachers take advantage of every opportunity to release students to discover the beauty of language. They do not think of students as belonging to a certain grade level or age group. They become familiar with the range of abilities described throughout this book. To this they add their knowledge and abilities in personal communication, their experience as people and as teachers, their judgment, and their observations of individuals and groups who communicate effectively.

PATHWAYS TO THE LANGUAGE-ARTS PROGRAM

The teacher:

▶ structures the learning environment to help ensure success for every learner.

▶ carries topics or themes throughout the day in order to keep instruction in context.

▶ works with children one on one.

▶ works with small groups of children.

▶ communicates clearly with parents.

▶ builds the program on language-based pillars.

FOUNDATIONS OF LISTENING AND SPEAKING

▶4 PATHWAYS TO INTEGRATING LISTENING EXPERIENCES

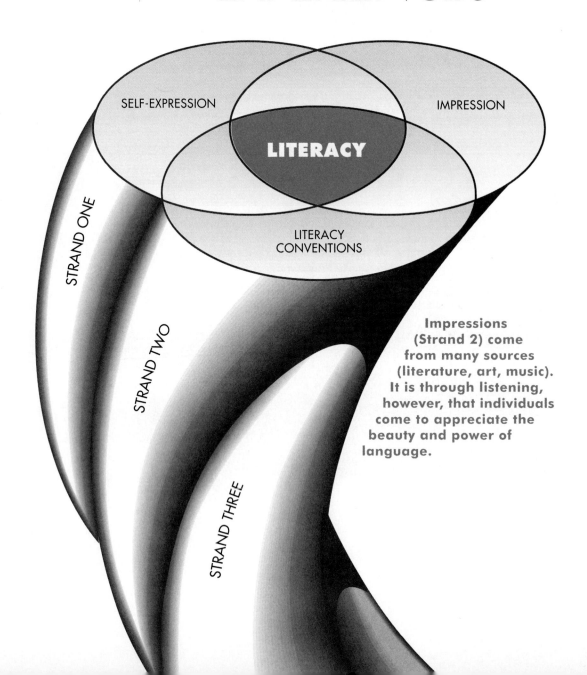

SELF-EXPRESSION

IMPRESSION

LITERACY

LITERACY CONVENTIONS

STRAND ONE

STRAND TWO

STRAND THREE

Impressions (Strand 2) come from many sources (literature, art, music). It is through listening, however, that individuals come to appreciate the beauty and power of language.

PATHWAYS TO PONDER

▶ **WHY IS IT IMPORTANT FOR STUDENTS TO BE GOOD LISTENERS?**

▶ **HOW ARE LISTENING AND LITERACY DEVELOPMENT RELATED?**

▶ **HOW CAN LISTENING ABILITIES BE CULTIVATED IN INSTRUCTIONAL SETTINGS?**

▶ **WHAT IS THE IMPORTANCE OF READING ALOUD TO STUDENTS?**

A GOOD LISTENER

Listening is perhaps the most important language art. We say that because oral language and written language have their foundation in the things we hear. Yet we are immersed in a sea of sound. Moffett and Wagner hypothesized that "the perpetual sound issuing from electronic media and urban bustle numb many children to the point of simply tuning out sound" (1983, p. 79). That means it's more important than ever for schools to provide students with specific training in the skills of listening. So much of what we learn from our environment, in school and out, comes from listening. Lundsteen (1976) provides a vivid metaphor that emphasizes how heavily biased our verbal intake and output are toward listening. She writes, "It might be said that we listen to a book a day; speak a book a week; read a book a month; and write a book a year" (p. 75).

Most of us think listening is something we do automatically—it needs no training. Not so. Listening is a participation skill and can best be learned in group activities and collaborative activities (Galda, Cullinan, & Strickland, 1993). To expect children to perform properly just because instructions are clearly given is to expect what is impossible for many of them. Patricia Van Metre (1972), in expanding a work by Carol Chomsky (1969), found that both bilingual and monolingual children who were poor readers at the end of third grade were confused consistently when listening to syntactic structures that included *ask/tell* constructions, *promise/tell* constructions, *easy-to-see/hard-to-see* constructions, and many constructions that include pronouns.

Teachers use these kinds of constructions all the time. Many children who have been in school for three and four years, however, have not mastered their meanings so they can function with information gained through listening. The Van Metre and Chomsky studies confirm the long-standing concept of teachers who function as linguists. Listening to language is more than listening to words. Pitch, tone, and volume are added to the syntactic characteristics of language during discussions and conversations. Children who are not exposed to a wide range of speech will be lost when looking at cold silent print that must be brought back to life through the reading process.

KINDS OF LISTENING

Listening is not just one thing. Listening is a transactive process that involves many elements, including receiving, focusing, attending, discriminating, assigning meaning, monitoring, remembering, and responding to auditory messages (Lundsteen, 1989). The teacher must be aware of many kinds of listening if children's abilities are to mature. Many kinds of listening may be observed and included in classroom instruction:

1. **Simple listening**   Hearing sounds without interpreting any particular meaning of the sound:

   a car going by

   the ring of the telephone

Devalin Drennon encourages the children in his class to prepare programs for the pleasure of others—songs, skits, plays, debates, travelogues, art shows, fashion shows, and musical recordings with live commentary. The programs themselves are important, but so is the opportunity they afford to discuss and practice listening courtesies that are appropriate throughout life.

Rachel Patterson uses oral sharing time as a base for discussing and practicing listening abilities. Rather than repeating over and over "Let's be quiet and listen while _____ talks," she speaks with the children about facial expressions that show pleasure or boredom, body posture that indicates participation or "cop out," and quiet attention to the person sharing, or quiet attention to some other appropriate activity. The be-quiet-and-listen routine, which she tried for too long, does not satisfy her present goals of developing good listeners for participation in discussions and conversations.

Judith Edgar watches for words, phrases, and sentences that undergo obvious changes of meaning when the pitch, tone, inflection, or volume of voice is changed. She will say something and then ask the children to interpret it in many ways. She writes some responses on the chalkboard to highlight changed emphasis and meaning.

Mother is here.

Mother is here?

MOTHER is here!

Mother IS here!

Mother is HERE!

Do you think I'll believe that?

Do YOU think I'll believe that?

Do you THINK I'LL BELIEVE that?

Do you think I'LL believe that?

Do you think I'll believe THAT?

As Judith works with discussion groups, she helps them develop sensitivity to the language along with ability to grasp simple meanings.

A child's ability to profit from school experiences and participate in a social life will depend as much on listening ability as on reading and writing abilities. No direct measure of progress may be possible or even necessary, but the teacher can always help by focusing children's attention on the need for careful, thoughtful listening as a basic ingredient in learning.

birds singing

water running

wind blowing

2. **Discriminative listening** Listening to hear and identify the likenesses and differences in sounds:

high-low sounds on a musical scale

soft-loud sounds at the same pitch

long-short sounds of the same tone

words that have the same beginning sound

words that have rhyming endings

words that have the same sound in internal syllables

words that are the same

3. **Listening for information**

repeating words that tell the names of things when listening to reading

repeating facts heard when listening to stories

understanding oral directives well enough to carry them out independently

recalling incidents from hearing discussions and from listening to reading

4. **Listening to organize ideas**

ability to hear and repeat happenings in the order they were heard

ability to summarize several points in a discussion

ability to arrange points from several discussions into a new organization

5. **Listening for main ideas**

understanding the important point of a story or discussion

discriminating between major points and illustrations to support and elaborate the points

6. **Listening for varied points of view**

developing a sensitivity to the language of agreement and disagreement

interpreting tones of voice that express controversy, sarcasm, irritation, reasonableness, and perplexity

watching for basic differences in ideas when listening to discussions

7. **Critical listening**

listening to analyze the purpose of the one speaking by recognizing bias, exaggerated statements, and false connotations

listening for conflicting ideas by the same speaker

being aware of propaganda techniques, half-truths, and name-calling

A fourth grader listens attentively as her teacher shares a story.

8. **Creative listening**

   visualizing characters, settings, moods, and situations while listening

   evaluating films and recordings in terms of personal feelings

   relating ideas in a television speech and mentioned in discussions

   putting several ideas heard on various occasions into a new whole

Other kinds of listening may be more available out of school than in school. Listening for relaxation and enjoyment can be a part of school programs and should be encouraged by suggestions for radio and television listening as a homework experience. Assigned programs for pure pleasure frequently lead pupils to broaden their listening interests and abilities. Such assignments give children a set time for listening to television other than the recreational time they or their family normally chooses.

FACTORS AFFECTING LISTENING AND LEARNING

Many factors affect listening, especially listening abilities that relate to classroom settings:

- ▶ physical environment
- ▶ psychological environment
- ▶ emotional factors
- ▶ physical factors

▶ poor language development

▶ preformed opinions

▶ high intelligence

These factors can be dealt with in a meaning-centered curriculum that includes flexible arrangements, continuous change of groups, diversified materials, and individualized instruction for specific skills and abilities. Several suggestions for dealing with these factors can be made:

1. **Physical environment**

   Furniture is arranged for face-to-face contact between speakers and listeners in large-group and small-group discussions.

   Speakers stand or speak so their facial and body expressions can be seen by listeners.

   Language from sources other than people talking is provided by tapes, records, films, radio, television, and sound filmstrips.

   Good manners on the part of the audience are studied and practiced to permit listening.

2. **Psychological environment**

   Children perceive themselves as members of the total group rather than as members of an ability group for reading.

   Ability grouping for reading is avoided as a daily systematic procedure that diminishes the self-concept of children to the point that low self-concept becomes a bigger problem than poor reading performance.

   Mutual trust is promoted as the teacher participates in reading, expressing opinions, and writing on topics along with the pupils.

   Divergent thinking is encouraged to promote participation with no fear of failure.

   Alternatives replace correctness as goals during discussions for problem solving and critical thinking.

3. **Emotional factors**

   Daydreaming is utilized as a time when a thought might emerge that can be captured for a poem or a story.

   A quiet place is provided in the learning environment to allow children to retreat into private thoughts with no questions asked as long as they are quiet.

   Children with low status in a group are helped to produce something significant so they can feel like active participants.

   Home influences that might produce barriers to participation in a listening-reading experience are considered in individual conferences at which inventories of progress are discussed.

A child's unpleasant associations can be recognized as barriers to effective listening and reading so that his or her difficulties can be assessed as personal problems needing positive support rather than as poor reading and listening skills.

4. **Physical factors**

Hearing loss or limited attention span may be confused with poor ability unless listening experiences are used as clues.

Inability to sit and listen for extended periods need not be treated as a severe disciplinary problem when movement among learning areas is possible.

5. **Poor language development**

Limited personal language makes listening to the language of others difficult, so the child's own language must be expanded in order to improve listening and to permit reading skills to develop.

Impaired speech that prohibits the reproduction of sounds selected for instruction can be a limiting factor in listening to the language of others.

6. **Preformed opinions**

Children who hear what they want to hear rather than what was actually said behave quite differently in listening and reading situations from children who are open to new ideas.

Inability to integrate new ideas into previous opinions and decisions limits listening and comprehension abilities.

7. **High intelligence**

Boredom caused by uniform expectations from teachers and by materials that repeat the same material year after year can create serious listening problems in children of high intelligence.

Requiring children of high intelligence to read and listen to reading in ability groups promotes regressive tendencies in attitude and school performance.

Environments with diverse learning opportunities accommodate high intelligence in a natural and normal way.

Children who think ahead of the main ideas of a topic can be furnished an audience to hear their ideas and views.

These environmental and experiential factors require the teacher's thoughtful attention. Variety of experiences is required for the variety of abilities in listening and reading. Particular activities planned for one group or for one individual can stimulate interest in others. Activities planned for one child may extend to others who may not have appeared to be ready for them. Each child's needs, when dealt with honestly and with trust, can positively affect the other children as they all set their own personal goals for improving their abilities in listening.

Ashley Harris _____ Name

_____ 13 _____ Age

listening to music, reading, Interests
mgazines and books,

What do you like most about school?

The pep ralleys and school dances.
But most of all I love to learn and
I like to be with my friends

What's your favorite subject? Why?

Mostly History and Math.
Well math, Is fun because M.Z. Allen
Makes geometry alot of fun.
Mrs. Laws makes Texas History fascinating.

What's your favorite book? Why do you like it?

My favorite book is The Witch from Blackbird
Pond. Its thrilling and I like kathrine in
this story.

What advice do you have for teachers?

My advise to teachers

Is that make teaching fun.

DEVELOPING LISTENING ABILITIES

Listening is a major aspect of communication and, as such, is an ability that should be cultivated in an instructional setting. An *intake* aspect of communication, it requires that the sound signals be produced by someone other than the listener. Listening is an ability close to that of reading print. The chief difference is that when "listening" to the language of others during silent reading, the "listener" must have enough ego strength to "hear without sound." Subvocalization may take place and be helpful in some cases, but the transfer from listening to the sound of language to silent reading is a development in communication that requires many literary transactions.

Listening as a participation skill can best be learned in situations in which every student has opportunities for class participation. Participation is a more challenging experience than merely being quiet while someone else talks, for example, the teacher giving directions. Throughout the day the teacher can use group discussions as a means of planning, problem solving, arriving at

◀ **THE BOOK MAKERS**

LYNNE CHERRY

1. Which book of yours has given you the greatest pleasure?

The Great Kapok Tree and *The Armadillo from Amarillo.* They are both very different books but I really loved doing them both. *Kapok* was such an easy book to write—I wrote it on the train going from Washington, D.C., to Connecticut. And I had such fun researching *Armadillo* because I had to spend so much time in Texas, which, I discovered, is a really beautiful state.

2. Which book has surprised you most in terms of its public reception?

A River Ran Wild. I had thought this book about the Nashua River would be of limited geographical interest. But people discovered that it tells the story of many rivers. Life really does imitate art—people who read the book started cleaning up the rivers in the places where they lived. It was really very gratifying to me to see this happening.

3. What would you like people to remember about your work?

I want people to remember the underlying reason for my books having been written at all—as motivators for children getting involved in cleaning up the environment where they live.

4. What impact do you hope your work will have on children?

I want children to realize that they have the ability to change the world around them.

Lynne Cherry's knowledge of and love for nature are evident in her beautifully detailed illustrations. Her books include *The Great Kapok Tree, Who's Sick Today?, A River Ran Wild, The Armadillo from Amarillo, Snail's Spell,* and *Where Butterflies Grow.*

Children use ▶
listening skills
throughout the
day.

decisions, and evaluating group and individual enterprises. Each student must thoughtfully listen to the other students in order to share ideas and effectively cooperate in achieving the goal of the discussion. A meeting of minds is difficult to achieve on a mature level, and children need many opportunities to sense the satisfaction that comes when they make an honest effort to interact with others. This ability, basic to silent reading, must be developed to the point that the reader is communicating with the author.

Numerous ways of organizing a classroom assure that every student will have opportunities to participate in listening:

1. Ensure that children have opportunities to respond to plans and instructions in meaningful ways. Work toward independence rather than dependence on assignments.

2. Use a portion of each school day for planning. Help students discuss the outcomes of plans formulated in group discussions.

3. Read *with* students each day on an individual or small-group basis. Help them hear how the story goes by taking turns reading orally. Participate in terms of the needs of students. Poor readers need especially to listen to models of good reading while they are learning how to recognize printed language. Those who struggle to recognize words seldom "hear" what the author has to say.

4. Read to students and let them participate from time to time by telling what they think the author would add if she or he were present with them. Help them understand in this way that the printed part is an imperfect representation of what the author had to say. Help them feel comfortable in thinking with an author. Help them recognize that

exact replication of the printed symbols is not the only measure of good reading.

5. Listen to music selections, and discuss the ideas and feelings they get when they listen to and view films without words. Follow up with discussions of what the children heard and saw when no words were spoken. Relate this type of experience to one of silent reading when the reader has communication clues other than sounds of words as the major resource.

6. Avoid assigning silent reading of print without some evidence that the students would respond meaningfully if they were to hear the same words.

LISTENING AND READING INSTRUCTION

The experience of most parents and teachers attests to the value of reading to children. The expanding market for children's literature reflects the concern of parents that children need an exposure to language and ideas that are not indigenous to the family and community where the child lives. Interest in television programs designed specifically to engage children in language acquisition has highlighted a need for rich listening and viewing experiences prior to and during the time when children are discovering the relationship of oral language to print.

Listening to and reading the language of others are inseparable in meaning-centered programs. This union of reading with listening results from both experience and research. Research that relates listening to language with success in reading suggests that when we improve certain specific skills in listening, those same skills improve in reading (Sampson, Briggs, & Coker, 1984).

Modeling of reading with "read along" and "echo" techniques has been employed by most adults when they read to young children for years. In recent years, however, such practices have been validated through research. Trelease (1989) reports that both language and vocabulary skills are significantly improved when children listen to good books being read.

Conversely, research indicates that when children are exposed to material that is not of high literary quality—such as textbooks—they often experience vocabulary regression (Nason, 1983). Serious questions must be raised concerning classroom practices that cause pupils to have to listen to inaccurate and boring models during the learning process.

READING ALOUD AND TELLING STORIES

Reading aloud and telling stories to students are basic strategies for developing literacy. Children must hear language as it is recorded by many authors if they are to be expected to read and write language that goes beyond their home-rooted variety. It's hard to communicate with an author when reading silently if the student is faced with language he or she has never heard. Listening to the language of authors is a basic language experience teachers can implement as they read aloud to students.

CLASSROOM VIGNETTE

   David Canzoneri sets aside 15 minutes a day for reading aloud. (Occasionally he might have to extend the time because stories are not written for timed reading.) He tries to choose stories and poems that can be read in the time allotted because he feels the total effect of a story or poem is important, especially for children who are not able to read whole stories or books independently. David feels his attitude toward reading aloud will be reflected in the attitude of the students. He wants them to know he really enjoys stories and poems and that reading them is important to him. David demonstrates he is willing to forgo something else in order to have time to communicate with an author who could not be

Continued

present. He wants his students to think of him as a reader, rather than a reading teacher. David wants reading to be a communicating experience first of all, and he provides lessons for those who want to improve their abilities.

Roger Fleming uses children's literature to increase students' love for the sounds of nature. He shares *The Other Way to Listen,* by Byrd Baylor and Peter Parnall, a beautiful story about an old man who was so in tune with nature that he could literally hear rocks murmuring, hills singing, and wildflower seeds bursting open (photo on p. 88). His students then write their own verses about nature's sounds—sounds they have heard or sounds they wish they could hear.

Dorothy Fielder believes that listening to good models of reading by the teacher who works with children on reading skills is so important she follows a checklist of procedures to assure a good situation for oral reading:

1. Dorothy rehearses the story or poem on a tape recorder if it is new to her. She listens to improve the tone and rhythm of reading.

2. She and the children put all other work away.

3. Special places are planned for the children to gather to listen. Some special places are a rug so children can sit on the floor, the lawn under a tree in warm weather, and a stage behind the curtain when special lighting effects are needed. She believes a good story deserves a good arrangement. Children need to sit near the reader in order to see illustrations and hear the subtle qualities of voice that portray mood and characters.

4. Selections that sparkle and have a touch of the dramatic are chosen. She knows the children are attuned to television and will resent babyish selections.

5. She is prepared to repeat favorites over and over.

6. She selects some books with only pictures—no text—and invites children to say their own story as she shows the pictures. She encourages them to select a setting and names for characters before they begin to develop the sequence of events suggested by the pictures.

7. As she reads along, she asks questions—not too many but enough to whet interest. She asks more predictive questions than comprehension ones. This tactic enables the listeners to compare their own ideas with those of the author as the story unfolds. Dorothy avoids any possibility of asking comprehension questions that can cause children to feel that they fail. Oral reading to children is a happy time and one of language influence more than one of specific skill development.

AMERICAN ENGLISH?

In Atlanta it's "Hi y'all,"
in New Orleans "Where ya'at,"
And both those cities are in the
*   south,*
Can you imagine that?

In Dallas it's "Howdy partner,"
In Los Angeles "What's happenin'
*   dude."*
And when New York says "Whata
*   ya want"*
It really isn't rude.

In Chicago it's "Hey yous guys,"
Yet another way to say
The very same thing in English
In a slightly different way.

"If you wanna tawk de rit way
Id's easy as can be,
Jus' listen very closely
An' try ta tawk like me."

READING ALOUD

Reading aloud to students increases the listening vocabulary. No part of literacy education is more important than this because students must recognize words by ear before they can recognize them by sight. They must understand the language of other people by listening to it before they can comprehend that language in print.

STORYTELLING

Telling original stories to students and having students tell their own original stories are as important an experience for literacy development as hearing stories read. It is a much more creative experience for the teacher and for students. It develops contact with an audience in a special way that few language experiences can do. Storytelling by the teacher serves as a model for children in their own storytelling and encourages them to do several things:

▶ Engage in a greater output of language than is required for daily sharing.

▶ Embellish language with descriptive terms that are not characteristic of ordinary conversation.

▶ Make up expressive dialogue.

▶ Use sound effects and physical movements to highlight meanings.

▶ Use voice inflections and emphasis that most children do not use when reading what someone else has written.

▶ Express ideas in thought units rather than word by word, which is characteristic of much oral reading by young students.

▶ Develop ideas in a sequence that reaches a climax and has an ending.

CLASSROOM VIGNETTE

Judy Embry, a Reading Recovery teacher in Louisville, Kentucky, believes storytelling makes literature come alive. She models storytelling because she wants to transfer her skills as a weaver of language to her students. She believes storytelling is the best tool classroom teachers have to help children develop listening abilities. She notices that children listen with rapt attention as their fellow classmates tell stories. Judy encourages every child to select a favorite book and develop it into a storytelling session. She suggests they follow these steps in preparation for sharing the story:

1. Select a story you like.

2. Read aloud.

3. Know your three-sentence challenge of the story:

   In the beginning . . .

   In the middle . . .

   At the end . . .

4. Retell.

5. Visualize story by making a silent movie in your head.

6. Practice! Practice! Practice!

Stories told from memory are usually more dramatic than those read aloud because of the freedom afforded the storyteller. It is still important to retain the way certain authors use words and phrases. When the beauty and uniqueness of the original language must be retained, a combination of telling and reading can be employed.

Variety should be the guide in selecting stories for telling and reading. Every teacher's repertoire should include nonfiction, fiction, legends, fairy tales, and every other kind of story from all over the world. They should be selected to please and entertain, to stimulate curiosity, to inform, to illustrate the power of the spoken and the written word, and to reveal beauty and truth.

Children must hear stories and poems from many authors if they are expected to understand the language of hundreds of authors as they move into silent reading experiences. They seldom understand what they see in print if they have not heard something like it prior to the silent reading.

ACTIVITIES THAT ENHANCE LISTENING ABILITIES

Every classroom experience that includes oral language can naturally and normally be a good listening experience. Listening abilities should be promoted, however, and not left to chance. A variety of activities can be made available from day to day as specific assignments or for self-selection:

1. Students who work with games need to listen for specific instructions in order to participate. The instructions can be on tape, read by an aide, or read by one of the group members. Listening to the reading of instructions and rules for games requires a level of attention to specifics that is not characteristic of most listening, but it is characteristic of the level of attention required for some school assignments.

2. Students who work in discussion-centered classrooms may respond in personal ways to what they hear and see. They can extend ideas to their own experiences with a "That reminds me of the time I . . ." kind of response. They do not need to listen at all times just to be able to repeat what they hear. That ability is important, but it is not more important than responding in personal ways.

3. Reading instruction activities should include reading to students on as regular a basis as listening to children read. Students need the experience of hearing good models of oral reading in individual and small-group conferences as much as they need to hear reading for pleasure in a large-group setting. "You read a sentence, then I'll read a sentence" or "You read a paragraph, then I'll read a paragraph" establishes a rapport for discussing some of the finer points of reading. This level of rapport seldom develops when teachers serve as judges of children's reading abilities.

4. Reading instruction situations afford an opportunity for students and teachers to relate personal language to language in the printed text. The teacher can read a sentence, then ask a child to tell how he or she might say the same thing. If the student's response is somewhat different in vocabulary and in syntactical structure, the teacher will know that reading from that author might be difficult for that student. However, if the student can mimic or repeat the language of the author, the "match" of language patterns probably indicates the child will be a fluent reader of that material.

5. Plan so that most oral reading by students to a group is prepared reading. Minimize the number of times that poor readers have to listen to poor readers read poorly. Poor oral reading should be a private affair with only the teacher listening.

6. Drama is an activity where children can act out stories and situations they have heard or read. It gives them opportunity to organize, sequence, and interpret characters from literature that are outside their life experiences. Through listening they pick up the feelings, moods, language patterns, and thought processes of characters.

7. Choral reading is an excellent activity for the refinement of listening. Students listen to each other to evaluate the total effect of their presentation. They make certain they can interpret the selections in a meaningful and dramatic way.

◀ Dramatic play provides an excellent opportunity for developing listening skills.

8. Students need a time and place to read their own compositions to an audience. When there is only one copy of a manuscript, everyone in the audience has to listen. Listening in an audience has purpose because there is little chance that some have read ahead and already know what they are to hear. The teacher becomes a member of the listening audience. This places a responsibility on the reader that is never felt in reading groups in which every student has a book opened to the same reading selection. Poor readers of reading textbooks have an equal chance with good readers when student authors are reading their original manuscripts.

9. Singing games and listening to singing and other music increases auditory discrimination. The experience also builds confidence in producing language with rhythm and rhyme. Students at all levels of achievement can participate in listening to music and in singing.

SUMMARY

Listening, like all learning experiences, benefits from collaborative teacher-student planning. There is more to it than the teacher commanding, "Now listen up!" dozens of times a day. There must be some aspiration for improving listening ability, some time for planning specific activities, and time for evaluating progress. Together, students and teachers can develop standards of listening to serve as a basis for relating listening to learning.

PATHWAYS TO LISTENING

The student:

DEVELOPING LISTENING HABITS

▶ makes use of past experiences and information in conversation.

▶ uses imagination in the formulation of original stories.

▶ follows simple instructions after hearing them.

▶ accepts worth of others' remarks.

▶ speaks in turn.

▶ realizes that different people speak in different ways and for different purposes.

▶ catches added meaning by noting gestures and intonations.

▶ thinks ahead while listening; anticipates what is coming next.

LISTENING TO GET INFORMATION

▶ understands, remembers, and responds to directions of increasing complexity.

▶ gets answers to questions from what is heard.

▶ relays messages accurately.

▶ takes notes from interviews and discussions.

▶ follows reading models heard in instructional conferences.

▶ organizes a sequence and assumes the role of a character to dramatize a story.

LISTENING TO EXCHANGE IDEAS AND FORM JUDGMENTS

▶ participates in group discussions.

▶ reads own compositions to an audience.

▶ grasps the central idea from listening to others read.

▶ recognizes subordinate ideas in stories heard.

▶ distinguishes between fact and opinion, fact and fantasy.

▶ realizes that one's feelings affect one's reaction to what is heard.

▶ seeks clarification of vague and ambiguous ideas.

LISTENING TO ENJOY AND APPRECIATE

▶ becomes aware of beauty in the rhythm and sound of language.

▶ appreciates poetry, stories, music, and dramatization enough to choose listening and reading in learning centers.

▶ develops an understanding of the role and responsibilities of the listener in different situations—face to face, audience to speaker, speaker to audience, radio, television, recordings, school programs.

▶ realizes how readers and storytellers achieve various effects.

▶ realizes the power of language to communicate.

▶5 PATHWAYS TO LANGUAGE GROWTH

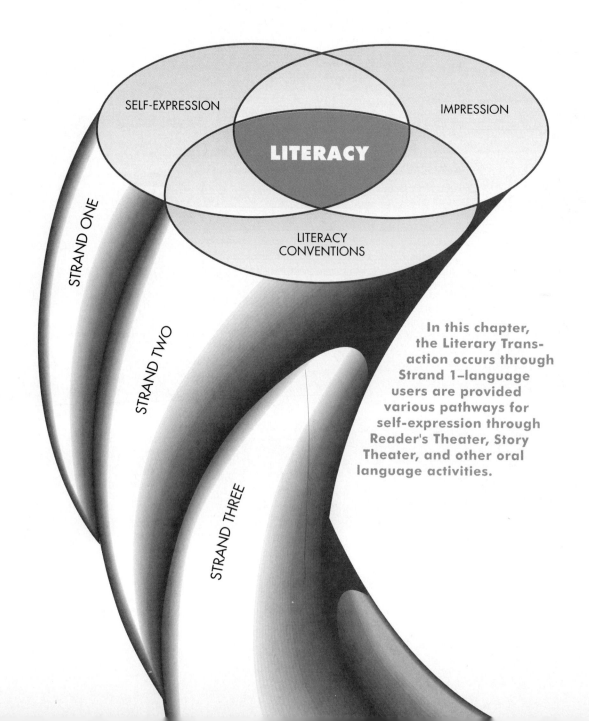

SELF-EXPRESSION

IMPRESSION

LITERACY

LITERACY CONVENTIONS

STRAND ONE

STRAND TWO

STRAND THREE

In this chapter, the Literary Trans-action occurs through Strand 1–language users are provided various pathways for self-expression through Reader's Theater, Story Theater, and other oral language activities.

PATHWAYS TO PONDER

▶ HOW CAN TEACHERS DEMONSTRATE ACCEPTANCE OF DIFFERENT LANGUAGE PATTERNS?

▶ WHY IS IT IMPORTANT FOR STUDENTS TO HAVE OPPORTUNITIES FOR ORAL SHARING IN THE CLASSROOM?

▶ WHAT IS THE RELATION BETWEEN STUDENTS' SELF-CONCEPT AND THE AMOUNT OF SELF-EXPRESSION THEY DEMONSTRATE?

▶ WHY IS DRAMATIZATION OF EXPERIENCES IMPORTANT IN MEANING-CENTERED CLASSROOMS?

ORAL LANGUAGE IN THE CLASSROOM

Oral language is often thought of as the forgotten language art. Perhaps this is because it's so easy for teachers and researchers to focus on reading and writing, and likewise, so easy to examine the results of writing programs or literature studies. And perhaps it's because children become oral language users so easily.

The most significant educational progress made over the last few years has been the move toward integration of the language arts and process learning. So do we want to focus on something as specific as oral language? The answer is a resounding yes.

Literacy skills and oracy skills should enjoy a reciprocal relationship. They reinforce each other. Teachers using a meaning-centered approach do not decide whether reading is more important than speaking or vice versa—they plan for both. They are aware that growth in oral communication is likely to represent growth in reading also. Research (Sampson, 1986) has indicated that the *quality* of oral language production is related significantly to a young child's growth in reading experiences and abilities. Children whose oral language production reflects a high level of mastery of the basic elements of phonological structure, syntactical structure, and morphological structure are the same children who read with minimum instruction. Conversely, children who do not possess a rich language base have difficulty becoming effective readers. The message is clear: We must include time in the curriculum for oral sharing of ideas.

ORAL SHARING

Oral sharing of ideas is basically a "getting acquainted" experience in communication. Students select topics, and timing is flexible enough to extend from the first greeting of the morning to the last good-bye of the afternoon. Time can be organized, but it need not be. Topics can be suggested but must not be mandatory. Freedom to use personal language is a prerequisite for oral sharing of ideas.

The oral language that children bring to school is a personal possession that, more than anything else, represents *who they are*. To deny the use of natural, home-rooted language is to deny children the right to function as the persons they really are. To degrade it is to degrade the person. To cast negative reflections on it is to cast negative reflections on the child and the family that language represents.

Oral sharing is a process of opening up communication between child and teacher and of the child's establishing rapport with the peer group. In the process, the child reveals interests and aspirations, fears and doubts. At the same time, the child shares influences that come from reading, observing, and imagining, and reflects home-rooted language with attendant strengths and weaknesses. Often the child tries out new ways of saying things. In this way the process furnishes anecdotal material to the teacher for follow-up instruction and provides evidence of children's growth in the quality of their language.

Oral sharing of ideas is the most basic process in communication available in classroom settings. It may be the most basic language experience in the

◀ Discussion
Centers offer
valuable
opportunities for
children to share
their thoughts
and ideas.

development of reading and writing abilities. It balances literacy skills with oracy skills, both of which are essential in communication. Many children have immature or divergent speech. A resolution is to provide opportunities for language growth through oral sharing.

CHALLENGE:	RESOLUTION:
1. Some children have unusual pronunciations for words that occur frequently in reading.	Unison reading and choral reading can emphasize phonological structure that is characteristic of reading materials but not characteristic of the oral production of the child. Chants and games that repeat language patterns give practice in pronouncing words. Recording reading and talking on tape provides immediate feedback for evaluation.
2. Some children use syntactical structure that will never be available for replication in reading textbooks.	Sing songs and play games that repeat sentence patterns standard in reading instructional materials. Chat with the child during dictation; offer alternatives rather than corrections. Select sentences to repeat during *reading* to the children. Ask children to read in natural language patterns what they have written and dictated.

3. Some children elaborate with descriptive words that reflect a literacy quality not characteristic of reading instructional materials.

To avoid causing boredom during the acquisition of basic reading skills, add descriptive language to the printed portion of the material—a color word or a size word to each sentence where appropriate, a phrase telling why or where. Make use of the full language power of the learner by substituting orally new nouns and verbs that make meanings more specific or language more creative. Encourage dictation and writing that use the quality of language characteristic of spontaneous expression.

4. Some children are slow in their progress in reading, yet they are confident in language use.

Remove the glory of being able to read every word correctly. Reduce emphasis on reading from textbooks with limited examples of sentence patterns. Relate writing more to speech production than to replication of reading books. Introduce poetry patterns, such as those of the haiku and cinquain, to provide opportunities for artful writing with a limited number of words. Read books of literary merit with repeating patterns that can be followed orally and that might serve as models for artful writing. Use dramatic play to keep language power functioning and alive during periods of learning specific skills.

5. Some children pronounce only portions of words that reflect tense and number.

Pronounce word endings that have meaning in language when reading with children. Model the whole word. Make games with root words that have meanings changed by adding sounds represented by -s, -es, -ing, -ed, -er, -est. Write dictation on the chalkboard. Erase all endings that have language meanings. Read the passage in unison. Restore the endings and discuss the improved meaning.

Only a few examples have been discussed to illustrate why it is important for teachers to hear individuals talk in natural ways. There is no substitute for gathering the information that a teacher must possess in order to do intelligent planning.

ORAL-SHARING ACTIVITIES

A meaning-centered curriculum stresses five major classifications of oral language activities: (1) storytelling, (2) spontaneous expression, (3) Reader's Theater, (4) Story Theater, and (5) reporting.

STORYTELLING

Telling and retelling stories are essential oral experiences in a language process approach. When a child is able—from real experience or from imagination—to choose characters, a setting, and fabricate a plot that contains a climax and an ending, that child has demonstrated the abilities required to comprehend stories written by other authors. Until such abilities are developed, reading is likely to remain word calling. There is no substitute for storytelling in the development of the intellectual base for *reading comprehension.*

The telling of stories, real and imaginary, is as important as listening to them. This creative experience develops audience contact that few language activities can do. It encourages voice inflections, sound effects, physical movements, and language embellishments that lend variety to the usual "reporting voice."

Storytelling about experiences develops such language abilities as expressing ideas in thought units, using colorful and descriptive language, developing ideas in sequence, and choosing good action words. All of these are essential communicating abilities of good readers and writers.

◄ **After repeated readings of the story "King Bidgood's in the Bathtub," kindergarten children present a Story Theater to a school audience.**

SPONTANEOUS EXPRESSION

Spontaneous expression is a priceless treasure in any learning situation. It may be the only avenue open in some classrooms for the establishment of rapport that is strong enough to support interaction. Without interaction it is doubtful that language learning will move forward. The child who is slow to start reading and writing must be made to feel secure in the learning environment. The acceptance of spontaneous expression is a sure way to establish security. Talking in the classroom helps children open up. It also sets the stage for future instruction that permits direct instruction in good faith at other times.

The fluent child who would probably be bored with preselected reading materials can have free rein of personal language power in spontaneous expression.

READER'S THEATER

Reader's Theater (often spelled *Readers Theatre,* with no apostrophe and the British *re* ending on *Theatre*) is one of the best ways to introduce students to the dramatic presentation of literature. The work read can be anything from a four-line poem to an adaptation of a novel. The production involves no sets, costumes, or physical actions. The readers simply sit or stand (usually sit) with scripts in their hands and expressively read their parts with minimal gestures and usually even without eye contact. The audience experiences Reader's Theater in very much the same way it would a radio or other audio presentation of a work of literature—the experience comes almost exclusively through the ears.

For younger readers, simple poems may be the best choices for Reader's Theater presentations. Depending on the poem, each line might be assigned to a different reader, or the parts can be divided in many different ways. The lines can be assigned according to any appropriate division: male/female, high-voice/low-voice, loud-voice/soft-voice, solo/chorus, and any other combination the individual poem might suggest.

THE POET ▶
PONDERS

FIRST STEPS

I read my first poem
And I felt like frowning
It sounded too much like Elizabeth
    Browning.

Then in my next poem
I noticed a change,
I was Emily Dickinson—
Quiet and strange.

Now it's happened again,
Please don't think I'm weird,
But today, I'm Walt Whitman,
Without the long beard.

As I read all my poems
I discover a rule:
I write like whomever
We're reading at school.

As the readers become more accustomed to Reader's Theater and their reading capacities increase, they can perform more complex poems and narrative works. As well as performing ready-made adaptations of short stories and plays and works written specifically for group reading, the students themselves can adapt other works of their own choosing and even write their own original Reader's Theater scripts.

In adapting works for Reader's Theater, keep in mind that actions may be expressed in words. Frequently a narrator is used to communicate complex actions, but new dialogue may be written to communicate brief actions expressed in other ways in the original. If the written description in a short story has the characters suddenly in the dark, and one has a flashlight, you could add lines such as, "What happened to the lights?" and "Shine that flashlight over here so I can see what I'm doing," to let the audience know what is happening.

The main virtue of Reader's Theater is that it requires the audience to use their own imagination to create the scene, costumes, setting, props, and actions of the work. Stephen, an 8-year-old boy raised on television, illustrates this virtue. He started listening to Saturday morning PBS radio drama with his father and was immediately hooked. When asked if he preferred the radio or TV shows, he said, "Radio." When asked why, he said simply, "The pictures are better."

Reader's Theater can provide an easy, enjoyable way for all readers to experience the potential power of the written word. Stimulated by both the words read and the vocal expressions of the reader, even students who are reluctant readers come to realize the potential life and excitement the written word can provide. A sampling of Reader's Theater scripts can be found in Appendix D.

◀ **First-grade students making hand puppets for dramatization.**

CLASSROOM VIGNETTE

Rick Kilcup, a primary teacher from Bellevue, Washington, makes frequent use of Story Theater. Before children are asked to perform, he gives them practice in a nonthreatening atmosphere. By starting out with games and warm-ups that have the whole class "up and doing" and progressing to activities that give small groups a chance to perform before their peers, he builds in students a feeling of confidence about performing. Some warm-ups include the following:

Picking cherries: Have them stretch up high, to the sides, behind them. This gets the blood flowing!

Statues: Give them a statue to become, such as the world's strongest person or a person catching a huge fish.

Rubber band: Their bodies are the rubber bands, and you stretch them by spreading your hands. Be sure to snap them a time or two, and shoot them too.

Rick finds that the imagination and the ideas of the children carry him quickly beyond these openers. Children rapidly get into the swing of things and join right in.

Rick has discovered that poetry works well for Story Theater, too. On the following poem, written by Rick Kilcup, paper bag masks add a nice touch to its enactment. He adds to the poem by asking the students to think of the sounds they can make as they bring the rusty, creaky old robot to life. His children love to act it out:

Continued

STORY THEATER

Story Theater allows students to pull the plot and characters right off the pages of books and bring them to life in the classroom. Stories are more "in the reader than in the book" (Martin, 1990), so Story Theater is a picture of what students are comprehending. Children act out the story while it is being read by a narrator or narrators. It may be performed before an audience after practice, but most sessions are impromptu.

Story Theater gives life to a story and allows students to live what they've read. History can come alive with Story Theater. Imagine the difference between reading about slavery and acting out a story that tells about the lives of slaves. Extensions of Story Theater are possible. You might try following a Story Theater performance by asking the class to write a letter home or make a diary entry from the point of view of one of the characters that they have just portrayed.

THE RUSTY ROBOT
There once was a robot, all rusty and stiff,
as jerky as jerky could be,
Who would lurch and glurch and wobble around,
it was a strange sight to see!

It would clank to the right and clunk to the left,
endangering everyone near.
Becoming a nuisance, a bother, a danger,
a downright pain in the ear!

Oh the noises which came from this rambling wreck
were enough to make sleeping dogs howl!
Those clanks, groans, and squeaks sounded oh so absurd
like loose nuts and bolts on the prowl!

It would rattle about, waving arms in the air,
tossing wild tin legs to each side.
We'd all screech and yell and holler for help,
then find a good safe place to hide!

So time passed as we lived in deep fear of this beast,
as we ran from its frightening sound.
'Til the day that it happened, oh wonderful day,
when its battery began to wear down!

Then it haltered and faltered and jerked to a stop,
falling down to the ground . . . kerplunk!
Now there's peace once again in the old neighborhood,
since we threw him out in the junk!

REPORTING

What one observes and hears can be reported. Awareness of the wonders of nature and of people is the basis for language growth. As one reports, formally or informally, there is need to name things, to tell how they move, and to describe them. Categories of description include color, size, shape, texture, sound, taste, smell, and feeling. The language of contrast and comparison enhances and clarifies meanings. Teacher-pupil interaction during reporting activities may be more specific than at times of spontaneous expression. Common experiences of a class group may be reported. Children may assume different roles when reporting the same experience—from the viewpoint of a scientist, an artist, a teacher, an architect, a musician, or from any other viewpoint possible because of an interest or an experience.

As children mature in reading abilities and interests, much of oral reporting may be related to self-selected and self-assigned reading. Such reporting can be unscheduled as well as scheduled. In addition to reporting bare facts from print, children should be expected to add: What else might the author have said if he or she could be here? What was hinted but not said? What would I have said or done under the same conditions? Other topics appropriate for personalizing and illustrating their influence on the reader can be woven into a report.

An important aspect of sharing and reporting is the ability to communicate accurately and with organization that the listener can follow. In the beginning stages these abilities can be developed and strengthened through questions that the teacher might ask: Did you really see or hear what you reported? Do you think the other children understood your explanation? Did the people in the class listen while you gave your report?

Good reporting can also be stimulated by several means:

▶ holding brief oral evaluations at the end of the day

▶ summarizing what happened in committee work

▶ describing how a construction project was carried out

▶ cooperatively planning the major activities of the day

▶ telling how to play games

Older children begin to learn to organize their ideas and thoughts by outlining or by listing major points of emphasis. They recognize that the purpose of reporting to the class is to supply information needed by the group as a whole, and so they try to give their reports, either oral or written, in a manner both clear and interesting to the audience. Skill in reporting increases as the teacher guides the children:

▶ to recognize and define problems

▶ to gather materials and evaluate their importance according to the problem

▶ to take brief notes and organize them in logical sequence for presentation

Abilities developed through sharing and reporting emphasize the value of individual contributions. These experiences characterize the real difference between a society that develops individuals who assume responsibility for contributing to the thought of its citizens, and a society that seeks to teach its youth by rote what officials deem important. Sharing experiences provides the openness, the motivation, and many of the ideas on which other language abilities are developed.

DRAMATIZATION

Dramatic play or dramatization is a natural activity of children in the classroom, on the playground, and at home. The classroom version of dramatic play, however, is a far cry from yesterday's classroom *dramas*. The most noticeable difference is the spontaneity of today's students engaged in creating their own plays. They have to have ideas before they can create. They must

P.J. Winston _____ Name

13 _____ Age

_____
In sports and
a Education _____ Interests

What do you like most about school?

What I like most about
school is sports and friend
around me. But I like my
class another thing I do take time out like reward time,

What's your favorite subject? Why?

My favorite subject is Soc St.
because like to learn about Texas History.
The other one is Science because
I like to dissect all kinds of animal and insects.

What's your favorite book? Why do you like it?

My book is Martin Luther King Jr. I like
it because I like to learn
about the great power and the
way he wasn't scared of anything.

What advice do you have for teachers?

To teach and help kids get
a education. Next you could
let them have a little free
time. That is what I think.

learn how to express their ideas in three-dimensional form in order to dramatize them.

For the majority of students, it is important to express most of their deepest feelings through vicarious experiences. In order to express the difference between being generous and selfish, brave and fearful, happy and sad, successful and failing, a child can become a character in a play and show real feelings. One experience in expressing such concepts may lead to confidence in other forms of self-expression and to continued interest in dramatizing an idea. As students play a great variety of roles, new interests are aroused and new problems are faced. These new aspects require the use of more materials and additional information in order to express clearly the basic ideas or situations. When used as a base for reading, the experiences in drama provide a backdrop for identifying and understanding characters that can never be understood from real-life experiences only.

Both assertive and timid children benefit from the opportunity to express themselves in dramatic productions. In addition to being an aid to speech production and refinement, realistic dramatic training improves listening, reading, and writing skills. It calls on the same basic mental abilities required for listening with comprehension; it exercises the same skills used for

THE BOOK ▶
MAKERS

BILL MARTIN JR

1. Which book of yours has given you the greatest pleasure?

Barn Dance. It appealed to children much younger than I had thought. I enjoyed both the poetry and the subtlety of the fantasy. It starts with dead realism and then the reader is several pages into the story before the fantasy begins when the scarecrow becomes a violinist.

2. Which book has surprised you most in terms of its public reception?

Brown Bear, Brown Bear. I never thought of it as being a book that would last or as an important book. It's not a storybook at all, but children see it as so. So many teachers have told me that they start their year with this book.

3. What would you like people to remember about your work?

I want them to remember a line or a combination of words that creates a lasting impression.

4. What impact do you hope your work will have on children?

My work revolves around coming to print through the sentence rather than through the letter.

Bill Martin's works delightfully "tune the child's ear to the music of language. . . ." He doesn't just write words, he creates lyrics that sing of the joys of life. His compositions include *Brown Bear, Brown Bear, What Do You See?, Polar Bear, Polar Bear, What Do You Hear?, Chicka Chicka Boom Boom, Knots on a Counting Rope, Barn Dance, Ghost-Eye Tree,* and *Old Devil Wind.*

organizing that are gained from silent reading; and it develops fluency and flexibility as an attribute requisite to creative writing. Yet all these skills and abilities can be developed without, or prior to, the acquisition of reading and writing skills. Dramatic experiences can keep learners in touch with language that is full and beautiful during processes of learning specific literacy skills. It can furnish teachers with valuable clues for planning direct instructional activities for the future.

In dramatic play students consciously pretend they are someone else. They extend their feelings, explore some of their emerging thoughts, seek relief from some of their frustrations, and become animals, people from another planet, persons earning a living, parents, teachers, and other characters who give them an opportunity to experiment with experiences and ideas before an audience.

Sociodrama is another creative technique of pretending. In spontaneous dramatic action children identify themselves with some personality described in some particular life situation. The acting is called role playing. Sociodramas are not written or memorized because their primary purpose is to open up new levels of awareness of how people feel or behave in a given situation. A simple form of sociodrama is to describe a true-to-life happening, stopping at the climax before the problems are resolved. Children can then choose various roles and create their own feelings about the problem or the situation while pretending to be someone else.

Pretending-to-be requires the use of voice inflections and vocabulary not typical of home-rooted speech. It offers repeated opportunities for children to practice using language they have never used before. It extends oral language experience toward the language found in many reading materials.

As a thinking reader and writer, every student will encounter a great variety of situations in responding to ideas. To have acted a part builds a base of experiences that help make reading and writing into thinking processes. Pretending is basic to literacy.

From their earliest days of listening to reading, students can indicate a level of understanding by simply acting out characters. This ability and interest can be continued and utilized in school to the advantage of students and teachers.

THE TEACHER AND DRAMATIZATION

The experience of dramatization as well as the dramatization of experience are an integral part of a meaning-centered classroom. It is important that children participate in activities that allow them to be someone (or something) other than themselves. It is through such experiences in communication that some psychologists believe self is enhanced (Carlton & Moore, 1971). If this theory is true, then teachers have an obligation to create learning environments that permit and promote dramatization. To retell a story in action is *not* a primary goal of dramatization in a language-arts classroom. Rather, the goal is to give children repeated opportunities to live through situations—to discover and improvise.

CLASSROOM VIGNETTE

Jonathan and Adrianne noticed an announcement on the A.C. Williams Elementary School bulletin board. Odyssey of the Mind teams were forming, and it looked exciting. The children attended a meeting at school that night, and joined Mary Beth, Christina, Ryan, and Ashley on a team. Their assignment? Write and perform an eight-minute play about an American legend or an American folktale.

As the children brainstormed about their topic, significant national attention was being directed at the U.S. Postal Service decision to issue a commemora-

Elvis. ▶

Continued

Teachers are wise to keep in mind several essentials to optimize use of dramatization to promote language growth for reading and writing:

▶   ESSENTIAL 1: A FRIENDLY RELATIONSHIP IN WHICH RAPPORT IS ESTABLISHED BETWEEN TEACHER
     AND CLASS   Mutual respect is fostered when the teacher is able to enter into

tive stamp for Elvis Presley. The team became intrigued about the attention the stamp received, and decided that Elvis must be an American legend. So they wrote their play with Graceland as the setting and with three children who would have a chance encounter with the "king of rock and roll." Here's their script:

ELVIS: THE LEGEND

CAST:

Boy:	Ryan Evans
Chrissy:	Mary Beth Crawford
Tour Guide:	Adrianne Jones
Girl 2:	Ashley Harris
Girl 3:	Christina Anderson
Elvis:	Jonathan Sampson

SCENE 1: GRACELAND

Tour guide: **Welcome to Graceland, the home of Elvis Presley. Elvis lives on here. You'll see him through the awards that he won and the hundreds of pictures that document his life. However, the Elvis of today is bigger than life. He's become an American legend, a character as famous as the American folk heroes Paul Bunyan and Johnny Appleseed. True, Elvis is bigger in death than he was in life, but the king of rock and roll left a legacy that changed American culture and music. Just how popular is Elvis? The Elvis stamp was the most popular of all time—five million were printed and sold!**

(Walks over, opens a curtain, and unveils "stamp." The stamp is the character Elvis, frozen in stillness.)

Tour guide: **More than one million votes were cast for the stamp design, and this is the way it looks.**

(Pulls cover back over stamp.)

Tour guide: **Let's move on to see more: Elvis's first golden record.**

(Tour guide moves on, but two girls and a boy lag behind.)

Continued

problem-solving situations as a learner. Experiences must be shared, desires must be revealed, ideals must be shared, and stands on moral judgment must be revealed but not offered as the right ones. There is no need for children to enter into personal problem solving when the result is always judged as right or wrong. The process of entering into possible solutions is the goal. In such

....

Chrissy: I must see that stamp one more time!

Girl 2: Chrissy, no! We'll get in trouble.

Chrissy: Come on, what are you, scaaared?

(Girls walk over and pull cover off. Elvis is still in a frozen pose.)

Chrissy: Oh, he's soooooooooo cute!

Elvis: *(Comes alive, and says, in Elvis dialect)* Well, thanks a lot, darling.

Girls: *(SCREAM!!!!)*

Boy: Elvis! But you're dead!

Elvis: Reports of my death are greatly exaggerated.

Chrissy: How do we know you're really Elvis?

Boy: Yeah, how do we?

Elvis: Well, this is thirty years old. *(Points to guitar, moves to keyboard)* Mind if I use the nineties to help me?

Elvis: *(Sings, with great soul and movement)*, "You Ain't Nothing But a Hound Dog."

Chrissy: More, more!

Elvis: *(Starts singing "Don't Be Cruel.")*

Girls: *(Dancing and clapping and going crazy)*

Girls: You are Elvis!!!

Elvis: Yep, I'm still me. But I don't get around as much as the tabloids say I do. There are a lot of people impersonating me. *(Elvis turns to Boy 1.)* What brings you to Graceland?

Boy: Well, my parents are here on vacation. They made me come! *(Sticks finger in mouth as if gagging himself)*

Chrissy: I learned in my history class that you invented rock-n-roll music and were a great songwriter. I am supposed to write my own song for my music merit badge in Girl Scouts. I thought being here might help me get some ideas.

Elvis: *(Moves and puts hand on shoulder)* Well, I hope it does, darling.

Boy: Say, since Elvis is here, why don't you get him to help you?

Chrissy: Oh, please will you help me? Please, please!

Elvis: Oh, you don't need *my* help. You can do it.

Chrissy: But I'm no songwriter.

Elvis: I think, therefore, I am.

Girl 2: What do you mean?

Continued

situations language production is real and natural. Teachers can gain clues from the performances that will guide in future encounters, but they cannot gain the privilege of passing final judgment.

▶ ESSENTIAL 2: AN ATTITUDE OF ACCEPTING CHILDREN'S LANGUAGE AS IT IS In dramatization there is no need to monitor the correctness of language. A major goal

....

Elvis: **Just what I said, you've got to believe in yourself. What do you want to sing about?**

Chrissy: **Oh, about love I guess.**

Elvis moves and strikes the keyboard. He begins to sing "Love Me Tender." Meanwhile, the girls are *really* excited. Boy is bored, until the girls start fainting. Boy runs from one girl to the next, catching them as they fall toward the floor. Finally, he starts dancing with one of the girls. When song ends, the girls express their amazement by clapping.

Tour guide: **(Reappears from offstage and says in an agitated voice) Elvis! Now you know you are not supposed to be out. (She grabs him by the arm and leads him back into the stamp.)**

Chrissy: **Wait, Elvis! But what about my song?**

Elvis: **You've got it in you, just do it.**

Boy: **Like Nike!**

Tour guide: **Elvis has left the stage!**

(Chrissy has moved to the keyboard and is starting a song.)

Chrissy: **At first . . . (pause) At first I thought . . . Oh, there's no hope.**

Voice of Elvis booms from backstage: **Just listen to the music inside you and let it out.**

Chrissy: **Hey, wait a minute, that's it. (The song comes to her and she begins playing and singing.) At first I thought there was no hope, but then you came along, and at that moment, I knew that I was all wrong. Cause Elvis, you are the one, and Elvis, with you, anything can be done. Cause Elvis, you are the one!**

Boy: **You sound just like Elvis!**

Girl 2: **(Faints.)**

Chrissy: **Yes! Yes! (Jumps up and down)**

All of the cast, including Elvis, joins together and holds hands. They sing Chrissy's song together. All take a bow.

THE END

The children rehearsed for six weeks. During this time, they built a backdrop for the play that depicted a wall at Graceland, complete with a picture of Elvis and two of his golden records. The highlight of the odyssey was an outstanding performance of the play at a regional competition. Oral language development? Yes, indeed. Dramatization of ideas is an excellent activity for language development.

for the teacher is one of creating opportunities to hear raw natural language coming from a "free spirit." No program of language instruction can be individualized until the chief planner knows individual potential and problems. Such information does not come from pencil-and-paper diagnostic tests or from listening to oral replication of someone else's language through reading.

It comes only when the individual is free to be himself or herself or to act as someone else.

▶   ESSENTIAL 3: AN UNDERSTANDING OF THE ESSENTIAL INGREDIENTS THROUGH WHICH DRA-MATIZATION FUNCTIONS   Dramatization, like other art forms, is dependent on contrast and comparison. There can be no drama without contrasts in stillness and motion, silence and sound, and darkness and light. A classroom does not need the equipment of a theater to provide actors with the resources necessary for a dramatic production. A Dramatization Center does need to have items for producing a variety of sounds not made by human voices. A flashlight or a lantern made of cardboard is all the equipment necessary for a shift from darkness to light when children are acting. Flicking an electric light switch might be enough. Motion is inherent in children's activities, but it may be refined with suggestions and practice in using hands, feet, facial expressions, and body motions to interpret a wide range of feelings.

▶   ESSENTIAL 4: A WILLINGNESS TO PARTICIPATE IN THE EXPERIENCE OF DRAMATIZATION   Children deserve to work *with* the teacher rather than *for* the teacher. Natural situations arise as new techniques and materials are introduced during dramatization. Beyond this, teachers must take character parts when stories are read for dramatization. In many classrooms it is essential that sometimes the teacher assume the role of a person who speaks with incorrect grammar and with a regional dialect. In some situations the teacher should be a character whose behavior is intolerable. Children who dramatize other character roles with the teacher come to understand the teacher as another human being.

▶   ESSENTIAL 5: AN AWARENESS OF LANGUAGE CONCEPTS THAT CAN BE EMPHASIZED AND EX-TENDED THROUGH DRAMATIZATION   Numerous objectives for dramatization can be enumerated:

▶   Experiencing the joy of being involved with others in human experiences.

▶   Understanding of self.

▶   Becoming self-directed.

▶   Discovering and selecting values to live by.

▶   Developing unique human potentialities.

▶   Developing interest in reading.

▶   Developing appreciation for well-written literature.

The major purpose of dramatization in a meaning-centered curriculum is that of extending language power in a variety of situations. Teachers are not satisfied to listen as one child after another replicates the language of someone else and call it reading. They are not satisfied to let one child—who raises a hand and begs for a chance to give an answer—answer for the whole class. Teachers in a language-centered curriculum must do several things:

▶   Hear children express themselves orally in an environment of free language use.

▶ Hear each child adjust his or her own language to fit a variety of characters.

▶ Observe expressions of feeling toward known and unknown situations.

▶ Mediate language growth toward the occasional use of literary language.

▶ Orchestrate groups of children into productions reflecting the influence of artist-authors and producers—phrases, sentences, rhymes, songs, and rhythms that fit naturally into spontaneous drama.

DISCUSSING AND CONVERSING

Because the fundamental business of public education is to train youth for active and worthwhile participation in the democratic way of life, any skill or experience that will contribute to one's ability to earn a living, to social and civic competence, and to the willing and intelligent exercise of the privileges and responsibilities of citizenry cannot be denied a place in the curriculum of our schools. One such skill slighted in emphasis is the art of conversation, including participation in group discussions. Even though it has been neglected in the past, educators are realizing that conversation furnishes a proven method for an intelligent and rational solution to community problems.

Conversation brings us more pleasure than dancing, golfing, going to the movies, or eating a favorite dessert. It not only brings pleasure in itself but also keeps alive memories of past pleasures. We would enjoy few activities if we were denied the satisfaction of talking about them.

Too many teachers continue to practice the policy of suppressing oral expression activities of children, preferring to judge their reactions through written expressions. Others are aware, however, of the need for a well-planned program built around realistic goals. These teachers have selected some broad abilities to be developed:

▶ To have something to talk about.

▶ To offer enthusiastic participation.

▶ To have a pleasing vocabulary.

▶ To observe common courtesies in conversation.

SOMETHING TO TALK ABOUT

Any classroom with normal children living in our rich language-filled environment affords many opportunities or topics for discussion. From kindergarten on, children come to realize that ideas for conversation come through listening to other people talk, wide reading, and experience that school life affords.

Teachers should utilize the experiences of children in periods of planned discussion and in periods of free conversation. Children consider all their content subjects as sources of information for conversation and discussion. An

CLASSROOM VIGNETTE

Jerry Watkins watches for items of interest to his class. At least once a week he arranges the learning space so when the children arrive there will be designated spaces for them to sit together and talk. Labels are arranged on the carpeted floor for topics that are listed at the entry on a poster with the headline "Let's Talk." In order to control size, tickets are placed in pockets opposite each topic on the poster. A ticket admits a student to a certain group. When all tickets for a topic are gone, students must select other topics. Popular topics are repeated. Children in the class anticipate the topics and try to keep abreast of current events through newspapers and news reports on TV and radio.

At the end of most school days, Julia Evans invites the children to sit comfortably on a rug to talk about what happened and did not happen during the day. Children are encouraged to talk about things they did in the learning centers. When a child reads a book or completes a poem, the group discusses it. Problems and ideas that need attention the following day are discussed. Behavior is a topic that comes up frequently. Children know that they can and must solve these problems together. The teacher is not the dictator of behavior but the administrator of policies developed through discussion by those concerned.

excursion or the viewing of a film for a class in social studies or science usually initiates talk among children, and the teacher takes advantage of such an experience to stress the abilities required for adequate conversation about the subject. In doing this the teacher has put discussion in its proper place in the curriculum. Assigned topics do not inspire students to talk as much about the things they know and want to share with others as do topics that grow out of everyday school life.

ENTHUSIASTIC PARTICIPATION

Because enthusiasm is usually evidenced by naturalness, children will use their natural language when they are enthusiastic. Thus the goal of enthusiastic participation in oral language can be met in several ways:

▶ When children whose home-rooted language is characterized by nonstandard speech speak naturally in discussion.

▶ When children whose first language is a distinct dialect use it in conversation.

▶ When children whose home language is not English use combinations of two languages when participating.

In classrooms where the children and the teacher live together and love each other enough to speak freely of their deepest feelings, alternative ways of saying things must be accepted.

Evaluation sessions follow frequently when enthusiastic participation is a goal of planned discussion sessions. These sessions are ones that are concerned about alternatives in speech rather than about correctness. The teacher does

CLASSROOM VIGNETTE

Marie Dominguez invites older children and adults to her class of young children to discuss hobbies, topics of special interest, and occupations. The invitation states specifically that they are coming for a discussion, not a lecture. In preparation for the discussion, the children talk about how they can participate and not about what questions to ask. Following the discussion, there is a period of evaluation at which time the group can discuss levels and quality of participation as well as the importance of having some information in order to participate. Marie feels a special responsibility to comment on enthusiastic participation on the part of children whose language needs massive refinement. She feels that instruction in refinement is futile for most of them apart from easy and enthusiastic participation.

Rick Kilcup reads something of his own choosing to the class almost every day. He uses short selections that he can read with enthusiasm. Then he leads a discussion centered around the main point or the writing style of the author. He demonstrates a feeling of ease and good personal involvement in this activity, which takes from five to seven minutes. He searches for materials well written in African-American dialects, in regional dialects, and in language characteristic of ethnic groups represented in the class. Also, he collects recordings of stories and songs illustrating many English dialects from the United States, Australia, Great Britain, Wales, and other places where English is the official language. His goal is to involve every student in discussion, regardless of the quality of the home-rooted language he or she brings into the classroom. Rick feels he is there to listen, to diagnose, and to offer alternatives. He cannot diagnose apart from hearing natural language.

not pose as the one final authority but participates in illustrating one or more ways of saying things.

Significant changes in oral language occur by choice—not by following lessons (Lindfors, 1987). Choice implies alternatives. Through enthusiastic participation in discussions and conversations, alternatives are illustrated in a meaningful way. A look at those that have been useful in the class may be a means of opening up choices for children who need to make significant changes in personal language if they are to enter into the mainstream of education and American life.

VOCABULARY

Having something to say and enthusiasm for saying it is not enough. Our choice of words and the way we use them mark us for what we are. Persons with meager vocabularies find depth of self-expression difficult; those with a broad vocabulary are able to express their feelings and ideas with clarity and power. Teachers do not expect perfection in the use of words that are difficult and strange to children, but they strive to develop rapport strong enough that children do not fear to try to use words they have never used before.

Simplicity and clarity are the keys to better language and are practiced by teachers in what they say and in the books they give children to read. Children are taught the basic principles of semantics rather than a list of meaningless words. They are led to realize that words do not represent things but that words represent thoughts. The eyes, ears, and hearts of children become sensitive to the breadth and beauty of language.

Many people are led to believe the large vocabulary is the one full of "big" and unusual words, but children should be encouraged to avoid affectations of speech when there are direct and meaningful ways of communicating. Outlandish phrases, unusual syntax, and vogue words should be evaluated against a backdrop of alternatives. Some children may use them because they lack other means of expressing themselves.

This possibility is substantiated in a research study, *A Word Count of Spoken English of Culturally Disadvantaged Preschool and Elementary Pupils* (Sherk, 1973). Sherk found the quantity of production was not a true reflection of the quality. Children in his study tended to use the same words over and over. Their inventory of nouns, verbs, adjectives, and adverbs was extremely limited when compared with lists generated from a broad segment of the population. Children with this problem do not possess personal language power that permits them to function in school tasks, especially in tasks of reading language as it is produced in written form. They must have many opportunities to try on a wardrobe of new words in a pleasant, easy environment. The acquisition of language may be a need greater than being able to recognize and analyze a few words from a simple reading text.

OBSERVING COMMON COURTESIES IN CONVERSATION

Everyone knows the desirability and importance of observing common courtesies in conversation and discussion. The rude, abrupt, and discourteous person is soon eliminated from a group and left alone, wondering why he or she has no friends. Some instruction in acquiring the knowledge and ability to practice common courtesies in talking with others can reduce the number of such cases in a school.

There are many ways to teach these abilities, but the most effective ones are derived from actual conversation practices that are noted and evaluated by the group. School social affairs offer opportunities for this instruction. Children can be brought together with adults or with other children they don't know as well as those in the immediate group in order to create a greater need for social competence in their talk. Activities can be planned and made an integral part of the school program to foster skills and courtesies in conversation.

Many desirable abilities and attitudes can be named in connection with this topic, and the following list includes some of the most useful:

CLASSROOM VIGNETTE

Anna Albritton has developed a Cooking Center over several years. With the help of parents who gave trading stamps, she has acquired the equipment needed to serve party refreshments as a follow-up of the cooking experience. Children plan a party appropriate for what they cook, and invite guests from within the school and from outside. Sometimes another class will be invited; at other times, only three or four special guests will be honored. Anna uses these occasions to develop the language of common courtesy in real situations rather than in workbook lessons. Dramatic play is used in practice, and the children evaluate progress in their abilities to carry on conversations with guests after each party.

Anna feels that language changes and improves when the environment in which it occurs changes and improves. She has collected beautiful dishes and serving pieces for the children to use at their many parties. They make decorations for their classrooms and are encouraged to wear suitable clothes when guests come. They discuss good grooming and appropriate dress for different occasions and how to adjust their language to various events.

Parents participate and are enthusiastic about Anna's program. They appreciate her efforts to do for the speech of their children what they cannot accomplish at home. Some of them try to follow up the school experiences with occasions to practice the language of courtesy at home.

A place in the Reading/Research Center is devoted to having and planning parties, and simple books of etiquette. These books would never be assigned as required reading, but they are extremely popular when a party is planned.

Ray Berg uses lunchtime to emphasize conversations that are polite and courteous. Host jobs are rotated, and each host can initiate, but not dominate, conversations. Although they are very informal, an effort is made to practice common courtesies and to develop language appropriate for social occasions. Tables accommodate six to eight, and the makeup of groups changes regularly so the same children do not talk together over an extended period.

Continued

▶ how and when to interrupt the person talking

▶ how to disagree with the speaker's statement

▶ not to be too demonstrative

▶ not to monopolize the conversation

▶ to avoid unpleasant topics

▶ not to whisper in the presence of others

▶ to include all members of the group in one's remarks

▶ to express likes and dislikes moderately

▶ not to be too personal

▶ to speak in a well-modulated voice

▶ to avoid futile argument

The class has an ongoing project of trying out ideas to stimulate good conversation. The children have a chart on which they list some of their guidelines:

Talk about things that interest people in your group.

Do not tell secrets during conversations.

Do not act as though you are smart when everyone knows you are dumb on a topic.

Do not argue. Change the subject.

Ask questions that will bring a new person into the conversation.

Do not talk just to please yourself.

Laura Howard was teaching a group of preschool Native American children when she realized that she was not hearing words of courtesy such as *thank you, please,* and *excuse me.* Even with urging, her efforts seemed fruitless. She felt the children should learn to use these words before they began their more formal school program, so she enlisted the help of her Native American aide, a college student who spoke the tribe's language. Lucia, the aide, confided there never have been words to say thank you in the Indian language. "We say it with our eyes," she explained.

Immediately Laura realized she had been receiving gestures of gratitude every time a child's eyes sparkled at the pleasure of new toys, the attractive classroom, and the good food. She knew she was participating in a culture that extended courtesies in ways different from her own. She wanted to preserve the culture at the same time she introduced one new to the children. She became gracious and loving when the children said thank you with their eyes. She imitated them and learned the pleasure of their gestures. She shared her way, too, because she knew that as the children grew older, they would need to use the expressions of both cultures. She built for herself a basic generalization out of the experience: There is no one right way to communicate common courtesies.

- ▶ to be considerate of people entering the group after conversation has begun
- ▶ not to hurt the feelings of others
- ▶ not to repeat needlessly
- ▶ to greet and to take leave of a host graciously

SUMMARY

In this chapter we examined classroom activities that engage students in self-expression through many media. The language children bring to school is a reflection of the language used in their home and community. School programs can expand children's language by engaging students in activities that involve speaking and listening. These activities offer students meaningful experiences with rich and beautiful language during processes of learning specific literacy skills.

PATHWAYS FOR ORAL SHARING IN THE CLASSROOM

The student:

ORAL LANGUAGE TECHNIQUES

- ▶ grows in ability to pronounce commonly used words correctly.
- ▶ tries to speak clearly and distinctly so others will hear and understand.
- ▶ extends and refines vocabulary.
- ▶ relates events in proper sequence.
- ▶ uses voice effectively to portray story.
- ▶ selects stories appropriate for audience.
- ▶ develops an easy, natural way for telling a story.
- ▶ develops skill in interpreting mood and character of a story.

SHARING AND REPORTING

- ▶ shares ideas and experiences with class and others.
- ▶ presents simple reports to class on observations, trips, reading, and other experiences.
- ▶ strives for accuracy in reporting.
- ▶ shows increasing skill in making announcements and explanations.
- ▶ increases skill in organizing and summarizing ideas to report.

▶ selects interesting and worthwhile material to report.

▶ uses notes and simple outlines for oral presentations.

▶ uses appropriate illustrative material to convey ideas more effectively.

▶ cultivates as a speaker clarity of speech, pleasing voice, and good posture.

▶ realizes need for presenting accurate information, giving sources.

DRAMATIC PLAY

▶ participates freely and willingly in dramatic play.

▶ is spontaneous and natural in oral expression.

▶ uses language appropriate to the character being portrayed.

▶ uses hands, feet, facial expressions, and body to interpret characters.

▶ uses conversation with another person to further the action of the play.

DRAMATIZATION AND READING

▶ shares favorite poems and stories by acting them out.

▶ shows originality in the interpretation of stories, poems, music, and dramatization.

▶ helps to plan and participate in class TV and radio programs.

▶ uses incidents in stories for dramatization.

▶ plans and participates in puppet shows.

▶ creates original plays with plot, characters, and setting.

▶ repeats words and phrases of characters in stories when dramatizing them.

CONVERSATION

▶ talks informally and easily with classmates, teachers, and other adults.

▶ increases skill in choosing interesting topics of conversation.

▶ develops confidence in asking and answering questions and in replying to remarks of teachers and others.

▶ develops understanding of some of the qualities of a good conversationalist.

DISCUSSION

▶ participates willingly in planned discussions to learn from others as well as to make contributions.

▶ takes turns in discussions.

▶ increases skill in participating in group discussions.

▶ practices social courtesies when participating in discussions.

▶ is not overly sensitive to criticism.

▶ reacts thoughtfully to the ideas of others.

LANGUAGE COURTESIES

▶ practices desirable social courtesies as a speaker and as a listener.

▶ develops sensitivity to others.

▶ makes introductions properly and graciously and responds to introductions in a similar manner.

PART

▶3

FOUNDATIONS
OF WRITING

CHAPTER

►6 PATHWAYS TO THE WRITING PROCESS

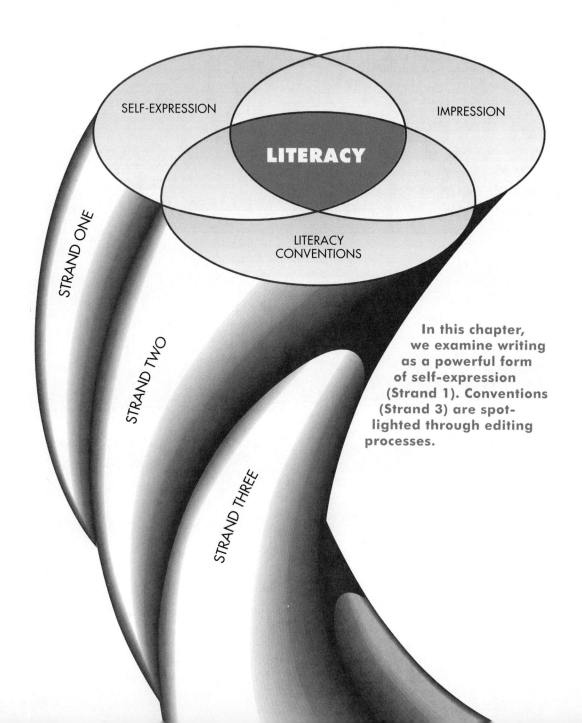

SELF-EXPRESSION

IMPRESSION

LITERACY

LITERACY CONVENTIONS

STRAND ONE

STRAND TWO

STRAND THREE

In this chapter, we examine writing as a powerful form of self-expression (Strand 1). Conventions (Strand 3) are spotlighted through editing processes.

PATHWAYS TO PONDER

▶ HOW DOES A TEACHER'S DEFINITION OF WRITING AFFECT THE WAY SHE OR HE TEACHES WRITING?

▶ WHAT HAPPENS TO STUDENTS' SELF-CONCEPT WHEN THEY VIEW THEMSELVES AS AUTHORS?

All children are writers. In this chapter we share numerous examples of the stories and poems that children have written. In the next chapter we look at literacy structures that provide formats for children's stories. We close Part Three with Chapter 8, which examines the different ways the writing classroom may be managed.

More than anything else, this chapter is about freedom—freedom to write without fear, embarrassment, or correction. We share stories that illustrate students' literacy growth as they write to convey information, as they share personal observations, as they use their imaginations, as they share feelings about themselves and life, and as they reflect the influence of literature on personal language and writing.

The scribbles of preschool children represent the first stage of writing. They convey meaning through these markings, and children can usually explain just what their writing "says." These messages may be refined into alphabetic writing as children move into meaning-centered classrooms that value self-expression through writing.

Young children must not feel they have to write correctly in order to begin. Eventually, however, they will come to realize that writing involves difficulties not encountered in oral expression. These appear in the form of handwriting, spelling, punctuation, and other elements of composition. However, if we begin too early to stress the mechanical and formal elements of writing or if we stress them at the expense of the quality of creative thought, we may create a distaste for writing. Our aim should be to develop genuine interest in writing and to promote as much writing as we can. Correct form must serve—never rule—writing.

By reading the writing of others in which standard forms of expression are encountered, children come to incorporate these forms into their own patterns (Graves, 1981; Martin & Sampson, 1994). As teachers, we must emphasize both writing and reading. They reinforce each other.

UNDERSTANDING WRITING

Current understandings about the writing process are being influenced by the theories of Lev Vygotsky. Vygotsky believed speaking and writing are linked—that, in fact, oral language is the springboard for writing. He observed that children's development of communication skills, including writing, evolved and matured from social speech (Vygotsky, 1962). This social speech includes what Vygotsky termed *communicative speech* and *egocentric speech.* Children use communicative speech for telling their mother they are hungry, writing a letter, or asking what time it might be. Egocentric speech is used as children plan and carry out activities. Egocentric speech helps students express, and sometimes overcome, difficulties: Two-year-old Bradley was overheard saying, as he was slipping off of a tree limb, "This boy's gonna fall, this boy's gonna fall!" He wasn't calling for help; he was merely vocalizing his thoughts.

Vygotsky (1962) viewed egocentric speech as a transition from vocal to inner speech. Inner speech is shortened and transformed speech—bursts of thoughts and insights that equate to pure meanings. These meanings or thoughts are a prerequisite to written communication. Writing takes place through the translation of inner speech into scribbles, drawings, words, or phrases. Figure 6.1 diagrams the relationships that exist between inner speech and its forms of expression—oral and written communication.

Inner speech may be used for many types of expression or communication. The expression may be in the mode of oral speech, thinking, or writing. Writers often use inner speech to "think out loud" or "talk through" what they want to express in written communication. Ideas may begin with images, but images soon are represented in inner speech with voice. Moffett (1981) asserts that writers must discover their "stream of consciousness," which is, in essence, their inner voice. Donald Murray, an accomplished writer, says, "I will not start writing until I hear or sense the voice of the text" (Murray, 1989, p. 85).

We often interfere with the natural cycle of self-expression by asking children to write about something they don't want to write about, or demanding that they write before they are ready to write. Vygotsky's theories have something to say to us here, too. Frank Smith (1993), in his book *Whose Language? What Power?*, summarizes Vygotsky's position clearly: "Anything the child can do with help today, the child will be able to do alone tomorrow. There is,

FROM THOUGHT TO COMMUNICATION   ◄ **FIGURE 6.1**

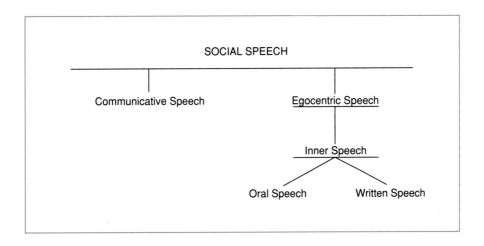

therefore, no point in teaching anything a child does not immediately understand or find relevant" (p. 66).

PROCESS WRITING RESEARCH

Writing as a developmental process has been an area of intensive research and interest. At the center of this focus has been Donald Graves and his research associates at the University of New Hampshire. Graves's ethnographic studies of young writers (1975, 1983, 1986) in primary classrooms have confirmed that students are creative artists who have both the ideas and language necessary to communicate through writing. Students need an opportunity to work independently as they conceive and plan their manuscripts, write drafts, revise, and refine to the point that the material is ready for classroom publication. Throughout the process, students may call on peers for advice and

KIDS' ▶
CORNER

_____ Name
Adam Spurlock

_____ Age
13

_____ Interests
Sports, reading, and going hunting.

What do you like most about school?
I like being and talking with my friends and just hanging out. I also like playing football and basketball outside.

What's your favorite subject? Why?
Math and Language Arts, because math is easy for me and I get to read alot in language arts.

What's your favorite book? Why do you like it?
My favorite book is Summer of the Monkey, because it is funny and exiteing.
I also like White Fang, because I like animals, and Jack london realy puts a picture in your mind when you read his writing.

What advice do you have for teachers?
Don't be realy strick, alow some slack. Have some fun with your lessons, play games, tak about it some, and let the students work in groups.

help. The teacher functions as an additional resource in encouraging the students to refine and elaborate their manuscripts.

In one important study, Graves and Hansen (1983) examined first graders' concepts of authorship and of the relation between reading and writing. They did so through the use of the "Author's Chair," a place where the children shared their "published work" or those of a professional writer. After reading a self-authored book, the author receives acceptance from the listeners: "I liked the part where you found the gold. I liked the way the story ended!" Then the questions begin. "Why did you choose this topic? Why did the spaceship blow up?" When a trade book is read and the author is not present, the questions are still asked as the teacher and children speculate on the answers the author might have provided. Through the use of the Author's Chair, Graves and Hansen (1983) observed that children grew into an understanding of the author concept.

Graves and Hansen (1983) broke the process of assimilating the author concept into three phases. The first phase, Replication, involved understanding that authors write books. In this phase this vague understanding is refined as students do what authors do—write books. As the children struggle to put their thoughts on paper, they experience what authors experience. As they read and listen to stories being read from the Author's Chair, they question the formation and meaning of stories and learn better how to communicate as authors.

The second phase, Transition, is marked by the child's developing concept of "I am an author." The children's books are displayed alongside those of professional authors. The children become more aware of the options they have as writers because of the questions they are asked as they sit in the Author's Chair.

The third phase, Option-Awareness, grows out of these questions. Students are aware of the content they want to include and the organization that will be needed to express their message. In addition, they become better readers because they become more assertive in dealing with other authors. Graves and Hansen (1983) clearly describe this process with this statement: "At first an author is distant, then an author is self, finally the self-author questions all authors and assertive readers emerge" (p. 181).

The results of a two-year study at Mast Way School in New Hampshire led Graves (1986) to focus on two capstones of highly successful classrooms: the role of the teacher as a literate leader or mentor in literacy, and the conditions for literate occasions that teachers set up in their classrooms.

In discussing the first capstone, Graves (1986) states, "It is the literate lives we lead, far more than methodology, that we bring to children." Teachers, then, must value literacy as a way of life, remaining active as readers and writers themselves.

In considering the second capstone, Graves calls on teachers to take an "inside-out" look at their classroom environment. This process involves a careful examination of teaching methods, student interactions, and literacy materials. Examination should lead teachers to a knowledge of what they need to do to "nurture, sustain and extend the literacy environment" in their classroom. Graves (1986) emphasizes that just as certain plants grow better in certain climates, different students and teachers learn together in different ways.

CLASSROOM VIGNETTE

Linda Lewis-White teaches third grade. Her students are in a bilingual program which recognizes that literacy develops as students have opportunities to communicate in both their native language and English. She uses journal writing as the cornerstone of her writing program. On the first day of school, Linda shared with her students that the purpose of keeping journals was to record their ideas, experiences, and feelings. She told the students that spellings did not need to be correct—they could invent spellings for words that they did not know how to spell. In addition, she promised not to mark or correct their journals. Instead, she said that she would read what they had written and write a response to their message.

As the year progressed, Linda fostered dialogue with her students through their journals. She used the opportunity to demonstrate through her responses how written language conveys meaning. She occasionally demonstrated standard spellings of the words a child might have spelled functionally by using the word or words in her response to the child. Sometimes the student would notice her standard spelling and would say, "So that's how you spell that word!" Usually, however, the entries would be received without comment.

Students generally started their journals in their native language, but moved to English by November. Linda usually responded to the students in English, demonstrating English syntax and construction. The journal entries started out very brief, but increased in length as the year progressed and the students gained confidence in their abilities to communicate their ideas through writing. The sample on the following page demonstrates the interaction between Linda and Jerry.

Journals provide a valuable opportunity for students and teachers to learn more about each other and the writing process. Students have an opportunity to write on a near daily basis and to receive quick feedback centered on the meaning of what they have written. Individual teachers adapt journals to the context of their classrooms and use them in many ways. Some teachers leave them as private writing, never responding to or reading them. Other teachers respond only when the student requests a response (Newman, 1984). Responding to journals is time consuming, but it is a good investment of time. Linda altered her journal schedule so the students wrote every Monday, Wednesday, and Friday. This enabled her to give back the journals Tuesday, Thursday, and Monday mornings.

Continued

Consequently, all teachers must create their own classroom environment, adapting what they have learned from others in order to capitalize on their own teaching strengths. We save the detailed discussion about how you can set up your writing classroom for Chapter 8.

The importance of conferencing with writers as they write was documented through the success of Lucy Calkins's (1986) Manhattan Writing Project. Calkins's (1991) further work focused on the significance of students' personal notebooks as a think tank for manuscript development.

And finally, the most important finding of process writing research—writers need an audience (Atwell, 1987; Thomason, 1993). Nancy Atwell expresses

9-2 Today was the frst day of skul,
     I was Japy dat I was in 3 grad.

     I am very happy that I am teaching
     third grade — and that you are in
     my class!! Welcome!! Welcome!!!
9-3 I always lak to wach tom and Jenny
     the in the monnin. It always maks
     me laf.

     You'll never guess what my favorite
     show is! It is Good Morning, America!
     Of course, sometimes they make me
     laugh.
9-4 I always lak to rede Buks we
     I am in the libere atskul,

     I am always reading and looking for
     new books to read. I just finished
     The River by Gary Paulsen. What are
     you reading? Any suggestions for a new book for me?
12-1 In cristmas I am going to have
     Legu toy, I want it becas it cud
     bild a lots of things.

Continued

it clearly: "A sense of audience—the knowledge that someone will read what they have written—is crucial to young writers" (p. 265). We share ways in which you can honor your young writers in Chapter 8.

SELF-EXPRESSION THROUGH JOURNALS

As with most literacy skills, writing is best learned by writing, not studying about how to write. One of the best ways of getting students involved extensively in writing is through journals. A journal is simply a notebook or tablet

Christmas is wonderful! There is always so much excitement and suspense.
It sounds as if you <u>know</u> what you want. There are so many different Lego sets; which one do you want? What are you planning to build?

178 Today at shcool at 8:30 we went ro the libere we met a man hou werks in a libere. And he told us haoo to get g libere card. And he had a dog and he told us about his fiusher.

Sounds as if you had a wonderful time! The library is one of my favorite places, and it seems as if it is one of your favorite places also. We have a lot in common.
Are you planning to get a library card? My library card is like my "ticket" to many new people and places!

in which students express themselves by writing about their thoughts, their ideas, their feelings. Journals let writers explore the writing process. Because journals are never corrected or edited, they represent the "least threatening of all writing activities" (Unia, 1985, p. 72). As students write about what is happening in their lives outside the classroom, teachers can monitor children's experiences and discover how they are growing as individuals.

Many teachers use journals as a means of responding to literature. Fuhler (1994) cites journals as an opportunity for students to mesh in a "thoughtful, personal engagement with trade books" (p. 400).

In summary, journal writing is an important tool in meaning-centered classrooms. They enable the teacher to understand their children in personal as well as academic terms, and provide an excellent opportunity for writing to be demonstrated as a meaning-centered process.

SELF-EXPRESSION THROUGH INDIVIDUAL STORIES AND POEMS

It's essential that children be given the opportunity for self-expression through writing every day. When children are allowed to write, you'll see their vocabularies spring to life. Consider Kelly, a bright first-grade student who wrote:

See the lightning!

Seagulls were twirling like kites.

The power of imagination is revealed in the pieces children write. Consider Carolyn's story:

THE ELEPHANT HAD A TOO-LONG TRUNK!!

Once there was an elephant with a very long trunk. In fact, it was too long. One day he heard about a contest.

The next day he saw a sign about it.

CONTEST*!*
> *The elephant that can eat the*
> *most peanuts will win a trip*
> *to Africa. For more information*
> *call 886-8844.*

He thought, oh I must enter that contest, so he called 886-8844.

The man who answered the phone was friendly. The man told the rules and that the contest was the next day.

The next morning the elephant with the too long trunk got up early and went to the contest spot. And to his surprise he won.

The next day he went to Africa. He had lots of fun playing tag with the snakes. He also had fun swinging from tree to tree with the monkeys. He stayed for a month and then he had to go home. He was very sad but he knew he would be back again.

The End

CAROLYN, AGE 9

Most students have tremendous language power that is never tapped for written self-expression. "Correctness" as a major goal forces them to rely on available materials and safe ideas. Teachers must create opportunities for students to express themselves through many genres and purposes. Some examples of these needs follow.

1. **Letters that will actually find their way to the intended reader.** Develop a postal system within the classroom with mail collection places for each person, including the teacher. Encourage communication through letter writing in a variety of forms. Write personal notes to absent members.

2. **Stories to be bound into books for the classroom library.** Somewhere in the classroom keep two or three folders to hold individual contributions for books. When 10 to 12 contributions have been made to a topic, edit them with the authors, bind them into a cover, and place the books in the classroom library following an oral reading in the Author's Chair or Discussion Center.

3. **A poem to preserve a beautiful thought.**

CLASSROOM VIGNETTE

Katie Hart read a Bill Martin Jr book to her class. Students liked it so much that she suggested they write one of their own using the same language pattern that was used in *My Days Are Made of Butterflies*. They decided on a title, *Spring Days Are Made of Blooming Flowers,* and composed the first page of the book. On days that followed, students contributed to the book. It was edited, illustrated, and bound into a book. Katie duplicated copies for every student. She left the space for illustrations blank for each student to fill in.

SPRING DAYS ARE MADE OF BLOOMING FLOWERS

(Adapted from *My Days Are Made of Butterflies*, by Bill Martin Jr)

Spring days are made of blooming flowers in my garden. *Joel*

Spring days are made of baby birds chirping in the trees. *Marcia*

Spring days are made of working bees collecting nectar in the desert. *Thomas*

Spring days are made of whispering breezes and waving leaves. *Maria*

ROCKS

Some rocks are round.
A streambed is where rocks are found.
Think of the years to get as round as that!
Even longer than nine lives of a cat.

Milton, age 10

Continued

Children, like adults, like to talk. The discussions children have represent excellent beginnings for collaborative stories. Writing a collaborative composition is an excellent opportunity to learn incidentally many conventions that carry over to the independent writing of students. As student editors capitalize a title or the beginning of a sentence, leave a margin, and supply quotation marks, they call attention to these literacy conventions. Thus conventions are learned as a natural part of writing, along with content and organization.

As teachers and students engage in talk about writing from group dictation or group response to a composition, writing skills and abilities emerge. They might include the following:

1. **Some words are used over and over, and others are not used very often.** Those that occur most frequently in group and in

---

MOUNTAINS AT DUSK

. . . The color was the deep purple of a hot day cooling.

Pam, age 11

Katie believed she should permeate the learning environment with lists of words in categories that help students say and write their observations and feelings in poetic language:

Color Words	Taste Words
Size Words	Smell Words
Shape Words	Rhyming Words
Texture Words	Similes
Sound Words	Metaphors

Keep the lists open so additions can be made. Pause when reading to students to savor a beautiful way of saying something. Keep available a "poet's corner" on a bulletin board on which students can pin contributions. Mount a branch from a tree for them to use to hang poetic expressions for others to read; it can be called the "Poet's Tree."

From the first year in school until the last, every student needs to feel the thrill of authorship. Individual contributions to writing should be treated with appropriate mountings and bindings and displayed to foster a feeling of authorship.

Students who experience authorship many times are likely to be those most interested in other authors. They appreciate good descriptive passages, the beautiful language of good poetry, and characters who seem to live. They can muse with an author rather than always seek to be amused. They know that good writing is not easy. The satisfaction of having personal ideas accepted, enjoyed, and appreciated builds a strong desire for contact with other authors.

MY POEMS

I write my dreams.
I discover the laughter.
I share the thoughts I think.
My body grows old and fails me,
But my soul lives on in ink.

individual compositions at any level in school are the same words that occur frequently in most writing. These are usually determiners (words that pattern like *the*), prepositions (words that pattern like *to*), pronouns (words that pattern like *I* and *you*), conjunctions (words that pattern like *and*), question words (words that pattern like *what*), auxiliaries (words that pattern like *be* and *have*), and an assortment of other words such as negatives and words of courtesy. Students should be made aware of the need to learn standard spelling for these words and to learn to use the spelling aids that will be furnished them in the classroom.

Other words that occur frequently in some compositions but not in all compositions may be nouns and verbs. Sometimes they are adjectives and adverbs. When students are writing compositions with the frequent use of the same word or words, the spelling should be furnished in a place that is easy to see.

2. **Some words begin alike.** The letters of the alphabet are used over and over in the initial position of words. If the first sound of a word is written with a consonant, it is likely to be the same sound–symbol relation for most works beginning with that letter. This is dependable information for writing.

3. **Some words end alike.** The endings that occur most frequently *(-s, -es, -ed, -ing, -er, -est, -ful,* and *-ly)* change the meaning of root words and may shift their positions in sentences. To recognize them and to understand their significance are essential to the finer points of meaning. It is through writing, much more than through reading, that students come to grips with this aspect of language structure.

4. **Only 26 letters are used to write all the words we use.** Each of the letters has a name that is useful in talking about spelling and in doing reference research. Each letter can be written with numerous configurations and must be recognized in its many forms. Each letter represents one or more sounds when used in writing. Consonants represent fewer sounds than vowels. Knowing the alphabet and being able to talk about the names of all the letters are useful in writing.

5. **Some syllables occur over and over in the language.** These syllables, when used with different consonants at the beginning of words

CLASSROOM VIGNETTE

Julia Gore was aware of some students' interest in football just before a Super Bowl game. She used this interest to invite groups of students to dictate to her their perceptions of "How to Play Football." The collaborative compositions were good enough that she duplicated them for students to take home. The parents of the kindergarten children encouraged her to submit the work of the students to the local newspaper for a Sunday edition special page.

All of the compositions were published. Two are reproduced here.

HOW TO PLAY FOOTBALL

They put on helmets, shoulder pads, knee pads and shoes with bumps.

All the heads go the same way and they hike the ball. They run and try to catch the ball. Then they jump all over each other.

They go back and do it all over again and try to make a touchdown.

When they make a touchdown, they win. They jump up and down and line up, shake hands, and say, "Good game!"

Then they change clothes and go to New York.

JULIE, SCOTT, TODD, JENNY, MONTY, AND CHASE

HOW TO PLAY FOOTBALL

First you get 6 or 7 or 20 or 38 people on your team.

You wear helmets and sport shirts and knee pads and arm pads.

You need poles so you can make a goal.

You hold the football and you run and kick and you throw the ball to one of your friends if someone gets too close.

You throw the ball to the other team to score points.

There is a defense, outfielders, frontrunners, offense, infielders, tackles and a scorpion.

You try to throw the football over the poles to make a goal.

Whoever gets the most points, wins and gets a cup and a treat and a free lunch.

BRIAN, MEREDITH, GUNNAR, EDDIE, SHARON, HEATHER, AND LARRY

and with different endings, form hundreds of words. The most frequent ones are:

-at, -an, -all, -am
-en, -ell, -et, -ed
-in, -ill, -ing, -ight, -it
-ook, -ot, -ow, -old, -oy
-un, -ug.

These syllables are found in all of writing and are useful in the analysis of unfamiliar words for spelling. Students enjoy games that contrast beginning sounds with these high-frequency syllables. After finding as many words as possible by changing beginning consonants and consonant clusters, students can add endings. For more mature students an added challenge might be to make columns and list words that become nouns, verbs, adjectives, and adverbs by changing the endings.

It is impossible to record collaborative compositions without illustrating the five characteristics of writing and spelling just described. The concepts related to these five must be understood and developed to support

FIGURE 6.2 ▶ AN 8-YEAR-OLD'S STORY

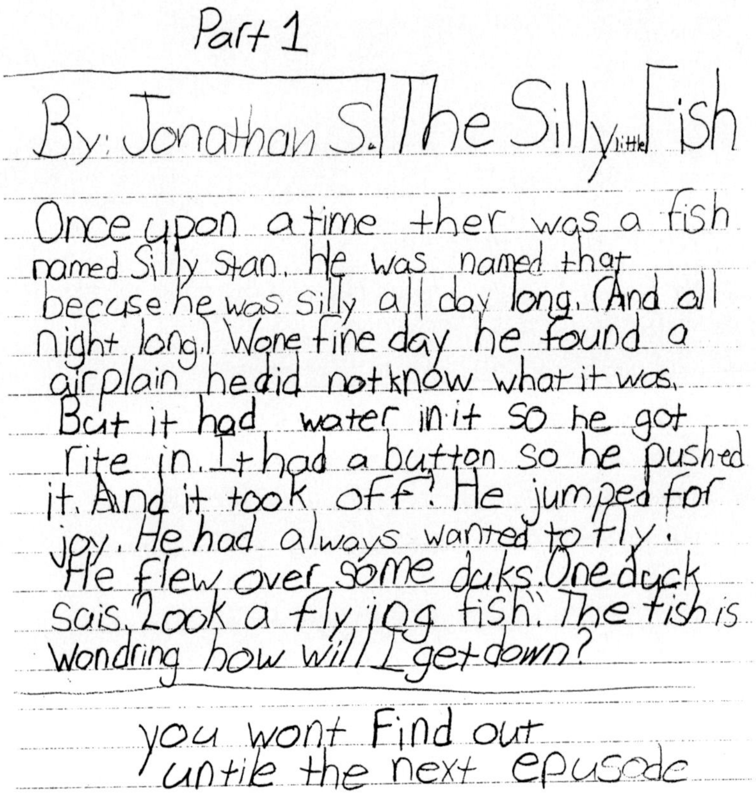

Part 1

By: Jonathan S. The Silly little Fish

Once upon a time ther was a fish named Silly Stan. He was named that becuse he was silly all day long. (And all night long.) Wone fine day he found a airplain he did not know what it was. But it had water in it so he got rite in. It had a button so he pushed it. And it took off! He jumped for joy. He had always wanted to fly. He flew over some duks. One duck sais, "Look a fly ing fish." The fish is wondring how will I get down?

you wont find out untile the next epusode

independent writing. However, too much emphasis on conventions without allowing for the personal, dynamic ideas of students may result in writing becoming a chore, not a joy.

FREEING STUDENTS TO WRITE STORIES AND POEMS

One of the most exciting aspects of teaching is the delight you feel when you read the stories your children write. Teachers are like sculptors—they have an opportunity to create beautiful treasures of art. Our creations are the manuscripts the children produce. Here are some examples in the genres of books, research reports, personal observations, aspirations, imagination, and self-concept pieces. You, too, can free students to write in personal ways that reflect their interests and concerns.

CHAPTER BOOKS

Students who begin to read whole books are aware they are printed on numbered pages. When they begin to write longer stories, they enjoy paging their manuscripts. Eight-year-old Jonathan discovered another division of stories—episodes. Figure 6.2 contains two episodes from his story "The Silly Little Fish."

◄ **FIGURE 6.2**
Continued

Part 2

By: Jon S. The Silly little Fish

Hay, wait a sekunt, what dose this button do? He wondrrd. So he pushed it it only made him go hire. (for one thing it was the same button). But then he saw a thing that looked like a wheel. He turned it he found out that he could drive! Then he pushed it up he went down he landed and he went home.

The End

Arrangement into chapters is another development in prose writing. Long compositions should have some breaking points in order to keep a plot sequenced and to take care of increasing complexity that develops as stories lengthen and deal with many characters. Kelly wrote *Paint's Adventures* at a time when the teacher was guiding students to notice that authors used chapter arrangements in many of the books they were reading. Kelly was beginning to write long and involved stories and was ready for some help in organizing her work. She tried writing with chapters. The text of her book is presented here as she presented it to her class. Some of her spelling is original, or invented.

THE ADVENTURES OF PAINT THE GOAT
. . . .
BY KELLY, AGE 9

Chapter 1

MOVING

PAINT

Today your new master is coming for you. And I'm glad!! And Paint whinned just as to say: I'm glad too. Paint finished her breakfast then the man come to take her to the mountains. It was a long trip to the mountains. And Paint fell asleep a few times. And she really missed a lot. She missed lots of beautiful flowers. Which were for-get-me-nots, violets, roses, gardenias, and camillias. There also was a pond that seemed to smile. And Paint missed that.

She woke up just when they got to the farm. At first she was scared. No longer was she in her stable in the city. But in a truck!! But when she got in the pasture and knew all the other goats were her friends, she wasn't afraid. Paint enjoyed the mountains and stayed many long years.

Finally the time came for her master to take Paint out of the countryside which was right next to a forest. Her master of course had to walk her through the forest. The soil was real good on the countryside and there was plenty of grass to eat. Painted like the countryside very much.

The countryside was practully made up of hills. Paint loved to slide down the hills, but she had to be careful. Because there was a beehive!!

Chapter 2

PAINT EATS FLOWERS

None of the goats up in the mountains liked to eat flowers. But Paint did! She liked violets!!!! When Paint was walked through the forest she saw what seemed like a acre of violets!! She was so excited she ate practully a half acre of flowers!!!! Paint ate so much that one day there weren't any flowers left. Paint was very sad. But finally she settled down and learned to eat grass again.

Chapter 3

AN ACCIDENT

One day Paint was sliding down the hill. but the third time down Paint was unlucky to bump right smack into the bee hive!!!!!!! Paint cried and cried. Her master didn't know what it was. He got his first-aid kit and looked all over. But he couldn't find who was crying. "The only place I haven't looked is out on the countryside," said her master. So he went out on the countryside and there was Paint lying on the ground crying. Down the hill the bees were swarmed, the bee hive turned over, and the honey running out. "Uh-ah, just as I thought. I warned you Paint. It is your own fault."

So the master whose name was Mr. Wooder went over and fixed Paint, and she stopped crying. Paint stayed away from the bee hive for 4 months. But then she couldn't resist it any longer. She had to slide down that hill. But this time Paint went off course and the 1st time down she again bumped smack into the bee hive!!!!!!!

Mr. Wooder heard her crying and said, "That's my clue to scadoo to the countryside." "Oh no! where's my first aid!?" He looked every place but he just couldn't find it. After a while Mr. Wooder couldn't hear the crying. "It must be my hearing," he said. "Oh no but it's not. I had a check-up and the Dr. said my hearing is fine. I'd better take a look." He went over and there was Paint, her body swollen but she was asleep! Now how did she do that!! He shrugged his shoulders and walked away.

Chapter 4

GOOD-BY TO THE FARM

Mr. Wooder had been thinking. I think I should sell Paint. I know she's a good goat and all, but I just can't keep her. I'll talk to Mr. Laboe. He's been wanting a good goat for over a year. Mr. Wooder called Mr. Laboe on the telephone. They talked it over and it was settled that Mr. Laboe was coming over to inspect Paint. He came the next morning. He came about 8:30 A.M. The next morning at 8:30 A.M. it was an exciteing moment at the farm. Mr. Laboe came right on time. He looked Paint over very carefully. He said, "How much do you want for her?" "She's worth about $150," Mr. Wooder replyed.

"You've got yourself a deal."

"Good!"

Chapter 5

LEAVING

It was the day before Easter and Paint was leaving the farm. A truck came to pick her up. It was dull up at the farm. All there was a dog, her, and Mr. Laboe. Paint didn't like the farm. She was planning to run away. She planned for months and finally she had it. One night when Mr. Laboe left the gate open Paint wandered out. She went into the forest thinking she could find her way home to the old farm. She went deeper into the forest and she got lost!! Paint had many miserable nights. All she had to eat and drink was sour grass and dirty water. One day Paint came to a clearing. She went over and drank some water and ate some grass. Then she went into the forest again. When night came Paint layed down under a tree and fell asleep. A boy came and saw Paint. He said, "hi!" Paint startled and got ready to butt the boy. The boy said, "No d-don't be afraid. Come w-with me." Paint and the boy went to the boy's farm. The boy went in and got his father. His father said, "H-m-m-m nice goat. Better call all the farms to see who it belongs too." "Oh no don't. I want to keep her." "On one condition. You milk and take care of her." "I will, I will!!!" "All right." So that's how Paint got a good home, new friends, and good pals.

RESEARCH REPORTS

As students travel down pathways to literacy, they are on a never-ending journey. They'll always be writers, and they'll always be doing research to support what they write. Or, as Lucy Calkins (1986) explains, "The writers begin with what they know, they learn more about the topic, and they

---

THE BOOK ▶
MAKERS

JANE YOLEN

1. Which book of yours has given you the greatest pleasure?
Three books have been especially meaningful, *Owl Moon, The Devil's Arithmetic,* and *Wild Hunt.* Each spoke to a deep part of me and each surprised me in a way. Also, there was not anything exactly like those books in my previous work or the work of other authors.

2. Which book has surprised you most in terms of its public reception?
Owl Moon. I thought it would be a quiet, gentle little personal book that might sell 10,000 copies over five years. There are now more than 300,000 copies in print. It struck a chord with families, I think, because it dealt with the relationship of a father and a child. There are lots of books about mother-child relationships, but not many about fathers and children.

3. What would you like people to remember about your work?
I want my work to be remembered for its honesty, the poetry of my prose style, my sense of story, and a versatile imagination.

4. What impact do you hope your work will have on children?
I want my books to be just a part of a much larger introduction to story in the lives of children, a part of their cultural upbringing.

Jane Yolen is a prolific writer of picture books and novels and a collector of nursery rhymes, lullabies, and songs. Her many works include the *Commander Toad Series, Owl Moon, The Piggins Books, Letting Swift River Go, Honkers, Encounter, Laptime Song and Play Book,* and the *Lullaby Songbook.*

teach their content to readers" (p. 274). This basis pathway from research to writing can begin in the elementary school. Here's how it happened for one student.

PERSONAL OBSERVATIONS

Some students fail to respond to instruction in how to read and write and so land in special classes with special teachers. This happened to Danny in school. His special teacher tried to relieve him of the feeling that he couldn't read and write. She showed Danny that he could "read" from his personal observations. He grew to the point that he could tell and dictate stories from real life and from imagination. The first story that he wrote independently and made into a book reveals he had been reading much nonprint during the time he was failing to read printed material in school. It had never occurred to him that he could write about what he observed and talked about. One of his stories in his language follows.

MY VERY OWN DOG

BY DANNY

One day my dog he got sick.

He sneezed a lot.

We gave him a lot of milk and he got well.

He played with us.

Then every day he went out looking for a girl friend because he wanted to see some baby dogs.

Then he found one.

Then he was the father of the dogs.

I don't know how many puppies.

Then one day this truck came by and ranned over him.

Then he had a broken leg.

We took him in the house and my father got a ruler and broke it and put it on his leg.

My dog is still alive—but he's tired of looking for girl friends.

Where did a "nonreader" and "nonwriter" like Danny get the information for his story? How is it that he could read this story but could not read a pre-primer in a reading series?

The answers lie in the ability of one special teacher to release Danny to say what he had to say in his own language patterns and with his own vocabulary. The writing process, though laborious to Danny, helped him internalize the vocabulary he used in talking so the printed forms were meaningful. Together, he and the teacher edited the story, paged it, illustrated it, copied it,

CLASSROOM VIGNETTE

Jonathan Sampson, a student in Linda Allen's sixth-grade class, became interested in Davy Crockett. In preparing a report on Crockett to the class, Jonathan demonstrated what he had learned about researching the writing process. He checked out books from the library on Davy Crockett. He read reports from an encyclopedia. He used the classroom CD-ROM multimedia encyclopedia. He kept notes of what he was discovering about Crockett, and used these to create a semantic web (see Chapter 5). Finally, he wrote the report. Here's his second draft:

DAVY CROCKETT

On August 17, 1786, Davy Crockett was born in the wild disputed frontier territory of Tennessee. Davy's mother and father, from the outside, looked pretty ordinary. They had a normal log cabin like anyone else. They ate normal food like anyone else. They even had a normal plot of land like anyone else. Yet, the Crocketts were far from ordinary. They had great talents and lived in a great place.

Davy learned how to do many things such as tell the weather for tomorrow by the signs of today, and to make animal like noises of almost any animal you can name. Davy also learned how to flip a tomahawk anywhere, and it would land any way he wanted it to.

To finish training Davy, the Crocketts had the best marksmen in the valley teach him all they knew about hunting. Along with the lessons, Davy figured out some ideas of his own. Then he finally made up a rule for the best way to shoot. The rule was: *Be sure you're right, then go ahead and pull the trigger.*

When Davy grew up, he finally got his first true love. You can take your choice of two stories about Davy's first sweetheart. His neighbors say that his first true love was the "pride of Old Kentucky." She lived up in Gum Hollow on Goose Creek. Every winter she got so plump on bear's meat that by the spring she was bigger around than a barrel. Some say that when she sneezed it took the hens right off of their eggs. There was never a girl who liked anyone the way that she did Davy.

Of course, Davy's story of his first sweetheart was *very* different. He said that he didn't like girls very much until he was about eighteen. This may have been because he had three sisters of his own. But after a time, he fell in love. He had been working for an trustworthy old Quaker, John Kennedy, who lived about fifteen miles from the Crockett cabin. When the Quaker's niece came back from North Carolina to pay the Kennedys a visit, Davy soon found himself head over heels in love. "I've heard people talk about hard loving," said Davy, "but I reckon

Continued

and then bound it into the first whole book Danny ever read although he had been in school for four years.

ASPIRATIONS

Inside many young students is the desire to be something—to be a contributor rather than always a consumer. Teachers need to know the aspiration no poor devil in all the world was every cursed with such hard love as mine. I thought if all the hills about there were pure gold and they all belonged to me, I'd trade them if I could only talk to her the way I wanted to." But Davy was too afraid to say anything to her because he was afraid he might say it wrong. Yet, Davy knew he had to talk to her. So he went and told her how much he loved her and how beautiful she was, but she was honest and said she was engaged to her cousin, the son of the old Quaker. This was even worse news for Davy than anything she could have told him. Fortunately, he finally got over her, and since he had heard that women liked men with an education, he went to school to get educated.

Then his life got onto a famous track. First, he fought in a few wars. Then when he returned, he decided to do something for the law. At first, he just wrote warrants and other documents as a scribe. But through the years he progressed until he became the colonel of the militia. Then Davy got elected to the legislature. He learned a good deal about the government and served his district well. We know he did well because when he moved to a new place where he thought his neighbors didn't even know him, they elected him to the legislature just as soon as an election came around.

When Davy went to Washington he had many interesting times there, but that is not the reason he is famous. During reelection he reportedly told voters in his district, "Elect me or not, if you don't, you can go to h---, and I'll go to Texas." I don't know if this is true or not, but it is a fact that before long, ex-congressman Crockett was going to Texas and the Alamo.

Texans by then were yearning for their independence. Davy did not go to Texas to get in a war, but to "look things over." When Davy got to Nacogdoches, he heard that the Texans had their revolution rolling and that they were asking Americans to come help and them. Davy decided to join the Texans and headed for the Alamo.

When Davy entered the gates of the Alamo, a young man came up to shake Crockett's hand. Crockett introduced himself, but the man explained that he needed *no* introduction. This man had a soft southern accent, and now Crockett knew why the newspapers called him "the gallant Travis." Just a little talk proved that the Texans were in a fix, but all of the Texans stayed to defend their country.

The battle of the Alamo continued until March 5, and then the soldiers of General Santa Anna caught the Texans off guard as they mounted a full attack. Every man tried to get to his post, but it was hopeless against the swarm of soldiers. Davy and his men held up their posts as long as they could. They were the last to be penetrated. As we know, the people of the Alamo died that day, but they still live on in our minds.

of students, but they never have access to that information when the daily routine consists of the exact replication of printed material followed by simple comprehension questions.

One way to assure some understanding of aspirations is to encourage self-expression through writing. Frequently this writing will reveal inner feelings and high aspirations. With this informal contact teachers can respond, support, and encourage growth.

First, let's consider the aspiration of Julie, a 7-year-old. She writes, *"I want to be a teacher. And why do I want to be a teacher? Cause a teacher makes your dreams come true."* Figure 6.3 is a copy of the piece; note her invented spellings on the following page.

Now let's look at a third grader, Lisa. She attended a school where she had had many opportunities to experience authorship. Her teacher organized the learning environment to promote self-expression through art, drama, and writing. She felt she had to have more information than that provided by test scores to do an intelligent job of grouping students for instruction in reading. Lisa wrote her book *When I Won $100,000,000.00* during the second week of third grade. Her book told the teacher much about Lisa. She was observant; she was interested in ecology, health, and peace; she gathered information from sources outside of school; she had made some contact with classical literature. But most of all, Lisa was a child with high aspirations that would be useful in her school program. Here is the text of Lisa's book without her illustrations and attractive binding.

WHEN I WON $100,000,000.00
BY LISA

When I won $100,000,000.00 I thought I was the president of the United States. Imagine me winning $100,000,000.00.

I bought two of the most expensive cars, ten large color television sets, five of the largest mansions, the Grand Canyon, ten bicycles, found a cure for muscular dystrophy, and gave our land freedom.

I stopped pollution and forest fires. I have a chauffeur-driven car.

Wow! It's a great feeling to win $100,000,000.00. I wish I could do more to help my country do the things it needs to do, but I ran out of money.

The greatest thing I won since the $100,000,000.00 was winning a teacher named Mrs. Allen. I think she's great!

(And just like Shakespeare said, "Money doesn't grow on trees.")

Lisa could never have revealed her high aspirations through diagnostic testing or by giving correct answers to an endless number of questions that she did not ask.

IMAGINATION

Perhaps the richest source for writing is the unlimited imaginations of children. The bulk of writing that children do is from this genre. Why is this so? Our theory is that this genre frees children from the requirement of being correct. After all, it's their imagination, and who can say something could or could not occur? Consider the story *The Time Machine,* by 10-year-old Josh (Figure 6.4).

Students who are reluctant to engage in writing from imagination can be teamed with other students for co-authored selections. Others can become illustrators for books produced by their classmates.

FIGURE 6.4 ▶

I had to be there by 5:30 I peddeld like a raging lion after his prey, woo!! Whats that, kuthud! I bumped into a cilver cilender the size of a hipo it had three bowny metal legs that started tap dancing when I aproched. I scrambld into the odd machine, and set down in a cosy coshin seat and pered at the dashboard. I glanced around, and saw a butten that said THE YEAR 5099 so I pushed it, and all of a sudent I heard a voice that said "O.K dude you got it im Nogo". Then I heard a zip boom ssssss zap and we were gone! Where are we goin? Exacly the year you pushed. But — no buts you push the buten we go!!

Soner than you could say jackrabit we were in the year 5099. I hoped out of the time machine, and Nogo gave me some mony and told me to come if the machine started tape dancing. First I went to

◀ **FIGURE 6.4**
Continued

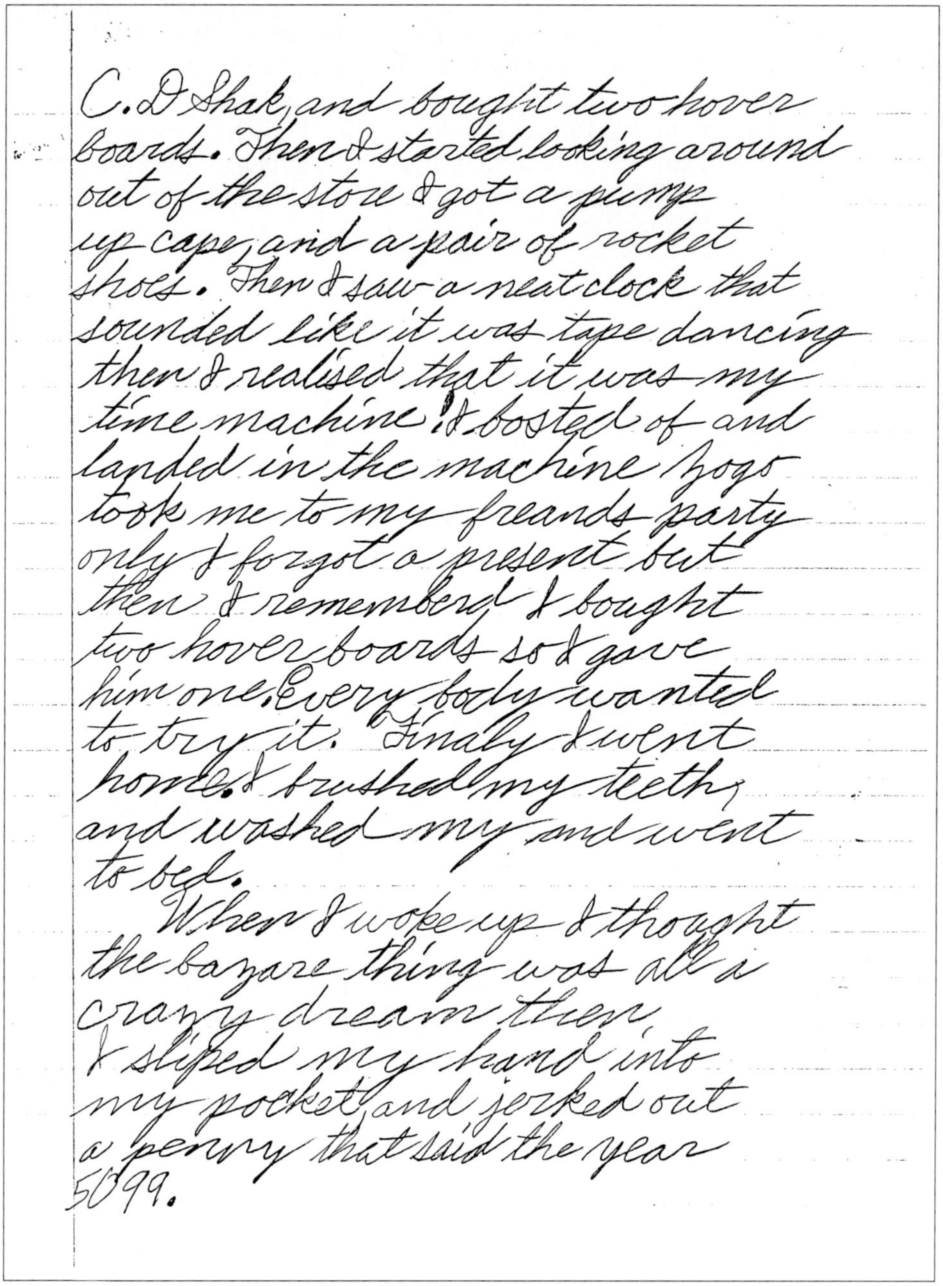

C. D Shak, and bought two hover boards. Then I started looking around out of the store & got a pump up cape, and a pair of rocket shoes. Then I saw a neat clock that sounded like it was tape dancing then I realised that it was my time machine! I bosted of and landed in the machine hogo took me to my freands party only I forgot a present but then I rememberd I bought two hover boards so I gave him one. Every body wanted to try it. Finaly I went home I brushed my teeth, and washed my and went to bed.

When I woke up I thought the bazare thing was all a crazy dream then, I sliped my hand into my pocket, and jerked out a penny that said the year 5099.

SELF-CONCEPT

Students reveal much of themselves as they write. The information, though subtle, helps teachers develop expectations for individuals. Johnny Gonzales revealed much about his basic character when he wrote "Why I Like Me." His teacher modified her feelings about Johnny after she read it. English was Johnny's second language and he had some difficulty with exact replication of the language in the reading curriculum. After knowing about Johnny's strong self-concept, she was able to help him without being concerned about fleeting errors in word recognition and in spelling. She trusted Johnny and his natural ability as a learner.

WHY I LIKE ME
BY JOHNNY GONZALES, AGE 7

Page 1—I like me because I clean the table and it makes me feel happy.

Page 2—Also I like me because I help my mom with the baby at night when she is tired.

Page 3—I like me when I understand my mom and dad speak Spanish, and I'm proud I speak English, too.

Page 4—I can make bookshelves all by myself, and my mom uses them, and when I'm finished my mom hugs me, and says, "That's great!"

Page 5—I like me because I finish my homework when my teacher tells me.

Page 6—I like me because I know how to drive a car. I learned from watching my dad drive.

Page 7—I like me because I am big and I could do almost anything my dad could do.

Page 8—Also, I like me because I do anything my mother says, and that makes me feel good.

Page 9—I like me because I like dogs and cats. I'm kind to them.

Page 10—And most of all I like me because I'm me.

Page 11—THE END

RESPONSE TO EXPERIENCES

Becky Davis took her first-grade class to the Shamrock Dairy. Something very interesting occurred while the class was there. See Figure 6.5 on the following page for Carson's response to the experience.

Here's how Carson read his story to the class during Author's Chair:

> We went to the dairy and I saw a baby cow be born. The mother cow just stood in her stall and mooed, and was she surprised when she turned around and saw her baby. She didn't even know what had happened!
>
> There was the baby, all wrapped up in a plastic sack, and the mother started to lick it off. I didn't know that baby cows came in plastic sacks! It was so cute!

By: Carson Barnes.

We weint to The dairy and
I saw a baby cow be born.

The mothr cow Juct
stued in her stfol and
Mued, and wos she surprizd
win she turnd aurind
and saw her baby.

Ther wos the baby, all
rapt in a plastc SAC, and the
moter startd to lic it of.
I didnt now tat baby cows
can in plastc SACS.
It wos sow net. The lade at
the daire didnt now the
cow wos going too hav her
baby whil we wer ter.
Boy, were we glad she did!

The lady at the dairy didn't know that the cow was going to have her baby while we were there. Boy, were we glad she did!

Three wonderful things had occurred. First, the children experienced a delightful trip to the Shamrock Dairy. Second, Carson had an opportunity to write his story using his language expressed with his own invented spellings. And third, Carson's story was honored as he shared it in the Author's Chair.

DESCRIPTIVE

One of the signposts we observe in developing writers is an attention to detail. Kyle received a pet lizard for his eighth birthday. The next day,

FIGURE 6.6 ▶

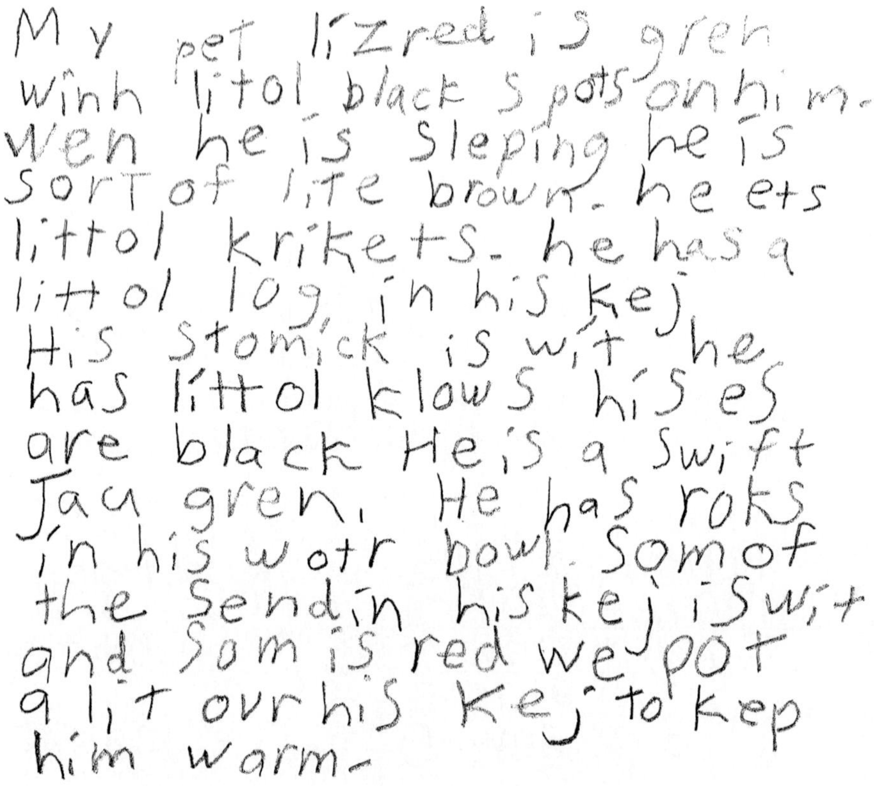

My pet lizred is gren winh litol black spots on him. Wen he is sleping he is sort of lite brown. he ets littol krikets. he has a littol log in his kej His stomick is wit he has littol klows his es are black He is a swift Jaq gren. He has roks in his wotr bowl. Som of the Send in his kej is swit and som is red we pot a lit ovr his kej to kep him warm.

My pet lizard is green with little black spots on him. When he is sleeping he is sort of light brown. He eats little crickets. He has a little log in his cage. His stomach is white. He has little claws. His eyes are black. He is a Swift Jade Green. He has rocks in his water bowl. Some of the sand in his cage is white and some is red. We put a light over his cage to keep him warm.

during Writer's Workshop, he described the lizard in great detail (see Figure 6.6).

CURRENT INTEREST

Students like to write about what is on their minds. While 8-year-old Kyle is excited about his new pet lizard, 13-year-old girls are daydreaming about other things (Figure 6.7)!

Students should be given the freedom to write about what they want to write about. Research has shown us that the more children write, the better they become at writing. Thus current interests are a fertile area for manuscript production.

◀ **FIGURE 6.7**

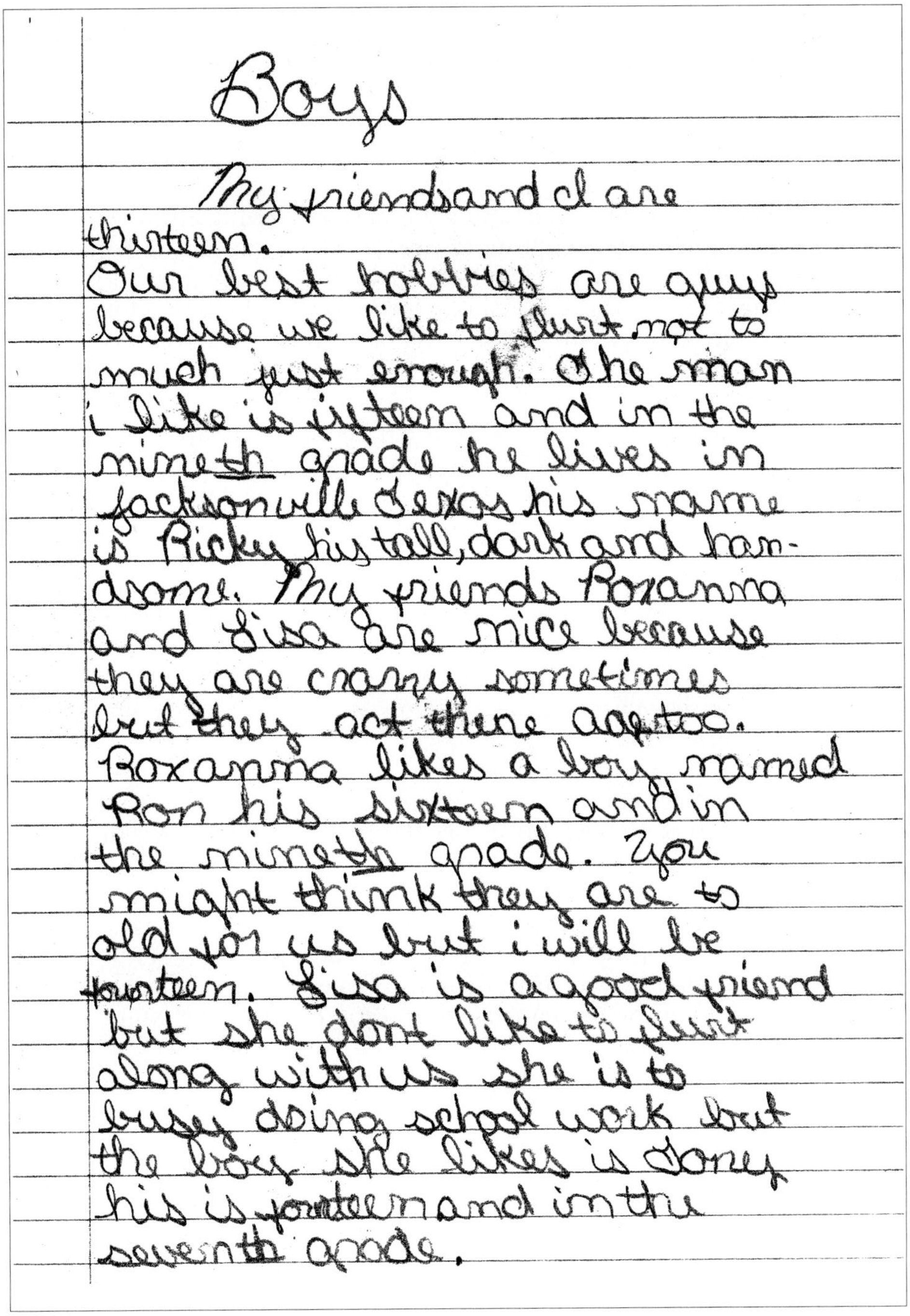

Boys

My friends and I are thirteen.
Our best hobbies are guys because we like to flirt not to much just enough. The man i like is ifteen and in the nineth grade he lives in Jacksonville Texas his name is Ricky his tall, dark and handsome. My friends Roxanna and Lisa are nice because they are crazy sometimes but they act there age too. Roxanna likes a boy named Ron his sixteen and in the nineth grade. You might think they are to old for us but i will be fourteen. Lisa is a good friend but she dont like to flirt along with us she is to busy doing school work but the boy she likes is Joney his is fourteen and in the seventh grade.

INDEPENDENT WRITING AND DICTATION

As children experience writing as a form of self-expression and are freed from the requirement of producing error-free work, they can and do write effectively. This independent writing is produced by preschoolers as well as elementary school students. This fact raises an important question: Is there a need for dictation (teachers operating as scribes for children), since students can write their own stories independently? The answer is "yes." Dictation involves different processes and has goals different from those of independent writing. Teachers don't take dictation "because children cannot write; they are using dictation as another form of writing" (Sulzby, Teale, & Kamberelis, 1989, p. 75). Dictation provides and demonstrates an important link among thought, language, writing, and reading for many children. In addition, dictation allows the teachers to reinforce the meaning and importance of writing skills, to offer alternatives to grammar, to demonstrate standard spelling, and to encourage elaboration that leads to clarity and interest.

We model reading by reading to children because we want them to read. In the same manner we model writing by writing down what children have to say because we want them to write. We validate the child when we take dictation; we enhance self-esteem as we accept the child's language and contributions to individual or group efforts. Furthermore, some children have not had many opportunities to write or scribble at home and really do not understand or value writing. Jacque Wuertenberg (1990) expresses the importance of dictation in school programs best: "Until you see your language valued through dictation you may not have the courage to write something down. Once you see your language written down you can't help but to want to write for yourself."

Independent writing of students can be slow because of the time it takes them to form letters and explore spelling. Dictation provides a technique that enables a writer to have his or her thoughts quickly turned into print, thus enabling the author to focus on stream of thoughts instead of surface features of print. Murray (1989), in discussing his own writing, takes note of the occasional need of authors to quickly capture their thoughts. Murray sometimes tapes his first draft to avoid the delays that letter formation entails. "Dictating is marvelously helpful, because it allows me to write at greater speed, and fast writing is extremely important for me" (Murray, 1989, p. 86).

Dictation is an efficient technique teachers can use to allow students to "discover" certain truths about language, writing, and reading. When children write independently, they represent their thoughts with spellings that may be unconventional or "invented." Over time, spellings become standard as children have repeated experiences with reading and writing. Dictation is one experience that aids in the acquisition of standard spelling.

However, teachers should be careful to balance dictation opportunities with opportunities for children to write independently. In independent writing, children should be encouraged to write without being concerned about standard spellings. Yes, teachers should avoid "telling" children standard spellings when they are involved in independent first-draft writing. To do so only makes children dependent on the teacher and results in children not having the incentive to try on their own.

Thus a combination of independent writing and writing through dictation is recommended. Both are effective avenues to self-expression.

FROM TALK TO WRITING

Relations between speech and writing exist, but writing, until it is refined through editing, is an imperfect representation of speech. It frequently lacks pitch, tone, emphasis, pause, and juncture. Whereas speech is highly perishable, written records have a degree of permanence. Refined writing represents the communication of thoughts with word order and patterns that are not characteristic of spontaneous expression; it raises language to a literary level.

THE DICTATION PROCESS

Procedures vary in instructional programs that help students progress from talk to writing, but a few basic steps are recommended.

FREEING STUDENTS TO WRITE PERSONAL POETRY

Poetry, because of its color, rhythm, and fresh approach to reality and fantasy, has a natural appeal. Poetry allows children to try out language characteristics used by many authors. These writing experiences move them closer and closer to the realization that much, if not most, of their writing is an extension of their own personal language.

How do we develop poets in our writing program? We believe two major emphases are key:

1. Read poetry daily in your classroom. Children internalize the structure and flow of poetry by hearing it through their ears. Be sure to read a variety of styles—from fun to serious—and a variety of authors as well.

2. Bring poetry to life by acting it out. Brod Bagert, author of *The Poet Ponders* section of this text, has developed what he terms "The Performance Method" as a means of leading children to confidence in their ability to act out poetry. Brod's method is printed in Figure 6.8 (see pages 160–161).

Nancy Larrick (1991) believes children come to poetry when teachers bring poetry to children. In her book *Let's Do a Poem: Introducing Children to Poetry*, she examines (1) the music of poetry, (2) the language of poetry, (3) the movement and dance of poetry, and (4) the drama of poetry. Like Brod Bagert, Larrick (1991) believes oral performance is the key. "Like a song, a poem is meant to be heard. Often the appeal of the song depends on the singer. We are captivated when the song flows melodiously, when the words are enunciated clearly, when the timing and tone seem to fit the mood. Once we hear the song from an appealing voice, we want to hear it again, even to try ourselves" (p. 2).

....

CLASSROOM VIGNETTE

Jane Goodall uses a procedure that works for most students. She follows seven steps.

STEP 1: Students talk about paintings they have made or experiences they have had. After the talk, Jane writes one or two things the student chooses for recording. As she writes, she talks to herself, not teaching directly but reminding herself in audible sound that:

▶ She is using alphabet symbols that have names;

▶ Some of the words use capitals for the first letter;

▶ The same letters are used over and over as first letters in words;

▶ Some words appear again and again; and

▶ Some ending sounds tell how many and when.

This talk is about the symbol system and how it works in writing.

STEP 2: Jane reads what has been written and checks it with the student who said it. If it is appropriate, she asks the student to read it with her.

STEP 3: Paintings with dictation are displayed around the classroom at levels that students can reach. With felt-tipped pens, students identify language characteristics that are essential to understand for independent writing:

▶ words that are alike (usually words of highest frequency)

▶ words that begin alike

▶ words with capital letters

▶ punctuation that is the same

▶ rhyming words

▶ other topics appropriate to what is displayed

Students mark each category with colored pens. Usually two, and not more than three, categories are used at any one time.

STEP 4: Words that appear five or more times are collected for a chart, "Words We All Use." This chart becomes a major resource for spelling in the Writing/

Continued

When students can enjoy hearing poetry and discussing what it means to them, they are interested in writing creative verses on their own. Class groups compose poems to describe or summarize a common group experience, but the heart and soul of poetry writing is in individual production. Individual compositions may first occur accidentally when young children are dictating their thoughts to the teacher. Simple poems of two lines occur in young children's compositions when their full free language is used in

Publishing Center. It is used for games that develop a sight vocabulary for reading. (Approximately half of the words young students use in writing, exclusive of proper names, will be on the list of 100 words of highest frequency.)

STEP 5: When a student indicates an interest in writing, the dictation is recorded very lightly, and the student traces over the letters. A model alphabet with arrows to show directions for strokes in writing is available in the Writing/Publishing Center.

STEP 6: Dictation is recorded with space beneath each line for copying. The writing is large enough so students have no difficulty copying beneath what the teacher has written.

STEP 7: Students write on their own, using resources from the Writing/Publishing Center—spelling lists of words of highest frequency, special lists of words of color, size, shape, smell, sound, texture, and motion.

Jane finds that with these procedures most of the students in her class improve as independent writers. In addition, when talking about writing, they can use names of the letters of the alphabet, can spell words and understand when someone else spells, and can talk about capitalization, punctuation, and other fine points involved in the writing process.

Charlene Chambers, a first-grade teacher, takes dictation on the chalkboard from one student each morning. The student is chosen ahead of time and comes prepared to tell about a real experience or to tell an imaginary story. The whole story is told orally, and then Charlene asks the author to select one or two things from the story for her to write. She wants young students to realize that what is written in most books for them to read is not all the author had to say. It is only a part of the whole story. In this way she helps them across the most difficult time in reading instruction when stories are short and incomplete and meanings are scarce.

As she writes, she chats about those characteristics of written language that everyone must know in order to be literate. This indirect teaching is an influence on students who would be reluctant to try to understand if they were confronted with the same information on a worksheet. She does this effective teaching of writing skills with materials that are understood by the learners. Comprehension is assured because the story comes from the students, not from an author who is not present.

self-expression. As they work in a nonthreatening language environment, they use language that is seldom used except in writing poetry.

Most students begin to write their thoughts in poetic forms when they live in a rich environment of poetry. From simple beginnings they want to express more and more of their thoughts and feelings in the poetic language they have been hearing and reading.

Teachers should bring poetry of many types into the classroom. Student interest in poetry is broadened by exposure to varied selections. Children

FIGURE 6.8 ▶

"The Performance Method"

Poetry is an oral art form. Encouraging children to perform poems is an effective way to introduce them to poetry, and the process begins with the selection of poems that are performable. Now comes the fun part–how to help children perform poems painlessly and well. Let me start by making a promise. This works, you're going to love it, and you may be in for a few surprises. There are many children whose ability to perform surprises their teachers. "But she's so quiet, I never would have dreamed she had it in her." So have faith in yourself and in your children, and let's do it.

Use the following method to make teaching poetry painless and fun. The steps should be spread out over time. You may for example do teacher performances for weeks or months before you proceed to group performance. When it feels right, go to the next step. Avoid doing whole classes on poetry. Sessions should be short. Always leave them wanting more. Poetry can be used as a break in classroom routine.

STEP 1: Teacher Performance:
Perform with full expression. Become the character. Be a little kid and hold nothing in reserve. Remember that you are the model. Your performance will license your children to perform. You know you've gone far enough when you forget you're teaching. If you feel utterly ridiculous, you're almost there.

> Note: Always evoke applause at the end of your performance. When you teach your class to be a good audience you create a performance friendly environment. A dramatic bow at the end of the reading will tell them to clap for you. If they do not respond, assume a pleading expression and clap for yourself. If they still do not respond, ask them to clap for you. By applauding for you they learn to applaud each other.

STEP 2: Group Performance:
Perform as a group. Recite single phrases with full expression and have the children mimic your performance. This is lots of fun and will serve as a confidence builder. There's safety in numbers and this is a painless way to help children discover the performer inside them. As they repeat the lines watch their faces, react to them with smiles and laughter, and stimulate applause at the end.

> Note: In the beginning, try to avoid choral reading of whole poems or long passages. Continuous choral reading forces children into expressionless sing song recitation and defeats your purpose.

STEP 3: Short Individual Performances:

Ask for volunteers to perform a poem for the class. You will have observed the "hams" in group performances. Encourage them, but be careful not to prematurely force a child into a pressure situation. Choose three for four children and have each perform a single line or short passage. Recite the line with full expression and have the child repeat after you. Reward each line with excitement and applause. Eventually you want each child in the class to have this experience and enthusiastic acceptance will encourage participation.

> Note: This is a big step. It takes courage for a child to "let go" in front of a class, and this is especially true for you first volunteers. I have found that it helps to kneel next to each performer. The more nervous the child is the closer I get. The physical closeness lends much needed support.

STEP 4: Individual Performance:

Take this very slowly and keep in mind that this may not be a good idea for every child in the class. Encourage the "hams" but do not force it. You may even develop a regular "troupe" and have one or two children perform a poem each day. The other children will not be left out. As members of the audience they are full participants in the process.

> Note: It is fine to memorize a poem but a performer should always have the text of a poem in hand. Though I have performed each of my poems a thousand times and can say them in my sleep, I always feel better with the book in my hand. If nothing else, it's a good prop.

STEP 5: Search and Share:

In this final step, you will perform your favorite "adult" poems, and explain why you like each poem. What feelings does each poem evoke in you? What experiences in your life does it relate to? How does the poem encourage or enrich you? Avoid an analysis of the poems. This is strictly personal sharing. You become the model for the relationship between poetry and human beings. Children begin to understand what poetry can mean to them.

> Note: If you do not have a few favorite poems, find a copy of *The Norton Anthology of Poetry* and begin the search. Feel free to dislike poems. Poetry lovers do not love all poetry. The object of the exercise is to find a dozen poems that move you deeply. They're there and you will find them.

move naturally from hearing poetry to writing poetry. Students often reduce complexity to simplicity, as Susan Hicks does here:

WHEN WINTER COMES

When winter comes a
noisy city seems to turn
into a winter wonderland.

Douglass, a 10-year-old, captures the intrigue of an old house he walks by on the way to school each day:

THE OLD HOUSE

The house is old and dark   *And the window shades are just torn*
And the trees are like a park.   *rags.*
It is damaged with no care.   *But the house has had its day!*
Stillness is in the air.   *Most things happen that way.*
The porch roof sags

You'll also receive some poems that will surprise, maybe even shock you. Consider the collaboration of seventh graders Susie and Kendra:

THE KISS

A peach is a peach,
a plum is a plum,
but a kiss ain't a kiss
unless there's a tongue!

Poetry writing brings together elements of style and form that lift ideas above communication of the common reporting type. It frees students to explore and experiment with language. Fears of being wrong are minimized. The language of poets is valued along with their ideas.

COMPUTERS IN THE WRITING CLASSROOM

Computer applications have changed the world. At the advent of the computer age, Toffler (1980) warned "an information bomb is exploding in our midst, showering us with a shrapnel of images and drastically changing the

◀ Good software involves students in collaborative sharing and learning.

way each of us perceives and acts upon our private world" (p. 156). This "explosion" is clearly visible in writing classrooms across the country today as children sit in front of monitors and interact with text through keyboards. Virtually every school district has invested in computers to keep pace with the changing world of technology.

Teachers must make wise use of the computer, being careful it does not replace creative teaching and child-to-child interactions as its capabilities are used to support children's growth as readers and writers. Computers cannot teach language or reading. Children learn language and literacy in the process of meaningful communications with the world around them. The computer is but one tool that may be used to provide these literacy interactions.

WORD PROCESSING AND THE WRITING PROCESS

One of the key advantages presented by computers is word processing. Many students are reluctant to write because of both their poor handwriting and the tediousness of recopying their stories and papers to make them "neat." In addition, good writing requires editing and rewriting, which results in even more recopying. When asked why his stories were so short, one third-grader replied, "I don't wanna write too much 'cause it takes to long to recopy." But writing is becoming less difficult because word processing enables text to be easily manipulated. It may be adapted, deleted, inserted, or moved

Margaret Blankenship's third-grade classroom is filled with children who love computers and computer software. In contrast to many classrooms, the computer is integrated into the content areas of science, math, social studies, and language arts. Software is used constantly throughout the day by her students as they learn, with the assistance of the computer, about topics related to their content studies. Margaret's students delight in encountering historical figures like Paul Revere and Joan of Arc as they solve mysteries while playing *Where in Time Is Carmen Sandiego?* Collaborative learning is evidenced as children work together in language-arts and science adventures like Sierra's *Space Quest* series.

Jason and Blake didn't want to go home one day until they had finished an exciting encounter in *Space Quest III.* They finally decoded an alien space message that led to the solution of the game. Their decoded message is pictured in Figure 6.9; notice Jason's writing at the top of the page and Blake's at the bottom. Notice the vocabulary generated by the boys—*inpenetrable, deactivated, jello pistols.* Such interactions and collaborations are the essence of meaning-centered learning.

FIGURE 6.9 ▶ **STORY GENERATED THROUGH STUDENT INVOLVEMENT IN COMPUTER PROGRAM**

about with ease (Dudley-Marling, 1985). Inexpensive dot matrix printers provide the students with nicely typed copies of their work. Zaharias (1983) reported that children are more willing to take risks as writers and to make more revisions when writing with a word processor. Perhaps the greatest contribution computers are making is the freedom they provide young writers through word processing.

CLASSROOM VIGNETTE

Josh Sonata, a third grader, had never used a computer before his teacher asked him to write using a word processing program. Within 20 minutes he had completed the first draft of "The Adventures of Mike," which is reproduced just as he wrote it in Figure 6.10. The computer freed Josh from concerns about his poor printing and allowed him to focus on story development. Josh corrected spelling and spacing problems in a later draft of the story. He soon became the third grade's most prolific writer.

FIGURE 6.10 ▶

The Adventures Of Mike

story and pictures by Josh Sonata

Once upon a time there was a sincetast his name was Mike. He had a cat named Sourpoos. He also had a dog named Wilber. As you know haveing a cat and a dog leads up to problems so the sincetast was not a happy one. But he was the worlds most best. He wanted to get away from the world and all the emotion. So he invented a srinking machine without knowing it. One day a day when he was esecialy curious he stepped in the srinking machine shut the door and pushed the red button and CLISH CLASH BING BANG ZINK ZANK and then he was small. Then his dog said "What happend to the professor?"

"I do not know"said the cat.

Well now we come back to are dear old professor. HELP he cried in his strongest-weakest voice I say that becose it was weak compared to his regular voice. But no one heard him. Luckly the door was light and not locked. So out he went into the real world. He was so small that his cat didn't even see him. But his dog did. " Hey" cried the dog look cat a rat. The professor started to say that he was the professor but he was afrad the dog might lick him. The professor happend to glance up at the clock and said "Oh my gosh! I can not bleve the time I have class in 12 minits." Now rember the cat he finaly found what the dog was talking about and when the professor looked up he found to his supprise he was being chsed by a cat. ....
TO BE CONTUED

CLASSROOM VIGNETTE

Scott Beesley is a fifth-grade teacher in a rural East Texas town. Recognizing the potential of the computer to motivate students in writing, Scott developed, with the aid of his students, an electronic mail system for his school. Students wrote more than 1,000 letters to one another during the school year. Scott found that the children's writing fluency improved by the year end and students made tremendous gains in spelling.

Gail Heather, a first-grade teacher who frequently took dictation from her children, decided to take the class to the school's computer lab and enter their dictation into a computer. The children were excited to see their spoken language appear on the screen, even more so than on chart paper. Students were eager to contribute their ideas to the collaborative story and to read the story when it was completed. The session was so successful that the dictation sessions using the word processor became a regular part of class activities. At the end of the year, Gail reported the following:

1. She was able to take dictation much faster with the word processor than by hand.

2. Stories dictated into the word processor were significantly longer than stories recorded on chart paper.

3. Realizing how easily changes could be made, children asked for more revisions than they normally did.

4. Dictated stories could easily be turned into typed class books by having the stories printed on the dot matrix printer and then bound.

Although Gail still takes group and individual dictation from children, she now has a valuable alternative for taking dictation. She reports that publishing has increased dramatically in her classroom and that the day she took the class to the computer lab was the dawn of a new era for her as a teacher.

TEACHERS AS WRITERS

The greatest leaders lead by example. It's one thing to tell children that writing is important and fun; it's even better to demonstrate that writing is important and fun by writing yourself. Writing will be valued where writing is honored. And we value writing when both students and teachers write together.

Teachers must be writers because only writers understand what writing is like (Wickwire, 1990). We must keep in touch with the writing process through writing, for when we cease to write we cease to understand the toils, frustrations, and joys that writing entails. Or, as Newman (1990) has said, we need to understand writing from inside the process.

How do we start writing again? Murray (1989) says it's simple—"writing begins when teachers give their students silence and paper—then sit down to write themselves" (p. 19). So remember to experience and discover with your students the joys of writing.

For a jump start, we recommend an excellent book by Tommy Thomason (1993), *More Than a Writing Teacher.* The book is designed as a writer's workshop for teachers. It includes sections ranging from "The best excuse" to "Time to write." Thousands of teachers credit Thomason's book with moving them from talking about the need to write to actually writing.

SUMMARY

Teachers in a process-centered environment use various methods and materials to stimulate students to develop as writers. They never set out to teach how to write by a prescribed system. They think of students as having the basic ingredients of writing and reading inside. They interact with students as they help each one to discover nonprint and printed forms of communication. When the ability to write independently is achieved, they do not say that they have taught the student how to write. They know what they did was to release something in the student that had always been there.

PATHWAYS TO DEVELOPING PERSONAL WRITING

A student:

▶   uses personal observations as a source for writing poetry and prose.

▶   draws on imagination as a source of topics for writing.

▶   shares aspirations through interesting topics and artful ways of writing.

▶   reflects the influence of good literature when writing.

▶   writes on a variety of subjects in interesting and creative forms.

▶   sees possibilities for artful writing in ordinary experiences.

▶   experiments with style and form in poetry writing.

▶   contributes copies of books to school and public libraries.

▶   enjoys writing more once he or she learns the ease of word processing.

▶7 PATHWAYS TO PATTERNED LITERACY GENRES

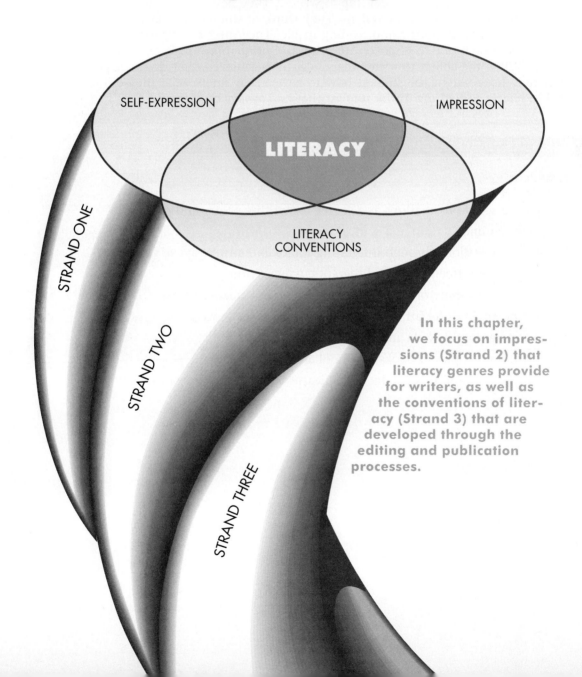

SELF-EXPRESSION

IMPRESSION

LITERACY

LITERACY CONVENTIONS

STRAND ONE

STRAND TWO

STRAND THREE

In this chapter, we focus on impressions (Strand 2) that literacy genres provide for writers, as well as the conventions of literacy (Strand 3) that are developed through the editing and publication processes.

PATHWAYS TO PONDER

....

▶ **WHAT ARE LITERACY GENRES?**
....

▶ **HOW DO GENRE MODELS MAKE WRITING EASIER FOR STUDENTS?**
....

▶ **WHAT IS THE VALUE OF GENRE POETRY WRITING IN A LANGUAGE-CENTERED PROGRAM?**
....

Genre refers to the different categories or types of stories we find within children's literature (Farris, 1993). Some examples are fiction, historical fiction, nonfiction, folktales, fantasy, poetry, and predictable. Within genres are subgenres. In this chapter, we explore the subgenres of predictable stories and patterned poetry. We start with the story patterns of the repetitive language subgenre, the rhyming language subgenre, the interlocking subgenre, the cumulative subgenre, the culturally familiar subgenre, and the circle subgenre. Then we move to the poetry subgenres of haiku, senryu, snapshot, tanka, sijo, couplet, cinquain, terquain, diamante, renga, limerick, and shape patterns.

These subgenres are important because they provide an excellent outlet for children's self-expression. In the last chapter, student stories illustrated what young authors can create when given an opportunity to develop their thoughts through stories and poems. In this chapter, through genre study and analysis, we see how students can go beyond their own personal writing styles.

As students read well-written materials that reflect the ways authors express themselves in beautiful language, they'll see how others write. From these patterns, they'll have opportunities to express their own thoughts and feelings

THE POET ▶
PONDERS

MY WRITER'S NOTEBOOK

It's a three hole spiral notebook,
A hundred pages
With blue lines
That await my words

Diamond Search
My Life lies before me
Like the bed of a shallow river,
My fingers sift sand and gravel.
For the rough diamonds that lie
    hidden,
And as I find them in this notebook.
I write... I cut... I polish...
And they shine.

My words . . .
On an empty page . . .
In an ordinary notebook . . .
The silver setting for the jewels of
*   my life.*

in similar ways. They'll notice that professional writers often use these patterns or genres in their writing. For example, 9-year-old Jennifer was excited to discover she had something in common with writer/illustrator Keith Baker—both had used a combination of repetitive and rhyming subgenres in their latest books. Jennifer had put the two subgenres to work in her book *Deep in the Woods;* Keith Baker had used the genres in his best-seller *Who Is the Beast?*

What is the value of genre patterns? Students are constantly learning, and the materials they read "demonstrate" to them what writing can be like (Smith, 1985). Consequently, students benefit when they come under the influence of a variety of writing styles and forms, including artful forms of expression such as predictable genre stories and genre poetry.

To write with the forms and patterns of others is to develop new means of self-expression because style includes intuitive choices by authors as well as studied ones. In verbal communication, style involves choices of words and ways of combining words to express ideas.

School programs should allow students to make choices, especially choices of words to express ideas and feelings. Language-arts programs can provide alternative means of self-expression, thus building students' confidence in their own writing abilities.

Although the focus of this chapter is on self-expression and the influence of other language styles on personal language, embedded within the process are elements of form such as spelling, punctuation, capitalization, grammar, handwriting, and sentence sense. These elements of form apply to the productive writing of students and are supports for clear and effective communication—not instructional lessons in themselves.

The teacher plays a crucial role in all aspects of the writing program. In a meaning-centered classroom she or he does not dictate standards and pass

◀ **Kindergarten children "chime in" as author Bill Martin Jr reads.**

Children ▶
collaborate on a
story.

judgment on students' creative productions. Rather, the teacher suggests and illustrates alternatives so students increase their awareness of variety in style and correctness in form. The teacher provides many models that give a measure of security to students who are exploring their communicative powers. This chapter describes some models that teachers may use to stimulate writing and literacy growth.

USING PREDICTABLE SUBGENRE STORIES TO EXTEND WRITING PATHWAYS

Research has shown that stories featuring patterned literary structures are easy for students to read (Bridge, 1979, 1986; Rhodes, 1981; Yellin & Blake, 1994). Such structures are sometimes called predictable books or structured language books. We use the term *predictable books* to highlight the patterns or genres contained in these books. When a story has an understandable structure, the students are free to use their knowledge about language to predict many of the events in the story. Such stories furnish an excellent pattern for young authors to emulate as they write stories for themselves and classmates. Many children will take the first step toward divergence in their writing as the pattern encourages them to go beyond their own writing style and adopt the style of the pattern.

The following examples can be used to stimulate the writing of many selections that have predictive characteristics. They can be used to extend students' writing beyond the personal styles discussed in Chapter 5.

THE REPETITIVE LANGUAGE PATTERN

Many stories for young readers feature a literary device called repetitive structure. Such stories present a pattern and repeat it, time after time, with only slight variations throughout the book. Bill Martin Jr, writing under the pen name Howard Wellesley, gives us such a structure in his "All Kinds of Neighbors":

> *Some neighbors play outdoors.*
> *Some do not.*
> *Some neighbors always hurry.*
> *Some do not.*
> *Some neighbors ask you to come in.*
> *Some do not.*
> *What kind of neighbor are you?*

CLASSROOM VIGNETTE

After reading and enjoying *All Kinds of Neighbors,* 7-year-old Angie used the pattern to write about her first love—horses.

Some horses neigh.
Some do not.
Some horses eat flowers.
Some do not.
Some horses are spotted.
Some are not.
Some horses run.
Some do not.
Some horses roll in dirt.
Some do not.
Some horses buck.
Some do not.
What kind of horse would you like?

Angie's story is one that even students who are considered nonreaders can read and is one of the most popular books in the classroom library. Note that Angie changed the pattern to "Some are not" to match the linking verb in the previous line. Her metalinguistic knowledge of language and her intuition told her to do so. Even nonreaders alter the pattern to make the language correct when they come to this section of the story. Repetitive structures like this one provide an excellent model for readers and writers.

THE RHYMING LANGUAGE PATTERN

Both the sound and syllabication of words are communicated to children when they encounter a story that utilizes a rhyme scheme. A story that has such rhyme and rhythm is the traditional "Whistle, Mary, Whistle." It begins:

> *Whistle, Mary, whistle.*
> *And you can catch a cow.*
> *I can't whistle, Mother.*
> *I just don't know how.*

A fifth grader's innovation about this story concerns reading.

> *Read, Meredith, read.*
> *And you will have some fun.*
> *I can't read, Teacher.*
> *I'd rather skip and run.*
>
> *Read, Jonathan, read.*
> *Of kings and queens and joy.*
> *I can't read, Teacher.*
> *I'm just a little boy.*
>
> *Read, Darcy, read.*
> *The frog just caught a rat.*
> *I can't read, Teacher.*
> *This book is just too fat.*
>
> *Read, Jared, read.*
> *Of lions and tigers roaring.*
> *I can't read, Teacher.*
> *I find it all quite boring.*
>
> *Read, Stephanie, read.*
> *Of travels to the zoo.*
> *I can't read, Teacher.*
> *I chose this book for you.*
>
> *Read, Joshua, read.*
> *Of trips to outer space.*
> *I can't read, Teacher.*
> *Its just too fast a pace.*
>
> *Read, Johnny, read.*
> *I've found a book for you.*
> *Oh, boy! Monsters!*
> *I want to read now, too.*

Students love rhyming language patterns such as *You Can't Hide a Hippopotamus,* by Elva Robinson. (See the following page.)

Predictable patterns that have a rhyme scheme are essential for the development of sensitivity to ending sounds that are alike. Most students can respond to rhyming whether they are good readers or not. They enjoy and benefit from selections that include rhyming.

Rhyme adds a poetic quality to text. However, rhyming schemes, regardless of position within the story, should not detract from the intention of the

YOU CAN'T HIDE A HIPPOPOTAMUS

You can't hide a hippopotamus.
It has too big a bottomus.
You can hide a chimpanzee
if you have a great big tree,
or a cuddly koala bear:
You'll hardly know it's there.
but . . .
You can't hide a hippopotamus.
It has too big a bottomus.

You can hide a little snake
in the grass beside a lake,
and a turtle hides quite well
it just crawls into a shell.
but . . .
You can't hide a hippopotamus.
It has too big a bottomus.

An otter thinks it's cool
to be hidden in a pool.
A beaver will not scram
if you hide him in his dam.
but . . .
You can't hide a hippopotamus.
It has too big a bottomus.

You can hide an old ground hog
stick him in a hollow log.
You can even hide a frog.
He'll stay happy in a bog.
but . . .
You can't hide a hippopotamus.
It has too big a bottomus.

If you hide a little quail
in a bush you cannot fail.
You can even hide a horse
in a barn, of course.
but . . .
You can't hide a hippopotamus.
It has too big a bottomus.

A squirrel can hide in a tree
where neither you nor I can see;
and it's not hard to hide a rabbit
'cause they hide out of habit.
but . . .
You can't hide a hippopotamus.
It has too big a bottomus.

A chipmunk scurries on the ground
so that he will not be found,
and a pigeon, I recall,
likes to hide out at city hall.
but . . .
You can't hide a hippopotamus.
It has TOO BIG A BOTTOMUS!

Elva Robinson

entire poem (Cramer, 1978). Rhyme has been undoubtedly overused, but should remain as one of the many styles that children may elect to use in their writing.

THE INTERLOCKING PATTERN

An intriguing variation of repetitive form is the interlocking pattern. Interlocking structures connect segments of the text and allow children to read each succeeding episode with confidence. One of the best known examples of interlocking structure is Bill Martin's (1983) *Brown Bear, Brown Bear, What Do You See?*. The story begins like this:

> "Brown Bear,
> Brown Bear,
>
> What do you see?"
> "I see a redbird
> looking at me."

> "Redbird,
> Redbird,
> What do you see?"
>
> "I see a yellow duck
> looking at me."

THE CUMULATIVE PATTERN

Cumulative story sequences allow students to hold lengthy phrases in short-term memory while concentrating on one new episode on each succeeding page. The Mother Goose tale "The House That Jack Built" is a well-known example of a cumulative structure.

> PAGE 1
>
> *This is the House that Jack built.*
>
> PAGE 2
>
> *This is the Malt,*
> *that lay in the house*
> *that Jack built.*
>
> PAGE 3
>
> *This is the Rat,*
> *that ate the malt,*
> *that lay in the house*
> *that Jack built.*

The pattern continues with an additional episode each page for an additional eight pages.

Crescent Dragonwagon uses the "Jack" pattern in *This Is the Bread I Baked for Ned:* "This is the Bread I baked for Ned, baked for Ned in the morning." Likewise, Michael Sampson and Ted Rand use the same pattern in *The Football That Won Super Bowl:* "This is the linebacker that sacked the quarterback that fumbled the football that won the Super Bowl."

Another example of the cumulative pattern can be seen in Bill Martin's *Old Devil Wind;* still another is evidenced in Don and Audrey Wood's *The Napping House.*

Joy, a second-grade student, used the "brown bear" interlocking pattern to create her own story, which she named "Woolly Lamb, Woolly Lamb." She modified the pattern by adding adjectives to describe the various creature sounds instead of just using colors for descriptive purposes:

Woolly Lamb, Woolly Lamb,
What do you hear?

I hear a green frog
croaking so near.

Green Frog, Green Frog,
what do you hear?

I hear a shaggy wolf
howling so near.

Shaggy Wolf, Shaggy Wolf,
what do you hear?

I hear a wild goose
honking so near.

Wild Goose, Wild Goose,
what do you hear?

I hear a sneaky snake
hissing so near.

Sneaky Snake, Sneaky Snake,
what do you hear?

I hear a little mouse
squeaking so near.

Little Mouse, Little Mouse,
what do you hear?

I hear a barn owl
hooting so near.

Barn Owl, Barn Owl,
what do you hear?

I hear a red rooster
crowing so near.

Red Rooster, Red Rooster,
what do you hear?

I hear a gentle donkey
braying so near.

Gentle Donkey, Gentle Donkey,
what do you hear?

I hear a woolly lamb
bleating so near.

Woolly Lamb, Woolly Lamb!

Joy could write "Woolly Lamb, Woolly Lamb, What Do You Hear?" because she knew so well the pattern of *Brown Bear, Brown Bear, What Do You See?* She knew the rhythm and the language well enough to make it her own. It is easy to see she could add many more stanzas, or she could change the focus to "What do you feel?" or "What do you smell?" or to other topics such as vehicles, insects, or bodies in space. This pattern is very useful in helping students extend their home-rooted language.

"Brown Bear,
Brown Bear,
What do you see?"

"I see a redbird
looking at me."

THE CHRONOLOGICAL PATTERN

This pattern uses enumeration to foster predictability, and alliteration to support predictability. Eric Carle's *The Very Hungry Caterpillar* is perhaps the most famous example of this genre:

In the light of the moon a little egg lay on a leaf.

One Sunday morning the warm sun came up, and . . . pop! out of the egg came a tiny and very hungry caterpillar. He started to look for food. On Monday he ate through one apple. But he was still hungry.

It can be extended with other stanzas, made into books, and read by students in their own classes and in other classes. Older students enjoy writing with this pattern to create books for kindergarten classes.

Additional suggestions for using patterns that involve numbers and days of the week are found in Chapter 16.

THE CULTURALLY FAMILIAR PATTERN

This pattern involves using stories that children will already be familiar with because they are a part of their lives and culture. We can't provide a list of such books because what's familiar to one culture may not be familiar to another. However, to many children in the United States, stories like *Little*

CLASSROOM VIGNETTE

Rosalinda Flores, a fifth-grade teacher in Dallas, Texas, uses patterned books as a mainstay of her writing program. She has developed a technique for using patterned language selections for literacy development that has become a model for other teachers in her school. She follows six basic steps (see Figure 7.1) that enable her students to produce beautiful adaptations of well-written books. Rosalinda believes quality is more important than quantity; consequently, she carefully orchestrates the movement of a patterned book from its introduction to its output as a new book.

When a new patterned book is introduced to the classroom environment, by students or by Rosalinda, she takes time to ensure the children have internalized the pattern before they attempt to adapt it. She shares the book with the students through choral reading and unison reading. The students do Reader's Theater presentations of the story. At some point, it becomes evident the children have claimed the pattern as their own.

Then the fun continues. Rosalinda invites the class to modify the pattern and create new books. Often one book is written from the pattern as a whole-class activity. After sharing Eric Carle's *The Very Hungry Caterpillar,* the class decided to write a book called *The Very Hungry E.T.* Verbs in the pattern were substituted to change the meaning in alignment with the new focus. Appropriate descriptive words were added and the vocabulary altered to make sense. After two drafts, the book was complete. Pictures were painted to illustrate the new version, and a Reader's Theater performance held. That was just the beginning. A host of authors started independent productions of new versions of the pattern. Within a week, Scotty, Yolanda, Stacey, and Mark had written and illustrated *The Very Hungry E.T.* Scotty had watched the movie *E.T.* 10 times and was the content expert of the group. Yolanda did most of the editing of the version, and Mark illustrated the book. It became the talk of the school and was featured on the community's cable television channel.

Continued

Red Riding Hood, The Three Little Pigs, Jack and the Beanstalk, and *The Night Before Christmas* will be culturally familiar. Steven Kellogg has illustrated a number of these books for today's readers. See page 182 for a classroom example of how children can use these familiar stories as a launching pad for writing.

THE CIRCLE PATTERN

Another noteworthy pattern for writers to emulate is the circle pattern. This pattern ends with a return to the first event of the book, hence the name "circle pattern." Laura Numeroff's *If You Give a Mouse a Cookie* is the classic example of this pattern. The story begins with a little boy who encounters a hungry little mouse. He gives the mouse a cookie, then has to give him milk to go with the cookie. The mouse and boy proceed through a series of cause/ effect events that culminate with the mouse wanting milk. The last line reads "and chances are if he asks for a glass of milk, he's going to want a cookie to

....

THE VERY HUNGRY E.T.

In the light of the moon, a little man stood in a field.

One Sunday morning the warm sun came up and—POP—out of a storeroom came a very hungry E.T.!

He started to look for food.

On Monday he ate one Reese's pieces . . .

BUT HE WAS STILL HUNGRY!

On Tuesday he ate two bowls of cottage cheese . . .

BUT HE WAS STILL HUNGRY!

On Wednesday he ate three pizzas . . .

BUT HE WAS STILL HUNGRY!

On Thursday he ate four slices of bread . . .

BUT HE WAS STILL HUNGRY!

On Friday he ate five bananas . . .

BUT HE WAS STILL HUNGRY!

On Saturday he ate a piece of lemon pie, a candy bar, one apple, a slice of meat . . . and a piece of strawberry shortcake!

That night he had a stomachache.

The next day was Sunday again and he drank a Coke and felt much better.

Now he wasn't hungry anymore—he was a BIG FAT E.T.!

E.T. went to Elliot's house and stayed for a month and then he went . . .

H O M E !!!

Rosalinda varies the procedure from time to time and always allows students freedom to choose what writing projects they wish to become involved in. The six basic steps that led to *The Very Hungry E.T.* are found in Figure 7.1.

go with it." Children enjoy composing books that feature this pattern, as illustrated on page 184.

THE VALUE OF GENRE WRITING

The use of highly predictive selections is a sure way to develop oral language abilities that are not natural in home-rooted language. These literary-level language abilities gained from reading predictable materials permit students to move into the reading and writing of sophisticated literature at a much faster rate. When stories with predictable language patterns are read with students, the patterns become a part of the students' language repertoire. What students hear and say can be used as a basis for writing, and patterns provide a framework for putting ideas into print.

USING PATTERNED LANGUAGE SELECTIONS FOR LITERACY DEVELOPMENT ◄ FIGURE 7.1

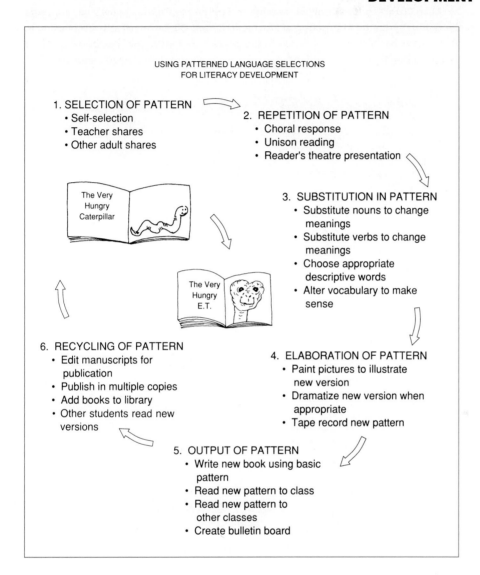

USING PATTERNED LANGUAGE SELECTIONS
FOR LITERACY DEVELOPMENT

1. SELECTION OF PATTERN
   • Self-selection
   • Teacher shares
   • Other adult shares

2. REPETITION OF PATTERN
   • Choral response
   • Unison reading
   • Reader's theatre presentation

3. SUBSTITUTION IN PATTERN
   • Substitute nouns to change meanings
   • Substitute verbs to change meanings
   • Choose appropriate descriptive words
   • Alter vocabulary to make sense

4. ELABORATION OF PATTERN
   • Paint pictures to illustrate new version
   • Dramatize new version when appropriate
   • Tape record new pattern

5. OUTPUT OF PATTERN
   • Write new book using basic pattern
   • Read new pattern to class
   • Read new pattern to other classes
   • Create bulletin board

6. RECYCLING OF PATTERN
   • Edit manuscripts for publication
   • Publish in multiple copies
   • Add books to library
   • Other students read new versions

The Very Hungry Caterpillar

The Very Hungry E.T.

Children who move toward self-selection of reading must have some prior experience in dealing with language that has characteristics of a predictive sequence. They must recognize the value and artistry of writing in comparing and contrasting patterns. They must know that many authors take a simple idea and elaborate to extend meaning. They must appreciate and enjoy the rhythm of language rather than be concerned at all times about recognition and comprehension abilities. Stories that are crafted with such patterns demonstrate to children what good writing is like and serve as an invitation to the student to emulate such a style.

Alice Cozart, a fourth-grade teacher in Commerce, Texas, knows her students have the rhythm and language of *The Night Before Christmas* deeply embedded in them. Thus her whole class wrote to the pattern, but with one modification. They were to rewrite the story with a future slant! Here's what Paul and Joshua penned:

> The year 3093 Night Before Cristmas
> Twas the night Before Cristmas
> and all throug the hightech
> house not a android was
> stering not evin a robot.
> The macanical soks were
> hung by the electical powderd
> chimny with care in hopes of
> that robot santy would
> soon be their. I woke frome
> my heted water bed and
> heard such a clater I got
> on haverbord and flew
> to the window to see
> whats a mater. I saw
> robat Santa and eight tiny
> batery powerd raindir
> more rapid than electrisity
> they flew in the air.
> He pressed his dorbell and
> called them by name
> now Twcher now Twahcee
> now Trong and Ting!
> on Yovo and Momo
> on Troxer and Witzen to
> the top of the porch to
> the topof the wall

As you can see, the boys had great fun with the poem. They succeeded because they started the writing with great confidence—they already knew the story. All they had to do was to modify it.

◀ A second grader shares her contribution to the class book, *I'm the King of the Backyard.*

◀ **THE BOOK MAKERS**

DONALD CREWS

1. Which book of yours has given you the greatest pleasure?

Bigmama's. This book meant a great deal to me personally and to my family. It was especially gratifying to me to see how excited my mother became over the book. A video was done on the book, and Mom and I got to travel back to where she grew up. It was fulfilling for me to share her feelings and her pride.

2. Which book has surprised you most in terms of its public reception?

Freight Train. I had done several books before, but this book was special from the beginning. Now there is a whole new crop of kids who have discovered the book. It was published in 1979, but for them, the book was just done yesterday.

3. What would you like people to remember about your work?

I want people to look at individual books and see that I have found ways to make the material exciting—and that it's not the same way all the time.

4. What impact do you hope your work will have on children?

Especially for black children, I want them to see that they can achieve a level of success by hard work and dedication. They have role models in sports, but I want to present another option for their talents, so they can find another way to achieve.

Donald Crews won the Caldecott Medal with *Freight Train* and has produced many stunning early childhood picture books. With *Bigmama's* and *Shortcut,* he has become a storyteller as well as an accomplished graphic artist. His books include *Ten Black Dots, We Read A to Z, Parade, Bicycle, Truck,* and *School Bus.*

Deeanne Barker's second-grade class enjoyed reading *I'm the Star of the Circus* by Michael Sampson. The circle pattern features a mouse who stands in the center ring singing, "I'm the star of the circus, I'm the star of the circus," only to be promptly pushed out of the center ring by the circus dog who demands, "Now who's the star of the circus?" The dog sings the song, but is soon pushed out of the ring by a larger circus animal. The book continues until the elephant is standing in the center ring singing the song. The mouse reappears, frightens the elephant away, and the mouse once again sings, "I'm the star of the circus, I'm the star of the circus!"

Deeanne's class incorporated this pattern into a book they wrote during their study of a thematic unit on pets. As children brainstormed different breeds of dogs, Deeanne recorded their dictations in the form of a semantic map (semantic maps are described in Chapter 11). The children then ranked the breeds according to size and incorporated them into the circle pattern of the book they called *Dogsong*.

Poodle stands on top of the doghouse
and sings,
"I'm the king of the backyard,
I'm the king of the backyard!"

Dachshund pushes Poodle off the doghouse
and says,
"Now who is the king of the backyard?"
"You are, big Dachshund," says Poodle.

Dachshund stands on top of the doghouse
and sings,
"I'm the king of the backyard,
I'm the king of the backyard!"

The book continues as it features a chow, a cocker spaniel, a german shepherd, a rottweiler, and a doberman. This is how the children closed the pattern:

Poodle was watching from behind a tree. He sneaks
up behind the doghouse and barks "Bow Wow Wow,"
and scares the Doberman away.

Poodle stands on top of the doghouse and sings,
"I'm the king of the backyard,
I'm the king of the backyard!"

The children edited, illustrated, and published the book. *Dogsong* is one of the most popular books in the library, and one that can be read by all of the students.

USING PATTERNED POETRY TO EXTEND LITERACY PATHWAYS

Poetry patterns that provide some security while offering openness to students' creativity are useful in launching children into new styles of talking and writing. These patterns provide guidelines but do not limit topics or choice of words. Here is a list of some useful writing patterns for children to use in the elementary and middle grades:

Haiku

Senryu

Snapshot

Tanka

Sijo

Couplet

Cinquain

Terquain

Diamante

Renga

Limerick

Shape Patterns (for example, triangle triplet or quadrangle)

These patterns require children to identify syllables in words, to rhyme, and to select predetermined forms of words such as nouns, verbs, and descriptors. In these forms the syllable is highlighted more than in some others. Its significance in studying language is summed up by Durkin when she states, "it is the syllable to which all [word study] generalizations refer" (1983, p. 164). The patterns of writing illustrated in this discussion suggest ways in which children can express their own observations, feelings, and imaginations with styles and forms they have not previously used at home and school. These patterns offer enough literary quality to help children appreciate the work of artist-authors who write in disciplined forms.

HAIKU

The pattern of haiku is three lines, 17 syllables, nonrhyming.

Line 1:   **Line 3:**
five syllables   five syllables

Line 2:
seven syllables

Haiku is an Oriental verse form of ancient origin. Its simplicity encourages children to say beautiful things in a new way. It is used to express observations and feelings about nature and the seasons. This form highlights the use of words of the form-classes—nouns, verbs, adjectives, and adverbs.

Here are two examples of haiku:

Winter's icy breath
Blows against the windowpane
Seeking warmth inside.

Jose

Beautiful mountains
Shimmering in the sunset
Day is leaving Earth.

Mike

CLASSROOM VINGETTE

Once Deanne Barker is sure most of her 8- and 9-year-olds can write their own ideas in language that is close to their talk, she combines brainstorming and dictation to illustrate other ways of saying things. She suggests rhyming words and records some the children know. She then introduces rhyming couplets, triplets, and quatrains. Rather than assign children to write in these patterns, she provides a common experience such as a picture or a film without words and then takes dictation from the group to illustrate the features of the patterns. Revisions are easy to make on the chalkboard, and the children suggest changes from original presentations until a satisfying pattern is illustrated. Nonrhyming patterns such as those of haiku and some cinquains are shown. Deanne hopes that from the experience the children will gain confidence to use new writing patterns on their own. And they do. They experience oral composition first and then move to writing.

She brought to the class a picture of a high mountain waterfall. It was a beautiful sight that inspired students to say things that were extraordinary. After talking for a while, she recorded on the chalkboard some of the things that individuals dictated. After she had seven or eight statements, she directed the attention of the class to the composition of a haiku to attach to the picture when it was put on the bulletin board. They had written haiku before and knew the basic structure. They knew they would have three lines. Line 1 would have 5 syllables, line 2 would have 7 syllables, and line 3 would have 5 syllables. Dee Ann knew a lot about the artistry of haiku, but she did not try to teach that at the time of composition. From all their dictated statements, these were chosen to represent the picture of the waterfall:

Slender waterfalls
From vast snow fields trickle down
Like long silver threads

This composition was satisfying and treasured by members of the class. They read it to each other and to visitors. Some students copied it in books of poetry that contained other poems they were collecting.

SENRYU

The pattern of senryu is the same as haiku. However, senryu is used to communicate topics that are not about nature and the seasons.

Some examples of senryu follow:

The ferris wheel turns *Taking me into the sky.* *I can see the World!* **Blake**	*Old fisherman sits* *On the pier early in day* *Catching his dinner.* **Meredith**

SNAPSHOT

The snapshot is a verse form developed by Claryce Allen in 1980. It gives writers more freedom than the haiku or senryu. Snapshots can be on any topic and "flow" more smoothly than haiku or senryu.

The pattern of snapshot is three lines, 19 syllables, nonrhyming.

Line 1:   **Line 3:**
seven syllables   seven syllables

Line 2:
five syllables

Examples:

The ocean waves lapping at *My feet come and go,* *Taking sand from between my toes.* **Yvonne**	*Double take:* *Late summer: six pelicans* *Led by two small birds* *Skimming over morning waves,* *Flying so low that each move* *Of birds is mirrored* *On the gray-blue waves.* **Bryan and Joshua**

Haiku, senryu, and snapshots use only a few syllables to express a thought that could become the main idea for an essay, a story, or a lyric. Children who have never expressed their thinking in these three complex forms profit from the experience of writing in the understandable, simple forms of a known pattern.

These forms, as well as other syllabic patterned poetry, require a functional understanding of structural analysis—syllabication, prefixes, suffixes, synonyms, contractions. The students must learn to eliminate many words of structure and depend on the reader to fill in the omitted words when they are useful for the flow of ideas. They focus on the words that carry the heavy load of meaning in communication, and thus build skills necessary for silent reading at a rate faster than speech.

TANKA

The pattern of tanka is five lines, 31 syllables, nonrhyming.

Line 1:
five syllables

Line 2:
seven syllables

Line 3:
five syllables

Line 4:
seven syllables

Line 5:
seven syllables

Tanka is another ancient Oriental poetry form. It is a haiku plus two lines of seven syllables each. Actually, the tanka is older than the haiku, and it is believed the more popular haiku is just a shortened form of tanka. The author of a tanka usually, but not always, expresses five thoughts on a topic. They may include the following:

The name of something

Its actions

Its location

Its usefulness

Its beauty

Something distinctive or unusual about the subject

A comparison

The color, size, shape, sound, and other features

Here are some examples of the tanka:

At morning sunrise
The ranch hands discuss the day.
Their work never ends:
Riding the rugged hillsides
Weathered crackling skin.

Carol

Gentle fields embrace
Chromatic-winged butterflies
On soft springtime days.
Their fluttering extension
Brings harmony to mankind.

Marcia

CLASSROOM VIGNETTE

   Kim Pearce uses tanka as group projects with her third graders, and encourages students to:

1. **Think about the topic.**

2. **Write what they think about the topic.**

3. **Edit, deleting words not required for meaning.**

4. **Add descriptive nouns.**

5. **Count syllables and change words to get more or fewer syllables.**

6. **Consult a thesaurus when new words with the same meaning are needed.**

   Kim collects tanka from several authors. The students illustrate them, bind them into a book, and place the book in the classroom library.

In guiding authors to try the tanka, haiku, and senryu, teachers can encourage children to record their observations in natural ways. Then they can count syllables. They will be surprised at how many natural utterances occur in phrases and sentences of five and seven syllables. Most of what is said can be recorded in measures of five or seven syllables, with a few adjustments. It is as natural for kindergarten children to dictate in these patterns as it is for older children to write in them.

SIJO

The pattern consists of six lines, six to eight syllables per line, 42 to 48 syllables total, nonrhyming, no limitation on topics.

Sijo (pronounced "she-djo") is a Korean poetry form of ancient origin. In the simplified form popularized for school use, it is much like the haiku and tanka but is not as restrictive. Although it is nonrhyming, sijo includes internal rhymes that occur frequently in Korean verse. Alliteration is used to produce a poetic quality. Observations can be recorded on almost any topic and then edited for the six lines of six to eight syllables each.

Here are examples of the sijo:

A wonderful time of year
Families coming together
Exchanging their gifts of love,
Enjoying the sights and sounds
Of a special celebration.
Christmas time is wonderful for all.

Fred

Intelligent, loving eyes,
Eyebrows expressing thoughts,
Tails wagging and thumping,
Bodies wiggling and hopping,
Barking, whining, sighing,
My labradors speak to me.

Christina

Writing the sijo gives children practice in elaborating, sequencing, and comparing. All of these abilities are prerequisite to comprehending when reading what others have written. Besides that, the sijo is a literary form that is easy and pleasurable.

POETRY PATTERNS THAT REQUIRE FORM-CLASS WORDS

Writing activities that require children to know classes of words to fit into a predetermined pattern are useful in vocabulary expansion. Children have the security of the pattern as a guide, but they are free to use any words they know to fill in the pattern. The couplet, cinquain, terquain, and diamante are examples.

COUPLET

The noun-verb patterns in sentences can be demonstrated with couplets. If students do not know what couplets are, assure them the meaning is about

Hard at work on a class book. ▶

the same as "couple." Most of them will know the meaning of the word and predict that "couplet" means "two."

A couplet is a short poem or part of a poem that has two lines that rhyme. A "quick couplet" (Allen & Allen, 1982) is an easy way to introduce this rhyming verse form.

Here are two examples of couplets:

Joshua cries
With his eyes.

Marsha

Bears growl
On the prowl.

Terri

....
CLASSROOM VIGNETTE

Linda Crane uses couplets with her kindergarten students starting from the first day of class. She uses the words the children generate from writing couplets in various ways, including the following:

1. She lists many of the words that are used as names in couplets on a chart called "Nouns We Have Used."

2. She lists many of the words in the first lines that are words of action on a chart called "Action Words." Students add rhyming words to these to generate new couplets.

3. She values couplets by collecting and binding them into books of couplets.

After children read, write, and enjoy couplets, the transition can be made to reading sentences with an effort to see the noun-verb pattern without looking at the other words. This is an introduction to skimming, but it also forms a basis for evaluating effective, clear writing.

CINQUAIN

The pattern of the cinquain is five lines, nonrhyming.

Line 1:
one word, the name of something
two syllables

Line 2:
two words that describe line 1
four syllables

Line 3:
three words, an action for line 1
six syllables

Line 4:
four words, a feeling about line 1
eight syllables

Line 5:
a synonym or a word referring
back to line 1
two syllables

The first cinquains were written by Adelaide Crapsey (1914). This American form has been widely used in schools because of its simplicity. The original form, just listed, has syllabic control, but this simplified form is usually used with younger authors:

Line 1:
one word, a title

Line 2:
two words, description of the title

Line 3:
three words, an action

Line 4:
four words, a feeling

Line 5:
one word, reference to line 1

Only 11 words are required to express the thought with a cinquain. Children who use it know when they have achieved their goal. Kindergarten children can dictate cinquains as group compositions, or individuals can dictate their own. Sixth-grade students enjoy writing them in the modified form as well as with the syllabic requirement.

Cinquain enables students to create beautiful and poetic language.

Here are two examples of cinquains:

Rabbit
Furry, quiet
Wiggling, listening, hopping
Cute and cuddly friend
Pet

Lisa

Football
Rough, rugged
Catching, crunching, collapsing
Fans are joyfully shouting
Fall

Cindi

Cinquain writing maximizes the use of nouns, verbs, and adjectives. It minimizes the use of words of structure. Children can compose them in group situations or on an individual basis before they have mastered English syntax. They are especially useful for children learning English as a second language because they can be used early and can be beautiful expressions of self.

TERQUAIN

The terquain is a simplified form of cinquain that was developed for recording artful language of young children who possess very little English. However, the form is excellent for all types of students. The pattern consists of three lines, four or five words, nonrhyming.

Line 1:
one word, the subject

Line 2:
two or three words, description of the subject

Line 3:
one word, a feeling about or a synonym for the subject

Here are two examples of terquain:

Children
Running, jumping
Playmates

Snow
Falling and drifting
Winter

DIAMANTE

The pattern is seven lines, nonrhyming.

Line 1:
one word, a noun

Line 2:
two words, adjectives

Line 3:
three words, participles

Line 4:
four words, nouns

Line 5:
three words, participles

Line 6:
two words, adjectives

Line 7:
one word, a noun

Lines 1 and 7 are opposites. Lines 2 and 3 and half of line 4 describe the noun of line 1. Lines 5 and 6 and the other half of line 4 describe line 7. A diamante challenges the writer to shift the description of one thing to its opposite within a pattern. It brings into play synonyms and antonyms and extends them with descriptive words. Line 4 is a transition line, and frequently the two middle nouns refer to both lines 1 and 7. Some examples of diamantes follow.

San Jose teacher Joan Hagan looks on as a second grader works on a terquain.

Elephant
huge, gray
trumpeting, stomping, rearing
giant performer / midget rodent
scurrying, scampering, squeaking
small, furry
Mouse

Bryant

Day
Bright, warm
Playing, working, swimming
Sun, clouds, stars, clear
Resting, sleeping, snoring
Dark, cool
Night

Sheila

CLASSROOM VIGNETTE

Shan Palmer, a resource teacher in Green Valley, Arizona, frequently uses terquains to record the language of her students. Shan introduces the form by composing terquains with the children as they make suggestions. They notice that everything around them has a name and can be described with language. They quickly move to composing their own terquains independently. Shan collects the poetry and uses it for bulletin board displays and classroom reading material. Because the focus of terquain writing is on nouns and descriptive language, Shan notices the language level of her students increases rapidly.

CLASSROOM VIGNETTE

George Gallegos frequently uses diamantes with his fifth-grade students. He leads them to talk about antonyms and how they form the key meaning of a diamante. He lists words of opposite meaning that students can use when they write diamantes. The students learn that participles describe nouns and function as adjectives. They discover that the root words of participles are usually found in verb slots in sentences and that participles have *-ing* endings.

George guides his students as they edit diamantes, using alliteration in some of the lines and progressing from fewer syllables to more syllables in lines 2, 3, 5, and 6. The class uses diamantes for choral reading. They enjoy reading half of the diamante in happy voices and the other half in sad voices when the subject is work/play or summer/winter.

George recognizes that diamantes are excellent as the basis for expansion to paragraphs. The students often expand diamantes in this manner, and remark that the key difference between a diamante and a good paragraph is that words of "empty" meaning or structure are needed in sentences, but not in diamantes.

RENGA

Renga is a chain of poems written by multiple authors. The first author writes with a pattern that the other authors are to follow. The first poem provides the topic. Some possibilities follow:

Haiku linked to haiku extended to tanka (tanka for two)

Tanka linked to sijo

Couplets linked to couplets

Here are some examples of haiku linked to haiku:

Bare branches outline
Against a flaming sunset
Winter's calm goodnight.

Christi

Snow begins to fall
Like a blanket of winter
Lasting until spring.

Ellie

Big branches blossom
to announce awakening
of nature's slumber.

Marcelino

Blankets of snow melt
As winter turns to springtime
Year after year after year.

Elliot

Here are two examples of couplet linked to couplet:

Owls whoo
In the zoo.

Shane

Rabbits run,
In the sun.

Amber

CLASSROOM VIGNETTE

Lila Bruton encourages collaboration among her young authors through highlighting rengas. She makes chain links that are large enough for patterned poems to be written on them. Links are added to the chain as the students work together and add sections to the length.

LIMERICK

The pattern is five lines, 34 to 39 syllables, rhyming.

Line 1:
eight or nine syllables—Rhyme A

Line 2:
eight or nine syllables—Rhyme A

Line 3:
five or six syllables—Rhyme B

Line 4:
five or six syllables—Rhyme B

Line 5:
eight or nine syllables—Rhyme A

Usually a limerick follows the syllable pattern of 8-8-5-5-8 or 9-9-6-6-9, but other combinations can be used. The rhyming scheme requires three words that rhyme and two words that rhyme. It is a triplet split by a couplet. Because limericks are written for fun and nonsense, rhyming words can be created. Some limericks follow.

There once was a farmer from Maine
Whose cow was in terrible pain.
He went to the vet
To care for his pet.
But then he got caught in the rain.

Carol

There once was a puppy named
*   Prince,*
Who guarded his owner's back
*   fence.*
He barked at the man
Who picked up the can
Stealing garbage just didn't make
*   sense!*

Mike

Writing limericks can create an interest in reading nonsense verse like that written by Edward Lear and Dr. Seuss. Students who write limericks will benefit from lists of rhyming words, which may be kept in the Writing/Publishing Area.

SHAPE PATTERNS

Writing patterns designed around shapes have been developed by Iris M. Tiedt (1983). Among those that bring new style and a dependable form to children's writing are the triangle triplet and the quadrangle.

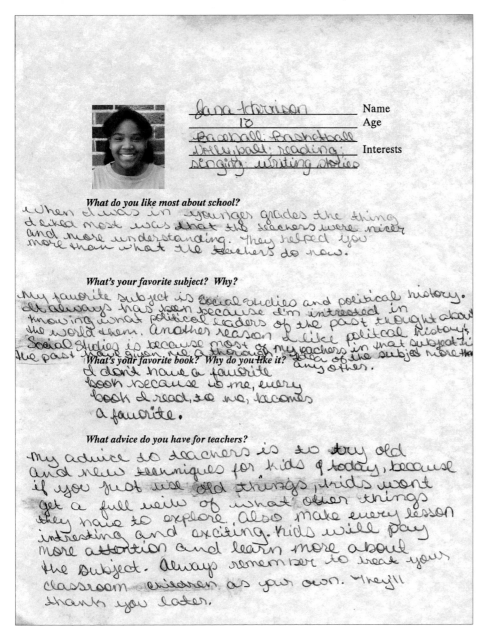

Name
Age
Interests

What do you like most about school?

What's your favorite subject? Why?

What's your favorite book? Why do you like it?

What advice do you have for teachers?

TRIANGLE TRIPLET

The pattern is three lines, rhyming. The three lines can be read by beginning at any point of the triangle. The challenge is to say three things on one topic that can be read in any order with essentially the same meaning.

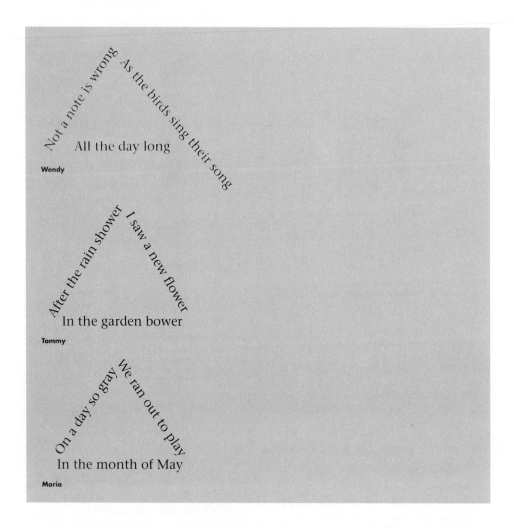

Not a note is wrong / As the birds sing their song / All the day long

Wendy

After the rain shower / I saw a new flower / In the garden bower

Tommy

On a day so gray / We ran out to play / In the month of May

Maria

QUADRANGLE

The pattern of a quadrangle is four lines, a quatrain. Rhyming schemes can be:

a a a a a a

a b b b a b

a a b a b c

a b a c b a

The lines are arranged around a quadrangle. They can be read beginning at any corner. The meaning remains essentially the same regardless of where the reading begins. The form requires a great deal of editing unless the author is lucky. This is a useful form for group writing as well as for individual authorship. An example follows:

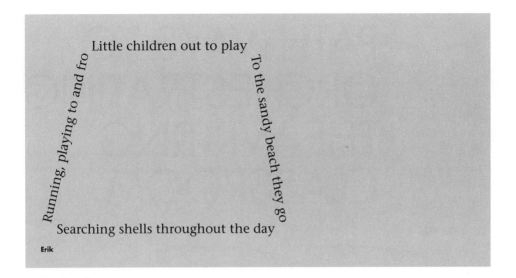

Little children out to play
Running, playing to and fro
To the sandy beach they go
Searching shells throughout the day

Erik

SUMMARY

Students' writing pathways are extended when they have opportunities to express themselves in one of the genres discussed in this chapter. Students and teachers alike will be amazed at the beauty of the expression that comes forth when one writes in patterned format and verse.

PATHWAYS TO EXTENDING PERSONAL WRITING

The student:

▶ elaborates basic sentences with descriptive words and phrases to denote:

Color	Sound
Size	Smell
Shape	Taste
Texture	Touch

▶ collects words and phrases from authors that may become a part of personal speech and writing.

▶ expresses own thinking in predictable story and poetry genres.

▶ is influenced by predictive language stories and becomes more self-expressive as an author.

▶ is the author of books that are shared with a wide range of readers.

▶8 PATHWAYS TO ORCHESTRATING THE WRITING CLASSROOM

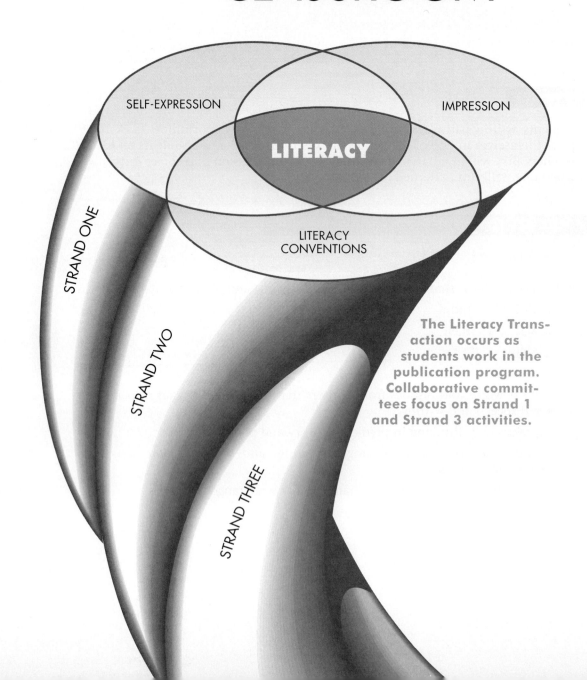

SELF-EXPRESSION

IMPRESSION

LITERACY

LITERACY
CONVENTIONS

STRAND ONE

STRAND TWO

STRAND THREE

The Literacy Trans-
action occurs as
students work in the
publication program.
Collaborative commit-
tees focus on Strand 1
and Strand 3 activities.

CHAPTER OUTLINE

A PSYCHOLOGICAL ENVIRONMENT FOR AUTHORS

PATTERNS OF INTERACTION
WRITER'S WORKSHOP
CONFERENCING
WRITING SEMINARS
COLLABORATIVE COMMITTEES

A PHYSICAL ENVIRONMENT FOR AUTHORS
THE WRITING AREA
THE PUBLISHING AREA
RESOURCES FOR AUTHORS

YOUNG AUTHORS' CONFERENCES

SUMMARY

PATHWAYS TO EDITING AND PUBLISHING

PATHWAYS TO PONDER

▶ **WHAT IS INVOLVED IN ORCHESTRATING A WRITING PROGRAM?**

▶ **HOW CAN TEACHERS BUILD A PSYCHOLOGICAL ENVIRONMENT FOR AUTHORS THAT ENCOURAGES CHILDREN TO BE RISK TAKERS?**

▶ **WHAT IS THE VALUE OF CONFERENCING WITH YOUNG AUTHORS?**

▶ **HOW DOES THE PHYSICAL ENVIRONMENT AFFECT STUDENTS' WRITING?**

W hen an orchestra plays together, the music they create collectively is much more beautiful than what any single musician makes. But there's one person who doesn't play at all. That person is the conductor. However, the conductor performs a very important role: She or he inspires the musicians to their ultimate level of performance.

And so it is with the writing classroom. The teacher serves as the conductor in that she or he seeks to inspire children to new heights in writing. But unlike the orchestra conductor, the teacher conductor gets to participate. Writing classrooms feature children and teachers writing together. In this chapter, we examine the roles of children and teachers in the orchestra of the writing classroom. We'll see classrooms where writers write and teachers and students learn together.

KIDS' ▶
CORNER

Sandra Hernandez ____ Name
13 ____ Age

Reading good books ____ Interests

What do you like most about school?

The thing I like most about school is when we play games. It's sometimes easier to learn things when the teachers let you play a game. It's not that easy to lose interest when you play a game.

What's your favorite subject? Why?

My favorite subject is math. I like it because you can make alot of games out of it. I also like working with numbers. Sometimes, it can be confusing but when you play a game, it makes it easier to learn. Also, there has been good teachers teaching me.

What's your favorite book? Why do you like it?

My favorite book is Courage Is Not Given. I like it because it talks about a girl that hides from the law. It also talks about her first love and all the places she is hiding in.

What advice do you have for teachers?

Advice I'd give to teachers is to let the children play more games, never grip at them, give treats everyday, praise the children alot and make the children feel comfortable with you, smile, don't fuss or frown.

The last two chapters were about the writing process. Chapter 6 examined the theoretical base and described the essays, stories, journals, books, and poems that can be produced when students are allowed the freedom to write creatively. Chapter 7 revealed the influence of genres or patterns on students' literacy development. In this chapter we describe how teachers can build environments where such writing can take place. We discuss teacher conferencing and collaborative student committees, the material resources needed for the Writing Center, and the orchestration that takes place between students and teachers in language-based writing classrooms.

A PSYCHOLOGICAL ENVIRONMENT FOR AUTHORS

In the process writing classroom, students have freedom to experiment with language. In fact, experimentation is essential if students are to reach their potential as language users and authors. Every oral exchange, every writing effort is an experiment in which students learn something about the effectiveness of that particular communication. In many classrooms, learning to be a successful language user is a trying situation and is very risky to students' self-esteem. Moreover, when the cost of making mistakes becomes too great, students stop taking risks and lose their opportunity for growth. The opposite is true in process-centered classrooms: Experimentation is the vehicle that carries students toward literacy. Students must feel free to try; otherwise there is nothing to refine, guide, or develop. An openness to efforts and an acceptance of invented or exploratory spelling, punctuation, and sentence writing are absolute requirements for budding authors. Students must be able to experiment with what they want to say and how they want to say it. When

◀ Hard at work on "Brite Spring" manuscript.

this situation occurs, creative efforts such as "Brite Spring" enter the classroom on scraps of paper and with supporting illustrations (see Figure 8.1).

Students who work in a strong phonics program sometimes develop generalizations about sound–symbol relations that, when applied, result in misspellings. Bobby furnishes an example (Figure 8.2).

To tell Bobby, age 7, that he misspelled the words *no* (know), *iny* (any), *thay* (they), *led's* (lettuce), *carits* (carrots), and *hi* (high) is in effect telling him that correct spelling is more important than content. At this stage acceptance and encouragement are high priorities. Children must produce manuscripts before they can refine them.

Some writing is difficult to interpret. Spelling often gives minimum clues, but with the author present to do the reading, comprehension is possible. Salvador gave a good example when he wrote, "dess June he is sic picos du munsr

FIGURE 8.1 ▶

Brite Spring

Once a time, it was winter but the people couldn't wate till spring. one day the people got an idea paint every thing spring colors. hey! that's a good idea lets do it yea! So they got all colors and strated to work it took seven days to do it but on the next day it relly was spring. But at night it rained and when they woke up it was warmer It was relly spring. The people said let's give it a name what shell we name it how about BriteSpring Yes! and from now on the people don't paint it spring and that how Spring go its name.

The End

> Rabbits
>
> This story is about Rabbits.
> do you no iny thing about them
> I will tell you something thay
> eat leds and carits and
> thay can jump hi

mk hm sic." When he read the story, the sound–symbol relation cleared up. He read, "This is Johnny. He is sick because the monster makes him sick."

A group of children wrote and illustrated stories following a seal show. Prior to writing, they created the following word cluster:

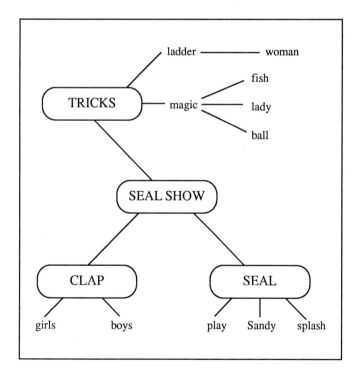

In addition to the 14 words the children suggested following the show, a list of about 100 words of highest frequency was visible from any place in the classroom. Abel wrote, "I sw a seal played wriz a ball and he make tricks." He read, "I saw a seal play with a ball and he makes tricks."

Harold wrote, "The seal was duen some trics. And the lade sent ot got a nedr seal. And the seal did not no trecs. And the lade hed some segy from the seal. Adn the seal clap hes hons. the seal got up on hes set. the seal et fsh. the fehes wer ded."

Harold's story is easy to read with his invented spelling. The only word that might give an adult reader trouble is *segy* (sausage). He made minimum use of the resources provided for spelling. At this point he was personally involved to the extent that his own resources seemed adequate—and they were.

Isabel wrote, "The seal had a ball on his nos. They he went up the ladder and down the ladder. The seal aet fish and all the doys and girls wour claping." Isabel used the resources but still had a problem copying from one place to another.

From the class of bilingual children the teacher had achieved major goals:

▶ Most students felt comfortable writing independently.

▶ A common experience, the seal show, provided a base for building a speaking, writing, and reading vocabulary.

▶ Every child could read his or her own writing.

▶ What was written was useful in reading.

▶ Children who volunteered their stories had them edited and published in a booklet with their own illustrations. One form of editing was to print what was written and then add how the author read it.

▶ Children used writing resources that were developed in the classroom to free themselves for independent writing.

PATTERNS OF INTERACTION

WRITER'S WORKSHOP

Stephanie Noland tells of the time Bill Martin Jr visited her Dallas, Texas, multiage classroom. After spending the day watching her and her students interact, he said, "Do you know what makes you such a great writing teacher?" Stephanie waited for Bill to continue, anticipating he would mention her knowledge base, her commitment, or perhaps her sensitivity to children. Instead, he said, "Because you're so extraordinarily organized!"

And Bill was right. Stephanie's classroom writing procedures are organized. Every child is familiar with the system the class uses and every child is independent of her. They simply "get to work" on writing when they arrive in the morning, picking up where they left off the day before. They can do so because of the predictable nature of her writer's workshop procedures. Lucy Calkins and Shelley Harwayne, in discussing their work with children in New York City, express the same concept. "In the writing workshop, both the schedule and the expectations are simple and predictable. Students can become strategic learners because they know when they will be writing, which supplies will be available, and what their writing time will be like" (Calkins & Harwayne, 1987, p. 33).

What is writer's workshop? It means different things to different people, but in general, it's simply a time when writers work. Their work may include journal writing, brainstorming, prewriting, collaborating with other authors, conferencing with collaborative student committees or the teacher, illustrating manuscripts, and celebrating authorship.

MINI-LESSONS IN THE WRITING WORKSHOP

Mini-lessons are short presentations on skills writers need and will use during their writing. They are generally presented just before writers write during writing workshops. Most teachers who use mini-lessons effectively make them short, focus them on one skill at a time, present them as options skilled writers frequently use (not mandates from headquarters), and tailor them to specific needs of the writers in the class at that time.

Mary Ellen Giacobbe (1991) categorizes mini-lessons into four categories:

1. *Procedures.* The operations and management of the writing workshop, such as a workshop on how to select a story for publication and the steps you must take to prepare a piece to "go to press."

2. *Strategies.* These include techniques real writers use, such as how to find a topic or what to do when you have writer's block.

3. *Qualities of good writing.* These include practical topics, such as writing strong leads, eliminating clutter, focusing the piece, and so on.

4. *Skills.* English conventions, such as capitalization and punctuation.

◀ **Bill Martin's books provide strong, dependable lines for young writers.**

CLASSROOM VIGNETTE

Bob Nottingham believes writers write best when they have time—time to work, time to share, time to dream, and time to turn their dreams into manuscripts. Here's his writer's workshop schedule:

BOB'S WRITER'S WORKSHOP

TIME	ACTIVITY
10 minutes	Journals
20 minutes	Uninterrupted writing
20 minutes	Committees meet Conferencing Writing seminars or mini-lessons
10 minutes	Celebration of writing Author's chair Whole-group share

Bob believes two factors are of great importance in the writing classroom: Children must have time to write every day and the writing his children do must be recognized. To that end, the classroom runs an "in-house" publishing center. His children work together in collaborative committees to receive, edit, and publish the writings of the children. The student committees formed are described in this chapter under the heading "collaborative committees."

Tommy Thomason (1994) recommends that mini-lessons fit the writing needs of the students. Here are some of his ideas for possible mini-lessons:

Establishing rules for the writing workshop

Managing your time in writing workshop

The mechanics of editing

Establishing procedures for illustrating a book

How to work in peer-editing groups

Choosing a topic

Using books as inspiration for topic choice

Rereading for clarity and completeness

Determining the focus of the writing

Avoiding plagiarism

Writing from another point of view

Sequencing information by cutting and pasting

Descriptive writing

How to write conversation

Adding information for clarity

Eliminating excessive adjectives

Writing effective titles

Writing good leads

How to show, not tell

Use of capital letters

Using a dictionary

Using exclamation marks

Using question marks

Using possessives

Plurals vs. possessives

Using contractions

Using nouns as antecedents for pronouns

Form for writing a letter

Using synonyms

CONFERENCING

Young authors learn more about writing through the actual process of writing and collaborating with other authors than by any other method. However, conferencing remains a very efficient method of guiding authors and

◀ At work on a story.

their writing. Conferences have been misused in the past because they were inflexible and teacher centered with set schedules: Choose topics and write first draft on Monday; Tuesday revise; Wednesday conference with teacher; final draft due on Thursday. This does more to damage fluency than to build writing strengths. Some papers do not need revisions; other papers need multiple revisions. Or, as Donald Graves and Virginia Stuart say, "It is just as hard to apply one timetable to twenty-five papers as it is to fit one assignment to twenty-five hearts and minds" (Graves & Stuart, 1985). Thus conferences must be individual matters and should be handled differently according to the context of the situation.

Powerful demonstrations stem from conferences—what the teacher emphasizes during the conference will affect how the students approach the writing act. In addition, teachers must be careful not to try to accomplish everything in one conference. Children will be overwhelmed if the teacher tries to address all the issues from punctuation to content in one setting. In some classrooms, teachers have overcome this problem by having different types of conferences, ranging from content conferences to editing conferences. Research has indicated that children learn best in classrooms where they have opportunities to talk with each other—not just to the teacher (Atwell, 1987, 1990; Dyson, 1987). Such collaborative talk and learning take place in peer writing conferences. Bissex (1982) suggests that teachers model conferences by leading them to demonstrate the conference process. Once children have internalized the process, they can conduct their own conferences, freeing the teacher to circulate and listen and serve as a resource if needed.

We find it best to do conferencing on an informal basis, giving feedback to students as we move through the room and as their questions arise. The important thing is that the first focus must be on content, with organization and conventions coming at a later time.

Teachers glean ▶ **valuable information about children's literacy growth through conferencing.**

WHAT DO I ASK DURING WRITING CONFERENCES?

Thomason (1994) cautions that "every conference is different." He does detail, however, the types of questions writing coaches might ask during conferences. His list will give you a feel for the types of questions you might want to ask at different stages of the writing process.

AT THE PREWRITING STAGE

1. What do you think you'll write about?
2. Why did you choose that?
3. Where will you start? What will your lead be about?

AT THE FIRST-DRAFT STAGE

1. Do you have more than one story here?
2. Underline the part that tells what this draft is about.
3. What is the most important thing you're trying to say here?
4. Explain how your title fits your draft.
5. Can you tell me more about this?
6. This part isn't clear to me. Can you tell me what you mean?
7. Can you describe this for me?
8. What next?
9. Are you happy with your lead/ending?
10. How does your lead grab your reader's attention?
11. Can you be more specific here?
12. Is this the best word here?
13. Can you think of a different way to say this?
14. What do you think you can do to make this draft better?
15. What works so well you'd like to try to develop it further?
16. What did you learn from this piece of writing?
17. Can you think of something you tried in this draft that you've never tried before?
18. How can I help you with this piece?

DURING PREPARATION FOR PUBLICATION

At this point, writers' conferences usually deal largely with form and mechanics. Ask what things need to be checked to get a piece ready for publication. You might ask the child to go back through the piece and circle all the words he or she thinks might be spelled incorrectly, box areas with punctuation and capitalization problems, and so on. You can use publication conferences to show the child progress made in spelling or show various rules the writer needs to know. After the writer has edited, you might have the piece passed on to an editing committee or to other writers who might specialize in spelling or capitalization, for example.

WRITING SEMINARS

Another method of influencing student style and form is through seminars (Sampson, Allen, & Sampson, 1991). Seminars may be whole class or

▶ Seminars afford opportunities for teachers and young authors to interact.

small group. Seminars conducted on a regular basis prepare students for ever-increasing abilities and responsibilities for editing their own manuscripts and for working on editorial committees. Students who lack confidence in making decisions about their own writing and that of others have opportunities to listen and participate without being graded. They get ideas to explore and gain insights into style and form that permit them to edit. As with conferences, the attitudes of teachers are crucial in seminar techniques.

Teachers are not the source of all information; rather, they guide and serve as reference sources. In some cases they serve as editor in chief when manuscripts in the seminar are to be published for use in the school program. The seminar is used to raise the level of awareness of style and correctness of forms. The first focus is on content and meaning, with conventions only a later concern. Such seminars result in improved writing by the students and an increased ability to appreciate effective writing by other authors.

COLLABORATIVE COMMITTEES

Students learn best when they are involved as editors and participants in the classroom publishing process. As students serve on committees, they

CLASSROOM VIGNETTE

Margie Thompson has a special place where students put their stories if they wish them to be used in a seminar. Stories selected for use in a seminar are duplicated for the fourth-grade students or they are put on transparencies. The authors know other students will make suggestions for changes and that they must be prepared for the change or to defend their work. Students gather around and listen to the author or teacher read the story. Then they comment on strengths and weaknesses.

Margie serves as the seminar leader in order to reinforce essential matters of form at the same time she seeks to preserve individual style. She encourages students to look for ways to increase clarity of meaning and organization.

The seminars lead students to avoid writing a story that is totally dependent on an accompanying picture with a beginning sentence such as "This is a . . ." or "Look at my. . . ." Rather, students learn to use sentences that are clear statements of their ideas: "My horse lives in a barn behind my house" and "I believe the President should have vetoed the bill because it was not fair to the farmers."

Ida Bohannan keeps informal notes on errors in form that she observes as children write. Periodically she calls for a seminar on a topic of need. She asks students to volunteer original manuscripts that can be made into transparencies. They are projected on the chalkboard so suggestions for improvement can be written in, discussed, and then changed if necessary. At other times she prepares transparencies with no punctuation or capitalization. Students edit as they discuss matters of form.

Other seminars deal with style. Ida will furnish a long and involved paragraph and ask students to experience the satisfaction of saying something ordinary in an extraordinary way. This is style in writing.

internalize the fine points of writing and develop an appreciation for the way other authors express themselves in beautiful language. Some committees on which students can serve fill several functions: editorial, printing, duplicating, illustrating, and bindery.

THE EDITORIAL COMMITTEE

The editorial committee accepts original manuscripts and reads them to identify mechanical and technical errors and to make suggestions for improving style and form. Some committees divide responsibility by assigning each member a specialty such as story sense, spelling, capitalization, punctuation, sentence sense, or paragraphing. Each specialist reads a manuscript and notes suggestions. Then the committee calls a conference with the author to review the suggestions. The author accepts or rejects the suggestions in terms of the purpose of the manuscript. In some cases the author then takes the manuscript to the editor in chief, who is usually the teacher. After review by the editor in chief, necessary revisions are made. Often rewriting is desirable before preparing a manuscript for duplication.

Editing of newspapers and magazines may involve other procedures. Contributors may place their rough drafts in designated places for editors to review. There might be editors for stories, reports, comics, sports, fashions, entertainment, editorials, interviews, puzzles, and any other sections included in the publication. In addition to attention to technical errors, editors have to plan the use of assigned space and recommend alterations to fit the spaces.

Reading of rough drafts may be used as an editing technique for contributions to a class book. Groups of five or six can read each other's manuscripts, marking anything that needs to be changed. When a manuscript returns to the author, it will have been reviewed by every editor and will be ready to rewrite in a refined version.

Never does the teacher serve as the *grader* of papers, mandating suggestions for corrections to be made when a manuscript is copied. If the teacher functions as an editor, it is *with the author.* And the author always makes the final decision or choice concerning revisions. Choices of topic, revisions, and illustrations lead to a sense of student accomplishment and pride (Hubbard, 1985).

THE PRINTING COMMITTEE

The author may type or print the manuscript for duplication or may choose a member of the committee to do so. Every printing committee should have at least one member who can use a typewriter or computer; however, expertise in typing is not required. A volunteer parent can be a committee member. Manuscripts can also be prepared with lead pencils on white paper and copied on one of the heat-process machines. If mimeograph machines are to be used, stencils can be cut on the typewriter or with a sharp pencil.

Most students, regardless of how young, like to try to do some of their own typing even though they type with only one finger. If someone else does the typing, the author, including many of kindergarten age, should be invited to strike a few of the letters to see what happens.

If pencil copies are being made for duplicating stencils, an adult can print lightly in letters similar to those used in the classroom, and the author can trace over the printing with bold strokes.

The author has the responsibility of paging the manuscript and deciding whether the book will be folded and stitched, stapled flat, held with ring binders, or put together by other means. Members of the committee serve as consultants and show mockups of different possibilities.

When preparing newspapers and magazines, each contributor may be assigned space or pages to prepare. The variety in printing and illustrating adds interest to the publication.

THE DUPLICATING COMMITTEE

In some schools, students learn to operate duplicating equipment to publish their own books, newspapers, and magazines. In others, teachers or parents are in charge of the machines. In all cases the author or authors whose work is being duplicated should be able to observe the process at least once. For some authors this is the most exciting part of the whole production.

Duplicating committee members have the responsibility for collating the pages into the order they will be in the binding. If pages have not been numbered before being duplicated, the committee members might number the pages.

THE ILLUSTRATING COMMITTEE

Authors may do their own illustrations or they may seek help from members of the illustrating committee in the Publishing Area. Children on the committee can offer suggestions for illustrations and read paged manuscripts

◀ An illustrating committee at work.

to make certain the text suggests an illustration at the point that space is provided for it.

Some members of each illustrating committee should understand the following points:

1. Nouns can be illustrated more easily than any other class of words. Because nouns carry the heaviest load of meaning in passages, good illustrations aid in word recognition and prediction of words and phrases. For easy reading materials, all nouns not on lists of words of highest frequency should be illustrated.

2. Color, size, and shape words can be illustrated. Illustrations can reduce the difficulty of the story and can add to an author's meaning.

3. Texture words can be illustrated with collage materials and with brush strokes. The tactile experience available from collage illustrations extends vocabularies whether the words are printed or not.

4. Taste and smell words can only be implied in most illustrations. (Some "scratch and smell" books are available commercially.)

5. Leaves, dried flowers, feathers, and other thin materials pressed between waxed paper with a warm iron make attractive illustrations.

6. Abstract designs such as blottoes, string paintings, sponge prints, and thumbprints are sometimes as effective as realistic representations.

7. Crayon rubbings that use templates prepared by the teacher for topics of interest such as Christmas can make "instant illustrations."

Some children like to take their manuscripts home for others to illustrate. The family team is a good unit for working on a publication.

In many classrooms some of the book-length publications are produced for every member. Spaces for illustrations are left blank during duplicating and binding. Each student does his or her own illustrations after receiving the book. Copies for the library are prepared by the illustrating committee.

THE BINDERY COMMITTEE

Many students volunteer for the bindery committee. They enjoy the process of assembling, sewing, stapling, cutting cardboard and cloth to size, gluing, and pressing. Most Publishing Areas have models of different bindings with step-by-step procedures to accompany them. An example of how to produce a hard cover book is detailed in Figure 8.3.

Explanations of several types of bindings should be available. Simple flexible bindings are useful, but they do not last long in libraries. Volunteer parents are very useful in the bindery. They can furnish materials and assist in making covers. A supply of covers for standard-sized paper can be made in advance, and the author can choose the binding and attach the book.

A publication program does not need to wait until a Writing/Publishing Area has been established. Simple recognition of student language productivity can be given by stapling a simple text to a painting for display on the chart rack or on a bulletin board. Attractive bindings can be made of

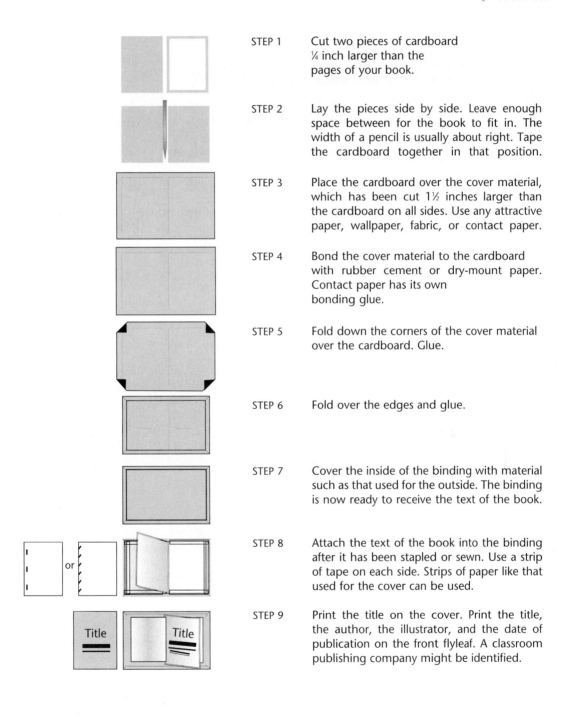

STEP 1   Cut two pieces of cardboard ¼ inch larger than the pages of your book.

STEP 2   Lay the pieces side by side. Leave enough space between for the book to fit in. The width of a pencil is usually about right. Tape the cardboard together in that position.

STEP 3   Place the cardboard over the cover material, which has been cut 1½ inches larger than the cardboard on all sides. Use any attractive paper, wallpaper, fabric, or contact paper.

STEP 4   Bond the cover material to the cardboard with rubber cement or dry-mount paper. Contact paper has its own bonding glue.

STEP 5   Fold down the corners of the cover material over the cardboard. Glue.

STEP 6   Fold over the edges and glue.

STEP 7   Cover the inside of the binding with material such as that used for the outside. The binding is now ready to receive the text of the book.

STEP 8   Attach the text of the book into the binding after it has been stapled or sewn. Use a strip of tape on each side. Strips of paper like that used for the cover can be used.

STEP 9   Print the title on the cover. Print the title, the author, the illustrator, and the date of publication on the front flyleaf. A classroom publishing company might be identified.

construction paper. Stories written on the chalkboard can be copied and placed in a folder and left unbound. Authors can read unbound and unedited stories to the class.

A PHYSICAL ENVIRONMENT FOR AUTHORS

In addition to the psychological and interactive aspects of the environment, some physical characteristics are helpful if productive efforts are to be attained with minimum help from a teacher or other adults. A Writing/Publishing Area must be available and well supplied.

THE WRITING AREA

The Writing Area is a part of the Writing/Publishing Center where students go to write. It can also be a place where materials are stored for students to check out and use in a variety of locations.

**THE BOOK ▶
MAKERS**

BYRD BAYLOR

1. Which book of yours has given you the greatest pleasure?

Actually, I could have said that about every one of my books at one time or another. If at any one given time I didn't think this was the most wonderful book, I wouldn't have written it.

2. Which book has surprised you most in terms of its public reception?

I wrote *The Best Town in the World* just for my father as a birthday present. I was surprised at the success of *I'm in Charge of Celebrations* because I thought that the celebrations in the book were such small celebrations that nobody else would care. What happened was that they were so small that they were in everyone's common experience and everyone related to the book.

3. What would you like people to remember about your work?

I honestly don't think that much about what I want people to remember about my work. It's more important to me what I get out of it as a writer. In fact, some of the books I've won awards for are not my personal favorites.

4. What impact do you hope your work will have on children?

If I write well, I hope they gain a sense of honesty in relationships of people to animals, to the earth, to other people, and to themselves.

Byrd Baylor's books are her private love song to her own part of the world. Her keen observations about the truly important things of life are found in *Everybody Needs a Rock, Hawk, I'm Your Brother, The Other Way to Listen, I'm in Charge of Celebrations, The Way to Start a Day, If You Are a Hunter of Fossils,* and *The Best Town in the World.*

The ideal Writing Area is developed cooperatively by pupils and teachers as they work together as authors. There are some supplies and components that can be planned and provided for before a class group is formed.

Paper should be available in a variety of qualities, sizes, and colors. Handwriting paper can be in supply for practice in handwriting skills, but it must not be a paper prescribed for authors to use. At all levels authors need a choice of paper, one suitable to what is being written. Large quantities of newsprint are handy for first drafts. The blank sides of printed sheets can be used for original manuscripts. Some classroom groups find a supply of computer print-out paper useful. Others supplement the school supply with end-of-roll newsprint from newspaper publishers and with printer's scrap from a print shop.

Markers of many sizes and colors should be available. Different kinds and colors of pencils, felt-tipped pens in a variety of colors, and crayons of all sizes and colors are needed so authors can get the desired effect for their manuscripts.

Writing models that show several configurations of capital and lowercase letters can be useful when authors are ready to refine and edit manuscripts.

Spelling aids need to be available in a variety of forms and in several places. Examples follow:

▶ lists of high-frequency words that develop as children analyze their own dictation and writing to discover the words all authors use (see Figure 8.4)

▶ lists of name words that accumulate for specific topics or that are used frequently by many students

▶ lists of descriptive words such as color, size, shape, texture, smell, taste, and touch

▶ lists of words of movement that are used as verbs in sentences

▶ proper names useful for special seasons and projects

▶ picture dictionaries that might grow from children's own language

▶ school dictionaries that offer a major resource for more mature authors

Idea starters have been misused by some teachers (Calkins, 1983). They tend to stifle children's creativity and freedom of choice as writers. However, a new form of literacy is emerging in the 1990s. Holistic writing tests are used to judge how good children are as writers and how effective writing programs are. Unfortunately, these tests are essays that children write cued by idea starters.

Children are given no choice; they must write an essay based on a picture or sentence stimulus. Good writers can fail such a task if they are not used to the form of such tests. Therefore, school writing programs must include activities that will enable students to succeed with this genre. Thus sentence or

FIGURE 8.4 ▶ **ALLEN LIST OF WORDS FOR SPELLING AND EDITING**

a	between	daddy	fellow	guess	is
about	big	dark	few		it
after	black	day	fifth	had	its
again	blue	dear	finally	hair	it's
all	body	did	find	half	
almost	book	didn't	fine	hand	jet
along	both	died	finished	happened	jump
alphabet	box	different	fire	happy	just
also	boy	do	first	hard	
always	bring	does	fish	has	keep
am	brother	dog	five	hat	kept
an	brown	done	fly	have	killed
and	but	don't	foot	having	kind
animal	buy	door	for	he	knew
another	by	down	found	head	know
any		drama	four	heard	
are		draw	fourth	help	language
around	cafeteria	dress	friend	her	large
art	call	drink	from	here	last
as	came		front	high	late
ask	can	each	full	him	laugh
asked	can't	early	fun	his	learned
at	car	ears	funny	hit	leave
ate	cat	eat		hold	left
aunt	chair	egg	game	home	legs
away	children	eight	gave	hope	let
	Christmas	end	get	hot	letter
baby	city	enough	getting	house	light
back	class	even	girl	how	like
bad	clean	ever	give	hundred	lips
ball	close	every	giving	hurt	little
be	coat	everyone	glad		live
beautiful	cold	everything	go	I	living
became	come	eye	goes	ice	long
because	coming		good	if	look
bed	cook	fall	got	I'll	lots
been	could	far	grade	I'm	love
before	couldn't	farm	gravel	important	
began	country	fast	great	in	made
best	cow	father	green	interesting	make
better	cut	feet	grow	into	man

many	oh	rain	sometimes	time	went
may	old	ran	soon	to	were
me	on	read	spring	today	what
meet	once	reading	start	together	when
men	one	ready	stay	told	where
might	only	real	stop	tongue	which
milk	open	red	story	too	while
mine	or	rest	street	took	white
minutes	orange	ride	study	top	who
Miss	other	right	such	town	why
money	our	room	summer	tried	will
more	out	round	sun	trip	window
morning	outside	run	supper	try	winter
most	over		sure	turn	wish
mother	own	said	swim	two	with
mouth		same			without
Mr.	paint	saw	table	under	woman
Mrs.	painting	say	take	until	women
Ms.	paper	school	talk	up	won't
much	part	second	teacher	upon	wood
music	party	see	teeth	us	world
must	pass	seen	tell	use	would
my	past	send	ten	used	wouldn't
myself	pay	sent	than		write
	people	seven	thank	vacation	writing
name	person	shall	that	very	wrong
near	pet	she	the	visit	wrote
never	pick	should	their	vocabulary	
new	pig	show	them		yard
next	pink	sick	then	walk	year
nice	place	side	there	want	yellow
night	play	since	these	war	yes
no	please	sing	they	warm	yet
nobody	pretty	sister	thing	was	you
none	principal	sit	think	wash	young
north	pull	six	third	wasn't	your
not	purple	sixth	this	water	yours
now	put	sleep	those	way	
		small	thought	we	zipper
of	quick	so	three	weather	zoo
off	quiet	some	through	week	
often	quite	something	till	well	

story starters may occasionally be used and serve as one aspect of the writing program. Activities include the following:

▶ Children may "jot" down ideas for stories in their writer's notebook, saving them for future writing workshop sessions.

▶ Story beginnings can be copied on cards with just enough story to suggest characters, setting, and a hint of plot.

▶ Story middles, copied on cards, can be developed in both directions to tell stories.

▶ Story endings, copied on cards, can give a hint of what might have happened in entire stories.

▶ Story pictures can be filed for personal interpretation by authors.

▶ Examples and explanations for riddles and jokes can be used as models.

▶ Headlines from newspapers, mounted on cards, can be used as ideas for stories and poems.

Students should be encouraged to make contributions to the resources in the Writing Area. It is their source of help and inspiration and they must understand what is there and how to use its resources.

Vocabulary enrichment resources must grow as the Writing Area is used, or there will be little improvement in the quality of writing. Lists, files, and posters can be started for enrichment resources. Here is a list of possibilities:

▶ figurative language files with examples of similes, metaphors, and personification as used by other authors

▶ lists of synonyms and antonyms, especially examples of words of two, three, and four syllables that are useful in writing poetry with controlled syllabic patterns

▶ Alliteration aids such as a list of words beginning with the same sound symbols that includes nouns, verbs, adjectives, and adverbs

▶ rhyming aids that include lists of two, three, and four words that rhyme

▶ how to say *said* in many ways as an aid to writing conversation that emphasizes characterization

▶ nonsense words that can be used or can serve as examples for making up new words for nonsense writing

As students mature as authors, each one should develop a personal writing handbook. A writing handbook contains many of the helps just listed for the Writing Area but features aids each author uses frequently. The main value of the writing handbook is that it serves as a place where students can jot down ideas for stories, leads for stories, or other ideas.

THE PUBLISHING AREA

The Publishing Area, a part of the Writing/Publishing Center, is a place in a classroom or school where students process their original manuscripts

HOW "PHONICS" GOT ITS NAME

*If B. . .O. . .M. . .B. . . says
"Bomb" as in "Tom,"
Why does T. . .O. . .M. . .
    B. . . say "tomb" as in
    "boom?"
Now please pay close attention,
Cuz your thoughts are bound to
    roam,
When I tell you C. . .O. . .
    M. . .B. . .makes a sound
    that rhymes with "foam."*

*Now H. . .O. . .M. . .E. . .
    says "home" as in "Rome,"
But S. . .O. . .M. . .E. . .
    says "some" as in "come,"
Both easy enough to say,
But how can words be spelled the
    same
But pronounced a different way.*

*Now I'm beginning to understand
How phonics got its name.
You see, the study of sound is sonics.
So they took off the "S" and added
    "PH,"
Cuz there ain't no sound in phonics.*

through editing, illustrating, paging, copying, and binding into forms for others to use. It may be an integral part of the Writing Area, or it may be at a separate location. Some schools with many authors maintain a Publishing Area for the whole school and invite parents to assist in the operation by supplying materials, typing, and helping with the binding process. In these schools, simple binding is done in the classrooms, and only manuscripts that are selected for production in multiple copies go to the school Publishing Area.

At Ben Franklin Elementary School in Littleton, Colorado, the students have established Beat Street Station, an area in the school's foyer that features the very finest of BE AUTHORS TODAY, their school's publishing house. This is a place for browsing, reading, and sharing.

The process of selecting manuscripts to be published in multiple copies should be well understood by students. A committee might develop criteria and publish them. It should emphasize that everything that is written does not need to be published in multiple copies. *Single original copies are enough for most of what is written.*

Publishing is the peak experience in a meaning-centered classroom. It truly integrates writing, reading, speaking, and listening. It brings into focus the mechanics of language. It draws on influences from many authors and publishers. It uses graphics as an essential ingredient in the language arts. It can be extended and interpreted through dramatization and choral reading. A meaning-centered classroom is impossible to maintain without publishing individual books, class books, individual story charts, newspapers, magazines, catalogues, and recipes. For these publications, supplies and aids are required that may not be typical of other communication and writing programs, including the following:

1. scraps of cloth, cardboard, wallpaper, braid, yarn, and leather for covers and illustrations

2. contact paper to use in bindings of hard-cover books

3. sewing equipment that includes a sewing machine, hand-sewing needles, an awl, and thread

4. laminator—a laminating machine or iron to use with laminating paper

5. computers and printers, especially when making multiple copies

6. lettering pens for printing with stencils and on title pages and covers

7. paper cutter to cut cardboard for covers and pages of different sizes

8. paper punch to cut holes for some bindings

9. glue and tape for securing books to bindings

10. art supplies for illustrating in cases in which the Publishing Area is far removed from the Arts and Crafts Center

The Publishing Area is of limited value unless students participate. Volunteer adults can help, and older students can work with younger children, but participation in process and procedures is of great significance when the ideas and language of the students are being made into reading material useful in the school program.

RESOURCES FOR AUTHORS

In addition to the patterns introduced in Chapter 6, teachers provide many resources to launch students into writing. These resources, which include language on the literary level and poetic forms of expression, are introduced and practiced so they can become a natural part of students' expression. Meaning-centered classrooms provide resources for helping authors get started. A few examples are given here.

Redundant patterns from children's books can launch a series of statements of personal experience or imagination. Students can copy the phrase and add a simple statement or a rhyme that is purely personal. The following were written in response to the pattern "the most important thing about . . ." from Margaret Wise Brown's *The Important Book*.

> *The most important thing about school is getting to play with friends at recess.*
>
> **Marie**

> *The most important thing about mommies is that they are good for kissing and hugging.*
>
> **Lynn**

Children may also use the entire pattern from *The Important Book* to write important things about themselves. Yesenia Tamez, a second-grade student, featured in Chapter 1, contributed a picture and stanza about herself, shown in Figure 8.5.

Redundant patterns provide:

▶ a structure that is dependable for each author

▶ repetition of the same sentence pattern with different content in each sentence

▶ repetition for easy reading

▶ spelling of many of the words

Students usually have more to say than just the printed part. They can elaborate on any accompanying illustration and thus keep full language in the classroom environment—naming things, telling how they move, and describing them. Home-rooted dialects are useful and welcome in oral elaboration even though they may have been denied by the nature of the model. Experience backgrounds are used with only slight variations in words.

Redundant patterns assure the introduction and repetition of words of highest frequency in the language. When bound into books, every page repeats phrases, but every page is different.

The *projection of self* to inanimate objects or to animals helps students say things and reveal frustrations that are not typical of sharing and reporting. Brenda illustrates this in her composition.

"OH NO, I'M AN ANT!"

One Saturday morning when I woke up I could not feel myself. I crawled out of my room and my house. I went to the end of the pool and I saw my reflection. I was an ant.

"Mom, Mom," I yelled.

"Where are you?" said my mom.

"I'm down here," I replied. She looked everywhere and then she found me.

◄ **FIGURE 8.5**

Important Me   Yesenia Tamez.

The most important thing about me is
I Like to do things and read for fun.
I am intelligent. I am good at the games
and I clean the house.
But the most important thing about
me is I like to do things and read for fun.

"Oh there you are," she said.

"Well, I have to put you in a jar," she said. She got a jar and punched holes in it as fast as she could. She carefully picked me up and put me in the jar.

"Can you breathe, dear?" she asked.

"Yes!" I yelled.

"Jennifer, I have to go to the store. You watch your little red sister," said my mom.

"My little red sister?" replied Jennifer.

"We will talk about it tomorrow," said my mom.

My sister did not know where I was but my little brother knew. He climbed on a chair and dropped the bottle. The lid came off and I fell out. My legs and I were not all there. I wanted to go one way but my legs took me another way. By the time I knew it I was already in the hall. My little sister came in the hall. She had big feet, but the worst thing of all was that we had red carpet! Her huge foot went right past me. Boy was I lucky. I heard the door slam. It was my mom.

"Where is your sister?" said my mom.

"I don't know. I was looking for her while you were gone," replied my sister.

"Oh no," yelled my mom. "Brenda, where are you?" she screamed.

"I'm in the hall," I replied. She got a flashlight and moved the carpet every which way she could. It was like she was parting my little sister's hair. I waved my little red legs high up in the air. She saw my legs and picked me up. She got me in the car and put my seat belt on. A police man came by and stopped my mom.

"Why do you have this seat belt buckled if no one is sitting there?" he said.

"My daughter is sitting there," my mom replied.

"Now you're going to tell me that she talks. Am I right?" he said.

"Well she does," said my mom.

"Oh yeah? Tell her to say something," he replied.

"Okay, say something, Brenda," said my mom.

"Hi, my name is Brenda," I replied.

"Okay, I'll let you go now," he said.

My mom rushed to my grandmother's house.

"Little Brenda has turned into an ant," said my mom.

"No need to worry. I know just the thing to do about it. Since little Richie turned into an elephant, I made a secret recipe. Now it runs in the family. You don't know this, but this happened to you when you were little," said my grandmother. She walked into the kitchen and told my mom to go watch T.V. in the living room. She came back in twenty minutes. It looked like chocolate pudding. She told me to eat it. I ate it as fast as I could. In nine minutes I was back to myself. Boy was I happy!

The next day when I woke up I was glad to see myself.

Mario reflects his aspirations to be a drag car driver in his composition.

WHY I WANT TO BE A DRAGSTER

I want to be a drag racer so I can be famous. And win a lot of money and stickers. I am interested in mechanical things. I want to be a mechanic, too, so I can fix my own car and I can help people by fixing their things like cars, go-carts, mini-bikes, and cassettes, too.

Feelings are an important part of life. Many students can express their feelings when they write with self projected into some inanimate object. Karla did this in a short poem.

FLOOR

Hi! I'm a floor!
People are always
walking on me.
Sometimes,
I feel like opening up
and swallowing them,
But I don't.

Personification is available to students as they project self into the world around them to express deep feelings and aspirations. Douglas wrote,

SUNBAKED SAND DUNE

I stand alone in the desert
Looking up at the sky.
I am dry and motionless,
Watching the clouds roll by.
My neighbor is a cactus plant,
Old and very big.
No other thing can you see

Not even a little twig.
You see why I am lonely?
Besides the cactus plant
I am the one and only.

Brief descriptions of things usual and ordinary help children use words that are not typical of conversation. As shown by the following examples, students can look for any object or word, think of its name, its use, its feelings, its size, its shape, its color, and other characteristics. Then they can write.

NIGHT

After the last traces of the sunset,
Night falls like a blanket of black
   velvet
Covering the world.

Geoffrey

BROOM

It sweeps
It keeps.
It falls apart.
It's big.
It's small.
It's any size at all.

Juana

JET

Soaring, roaring, flying
Through the polluted sky.
Turning engines breathing
Black, smoky fumes.

Carl

Alphabet books of all kinds promote the development of reference skills, stimulate dictionary use, and provide experience with sound–symbol relations. Alphabet books such as Bill Martin and John Archambault's *Chicka Chicka Boom Boom* (1989) may serve as a model that highlights the form.

Each student can choose a category of some kind, such as zoo animals, foods, people I know, homes, and vehicles. These can be made into a book such as *All Kinds of Things from A to Z*. Words for each letter of the alphabet can be accompanied with illustrations. Older students can serve as scribes to younger children who need help. Books can be bound and used for reading.

Alliterative language highlights the use of repetitive sounds as a literary device. Simple statements made around a topic such as "Piles of Presents" can involve students in alliterative language.

A jolly, jumping jack-in-the-box.   *A beautiful, big, buzzing bike.*

Rosa   **Jerome**

Alliteration can be promoted through nonsense writing. The teacher or a student can produce a nonsense title and an introduction. Nonsense statements from other students can follow.

> *Is that a cow crunching crackers on*
> *   the couch?*
> *There's a thumping and a thrashing,*
> *There's a crashing and a cracking,*
> *There's a banging and a bumping*
> *All over the place.*
> *Could it be*
> *Bats batting butter in bibs in the*
> *   bedroom?*
> *Or a*
> *Goat giggling in the garage?*
> *Maybe it's*
> *Swans sweating while swimming in*
> *   sweaters,*
> *Or*
> *Penguins popping popcorn in the*
> *   pantry.*

Each student can add an illustrated page for a book that can be used for reviewing initial consonants and consonant clusters. The pride of authorship inherent in this type of production is enough motivation for active participation in the learning experience.

Comics from newspapers are useful in promoting clever and creative language. Comic strips can be collected, and the "talk" can be cut out. Then the remainder of the comic strip can be mounted in books with one frame to a page and the talk can be restored by the students. The talk written can be their own and may include dialects typical of home-rooted language. Often this language is clear, forceful, and creative, and it needs to be recognized as useful in some types of communication.

Some students like to cut out characters from several comic strips they know well and combine them into one of their own. Those who are able to retain the language and personalities of the characters in new and mixed up settings get results that are entertaining and highly creative.

Classic stories and poems are useful as models for language and characterization. Several versions of "Peter Rabbit" were read before Patricia wrote her own while in second grade. She paged and illustrated the story and bound it into a book for the classroom library.

PETER RABBIT
. . . .

Peter Rabbit's mother called him and told him to go to the store to get some
*   lettuce and carrots for dinner.*

When Peter was on the way to the store, he fell and skinned his knee on a sharp rock. He cried because it hurt him.

Then he got up and went to the store. He was hopping on one leg.

When he got to the store, he got the wrong things because he forgot what his mother told him. He got ice cream and Cokes because he liked them.

I'll bet his mother is going to be mad.

He hopped all the way home with the Cokes and ice cream.

When he got home, his mother looked at him and shouted, "What's the matter, Peter? What happened to you?"

"I fell down on a sharp rock," he cried.

"Oh, you poor baby! I shouldn't have sent you to the store!"

Mother Rabbit carried Peter into the bathroom and fixed his knee with a Band-Aid.

And then she looked into the bag and saw the Cokes and ice cream, and she shouted, "Peter Rabbit! I told you to get some carrots and lettuce for dinner!"

Mother Rabbit was mad! She sent Peter to his room and said, "Get your pajamas on and get to bed!"

She was mad!

The End

Types of literature can be used as models for writing that bring variety into the publications program. These include fables and short stories. Fables are of ancient origin and are in many reading collections. It is one thing to read a fable well enough to understand it; it is quite a different and more demanding ability to be able to write one. After reading and enjoying Arnold Lobel's (1980) Caldecott Award-winning *Fables*, Eric decided to try to write a fable. This is what resulted:

THE MAN WHO GREW PEACH TREES FROM HIS EARS

Many years ago there was a man who never cleaned his ears.

The same man owned an orchard of peach trees.

One winter when the seeds were falling, one seed fell in each of the man's ears while he was asleep under a tree.

Naturally, the man thought he was deaf.

One night the man took a shower and water got in his ears.

About one month later a little green plant grew from each ear.

When he transplanted the plants, he could hear again because the plants had stopped up his ears.

The next summer he had grown some fine peaches from his ears.

Never sit under peach trees with dirty ears in the winter.

Kemi, a second grader from Seattle, demonstrates the influence of the fable genre on her personal writing with the story shown in Figure 8.6.

Recipes, real and imaginary, require specific language. The results can be a product you cook, a hug, or a good laugh. It all depends on the purpose.

Joshua Sampson wrote a recipe for a good mom (Figure 8.7).

◀ **FIGURE 8.6**

How Parrot Got Her Pretty Colors

One day a new parrot was born. You know that parrots used to be white. One day she was playing in the jungle, and she saw a rianbow. She flew though. It. Then all the colors got in her feathers. And that is how the parrots got her colors.

by
Kemi
Kilcup

FIGURE 8.7 ▶

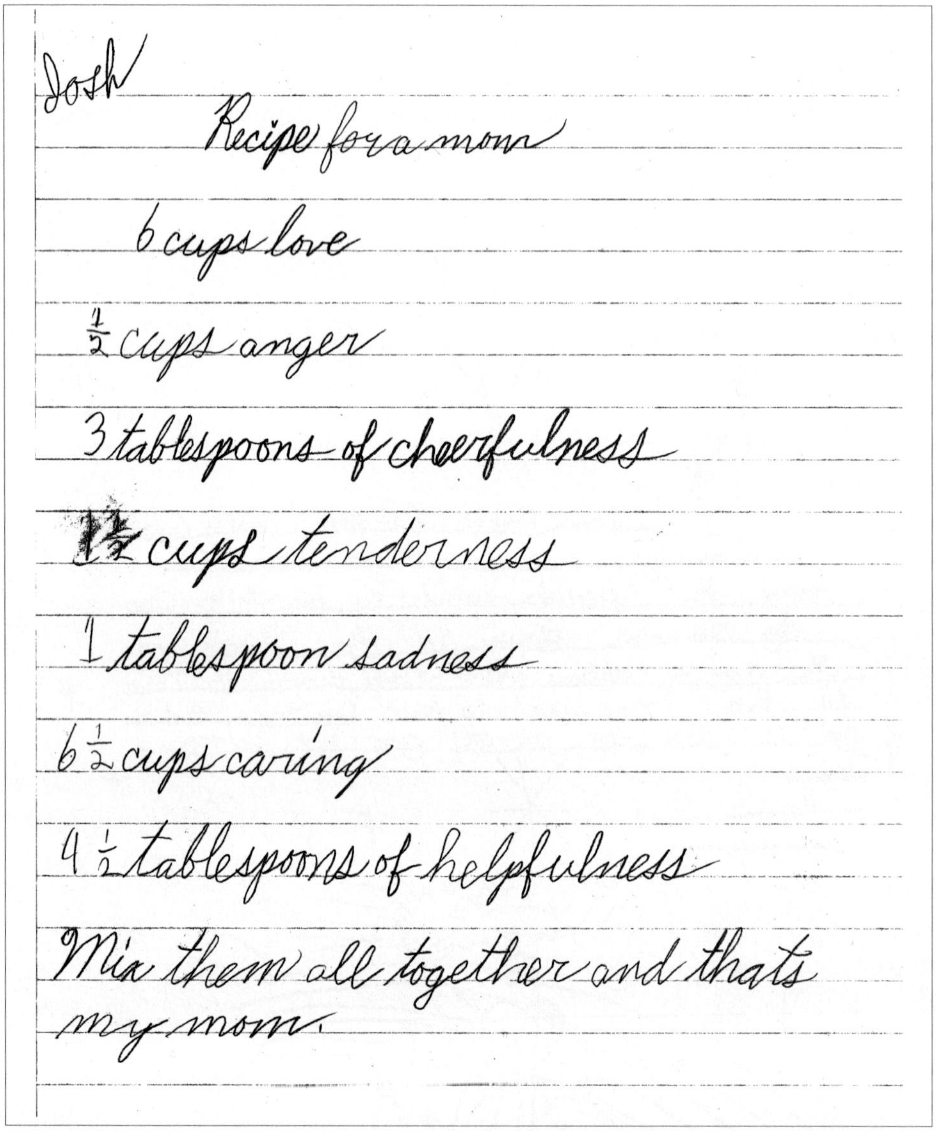

Josh

Recipe for a mom

6 cups love

½ cups anger

3 tablespoons of cheerfulness

1½ cups tenderness

1 tablespoon sadness

6½ cups caring

4½ tablespoons of helpfulness

Mix them all together and thats my mom.

When teaching a unit on foods that are good for your health, Marlene Shaever asked her first-grade students to write or dictate the recipe for their favorite food. The results were duplicated, made into class books, and sent home as gifts for the parents. Some of the results appear on the next page.

Charles Mendez interested his sixth-grade class in writing "Ridiculous Recipes" at Halloween time. This activity gave students a chance to organize their ideas and communicate them (see page 234).

Elva decided that Tarantula Cookies would be tasty (Figure 8.8).

APPLE PIE

Cut 7 apples in small pieces.
Make dough flat on the
*   outside—bumpy on the inside.*
Put apples in dough. Put dough over
*   apples.*
Bake in hot oven 'till done.
It is done when the dough turns to
*   crust—about 2 hours.*
Let it cool. Then eat it.

Kelly

PIZZA

Put dough in a bowl and mix up
*   with your hands.*
Put it in the oven and cook it for 5
*   minutes at 100.*
Cut up sausage and add one cup of
*   salt.*
Serves 4 people.

Julie

LASAGNE

Fry the lasagne in a pan.
Add 1 pound of salt
Add 1 pound of red pepper and
*   black.*
Cook for 20 minutes.
Pour 1 pint of cream and sugar over
*   the lasagne.*
Put in a bowl and 3 people can eat
*   out of it.*

Robert

When cooking in the classroom, students can learn to write real recipes. When they don't follow the recipe, they can see the results are not what were expected. They can also be sure to use all classes of words as they write recipes and do follow-up writing about the results.

By writing recipes and using them, students learn to write directions and follow them. This is an ability required for success in any classroom and in life itself.

TOAD STEW

*Cut enough toads to melt a pint of
  toad fat.
Cut toads in pieces.
Dice 5 poison mushrooms.
Add ingredients to broth from fat.
Season to taste with dragon claw
  powder.
Cook until bubbling rapidly.
Serve to ghosts and goblins on
  Halloween.*

Brad

FIGURE 8.8 ▶

Tarantula Cookies

Grind 5 tarantulas &
season to taste with
spider webs. Add ½ lizard
tails ground very coarse.
Mix in ½ cup of gasoline.
Drop on cookie sheet &
watch them flame.
  Cook for 10 minutes.
Makes 1 dozen cookies.
Eat to cure warts on your
  nose.

YOUNG AUTHORS' CONFERENCES

Young authors' conferences are sponsored by many schools. They help students learn to select story lines representative of their goals for personal writing. They also help children gain the accompanying skills required for publishing. Students who are selected to represent their classrooms or school groups at areawide book fairs usually have opportunities to participate in writing seminars conducted by well-known authors and by college teachers of writing and children's literature. This experience is highly motivating and helps young writers set goals for future productions.

Getting ready for a young authors' conference involves much more than writing books. Parents, school administrators, and school board members are involved in planning and decision making. In the process they come to appreciate the work of teachers and students who are involved. They discover the students have responsibilities that are very demanding. They learn that selections are made on the basis of criteria that students consider important. And in applying the criteria, the young authors find out much about the mechanics of writing and publishing. A group getting ready for a young authors' conference needs:

▶ students with the attitude of scientists to check the validity of facts

▶ students interested in the mechanics of editing

▶ students sensitive to language who can consult with authors about style and form

▶ students talented as artists who can illustrate books when an author does not choose to do so

▶ students who can type manuscripts

▶ students who can bind books with sturdy and attractive bindings that withstand much handling

▶ students who can organize parents into working groups to support the publishing enterprise with scrap materials and needed equipment, such as sewing machines and computers

▶ students who can represent the class project to the school principal and the local school board

▶ students who can share their books with audiences by skillful oral reading

▶ students who can contribute to writing seminars that will be helpful in setting new goals and raising aspirations for improved publications

Because a book will be shared in a young authors' conference, students produce stories that represent their finest writing. This writing reflects the research and editing efforts of the students and demonstrates what happens when children extend their imaginations in new and creative ways.

Young authors' conferences require much work, but the rewards far outweigh the costs. When children's books are honored, children are honored—and when children are honored, they will be motivated to write time and time again.

CLASSROOM VIGNETTE

Ley Yeager, a bilingual fifth-grade teacher from Riverside, California, has been involved in honoring the writings of his school's young authors for many years. Consequently, Longfellow Elementary School's Young Authors' Conference is a highpoint of the school year.

Ley has discovered that a literacy-rich environment results when children's books are integrated throughout the school day. When students read books like Lois Lowry's (1994) Newbery Award-winning *The Giver,* they want to write their own. An additional motivation for writing is the opportunity to have the book admired by others at the Young Authors' Conference.

One secret to a successful conference is parent involvement and support. Ley writes each parent, telling them what a young authors' conference is like, and asks for their participation. A sample letter follows:

Dear Parent,

You are invited to participate in the celebration of Longfellow's 9th Annual Young Authors' Conference on Friday, April 28, from 8 to 11:40 a.m. It's an exciting day for students, teachers and parents as our young writers share their books and meet John Archambault, a noted author.

First, the children are placed in small sharing groups where they share the books they have written with nine other children and an adult leader for about 30 minutes.

After the sharing groups, one-third of the students will go to an assembly to meet a famous author, one-third will go to activity groups, and one-third will make new books. Each group will rotate through all three sessions. Each session will last about 45 minutes. A leader will stay with the same group all morning.

We would like to invite you to participate in the conference as a sharing-group leader and/or an activity-group leader. Sharing-group leaders will guide small groups in which students read their own books. Activity-group leaders will plan and conduct activities designed to encourage student creativity. These may include games, arts and crafts, music, drama, cooking and more. This year we want one adult for every ten students. Some of the adults may assist in an activity directed by someone else.

If you can participate, please respond below and return by Friday, April 7. We know you will be glad you did!

(Please check one or more.)

_____ I will conduct a sharing group only.

_____ I will conduct a sharing group and will stay with a group of ten students throughout the three morning sessions.

_____ I will conduct an activity group.

Activity planned _____ Number of students (circle) 10 20 30

Grade level preferred _____ Language of students preferred _____

_____   _____   _____

   Signature   Student's Name   Rm. #

SUMMARY

This chapter provided the how-to aspect of orchestrating the classroom writing program. However, the key to excellence in guiding a literacy program is not in procedures, but in attitude. An attitude that values student self-expression releases authors to write in creative and beautiful ways. This freedom of expression is the ultimate goal of meaning-centered classrooms.

PATHWAYS TO EDITING AND PUBLISHING

In the editing of manuscripts, students:

▶ assume responsibility for self-editing at a level appropriate to ability.

▶ participate on editorial committees in the editing of group projects.

▶ use spelling resources available in the Writing/Publishing Center.

▶ use descriptive vocabulary to elaborate simple language.

▶ page manuscripts for illustrating and printing so each page has at least one contributing idea.

▶ edit poetry for spacing and selection of print as well as for spelling, capitalization, and punctuation.

In publication of manuscripts, students:

▶ make a variety of bindings for books.

▶ participate in the production of class publications such as newspapers and magazines.

▶ serve on committees responsible for producing finished books:
  ▪ the editorial committee
  ▪ the typing or printing committee
  ▪ the duplicating committee
  ▪ the illustrating committee
  ▪ the bindery committee.

In selecting ideas and patterns, students:

▶ find topics for writing in the immediate environment.

▶ find topics for writing from imagination.

▶ use classic stories as models for writing.

▶ extend the concept of the alphabet into book-length production.

▶ select a variety of literary forms to express personal ideas.

▶ choose imaginary and nonsense topics as well as real-life topics.

▶ adapt predictive language patterns to own topics and interests.

4

FOUNDATIONS OF LITERACY CONVENTIONS

CHAPTER
▶9 PATHWAYS TO SPELLING DEVELOPMENT

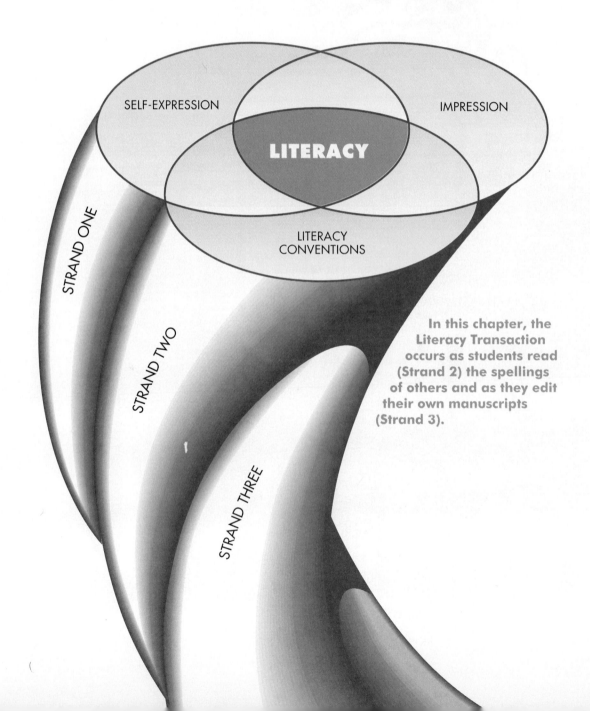

SELF-EXPRESSION

IMPRESSION

LITERACY

LITERACY CONVENTIONS

STRAND ONE

STRAND TWO

STRAND THREE

In this chapter, the Literacy Transaction occurs as students read (Strand 2) the spellings of others and as they edit their own manuscripts (Strand 3).

PATHWAYS TO PONDER

▶ WHAT ROLE DOES WRITING PLAY IN SPELLING ACQUISITION?

▶ WHAT ROLE DOES READING PLAY IN SPELLING ACQUISITION?

▶ WHY IS THE FREEDOM TO EXPERIMENT—TO USE INVENTED SPELLINGS—IMPORTANT IN MEANING-CENTERED CLASSROOMS?

▶ WHAT ROLE DOES DICTATION PLAY IN THE PROCESS OF SPELLING MATURATION?

▶ WHY IS IT IMPORTANT FOR SPELLING PROGRAMS TO AFFORD MANY OPPORTUNITIES FOR WRITING?

▶ WHAT INSIGHTS INTO SPELLING DO CHILDREN GAIN THROUGH READING AND WRITING ACTIVITIES IN MEANING-CENTERED CLASSROOMS?

▶ HOW DO LINGUISTIC FACTORS AFFECT SPELLING?

Spelling is one of the most researched, most discussed language arts. Unfortunately, misconceptions abound on the topic of spelling. We take an in-depth look at spelling in this chapter and leave you with suggestions that will help you free students from the fears of spelling and help them become excellent editors of their own work.

How do children become good spellers? By writing! And by reading. Children who feel an urge to communicate, who experience the thrill of authorship, and who know the satisfaction of writing something that is important to other people are the ones most likely to develop skill as spellers.

Spelling is an inseparable part of meaning-centered programs that keep speech, writing, and reading related in instruction. Children must learn common spellings of words they write because other students—not just the teacher—read much of what they write. Children must learn to edit their writing for correct spelling because many stories or poems are published and become a part of the instructional materials. However, as teachers, we must be sure concern for spelling does not hamper the creative composing process of the writers in our classrooms.

Thus, as children write, they should be encouraged to use whatever words are most appropriate to express the feelings or moods they wish to create, regardless of how they might spell the words they use. These natural or "invented" spellings are developmental in nature and are an indication that children feel, as Clark (1989) says, "free to write." Simply expressed, communication is the primary objective of writing. Correct spelling is a secondary objective, a supporting one. Children must feel secure in exploring the spelling of new and unusual words. Kasten (1993) has gleaned the following principles for teachers concerning spelling:

1. Children learn to spell words they need to know how to write in everyday writing.

2. Learners forget how to spell words they have little occasion to use.

3. Spelling is a developmental process. It develops along the same lines as oral language, and children have a natural desire to spell like grown-ups (as they want to talk like grown-ups also).

4. Having children work out their own invented spellings of low-frequency words reinforces their knowledge of phonics and English orthography, and enables them to make and test hypotheses about how language works.

5. Always giving children the spelling of words they ask for takes away valuable learning opportunities.

6. Expectations about spelling should be realistic. Expectations should be consistent with the child's development and experience. Spelling should be a low priority when students are new or emerging writers.

7. Spelling skills will develop through consistent writing, such as keeping journals, with no direct instruction.

8. Spelling is a subset of writing. It should never be more important than writing, a prerequisite to writing, or taught in place of the teaching of writing.

9. Some people are naturally good spellers; some are not. There is no relationship between ability to spell and intelligence. A perfect speller is extremely rare.

10. The most important aspect of spelling after one is a fluent writer is learning what you know and what you don't know. This enables one to develop strategies to spell difficult words and utilize available resources.

CLASSROOM VIGNETTE

After five years of teaching third grade, Susan Tollison had developed a love for the language arts. She enjoyed children's literature and loved sharing her favorite books with her children. She loved music and enjoyed the daily sing-along sessions in her classroom. But there was one thing she didn't enjoy—the school's spelling program. The very traditional program required that children be given 20 words to learn each week, and that a test be given every Friday. Many of her children struggled with the test and failed the Friday quiz week after week. Other students quite easily memorized the words, scored an "A" on the test on Friday, then forgot the words. Parents complained to Susan they would spend hours each week working with their children on the spelling list at home. Finally, after five years of having the spelling curriculum rule Susan and her students, things changed. Susan attended a whole-language workshop led by Bill Martin Jr. In the session she became intrigued with process writing and vowed to change her language-arts block when she returned to school in the fall. And change she did. Spelling ceased to become a subject in school and became a part of her writing program. After one year of children writing and editing every day, Susan discovered she had a classroom filled with good spellers. But more importantly, she had a classroom of children who were not afraid to write. They used much more advanced vocabulary in their compositions. And the final drafts of their manuscripts contained very few spelling errors. By trusting in the children and the process, Susan transformed her classroom and triumphed over the one aspect of school she disliked the most.

SPELLING: THE BEGINNINGS

Young children's scribbles are a form of self-expression. This early writing is a process that will evolve as the child matures. Consequently, adults should be patient with their letterlike forms that look only slightly like writing. In effect, children can write before they can read if given the opportunity. These young children use "invented spellings" (Bissex, 1980; Cambourne & Turbill,

Children develop ▶
spelling abilities
through writing.

1988) and learn to write in the same manner and for the same reasons they learned to talk.

After hearing his mother share *Read About Spiders*, 5-year-old Joshua wrote, "I LIC SPIDRS CS' SPIDRCR GUD" [I like spiders because spiders are good] (Clem & Feathers, 1986). His message reveals his understanding that writing may be used to express feelings and to record thoughts and opinions (see Figure 9.1). His story confirms what Bissex (1985) has noted: Children invent their own systematic spellings in their "active search" for the rules that govern our

FIGURE 9.1 ▶ **A 5-YEAR-OLD WRITES, "I LIKE SPIDERS BECAUSE SPIDERS ARE GOOD"**

ILIC SPIDRS
CS'

SPIDRCR
GUD

writing system. Joshua's experimentation demonstrates he has comprehended that letters represent speech sounds and he is well on his way to becoming a proficient speller. The first step in spelling is to recognize its role in communication.

The importance of invented spellings and the role they play in children's pursuit of literacy has received widespread attention in recent years (Bissex, 1980; Chomsky, 1971; Farris, 1993; Henderson, 1986; Henderson & Beers, 1980; Kami & Randazzo, 1985; Read, 1980; Yellin & Blake, 1994). This recognition is leading teachers to the understanding of the importance of allowing young children to represent their thoughts on paper, and of not correcting invented spellings because "corrections stifle children's confidence and desire to write" (Kami & Randazzo, 1985, p. 124).

These "errors" are, in fact, a step toward the child's construction of a coherent system of spelling and writing. These representations of meaning constantly evolve toward standard forms (Bissex, 1980). In addition, it must be remembered that most writers, including adults, encode meaning on the first drafts of a message without allowing spelling or grammar to interrupt the process (Harste, Burke, & Woodward, 1983).

The writings of 6-year-old Angel illustrate an evolving maturity (Figure 9.2). Notice that in this story, authored in December of her first-grade year, she has already mastered the high-frequency words that all writers use most frequently (*is, the, a, I, like, play, have, fun*). However, she continues to use invented spellings of words like favorite *(favrite)*, time *(tim)*, year *(yire)*, because *(cus)*, flakes *(flaxs)*, build *(bilde)*, and out *(alt)*. What strategies did Angel use in her attempt to spell these words? Table 9.1 contains six spelling strategies

◀ **TABLE 9.1**

STRATEGIES	EXAMPLES
Spelling the way it sounds	**U—you** **DA—day**
Spelling the way it articulates	**BRIF—brief** **USLIP—asleep**
Spelling the way it looks	**FRO—for** **WHIT—with** **TIMSE—times**
Spelling the way it means	**REFRIGERATORED—refrigerated** **WASUPONATIM—once upon a time**
Spelling the way similar spellings have been solved	**TOOL UP—tulip** **REALISTICK—realistic** **FINELY—finally**
Spelling by rules	**PIZZIE—pizza** **ALSOE—also**

FIGURE 9.2 ▶   STORY BY A FIRST GRADER

identified by Harste, Burke, and Woodward (1983) that young children use as they encode meaning in graphic form. Examine the table to see if you can determine some of the strategies Angel was using as she wrote "Christmas."

These six strategies do provide insights concerning why children spell some words the way they do. However, as Harste, Burke, and Woodward (1983) emphasize, "each spelling reflects a complex orchestration of language decisions" (p. 310). Consequently, it would be an oversimplification to expect a child's spelling to reflect one of the six rules listed here. Rather, the rules provide insights into the spelling of some children on some occasions.

The most important thing to note in Angel's story is that she had the freedom to experiment—to write down what she wanted to communicate—without the fear of misspelling a word. This freedom must be the goal of all meaning-centered programs.

◀ **FIGURE 9.2**
(cont.)

STAGES OR EVOLUTION OF SPELLING DEVELOPMENT

Over the past six years we've had an extraordinary opportunity. We followed a class of 24 children from kindergarten through fifth grade. During that time, we saw the children blossom into readers and writers. Along the way, we also observed their development and transition as spellers. We share what we learned, because teachers often only see the grade level they work with and do not have the opportunity to view children along the developmental pathways we observed.

Others have defined stages of spelling development (Beers & Beers, 1981; Gentry, 1984; Henderson, 1985). However, we describe to you exactly what

FIGURE 9.2 ▶
(cont.)

we saw as these children developed in the holistic program in which they participated. Keep in mind that we are describing the group and not necessarily individuals. The developmental stages we observed (see Table 9.1) were (1) Scribble-Pictorial, (2) Letter, (3) Phonetic, (4) Approximal, and (5) Standard. While most children follow this pattern, not all will. Table 9.2 (see page 250) provides examples of these developmental stages.

1. **The Scribble-Pictorial Stage.** We observed that some of the children, upon arriving at kindergarten, would simply scribble or draw pictures when asked to "write a story." Typically, children ages 1 to 5 tend to be in this stage. During this stage, children are becoming aware that speech can be recorded with graphic symbols, but do not have a clear understanding of the relationship between sounds and letters.

2. **The Letter Stage.** Many children arrive at kindergarten in this stage. They tend to "write" using one to three consonant letters to represent each word. Often children will spell with two letters here—one letter to begin the word and one letter to end it. Children in this stage have made a major leap toward literacy. They have formulated the concept of words and are attempting to represent words with letters (Raine, 1994). With some effort, you can read what children have written.

THE POET ▶
PONDERS

TURN THE TV OFF!

I never felt the terror
Of nature in the night
Till the hurricane came with wind
*   and rain*
And took away the light.

But my Mama had a match
And it made a little spark
That turned itself into a flame
And burned away the dark.

Now the house is a cozy candle-glow
As quiet as can be,
And I wonder . . .
Why did it take a hurricane
To turn off my TV?

3. **The Phonetic Stage.** You can easily read what children write in this stage. The letters in words closely resemble the way the words "sound,"—*for* is spelled *fro* and *with* is spelled *whit*. Children have started adding vowel sounds as they attempt to represent words.

4. **The Approximal Stage.** Many of the high-frequency words are spelled correctly; many others are almost correct. Spellings still tend to be phonetic, but editing processes have "kicked in" and almost weekly growth toward standard spellings is observed.

TABLE 9.2 ▶   STAGES OF SPELLING DEVELOPMENT

STAGE	CHARACTERISTICS	EXAMPLES
Pictoral-Scribble	**Draws pictures; scribbles**	**Example on pages 246–249**
Letter	**Recognizes that words are made up of letters**	**Rd for Read**
Phonetic	**Spells words the way they sound** **Uses some vowels**	**sekunt for second**
Approximal	**Many words correct** **Some words spelled phonetically**	**wondring for wondering**
Standard	**Spelling is usually accurate; some spelling errors made**	

RUTH HELLER

1. Which book of yours has given you the greatest pleasure?

Color, Color, Color, Color. It's my current favorite because I'm working on it right now. It deals with how the printer puts the colors in books.

2. Which book has surprised you most in terms of its public reception?

I guess I was most surprised in a negative way by *Plants That Never Ever Bloom,* my fourth book. I liked it so much and was surprised by its slow sales. It could be because the color on the cover was brown.

3. What would you like people to remember about your work?

I want people to remember my sincerity in trying to give as much information in my books as possible. It pleases me to know how much people feed on the information I present in the books.

4. What impact do you hope your work will have on children?

I want my work to continue to educate children. I also want children to realize, through my books, that learning can be both enjoyable and exciting.

Ruth Heller tries to make her writing succinct and let the illustrations convey as much information as possible. Her delightfully rhyming, intricately drawn books include *Animals Born Alive and Well, Chickens Aren't the Only Ones, Reason for a Flower, Plants That Never Ever Bloom, Cache of Jewels, Kites Sail High, Up, Up and Away, Merry Go Round,* and *Many Luscious Lollipops.*

5. **Standard Spelling.** This level is achieved by most children no sooner than fifth grade. For some children, spelling is natural at this point and they spell most words correctly. For many children, as with adults, standard spelling will occur through editing, not first draft attempts.

We noticed that some of our brightest students were poor spellers, and that some of our weaker students were good spellers. We conclude that spelling is a talent, just as music and art are talents. However, all children can become better spellers through writing, reading, and editing.

SPELLING AND THE DICTATION PROCESS

In our work with young children, we've noticed one key strategy that enhances children's move toward standard spellings. We're talking about dictation. Through dictation, children can see the relationships that exist among thoughts, language, reading, and writing. Dictation also demonstrates to young children the accurate spelling of words. Smith (1985) states that the first key component in learning is observation. He calls these observations "demonstrations," and says they tell the learner "this is how something is done" (p. 108). As teachers take dictation from children and write their

The process of ▶
writing and
editing books
significantly
influences
spelling
acquisition. Here,
a first grader is
proud of her new
"Batman" book.

language on the board, they are "demonstrating" to the children "this is how this word is spelled." Children will receive additional demonstrations concerning spelling as they become proficient readers and see the words playing in the movie of their minds time after time. The schemata that are constructed through these demonstrations enable us to "look" at a word and, using the visual feedback, know if it is spelled correctly or incorrectly.

Some have argued that the practice of taking dictation should be replaced with the opportunity for children to do independent writing using invented spellings (Kami & Randazzo, 1985). As we discussed in Chapter 5, both practices are valuable classroom tools for the development of literacy skills—both allow children to supply the language and the words that are a part of that language. Invented spellings enable children to write independently. Dictation, however, is very efficient because it points children toward the use of standard spellings and is, therefore, a valuable part of language-arts classrooms in the primary grades.

Estelle Valdez introduces spelling during processes of dictation. She talks to herself as she writes as if to remind herself of how to spell. She invites children to help with spelling. At first, she might ask for help with initial consonants because most consonants in initial positions in words have stable phoneme-grapheme relations.

She begins to involve children in spelling whole words. These are usually structure words that occur frequently in language. She hopes every child will learn to spell the words of highest frequency in an informal, practical setting because many of them defy phonetic analysis.

When one child is ready, Estelle spaces the dictated story so it can be copied directly beneath her writing. Once the process is initiated, one child after another asks to copy. Words in the child's speaking vocabulary are sure to be ones used for the early spelling-writing experiences because they are the ones spoken in dictation.

Words that occur in the work of several children are collected on a chart for spelling review and for sight vocabulary. The chart is kept in a place where the children can use it as a spelling reference from the earliest days of exploratory writing. There are no spelling workbooks or lists on which children drill to make "hundreds" on spelling. All work to master the correct spelling of words useful in writing.

Glen Murphy encourages children to try to write any word they can say when preparing original manuscripts. He helps them to see that most of the spelling errors involve only one or two letters in a word, and that if a word communicates the desired sound, it can be edited for correct spelling.

Many children in Glen's class will use first letters and a line—for example, b___, g___, or t___—to hold space for correct spelling. If the context is strong enough to carry the meaning, the correct spelling can be handled in a few minutes after the flow of ideas has been recorded. Lists of words may be provided as aids in editing spelling. Most children at this stage do not need to spend time hunting words in dictionaries for spelling. They do not need definitions because they are editing their own writing.

SPELLING IN WRITING AND READING

Meaning-centered approaches assure active involvement in writing, helping children learn spelling as a part of the process (Stetson, Seda, & Newman, 1988). Although spelling is typically taught as a subject in school, most spelling is learned outside of spelling class. Consider, for example, that the average educated adult has a vocabulary of more than 100,000 words. Spelling curricula provide 36 weeks of spelling lists that contain approximately 20 words each. Over eight years of instruction, students are asked to learn only 5,760 words—far short of the 100,000 they need. Spelling is learned through using language in reading and writing. As children read and write, many words and patterns are learned largely at the subconscious level.

When correct spelling becomes an issue of prime importance, it can hinder the creative process and discourage effective communication. Classroom policy that establishes spelling as an aid to effective written communication rather than as an equal to it is one that yields manuscripts worthy of being edited and published.

Spelling that is related to personal writing is not random. Certain forms of written expression occur routinely in children's writing:

▶ words of highest frequency, the correct spelling of which is highly desirable, if not mandatory, in writing

▶ words that begin alike in phoneme-grapheme relation

▶ words with suffixes that appear frequently, that modify meanings (examples: *-s, -es, -er, -ed, -ing*), and that change the part of speech of many words (examples: *-ly, -est, -ful*)

▶ root words with prefixes that modify meanings (examples: *re-, un-, dis-, bi-, tri-*)

▶ syllables that occur over and over in words—beginnings, endings, and middles (examples: *an, on, in, ill, all, at, it, ut*)

▶ each vowel in multiple phoneme-grapheme relations.

FUNCTIONAL SPELLING

Children don't go to school to learn to make the basic sounds of their native language. They already know how. At school most of them learn how to represent their language sounds with an alphabetic code. This link between speech and written composition involves spelling directly and constantly.

Some believe the key to spelling is an early mastery of phonics. But programs that attempt to link basic concepts of spelling with reading through what most teachers call phonics may deny children an understanding of how their natural language works when written. Process-centered approaches build bases for understanding of:

▶ the relations of personal language production to an alphabetic system of writing

▶ the relation of personal meaning expressed in speaking and writing to others' meaning through reading

▶ the predictive ability that permits a reader to anticipate most printed words and patterns so the thinking process can be active during reading

Meaning-centered approaches and programs provide enough functional spelling situations that in many cases the development of spelling skills exceeds normal expectations. Movement toward standard spellings may be enhanced by creating "word spokes" from children's dictation. As children brainstorm, the teacher lists the words in a circular or spoke shape. Active

◀ **Word spokes and dictation demonstrate standard spellings of words.**

writing situations provide needed practice in spelling, and a continuing program of publishing children's writing for classroom use requires a high level of refinement of spelling.

CLUES FOR INSTRUCTION

Make crossword puzzles, word-step puzzles, homonym games, words-that-begin-alike games, and card games for and with your students. Develop activities that require an understanding of syllabication, suffixes, prefixes, contractions, and compounds. Include activities that involve the use of specific vocabulary—alliteration, conversation, riddles, shopping lists, catalogues, rhyming poetry, and other writing forms using language structure that repeats spelling structure.

INTERNALIZING SPELLING PATTERNS

How do children learn to spell the thousands of words needed for communication? Through reading and writing they naturally internalize spelling patterns. Children who develop phonological relations between *sounds* and

Roberta Parish uses frequent walking trips in the school community to introduce children to vocabulary appropriate for writing their observations. She invites a fifth-grade class to accompany her first-grade class and to act as private secretaries. They usually concentrate on one or two categories of words such as sound words, shape words, smell words, and, perhaps, "words for green." Master lists are made from the secretaries' records. A copy is published for a chart to go in a writing center of the first grade, and copies are reproduced to go into the writing handbook that each fifth-grade pupil keeps.

When children write, they are encouraged to use the lists as spelling references. They also have available the growing list "Words We All Use." The combination of visible spelling sources encourages children to spell correctly when writing, rather than just to guess.

At the same time, Roberta encourages children to attempt to spell any word they need to use. She wants them to feel their ideas and personal language are more important than correct spelling. By continual demonstrations, she shows that original manuscripts can be edited if they are to be published.

In functional writing situations in which children are secure in exploring spelling, the teacher has opportunities to observe spelling behavior and to note points that need direct instruction. As children call for help in spelling words, the teacher can ask questions and make points that assist them to generalize certain principles about spelling.

As children work in various learning centers that require writing, their spelling behavior can be observed, and teachers can visit informally to help them gain basic insights into spelling and to understand consistency in and variability of spelling patterns.

letters of the orthography can spell literally thousands of words they use in oral language because of the consistency of spelling patterns. Repeating patterns of sound and spelling occur frequently in syllables such as these:

at	en	in	ook	un
an	ell	ill	ot	ug
ay	et	ing	ow	up
all	ed	ight	old	ull
am		it	oy	

These basic phonograms, contrasted with initial sounds represented by consonants, generate hundreds of words. When morphological characteristics such as affixes are added to root words, hundreds of additional words can be spelled.

The cues from linguistics provide children with clues to spell most of the words in their oral vocabularies in an open environment that permits invented spelling. They may spell correctly phonetically and not use standard spelling: *hi* for *high, brite* for *bright, thay* for *they,* and *rong* for *wrong.* Such explorations should be encouraged.

IRREGULAR SPELLINGS

American-English spelling is often inconsistent with sounds—these exceptions must be learned by anyone who writes for others to read. When children find words that require special treatment for correct spelling, they add them to a growing list of words. They try to locate the place in a word that requires irregular spelling, and find that in most cases one or two letters cause the spelling trouble.

Lists of words with irregular spelling can be placed in a game center. Children can be encouraged to use these words to make spelling games to play with friends. A master alphabetic list may be provided as an aid in editing.

◄ **KIDS'
CORNER**

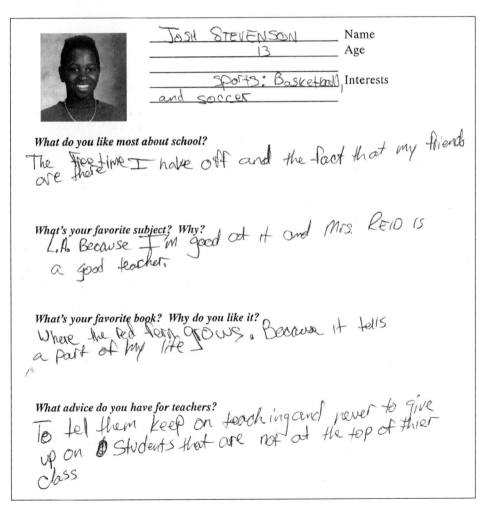

Josh Stevenson _____ Name

13 _____ Age

Sports: Basketball, Interests
and soccer

What do you like most about school?
The free time I have off and the fact that my friends
are there

What's your favorite subject? Why?
L.A. Because I'm good at it and Mrs. Reid is
a good teacher.

What's your favorite book? Why do you like it?
Where the red fern grows. Because it tells
a part of my life

What advice do you have for teachers?
To tel them keep on teaching and never to give
up on students that are not at the top of thier
class

LINGUISTIC FACTORS THAT INFLUENCE SPELLING

Some linguistic factors that influence spelling during writing processes are phonological, morphological, and syntactical (Henderson, 1986).

Phonological factors deal with the position of a sound in a word, with stress, and with internal constraints that certain sounds put on others when pronounced together. (Example: The beginning sound of words like *foot, finger,* and *fat* is almost always spelled with an f. At the end of a word it can be spelled *ff* as in *cuff, off, gh* as in *cough* or *laugh,* or *lf* as in *calf.*)

CLASSROOM VIGNETTE

Claryce Allen composes rhymes and jingles to interest children in some of the linguistic factors in spelling. For *compound words* she makes cards that suggest the collection of compound words.

Here is a finger.

Here is a nail.

Put them together.

You have a *fingernail!*

For *rhyming words* she sets a pattern that children can follow.

This is a pup.

This is a cup.

This is a pup in a cup.

For words of *enumeration* she provides an example for children with their own ideas.

The first cook cooked one cookie.

The second cook cooked two cookies.

The third cook cooked three cookies.

The fourth cook cooked four.

Were there any more?

For *alliteration* she suggests a pattern of adding descriptive words to a base sentence.

This is an ant.

This is an angry ant.

This is an angry ant acting.

This is an angry ant acting atrociously.

Morphological factors deal with word formation and include compounding, affixation, and word groups that have partial phoneme similarities such as *dog, log,* and *hog.*

Syntactical factors that affect spelling deal with words that are pronounced alike (homophones) but differ in meaning, derivation, and often spelling. Some words are spelled alike (homographs) but differ in meaning, derivation,

◀ **FIGURE 9.3**

Words Often Spelled and Pronounced Incorrectly

above	couple	give	machine	ranger	tongue
across	cousin	gives	many	ready	too
again	cruel	gloves	measure	really	touch
against	curve	gone	might	right	two
aisle		great	mild	rough	
already	dead	guard	million		use
another	deaf	guess	mind	said	usual
answer	debt	guest	minute	says	
anxious	desire	guide	mischief	school	vein
any	do		mother	science	very
	does	have	move	scissors	view
bear	done	head	Mr.	sew	
beautiful	don't	heart	Mrs.	shoe	was
beauty	double	heaven		should	wash
because	doubt	heavy	neighbor	sign	weather
been	dove	here	neither	snow	weight
behind	dozen	high	night	soften	were
believe			none	soldier	what
bind	early	idea		some	where
both	earn	Indian	ocean	someone	who
bough	eight	instead	of	something	whom
bread	enough	isle	office	sometime	whose
bright	eye		often	son	wild
brought	eyes	key	oh	soul	wind
build		kind	once	special	wolf
built	father	knee	one	spread	woman
bury	fence	knew	onion	square	women
busy	field	knife	only	steak	won
buy	fight	know	other	straight	would
	find		ought	sure	wrong
calf	folks	language		sword	
captain	four	laugh	patient		you
caught	freight	laughed	piece	their	young
chief	friend	leather	pretty	there	your
child	front	library	pull	they	
clothes		light	purpose	though	
colt	garage	lion	push	thought	
coming	get	live	put	to	
cough	getting	lived		together	
could	ghost	love	quiet	ton	

and sometimes pronunciation. The spelling and/or pronunciation of these words can be determined only in context.

Homographs:	**Homophones:**
tear on your cheek	*pool* of clear water
tear in the paper	game of *pool*
	reed instrument
	read a book

Both homographs and homophones are homonyms. They offer a special challenge to spelling and reading.

WORDS LISTS FOR SPELLING AND EDITING

Children who can read words on lists are able to improve their spelling by the use of the lists during writing and/or editing. Here are three lists that can be supplied on an individual basis or on charts in a Writing/Publishing Center:

1. A List of Words for Spelling and Editing
2. Words Often Spelled and Pronounced Incorrectly
3. The "Yucky" List

The List of Words for Spelling and Editing may be created using the Allen List of 100 High-Frequency Words (Chapter 7). Arrange these words alphabetically so students can locate words quickly.

Words Often Spelled and Pronounced Incorrectly (Figure 9.3) is a useful editing resource because it shows children words they may think they spell correctly but don't. The "Yucky" List (Clark, 1989) is a list the classroom teacher creates for each class. The list is comprised of words the teacher notices children constantly misspell. Thus this list will be different for each grade and will change during the school year as children progress as spellers.

SUMMARY

Spelling is best learned through the processes of reading and writing. As children engage in meaningful communication activities, they internalize spelling patterns. Our focus in this chapter has been on the relationships among oral language production, writing, and reading and the functional nature of spelling.

PATHWAYS TO EXPLORING SPELLING

Spelling in communication
The student:

▶ writes original stories without fear of misspelled words.

▶ writes poetry that uses rhymed and nonrhymed patterns.

▶ writes directions and instructions for classroom activities.

▶ chooses writing as a recreational activity.

▶ edits own manuscripts for spelling before publishing.

Spelling attitudes and skills
The student:

▶ uses spelling resources when writing and editing.

▶ is interested in spelling new words.

▶ wants to spell correctly.

▶ accepts responsibility for accuracy and legibility.

▶ has no fear of trying to spell new and unusual words in original writing.

▶ studies words spelled in unexpected ways to achieve mastery of those used frequently.

▶10 PATHWAYS TO LANGUAGE REFINEMENT

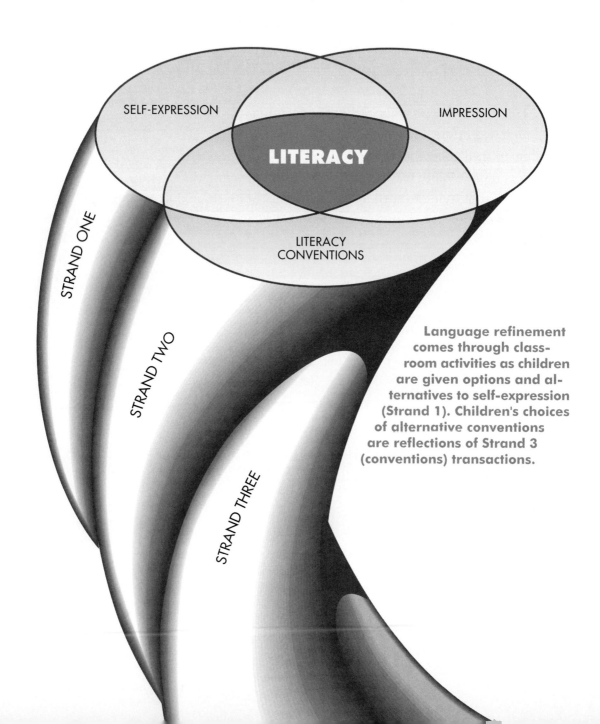

SELF-EXPRESSION

IMPRESSION

LITERACY

LITERACY CONVENTIONS

STRAND ONE

STRAND TWO

STRAND THREE

Language refinement comes through classroom activities as children are given options and alternatives to self-expression (Strand 1). Children's choices of alternative conventions are reflections of Strand 3 (conventions) transactions.

PATHWAYS TO PONDER

▶ WHY IS IT IMPORTANT TO DEMONSTRATE RESPECT AND ACCEPTANCE OF THE HOME-ROOTED LANGUAGE THAT CHILDREN BRING TO THE CLASSROOM?

▶ CAN GRAMMAR BE TAUGHT IN AN INFORMAL, MEANING-CENTERED WAY? OR MUST IT, BY NECESSITY, BE PRESENTED IN A PREDETERMINED SEQUENCE?

▶ HOW HAS HANDWRITING LOST ITS "TOOLNESS"?

▶ HOW SHOULD HANDWRITING BE TAUGHT IN MEANING-CENTERED CLASSROOMS?

▶ IF CORRECTNESS IS NOT AN END OF LANGUAGE INSTRUCTION, THEN WHAT IS IT?

How do we help children improve their language skills? In this chapter we examine several different methods that have been tried, and we recommend one approach that is developmental in nature.

Remember the linguistic guidelines we shared with you in Chapter 1? Those guidelines will certainly come into play as we ponder ways that children can expand on their personal language. We want you to know that language change is a choice—we can't make children change the way they speak. And we want you to know that the Literacy Transaction Model is the key for language change. Children learn new ways of saying things through Strand 2: impression. Therefore, we want our classrooms to be rich sources of new language. What comes in the students' ears and eyes will soon come out of their mouths if the language touches their hearts.

Traditional language education has been rule based. Rules have been taught to children with the expectation that function would follow form. It doesn't.

We share this language story with you to illustrate what we mean. In 1980 the Sampsons moved from their Tucson, Arizona, home to Commerce, Texas. In Tucson, they had a rock-covered yard. In East Texas, they inherited a grass yard. Here's how Michael tells the story:

> Our yard looked so beautiful and green. After three days, however, it needed mowing. We had no use for a lawn mower in Arizona, so we were without one. I had to make a trip to Wal-Mart to buy one. I spent two hours mowing that Saturday afternoon. Afterwards, I felt so proud of myself, and our yard looked so nice. However, two mornings later I got a big surprise. As I walked out to pick up the morning paper, I felt something brushing against my blue jeans legs. I reached down, touched my leg, and found my hand covered with brown, sticky juice! Weeds had sprung up, and the juice was coming from the seeds that covered the ends of the weeds. Later that morning I mowed again—it wasn't fun this time! And for the next three months I mowed that yard twice every week. I prayed for an early frost; in November my prayers were answered. The frost came and the yard turned brown.
>
> I dreaded the coming of spring. But come it did, and I found myself pushing the lawn mower again. But then I noticed something. My next door neighbor, Jay, only mowed once a week. I asked Jay what the difference between our yards was. Jay replied, "Dalis grass." Dalis grass, I cried. What's that? Jay pointed at the weeds in my yard and said that I needed to get rid of the Dalis grass, so the Bermuda grass could take over. He recommended that I use Round Up, which I soon discovered was an expensive but highly effective weed killer. I sprayed the spots where the Dalis grass was, which was about everywhere, and the Dalis grass died. Soon I had a lovely, green Bermuda grass lawn that only needed mowing every week or so.

Why do we tell you this story? Because there's a connection between the Dalis grass and children's language. In cutting the grass twice a week, Michael made no real progress in his battle with the grass. It was only when he went beneath the surface and dealt with the roots that he made progress. No, we aren't going to tell you to spray your children with Round Up! But we are going to tell you that like grass, language has a surface structure and a deep structure.

The language that flows from children's mouths represents their language surface structure. Surface structure language is composed from the roots, or deep structure of the child's language. You can correct a child when she makes a grammatical error, but when you do you are actually only cutting off the surface structure of the child's language. If you really want to change the child's language, you have to change the deep structure. And the deep structure will only change as children, through Strand 2 transactions, acquire different ways of saying things.

We must allow students the freedom of self-expression through Strand 1 activities, while trusting that language refinement will occur as students come under the influence of the communications of others through Strand 2 experiences or activities. We must understand that criticizing an individual's dialect is understood by students to be an attack on the person, the family, the language community, and the cultural heritage of the student.

In process-centered classrooms, students are free to express their ideas without fear of rejection. The home-rooted speech and dialects of the students serve as the foundation for their literacy instruction. Students in language-based programs do NOT need to acquire a new dialect or a new set of noun and verb endings before they engage in writing and language refinement. Contrary to popular assumptions, language users are able to read the sounds of their own speech from standard, printed English, regardless of dialect (Goodman, Smith, Meredith, & Goodman, 1988; Lefevre, 1970). Therefore, language instruction must be centered on communication, with refinement as a secondary goal.

As students write, they acquire a desire to share their work with others outside the classroom. This desire can be used by meaning-centered teachers as a pathway by which students can come in contact with certain conventions of print and communication. Each student will discover basic structural elements in his or her personal language and then will contrast them with those of other dialects, especially those that are required for writing.

The teacher's goal is for students to refine their communication so they can understand, enjoy, and interact with the ideas and language of other dialect communities. Consequently, process-centered teachers structure the classroom environment so students can choose to expand and refine their oral and written discourse by the influence of the communication of others.

REFINING GRAMMAR

By the time they start school, most children use all the basic language patterns common to good English speech *without having had any formal instruction.* Their speech approximates fairly accurately the adult language of their families and others in their environment. Adults usually do not realize how phenomenal this is. They are aware their children are growing and developing, but they do not recognize the complexity of the learning taking place as they supply models of speech for their children in the course of everyday living. They often notice "cute" mistakes their children make in the use of

language much more than they do the many correct and often sophisticated usages that occur.

Beginning schoolchildren have vocabularies ranging from 8,000 to 20,000 words and are actively using the simple sentence, the complex sentence, the compound sentence, and modifiers of all descriptions. These sentences may contain occasional errors, but essentially they conform to the grammatical usage standard in the child's environment.

The mistakes the child does make are usually overgeneralizations of the rules of grammar. For example, a child, knowing that in many cases one expresses the past tense by adding "ed" to the end of the verb, may come in and announce, "Mom! Dad! I hitted the ball." The parents think this is a cute error, not realizing it actually demonstrates the child's growing awareness of the "time" context of verbs and how time is expressed.

Four of the most important reasons children make such amazing strides in learning language follow:

They have been free to imitate what they hear.

They have been encouraged to try to say new things—to experiment.

They have received adult praise and approval for what they have said.

They have found they can secure many of the things they want by using language correctly.

Because these factors have been highly effective in teaching language grammar to children, it makes no sense to suddenly shift the methods and motivations of learning language. Grammar does not need to be taught in the same ways as history, for example. The teacher of history must, of necessity,

◄ Children's vocabulary is influenced through oral discussion with other students.

present the students new facts and details, which they are asked to remember. Language grammar, however, has already been internalized in amazing complexity and should not be taught as new material. Children should receive help with specific problems in their use of language grammar as they use it to work on other areas of study. In addition, they should be helped to learn to write their thoughts and use language in its written form to communicate with others.

By taking part in these activities, children can continue to learn about the structures of language usage through the same natural learning processes that allowed them to learn so much in their first five or six years of life.

THREE TYPES OF GRAMMAR

Before a teacher can decide how to teach grammar, he or she must first decide *which* grammar or combination of grammars to teach. There are many types or models of grammar, but the three best known are *traditional, structural,* and *transformational-generative.* Roughly speaking, traditional grammar is prescriptive—it tells you what you should do when you speak and write. Structural grammar is descriptive—it describes what is *done* in actual language usage by describing the surface structure of language. And transformational-generative grammar analyzes the subconscious meaning structures beneath the spoken or written words that determine what can and cannot be used and be comprehensible.

TEACHING GRAMMAR

Once the teacher has decided which grammar to teach, he or she must decide *how* to go about teaching it. The matter of how to teach grammar in the

Sharon Ann Tandy _____ Name

13 _____ Age

Birthday - February 21, 1994

Music (Classical), Poetry, Art, Interests (to draw)
and well being of others

What do you like most about school?

I like the fellowship with my classmates. I like to learn, to move on, to inhance and develop my knowledge. I like receiving new information. It makes me feel more understanding.

What's your favorite subject? Why?

Math is my favorite subject because it is always a challenge. You always have to work for the answer in Math. Once you understand the challenge it becomes fun.

What's your favorite book? Why do you like it?

My favorite book is The Vision by Dean R. Koontz. I like this book because it is a mystery, a thriller, and it is also a poetic book. I suspends you and then it drops the truth. It is very exciting.

What advice do you have for teachers?

I advise my teachers to get out of their time and put it in our time. When they give us notes put them in our language so we will learn and understand it.

elementary grades has concerned teachers for a long time. Three major differing points of view exist:

1. Those who are convinced from teaching experience and research findings that the teaching of grammar as a systematized body of information does little or nothing to improve the actual grammar usage of young people.

2. Those who insist on grammar as an organized body of knowledge that children must learn in a logical sequence. They continue to measure children's knowledge of grammar in terms of what they know about grammar rules rather than in terms of how well they observe those rules in speech and writing.

3. Those who have devised means of teaching grammar in situations in which grammar really means something to the students.

Our view of grammar corresponds to the third category. In this approach, grammar is taught but not as a separate subject matter. Rather, specific grammatical rules are explored as the occasion arises. The editing and publishing of student-produced writing and the use of some of that production in the school curriculum assure real situations for learning basic grammar. Thus this third approach combines the best characteristics of the first two.

This process allows the child to learn correct grammar without feeling criticized for using the "incorrect" grammar learned in the home environment or for making the mistakes that are inevitable in the complex process of learning to speak and write English. The child is not constantly criticized for making mistakes in ordinary speech or even casual writing. Instead, teachers help students find errors as they prepare their written work for in-class publication or as they prepare for formal oral presentations. Then, in the process of explaining and helping the student correct those errors, the teacher gradually teaches the child the rules of correct formal grammar.

Children's literature is a valuable resource to use to furnish examples of how the parts of speech are used in meaningful language. Ruth Heller has a series of books that use beautiful artwork and language to furnish examples which enhance children's understanding of the parts of speech. Heller's books include *Many Luscious Lollipops: A Book About Adjectives* (1989); *A Cache of Jewels and Other Collective Nouns* (1989); *Merry-go-round: A Book About Nouns* (1990); *Kites Sail High: A Book About Verbs* (1991); and *Up, Up, and Away; A Book About Adverbs* (1991). Marvin Terban's *Your Foot's on My Feet! And Other Tricky Nouns* (1986) and *I Think I Thought and Other Tricky Verbs* (1984)

Heller's *Many Luscious Lollipops* brings adjectives to life.

▼

An adjective's terrific
even when it's not specific...

SOME jellybeans
a FEW gum drops
and
MANY luscious lollipops.

address the irregularities of many of the nouns and verbs in English in a humorous and memorable manner.

GUIDELINES

Several guidelines should be observed by teachers when working with students on grammar:

1. The study of grammar is functional when it is derived from a study of errors in usage. It includes training in principles and definitions that may help pupils with difficulties of expression and in the correction of errors.

2. In the process of building sentences and paragraphs to express ideas clearly, students notice change of meaning with change of form and position of words, learn how meaning is affected by change in position of various parts of a sentence, and discover classes of words.

3. The definitions and principles to be developed in the grammar part of the language program are those related to clear thinking and clear expression. They include:

   ▶ use of a simple sentence in the expression of a complete thought;

   ▶ the relations involved in the expression of a series of closely related ideas in a compound sentence;

THE BOOK ▶
MAKERS

LEE BENNETT HOPKINS

1. Which book of yours has given you the greatest pleasure?
Mama. I had done anthologies and picture books before, but this was my first novel. It was very autobiographical and I got a great sense of pride from doing it.

2. Which book has surprised you most in terms of its public reception?
The Sky Is Full of Song. I hadn't anticipated the unbelievable reaction to this poetry collection, both on the part of the reviewers and the children. I think it was an unusual collection for this age group, some poems that hadn't been published before.

3. What would you like people to remember about your work?
I want people to think I was dedicated to get every child in the United States into poetry—and not miss a single one of them!

4. What impact do you hope your work will have on children?
I want children to gain both a love of poetry and a love of language by coming to poetry.

Lee Bennett Hopkins is one of the great chroniclers of poetry for children of our day. His books include *Extra Innings, Side by Side, The Sky Is Full of Song, Pass the Poetry, Please, Through Our Eyes,* and *Do You Know What Day Tomorrow Is?*

▶ recognition and understanding of the classes of words, for example, how adverbs and adjectives add vividness and color to expression.

4. Grammar work in any of its details is neither concentrated in any grade nor presented in isolated lessons. It represents the building of a body of concepts that begin to take form in preschool years and develop gradually through the grades with pupils' increasing maturity and expanding needs for detailed communication.

5. Formal grammar is not needed by children or by average adults to carry on their vocational and personal lives. It is the professional tool of the editor, the copy editor, and the linguistic specialist.

6. The goal of grammar instruction in the elementary school is to help children participate with others in all types of activities without being conspicuous and without having to give thought to their use of language.

7. Writing, more than listening, speaking, or reading, offers meaningful situations in which to discuss and change ways of saying things with reasons that are derived from grammar.

GRAMMAR SUMMARY

We close our discussion of grammar with another lauguage story. Ken Goodman tells the following tale:

> A group of second graders were reading in round-robin fashion. It was Jim's turn. "There was a lot of goats," he read. "There was black goats and white goats."
>
> His teacher smiled encouragingly. "Would you repeat that please, Jim," she said.
>
> Somewhat puzzled, Jim reread: "There was a lot of goats. There was black goats and white goats."
>
> Still smiling, his teacher stepped to the board. In excellent manuscript she wrote two words. "Do you see a difference in these two words?" she asked.
>
> "Yes, they have different endings," said Jim.
>
> "Can you read these words?" the teacher asked.
>
> "Was, were," Jim read.
>
> "Good," said his teacher.
>
> "This is *was,* and this is *were.* Now, read again what you just read from the book."
>
> "There was a lot . . ." Jim began.
>
> "No, no!" his teacher said with some annoyance. "It's *were*. There *were* a lot of goats." Now, please reread."
>
> "There were a lot of goats. There was black goats and . . ." (Goodman, Smith, Meredith, & Goodman, 1988, p. 62)

Once again, this story points out that children actually "read" from their deep structure, not the surface structure of the book's print. Jim will only meet his teacher's expectations when his deep structure is modified. And deep structure changes take time and thousands of encounters with language.

CLASSROOM VIGNETTE

Paul Wheat uses editing procedures connected with publishing a newspaper, a magazine, and class books to furnish raw material for dealing with functional grammar. As students work on editorial committees to which they are assigned, they use their language textbooks and writing handbooks as resources. A chart is posted in the room with editing marks for the children to use during the editing process. As they prepare for conferences with authors, they are expected to have reasons to accompany their suggestions for change. When a newspaper edition or a magazine is in progress, Paul prepares envelopes for students to deposit their original manuscripts. Each envelope is designated by a major section. For newspapers:

Editorials	World news
Sports	Local news
Fashions	Supermarket specials
Arts	School news
Comics	Book reviews
Motion picture reviews	Television listings

For magazines:

Short stories	Poetry
Mysteries	Games
Biographies	Puzzles

Students are assigned to one committee at a time. When there is a contribution or two in the envelope, the chairperson calls a meeting. Manuscripts are read by each member, and suggestions are made for corrections and improvements. The committee has a meeting with the author to go over the suggestions. The author can accept or reject the suggestions. During the whole process Paul serves as editor in chief.

Each week, Marsha Bryan puts a word on the bulletin board such as *act, bank, cast, block,* or *check* that demonstrates most words have more than one meaning and the word's position in the sentence determines its grammatical class. She invites her students to compose sentences using the word as a noun, verb, or descriptive word. Suffixes are allowed. At the end of the week the class discusses

Continued

Formal grammar is simply a system for analyzing our language and coming up with a set of rules for or consistent descriptions of the way language works. It is merely a tool to help us, not an end in itself. Realizing this, the teacher must introduce grammatical rules gradually as they are needed and present them in enjoyable, nonthreatening ways. The teachers should never correct a student's grammar in a way that embarrasses or humiliates the child the variety of meanings. The activity demonstrates that it is the position of the word in the sentence that determines its class, not the word itself. Examples:

Priscilla put on a big act when she hit a home run.

My brother acted like a baby when he didn't get his way.

An action-packed show was on TV last night.

I acted as if I did not understand.

I was accused of being in the act, but I was not.

Some day I may go to acting school.

This activity causes students to wonder about meanings and classes of words. Therefore, they go to dictionaries and thesauruses to gather information about their language. Composing the sentences provides a functional format to share and discuss their information with the entire class.

About once a week Cindy Jones writes a two-word sentence on the chalkboard to illustrate the simple noun-verb pattern. She involves her students in expanding the sentence. An example:

Birds sing.
Add an auxiliary.
Birds *can* sing.
Add a determiner.
The birds can sing.
Add an adverb.
The birds can sing *noisily.*
Continue to expand.
The *flock of* birds *in our back yard* can sing noisily *when they think it is time for their breakfast.*

Jason Barnes encourages students to write stories using some simple sentences. Stories are exchanged and the readers are asked to make additions that elaborate the language of the story.

The first reader tries to add an adjective to each sentence.

The second reader tries to add a prepositional phrase.

Continued

or implicitly criticizes the dialect spoken in the child's home. Instead, grammar should be presented positively—how to say something more clearly, not how not to say it. In this way, children will acquire universally intelligible speaking and writing abilities and will come to view grammar as it should be viewed—as a friend, not an enemy.

The third reader adds an adverb where appropriate.

The fourth reader makes a complex or a compound sentence to improve the effect of the language.

The story then goes back to the author for oral reading to the group.

This same procedure can be used with stories written by young children and expanded by older students in the school.

As the students in Linda Blair's fourth grade gain awareness of the words in their stories that are in positions of nouns and verbs, she asks some of the students to go through their stories and underline the words used as nouns. Then she asks them to read the words they have underlined to the class. After hearing just the nouns, students predict what the story is about. After a few predictions, the author reads the story. Listeners compare and/or contrast the predictions with the actual story. They are surprised at how close their predictions were to the actual story. Students can see how much of the meaning of the story is conveyed by the nouns.

After students identify the nouns, they identify the nouns *and* the verbs. They follow the procedure of reading, listening to predictions, and then hearing the total story. This activity focuses attention on words that are basic to sentence structure and clarifies the difference in the use of a word as a noun and as a verb. Readers realize the noun-verb combination carries the bulk of meaning in passages.

Edward Martin, like many other teachers in his school, uses the writing of patterned poetry to establish some of the understandings of grammar required for literacy. He finds the simple form of the cinquain to be the easiest form to develop in the classroom.

He asks for the name of something.

Then he asks for two words to describe the word selected.

Next, he asks for a three-word phrase that expresses an action.

The fourth line has four words and expresses a feeling. It might contain an adverb or an adverbial phrase that would modify the verb in line 3.

The fifth line is a synonym of line 1 or refers back to line 1.

Continued

REFINING HANDWRITING

Handwriting is an important part of the language-arts curriculum. The purpose for writing is communication; therefore, students must strive for legible handwriting that can be read by others. However, like grammar, handwriting must not be an end in itself. Instead, it must be taught within the broader context of communication and not through isolated drills. Graves (1978)

An example:

Music	**Noun**
Peaceful, pleasing	**Adjectives**
Rising and drifting	**Verb phrase**
Carrying my troubles away	**Feeling phrase**
Rhythm	**Synonym (or near-synonym) of line 1**

Once Edward's students can write cinquains on their own, he introduces them to the diamante, a poetry form that does not have any structure words. With this form he helps students see that the words of the form-classes— nouns, verbs, adjectives, and adverbs—carry the bulk of meaning in language.

In developing the diamante as a class discussion, he illustrates it on the chalkboard.

Lines 1 and 7 are names of things that are opposites.

Line 2 is two adjectives describing line 1.

Line 3 is three participles related to line 1.

Line 4, the first two adjectives relate to line 1.

Line 4, the third and fourth adjectives relate to line 7.

Line 5 is three participles related to line 7.

Line 6 is two adjectives related to line 7.

One of the things many students like about the diamante is that the writing is random. You can write a word for any line at any time. In fact, lines 1 and 7 need to be written first in order to have the reference points.

An example:

> birds
> beautiful graceful
> gliding flying soaring
> shy silent / brave bold
> crunching creeping crawling
> ugly clumsy
> bugs

complains that handwriting, the proper formation of letters, has become the "main event" in many language-arts classrooms, leaving composition as the "side show." When handwriting loses its "toolness," it can interfere with composition or the creative presentation of ideas and thoughts.

When handwriting is divorced from composition and content, significant problems may develop. Graves (1983) has found that "One group of writers feel that their information is good because the handwriting is clear" (p. 180). In contrast, he found other writers who "dismissed their experiences and their

views about issues because their handwriting had been deemed unacceptable" (p. 180).

Consequently, teachers must place emphasis on what is being said, and not on the physical appearance of the manuscript. However, our society does place great value on the appearance of handwriting—tending to judge writing by how neat or messy the paper is while sometimes overlooking the underlying quality of the composition. Because of this discrimination, good handwriting is a goal for which students should strive. When clearly viewed as a mechanical skill, handwriting may be taught within the act of composition without interfering with the process of writing.

HELPING STUDENTS REFINE HANDWRITING

The physical environment is important when students are attempting to produce handwriting that has a pleasing style. The students must be comfortable and relaxed. Teachers should be sure desks and chairs are the proper height. This will enable students to place both feet on the floor and rest their arms comfortably on the desks.

Students' handwriting is improved when the paper is positioned correctly. The edge of the paper should be perpendicular to the front edge of the desk when the student is printing. In cursive writing, the paper should be tilted at a 30-degree angle to the left. Left-handed students should tilt their paper the opposite direction with even more of a slant than right-handed students (Fox & Allen, 1983).

The teacher should provide areas for students to explore and practice the forming of letters. An area of the chalkboard or an easel set up in a corner of the room may be designated for writing practice and will attract students' attention. Guides (see Figure 10.1) that demonstrate the correct form of the letters should be readily available. Many teachers have found it valuable to attach small copies of writing guides to each child's desk for easy reference.

In addition to comfortable and attractive places in which to write, a variety of writing materials should be provided. Writing is traditionally thought of as a pencil-and-lined-paper task; however, students should be given the opportunity to use many different types of media. Whether using a pen, chalk, marking pen, paintbrush, or fingers in fingerpaint, a child is still internalizing ways to use print to convey a message. Small pieces of cardboard or plyboard sprayed with chalkboard paint provide students with personal chalkboards on which to practice and perfect their penmanship. The "lift and erase" tablets are also useful. Teachers should realize that the way handwriting is "taught" to students will help determine their views on the entire process of writing. If students form negative views concerning the mechanical aspects of writing, the creative aspect of the process is directly impacted. Fluency is forgotten in the struggle to "draw" the letters to match a model.

Most school districts have adopted a commercially prepared writing program that gives teachers guidelines on teaching handwriting. Letters are usually grouped for presentation by similarities such as *i*, *l*, and *t*. The programs usually provide workbooks for the students. Activities in these workbooks emphasize the copying of isolated letters, words, and phrases.

MANUSCRIPT GUIDE ◀ **FIGURE 10.1**

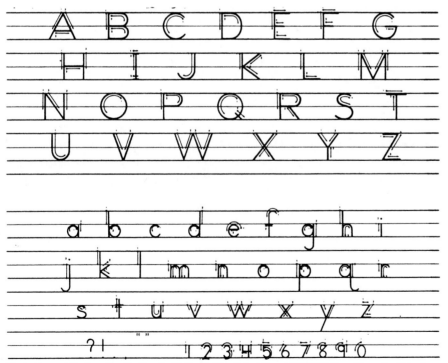

PENMANSHIP

She was the girl of my dreams,
So I wrote her a note to sing my
    love:

I've seen canyons deep and
    dangerous,
I've seen mountains white and
    high,
I've seen oceans blue and clear,
And deserts flat and dry,
But in all the world, my darling,
There shall never be
A vision quite as beautiful
As you appear to me.

And the girl of my dreams wrote
    back to me:

You seem to be real nice,
But your penmanship's a sight!
Your cursive is so messy,
I can't read a word you write.

A beginning writer needs to experiment with and manipulate print that has personal meaning. Copying of isolated letters can easily disintegrate into an art lesson, and the bridge between meaning and print is destroyed.

One way of assuring that handwriting is linked with meaning is to incorporate the child's language into the process. Using a child's dictation is an effective way of doing this. The following classroom vignette describes the process:

CLASSROOM VIGNETTE

Judy Embry uses group dictation to let her first graders construct their own daily "writing" lesson. After the selection of a topic, students volunteer sentences to form a story or provide information concerning the topic. Judy records these sentences on a large chart tablet in front of the group by using a marking pen to write a sentence in the child's favorite color. The child's name is included at the end of the sentence. The chart is left on display in the room, and a ditto master of the print is prepared with space left for illustrations. Students decide whether they will trace over the print or recopy it on another line.

As the year progresses, many students decide to use the chart rather than wait for a ditto master to be made. They copy their own sentences, or others, and sometimes combine them to construct an individual story or create their own sentences and/or story. Often students decide to illustrate their work and produce an individual, group, or class book.

Beginning writers generally use a form of manuscript. As students become older, they begin to express an interest in cursive writing, since this is what they see adults using. In past years, controversy has abounded concerning the optimum time to introduce the cursive form of handwriting to students. Currently, flexibility is the key. The practice of moving all second- or third-grade students into cursive at the same time is inappropriate. Just as all literacy processes are developmental and different students acquire them at different ages, students will be ready for cursive at different times.

Introducing cursive writing to students involves the same linguistic principles discussed in the instruction of manuscript. As is true for manuscript materials, many commercially prepared programs for the teaching of cursive are available. These programs include workbooks, charts, and teachers' manuals that delineate the proper way to make the letters and give teachers instructional advice concerning special difficulties that students may encounter with certain letters.

While teaching the forms of cursive, teachers must keep the emphasis on fluency of expression and meaning. If a child is asked to focus all energy on the task of abandoning a familiar writing form in favor of a new one, it means the emphasis is once again being focused on the mechanical aspect of writing rather than the communicative aspect. The transfer from manuscript to cursive must, therefore, be a natural process that stems from the need to communicate.

The teacher can facilitate this transfer by using the cursive form to write meaningful messages to students concerning everyday announcements, schedules, and information necessary for the normal operation of a classroom. In addition, cursive writing may be utilized to share riddles, rhymes, and special events with the students. Soon, many students will begin to experiment with this style and to incorporate it into their writing. This is the time to begin "formalized" instruction by providing students with writing models. Instruction should then be provided by the teacher concerning the method of making the letters in the most legible and efficient way.

In an effort to bridge the gap between manuscript and cursive writing, Donald Thurber developed D'Nealian manuscript in the mid-1960s. This writing system consists of characters that are lowercase and simple to write. As illustrated by Figure 10.2, most of the letters contain the same slant as cursive and are made with one continuous stroke.

EVALUATING HANDWRITING

At one time, handwriting was evaluated on the basis of its beauty, and elaborate penmanship was highly valued. However, because the primary purpose of writing is to convey a message and not to be aesthetically pleasing, this emphasis has faded. On the other hand, writing cannot fulfill its purpose if it is not legible. Therefore, norms of acceptability exist. However, the teacher's understanding of writing as a developmental process that is constantly in the midst of change is crucial. For example, neatness is undoubtedly a consideration because it directly influences legibility; however, neatness may suffer as a child struggles to erase and perfect a letter. At times, a lack of neatness may reflect a movement toward legibility.

Change and progress are achievable goals that enhance students' attitudes toward writing as a communicative tool. When perfection becomes the goal, the medium—not the message—becomes the primary concern (Yellin & Blake, 1994). Evaluation must be a process in which teachers help students develop

FIGURE 10.2 ▶ **D'NEALIAN MANUSCRIPT ALPHABET**

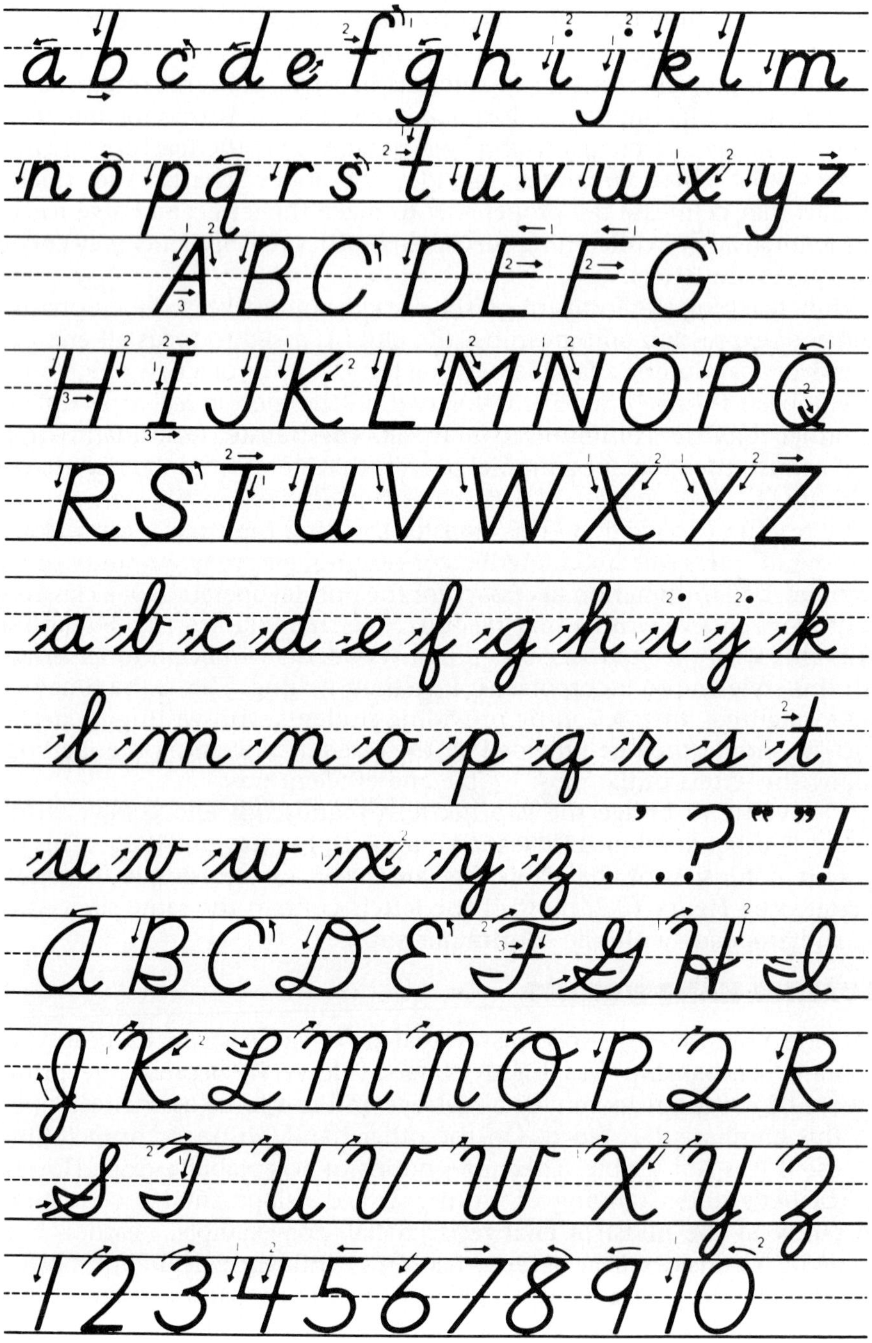

habits that will aid them in writing legibly and efficiently (Fox & Allen, 1983). By demonstrating the most effective way to make a letter and assisting students who are using inefficient movements in their writing, a teacher can use evaluation as a teaching aid. The teacher must keep in mind that each writing system has certain arbitrary rules. A handwriting system must have a certain number of unique characteristics to be copyrighted. Regardless of what handwriting system is utilized in a classroom, a teacher must realize that efficiency and legibility are the key factors, not "slavish imitation" (Smith, Goodman, & Meredith, 1976, p. 254).

As older students progress in their writing ability, they will begin to develop individuality in their handwriting style. Students may begin to use embellishments as they cross the "t's" and dot the "i's." Slant and size may vary. Although students should be encouraged to develop their own style of writing, they must realize handwriting cannot be stylized to the extent that legibility suffers.

Teachers can emphasize the need for continuous concern about legibility by giving students the opportunity to evaluate handwriting samples. Students can place samples into categories such as "easiest to read" or "most difficult to read" and "neatest" or "messiest." The learning process should be extended as students are given the opportunity to identify the factors that make one paper easier to read than another. The characteristics of size, slant, spacing, and formation of letters will be identified.

Students must apply these same principles of evaluation to their handwriting. By keeping samples of their handwriting, the students become aware of changes in its readability. Individual folders are useful for storing samples. Models of handwriting should be available (see Figure 10.3) and time provided for students to compare their handwriting to the models and to identify problem areas (Fox & Allen, 1983).

The acceptability of handwriting depends on its purpose. The legibility and neatness of a paper will vary depending on whether it is a first draft, a scribbled reminder, or a final copy of a paper to be graded. When students learn to adapt their writing style to match their needs, they will view handwriting as a communicative tool rather than a product in itself.

REFINING MECHANICS: PUNCTUATION AND CAPITALIZATION

PUNCTUATION

Punctuation is a matter of courtesy in making meanings clear to the reader. Modern writers take a great deal of liberty with punctuation and capitalization, but there are certain standard forms that everybody should know. These forms should be taught as students become aware of the need for help in making their early writing and dictation meaningful to the reader.

The following list is one that teachers can use as a guide for teaching punctuation. Student editing committees (see Chapter 7) will find these suggestions useful as they help others refine manuscripts. The list is *not* a sequence for teaching skills in punctuation, but suggests the areas of punctuation with which students should be familiar as they mature in creative expression.

FIGURE 10.3 ▶ **CURSIVE ALPHABET**

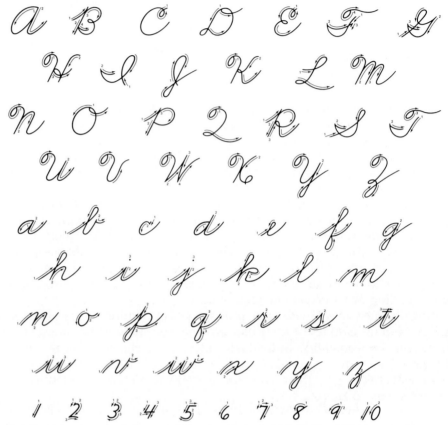

Used with permission of the publisher, Zaner-Bloser, Inc., Columbus, Ohio; taken from *Handwriting: The Way to Self-Expression*, copyright, 1991.

1. Use of a period
   at the end of declarative sentences
   after initials and common abbreviations
   after letters and figures prefixed to points in outlines
   after numerals in lists of words or sentences
2. Use of a question mark following a question
3. Use of a comma
   between days of month and year
   between name of city and state
   after salutation and complimentary close of a personal letter
   to replace "and" in a series of words, phrases, and clauses
   to separate a direct quotation from the rest of the sentence

following "yes" and "no"

to set off the name of the person addressed

4. Use of an exclamation point after expressions that reflect strong feelings

5. Use of quotation marks

    around direct quotations

    around titles of stories and poems

6. Use of a hyphen to separate parts of a word split at the end of a line

7. Use of an apostrophe

    in common contractions

    in possessives

8. Use of a colon after the salutation of a business letter

CAPITALIZATION

Capitalization, along with punctuation, is a matter of courtesy to help make meanings clear to the reader. Although some options do exist in capitalization, some standard usages also exist with which students should be familiar. As with punctuation, these should not be directly taught to students; rather, they should be mastered through the actual practices of writing and refinement.

1. Capitalization of the first word of a

    sentence

    line of poetry

    direct quotation

2. Capitalization of the important words in a title

3. Capitalization of names of

    particular places: schools, streets, cities, nations, and important geographic localities

    days of week, months, and special days

    persons and pets

    initials and abbreviations of proper names

    organizations

    races, nationalities, and school subjects

    companies and firms

    brands and special products

4. Capitalization of

    the pronoun "I"

    the topics of an outline

the first, last, and each important word in titles of books, pictures,
magazine articles, and so on

LINGUISTIC GUIDELINES FOR REFINING COMMUNICATION

Language usage seldom improves without the influence of instruction; yet instruction in skills does not assure improvement. Skills do not emerge by leaving out all other aspects of instruction. Awareness of acceptable usage can be
raised when teachers follow a few guidelines.

1. Improved usage is essentially a problem of enlarging and refining vo-
    cabulary so the speaker or writer has alternatives from which to choose.

2. Correctness is not the end of language instruction. Willingness to par-
    ticipate in useful language activities is far more important. Productive
    language can be refined, but one cannot refine what does not exist.

3. The English language is changing. Some traditionally objectionable
    forms of expression are now acceptable.

4. Language is a living, growing instrument of communication. It must
    remain flexible and adaptable to a variety of life situations. Every
    person needs a "wardrobe of languages" to meet the demands of chang-
    ing relationships.

5. Standards of acceptable usage vary within communities and with stu-
    dents of different capacities. Efforts of teachers to raise the levels of us-
    age far above the standards of the community are usually futile and
    may be harmful, unless the teacher values the community standards
    and approaches instruction as providing alternative ways of expression.

6. The usage program should concentrate on a relatively few serious er-
    rors at any given time. Which ones to emphasize should be determined
    by the standards prevailing in the community and by the basic require-
    ments for success in writing and speaking.

7. Improvement in usage requires much oral work. Correct forms of expression must be repeated sufficiently to cause the correct forms to sound right.

8. Refinement of oral language as a base for written language is accelerated through the use of the dictation process, editing for publication, and the use of student-produced material in the school curriculum.

SUMMARY

Meaning-centered programs structure the classroom environment so students can *choose* change under the influence of the communication of others. Grammar and handwriting skills can be improved as students strive to communicate in clear and effective ways in classrooms where communication is the instructional goal.

PATHWAYS TO LITERACY CONVENTIONS

Usage
The student develops standards of correct usage as needed and attempts to meet them in the following ways:

▶ increases skill in using correct forms of verbs.

▶ names self last (John and I).

▶ avoids double negatives.

▶ uses comparative forms of adjectives correctly.

▶ uses subject-verb agreement.

▶ uses forms of pronouns for subject and object.

▶ uses possessive pronoun forms.

▶ uses personal pronoun forms in compound subjects, objects, and predicate pronouns.

▶ has pronoun agree with noun and pronoun antecedents.

▶ uses objective form and infinitive.

Grammar
The student develops an understanding of grammar as *the orderly description of what is said by certain groups of people*. The student:

▶ begins to recognize and write sentences.

▶ realizes a sentence tells or asks something.

▶ recognizes the kinds of sentences:
statement
question
command
explanation

▶ develops an understanding of the sentence as a structural unit.

▶ develops an understanding of the functions of the subject and the predicate.

▶ develops an understanding of the functions of words that modify and words that connect.

▶ develops an understanding of:
simple sentences
compound sentences
complex sentences
clauses

▶ uses regular and irregular verbs correctly.

▶11 PATHWAYS TO AUTHENTIC LITERACY ASSESSMENT

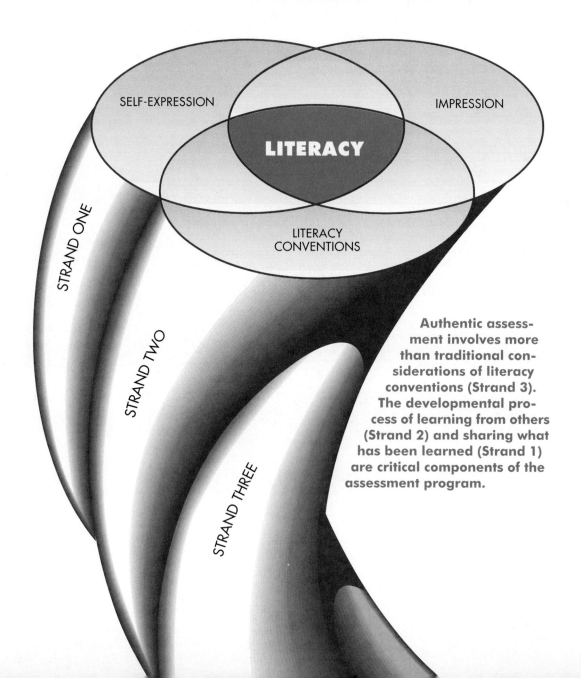

SELF-EXPRESSION

IMPRESSION

LITERACY

LITERACY
CONVENTIONS

STRAND ONE

STRAND TWO

STRAND THREE

Authentic assessment involves more than traditional considerations of literacy conventions (Strand 3). The developmental process of learning from others (Strand 2) and sharing what has been learned (Strand 1) are critical components of the assessment program.

PATHWAYS TO PONDER

....

▶ **HOW DOES ASSESSMENT INFLUENCE INSTRUCTION?**
....

▶ **WHAT OBSERVATIONAL TECHNIQUES CAN TEACHERS USE TO GAIN BETTER UNDERSTANDINGS OF THEIR STUDENTS' LITERACY GROWTH?**
....

▶ **WHAT IS THE VALUE OF STUDENT INTERACTION IN TERMS OF ASSESSMENT DATA?**
....

▶ **HOW CAN STUDENTS' WORK SAMPLINGS DEMONSTRATE THEIR LITERACY GROWTH?**
....

▶ **HOW IMPORTANT IS IT FOR STUDENTS TO DO SELF-ASSESSMENT?**

▶ **WHAT FEEDBACK DO TEACHERS IN MEANING-CENTERED CLASSROOMS RECEIVE CONCERNING THEIR OWN TEACHING AND LEARNING?**

Jonathan, a bright second grader, became very anxious on a Monday evening during the third week of school. When he was questioned by his mother, the problem surfaced. Achievement tests would begin the next morning and continue for the rest of the week. His teacher's anxiety about the test was clearly comprehended by her students, despite her reassurances of "Just do your best and don't worry. This is our chance to show how good we are." That night Jonathan had a stomachache and couldn't sleep. Jonathan, however, didn't have a *reason* for his worry—he had scored at the 98th percentile on the previous year's standardized test. It was a rough week for Jonathan and his classmates as they answered questions asked by the test writers and struggled with the format of the test. At home the pale little boy worried every night about how he was doing on the tests. On Friday, when the tests were finished, Jonathan sang his teacher this song:

> *Let's have a celebration,*   *Let's have a celebration,*
> *A big wing ding, a jubilation,*   *give our teacher a big ovation*
> *send out the invitations,*   *send out the invitations,*
> *we finished all of our tests!*   *we finished all of our tests!*

Did Jonathan worry needlessly? No. His test results will determine what programs he can participate in, including the school's gifted and talented program. The results will influence his educational options all the way to which college he can attend. In effect, children are being told to put their curiosity away, contain their imagination, and answer other people's questions instead of raising their own. Testing is the culprit.

When you enter the teaching profession you become a member of a culture with deeply anchored beliefs, philosophies, values, organizational frameworks, and established goals (Stewart & O'Brien, 1989). Many of these involve testing, or evaluative practices. As you begin to examine assessment techniques and make decisions concerning what type of evaluative system you will use in your classroom, remember that many fallacies surround assessment.

FINAL EXAMS

*I would ride a wave
To an island of pleasure,
Or search the deep
For a chest full of treasure,
Or float alone
In a hot air balloon
To follow the fog
All the way to the moon,
Or ride a camel
Through cold desert night,
Or walk through a forest
Lit with green fairy light.*

*I'm ready for life's journey
Through happiness or sorrow,
Just save me from this stupid test
I have to take tomorrow.*

Is testing fair? Not really. Research has documented the cultural bias of many standardized tests (Costa, 1989; Eisner, 1990) and the view that they do not measure cognitive skills (Marzano & Costa, 1988) or higher level literacy abilities (Hiebert, Valencia, & Afflerbach, 1994).

Some believe tests that require one right answer are objective. This is a false notion. By the selection of the items and the correct answer, the test maker has subjectively decided what the important information is concerning that subject and how the information should be reported. Have you ever been ready to take a test, yet done poorly? Perhaps after taking the multiple-choice exam you realized you had not been able to convey your understanding in that particular mode of evaluation. In essence, the test did not ask what you knew and/or considered and therefore remembered as important! Such testing ignores the context of the student, or what the student is thinking, and often fails to tap into the knowledge base of the child (Messick, 1989, Wiggins, 1993).

Let's consider Jonathan again. When he was in kindergarten he was given a standardized test in order to determine his readiness for first grade. When the teacher shared the results with the child's parent, she noted that Jonathan had lost points on the section of the test that required a self-portrait. He had neglected to put fingers and thumbs on the hands and in accordance with the scoring mandated by the test was penalized. In conversation with the child, the parent asked the child about his day. He responded by saying, "Well, they said we were going to play games today, but it was really a test." When asked to describe the test, he did so in detail. After discussing the figure he had drawn, the parent asked him why he did not put fingers and thumbs on the two hands of his drawing. "Mother!" Jonathan said with some exasperation, "he (referring to drawing) was taking a test—so his hands were like this!" The child then clenched both of his hands, and obviously no fingers or thumbs were in evidence. The context of the testing situation had determined

Jonathan's response, yet the evaluative process did not include any input from the child, only a marking system that allowed for one right answer. The cognitive processes that generated Jonathan's answers were ignored.

In reality, very few problem situations in the real world have only one correct solution; therefore, we do students an injustice if our evaluative system relies heavily on tests that require convergent answers for success. Perhaps Grant Wiggins says it best when he states, "Understanding is not cued knowledge: performance is never the sum of drill; problems are not exercises; mastery is not achieved by the unthinking application of algorithms. In other words, we cannot be said to understand something unless we can employ our knowledge wisely, fluently, flexibly, and aptly in particular and diverse contexts" (Wiggins, 1993, p. 200).

Therefore, it is critical to use assessment techniques in our classrooms that are an integral part of the ongoing instructional environment. Children must participate in the evaluative process by engaging in self-evaluation, determining what goals should be set, and planning how to reach these goals. By involving children in this active process of self-evaluation, goal setting, and planning action, we are exposing them to a process that will increase their productivity as literate adults.

Yet even though we know testing can have a negative impact on learning, testing seems to demand more instructional time each year. For many students one week is spent on standardized tests at the beginning and end of the school year. Another week is spent on the locally developed skills test, still another week on state-mandated criterion references.

In addition, children are confronted with end-of-unit basal tests, weekly spelling tests, end-of-story skill and comprehension tests, tests of isolated writing and grammar skills—the list continues indefinitely. These tests are then evaluated to determine if children have mastered isolated skill areas such as "initial consonant c" or "the use of plurals."

In this chapter we briefly examine and comment on standardized tests. Then we provide alternatives to such testing—authentic assessment that is compatible with meaning-centered classrooms and will complement, not hinder, the literacy learning of students.

STANDARDIZED TESTS

The format and content of standardized tests have remained uniform for the past 50 years and do not reflect the current research and practices in language development and instruction. Standardized tests depict views formed by behavioral researchers more than 30 years ago, which assume that literacy is acquired by teaching isolated skills one at a time and testing for mastery of the individual skills (Farr & Carey, 1986; Pearson, 1985; Valencia & Pearson, 1987).

In most scenarios, standardized tests consist of questions involving isolated skills in decontextualized settings rather than situations that give children the opportunity to function as real readers and writers. What do such tests communicate to children about reading and writing? Morrow and Smith offer a condemning description of the message that is sent to emerging writers and readers:

> First, the examples presented to illustrate skills tested portray a picture of isolated, not integrated, reading skills. Second, recognition, not production or even identification, dominates as the primary mode of cognitive processing. One wonders what happened to the theory of reading as a constructive process. Third, when they recognize things, children are usually asked to respond to either a picture or something the teacher says. At the very least, real reading involves identification of words in sentences. Finally, what dominates the whole enterprise when children actually take the test is test-taking behavior—filling in bubbles, moving the marker, making sure everything is in the right place. These activities may be related to test taking, but they have nothing to do with reading. An important final point to consider in regard to these formal measures of early literacy is the message they are sending about what really counts. If you take the tests to be a reflection of the field's priorities in early literacy instruction, then what matters most is the child's ability to recognize pictures, letters, and sounds so they will be ready, someday, for the real thing. (Morrow & Smith, 1990, p. 38)

What are schools doing in response to standardized testing? In some cases, program content that does not meet the child's social, emotional, and developmental needs is adopted in order to attempt to raise scores on standardized tests. In many instances, activities are substituted that do not foster the development of curiosity, critical thinking, or creative expression. Conversely, programs developed on the basis of current research are often abandoned on the basis of results of standardized test scores (Valencia & Pearson, 1987). Tests encourage or reward convergent thinking and, in effect, penalize divergent thinking. The loss of an emphasis on divergent thinking is particularly disturbing because divergent thinking is the basis of all higher order thinking skills (Kasten, 1989).

Perhaps the most subtle yet potentially most dangerous result of test-centered evaluation is that the teacher and students are cast in primarily adversarial roles. When undue emphasis is placed on scores of standardized tests, end-of-unit basal tests, or teacher-constructed tests, teachers assume the role of judge, not advocate. Confusion results for children when they receive mixed messages from teachers' assurances that creativity and risk taking, which often result in "mistakes," are part of the learning process, yet are tested in ways that penalize this type of thinking. The environment is contradictory, and process-oriented instruction is negated (Graves, 1983).

A dilemma, therefore, is present. Common sense indicates that evaluation must be a part of effective instruction because the information evaluation yields may be used to modify instruction to fit the needs of learners. Parents and administrators want information concerning what and how students are achieving, yet traditional formal measures often negate or supersede the learning process.

The International Reading Association has long been concerned with the issue of literacy assessment. At their 1988 conference in Toronto, Canada, the IRA Delegates Assembly unanimously passed the following resolution:

> Reading assessment must reflect advances in the understanding of the reading process. As teachers of literacy we are concerned that instructional decisions are too often made from assessments which define reading as a sequence of discrete skills that students must master to become readers. Such assessments foster inappropriate instruction. We are concerned that inappropriate measures are proliferating for the purpose of school by school, district by district, and province by province comparisons. The expansion of such assessments aggravates the issue of educational decision making based upon an inaccurate definition of reading. Be it therefore RESOLVED that the International Reading Association affirms that reading assessments reflect recent advances in the understanding of the reading process; be it further RESOLVED that assessment measures defining reading as a sequence of skills be discouraged and the International Reading Association opposes the proliferation of school by school, state by state, and province by province comparison assessments.

This resolution is but one indication that attitudes toward standardized assessment are changing. We are optimistic that better times are ahead for children like Jonathan.

Fortunately, assessment and learning do not have to be at odds with one another. Instructional planning is enhanced by evaluation of the learning of the children and the success of instructional activities. Programs become better when teachers continually assess the effectiveness of the learning environments they have designed as well as the academic progress of their students. We now turn to the kinds of assessment that are positive and powerful—types of evaluation that do not disrupt or supplant children's learning, but enhance it. We start with authentic factors that teachers should consider in evaluating students. We then share one way of collecting or showcasing student knowledge: portfolios.

ASSESSMENT THROUGH OBSERVATION

Evaluation can tell us how comfortable children are in the literacy environment and how successful they are in their literacy endeavors. One of the most effective methods of evaluation is simply observing what students are doing as they engage in literacy activities. As a teacher moves about the classroom, intuitive impressions are formed concerning an individual or class. A teacher can quickly jot concerns and evidence of growth in an impressions journal in which notes are recorded on student development. This record is useful to jog the memory if the teacher decides to transfer some information to a more formal account such as an anecdotal record (Figure 11.1) or a checklist (Figure 11.2).

ANECDOTAL RECORDS

Anecdotal records are one cornerstone of the assessment program in meaning-centered classrooms. Such records are an ongoing study of classroom happenings that center on student and teacher learnings. Teachers note significant events in the record, and react to their own recordings with observations or musings as insights develop (Bird, 1989).

AN ANECDOTAL RECORD ◀ **FIGURE 11.1**

FIGURE 11.2 ▶ **A LITERACY CHECKLIST**

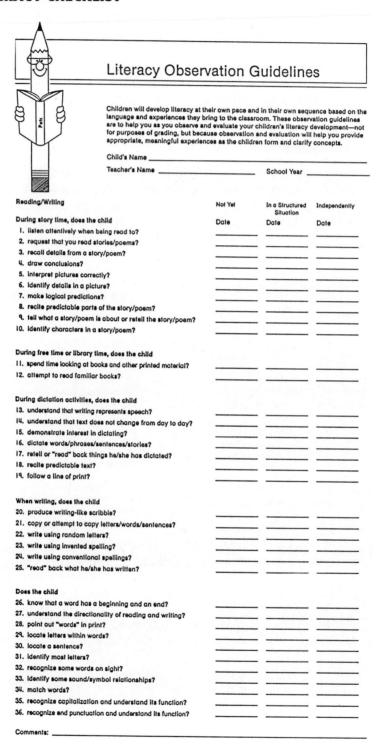

Literacy Observation Guidelines

Children will develop literacy at their own pace and in their own sequence based on the language and experiences they bring to the classroom. These observation guidelines are to help you as you observe and evaluate your children's literacy development—not for purposes of grading, but because observation and evaluation will help you provide appropriate, meaningful experiences as the children form and clarify concepts.

Child's Name _____

Teacher's Name _____   School Year _____

Reading/Writing	Not Yet	In a Structured Situation	Independently
During story time, does the child	Date	Date	Date
1. listen attentively when being read to?	_____	_____	_____
2. request that you read stories/poems?	_____	_____	_____
3. recall details from a story/poem?	_____	_____	_____
4. draw conclusions?	_____	_____	_____
5. interpret pictures correctly?	_____	_____	_____
6. identify details in a picture?	_____	_____	_____
7. make logical predictions?	_____	_____	_____
8. recite predictable parts of the story/poem?	_____	_____	_____
9. tell what a story/poem is about or retell the story/poem?	_____	_____	_____
10. identify characters in a story/poem?	_____	_____	_____
During free time or library time, does the child			
11. spend time looking at books and other printed material?	_____	_____	_____
12. attempt to read familiar books?	_____	_____	_____
During dictation activities, does the child			
13. understand that writing represents speech?	_____	_____	_____
14. understand that text does not change from day to day?	_____	_____	_____
15. demonstrate interest in dictating?	_____	_____	_____
16. dictate words/phrases/sentences/stories?	_____	_____	_____
17. retell or "read" back things he/she has dictated?	_____	_____	_____
18. recite predictable text?	_____	_____	_____
19. follow a line of print?	_____	_____	_____
When writing, does the child			
20. produce writing-like scribble?	_____	_____	_____
21. copy or attempt to copy letters/words/sentences?	_____	_____	_____
22. write using random letters?	_____	_____	_____
23. write using invented spelling?	_____	_____	_____
24. write using conventional spellings?	_____	_____	_____
25. "read" back what he/she has written?	_____	_____	_____
Does the child			
26. know that a word has a beginning and an end?	_____	_____	_____
27. understand the directionality of reading and writing?	_____	_____	_____
28. point out "words" in print?	_____	_____	_____
29. locate letters within words?	_____	_____	_____
30. locate a sentence?	_____	_____	_____
31. identify most letters?	_____	_____	_____
32. recognize some words on sight?	_____	_____	_____
33. identify some sound/symbol relationships?	_____	_____	_____
34. match words?	_____	_____	_____
35. recognize capitalization and understand its function?	_____	_____	_____
36. recognize end punctuation and understand its function?	_____	_____	_____

Comments: _____

_____

_____

_____

_____

From *Experiences for Literacy* by R.V. Allen, M. Sampson, and B. Teale. Used with permission of DLM, Incorporated.

Sylvia Riojas, a first-grade teacher, noted that Carlos seemed tentative in his journal entries. Later, she interpreted her observation:

> At the beginning of the year, I noted that Carlos was tentative in his writing. Now I know that he was insecure because he didn't know what or how to write—he was trying to write for me instead of for himself! Now he knows that what he writes is up to him and that it will not be shared with other kids. Since that realization, Carlos has learned that he can write. His journal entries reflect this as he now processes what's happening in his life and expresses it through writing.

Through Sylvia's notes, she knew that Carlos needed to discover and value the personal nature of writing. She was able to help Carlos, and she helped herself to become a better teacher in the process. As demonstrated in this case, anecdotal records help teachers evaluate their own learning and emerging insights about children and instruction.

CHECKLISTS

Checklists can record much of the same information that is found in anecdotal records. Some teachers prefer the checklist format, for after the initial development of the list, less time is required to use this format. Of course, the teacher must be constantly aware of revisions and additions that need to be made as children develop and progress. The comments section of the checklist is perhaps the most crucial aspect. Checklists are convenient and provide at-a-glance information on each child. Figure 11.2 provides a checklist of early reading/writing behaviors that can serve as a basis for teacher-designed checklists.

ASSESSMENT THROUGH INTERACTION

While observation is a sound assessment procedure, our greatest understanding of student progress and comprehension comes through direct communications with students. These communications can take many forms—talking with students about their work, conversing during writing conferences, and written conversations with students as teachers respond to their journals.

Unlike observation, this type of assessment goes one step further: Teachers may challenge, encourage, or stimulate children as they interact with them. Goodman (1989) states that interaction may be "the most powerful aspect of the process of evaluation in whole language classrooms because of its immediate relationship to instruction" (p. 11).

Teachers may model higher level thinking strategies during these interactions by asking open-ended questions, or they may choose to have children examine their assumptions by asking "why" they chose a specific answer to a question or "why" they took a specific stance on an issue.

Most interactive assessment is informal and produces a general sentiment in the teacher of how a student is doing. This useful information can be made more formal, however. A student progress diary may be kept by the

Listening to ▶
children describe
their work is a
valuable
assessment
procedure.

teacher that records evidence of student growth and provides a written record or discussion of insights concerning students' growth in cognition and literacy.

COACHING VS. EDITING

Conferencing with students about what they've written offers an invaluable opportunity for assessment through interaction. And student growth and development in writing can best be observed by teachers who view themselves not as editors, but as coaches (Thomason, 1990).

An editor is a fixer. Teachers who view themselves as editors see their primary responsibility as working with a student's finished product. Teacher-editors are diligent in fixing grammar, spelling, and punctuation errors. They red-mark writing mechanics, mistakenly believing this will either motivate the writer to do better next time or help the writer to eliminate the errors. It does neither. What it *does* do is to discourage the writer and introduce a fear of writing (Thomason, 1990). A sad example of such editing is seen in 8-year-old Michael. He was saddened by the deaths of two squirrels on his street and was motivated to write a song about squirrels one evening.

He sang the song to his parents and was praised for his creative efforts. The next morning, with great excitement, he took his piece to school to show his teacher. That afternoon he came home dejected. His teacher had immediately assumed the role of editor. Her first thought and action was to "correct" spelling with "a big red marker!" Michael reported, "She didn't even know it was a song." Fortunately, Michael's mother was a teacher, too. And she functioned as a coach, not an editor. After much encouragement she was able to restore Michael's confidence and self-esteem. He was persuaded to reconstruct the poem; the second version is pictured in Figure 11.3 (see page

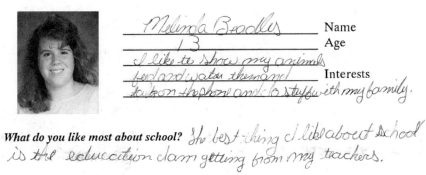

Name *Melinda Bradley*

Age *13*

Interests *I like to show my animals feed and water them and talk on the phone and to stay with my family.*

What do you like most about school? *The best thing I like about school is the education dam getting from my teachers.*

What's your favorite subject? Why? *My favorite subjects are Math, Atheletics and Reading. I like these subjects the best because they are the most intrusting and I like the teachers.*

What's your favorite book? Why do you like it? *My favorite book is Roots because it explains the hardships that the inslaved people had and what happened to them.*

What advice do you have for teachers? *The advice I have for teachers is, to do more things in our classroom. Teach the lesson like you want it to be taught and above all just play it cool and enjoy having the kids, the classroom and the job.*

300). The first version has never been seen again. Michael continues to write, but what about all the children who don't have a parent who functions as a teacher-coach?

But let's return to the classroom and look more deeply at differences between editors and coaches. If the editor works with the product, the coach works with the writer. In individual conferences, the coach becomes the first "audience" for student writing. Teacher-coaches motivate students by finding positive aspects of their writing and asking questions and encouraging them to expand undeveloped sections. Instead of taking responsibility to mark everything that needs correcting (as the teacher-editor does), the coach helps student writers discover areas that need improvement—anything from a lack of description to a number of misspelled words. Correction is the student's responsibility.

FIGURE 11.3 ▶ A THIRD GRADER'S SONG

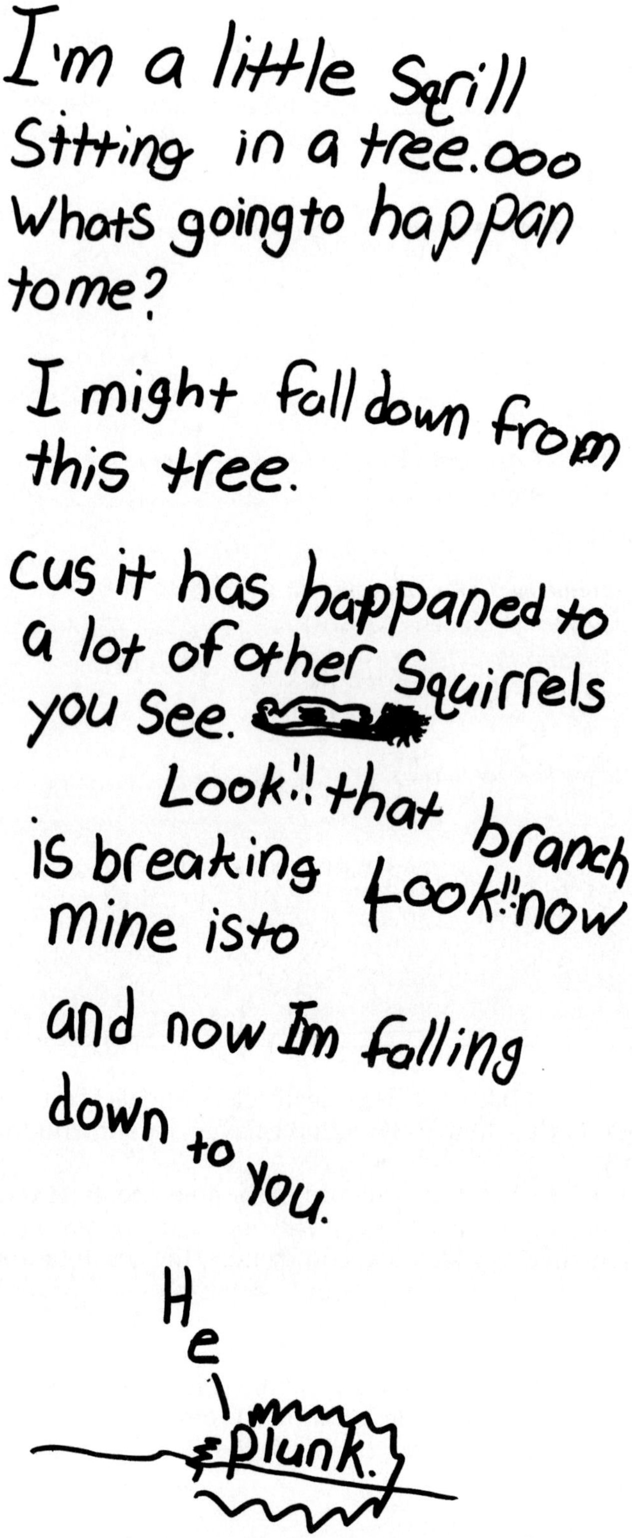

I'm a little Sqrill
Sitting in a tree.ooo
Whats going to happan
to me?

I might fall down from
this tree.

Cus it has happaned to
a lot of other Squirrels
you See.

Look!! that branch
is breaking   look!!now
mine is to

and now Im falling

down to you.

He
e
i
Plunk.

The teacher who functions as a coach finds evaluation much easier because it is easier to trace the student's development. Coaches encourage rewriting and movement toward publication. The student's writing folder frequently includes many different versions of a piece, allowing the teacher to trace the development of both writing skills and mechanical skills. This work may be shared with parents and administrators to document children's literacy growth.

ASSESSMENT THROUGH ANALYSIS OF STUDENT WORK

While observation and interaction constitute two forms of assessment, a third type used in meaning-centered classrooms involves analysis of the work that children do. Children should be involved in this process—choosing the pieces of writing or other work the teacher will examine or meeting with the teacher to show the progress the student is achieving. The collections are called *work samplings* because they represent but a small part of the activities in which the students are involved.

WORK SAMPLINGS

For detailed analysis of an individual's development, it is very beneficial to keep periodic samples of the child's work, which provide examples of growth in a child's sense of story and the use of different genres of writing. In addition, documentation is provided that reveals student progress, which may include the development of mechanical and refinement skills such as spelling, handwriting, punctuation, and grammar conventions. In addition, tape recordings of children's language while dictating, dramatizing, or storytelling

◀ Children collaborate on a project.

show evidence of growth in language development (Heald-Taylor, 1989) (see Figure 11.4). Taking samples of writing early in the year provides a base point for determination of individual growth.

A close look at Vincent's work (Figure 11.4) shows his progress as a writer from September through November. Such samples document to the child and the parents the progress the student is making in literacy development. Sometimes children's writings document nationally significant news from the local perspective. Note that Vincent wrote about the San Francisco earthquake of 1989, a mammoth earthquake measuring 7.1 that collapsed the Bay Bridge. Was Vincent "shaken"? Notice that he took an opinion poll in his classroom (Figure 11.4), and that he "liked" the earthquake!

HOLISTIC SCORING OF WRITING

The emphasis on process writing has led to holistic evaluation criteria for student writing. The holistic approach purports that writing is an evolving process and that samples of writing taken under testing situations should be viewed as first drafts. Consequently, the criteria focus on the whole, or message conveyed by a writer.

Many states evaluate students' writing with holistic tests on an annual basis. Holistic scoring is based on the total piece of writing and evaluates in terms of how organized the essay is and how appropriately the student responds to the purpose and audience of a given writing situation.

FIGURE 11.4A ▶ VINCENT—SEPTEMBER

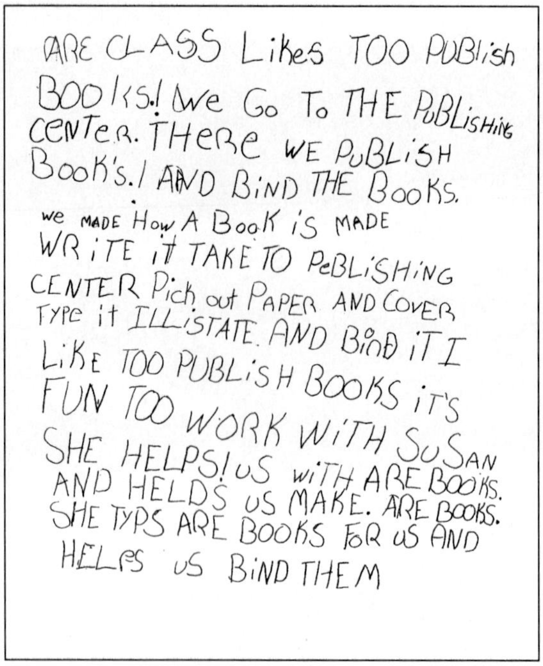

VINCENT—OCTOBER ◀ FIGURE 11.4B

ERTHQUAKE! IN OUR CLASS
CLASS ONE BOOK FELL OFF THE
SHEL iN ARE HOUSE MOST OF
ARE CHINA BROKE AND ALLOT
GLASS BROKE'S MY MOM SCREAM-
ED BECAUSE THiNGS WER
FLYiNG EVERY WERE MY HAMSTER
TRiED TO SLEEP THROugh it Its
SCaRy When a earThQuake HAPPens
it is scary. SOME PEOPLE DieD iN THiS
one OCTOBER i7 19-89 SeVeN PoiNT ONE
THE BAY BRHGE. CIAPEST DiD
YOu LiKE THE earTHQUAKE

YES	MAYBE	NO C9 HOA
VINCENT MATTHeW MAX	PHiLiP ReBeKAh	Phamd veronica B. DAVID HOH etiennekiAK Otto

VINCENT—NOVEMBER ◀ FIGURE 11.4C

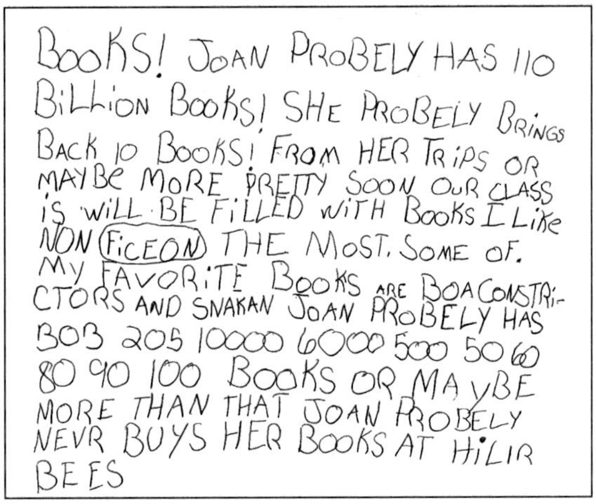

BOOKS! JOAN PROBELY HAS 110
BiLLiON Books! SHE PROBELY BRiNGS
BACK 10 BOOKS! FROM HER TRips OR
MAYBE MORE PRETTY SOON OuR CLASS
is WiLL BE FiLLED WiTH Books I LiKe
NON (FiCEON) THE MOST. SOME OF.
MY FAVORiTE Books ARE BOA CONSTRi-
CTORS AND SNAKAN JOAN PROBELY HAS
BOB 205 10000 6000 500 50 60
80 90 100 BOOKS OR MAyBE
MORE THAN THAT JOAN PROBELY
NEVR BUYS HER BOOKS AT HiLiR
BEES

For example, the Texas Education Agency (1989) reports "since the responses elicited are first-draft compositions, problems with writing mechanics, such as punctuation and spelling, are considered only if they are so serious that they interfere with the communication of the writer's ideas" (p. 16). In a negative vein, the test requires writers to write from an "idea prompt," denying personal choice of a writing topic. The idea prompt may ask for students to write in a persuasive, informative, or expressive mode.

In holistic scoring, each composition is scored independently by two trained readers who assign the paper a score of 1 to 4. If the two scores do not match, the paper is given to a third reader, who also evaluates the response independently. If the third score matches one of the previously assigned scores, this matched score becomes the paper's score. If the third score does not match either of the other two, the paper is given to a fourth scorer for resolution.

Measurements of writing on tests reflect a new style of literacy required of today's students. Meaning-centered programs prepare students for this style of writing as well as other more practical, relevant, or creative styles. In states where students' writing is scored with holistic criteria, it is important to provide occasional opportunities for writing in the genre under which they will be tested. Good writers should do well on tests scored holistically, but they do need to know how specific such tests are in the prompts they use. Students should also know that the evaluators are looking for organization and clear communication when they score the test, not just creativity.

ASSESSMENT THROUGH STUDENT SELF-EVALUATION

The greatest goal of meaning-centered classrooms is for students to take charge of their own learning and to become responsible for their own progress (Hansen, 1989; Newman, 1990). When students become responsible for their own learning, they should also become actively involved in the evaluative process. The teacher's role changes from being a judge to being an intellectual agitator. Teachers help students to ask themselves questions: "Do I really understand this?" "How does this relate to what I learned yesterday?" "What can I do to make sure I do better next time?"

Perhaps this interaction is the key difference between evaluation in traditional and meaning-centered classrooms. In the first, evaluation is viewed as something the teacher "does to the students." In the latter, monitoring of literacy growth is viewed as an interaction in which the growth of the students is being evaluated while the learning environment is being monitored and revised to meet the ever-changing needs of the student.

Glasser (1992) lauded the benefits of self-evaluative behavior by stating there are basically two types of people in the world. One group consists of those who are productive, growing, contributing members of society. The second group consists of nonproductive individuals who are actually a detriment to society. The productive group is actively engaged in self-evaluating, reflecting on their self-evaluation, making decisions such as goals, plans of action, or corrective behavior based on their reflections, and then moving forward in a growth cycle. In contrast, the nonproductive group is constantly evaluating others and assigning blame to others for their own lack of success.

It is critical that we look at our evaluative system and determine if we are providing opportunities for children to participate in the assessment process by engaging in self-evaluative behavior. Children must not feel that evaluation is something "done to them" for the purpose of finding deficits.

This all-too-familiar model of assessment has been termed "teacher as examiner" (Britton, Burgess, Marin, McLeod, & Rosen, 1975) or what Glasser (1992) referred to as the "boss" mentality in which one is dependent on someone else to determine if a job is completed to satisfaction. This is probably the method of assessment that most of us were subjected to during our elementary and secondary school careers. An assignment was given, we completed it, turned it in, and then waited with anxiety for the teacher to "grade" it. If we were successful, we were given a good grade—if unsuccessful a poor one. If a poor grade was received, there was little or no opportunity for dialogue concerning the strengths and weaknesses of the assignment or opportunity to learn from mistakes and revise and resubmit. In essence, that assignment was a "done deal" when it was returned with a grade, and we moved on to the next task, hoping we would improve and "do what the teacher wanted."

◀ THE BOOK MAKERS

TOMIE DEPAOLA

1. Which book of yours has given you the greatest pleasure?

My greatest pleasure has come from writing those books which are autobiographical, like *The Art Lesson* and *Tom*. In those types of books, I try to connect with the feelings of what went on in my own life and translate those feelings into art. Then I try to make the test as "bare bones" as possible.

2. Which book has surprised you most in terms of its public reception?

I was surprised at first at the public reception to the character of Strega Nona, who now appears in five of my books. I think her popularity can be attributed to the fact that she's the archetypal grandmother.

3. What would you like people to remember about your work?

I want people to remember that my books were full of hope.

4. What impact do you hope your work will have on children?

As a child, I loved to read. I want my books to invite children to become readers and book lovers. If a child comes to reading and falls in love with books through my work, I'll call myself successful.

Tomie dePaola has brought his distinctive style of illustrating to more than 200 books. He has won numerous awards, including the Caldecott, as well the hearts of children around the world with titles such as *Strega Nona, Now One Foot, Now the Other, Legend of the Bluebonnet, Legend of the Indian Paintbrush, Pancakes for Breakfast,* and *Legend of the Persian Carpet.*

This model of assessment has several drawbacks. As mentioned earlier, it places teacher and students in adversarial roles (Dobbyns & Crawford-Mason, 1991; Glasser, 1992; Graves, 1993; Johnston, 1992). When the teacher is the sole evaluator and the job is to find the errors and deduct points, the collaborative relationship is usurped by an adversarial one. Second, it tends to separate subjects for the goal of evaluation. Tests are given in discrete areas such as spelling, science, social studies, math, writing, and reading. In the real world, solving problems requires the integration and concurrent use of all of one's investigative, literate, and content skills and knowledge (Altwerger & Flores, 1994). When subject areas are artificially divided for the purpose of testing, children are not given the opportunity to develop problem-solving strategies that will serve them in later years.

STUDENT LOG BOOKS

Student log books are records children keep that document the literacy activities they are involved with and the things they are learning. Most important, they allow students to become actively involved in the evaluative process. As teachers strive to move their students toward independence in learning, it is important the students engage in the monitoring of their own growth or self-evaluation. When students participate in this documentation of their language development, they are utilizing crucial metacognitive (knowing what and if you know) skills. As active participants in monitoring their own learning, children quickly become aware that learning is a lifelong activity that is not dependent on another person such as a teacher. While student log books are valuable ways for children to record information concerning their literacy activities, they provide a valuable format for teacher and student interaction when they both make comments in the log book. As dialogue occurs, progress is seen from the eyes of both teacher and student. In many instances, an interactive log book becomes a method of self-evaluation for the teacher as well as the student (Figure 11.5). Note that Vi Nguyen, a second grader, has decided to "edit" his own writing by circling words he wishes to "check the spelling on."

ASSESSMENT THROUGH PORTFOLIOS

During this decade, there has been a call for alternative methods of assessment that allow student input and are part of the ongoing instructional environment (Harp, 1991; Palinscar & Brown, 1986; Slavin, 1983; Wolf, Bixby, Glenn, & Gardner, 1991). The use of portfolio assessment has been one response to this call. When portfolio assessment is incorporated, children have opportunities to become an integral part of the process of evaluation as they participate in decision making concerning the ongoing documentation of and reflection on their work (Gardner, 1991; Tierney, Carter, & Desai, 1991; Valencia, 1990; Valencia, McGinley, & Pearson, 1990). Student and teacher dialogue becomes an integral part of the assessment process as both child and instructor collaborate and cooperate to determine the contents of the portfolio and then examine and reflect on those contents (Calfee & Perfumo, 1993).

STUDENT LOG OF A SECOND-GRADE VIETNAMESE STUDENT ◀ FIGURE 11.5

WHAT IS A PORTFOLIO?

The word *portfolio* traces its origin from the Latin verb *portare,* which means to carry, and the Latin noun *foglio,* which means sheets or leaves or paper. The concept of a portfolio to provide information concerning the strengths and skills of a person is a familiar notion in the business and art worlds. Artists have prepared portfolios that best display their diverse talents and strengths, and executives have compiled portfolios representing their skills and successful projects.

In education, definitions abound for portfolios: collections of children's work for the purpose of demonstrating progress (Sampson, Allen, & Sampson, 1991); a collection of student's work over time that shows development in a particular subject area which is utilized as a vehicle for engaging students in the process of self-evaluation and goal setting (Clemmons, Laase, Cooper, Areglado, & Dill, 1993); a collection of all different kinds of things that provide a history of one's learning (Graves & Sunstein, 1992); documentation that paints a portrait of one as a reader, writer, learner, and literate individual (Hansen, 1992); a systematic, purposeful, and meaningful collection of students' works in one or more subject areas (DeFina, 1992, p. 13); collection of students' writing and other materials, reflecting student reading and thinking as much as writing (Farr & Tone, 1994, p. 2).

So, exactly what is a portfolio? The good news is there is not one right answer. Just as definitions vary, remember that one of the strengths of portfolio assessment is that there is not a predetermined format. The possibilities for portfolios are endless (Graves & Sunstein, 1992). Much of the value of portfolio assessment is derived from the collaborative process in which the student and teacher work together to select and reflect on work to be included in the portfolio, rather than the display of the final product (Gardner, 1991; Hansen, 1992; Tierney, Carter, & Desai, 1991; Valencia, 1990; Valencia, McGinley, & Pearson, 1990). Portfolio assessment centers on the evaluative process as a documentation of the strength, growth, and accomplishments of a student rather than emphasizing the deficiencies. Therefore, the challenge for teachers and students is to find the format that best "paints a picture" of the literate growth of the students in the classroom while involving students in the continual process of self-evaluative reflection on their work and setting goals for growth (Clemmons, Laase, Cooper, Areglado, & Dill, 1993; Tierney, Carter, & Desai, 1991).

The portfolio process must include the opportunity for students to reflect on their work, make self-evaluative judgments, and set goals for future development. Both theory and research have advised that humans function at their optimal levels of performance if they are striving toward goals which they have been involved in determining and are meaningful to them (Glasser, 1992; McCombs, 1991). This process of goal setting occurs only when one has had the opportunity to self-evaluate and reflect on strengths and areas that need growth. Students know more about their own talents and abilities than anyone else; therefore, their judgment should be valued and sought as part of the assessment process (Goodman, 1989; Hansen, 1992; Valencia, Hiebert, & Afflerbach, 1994).

However, assessment must not be confined to a review of one's work. Students make movement toward becoming independent lifelong learners when they have the opportunity to determine goals based on reflective review. As stated by Gardner, reflection means being able to say," What am I doing? Why am I doing it? What am I trying to achieve? Am I being successful? How can I revise my performance in a desirable way?" (Gardner, quoted in Brandt, 1988, p. 32). Only when students are involved in this process of reflective self-assessment does assessment become part of the ongoing learning environment and students are doing far more than acquiring facts—they are *learning how to learn* (Wiggins, 1993).

WHAT'S IN A PORTFOLIO?

The vital ingredients to successful portfolio evaluation in classrooms, then, are the components of *voice* and *choice*. Teachers and students must remember that portfolios should first enhance the student's understanding of his or her learning, and the student obtains ownership and optimal benefit from participating in portfolio assessment when she or he assumes the role of active participant in the process. This student participation includes involvement in choosing what makes up the portfolio and reflecting on and responding to the contents. As this process occurs, teachers can survey the individual growth framework of each student through conferences concerning the components of the portfolio and the student's responses, reactions, and goals (Farr & Tone, 1994; Graves & Sunstein, 1992; Murphy & Smith, 1991; Pils, 1991; Tierney, Carter, & Desai, 1991).

Therefore, the contents of a portfolio vary. Children should have the opportunity to utilize a variety of sign systems (Harste, 1993) such as music, art, drama, writing, and reading to demonstrate their knowledge and skill as literate individuals. Some of the items that can be included in a portfolio include the following:

1. Baseline samples of writing and reading
2. Student's reading log and reactions/responses
3. Student's learning log entries
4. Writing samples such as: both edited text with all drafts attached and unedited text of stories (different genres), poems, raps, songs, retellings, letters, essays and reports, story spin-offs, interviews, and posters
5. Attitude surveys
6. Self-reflective notes
7. Records of portfolio conference
8. Student-composed list of goals and progress of accomplishment/teacher input added at conference
9. Student-composed list of strengths or what student has learned/teacher input added at conference
10. Art projects with attached notes
11. Evidence of literate activity from outside class
12. Audiotape of child reading a favorite text with photocopy of text
13. Audiotape of child reading an unfamiliar text with photocopy of text
14. Audiotape of retelling of a story
15. Projects from thematic units
16. Table of contents
17. Explanation of portfolio contents and organization
18. Comments about portfolio from teacher, peers, parents/guardians, visitors to classroom

The teacher may feel that all students should have specific items in their portfolios, such as specific baseline data or a completed writing piece with all of the rough drafts attached. Teacher-determined "external" criteria may be established for this purpose. However, in order for the portfolio process to be most effective, it is critical that students be given an opportunity to develop "internal criteria" by selecting certain pieces for inclusion into their portfolios and giving their reasons for the selection (Rief, 1990). When students have the opportunity to self-select pieces and reflect on them, they give us a view of who they think they are as readers and writers.

PORTFOLIO CONFERENCES

Portfolio conferences are opportunities for teacher and student dialogue, collaboration, and goal setting concerning the contents of the portfolio and the processes that were involved in producing the contents and selecting them for inclusion in the portfolio. This is in marked contrast to the dominant pattern of interaction between students and teacher that "consists of the following moves: the teacher solicits a student to answer a question; the teacher listens to the student's response; and the teacher evaluates or modifies the student's response" (Alvermann & Moore, 1991, p. 969). As students reflect on and evaluate their learning with their teacher, their role in the instructional environment is valued. Sample questions that facilitate a discussion of this type include the following:

How did you organize your portfolio?

Why did you choose this piece of writing? or What makes this piece of writing best show your strengths? Or growth?

What are its strong points?

What did you struggle with?

What did you learn from this experience?

How have you progressed as a reader?

What shows this?

How have you progressed as a writer?

What goals have you reached?

What documents this?

What does this show about you as a learner/reader/writer?

Tell me more about how you did this.

What makes this your best piece?

How did you go about writing it?

What problems did you experience?

How did you overcome them?

What makes this best piece different from your worst piece?

What are you doing as a reader/writer that you were not doing before?

What documents this?

What are you able to do as a reader/writer that you were not able to do before?

What shows this?

In what ways are your reading and writing connected?

How has growth in one affected the other?

How have you met your reading/writing goals?

What are your reading/writing goals for the next semester?

How do you plan to meet them?

The questions just listed are only a sampling of the types of questions that might be appropriate for portfolio conferences in your classroom, and obviously you would select only a few of the questions for one conference. Remember, the conference is a time for *student* reflection on writing and reading progress during the semester and for interactive dialogue that allows the teacher to learn about the student as a reader, writer, and literate individual. Therefore, *both* student and teacher should review goals and determine the progress that has been made, and then collaboration can occur on the revision and extension of the goals and on a plan for meeting them. During this cooperative experience with the teacher it is crucial to place the student in the role of articulating the self-evaluative process and making educational decisions based on that self-evaluation. Through this process, the student's learning is anchored and extended. As stated by Glasser (1992, p. 202), "Without detailed self-evaluation followed by more learning based on that evaluation, little of permanent value will be learned and the purpose of education—to improve the quality of our lives—will be defeated."

The portfolio conference should be documented and included in the portfolio for future reference. A sheet containing the date and highlights of the conference such as student comments or notes, teacher comments or notes, and determination of future goals can be designed to reflect the needs of teacher and student(s). When conferencing, student and teacher can look at the record of the last conference to determine progress toward goals. Figure 11.6 shows a sample of a portfolio conference record form. Note the signature line for both student and teacher. This signifies that both participated in the conference and are aware of the observations made by each other.

REPORT CARDS

Classroom teachers place a priority on communication with parents. They talk with them by phone, invite them to sessions to explain process-centered instruction, and send letters and notes home. Teachers who use portfolios have clear communication with parents and children concerning the educational progress of the children. However, for many parents, the report card is the major signpost that keeps them informed about how their children are doing in school. Parents may glance at daily work children bring home from school, but report cards are carefully scrutinized.

Unfortunately, the report cards issued by most schools do not reflect the latest research findings and thinking concerning what's important in learning. Thus most report cards typically identify bits and pieces of the language arts and present a fragmented picture of children's literacy development.

Conflicts arise when teachers and school districts do not agree on the variables that reflect literacy growth. Report cards in such schools may readily accommodate letter or number grades, but limit descriptive data or even teacher comments. Teachers become frustrated when their classroom observations of students' literacy growth are overlooked and they are unable to share their knowledge about students (Afflerbach, Norton, & Johnston, 1989).

FIGURE 11.6 ▶   **PORTFOLIO CONFERENCE RECORD FORM**

PORTFOLIO CONFERENCE RECORD

date
_____

Student's Observations	Teacher's Observations	Goals
Progress toward goals	Progress toward goals	
Strengths	Strengths	
What I learned	Learning demonstrated	
Other observations	Other observations	

_____   _____
          student signature   teacher signature

Fortunately, this is a decade of change in education. Many districts simply use traditional report cards because they have not been presented with options. Informed teachers can bring about changes in report card formats by proposing alternate formats to the appropriate decision makers in a district. Some districts require a combination of the traditional and new (Figure 11.7); other districts are ready to move entirely to report cards that more completely reflect children's academic growth (Figure 11.8). Still other districts have an open format for report cards (Figure 11.9), providing a comfortable interchange of information in note form.

In situations where improvements in report card formats are not possible, teachers may convey information similar to the data listed in Figure 11.9 through letters to the parents and written comments on children's work.

EVALUATING THE MEANING-CENTERED CLASSROOM

Evaluation doesn't end with the students. We must remember that when we point one finger at the students, three fingers are pointing back at us! Therefore, in order for a meaning-centered curriculum to evolve, the teacher must be as actively involved in self-evaluation as in student evaluation. Educators

REPORT OF PUPIL'S PROGRESS

Pupil _____

School _____

Teacher _____

Principal _____

TRANSFERRED TO:

_____ School

Teacher _____

Principal _____

TO PARENTS:

This report card is sent to you four times each year at the conclusion of each grading period. A parent-teacher conference is held the first semester of each year. You are encouraged to initiate additional conferences whenever a need arises.

When a home and school are communicating and supporting each other, quality education can take place for your child. I appreciate your support of your child and school.

Student _____

PARENTS COMMENTS

FIRST QUARTER

_____
Parent's Signature

☐ Conference Requested

SECOND QUARTER

_____
Parent's Signature

☐ Conference Requested

THIRD QUARTER

_____
Parent's Signature

☐ Conference Requested

FOURTH QUARTER

ASSIGNMENT:

Math Level

Reading Level

Student _____

TEACHER COMMENTS

FIRST QUARTER

☐ Conference Requested

SECOND QUARTER

☐ Conference Requested

THIRD QUARTER

☐ Conference Requested

FOURTH QUARTER

FIGURE 11.7 ▶
(cont.)

EXPLANATION OF SYMBOLS

◇ below grade level   + Outstanding
☆ on grade level   ✓ Satisfactory
△ above grade level   – Unsatisfactory

EXPLANATION OF PROGRESS

E - Student is making outstanding progress and needs a minimum of teacher direction on independent activities and is involved in teacher-assigned enrichment activities.

V - Student is making very good progress and needs a minimum of teacher direction on independent activities.

S - Student is making satisfactory progress and needs teacher help on independent activities and/or needs some skills to be retaught.

N - Student is placed at the proper level of instruction and is making progress but has not mastered needed skills for that level.

READING	1	2	3	4
LEVEL				
PROGRESS				
EFFORT				
Applies reading strategies				
Reads independently				
Makes choices about reading material				
Responds to literature				
Displays awareness of authors and literacy forms				

WRITING	1	2	3	4
PROGRESS				
EFFORT				
Uses writing process and other writing strategies				
Writes to learn				
Uses varied print formats				
Shares writing with classmates				
Proofreads to locate/correct mechanical errors				

SPELLING	1	2	3	4
PROGRESS				
EFFORT				
Uses invented spellings for unfamiliar words				
Applies spelling strategies				
Uses learned spellings in writings				

LANGUAGE	1	2	3	4
PROGRESS				
EFFORT				
Uses appropriate grammatical constructions				
Applies language skills in reading/writing				
Participates in oral language activities				

HANDWRITING	1	2	3	4
PROGRESS				
EFFORT				
Prints/writes fluently and legibly				

MATH	1	2	3	4
LEVEL				
PROGRESS				
EFFORT				
Displays understanding of numerical concepts				
Applies mathematical concepts to solve word problems				
Uses number facts, basic operations, and problem-solving strategies in computation				

SOCIAL STUDIES	1	2	3	4
PROGRESS				
EFFORT				
Displays understanding of history, geography government, and economic systems appropriate to grade level				
Uses maps, globes, charts, time lines, and graphs in learning about the world				
Displays knowledge of concepts through reading and writing				

SCIENCE	1	2	3	4
PROGRESS				
EFFORT				
Displays understanding of grade appropriate concepts in the biological, earth, and physical sciences				
Uses experiments to increase understanding of scientific concepts				
Displays knowledge of concepts through reading and writing				

	1	2	3	4
P.E.				
Music				
Art				

PERSONAL GROWTH

YOUR CHILD:	1	2	3	4
Listens and follows directions				
Completes work on time				
Does careful work				
Works independently when he should				
Takes care of books and supplies				
Can control talking				
Keeps work areas neat and orderly				
Respects rights of others				
Respects property of others				
Is polite in speech and manner				
Gets along well with others				
Has necessary supplies				
Displays positive attitude toward school				

ATTENDANCE

	1	2	3	4
Days Present				
Days Absent				
Days Tardy				

HOLISTIC REPORT CARD FORMAT ◀ FIGURE 11.8

Stratham Memorial School
Stratham, New Hampshire

PROGRESS REPORT

Name _____

Grade _____ September,19 _____ to June, 19 _____

Teacher _____

PHILOSOPHY

In student-centered classrooms, children are encouraged to explore, manipulate objects, question, take risks, work cooperatively with others, think, speak, trust, and feel. The teacher's role is to guide the child's emerging identity, to clarify appropriate social norms, and to create learning experiences which motivate and provide structure. Individual progress is measured within this context. The purpose of this report is to give your child and you a picture of his/her performance and development.

ATTENDANCE

	1	2	3	4
Days Absent				
Days Tardy				
Times Dismissed				

ENVIRONMENT
(Science and Social Studies)

	1	2	3	4
Contributes to classroom discussions and activities				
Classifies and records information				
Questions and investigates concepts				
Demonstrates an understanding of new facts and concepts				

COMMENTS:

WORK HABITS

	1	2	3	4
I am a good listener				
I follow directions				
I work independently				
I organize time and materials				
I work carefully and accurately				
I work neatly and legibly when appropriate				
I apply spelling strategies				
I complete work on time				

SOCIAL DEVELOPMENT

I demonstrate self-confidence				
I demonstrate verbal control				
I demonstrate physical control				
I accept correction				
I work cooperatively in a group				
I respect the rights and property of others				
I obey classroom and school rules				

My program also includes art, enrichment, library, physical education, and music.

FIGURE 11.8 ▶
(cont.)

E – Excellent Progress
W – Working Toward; Making Progress

N/P – Not Progressing as Expected
N/E – Not Evaluated at this Time

READING

	1	2	3	4
Initiates own reading				
Chooses reading materials with confidence				
Requests meaningful help in reading				
Actively participates in reading discussion groups				
Shares own reading				
Writes effective journal responses to literature				
Uses appropriate comprehension strategies to develop meaning				
Uses appropriate print cues to develop meaning				
Reads materials developed for his/her grade level				

COMMENTS:

WRITING

	1	2	3	4
Initiates own writing				
Chooses writing topics with confidence				
Requests meaningful help in writing				
Actively participates in writing conferences				
Shares own writing				
Produces meaningful writing				
Revises ideas when appropriate				
Edits when appropriate (Mechanics)				

MATHEMATICS

Note: Only areas focused on each quarter will be marked.

	1	2	3	4
Is developing concepts of:				
Patterns				
Place Value				
Problem Solving				
Graphing and Mapping				
Measurement				
Geometry				
Fractions				
Time and Money				
Computes in:				
Addition				
Subtraction				
Multiplication				
Division				

SUDBURY PUBLIC SCHOOLS
SUDBURY, MASSACHUSETTS

Dear Parents:

This report communicates as clearly as possible your child's performance in school. Our major goal in educating Sudbury's children is to help produce resourceful, thoughtful, and creative adults. Our desire is to foster self-confidence in our students and assist them in developing a positive attitude about themselves and learning to work for success after accepting some failures. This report, based on the growth and development of your child, reflects performance in accordance with ability.

Dr. Henry W. DeRusha, Jr.
Superintendent of Schools

DEVELOPMENTAL ASSESSMENT

Pupil _____

Teacher _____Grade ____1____

School _____

Date _____ Academic Year_____

FIGURE 11.9 ▶
   (cont.)

SOCIAL/EMOTIONAL: _____

_____

_____

_____

ACADEMIC: _____

   Reading: _____

   _____

   _____

   Writing: _____

   _____

   _____

   Math: _____

   _____

   _____

STRENGTHS: _____

_____

CONCERNS: _____

_____

_____

SUGGESTIONS: _____

_____

_____

PARENT COMMENTS: _____

_____

_____

Participants' Signatures: _____

should be constantly discovering how children learn and how to be most effective in guiding their learning. Teachers who engage in reflective self-evaluation are in a better position to implement an evaluative system in their classrooms that provides students opportunities for reflective self-evaluation.

How can you identify a meaning-centered classroom? Excited students and enthusiastic teachers are two variables. However, to be more objective, classrooms may be examined and compared with the goals of the Literacy Transaction Model defined in Chapter 1. That curriculum model involves three aspects or strands that should be present in the classroom environment and interactions:

1. **Research indicates that the real language of the learners should be valued by the teacher and used in building students' skills for communication.**

PATHWAYS TO SELF-EXPRESSION

- Students participate freely and comfortably in their home-rooted language.

- The real language of students is used as part of the room environment in reading charts, posters, talking murals, and books they have written and published.

- Students are free from the fear of using incorrect language to express themselves.

- Space and time are provided for students to communicate their ideas through many arts-and-crafts media and through dramatization, puppets, rhythmic activities, and discussions.

- Recordings of students' own language are included in the listening activities.

◀ **Meaning-centered classrooms are places for laughter, as well as literacy.**

- Edited and unedited stories and poems written by the students are part of the oral reading program.

2. Research indicates that students' language is influenced by the language and ideas of other people.

PATHWAYS TO IMPRESSION

- Many books are available for recreational reading, browsing, locating information, and improving reading skills.

- Books written and published by the students are a part of the classroom library.

- Computers and videos bring students who are not necessarily good readers in contact with the language and ideas of others.

- Books with records and/or tapes of the printed text are available to students to provide models of good reading and enjoyment of the ideas of others without their having to be good readers.

- Oral language activities include language patterns of authors that may not be typical of the home-rooted language of the learners.

- Art prints, musical compositions, sculpture, and other creative products are available for individual interpretation.

- Students have opportunities and resources for research on topics of interest.

3. Research indicates that skills, or conventions of language, are learned in the process of actual reading and writing.

PATHWAYS TO CONVENTIONS

- Students fine-tune their writing abilities with repeated opportunities for writing.

- Speech-to-print relations are discussed in informal and friendly ways that permit the natural internalization of a phonetic system for one's own dialect.

- Traditional skills such as sequencing are learned in the context of real literacy activities like Reader's Theater, not by isolated study.

- The classroom instructional environment reflects an emphasis on the increase in vocabularies of nouns, verbs, adjectives, and adverbs.

- Students participate in editing manuscripts for publication of their stories and poems.

Figure 11.10 is a scale for rating levels of implementation of meaning-centered instruction. Rating scales provide scores that can be interpreted in light of the goals for the program. The scale may be used by teachers for self-evaluation, by a principal or supervisor for external evaluation, or for cooperative evaluation through conferences that compare and contrast teacher self-evaluation with evaluation by an observer using the rating scale.

To date, use of the scale indicates that students in classrooms where teachers score highest are classrooms where students score highest on reading

CHECKLIST FOR ELEMENTARY LEARNING ENVIRONMENT   ◄ FIGURE 11.10
(cont.)

CHECK LIST FOR ELEMENTARY LEARNING ENVIRONMENT

This check list is to be used in rating the extent to which any learning environment has visible evidence that the three strands of a meaning-centered curriculum are being implemented. It does not deal with the nonvisible aspects of a program.

Tentative conclusions from the use of this rating scale indicate that children who live and learn in an environment with a rating above 3.0 score higher on reading achievement tests than those in classrooms with lower scores.

THE SCORING SCALE
0—*Does not exist* at the time of the observation
1—*Present* but on a restricted bases—by permission only or after completion of "regular work"
2—*Present during observation period* but little or no evidence as a continuing part of the program
3—*Present during observation* with visible evidence that the condition is a continuing part of the program
4—*Superior performance of part observed* and/or visible evidence that the condition is an essential part of the program

OBSERVATION TIME
Minimum of 30 minutes recommended for external evaluation. No time limit for self-evaluation

SUMMARY

Mean score Strand One	
Mean score Strand Two	
Mean score Strand Three	
TOTAL Mean scores divided by 3	

INTERPRETATION

The closer the total mean score is to 4.00, the nearer the classroom environment is to satisfying basic requirements for a meaning-centered curriculum.

Scores below 3.00 reflect a need for improvement in communication opportunities that are required of a meaning-centered curriculum.

---

achievement as judged by standardized tests. The students in a high-scoring environment discover literacy in various places and forms in the classroom. If they fail to comprehend in one setting, another setting or opportunity is available. The interrelations of language and an environment that promotes literacy development are illustrated in Figure 11.11 (see page 324).

SUMMARY

Traditional evaluation has been external—mandated outside the classroom, administered with instruments that may not reflect the instructional

FIGURE 11.10 ▶
    (cont.)

STRAND ONE

SELF-EXPRESSION

MAJOR IDEA
This strand emphasizes the real language of the learners as basic to communication skill development.

	0	1	2	3	4
Superior performance of part observed. Essential part of program					
Present during observation. Continuing part of program					
Present during observation. Not a continuing part					
Present but on a restricted basis					
Does not exist at time of observation					

ITEMS TO BE CHECKED

1. Is there obvious opportunity for each child to participate comfortably with home-rooted language in both talking and writing?
2. Is the real language of the children used as a part of the room environment?
3. Are children free from the fear of using incorrect language?
4. Is space and time provided for children to express their ideas with many media?
5. Do children have opportunity to listen to their own language on tapes and/or through oral reading of their own stories and poems?
6. Is space and time provided for children to participate in puppetry, pantomime, and dramatization?
7. Is there opportunity for children to respond rhythmically to music?
8. Do children produce original manuscripts of poems and stories that are useful in the reading program of the classroom?

Raw score totals
TOTAL RAW SCORE
Mean score (raw score divided by 8)

STRAND TWO

IMPRESSION

MAJOR IDEA
This strand emphasizes the influence of the language and ideas of many people on the personal language of children.

	0	1	2	3	4
Superior performance of part observed. Essential part of program					
Present during observation. Continuing part of program					
Present during observation. Not a continuing part					
Present but on a restricted basis					
Does not exist at time of observation					

ITEMS TO BE CHECKED

1. Are many types of books available for browsing and reading—recreation, information, reading skill development, own publications?
2. Are films and filmstrips used to bring children in contact with the language and ideas of others?
3. Do children have access to records and tapes that accompany books?
4. Do children have opportunities to repeat words, phrases, and sentences of other authors as they listen to reading of stories and poems that are different from home-rooted language?
5. Do children have opportunities to add to the ideas of others as they listen to and read stories and poems?
6. Are art prints, musical compositions, photographs, and other creative materials available for personal interpretation?
7. Is choral reading a part of the reading program that brings children in contact with language and ideas of others without requiring excellent reading skills?
8. Do children have the opportunity to research on topics of interest and relate findings to their personal questions and observations?

Raw score totals
TOTAL RAW SCORE
Mean score (raw score divided by 8)

◀ **FIGURE 11.10**
(cont.)

STRAND THREE
CONVENTIONS

MAJOR IDEA
This strand emphasizes an
understanding of how lan-
guage works for individ-
uals.

	0	1	2	3	4
Superior performance of part observed. Essential part of program					
Present during observation. Continuing part of program					
Present during observation. Not a continuing part					
Present but on a restricted basis					
Does not exist at time of observation					

ITEMS TO BE CHECKED

1. Are children given opportunities to write using natural or invented spellings?
2. Do students have the opportunity to share knowledge of conventions by collaborating on work?
3. Do children have conversational abilities to discuss topics such as names of letters, words, sentences, and spelling?
4. Is there evidence that children are using vocabularies of the form-class words (nouns, verbs, adjectives, and adverbs) as a part of the planned program for extending language?
5. Is there opportunity for the development of a high-imagery, descriptive vocabulary?
6. Are skills explored within the context of meaningful activities?
7. Do children participate in editing manuscripts for publication?
8. Do children have opportunities to respond to meanings in their environment not represented by symbol systems—weather, color, shape, emotions, motion, sound, size, texture, etc?

Raw score totals
TOTAL RAW SCORE
Mean score (raw score divided by 8)

program's philosophy, and yielding results that are meaningless for the day-to-day instruction of the students.

Conversely, assessment in meaning-centered classrooms is practical and relevant. Responsibility is shared between student and teacher; the teacher documents student literacy growth with checklists, anecdotal records, interaction, and analysis. Students share in their own assessment by keeping a portfolio of their work and choosing pieces of work they wish to have evaluated. Teachers are constantly involved in self-evaluation in meaning-centered classrooms, constantly seeking better ways of leading their students to literacy. The evaluation includes the entire learning environment as teachers step back and examine their classrooms to see if they indeed are havens for developing authors, artists, and learners.

PATHWAYS TO AUTHENTIC ASSESSMENT

The teacher:

▶ recognizes the limitations of standardized tests.

▶ observes students as they interact with literacy tasks.

FIGURE 11.11 ▶ LANGUAGE ENVIRONMENT AND LITERACY

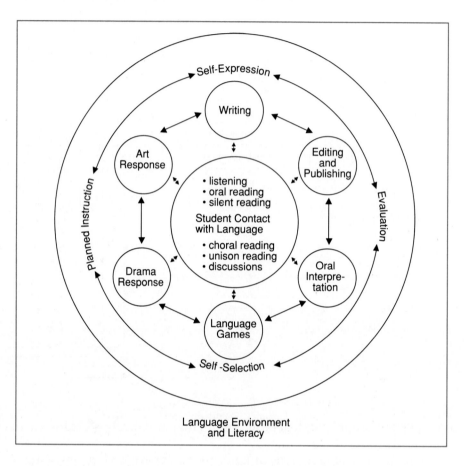

Language Environment
and Literacy

▶ records student progress with anecdotal records and checklists.

▶ helps children present their learning through portfolios.

▶ functions as a coach, not a "fixer."

▶ understands the nature of holistic scoring of essays.

▶ uses portfolios as a means of showcasing student accomplishments.

▶ evaluates teacher learning as well as student learning.

▶ evaluates classroom atmosphere and organization on a regular basis.

▶ reports student progress to parents in a relevant manner.

PART

▶5

FOUNDATIONS
OF READING

12 PATHWAYS TO READING: THE PROCESS

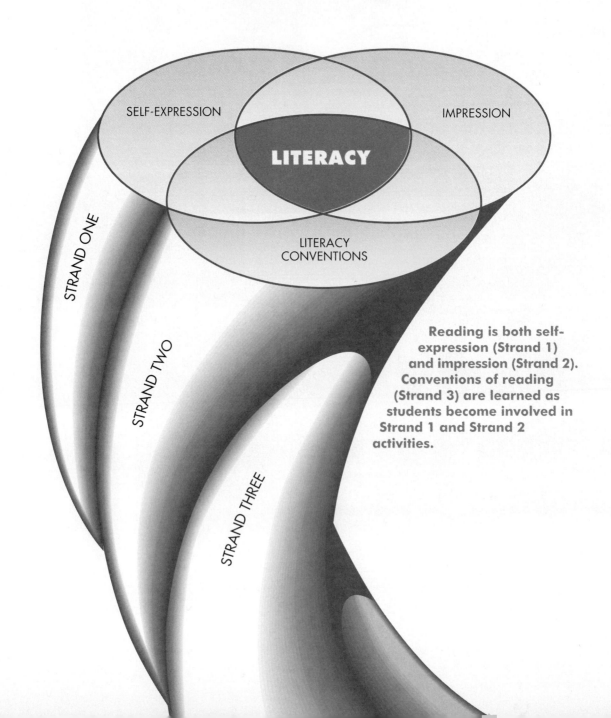

SELF-EXPRESSION

IMPRESSION

LITERACY

LITERACY CONVENTIONS

STRAND ONE

STRAND TWO

STRAND THREE

Reading is both self-expression (Strand 1) and impression (Strand 2). Conventions of reading (Strand 3) are learned as students become involved in Strand 1 and Strand 2 activities.

PATHWAYS TO PONDER

....

▶ **HOW IS READING A TRANSACTION ?**
....

▶ **HOW DO READERS USE THE THREE CUEING SYSTEMS IN THE READING TRANSACTION?**
....

▶ **WHEN ARE MISCUES A SIGN OF COMPREHENSION?**
....

▶ **WHAT IS THE IMPORTANCE OF SCHEMA THEORY TO THE CLASSROOM TEACHER?**
....

I n this chapter on the reading process, we explore what reading is and how it happens. You'll come away with an appreciation for the complexity of the reading process. But you'll also come away confident that children have within themselves all that is necessary to become good readers.

Reading is exploring and comprehending life. We explore life through listening; we explore life through talking; we explore life through writing. Reading is simply another aspect of our exploration. Without the pillars of language and writing, we could not be readers.

WHAT IS READING?

Reading is a transaction that occurs between human beings and their environments. A great fallacy exists, however. Many take a simplistic and erroneous view that reading is decoding, or constructing meaning from language as represented by graphic symbols.

The literacy transaction is much more involved than simply encoding language. Reading is communication. Before children can comprehend written language, they must first be able to comprehend the feedback their environments provide. They must be able to "read" the faces of people and their emotions. They must be able to comprehend the sounds, actions, smells, and changes of the world that surrounds them. According to Piagetian theory (Piaget, 1959), these life experiences are the very foundation of thinking and comprehending.

Reprinted with special permission of Cowles Syndicate. Inc.

These experiences are what enable children to bring cold silent print to life when they are asked to read from the decontextualized reading exercises that are so common in the early grades. Peter Spencer (1970) terms this environmental reading *primary reading* and states that it is "fundamental to the giving of meaning and significance to the reading of symbols." Thus we can conclude that most children feel a sense of accomplishment in being able to "read" their environment and their experiences. Once that confidence is established, they are ready for the reading of school-type reading activities, or what Spencer (1970) terms reading from "secondary sources." This primary reading should continue as a part of the school program and should form the foundation of instructional activities. It is essential that those children who are slow to read the language represented by alphabetic symbols have repeated opportunities to be affirmed through "primary" reading experiences. Such activities must be important enough in day-by-day operations for children to feel a sense of reading achievement when they are participating. Teachers must demonstrate (Smith, 1985) to the children that they feel such primary reading is an important part of the school curriculum.

THE CHILD'S VIEW OF THE READING PROCESS

Children spend the first years of life experimenting with and manipulating language and print. As we discussed in Chapter 2, this is a time when children come to understand the nature of communication. Thus, when children arrive at school, they already possess vibrant oral language, a strong sense of the syntactic and semantic structures of language, and a rich oral tradition of stories and rhymes (Sampson, Briggs, & Sampson, 1986).

Some children will enter school already reading, and others will be well on their way to becoming readers. Wise teachers will capitalize on the strengths young children have as language users as they begin formal reading instruction. In addition, they will realize that learning to read and learning to become better readers are things children do throughout the school day—not just during the period set aside for "reading."

What do children think reading is? In far too many cases, children view reading as a subject in school or "sounding out words" (Harste, Burke, & Woodward, 1982). They fathom reading as being a mysterious activity in which words appear magically to the reader. They don't understand that reading is related to talking; that reading is simply language which has been preserved with a symbol system.

The pathway to becoming a good reader is made easy when teachers help children understand the link between reading and other communication forms. Of vital importance is the responsibility of the teacher to help children conceptualize and internalize the following truths about self and language.

"I can think about all the experiences I've had in life." Children live in an exciting world. Their minds are filled with past experiences and memories, as well as a world of daydreams and imagination.

"I can talk about what I think about." And talk they do! Children love to talk about their life—ask any kindergarten teacher. Children have no problem translating their thoughts to oral language.

THE POET ▶
PONDERS

THE READER VOICE

She took me to a forest
Full of fairies, elves and trolls.
We watched a hunter's campfire
Burn low to a glow of coals.

We met this kid who was just like
*   me,*
He tried to win a race
And he cried alone in his room at
*   home*
When he finished second place.

I listened as she read each tale
And made each tale my own,
And now my soul still hears her
*   voice,*
Though my body's old and grown.

"What I can talk about or think about, I can communicate to others in many forms." Children become storytellers through writing, or scribbling, as preschoolers. They love to mark paper up with their stories, and are quick to "read" to you the meanings behind their scribbles. They also communicate in other formats—painting, dramatizing, singing. Teachers can also record children's language—through the webbing of brainstorming activities or through taking dictation.

"I can read what I write by myself and what others write for me to read." Children can read what they've written—be it scribbles or be it stories written with invented spellings. And because others write using the same symbol system, the child can read their writing, too.

Children need to know that reading is "talk written down." Yes, it's more than that—writing is usually refined while oral language often is not. But it's very important for children to make the connection between oral and written representations of language. Children need to see the connection or link between their oral language and the written language of others.

THE TEACHER'S VIEW OF THE READING PROCESS

We have just presented our rationale of how we feel children should view the reading/writing process. Now we turn our attention to you, the teacher, as we consider the question "What is reading?" Although we present our views of the reading process, our intent is to show you that the view you hold of the reading process affects what children do as readers in your classroom. You need to think through your feelings about reading. As you do, you will become a better teacher as you trust in your own intuitive feelings about the children you instruct. You'll come to trust more in the transactions children have with reading and writing processes as they engage in meaningful literacy activities. And, you'll rely less on published materials.

THE THREE CUEING SYSTEMS

The reading of printed material such as books, newspapers, and even billboards involves the construction of meaning by the reader. Readers arrive at meaning by using their background knowledge or scriptal information about the topic and by using three basic cueing systems. These cues consist of (1) cue systems within words (graphophones), (2) cue systems within the structure or flow of language (syntax), and (3) cue systems within the person reading the message (semantics) (DeFord, 1985; Goodman, 1985; Goodman, Smith, Meredith, & Goodman, 1988; Smith, 1982). All of these cue systems are influenced by the environment in which they are found and the circumstances of the reading act.

An understanding of these three language systems—graphophonic, syntactic, and semantic—enables the teacher to understand how readers process text as they reconstruct an author's ideas.

GRAPHOPHONIC CUES

The *graphophonic system* consists of the relations that exist between the graphemes a reader encounters in print and the phonemes or sounds of the spoken language. Children internalize these relations naturally as they are exposed to language and reading. Illustrating this process is the example of Michael and Mary Beth Sampson's 3-year-old son Jonathan. When author Jim Trelease from New England visited Jonathan's Texas home, he asked what the dog in the backyard was named. Jonathan replied, "Prince." However, because Texans and New Englanders differ in phoneme pronunciation, Jim Trelease thought Jonathan had said "Fritz." Jim walked into the backyard and called "Here, Fritz, here, Fritz!" "No!" a concerned Jonathan replied, "His name is not Fritz, it's *Prince*. Prr- Prr- Prince!" Jonathan had never received any type of phonics instruction or emphasis on the graphophonic system, yet he was learning language orally and auditorily and was making fine discriminations between speech sounds at age 3.

For Jonathan's fourth birthday he received a copy of Donald Crew's award-winning book *Freight Train*. His interest started with the story being shared. Soon he was chiming in with the reader. Finally, his learning of the relations between phonemes and graphemes was demonstrated as he read the book to his little brother. His added emphasis on the initial phonemes "Fr" and "Tr" was obvious as he read "*f*reight *t*rain!" Jonathan provides a good example of the message communicated throughout this book: Learning moves from whole to part, not part to whole. Thus graphophonic cues are useful to readers and they are internalized by children as they come to understand the English language. Proficient readers, however, rarely rely on graphophonic information alone. Consequently, our emphasis should be on demonstrating

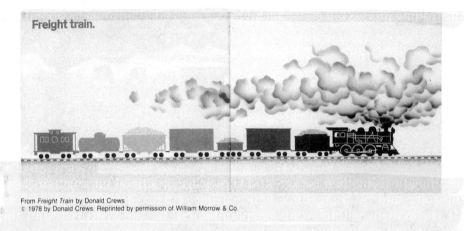

Freight train.

From *Freight Train* by Donald Crews
© 1978 by Donald Crews. Reprinted by permission of William Morrow & Co.

to children the joy and importance of reading—not isolating the study of word parts.

SYNTACTIC CUES

The *syntactic system* consists of the interrelations among words and among sentences based on the grammar or language rules of the speaker or writer. Syntactic knowledge is implicit (see Chapter 10)—the language user may not be able to verbalize grammatical rules, but the mastery of the rules is demonstrated regularly in language use of the person. This cue is very useful in reading. It enables readers to know what part of speech might be used next in a sentence and enables them to finish a sentence someone else has started. All of this is done at the subconscious level—the words just seem to "pop" into one's mind.

Syntactic cues are valuable because they enable children to monitor their reading. When a miscue disrupts the normal flow of language, an "alarm" goes off in the reader's mind and she or he backtracks to find the source of confusion (Goodman, Smith, Meredith, & Goodman, 1988).

Although syntax involves the placement of words into sentences according to grammatical rules, words may still be in the correct grammatical position and yet cause confusion to the reader. Syntactic cues are disrupted when the language flow is artificial or contrived. Researchers have found that children who read material with simple syntax do not read that material as well as they read more complex material which features a natural language flow (DeFord, 1981; Sampson, Briggs, & Sampson, 1986).

SEMANTIC CUES

The *semantic system* is the most basic and valuable of the three cueing systems and involves the relations among language and experiences that establish meaning for a reader. This process occurs as the reader interacts with the ideas presented from the text to construct meaning according to existing schemata. Understanding occurs as prior experiences are brought into play in response to graphic input.

The semantic cueing system enables readers to monitor their reading by demanding that the text make sense. When the text does not elicit understanding, a short circuit occurs and the reader retraces the message or print in an attempt to find out *why* the text did *not* make sense (Goodman & Goodman, 1978).

REDUNDANCY AND THE CUEING SYSTEMS

As readers process print they may use all three of the language systems in their search for meaning. However, because our language is redundant, more information is provided than necessary for comprehension to occur. We define *redundancy* as the characteristic of language (1) to restrict the ordering in which language symbols occur and (2) to provide several clues concerning the same piece of information. The graphophonic system provides redundancy through a narrowing of the elements of sounds. For example, only certain sounds can follow the *b* in boat. In addition, the unseen rules of spelling help the reader. The reader has internalized these rules through interaction with language and utilizes them in making predictions while reading.

The syntactic system also provides redundancy. Pearson and Johnson (1985) provide the following example of how this redundancy operates:

1. The boy thanked the girl.
2. The girl was thanked by the boy.
3. Girl was the by thanked boy the.
4. Thanked girl boy was by the the.

Our knowledge of syntax is demonstrated when we recognize that numbers (1) and (2) are acceptable English sentences; (3) and (4) are not. Our knowledge of syntax is evident when we recognize that sentences (1) and (2) hold the same meaning.

Syntax can also enable us to answer questions when reading. It is this understanding of sentence structure that enables us to read (5) and then answer questions (6), (7), and (8) (Pearson & Johnson, 1985).

5. The argle zoolked the bordiddy in the ershent because the bordiddy larped the argle.
6. Who zoolked the bordiddy?
7. Why did the argle zoolk the bordiddy in the ershent?
8. What did the bordiddy do to the argle?

The redundancy of our language enables us to answer many such questions. However, it is not clear if our ability to answer questions like (6) and (8) indicate comprehension. Could it be that students often only appear to be comprehending—that, in fact, they are simply getting by through using the syntactic system of language to provide the answers to questions?

The semantic system enables us to know what meaning of a word is intended by an author when the word is a homograph and has different possible meanings. For example, does the word "light" mean "the opposite of dark" or "pale or whitish in color"? Or does it mean to "start a fire"? Context alone can answer the question.

In addition, semantic cues enable readers to predict what will come next in the story. These predictions are sometimes possible because of cultural experiences (hearing the story of "The Three Little Pigs" for the fifty-eighth time) and life experiences (the story is about a camping trip and the reader is an experienced camper).

These three cueing systems or sources of information offer, to a degree, overlapping information. Smith (1982) states that cueing systems and the redundancy they offer eliminate many alternatives.

Redundancy lessens the need for careful attention to every tiny detail in the print setting—it represents information the reader does not need because

**THE BOOK ▶
MAKERS**

STEVEN KELLOGG

1. Which book of yours has given you the greatest pleasure?

Making a book is like making a friend. Each one is different, each one is special, and it is very difficult to choose a favorite. I have received enormous pleasure from all the books I've worked on, but two that I could mention are Margaret Murphy's *The Boy Who Was Followed Home,* which was a particularly magical story to illustrate, and *Jack and the Beanstalk,* which gave me the chance to retell and illustrate one of my childhood favorites.

2. Are you sometimes surprised by the way your work on a book evolves?

The element of surprise is an important ingredient of a book. Literature, like life, is most compelling when it confronts us with the unexpected and demands a spontaneous reaction. These experiences challenge us to grow and to expand our personal horizons. In the writing and illustrations of a book I am never sure exactly where the characters or their story are going, and so there are a constant series of surprises for me as the words and pictures go together, and that is an important part of the fun.

3. What would you like people to remember about your work?

I would like people to think of my books as a feast for the eye and a feast for the ear, and I hope that they will be happy that my stories and pictures have been, for a brief period, a part of their lives.

4. What impact do you hope your work will have on children?

I want the time that the young reader shares with me and my work to be an enjoyable experience—one that will encourage a lifetime association with pictures, words, and books.

Steven Kellogg's almost hyperkinetic illustrations threaten to jump off the page and run amok. Certainly his characters do run wild in the imaginations of millions of children because of books such as *Best Friends, Island of the Skog, Christmas Witch,* several *Pinkerton* books, and legends of Mike Fink, Johnny Appleseed, Pecos Bill, and Paul Bunyan.

he or she already knows what the author is saying and where the author is attempting to lead. Or, as Smith says, "the more redundancy there is, the less visual information the skilled reader requires" (1982, pp. 18–19).

READING AS TRANSACTION

Reading, as we have seen in the section on semantic cues, is a transaction. As readers read, they simultaneously move from mental predictions to surface features of text, monitoring understanding and moving forward as meanings are confirmed.

Comprehension is influenced by each reader's experiences and belief system. Experiences build cognitive schemata. A *schema* is an organized "block" of experience and knowledge, usually accompanied by feelings or attitudes (Rumelhart, 1980). People comprehend differently partially because they have varied experiences and schemata. No two people have identical thoughts, experiences, or feelings. Therefore, a writer cannot communicate a message; meaning does not reside in the written word or text. Instead, meaning arises during a transaction between the text and a reader.

The concept of transaction was introduced by Dewey and Bentley (1949). Rosenblatt (1978) elaborates on it by describing the product of the interaction of reader and text as being a "poem." This poem, or literary work, is created in the mind of the reader. The work created is influenced by which schemata are activated by the reader, which are selected according to the social or situational context of the reading event. This transaction is depicted in Figure 12.1. In this figure, the sociolinguistic context represents the language schemata activated by the reader. Schemata are influenced by the context or situation in which the reading takes place.

Different "poems" may be created based on the richness of the schemata that are activated. Sampson and White (1983) found that reading in school environments results in different schemata activation than does reading in nonschool situations, which validates the influence of the sociolinguistic and situational context during reading.

The discussion of miscues, which follows, illustrates in greater depth certain sociolinguistic aspects of these transactions.

MISCUES AND READING PROFICIENCY

We now turn our attention to oral reading and to the lessons children can teach us about the reading process. Thus far we have stated that reading involves a transaction with print and that readers use the three cueing systems simultaneously and interactively in their search for meaning. During this process, effective readers use the strategies of sampling, predicting, confirming, and correcting as they construct their personal representation of the author's message. Goodman (1985) sees effective reading as a search for meaning that involves selectively using the fewest most productive cues to confirm what the reader expects to find. As readers search for meaning, they personalize the author's message by sometimes changing the surface representation of

FIGURE 12.1 ▶   **THE LITERACY TRANSACTION**

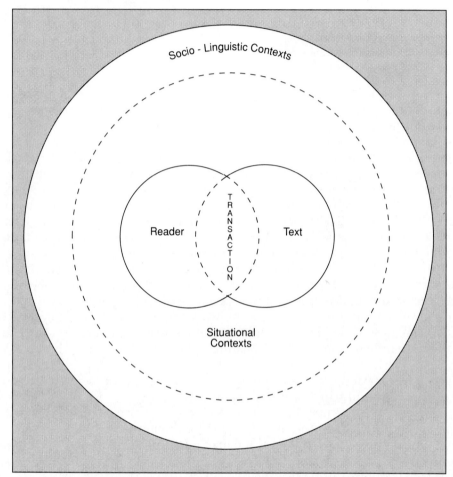

Reprinted with permission of Jerome Harste and the International Reading Association.

text to reflect their own language patterns and word choice. For years educators corrected all such "mistakes" because they believed they indicated an inability of the reader to respond to an unknown word, a lack of proper word-attack skills, or carelessness. Miscues in the reading process are illustrated by Jason, a first grader.

> Jason read, "The cat was in the home." The text read, "The cat was in the house." As he started to read the next sentence, his teacher stopped him. "Jason, read that last sentence again, carefully. Be sure to look at the last word."

The teacher's emphasis on the "mistake" indicated a great deal to Jason about "what" reading is. He was exposed to the concepts that reading is an exact process and that the goal of reading is saying the words correctly. Receiving meaning from the print was not emphasized.

Correcting the oral reader's "errors" has long been recognized as an important part of the reading teacher's role. However, the indiscriminate practice of correcting all textual deviations, or miscues, by having the pupil stop and reread, should not be done because of its effect on the child's view of reading (Phinney, 1989).

"ERRORS" AND LANGUAGE GROWTH

Children know that language conveys meaning (Goodman, Smith, Meredith, & Goodman, 1988; Holdaway, 1979). Their early years are spent

Name: Christina Anderson
Age: 12 years
Interests: Drawing, Writing and Creating things on my own.

What do you like most about school?
I like getting to use my imagination in my school work. I think creativity makes learning easier and more fun.

What's your favorite subject? Why?
The geometry section in our math classes is my favorite. I like it because I think it's neat how everything works out and all the angles equal one certian number even if the shapes are different.

What's your favorite book? Why do you like it?
My favorite series of books is the Little House collection by Laura Ingles. I like them because they describe life in Laura's time from someone who really knows what it was like.

What advice do you have for teachers?
Let your students use thier imagination in thier schoolwork but still learn what they need to know. If you let them do a short creative activity before class then that will get their brains to start thinking.

experimenting with and manipulating language as they seek to bring meaning and order to their world. This manipulation involves forming new ways of saying things, molding existing language into new constructs, and experimenting with language patterns. This learning process, on many occasions, results in the child's making "errors." However, these communications should be recognized as signs of growth, and such language manipulation should be applauded. When a young child experiments with language and says "mouses" instead of "mice" and "goed" instead of "went," parents usually realize these "errors" are a sign of immaturity and that the child, through growth and practice, will eventually become a proficient user of language. Thus the child receives positive feedback from understanding parents and continues to grow in the language-learning process (Dale, 1976).

Unfortunately, when the child moves into the educational environment, this reinforcement does not always continue. One needs only to observe reading instruction practices to realize that, all too often, "correctness" becomes the overriding goal. Any manipulation of the text by the reader is regarded as an "error" and is penalized. The divergent risk-taking language techniques that the child very successfully utilized in preschool oral language learning may not be applicable to the contrived school situation.

Miscues, therefore, should be looked on as "windows on the reading process," for they allow one to "infer what the reader is thinking" (Goodman, 1976, p. 71). An analysis of these miscues may provide valuable information concerning the strategies readers utilize in discovering meaning.

Remember Jason? When he read "The cat was in the home" instead of "The cat was in the house" and continued reading, he showed an awareness of the semantic and syntactic flow of the sentence. His emphasis seemed to be on meaning.

Books are the ▶
framework of
meaning-
centered literacy
programs.

The same emphasis is indicated if a child reads "The cat were in the house," when the child is using a dialectal pattern he or she normally uses in spoken language. In this construct, the child has transformed the text into a meaningful form.

If another child read the passage as "The cat was in the horse" and continued reading, the child's emphasis would seem to be on the decoding of individual words rather than the meaning of the complete passage. The oral construct distorted the meaning.

Bettelheim and Zelan (1982) carried this concept a step further by suggesting that at times miscues can indicate a reader's sophistication and expertise with text. Often, the miscues make equal or more sense than the original text.

Weber (1970) studied the miscues that first graders made when reading and found that substitutions constituted 86% of the miscues. The substitute words, however, maintained the meaning of the text. Furthermore, Weber found that nearly all of the beginning readers' substitutions made the text "more colloquial and less stilted, or more sensible" (p. 132). The children's search for meaning was very obvious.

When looking at children's miscues, one soon realizes that all "mistakes" are not "created equal." Teachers tend, however, to solve the problem of miscues by using one approach—having the child stop and reread (Goodman & Burke, 1972). Miscues that maintain or improve meaning give us different information about the child's proficiency in reading than do miscues that cause the semantic and syntactic flow to be disrupted or destroyed. The latter miscues should be viewed differently.

Teachers must realize what concepts about reading are being formed as "errors" are being corrected. When teachers indiscriminately correct all miscues, children assume that reading orally must involve reproducing "exactly what is on the printed page" (Goodman & Burke, 1972, p. 4). This view of reading forces children to become passive reproducers of the author's words. Thus the concept portrayed to children concerning "what reading is" becomes distorted. The individual words assume prime importance, and meaning is subordinated. Unfortunately, this emphasis on the "correct" word places undue importance on the graphophonic cues at the expense of the semantic and syntactic cues, and comprehension suffers.

If we look at accomplished readers, however, we find that they read in chunks of meaning rather than letter-by-letter or word-by-word. Proficient readers become involved in the text and begin to predict words and anticipate thoughts. As stated by Smith (1973, p. 188), "Fluent readers do not read words, they read meanings . . . [and] make maximum use of a minimum of visual information."

MISCUE IMPLICATIONS FOR TEACHERS

As you've seen, reading cannot be viewed as a one-way street of correctly pronouncing words. Rosenblatt (1978, 1983, 1993) stated that the reader's textual interaction should be active rather than passive in order to cue thinking and derive meaning. Like other communicative processes, reading is not exact, for a reader is "not a blank tape registering a ready-made message" (Rosenblatt, 1978, p. 10). The reader brings a wealth of ideas, emotions, experiences, and expectations to the printed page. This has an effect on the reader–text interaction.

Miscues can tell us a great deal about what children think reading is, what they know, and what they need to learn. A teacher must be linguistically aware of the information that is available through the analysis of miscues and must not perceive the child who makes miscues as being deficient, but rather as an emerging learner.

As stated by Donaldson (1978, p. 110), "The learner, if . . . an active discoverer, will make mistakes." In order to be a dynamic learner, the child must be an active risk taker and must realize that reading is much more than word-by-word processing. The child must interact with the text through predicting and confirming, with the end result being meaning. In this "risky" process, miscues will occur, but miscues happen in the reading process as an effect of the interaction between reader and text. The teacher's role is to provide reading instruction that makes the child realize that "saying the correct word" is not the reason for reading. Rather, for each individual student the "why" of reading must involve thinking, which leads to comprehension.

FACTORS THAT AFFECT READING COMPREHENSION

Teachers are increasingly aware that comprehension is a process students experience rather than a product consisting of numerous memorized comprehension skills. We now know that comprehension resides in the reader, not in the text being read. We now examine factors that affect reading comprehension; then we move in the next chapter to a discussion of strategies that enhance students' understandings.

SCHEMA THEORY AND COMPREHENSION

Comprehension occurs when readers relate new information to existing knowledge (Anderson & Pearson, 1984; Pearson & Johnson, in press). This existing information store is known as the reader's *schema,* an important concept in helping us understand the process of reading comprehension.

As human beings, we have a schema for each of the things we experience in life. This schema includes single events, situations we have encountered, things we have learned, and even sequences of events (Rumelhart, 1980, 1984). The central function of this schema is the "interpretation of an event, object, or situation—in the process of comprehension" (Rumelhart, 1984, p. 3).

Therefore, it is the activation of the schema we hold for a given situation that enables us to comprehend the situation. For example, we feel very comfortable when we check into a Holiday Inn during a long road trip because our schema for Holiday Inn is quite complete. We know what to expect from the desk attendant and what will be in our room. As we walk into the room we *expect* to see familiar objects—beds, a color TV, drapes on the window, and a table. We also expect to find certain things in the bathroom—clean glasses wrapped in paper or plastic, towels, soap, and perhaps even a plastic shower cap. We have learned these things about motel rooms by experiencing them firsthand, by watching television commercials, or perhaps through reading.

Schemata are constantly being updated and revised. For example, one day we went tuna fishing off the coast of Maine and, during the course of the day, drastically altered our schema for tuna. Having never seen a live tuna before, we had been influenced by the "Charlie the Tuna" ads on television. To our surprise, however, we found that fishing poles and hooks were not used to catch the tuna, but harpoons! The fish harpooned that day were the size of small cars, not the 10-inch fish that existed in our schema. The result of the fishing trip was a revised schema concerning the size of tuna. Now that you've read this story, you too may experience a change in schema.

What is the importance of schema theory to the classroom teacher? The answer is quite emphatic: Readers comprehend text when they are able to "find a configuration of hypotheses (schema) which offer a coherent account for the various aspects of the text" (Rumelhart, 1984, p. 3) and then activate that schema. When readers fail to find such a configuration, the text appears incomprehensible. However, when those configurations are recognized, comprehension occurs as new information enters the reader's cognitive realm and interacts with an existing schema. This allows readers to form a framework of "known information" so they can hook the "new" information into it. The result is an understanding of the passage and an expansion of the existing schema.

What about you? What happens when you activate a schema? Let's try an experiment. First read the following passage and rank your understanding of the passage from 1 to 10, with 10 signifying you have complete and thorough understanding of the passage, and 1 designating you do not have a clue concerning the meaning.

> The procedure is actually quite simple. First you arrange things into different groups. Of course one pile may be sufficient depending on how much there is to do. If you have to go somewhere else due to lack of facilities that is the next step, otherwise you are pretty well set. It is important not to overdo things. That is, it is better to do too few things at once than too many. In the short run this may not seem important but complications can easily arise. A mistake can be expensive as well. At first the whole procedure will seem complicated. Soon, however, it will become just another facet of life. It is difficult to foresee any end to the necessity for this task in the immediate future, but then one never can tell. After the procedure is completed one arranges the materials into different groups again. Then they can be put into their appropriate places. Eventually they will be used once more and the whole cycle will then have to be repeated. However, that is a part of life. (Bransford & McCarrell, 1974)

Now consider the title of the passage: *Washing Clothes.* Reread the passage and rank your understanding by using the same numerical system you did previously. Did the number signifying your comprehension increase? What made the difference? If your score increased, it was due to the activation of your schema. After you were given the title *Washing Clothes,* you were able to construct a framework of "known" information. That in turn facilitated your ability to connect the "new" information in the paragraph to the "known" information in your schema and understand the passage. Scenes probably "played in your mind" as the text triggered experiences of personal laundry drudgeries, successes, or disaster, which increased your comprehension of the text. Your lack of understanding during the first reading was not due to lack of decoding skills, it was because you were unable to activate your schema; therefore, you were only "calling words" and optimum comprehension was circumvented.

Teachers must remember the importance of facilitating conceptual development in students, and must provide them with opportunities for schema activation and expansion. Above all, we must demonstrate to students that reading involves a semantic transaction with text, that a passage does not have a meaning by itself. Meaning must be created by the students through interaction with the material they read.

TEXTUAL FACTORS

In addition to schema considerations, teachers must be aware that other factors affect the reading comprehension of students. Often comprehension is hampered because of poorly written text, sometimes referred to as inconsiderate text—passages written in ways that disrupt the natural flow of language and thought and are incompatible with the language of the reader. The preprimers of most basal series are texts with very restricted vocabulary and awkward syntax. Students have more difficulty comprehending such simple, dull material than they do reading and understanding more complex, but better written material (Sampson, 1982).

Writers can help readers comprehend by providing headings, subheadings, summaries, definitions, graphs, and tables. And teachers can help students by demonstrating the usefulness of such textual aids.

CONTEXTUAL SETTING

Reading and reading comprehension always occur in the rich context of a literacy event. Reading events are multisituational and ever changing. The same book being read by a fourth-grade student on the sofa of his or her living room will be read in a different manner when the context is changed to the student's classroom at school. The reading event is different not only because of the location change, but also because of emotional or physical changes within the reader. Thus a poem read in the morning will be read differently in the afternoon. Different schemata will be engaged, and different interpretations reached. This phenomenon of the language setting and mental setting interacting to create divergent environments is well documented (Harste, Burke, & Woodward, 1982; Harste & Carey, 1979; Rosenblatt, 1978, 1983).

Strategies for reading also change from situation to situation and from reading to reading. Sampson and White (1983) found that children read school-type materials differently from story-type materials. Interestingly, the students used more effective strategies when reading was removed from the formal school environment. Figure 12.2 (Harste, Burke, & Woodward, 1982), which details a sociopsycholinguistic view of language processing, gives the likely explanations for these findings.

The term *language setting* means both oral and written language contain many cues (linguistic, situational, cultural) that may be processed. These, in turn, modify the mental setting. The mental setting alters the schema the

SOCIOPSYCHOLINGUISTIC VIEW OF LANGUAGE PROCESSING ◀ FIGURE 12.2

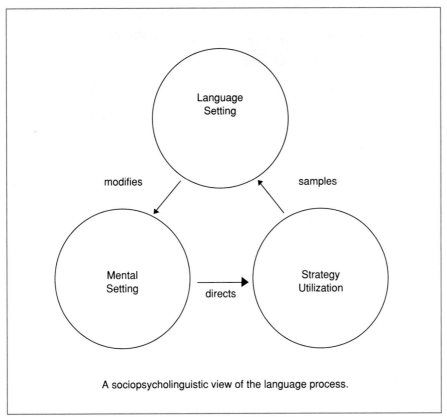

A sociopsycholinguistic view of the language process.

Reprinted with permission of Jerome Harste and the International Reading Association

reader uses, which in turn determines the strategy the reader uses (Harste, Burke, & Woodward, 1982).

COMPREHENSION MODES

Related to the discussion of language setting and context is Rosenblatt's theory of reading *stance*. She states that all readers select a purpose or mental set for reading that determines what they seek to comprehend in the reading session. These positions vary along a continuum, ranging from an efferent to an aesthetic stance (Rosenblatt, 1978, 1983). *Efferent reading* focuses on meaning and includes information to be remembered, conclusions to be drawn, and propositions to be tested. Thus the reader's attention is on what is to be retained or applied *after* the reading.

In contrast, *aesthetic reading* focuses on what is being lived through *during* the reading. The reader's attention is expanded to include both the images and associations that make the reading enjoyable and an awareness of the sound and rhythm of the language as it resounds in the inner ear. Rosenblatt terms the comprehension that results from this type of pleasurable reading act a *poem* (Rosenblatt, 1983).

THE FAMILY CIRCUS®   By Bil Keane

"I'd like to watch TV, but
I don't dare."

When students read, they may adopt an efferent stance, an aesthetic stance, or some position on the continuum between the two. The previous discussion of schemata detailed the importance of readers' tapping the schema during the comprehension process. Efferent reading, however, tends to place more emphasis on what is on the page and less on what is within the reader. Thus the teacher's goal is to promote the aesthetic stance by freeing students to contribute personal knowledge as they seek to comprehend. Instructional practices that allow this reader contribution, such as Directed Reading and Thinking Activities (DRTA), are discussed in Chapter 13.

In summary, aesthetic reading and the creating of personal "poems" require a context or reading environment that allows freedom for the reader to contribute to the text. However, many school environments stress the exact reproduction of the story as the child reads orally. This places the student into the efferent stance and discourages the aesthetic stance. Such practices focus on what students *do* comprehend instead of tapping what they *might* be able to comprehend if they were given more freedom while reading (Tuinman, 1979).

COMPREHENSION INSTRUCTION AND ASSESSMENT

Comprehension has typically been taught through the presentation of various subskill exercises. Such instruction does not usually take into consideration the contribution language users have to make to the process of reading comprehension. In fact, research indicates that basal readers and their subskills approach to comprehension instruction have a very serious shortcoming: They assess, rather than teach, reading comprehension (Durkin, 1978–1979, 1981, 1983).

Distinctions must be made between the practice of asking students questions about what they have read—comprehension assessment—and teaching students how to comprehend—comprehension instruction. Because basal reader series and commercially prepared materials often equate the two, teachers must use alternative strategies if they are to show students that comprehension is a process in which meaning is created, rather than a recall test of what they have read.

The most effective way of evaluating students' comprehension is through teacher observation, not testing. These teacher observations are less expensive than standardized tests and provide better information. Yetta Goodman (1985) has called these informal observations *kid watching* (see Chapter 11). The thrust of such observations would be to find answers to two questions: (1) What evidence is there that comprehension is taking place? and (2) Do students' actions, such as choosing to do independent reading, indicate they are successful in the classroom reading environment? The latter is easily answered by simple observation of student choices during free times. The first question may be answered by observing students as they encounter the comprehension activities described in the next chapter.

SUMMARY

We examined the reading process and found it to be an artifact of the other communicative processes. Reading and writing are based on language and are driven by the human need to communicate. We find reading to be a process that involves a transaction between a reader intent on establishing meaning and a text. This search for meaning will be directed by the ever-learning mind of the reader and involves a transaction between language and thought. Thus reading truly is a psycholinguistic "selection" process.

Teachers must aid students by helping each child conceptualize the truths about language in the communication process that have been discussed in this chapter. In addition, teachers have a fundamental responsibility to establish a conceptual framework that will serve as their guide in selecting activities, experiences, materials, and evaluative procedures.

PATHWAYS TO UNDERSTANDING READING

The student:

► appropriately utilizes semantic, syntactic, and graphophonic cues.
► samples, predicts, confirms, and corrects while reading with meaning or "making sense" as a basis for continuing the process.

▶ is more concerned with getting meaning from the text than decoding each word.

The teacher:

▶ views children as emerging learners.

▶ realizes that students learn to read and become proficient readers by having many opportunities to interact with meaningful texts.

▶ does not indiscriminately correct all miscues but looks on them as "windows on the reading process" and makes instructional decisions based on this information.

▶ provides an instructional environment that emphasizes the foundation of reading is not to just "say the right word" but to get meaning from the print.

▶13 PATHWAYS TO READING: COMPREHENSION STRATEGIES

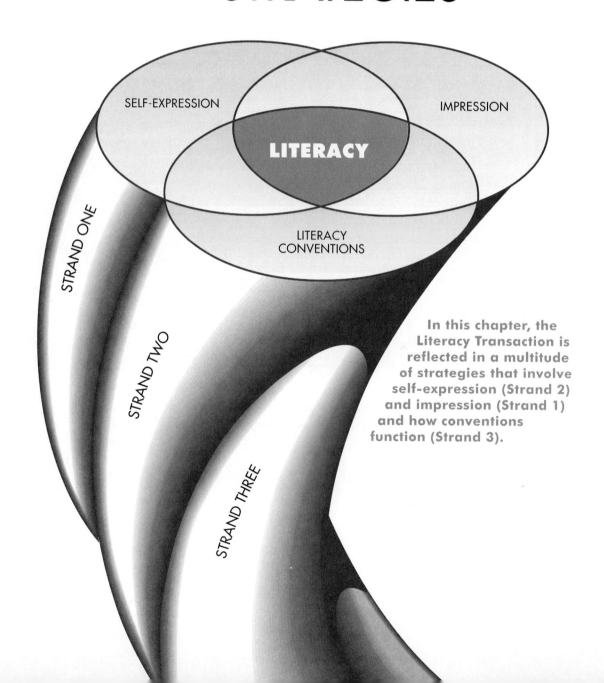

SELF-EXPRESSION

IMPRESSION

LITERACY

LITERACY
CONVENTIONS

STRAND ONE

STRAND TWO

STRAND THREE

In this chapter, the
Literacy Transaction is
reflected in a multitude
of strategies that involve
self-expression (Strand 2)
and impression (Strand 1)
and how conventions
function (Strand 3).

CHAPTER OUTLINE

STRATEGIES FOR COMPREHENDING
    TEACHER-DIRECTED STRATEGIES
    READER-DIRECTED STRATEGIES

MAKING STRATEGIES WORK FOR YOU

SUMMARY

PATHWAYS TO READING COMPREHENSION

PATHWAYS TO PONDER

▶ **WHY IS IT IMPORTANT TO INVOLVE STUDENTS IN THE PROCESS OF THINKING AND PREDICTING DURING READING?**

▶ **HOW CAN A MEANING-CENTERED CURRICULUM CAPITALIZE ON THE DIVERSE SCHEMATA THAT STUDENTS BRING TO THE CLASSROOM?**

▶ **HOW CAN TEACHERS SHIFT THEIR STUDENTS' COMPREHENSION STANCE FROM EFFERENT TO AESTHETIC MODES?**

▶ **WHAT ARE THE ADVANTAGES OF STUDENTS' MASTERING READER-BASED STRATEGIES?**

▶ **WHAT IS THE VALUE OF STUDENTS' CREATING CONCEPTUAL MAPS?**

In Chapter 12 we explored the reading process and students' interactions with text. This chapter focuses on strategies that help children comprehend text. Some of the strategies are teacher initiated; others are student initiated. Above all, we must remember the value of a strategy should be evident to the students. We must never make reading a chore; instead, we should strive to make reading a delight. Thus strategies should be a resource that children can call on when they need help in understanding text. They should be a means to the end of better comprehension: They must never become an end in themselves.

STRATEGIES FOR COMPREHENDING

As you examine strategies, it is important that you focus on the process rather than the individual steps of the strategy. Ask yourself, "Does this strategy allow my students to 'act like real readers'?" Think about the processes that "real" readers are involved in and determine if the strategy provides opportunities for your students to engage in those processes. Does the strategy engage students in active interaction with the text? Do students have opportunities to predict and revise, confirm, or reject their predictions? Does the strategy allow students to determine purposes for reading and then read to fulfill those purposes? Are students involved in forming questions about the text and searching for answers to those questions? Do students have the opportunity to share and discuss their views? These and other questions must be asked as you determine if a strategy will be worthwhile for your students.

Your examination and decision-making process is rather like the old story concerning a sculptor. When asked how he was able to sculpt such a realistic elephant out of granite the sculptor replied, "Well, I just decide what an elephant looks like, look at the block of granite, and chip away everything that doesn't look like an elephant." As a teacher, your challenge is to decide what real readers "look like," and chip away everything from your reading program that does not allow your students to "look like" or "act like" real readers.

TEACHER-DIRECTED STRATEGIES

THINK-ALOUDS

In think-alouds, teachers reveal the mental processes they are engaging in while reading by sharing their thoughts about the text and their comprehension while reading orally to their students. The strategy was devised by Beth Davey (1983), and involves teachers in modeling a process they hope their students will internalize. The strategy consists of the following steps:

1. Select a text to read aloud to your class. Decide which places in the text you consider important, and then pause at those places.

◀ Students demonstrate their comprehension of *Each Peach Pear Plum* with a mural.

2. When you pause, predict what you think will happen next. Verbalize the process you went though in order to make those predictions. What in the text triggered your response?

3. Describe the "picture" that the text has painted in your mind. Tell children how that picture changes as you receive more information from the text. Talk about how the mental picture stays in your mind throughout the story.

4. As you continue to read, talk about the schemata the text has triggered. If the story reminds you of particular people, events, scenes, or other stories, tell the students what you are thinking about and why. You may want to use analogies to explain your comprehension by stating, "Oh, I understand, this is like . . ." and then giving an example or illustration.

5. Stop occasionally and share a comprehension problem with the class such as something that has puzzled you or that you don't understand. Elicit students' help in formulating a plan of action that will aid in clarifying your confusion or "fixing" the problem. Talking about comprehension problems is a very important part of a think-aloud. The teacher and students have the opportunity to explore varied ways to aid in the comprehension of a text, and then to discuss what was effective and what wasn't. Students will also learn that sometimes it is effective to just keep on reading. The point of confusion will often become clearer as the reader moves on into the text.

Modeling the strategy is important, but students need the opportunity to practice verbalizing their interaction with the text. Students may work in pairs and "talk through" text as they monitor their understanding.

SHARED BOOK EXPERIENCE

Shared Book Experience (Holdaway, 1979) originated in New Zealand in the late 1960s, to provide emerging readers with the opportunity to have successful, meaningful interactions with text. Big Books containing enlarged pictures and text are used so children may be able to visually and auditorially experience the book as the teacher shares it. Patterned or predictable stories are often used so children may participate in the sharing experience by repeating patterned lines and predicting story development. The stages in using a text for Shared Book Experience are listed below (Ward, 1993).

1. **Discovery.** This is the introduction of the text to the students. This presentation includes sharing the title and author, previewing and discussing the book, and providing opportunities for the student to use their prediction skills. This phase includes an enthusiastic reading of the text, during which the teacher points to the words; the children have an opportunity to see the words as they are being read. In addition, this is an opportunity for the teacher to verbalize predictive aspects of the story with phrases such as, "Do you think his parachute will open?", "What makes you think that?", "What do you think will happen next?", and "What in the story makes you think that?"

2. **Exploration.** This stage may involve many visits to the text for varied purposes. From the Literacy Transaction Model you might incorporate Strand 1 (Self-Expression) activities such as unison reading, role playing, or dramatization during this phase. Strand 3 (Conventions) activities like examining textual features or print details or identifying and categorizing letter–sound relationships are possibilities. Favorite words and phrases could be identified and added to the word wall. It is important to remember that all of these activities utilize the text, not worksheets.

3. **Independence and Expression.** This phase intertwines with the second. Many Strand 1 activities fall in this category as children bring their own understanding to the text. Activities such as dramatization, independent writing, art and music activities, contrast and comparison with other texts, and innovations on the text provide opportunities for children to demonstrate and anchor their knowledge of the text.

These phases represent how one book might be shared with a class; when you use Shared Book Experience in your classroom, the phases may overlap as you continually expose your children to new books. The following classroom vignette shows how one teacher utilizes Shared Book Experience in her classroom, based upon suggestions by Geoff Ward (1993).

Continued

DIRECTED READING AND THINKING ACTIVITY (DRTA)

The DRTA was developed by Russell Stauffer (1976) to involve students more actively with the material they read. The procedure involves the students in divergent thinking by asking them to read, make predictions, and think about what they are reading. The DRTA motivates students because it arouses their curiosity and lets them become involved in stimulating explorations of plot developments.

The teacher can adapt the DRTA for most types of reading material and for just about any grade level. While the procedure may also be used with individual students, Stauffer (1980) suggests the procedure is most effective when used with a group. The DRTA attempts to develop several abilities:

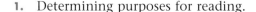

1. Determining purposes for reading.

She then introduces a new Big Book or chart, and children have an opportunity to engage in the discovery phase of the book by using their predictive skills. During the initial reading, the children begin to chime in and say predictable phrases with her. She sometimes uses small pieces of paper to cover up words or parts of words and encourages children to discuss how they can determine which word is covered. Children utilize the semantic, syntactic, and graphophonic cueing systems in unison during this contextualized activity. If the children are enthusiastic about the book, Sue reads it with the class again, and children volunteer to dramatize portions of the book during reading. This often leads to expressive activities centered around the book: innovations on the text, art activities, thematic studies, musical adaptions of the text, Reader's Theater presentations, contrast and comparison with other texts, or other activities determined by collaboration between the teacher and students. Not every text becomes an extended study for every student. The students continually have voice and choice in determining texts that spark their interest.

Sue weaves a time for independent reading into every day. Some children may revisit books or charts which have been shared in Big Book format and have become old favorites. Other children may work in self-chosen small groups. During this time, Sue has the opportunity to observe the children's reading and record her observations. She occasionally joins in or provides assistance, but she is careful not to destroy the self-monitoring reading behavior that the children are developing during this time.

Sue may vary the order and grouping of the instructional activities. For instance, the independent reading time may occur earlier in her schedule so she will have an opportunity to work with small groups who have shown a need for mini-lessons in specific areas. At times, some children might be working on expressive activities inspired by a specific text, while others are engaged in independent reading of favorite texts. Some text receives such an enthusiastic response that the entire class collaborates to write an innovation. Sue strives daily to provide her emerging readers with depth and breadth of exposure to a variety of text through the flexibility of Shared Book Experience.

2. Extracting, comprehending, and assimilating information.

3. Examining reading material based on purposes for reading.

4. Suspending judgments.

5. Making decisions based on information gleaned from reading (Tierney, Readence, & Dishner, 1990, p. 12).

A group DRTA is conducted in the following manner:

1. The teacher begins the lesson by sharing the title of the selection to be read. Asking, "What do you think a story with this title might be about?" the teacher then accepts the answers of four or five students before proceeding. The teacher may want to write these predictions on a chart or overhead transparency, or may choose to share them at the oral level.

2. The teacher invites the students to read the first paragraph or to the point that the predictions will be confirmed, rejected, or modified. Asking the students if they still think the same as they did earlier, the teacher may focus on specific responses. "Do you still think the story is about a bank robber?" After students are allowed to respond, new predictions are elicited.

3. Students continue through the text—predicting, reading, and reacting to their predictions. The teacher continues to ask questions such as "Were you correct?" or "What do you think now?" or "What do you think will happen?"

At this point the teacher has completed the first phase of the DRTA, stimulating the reading–thinking of the students during the story. Now the emphasis changes to specific skill development and a reexamination of the story. Stauffer refers to this stage as "skill training of a different kind" (Stauffer, 1969, p. 64). The format of this stage may vary, but components usually include concept clarification, personal reflection, and semantic analysis (Tierney, Readence, & Dishner, 1990).

Vocabulary extension comes during this final stage rather than before the reading of the story. The teacher asks questions like "Was there something you didn't understand in the story?" Some students will bring up concept-level questions, and others will ask about specific vocabulary words encountered in the story. This method of vocabulary study makes more sense than the preselected method used in the Directed Reading Activity because it allows for self-selection by the student and vocabulary discussion in context. Furthermore, this discovery technique of vocabulary development is more effective because the words are encountered in the context of the story rather than in isolation (Cunningham, Moore, Cunningham, & Moore, 1983).

The teacher's role is quite different in a DRTA than when presenting a Directed Reading Activity. In a Directed Reading Activity the teacher operates from a script provided by a basal reader and serves as questioner and judge of the students' answers. In contrast, the role of the teacher during a DRTA is as moderator and "intellectual agitator" (Petre, 1969).

The Directed Listening and Thinking Activity follows basically the same process as the Directed Reading and Thinking Activity except that instead of the students reading the text, the teacher reads the text aloud to the students. Step 1 of the process is the same as the Step 1 previously discussed for the DRTA. Steps 2 and 3 of a DLTA copy steps 2 and 3 listed for a DRTA except the teacher is reading the text aloud instead of the students silently reading the text. The discussion and the opportunity to confirm, reject, extend, or offer a prediction engage children in the interactive process with text offered by the DRTA. Vocabulary extension is addressed in the same way for a DLTA as for a DRTA. Students have the opportunity to identify words and phrases that captured their attention by puzzling them or saying things in a new way.

The DRTA and the DLTA place a major emphasis on the relations among reading, thinking, and predicting. Because they encourage students to initiate their own reading goals, reading becomes more meaningful and comprehension is facilitated. DRTAS are a useful alternative to Directed Reading Activities

THE POET-TREE

One day I saw a cypress tree
With bumpy knees like you and me.
I saw a pine tree tall and green
That made the air feel fresh and
*   clean.*
An oak tree,
A red-leaf maple,
A hickory
And a palm
With leaves like fans to cool the sky
In places where it's warm.
But in all the world from pole to
*   pole*
I think I may never see
Branches with leaves that sing to me
Like our lovely poet-tree.

and are claiming larger shares of instructional time in elementary classrooms. DLTAS help teachers allow their students to become involved in the processes of predicting and then confirming, rejecting, extending, or revising those predictions based on information revealed in the text during times when the teacher is reading aloud.

BRAINSTORMING

The importance of a reader activating his or her schemata before reading in order to maximize comprehension has been discussed previously. Brainstorming is one of the simplest ways to aid children in activating their schemata or prior knowledge before reading. This "what-do-you-think-of-when-I-say" activity is the cornerstone for many of the more sophisticated prereading activities, such as conceptual mapping or K-W-L (described later in this chapter). As the teacher records students' responses, assessment of the knowledge base of the students is possible. As the students brainstorm items, the teacher may extend concepts or define terms the students will encounter when reading the text. Because brainstorming is a flexible strategy that requires marginal manipulation of information, it is useful when students have little prior knowledge of a subject. The Classroom Vignette about Laurie Mattox's class on the following page illustrates this point.

By using brainstorming as a prereading strategy, Laurie involved her students in activating their schema concerning eagles. Using the children's information as part of her instruction caused the students to realize their input was valued. By using the words the children had originally brainstormed as a basis for the introduction of new terms and concepts, a framework of "known"

Laurie Mattox frequently uses brainstorming with her sixth graders before they read science text. One lesson dealt with the physical characteristics of eagles, their habitat, and the problem of eagles becoming an endangered species because the chemical thallium sulfate weakens the shells before the eaglets could hatch. She was concerned that students would not be familiar with some of the terminology used in the text although they might have heard the concepts referred to in different terms. Therefore, she asked students to close their eyes and think about "eagles"—any places they had ever seen eagles, how they would describe an eagle to someone who had never seen one, and any information they had read or heard about eagles.

After two minutes of thought time, she asked students for their ideas. She recorded the information on an overhead (Figure 13.1) as students shared. When all of the responses were recorded, she asked students if any of the terms seem to refer to the same thing or category of things. Students identified words and phrases that seemed to address the same topic and assigned the following categories: feeding habits of eagles (carnivorous, eat rodents, hunters); descriptions of eagles (claws, beak, long wings, strong, powerful, not really bald but white feathers, feathers, large wingspan, majestic, soar, fly high); different types of eagles (bald, golden); where eagles lived (mountains, big nests); ways eagles used as symbols (symbol of freedom, symbol of USA, national bird, on Mexico's flag, on USA money); threats to the eagles (endangered, pollution harmful to them, being poisoned by chemicals); and other information. As the students categorized the information, Laurie wrote it on another overhead (Figure 13.2). After the students were finished with their categorizations, she said, "I am impressed. It is obvious you already have a lot of knowledge about eagles. The pages you are going to read tell about three things you have generated information about, what the eagles look like, where they live, and what is causing them to become endangered. Let's look at what you said."

Laurie then used the students' knowledge as a basis for extension. "You talked about 'where the eagles live.' When you read your text, the authors are going to use a word that means the same thing. Does anyone have an idea about what that term might be?" When a student volunteered "habitat," Laurie wrote it by the appropriate phrase. She then commented, "The book is also going to describe the eagle's claws, but will use another word that means the same thing as claws. Remember that word and we will talk about it later," and drew a line by "claws" to provide a reminder to write the new term on the overhead. She mentioned that the text would give many details concerning the ways the eagles looked, but it would be referred to as "physical characteristics" in the text, and then she wrote that label on the overhead. She continued, "You will also find out more information about why some eagles are endangered species. One chemical that will be talked about is thallium sulfate. Be sure to note why this chemical is dangerous to eagles," and she wrote the term by the comment "being poisoned by chemicals."

Continued

Eagles

fly high
soar
claws
beak
carnivorous
eats rodents
majestic
mountains

babies are eaglets
hunters
bald
golden
long wings
strong
powerful
not really bald, just
white feathers

endangered
feathers
Symbol of freedom
Symbol of USA
national bird
large wingspan
protected by law
big nests
pollution harmful
to them
being poisoned by
chemicals
on Mexico's flag
on USA money

Laurie concluded by stating, "I will leave this overhead up during your reading so you can jot anything down that you want to add to the information we have, or if you read something that confirms information we have listed. Be sure to note the page number, so we will have it for a reference. We'll have a chance to see if our information is the same as the book's."

information was formed to "hook" the "new" information onto so it would be easier to understand and remember. Because the brainstorming was recorded on overhead transparencies, the information was available throughout the study for refinement and extension.

Laurie's framework for brainstorming is that thinking and creativity are the keys. Therefore, all brainstormed information will be recorded and will never be challenged or ridiculed. However, the class is not allowed to accept *any* information as fact until it can be documented. Therefore, as students find information that proves brainstormed information, they jot down the source and page number and that data is added to the overhead. Then—and only then—will that information be stated as factual. Laurie has found that this has motivated her students to continue their exploration of a topic beyond the time spent in class and outside of the school environment. Students often bring in magazines, books, or newspaper articles that "document" a brainstormed item as factual. Through extending and refining brainstormed information, students are becoming aware that learning is not confined to the classroom, but is a lifelong journey!

LINK

Link is a variation of brainstorming. The strategy was developed by Joseph Vaughan and Thomas Estes (1986) and is ideal when you suspect that only some of your students have background knowledge on the topic.

◀ **FIGURE 13.2**

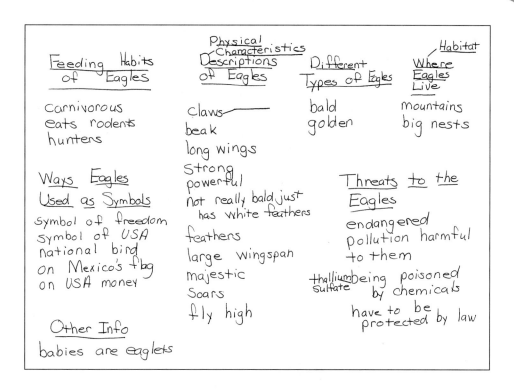

Here are the steps:

1. Write the topic or key term on the board or overhead transparency. Then give students three minutes to *list* what they know about it in brainstorm fashion on their own paper.

2. Go around the room and let students share their responses. Write these responses on the board or overhead transparency. After all responses are given, invite the students to interact with students who provided items in order to *inquire* and ask for clarification about the items.

3. Next repeat the first step, but limit the time to one minute. (Students usually write more.) Have them note all they now *know* about the word based on the previous discussion.

This format incorporates writing before students share and allows students to explore the reason behind certain contributions. The opportunity for discussion, reflection, and clarification enhances the students' understandings of the topic, and usually enables them to think of more information when they move to step 3.

CIRCLE OF QUESTIONS

Circle of questions (Sampson, Sampson & Linek, 1994) is a strategy that was developed to engage students in brainstorming, predicting, generating questions about text, categorizing, and interacting with text to answer those questions. When used with content material, the steps are as follows:

1. Divide students into groups of four. Groups should have a timekeeper, a recorder, a reporter, and a leader. Introduce the topic and allow students 3 to 5 minutes to brainstorm questions they have about the topic.

2. Draw a circle on a chart, an overhead, or the board. Allow students 2 minutes to rank-order their questions from most important to least important.

3. Each group then shares their most important question and the teacher draws a line from the circle and writes the question. If a group's number one question has been shared, the group shares their number two question. The sharing and recording of questions continues until all of a group's questions have been shared by that group or another one. The group may then "pass." Recording of questions continues until all groups have "passed."

4. The questions are reviewed and examined to determine categories. The teacher may use colored markers or chalk to designate items that belong in specific categories.

5. Each group then chooses a category to become an "expert" in. As they read, they search for answers to the questions in that particular category. The recorder writes their answers and where they were found in the text and shares the information with the class. The teacher then writes the answers and where they were found by the appropriate

◀ Mary Beth Sampson introduces the "circle of questions" procedure to third graders.

question. Discussion can then occur concerning the answer and if the text adequately addresses the concern. If not, additional research may be needed.

Try this strategy *after* students have read a challenging or controversial text. Students can divide into groups and generate questions they have about the text after reading it. The procedure can then continue with step 2.

As students engage in this strategy, they begin to realize that not all questions are answered by a particular text, and sometimes more questions are raised. Even more importantly, they are actively constructing their own questions about a topic and then exploring the text to find answers, just as "real readers" do.

CONCEPTUAL MAPPING

Because reading is a transaction between a reader and a text, comprehension may be facilitated when students think about what they are about to read. *Semantic* or *conceptual mapping* is a strategy that enables students to associate what they know with what they read, thus bringing stories to life (Heimlich & Hittleman, 1986; Hittleman, 1988).

Conceptual maps may involve groups or individual students; the procedure is appropriate for use with ages ranging from preschool to high school. Matthew, a 5-year-old with an interest in dinosaurs, received a copy of *Dinosaurs and Other Prehistoric Animals,* by Darlene Geis, for his birthday. His mother Pat, who had just studied conceptual mapping in an education class, tried out the procedure with him. She started by writing "DINOSAURS" on a large sheet of paper, and then asked him to think about dinosaurs and how they lived. Matthew quickly took charge of the "lesson" by stating, "They had a lot of different names." After Pat wrote the word "NAMES," Matthew asked how to spell Hesperornis, and insisted on writing down the letters himself, one by one. He then allowed his mother to print Coelophysis, Plateosaurus, and Teratosaurus. He then brainstormed about where the dinosaurs traveled, how they died, where their bones and fossils are found today, and much more. From time to time, Matthew insisted on printing letters and adding pictures to the conceptual map. Figure 13.3 shows the completed map.

Matthew was now prepared to read his new book, with all of his stored knowledge about dinosaurs at hand to assist him when the book presented new information about dinosaurs and their lives. When the story was over, Matthew wanted to add new categories and information to his dinosaur "map."

When conceptual maps are created in group situations, the students can assist in organizing their knowledge about the subject. The creation of the map brings out the key vocabulary words and concepts, enabling many students to learn about the subject even before they read.

Conceptual maps are also excellent postreading activities. After reading, constructing maps allows students to remember and represent graphically the information read (Pearson & Johnson, in press). In addition, if students have constructed conceptual maps before reading, they have the opportunity to extend and refine those maps with information they gleaned from the text. If desired, information that has been confirmed by the text can be highlighted and page numbers can be noted. These maps reveal significant information concerning students' comprehension and their conceptual organization of the

FIGURE 13.3 ▶ **A YOUNG CHILD'S CONCEPTUAL MAP**

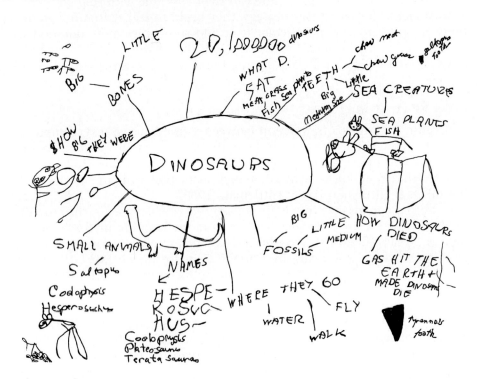

text, and often encourage children to engage in further study concerning a particular topic or character.

STORY MAPS

Story maps involve students in constructing "a basic framework for organizing and storing information" (Idol-Maestas & Croll, 1985, p. 4), which in turn anchors and extends their comprehension (Gordon & Pearson, 1983; Short & Ryan, 1984; Singer & Donlan, 1983). Story maps can consist of a very basic format in which students draw, write, or do a combination of both to represent their understanding of the beginning, middle, and end of a story. They may be developed to portray the different elements of story grammar that refers to the components of a story: characters, setting, problem, series of problem-solving events, resolution. Or, as demonstrated in the vignette on the next page, a story map may portray a child's conceptualization of a story and character relationships.

K-W-L

K-W-L is a strategy that involves students in activating their mental schema concerning a topic, developing questions about and a purpose for reading text

◀ **TABLE 13.1**

Dee Finley, a third-grade teacher, became interested in story maps as a "window" through which she could view her students' comprehension. Before reading a version of the "Three Little Pigs" in the basal reader, she asked her students to share what they remembered about the classic story. This information was organized into a conceptual map as the students shared. Next, Dee allowed the students time for silent independent reading of the story. Finally, the students created their own story maps. Table 13.2 shows Shannon's conceptualization of the story.

Interestingly, the map clearly shows the major characters in the story and their relationships with one another. The map demonstrates to Dee that Shannon has comprehended the story. In addition, the creation of the map probably deepened Shannon's knowledge of story structure and should help him the next time he creates a story of his own.

TABLE 13.2 ▶ STORY MAP OF THE THREE LITTLE PIGS

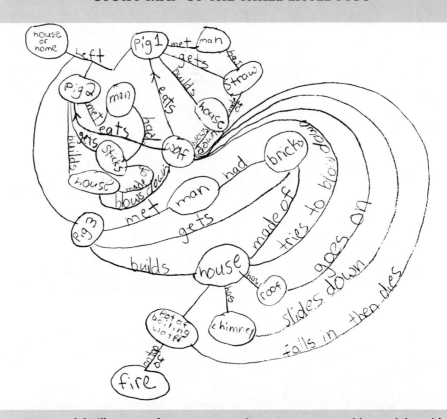

Tomasa del Villanueva often uses semantics maps as a prewriting activity with her third-grade students. Children in her class were writing "letters" or "poems" of appreciation to their caretakers: Bryan Capehart, for example, incorporated his knowledge of semantic maps into the second page of his birthday poem to his father. The unedited poem is found in Figure 13.4.

Continued

FIGURE 13.4 ▶ **BIRTHDAY GREETING FROM A THIRD GRADER**

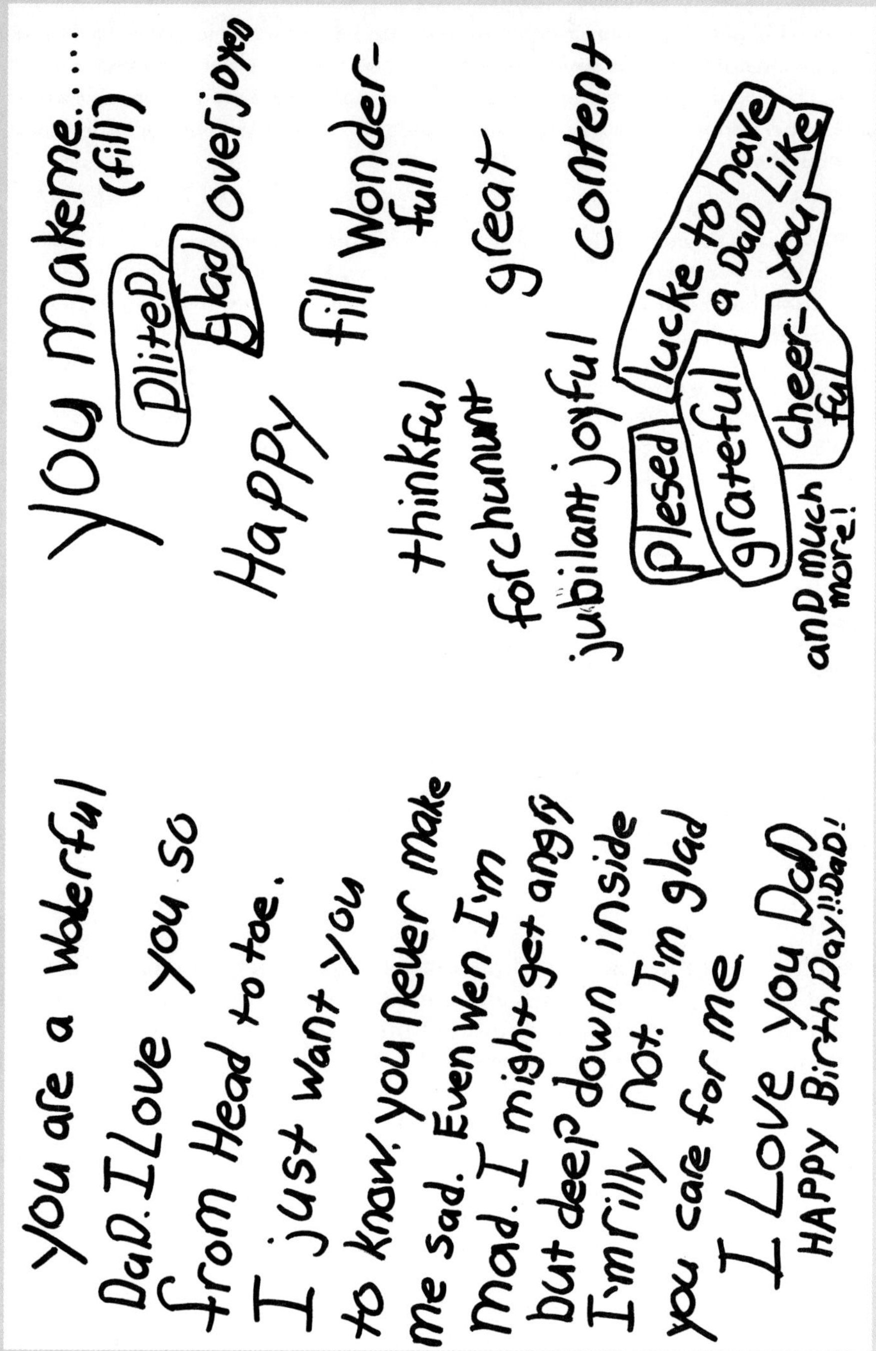

You make me..... (fill)

DliteD
glaD overjoyeD
Happy
fill Wonder-full
great
thinkful
forchunint
jubilant joyful
content
lucke to have a DaD Like you
PleseD
grateful
Cheer-full
anD much more!

you are a woderful DaD. I Love you so from Head to toe. I just want you to know, you never make me sad. Even wen I'm Mad. I might get angy but deep down inside I'm rilly Not. I'm glad you care for me. I Love you DaD HAPPY Birth Day!! DaD!

TED RAND

1. Which book of yours has given you the greatest pleasure?

Cabin Key. It's a new book published by Harcourt Brace. It began as a conversation with an editor—Gloria and I were telling her about a mountain cabin that has been in our family for four generations. She suggested that there was a book there. Writing and illustrating the book turned out to be a labor of love. We first took our children there when they were in diapers and now they are taking their children there.

2. Which book has surprised you most in terms of its public reception?

Knots on a Counting Rope. We were apprehensive at first because the Native American boy in the story is blind and we wanted to handle that with sensitivity. That book has been so well received and is used by many teachers in talking about attitudes toward people with handicaps.

3. What would you like people to remember about your work?

I want people to remember the authenticity. We do a lot of research so our artwork accurately represents the images in the text. Our goal is to thoroughly connect words with pictures, to so interlock text and illustration that they cannot be separated.

4. What impact do you hope your work will have on children?

More than anything, we want to produce books that children will love, in the hope that they will come to love reading itself.

Ted Rand excels in portraying the emotions of the characters in his books. While his paintings are painstakingly researched and accurately rendered, his masterful use of light and darkness brings a magical quality to his work. His books include *The Night Tree, The Football That Won the Super Bowl, Here Are My Hands, Knots on a Counting Rope, Barn Dance, Ghost-Eye Tree, Once When I Was Scared,* and *Paul Revere's Ride.*

concerning the topic, and recording what information they gleaned from the text that answers their questions and concerns about the topic. Developed by Donna Ogle (1989), this strategy models processes that proficient readers utilize when attempting to learn from text. Here is a list of the steps for implementing K-W-L with a class:

1. Introduce the new topic and solicit through brainstorm fashion what the students think they *know* about the subject. The teacher should divide a chart or overhead into four categories labeled K—What We Know; W—What We Want to Know; and L—What We Learned; and Categories of Information. The teacher should write the brainstormed information in the column labeled K—What I Know on the chart or overhead so it can be utilized throughout the study. It is important that *all* brainstormed information be recorded on the overhead or chart—

this is not the time to correct misconceptions but for students to activate their schema or knowledge base concerning the topic. However, students may be given a sheet with the K-W-L categories so they can record their personal brainstorming.

2. Pose the questions "What do you have questions about?" "What do you want to learn more about?" "What do we need to find out about this topic?" As students begin to generate questions, the teacher records these on the chart or overhead in the column labeled W—What We Want to Know. This questioning process models what lifelong learners are consistently doing—developing questions and purposes for reading. If students have been given a personal K-W-L sheet, they should be encouraged to write questions they have about the topic.

3. In order to extend the students' readiness to read the text, the teacher can ask students to look at their knowledge about the topic and the questions they have. They then categorize their prior knowledge into categories the teacher writes on the overhead or chart and students may write on their own K-W-L sheets. Students should then be asked to predict if and how the author might address these categories in the text.

4. The students then read the text selection. As they read, they answer the questions they have generated and make notes about new information or concerns in the L—What We Learned column. In addition, we have found that if students encounter information in the text which confirms items that were brainstormed in the K—What We Know column, it is important for the students to mark the items and note the page numbers of the text where the confirming information was found. This activity aids students in realizing the importance of documenting the validity of items.

After the students have read and recorded information on their sheets, debrief with the class. Ask them to share the answers they found to questions in the W column, and the information they were able to confirm in the K column. Record their responses on the class K-W-L form. During this time, you may find that students confirm, reject, or extend some of the information that was brainstormed in the K column. Remind them that this revision and extension of knowledge is part of the learning process. Continue the process by asking students to share any new ideas or information they found in the text that they did not expect. Record students' responses on the class K-W-L sheet and ask if they now have further questions. We have found that this discussion will often lead to an extension of the K-W-L form as shown in Figure 13.5 (see page 370).

ANTICIPATION-REACTION GUIDE

Anticipation-reaction guides (Head & Readence, 1986) are designed for prereading anticipation and postreading contemplation. They consist of a series of teacher-prepared statements related to the topics of a book or chapter. Students agree or disagree with the statements *before reading,* and discuss the reasons for their answers. (Students might write down their reasons, in pairs,

FIGURE 13.5 ▶ **EXTENDED K-W-L**

K-W-L

K What We Know	**W** What We Want to Know	**L** What We Learned and Where We Found It	**W** What We Want to Know Now	**W** Where We Might Find It
Categories of Information				

before discussing them as a group.) After reading, students decide what they think are the author's feelings or thoughts about the statement, and what in the text makes them attribute this viewpoint to the author. During class discussion they compare their responses with their classmates and have the opportunity to reread and cite evidence that supports their responses. Figure 13.6 is an example of an anticipation-reaction guide based on *Who Put That Hair in my Toothbrush?* (Spinelli, 1984).

Using this technique causes students to draw on their background experiences in responding. Prereading discussions are facilitated because there is no right or wrong answer. A framework is formed by the activation of students' schema for new information to "hook" onto. As students compare and contrast their views with the views they perceive to be those of the author, they have the opportunity to discuss what passages in the text support their beliefs. Because there are no "right" or "wrong" answers, students have the opportunity to discuss text and defend divergent viewpoints.

CONFERENCING ABOUT TEXT

As we have discussed earlier, it is important for students to have the opportunity to talk about the text they are reading. This is a literate activity that people who love to read naturally engage in—they are always telling you

ANTICIPATION-REACTION GUIDE ◀ **FIGURE 13.6**
WHO PUT THAT HAIR IN MY TOOTHBRUSH?

ANTICIPATION-REACTION GUIDE
Who Put That Hair in my Toothbrush?

Read the statements. Write yes if you agree. Write no if you disagree.

What I think   What the author thinks

_____   It is difficult to be a middle child.   _____
_____   Parents treat all their children fairly.   _____
_____   Sometimes getting what you wished   _____
                         can be painful.
_____   Sibling rivalry is natural.   _____
_____   Treating others like you want to be treated   _____
                         is very important.
_____   Sometimes it is difficult to be a parent.   _____

about the book they are reading, the new author they have discovered, the interesting article they just read—the list goes on. When reading is an interesting and integral part of our lives, we want to share our excursions into text with others. Conferencing allows students to engage in this behavior in the classroom.

Students may conference with a peer or with the teacher. If a child is conferencing with a peer, the conference may be recorded so the teacher can sample bits of the conference and determine what interactions with the text were being discussed. Older children can utilize Carolyn Burke's strategy of written conversation to conference (Harste, Short, & Burke, 1988) and write their conversation rather than discussing orally. In order to accomplish this, a student would write a comment or question about the text on a piece of paper and hand it to a partner. The partner would read the question or comment, respond in writing, and return the paper to the first student. The process would continue in this manner with students shifting roles of questioner and responder.

Sample questions that aid in oral or written conferencing about stories include the following:

1. Who are the most important characters? Why do you think so?
2. Describe what kind of place the story happened in.
3. What is the main problem or conflict in this story? How was it solved? Can you think of another way it could have been solved?
4. Who do you think is the main person in the story? Why?

Name: JOSH GODWIN

Age: 13

Interests: SPORTS, OM, PARTIES, FRIENDS, SCHOOL

What do you like most about school? I THINK WHAT I LIKE MOST ABOUT SCHOOL IS BEING AROUND FRIENDS. I USUALLY AREN'T AROUND THEM MUCH DURING THE SUMMER. IN SCHOOL I GET A CHANCE TO REUNITE WITH THEM AND TO MEET OTHER FRIENDS.

What's your favorite subject? Why? I LIKE S. STUDIES AND ATHLETICS BEST. STUDYING HISTORY IS REAL AMAZING. THE TEACHERS I HAVE HAD NOT ONLY READ FROM THE BOOK BUT ALSO PUT IT IN PERSPECTIVE.

What's your favorite book? Why do you like it? MY FAVORITE IS A WRINKLE IN TIME. ITS WIDE VOCABULARY AND EXCITING FUTURISTIC PLACES APPEAL TO ME GREATLY. THE AUTHOR LETS YOU BELIEVE ITS REAL, TOO.

What advice do you have for teachers? I ONLY HAVE TWO ADVICES FOR TEACHERS. BEFORE THE SCHOOL DAY PUT YOURSELF IN THE STUDENTS' FEET. WHAT WOULD YOU LIKE TO DO FOR THE DAY? ALSO, GET ALONG WITH YOUR STUDENTS AND IT WILL BE A MUCH FUNNER YEAR!

5. How does the main character change or how is the character different at the end of the story? What do you think caused this change?

6. What do you think is the most important event in the story? Why?

7. Would you recommend this book to other readers? Why or why not?

8. If you were the author of the story, would you rewrite any parts? Why?

9. Does this story remind you of any other stories you have read? Why? What parts?

10. What is your favorite page? Why?

Sample questions for use with content text include these:

1. What was the most important thing you learned from this text? What made it the most important?

2. What was the most confusing part of the text? What seemed to cause it to be confusing?

3. What new terms did you find in the text? Were you able to figure out what they meant? How did you do this?

4. Was there information you already knew? What was it?

5. Was there anything you thought you knew, but the text had different information? What was it? Do you believe the text is right? Why?

6. What would be a good question about this text? What is the answer?

7. What in the text would you like to know more about? Where do you think you might find the information?

As children engage in oral or written conferencing, they have the opportunity to explore their perceptions of the text and gain exposure to the perceptions of others.

RECIPROCAL QUESTIONING TECHNIQUE

Are you interested in ways to involve your students in the reading process—to help them interact mentally with the printed page in such a way that the text becomes more than mere words on paper? One strategy proven effective in facilitating this interaction is the *Reciprocal Questioning Technique—ReQuest.* Tony Manzo's procedure (1969) enables students to approach reading with an inquiring attitude. The strategy is particularly effective for students with poor comprehension skills. ReQuest can be used at any level, from first grade through university classrooms. The basic steps of the procedure remain the same, regardless of the class. The teacher simply adjusts the difficulty of the material and length of the text according to the abilities of the students. Originally, ReQuest was designed to be used on a one-to-one basis, but the procedure has proven to be equally effective with groups ranging from two to eight students. However, participants in the group must have approximately the same reading level because they will all be reading the identical passage.

The first responsibility of the teacher when using ReQuest is to select well-written and level-appropriate reading material. Contrived basal stories that contain no real plot are ineffective. However, some basal stories are perfect candidates for ReQuest. Other material sources include content-area textbooks, newspaper articles, and magazine pieces. After selecting the material, the next step is to identify good break points within the story where the group will pause from their reading and ask questions. When using ReQuest for the first time, it is very important to explain to students what is expected of them. Most students have had very little instructional variation from the traditional Directed Reading Activities that accompany basal readers. Therefore, students should be told they will be reading the story in a different way, and that the purpose of the lesson will be to improve their understanding of what they read. In addition, students will be told that *they* will be required to ask both teacher and other students questions about the passage. Further, these should be the thought-provoking kinds of questions that teachers ask. At this point the teacher is ready to begin and should adhere to the following basic steps:

1. Teacher and students silently read the first section of the material. This section might be as short as a few sentences for second graders, or as long as several pages for high school students.

2. When all have completed the section, books are turned face down and the questions begin. As originally designed by Manzo (1969), one student asks the teacher as many questions as desired. Then the teacher asks that same student questions. However, Tierney, Readence, and Dishner (1990) recommend that a good alternative to this procedure is to have "the roles of questioner and respondent either alternate around a circle or proceed at random within the circle" (p. 57). This works quite well, resulting in intragroup discussions about the quality and appropriateness of certain questions and responses. The teacher's role during this question-and-answer time is to model more provocative questions and to provide positive feedback to students by commenting on their questions. Such comments might include, "Good question," and "That's a good way of thinking about that." If a question is not clear during the question–answer procedure, the student can ask for clarification. An answer of "I don't know" is unacceptable. The student (or teacher) must at least try to explain why he or she doesn't know the answer. If necessary, the question can be rephrased and reference to the text can be used to justify an uncertain response. Should the question a student intended to ask be posed first by someone else, that student is allowed to refer back to the material and select another question. Teachers must, of course, be sure to have the students read the next section of the story when it appears the material has been "milked" of all useful information.

3. The students and teacher proceed from section to section, following the same procedure. This continues until the teacher observes that questions are being asked that show the students are in command of their comprehension of the story. At this point, the teacher moves the group from the development of questioning behaviors to the development of student-predictive behaviors. The teacher can make inquiries such as "What do you think will happen next?" and "Why do you think so?" Such questions guide the silent reading of the students as they read the next section of the story. After reading the section, the teacher discusses individual predictions of the students. Questions like "Did your prediction occur?" and "Do you still think . . . ?" help stimulate further consideration of the text. This process is modeled through several sections of the book, or until the teacher feels the students are making sensible predictions and are comprehending the text. From this point, the remainder of the selection is read silently, with the teacher

offering assistance to the students when necessary without interfering with their reading.

4. After the selection has been completed, the students and the teacher may discuss specific predictions that were made by members of the group. Information or concepts not understood in the story may then be clarified. Through this interaction, students often gain a clearer understanding of the selection.

Students who participate in ReQuest will quickly assume more responsibility in asking questions. Searfoss and Readence (1985) state that the ReQuest procedure "provides a format to fill the gaps between instructional lessons in which teachers direct children's comprehension processes by questioning, and lessons that allow for children to direct their own learning through active comprehension" (p. 246).

When using ReQuest for the first time, some teachers make the common error of dominating the discussion. The teacher should be patient with the students and allow them to create and answer the questions at their own pace. Group interaction is essential. The silence that may occur during this procedure could be an indication that the students are thinking, and that's what they must do in order to comprehend. Goodlad's (1983) research indicates our schools are in critical need of instructional practices that provoke students to think. The ReQuest procedure offers an important step toward that goal.

CLOZE PROCEDURE

The *cloze procedure* requires readers to respond to a reading passage by supplying words that have been deleted from the text. It demands that the reader search for information clues in order to predict what word or type of word would be syntactically and semantically appropriate for the deletion. Thus students are required "to complete a familiar—but not quite finished pattern—to 'see' a broken circle as a whole one . . . by mentally closing the gaps" (Taylor, 1953, p. 415). As a teaching technique, cloze may be used to encourage the use of contextual clues, strengthen vocabulary, encourage divergent production, and improve reading comprehension (Bortnick & Lopardo, 1976; Rankin, 1977; Sampson, Valmont, & Allen, 1982).

The cloze procedure is appropriate for use with students of all ages. The materials selected for use as cloze materials should be relatively easy reading for the students. Selections may be taken from poems, stories, subject matter texts, or even from language experience stories (Tierney, Readence, & Dishner, 1990).

After selecting the passage the teacher wants to develop into a cloze exercise, he or she will need to determine instructional objectives before making the cloze deletions. Adjectives or some other part of speech may be deleted, but, whatever is decided, the difficulty of the passage will be affected.

The passage may be read and completed individually by the students. However, it is important that the students come together in small groups to discuss the various words selected to complete the cloze blanks. Such discussions should focus on the variety of answers that could be used in most cloze blanks and on the reasons for a particular response within the context surrounding the deletion (Sampson, Valmont, & Allen, 1982). Semantic consistency should be the determining factor concerning the appropriateness of the responses (Sampson & Briggs, 1983).

Cloze is a worthwhile instructional activity when used appropriately. However, cloze lessons must include more than just the completion of cloze deletions. Group discussions are imperative. Comprehension and vocabulary improvements will result only when student involvement and teacher follow-up are included.

READER-DIRECTED STRATEGIES

Students who excel in school usually share a common characteristic—they are good readers. What is a good reader? Perhaps the best definition is revealed by examining characteristics of successful readers. Good readers know how to extract information from their textbooks, to evaluate its importance, and to link new information with old. In addition, they monitor their understanding and retention and evaluate their progress in terms of their purpose for reading.

Unfortunately, content-area materials are often quite difficult for some students to comprehend. Consequently, students may experience continual frustration from their inability to understand their text. Their study time often involves nothing more than passive—sometimes desperate—rereading.

So what can a teacher do to help students learn from reading? One answer is to provide them with workable strategies to guide their reading. This section of the chapter details several techniques that have been proven successful in improving the comprehension of individual readers.

SMART

Study strategies for content-reading books have been available for years. However, most of these strategies share a common fault: They stress remembering and place little emphasis on understanding. The *Self-Monitoring Approach to Reading and Thinking* (SMART) was developed to emphasize understanding—and, as a by-product, remembering (Vaughan & Estes, 1986). The strategy is effective because remembering naturally follows understanding, and understanding often eliminates the need to memorize.

The steps involved in SMART are discussed next. We recommend you try out the procedure with the next reading assignment. The following instructions are for the students:

▶ STEP 1 Survey the material to get a general idea of what the passage is about. When surveying, look at the title, subheadings, pictures, graphs, and summary of the section. Identify and note logical breaking points; you will be stopping at these points to check your understanding. These breaking points often are between subheadings in the textbook.

▶ STEP 2 Read each segment of the text, placing a plus (+) by material you understand (place this "+" in the margin in pencil, using a separate sheet of paper if marking in the book is not permissible). Place a question mark (?) in the margin beside material you do not understand.

▶ STEP 3 As you read each section, pause to clarify your understanding. Do so by completing the following steps:

▶ 1. Explain to yourself in your own words what you understand. Looking back at the material as you do so is allowed.

▶ 2. Examine what you do not understand. Use the procedure listed below.

▶ a. Reread the portions you do not understand.

▶ b. Try to identify what might be causing the problem. It might be a word, a phrase, or a relationship.

▶ c. Try to think of something that might help you to understand, such as reviewing similar information in another portion of the text, using the glossary, or perhaps examining graphic aids and illustrations.

▶ d. Try your idea out. If it works and you now understand, change the question mark (?) in the margin to a plus (+).

▶ e. Explain to yourself what you do not understand (for example, "I still don't understand how investment casting of metal is done").

▶ f. If a formula is creating the problem, reread the explanation of the formula. Next, reread the example that illustrates the formula; this will often clarify hazy notions you might have. Your goal should be to comprehend the formula, the example of the formula and its answer, and, most important, the generalization or conclusion at the end of the section.

▶ STEP 4 Go on to the next segment of the text. Repeat steps 2 and 3.

▶ STEP 5 As you proceed through each section of the reading assignment, turn back and reexamine concepts you did not understand earlier. Ask yourself, "Does it make sense now?" If it does, it is probably because you learned something new as you read the latest section, or were able to relate the new information to old information you already knew. If the content still does not make sense to you, don't be concerned. Just keep reading.

▶ STEP 6 After reading the entire assignment, do the following: (1) With your book closed, explain to yourself what you understand about what you read. (2) Open your text and look back over the material to refresh your memory. Do not be concerned about things you don't understand. You can ask a classmate or your teacher about them later. (3) Rethink what you do not understand. What could they mean? Are they related to other things that you do understand?

▶ STEP 7 With the book closed, explain to yourself one final time what you do understand.

Content-area materials are often difficult for students to read. Their difficult readability levels and complex explanations of concepts, formulas, and procedures frustrate many students. Consequently, many students decide that taking notes and observing the teacher are the best ways to obtain information about content. The solution to the problem is for you to help students overcome their fears of their texts. SMART is an excellent first step toward that end. As students learn to monitor their own comprehension and learn *what* to do when they don't understand, they will develop a new respect for their text and their ability to manipulate it. The result will be successful students who learn from reading.

REAP TECHNIQUE

The *Read, Encode, Annotate, Ponder* (REAP) *Technique* is based on the premise that comprehension is facilitated when students have to communicate their understanding of text to others. Specifically, the procedure is designed to improve the comprehension skills of students by having them synthesize an author's message in the form of annotations (Eanet & Manzo, 1976). Research indicates that comprehension is significantly improved by this postreading activity (Eanet, 1978). However, Vaughan (1982) cautions that the technique requires students to become "adept at constructing" the various types of annotations if the activity is to be of value.

REAP is appropriate for use with intermediate-grade students and higher. The activity consists of the following four stages:

R—READING to uncover the ideas of the author

E—ENCODING the ideas of the author into the student's own language

A—ANNOTATING those ideas into written form

P—PONDERING the significance of the annotation

When your students write annotations, they will be interacting with the ideas of the author, synthesizing those ideas into their own language and putting that synthesis into writing. This demands interaction with the text, which results in comprehension.

Students may use several different forms of annotations. Eanet and Manzo (1976) suggest that these types should include summary, critical, question, motivation, intention, heuristic, and thesis annotations.

The Ponder stage of REAP involves the use of annotations for classroom activities or personal study. Eanet and Manzo (1976) suggest several possible uses of annotations. Students might write annotations of library books they have read. These annotations can be filed in the library as a source of review for prospective readers of the book. Another possibility is for students to review past reading assignments by consulting their annotations and the annotations of others.

REAP does a good job of interrelating reading, writing, and thinking. When used selectively, it can facilitate reading comprehension and improve study skills.

SKETCH TO STRETCH

The Sketch to Stretch strategy was devised by Jerry Harste, Carolyn Burke, Marjorie Siegel, and Karen Feathers (Tierney, Readence, & Dishner, 1990) and provides students with an opportunity to represent the most important "picture" that played in the mind when they read a selection. It also gives students the chance to view what varied meanings were constructed by different class members as they share and discuss their drawings. The strategy is useful for both content and narrative texts and consists of the following steps:

1. Students read text. (If desired, students may divide into groups of four to five and read the same selection. This strategy may also be implemented with a story the teacher reads aloud to the class or a small group of children.)

2. Draw a sketch of "the picture that you see in your mind when you think of the story." Remind students there is not a "right" or "wrong" picture. There are many ways of depicting the meaning of an experience.

3. If all students have been reading the same text, they should divide into groups of four or five after completing their sketches. Each person shows his or her sketch to the others in the group. Group members have a chance to express what they think the artist/student is trying to say.

4. After all the group members have had the opportunity to indicate what they think the drawing represents, the artist/student gets the last word.

5. All of the groups share. Groups may collaborate and construct a group sketch after sharing, choose one from the group to share, or share all of the sketches. Sketches may be put on the overhead projector or displayed on poster board.

This strategy provides students with an opportunity to discuss the impact the text had on them by deciding on and then sharing the most important mental image that was formed as they interacted with the text. During this sharing, the concept is reinforced that reading text is much more than just "saying the words." Mental images must be formed.

SAVE THE LAST WORD FOR ME

Save the Last Word for Me is a strategy developed by Carolyn Burke (Harste, Short, & Burke, 1988) to involve students in making decisions about text and sharing the basis for those decisions. As students discuss their views, they are exposed to the concept that there is not one "right way" to comprehend.

Save the Last Word for Me consists of the following steps:

1. Students are given 3 x 5-inch cards and instructed to read the text.

2. As they read, they are encouraged to write any words, phrases, or segments from the text that they feel are particularly important, interesting, surprising, or warrant further discussion. We have found it useful to limit the number of cards so children are involved in making decisions about text. Otherwise, children begin writing everything down and do not have time to complete the reading. The number of cards you give will depend on the grade level of the students, but we usually limit it to five. We also ask children to write the page number where the segment of text was found so it will be easy to find the portion for future reference.

3. On the back of the cards, the children compose what they want to say about the segment of text they selected. (See Figure 13.7.)

4. Students rank-order their cards from most important to least important.

5. Students divide into small groups and share their number one quote. During this time of sharing and discussion, if a student's number one quote has been shared by another student, he or she shares the second-ranked quote. As each student shares, the other students in the group react to the segment of text. After students have responded, the sharer of the quote has the "last word" and reads from the back of the card what he or she wrote as the reason for choosing that particular segment of text. The process continues until all quotes are shared or time runs out.

6. Students in the group may collaborate and rank-order several quotes they would like to share with the entire class and develop reasons for their choices. The same procedure for group sharing as for individual sharing would be followed. After the other groups had given a group response to shared quote, the sharing group would have the "last word."

As students engage in this process, they have the opportunity to make decisions about text, justify those decisions, and then discuss. When this process occurs, students are actively involved in bringing personal meaning to text. See Figure 13.7.

MAKING STRATEGIES WORK FOR YOU

After looking at a sampling of strategies, we hope you are thinking of ways you could adapt or modify them to utilize in your classroom. Once again, the emphasis must be on involving your students in the *process* of "acting like real readers." Activities must place students in the position of actively interacting with the text, synthesizing the material, and producing something that demonstrates *their* understanding, rather than being in the position of answering questions they never asked. Here are some examples of activities that students might do that would provide avenues for reflection, sharing, and discussion:

1. Make a newspaper out of the important events of a story or a selected part of the newspaper such as a comic strip, editorial cartoon, want ad, lead story, editorial, help wanted ad, classified ad, letter to the editor— the list goes on and on.

2. Write to the author about his or her story, write to a character in the story, assume the role of a character in the story and write to a classmate, assume the role of one character and write a letter to another character in the story, assume the role of a character in one story and write to a character in another story, assume the role of a character in

SAVE THE LAST WORD FOR ME STRATEGY ◄ FIGURE 13.7

SAVE THE LAST WORD FOR ME
based on HATCHET by Gary Paulsen

The very core of him, the very center of Brian Robeson was stopped and stricken with a white-flash of horror, a terror so intense that his breathing his thinking and nearly his heart had stopped. p.12	When I read this — I knew the pilot was really dead and I knew Brian was in big trouble. What was he going to do now I thought!!!
When I threw the hatchet at the porcupine in the cave and missed and hit the stone wall it had showered sparks, a golden shower of sparks in the dark, as golden with fire as the sun was now. p.86	This was important because he figured out how to start a fire!! You know he thought it was bad when he missed the porcupine, but if he had hit it he wouldn't have made sparks so what seemed bad was good.

the story and write a letter to the editor of a newspaper—once again you are only limited by your imagination.

3. Make a wall story out of the story. Select the important events that tell the story and illustrate and write a short description. Attach to the wall or bulletin board in sequential order. This project could be done in groups.

4. Create time lines from a story or chart the sequence of important story events.

5. Illustrate favorite scenes and characters from the story and write or tell why they were chosen.

6. Rewrite a story into a play or Reader's Theater.

7. List alternative solutions for a problem in a story.

8. Create puppets for a dramatization. Dramatization may be impromptu or students may write a script.

9. Do writing activities on the story—journal responses, letters, poems, patterned books, critiques.

10. Write a "concise summary" of the story. Teacher and students should collaborate to determine the maximum number of words that may be

used. This limitation causes students to write precisely with words of high imagery. Students may edit their summaries, illustrate them, and make a class book.

11. Have a panel discussion. Topics could vary—actions of a character, alternative endings of story, believability of story, contrast and comparison with other stories, writing style. Topic would depend on story and age of students.

12. Prepare a book jacket that would represent the story.

13. Decide on three new titles for the story. Give a rationale for your decision.

14. Write a publisher's blurb or advertisement for the story.

15. Create a poster advertising the story.

16. Write a review of the story. Teacher should bring in book reviews from magazines and newspapers so students can become acquainted with the critical style of writing. Students may also follow a pattern such as: (a) title; (b) author; (c) where and when the story takes place; (d) main characters; (e) the most interesting thing that happened; (f) if you did or did not enjoy the story—why or why not; (g) would you recommend this story to someone else—why or why not?

17. Write a letter recommending the story to a friend.

18. Assume the role of a character in the story and write a letter to a friend or family member describing your situation/problem.

19. Write a personality sketch of one of the story characters.

20. Compose a "rap" about a story character.

21. Construct a mobile of the story characters. On the back of each character write five adjectives that describe the character.

22. Construct a flip chart depicting the important scenes in a story. Students may also write a one- or two-sentence description on each page.

23. Think of a new character that could be added to the story and assume the role of that character. Then write or discuss the following: What would the character do? How would the character fit into the story? What would the character contribute?

24. Write a sequel to the story. What happens to the characters?

25. Identify the turning point in the story and rewrite it. Then finish the story with the new ending.

26. Write an interview between a character in the story and the author, between student and a character in the story, between student and the author, between two characters in the story—once again the list goes on and on.

27. Play story charades. After numerous stories have been read, put the names of the various stories and characters into a box. Draw the titles of the stories or names of characters out of the box and then pantomime actions to convey the answer.

28. Try the "never-ending story review." Start a sheet around the room with each student giving a one-sentence response to the story. Sentences cannot be duplicated.

SUMMARY

Comprehension should be the major focus in all language activities. Because it involves a transaction between language and thought, instructional activities must be meaningful and representative of the kinds and types of language experiences students encounter in life. Contrived language and instructional practices are confusing and counterproductive for students.

We must shift instructional priorities from regurgitation of information to demonstration that what is important in reading is the personal meaning created when a reader and a text interact. The comprehension strategies presented in this chapter were developed toward that end. They will serve as a valuable resource as you seek to build and enhance the reading comprehension skills of your students.

PATHWAYS TO READING COMPREHENSION

The student:

▶ applies personal experiences and background knowledge to text in order to facilitate comprehension.

▶ adjusts comprehension mode and utilizes various strategies based on purpose for reading and difficulty of text.

▶ monitors own understanding of text and takes appropriate measures when comprehension breaks down.

The teacher:

▶ has a repertoire of teacher-directed and reader strategies that may be modeled to assist students in comprehending text.

▶ realizes that students have individual schemata or background experience, which affects their comprehension of a text.

▶14 PATHWAYS TO CHILDREN'S LITERATURE

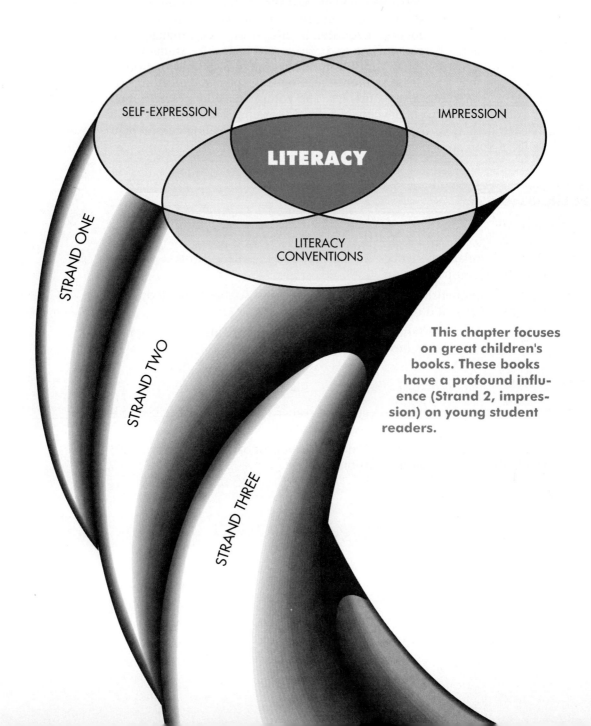

SELF-EXPRESSION

IMPRESSION

LITERACY

LITERACY
CONVENTIONS

STRAND ONE

STRAND TWO

STRAND THREE

This chapter focuses on great children's books. These books have a profound influence (Strand 2, impression) on young student readers.

CHAPTER OUTLINE

PATHWAYS TO PONDER

▶ WHAT CAN TEACHERS DO TO HELP CHILDREN DEVELOP A LOVE OF BOOKS?

▶ WHAT ARE YOUR FAVORITE BOOKS? WHY?

Authors' Note: Bill Martin Jr, the author of this chapter, has written more than 300 books for children, including the classics *Brown Bear, Brown Bear, What Do You See?* and *Chicka Chicka, Boom Boom.*

Bill Martin began his career as a teacher in Kansas. His teaching was interrupted by World War II and his subsequent service in the army. In the military, he served as a journalist.

After the war, Bill wrote children's books with his brother, Bernard. His quest to learn more about children and how they learn led him to Northwestern University, where he received a doctorate in elementary education. He then returned to the public schools where he served as an elementary principal.

Bill Martin Jr ▶

In 1961 he moved to New York to work for Holt, Rinehart and Winston, where he developed the literature–based reading programs *Sounds of Language* and *The Instant Readers*. Seven years later, he left Holt and launched his career as a writer of children's books.

Through the years he has given children some of their favorite books, including *Polar Bear, Polar Bear, What Do You Hear?*, *The Ghost-Eye Tree*, *Barn Dance*, *Knots on a Counting Rope*, and many more.

Dan Darigan of West Chester University also contributed to this chapter.

CHILDREN LEARN BEST WHEN THEY COME TO BOOKS EXPECTING ADVENTURE

What's the difference between children who like to read and those who don't? Surprisingly, it's not ability. Rather, the answer is that some children have discovered the joys of reading and others have not.

Children are born into a world that swirls with print. Even before a child can talk, that child has favorite books and favorite reading companions. Children fall in love with the sweep of the sentence and the music of the poetic line. They nestle in the arms of a loved one, mesmerized by the cadence of endearing words falling into comfortable patterns. Soon, books become children's best friends. Children get hooked on stories—the spinning of dreams and imaginative releases into a world that beckons them to enter.

These early experiences with stories form the foundation for a lifelong love of reading. But a transition must occur. Children must move from being a hearer of language to the role of being an independent reader and recreator of language and stories.

◀ A young girl enjoys a good book.

And there's good news. The secret of keeping children's love for story alive does not reside in a reading method or in the intellect of the child; rather it resides in children's continuing encounters with stories that bring them to the brink of the best things life has to offer—adventure, intrigue, suspense, love, and excitement. That's what books have to offer.

This chapter examines ways we can help children become lifelong readers. As teachers we have the opportunity to introduce children to literature—from the classics to this year's best-seller. We must choose with care; each book a child engages with becomes a part of that child—its language, its visions, its excitement. So join me as I share with you my love for books. I'll lead you down a pathway rich with literature. Along the way I'll introduce you to classroom teachers who are successful in maintaining children's love for books through their daily teaching. And I'll share with you my favorite books and my ideas for how these books can entice children into a lifelong love of reading.

MAKING CONNECTIONS WITH BOOKS IS THE KEY TO A LIFETIME OF READING

I'll always remember Miss Alice Davis, my fifth-grade teacher in Hiawatha, Kansas. She's the first teacher I remember as a reading teacher. All prior reading instruction had left no imprint, either positive or negative. Miss Davis loved books, and she loved sharing this love with us. She enriched us, enabled us, expanded us by reading aloud twice a day. She read to us in the morning to neutralize the worldly rush we brought to school. And she read to us at day's end to depressurize us from the day's accumulation of scholastic anxieties.

It was under her spell that I came to know and love Rudyard Kipling, Charles Dickens, Jack London, Robert Louis Stevenson. Their dreams became my dreams, their loves became my loves. Miss Davis had convinced me that books are essential to human enrichment and fulfillment. Like a good whole-language teacher of today, she knew precisely what she was doing. Her love for books was contagious, and her reading of favorite books inculcated a view of life that gave us ways of passage. I became a reader that year. Oh, I didn't have the skills of reading that present-day tests measure. But I became a reader because I was filled with a thirst for the excitement and adventures that beckoned to me from books. I developed the skills of reading through encounters with books in the years that were to follow. Books have indeed been for me a way of passage. I hope you can carry on the tradition of Miss Davis by introducing your students to books that will launch them into a lifelong adventure through literacy.

BOOKS I'VE COME TO LOVE

By category, I'll now share the books that I've come to love, and the books that seem to have tremendous impact on readers.

BOOKS TO START WITH

Tomie dePaola's Mother Goose by Tomie dePaola
The Tale of Peter Rabbit by Beatrix Potter
Where the Wild Things Are by Maurice Sendak
Charlotte's Web by E.B. White
Sarah, Plain and Tall by Patricia MacLachlan
Treasure Island by Robert Louis Stevenson
Island of the Blue Dolphins by Scott O'Dell
Indian in the Cupboard by Lynne Reid Banks
Mississippi Bridge by Mildred Taylor
The Cat in the Hat by Dr. Seuss
The Magic School Bus Lost in the Solar System by Joanna Cole

HUMOROUS BOOKS

Miss Nelson Is Missing! by Harry Allard
The Stinky Cheese Man and Other Fairly Stupid Tales by Jon Scieszka
Homer Price by Robert McCloskey
Martha Speaks by Susan Meddaugh
Lizard Music by Daniel Pinkwater

POETRY

Where the Sidewalk Ends by Shel Silverstein
Talking Like the Rain by X.J. and Dorothy Kennedy
The Random House Book of Poetry for Children by Jack Prelutsky
Pass It On: African American Poetry for Children by Wade Hudson
A Child's Garden of Verse by Robert Louis Stevenson

WORDLESS PICTURE BOOKS

The Snowman by Raymond Briggs
Deep in the Forest by Brinton Turkle
Tuesday by David Wiesner
Anno's Journey by Mitsumasa Anno
Moonlight by Jan Ormerod

FOLKTALES

Little Red Riding Hood by Trina Schart Hyman
Puss in Boots by Charles Perrault, illustrated by Fred Marcellino
Snow White by the Grimm Brothers, illustrated by Nancy Ekholm Burkert
Rapunzel by Amy Ehrlich, illustrated by Kris Waldherr
Rumpelstiltskin by Paul O. Zelinsky

BOOKS OF ARTISTIC MERIT

Grandfather's Journey by Allen Say
Chanticleer and the Fox by Barbara Cooney
Lon Po Po: A Red Riding Hood Story from China by Ed Young
The Fortune-Tellers by Lloyd Alexander, illustrated by Trina Schart Hyman
Jumanji by Chris Van Allsburg
Round Trip by Ann Jonas

INFORMATIONAL BOOKS

The Way Things Work by David Macaulay
Across America on an Emigrant Train by Jim Murphy
Freight Train by Donald Crews
Bugs by Nancy Winslow Parker
Appalachia: The Voices of Sleeping Birds by Cynthia Rylant
Neptune by Seymour Simon

REALISTIC FICTION

The Pinballs by Betsy Byars
Nothing But the Truth by Avi
Maniac Magee by Jerry Spinelli
Dear Mr. Henshaw by Beverly Cleary
Shiloh by Phyllis Reynolds Naylor

HISTORICAL FICTION AND BIOGRAPHY

Across Five Aprils by Irene Hunt
Devil's Arithmetic by Jane Yolen

Lincoln: A Photobiography by Russell Freedman

John Brown: One Man Against Slavery by Gwen Evert

Roll of Thunder, Hear My Cry by Mildred Taylor

BOOKS FOCUSING ON SOCIAL ISSUES

Fly Away Home by Eve Bunting

An Angel for Solomon Singer by Cynthia Rylant

At the Crossroads by Rachel Isadora

Wilfrid Gordon McDonald Partridge by Mem Fox

A River Ran Wild by Lynne Cherry

STORYBOOKS

Strega Nona by Tomie dePaola

Owl Moon by Jane Yolen

The Napping House by Audrey Wood

Hiawatha by Susan Jeffers

The Orphan Boy by Tololwa Mollel

PICTURE BOOKS

Ira Sleeps Over by Bernard Waber

Chrysanthemum by Kevin Henkes

The Keeping Quilt by Patricia Polacco

The Very Busy Spider by Eric Carle

The Mitten by Jan Brett

CINDERELLA FOLKTALE VARIANTS

Cinderella by Diane Goode

Yeh Shen: A Cinderella Story from China by Ai-Ling Louie

The Rough-Face Girl by Rafe Martin

Mufaro's Beautiful Daughters by John Steptoe

The Talking Eggs by Robert D. San Souci

FANTASY

The Lion, the Witch and the Wardrobe by C. S. Lewis

Tuck Everlasting by Natalie Babbitt

The Wish-Giver by Bill Brittain

The Remarkable Journey of Prince Jen by Lloyd Alexander

Redwall by Brian Jacques

READ-ALOUDS

Where the Red Fern Grows by Wilson Rawls

Crow Boy by Taro Yashima

Angel Child, Dragon Child by Michele Maria Surat

In the Year of the Boar and Jackie Robinson by Bette Bao Lord

My Father's Dragon by Ruth Stiles Gannett

Mr. Popper's Penguins by Richard and Florence Atwater

The Fantastic Mr. Fox by Roald Dahl

Matilda by Roald Dahl

The Jack Tales by Richard Chase

Hatchet by Gary Paulsen

The Castle in the Attic by Elizabeth Winthrop

Hubert's Hair-Raising Adventure by Bill Peet

Alexander and the Terrible, Horrible, No Good, Very Bad Day by Judith Viorst

Sylvester and the Magic Pebble by William Steig

American Tall Tales by Mary Pope Osborne

Frog and Toad Are Friends by Arnold Lobel

A Rose for Pinkerton by Steven Kellogg

The Borrowers by Mary Norton

THE BEST READING ENVIRONMENT WE CAN OFFER CHILDREN IS A CLASSROOM FILLED WITH BOTH BOOKS AND READERS OF BOOKS

So far we've talked about the importance of introducing children to books, and we've looked at titles that should intrigue them. Now let's take a look at the marriage between literature and teaching, and how books can be the cornerstone of the classroom environment.

◀ **THE BOOK MAKERS**

GLORIA HOUSTON

1. Which book of yours has given you the greatest pleasure?

Mountain Valor. This Civil War book was the greatest joy of my writing career. My editor was satisfied with the book, but I couldn't let go—I just had to keep writing, revising, and playing with the language. I've never enjoyed working with characters so much. In fact, it has a character who's an 80-year-old woman who is no doubt who I'll be and what I'll be like when I reach 80 myself.

2. Which book has surprised you most in terms of its public reception?

My Great Aunt Arizona. I thought adults would like this book, but I have been blown away by the response of children—even young primaries. The book traces Arizona's life from her birth through her old age, and I don't think children get much of that. Most children's stories deal with an incident or a day or a few days. *Arizona* gives them the scope of a life. And they seem to have responded to that.

3. What would you like people to remember about your work?

First, I want to be remembered for my teaching more than my writing. But as for my writing, I want people to recognize the fact that I respected children and tried to give them rich characters to enjoy.

4. What impact do you hope your work will have on children?

I want to provide strong female role models for little girls. I did that for boys also in *Littlejim,* but I especially want to give girls characters they can identify with.

With an ear to the language of the Appalachian Mountains where she grew up, Gloria Houston weaves rich tapestries of language into stories of families, friends, and love. Her books include *My Great Aunt Arizona; The Year of the Perfect Christmas Tree; But, No Candy;* and *Littlejim.*

CLASSROOM VIGNETTE

The children in Randy Methven's first grade at Moriches (Long Island, New York) Elementary School are brought to reading by two powerful forces: (1) the teacher has complete confidence that each of them will learn to read easily, and (2) the children themselves are their own teachers. "Children like to be in on the planning," Randy said as he gathered a group of children around a poem hand printed on a large cardboard. "The final decision whether this poem, which is a favorite of mine, will become part of our reading and language fare depends on their reaction." Then he suggested, "Children, let's read through this poem to see if you like it." They read from the A. A. Milne poem *The End:*

When I was one, I was just begun,
When I was two, I was nearly new,
When I was three, . . .

The young readers reacted with excitement. Yes, yes, they liked the poem. "That's neat! Let's read it again!" And they did. And again. And again. With each chorusing of the poem, the children's reading became more secure, and the structural play of the poem became more cerebral. Every child in this typical class was deeply invested in the act of reading. Every child was mesmerized with reading success.

This was only the beginning of making the Milne poem and all its components (sentences, words, punctuation, rhythmic words, meanings, humor, inferences, nuances) available to each child for the mental and verbal interaction that leads to reading and other language acquisitions.

Each day for about two weeks, the children read the poem in chorus, along with 10 or 15 other poems they had previously given their "thumbs up." Each poem demanded a different mind-set, a different window on the world. They were not apprehensive about it. They were excited about it! In just a couple of days, they had learned each poem and its game plan and had them imprinted in long-term memory for a lifetime of repetitions and transpositions. Regardless of its thematic and verbal and structural intricacies, any poem the children like can become part of their reading program.

Continued

LITERATURE STRATEGIES THAT FACILITATE CHILDREN'S INTERACTIONS WITH BOOKS

Let's talk about ways we can help children enjoy and explore books. First, a word of caution. We must be very careful to only lightly touch literature through literature strategies. We have just completed the basal era—three decades in which children were subjected to drill after drill with literature. This era left us with millions of readers who choose not to read. We learned from this "experiment" a terrible lesson. It doesn't pay to tear literature apart

The class poems are stored hanging on the wall, hanging from the ceiling, hanging in clusters like large flip-page books. Any poem the children want to read can be lifted from its storage place and hung in the open for all to see.

In the course of the school year, 183 days, Randy's first graders select and learn to read 80 to 90 poems. The poems range from the ever-popular childhood lilt

1,2, buckle my shoe,
3,4, shut the door,
5,6, pick up sticks,
7,8, lay them straight,
9,10, a big fat hen.

Mother Goose

to the lyrical meditation

TREES

Trees are the kindest thing I know.
They do no harm, they simply grow.
They make a shade for sleepy cows.
They shelter birds among their boughs.
They give us fruit in leaves above,
And wood to make our houses of.
And leaves to burn at Halloween,
And in the spring new buds of green.
They are the first when day's begun
To catch the glimpse of morning sun.
They are the last to hold the light
When evening changes into night.
And when the moon floats on the sky,
They hum a drowsy lullaby
Of sleepy children long ago.
Trees are the kindest things I know.

Harry Behn

Continued

because children will lose their love for reading when we make readers toil over books. So literacy strategies must be practiced only under the watchful eye of the teacher. Be prepared to move on when children show signs of growing weary of the activities.

LITERATURE CIRCLES

As adults, we love to talk about an exciting book that we are reading. Children deserve the same privilege. An effective way of facilitating this "book talk" is through Literature Circles (Kasten, 1994). Literature Circles provide a

The range, breadth, and impact of all the language models the children have impressed in their long-term memory through their association with the poems are the fastest and best way they can possibly come to language usage.

Besides the emphasis on poetry in his classroom reading program, Randy Methven has a second daily reading focus—on children's books, at school, and at home. Randy and his 24 pupils and all of their parents are involved. The program works like this: First, on each Monday morning Randy introduces the four children's books of the week. He reads each one aloud and remarks about it in a way that helps the children anticipate the book and the pleasure of the reading.

A special place
for reading.
▼

Continued

stimulating opportunity for students to discuss chapter books or novels they are reading. They are excellent for grouping children of mixed abilities and are rapidly replacing the traditional grouping procedures of basal-oriented classrooms (Kasten, 1993).

Literature Circles make reading a family affair. The excitement of reading a book together binds the groups together and improves the reading/thinking/predicting abilities of all. And you'll notice another miracle during the sharing time—a miracle of courtesy as kids are attentive to one another. But the greatest thing you'll notice is growth: growth in confidence, growth in writing

The chosen titles have a significant relationship—all are written by the same author, all are illustrated by the same artist, or all four books are thematically related. The reading fare for one week is four Ezra Jack Keats titles: *Snowy Day, Whistle for Willie, Goggles,* and *Pet Show.*

Each day each child chooses a title to take home that evening for a family read-aloud. The act of choosing divides the class into four reading groups, there being six copies of each title.

"It is not enough that we ask parents to read aloud to their children," Randy said. "Not all parents have books and the wherewithal to buy books. I send home a book each night to read aloud. This is a book the child has already heard and can discuss, perhaps even read, with the parents and siblings. Every day of the school year, 183 days, I send a book home to be read aloud and enjoyed."

The second step of the children's literature/reading program occurs the next morning, Tuesday, when the children return to school bringing back the chosen book to the classroom. Randy unites each group of six children having the same book to meet around the reading table, where the book is again read aloud and discussed. The insights and opinions of each child are valued and encouraged, as are the sharing of writing, singing, storytelling, drawing, painting, and other talents that were activated by the book experience.

The third step of the literature/reading program is selecting another title from the week's chosen four, to take home for the family evening read-aloud—and the whole process begins again. On Friday nights each child takes home any book he or she wants for a parent-child-family weekend read-aloud.

"There is an increasing difficulty in the books chosen for the children to read," Randy said. "At the beginning of first grade I use Douglas Florian's *Beach Day,* and Mira Ginsberg's *The Chick and the Duckling.* By year end, it's Leo Lionni's *Swimmey* and *Frederic* and Arnold Lobel's *Frog and Toad.*"

Randy never doubts the skill development of the children. "They learn by involvement," he said. "Children who can read 80 or 90 wide-ranging poems and more than 175 books obviously are developing the skills of literacy."

ability, growth in knowledge about how writers put stories together, and most of all growth in appreciation for books and reading.

ACTING OUT STORIES

To love a story is to live it. And to live a story is to act it out—to become the characters and to take on their characteristics, their nuances, their views of life.

In the process of becoming actors, children become writers. They study the structure of stories in order to discover how to modify structure to fit the

CLASSROOM VIGNETTE

   Gary Bowman is a sixth-grade teacher in Covelo, California. Gary follows Kasten's (1993, p. 380) recommendations for Literature Circles, as his students Read, Write, Discuss, and Share. First, Gary selects, with input from his students, 10 books. Next, he shares something about each book with the class. He shares from his own knowledge of having read the book, or from the reviews of the books. He randomly breaks his class into six groups, and allows each group an opportunity to sign up for a book the group would like to read, indicating a first and second choice. He's now ready for the first step.

   Read: Students are given 20 minutes each day to participate in Literature Circles. Gary has volunteers from each book circle read aloud to the group. At the end of the reading period, the students move to step 2.

   Write: Students write whatever they are thinking as a result of what they've heard or read that day. Each student keeps a personal Literature Circle journal (see Figure 14.1). Then the groups move to step 3.

FIGURE 14.1 ▶

> 2-20-94
>
> I'm liking a Wrinkle in Time. The Charactors had weird names. I'm trying to figure out the language on page 40. I think that it is neat.
>
> Ryan

   Discuss: Using their journal entries, students share their reactions and discuss the different ideas and reactions. Students continue the Read, Write, Discuss cycle until the book is completed. This leads them to the most important step in the process, step 4.

   Share: The Literature Discussion group meets to decide how they can share their book with the entire class without revealing the conclusion of the story. Sometimes groups design an advertisement, act out a skit, or create a video. These presentations serve to make the book memorable to the group and lead others to want to read the book.

◀ Drama provides an excellent opportunity for developing listening and speaking skills.

constraints of moving from print to action on the stage. In short, they ask themselves, "How is it put together and how can we act it out?" And "What will act out and what will not?" They may discover they want more speaking parts so they add new characters. In the process, they discover the need to be flexible—what looks good on paper may not work as well on stage.

KEEPING ABREAST OF CHILDREN'S BOOKS

More than 5,000 new children's books are published each year. How do busy teachers keep abreast of these new titles? Here are six suggestions:

1. Form a literature share group with other teachers in your district. Schedule one evening per month to get together over snacks at someone's home, with the discussion dedicated to children's books. You might ask

CLASSROOM VIGNETTE

Rick Kilcup, a third-grade teacher from Renton, Washington, is a firm believer in the value of drama in the classroom. Every week his children adapt books into scripts. He calls his classroom productions Story Theater, and he believes four major benefits are achieved when children make books come alive: (1) it brings a story right off the pages and into the kids' lives, (2) it gives kids a chance to perform for an audience, without having to memorize a lot of lines! (3) Story Theater is a wonderful way to get nonreaders involved, and (4) it brings art into reading through the use of masks and simple costumes.

one person to moderate the evening, but the important thing is that every teacher who comes brings his or her favorite new book to share. It's fine to ask a special guest to share, such as the manager of the children's section of the local bookstore, but the emphasis should be on teacher-to-teacher sharing.

2. Examine resources that publishers use to alert bookstores about new titles. Baker & Taylor book wholesalers publishes the *Book Alert*. Ingram book wholesalers publishes a similar resource titled *The Advance*. You can also write to publishers of children's books and ask to be placed on their mailing lists.

**KIDS' ▶
CORNER**

Kristi Stobbs _____ Name

12 (April 24, 81) _____ Age

_____
_____ Interests

What do you like most about school? I enjoy playing games while learning. That always makes it more interesting to use when a teacher just lectures over and over you get in a daze and don't learn a thing. When you have to do a ton of worksheets that is just flat out boring. When you get to play bordoves of some other interesting is alloy more enjoyable, and holds your attention

What's your favorite subject? Why? I don't really have a favorite subject, just a favorite teacher. Who ever makes class the most exciting, and will hold my attention my the best is my favorite subject.

What's your favorite book? Why do you like it? Now I don't have a favorite book, just one that holds my attention, and something different happens in every chapter. One of my favorite books a while back was *Where the Red Fern Grows*. It was really exciting and I liked it alot.

What advice do you have for teachers? Just try to make learning fun because if it isn't children will come to your class and be in a daze the whole time. If your class is interesting and exciting than students will come in wide eyed and ready to learn.

3. Subscribe to magazines that review books. The University of Illinois publishes *The Bulletin of the Center for Children's Books,* in which they review more than 900 new books each year. *The Horn Book* also has outstanding and extensive reviews, as well as informative articles about children's literature. *The New Advocate* likewise has articles about children's literature and reviews 50 recommended books in each issue. *Booklist* is a biweekly journal that not only reviews children's books, but also other media and computer programs. *Book Links,* another publication from the American Library Association, provides teachers with comprehensive lists of books centered around themes and current issues.

4. Take advantage of the National Council of Teachers of English and The International Reading Association, professional organizations that promote literacy acquisition through a number of publications. The International Reading Association publishes *The Reading Teacher* and *The Journal of Reading,* which review new books. In addition, *The Reading Teacher* publishes a list in the October issue of new books that children consider their favorites. The National Council of Teachers of English publishes two outstanding journals, *Language Arts* and *English Education,* which feature book review columns.

5. Make friends with the manager of your local children's bookstore. Bookstores often receive information about author visits to your area; don't let your children miss their visits and storytelling sessions.

6. Consult a comprehensive source, such as textbooks designed for college-level children's literature courses. Bernice Cullinan's *Literature and the Child* is an outstanding resource, as are *Children's Literature in*

◄ Watch for author appearances at children's bookstores. Here, Bill Martin Jr shares with children at the Cornerstone Bookstore.

the Elementary School by Charlotte Huck and *Children and Books* by Zena Sutherland. Lively interest is also buoyed by the annual announcement (in February) of the best illustrated children's book and the best written children's book of the preceding year. These awards are known as the Caldecott Award and the John Newbery Award, respectively.

SUMMARY

Children's literature and the ways teachers use children's books in the classroom have been explored as productive methods of helping children develop the habits of lifetime readers. As certain books become young children's best friends, they lure the children on into an ever-enlarging world of reading and writing, with adventure, intrigue, suspense, love, and excitement. Books become times of temporary escape. They become "treasure islands" to search and explore for guidance, information, and "new worlds to conquer."

For teachers who are just beginning their association with children's books, I presented a carefully chosen list of titles, old and new, that hopefully opened doorways to continued reading. There also was a list of publications to help you keep abreast of what's new in children's books.

For teachers who have already followed Alice "down the rabbit hole," there was association with master teachers who have created dynamic language skill-building programs with poetry readings, family read-alouds, Literature Circles, and creative dramatics, which are but a few of the many uses of books in a meaning- and child-centered classroom.

Children's literature and active use of themes, aesthetics, knowledge, and humanity conveyed by those books were envisioned as a lively curriculum involving all subject areas and the whole spectrum of children, young and old.

The children's librarian is seen as a facilitator of curriculum, and friend of both children and teachers. Children themselves are seen as their own teachers, buoyed by the continued impact of great literature.

PATHWAYS TO CHILDREN'S LITERATURE

Children:

▶ inherit their teachers' love of books.

▶ develop appreciation of different genres of books.

▶ discuss favorite books and authors.

▶ bring stories to life through Story Theater.

Teachers:

▶ read aloud to children every day.

▶ introduce children to different categories, or genres, of books.

▶ allow time for silent reading of books every day.

▶ involve children in interactive strategies with books and other readers.

▶ keep abreast of new children's books.

FOUNDATIONS
OF
INTEGRATION

15 PATHWAYS TO THEMATIC APPROACHES TO LEARNING

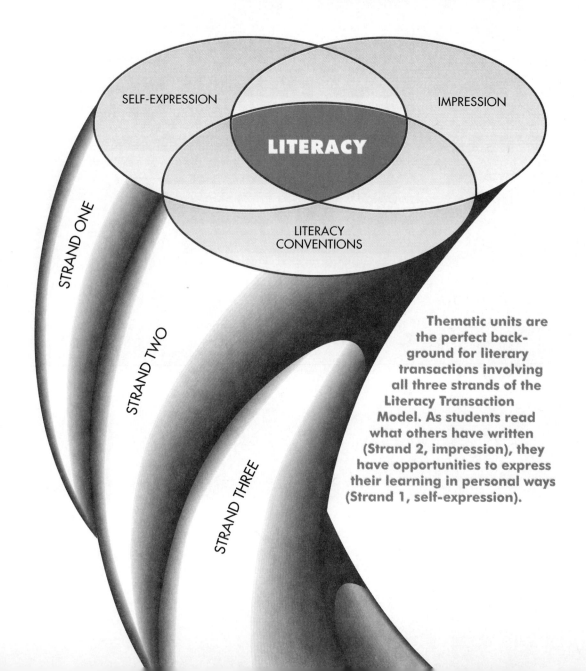

SELF-EXPRESSION

IMPRESSION

LITERACY

LITERACY CONVENTIONS

STRAND ONE

STRAND TWO

STRAND THREE

Thematic units are the perfect background for literary transactions involving all three strands of the Literacy Transaction Model. As students read what others have written (Strand 2, impression), they have opportunities to express their learning in personal ways (Strand 1, self-expression).

PATHWAYS TO PONDER

▶ WHAT ARE THE ADVANTAGES IN SEEING KNOWLEDGE FROM DIFFERENT FIELDS OR DISCIPLINES AS RELATED?

▷ **HOW DO THEMATIC APPROACHES MAKE LEARNING OF SKILLS MORE ACCESSIBLE?**

▷ **WHAT ROLES DO STUDENTS PLAY IN MAKING THEMATIC UNITS EFFECTIVE?**

▷ **WHAT ROLES DOES THE TEACHER PLAY IN MAKING THEMATIC UNITS EFFECTIVE?**

▷ **WHAT DIFFERENT STYLES ARE POSSIBLE FOR THEMATIC APPROACHES?**

Authors' Note: Geoff and Cherry Ward are the authors of this chapter. Geoff teaches at James Cook University in Queensland, Australia, and serves as the secretary of the Australian Reading Association. He is the author of two books and many articles for professional journals. Geoff began his teaching career in New Zealand, where he taught in the elementary grades. He is known internationally for his outstanding conference presentations and his ability to bridge from theory to practice. Cherry Ward is an authority on natural literacy acquisition, art, thematic teaching, and writing process. She has taught in New Zealand and Australia, where she has served as a classroom teacher and principal. She now leads a multiage classroom in Townsville, Queensland, Australia.

THE VALUE OF THEMATIC APPROACHES FOR REAL LEARNING

In classrooms around the world, we find students engaged with thematic units. Children love thematic units, and meaning-centered teachers believe thematic units are extremely effective in integrating the curriculum and in teaching skills in context. In this chapter we examine the concept of thematic teaching and its artifacts—thematic units.

Teachers use many different approaches to thematic learning. However, all forms of the thematic approach have something in common: an emphasis on making connections. When we learn we connect new information with what we already know, tying it in with our existing knowledge structures or attaching it to concepts we control.

When we look at very narrow aspects of knowledge, it is difficult to do more than make our own particular connections. But when we look at wider and more complex representations of meaning, we can see more of the variety of ways in which people make sense of the world. Wurman (1990) has demonstrated how easily people become anxious about the overload of having too much information to deal with. He shows that understanding how things are connected to our uses makes them easier to organize and understand. Dalton and Boyd (1992) explore ways in which teachers can make choices about leadership in the classroom:

> Instead of choosing to feel overwhelmed by the knowledge explosion, the pressure of external forces and "more and more to teach," they are choosing to move to an economy of learning—learning and teaching that is more economical because it is centered on principles that underpin the way they operate as teaching professionals. Unlike packaged programs, models and activity books, such principles offer guidelines against which to measure the worth of external resources. They provide a holistic or "big" picture for us all to work towards in terms of leadership, learning and human growth, relationship with self and others, individuality, interdependence and harmony. (p. 3)

Thematic units are studies that begin by making connections among various aspects of the world we live in. They may, for example:

▶ connect different books by the same author,

▶ connect books by different authors on similar topics,

▶ connect different animals by looking at their shared common environment,

▶ connect a range of different kinds of information about a particular topic,

▶ compare different parts of the world, or

▶ explore different stages or the sequence of processes.

Whatever the nature of a thematic unit, it will enable students to make significant connections among things, people, or events that enhance their real knowledge about the world and themselves. Much of what takes place in education at all levels, and particularly in schools, has been cut up into manageable pieces to be presented to students. In the process, it has lost much of its connections with the real world. Subject boundaries are often imposed artificially to make information easier to handle; the pieces may seem to be more easily sorted out and identified. But the result can be like a jigsaw puzzle where the little pieces may actually be harder to place because they are not seen in relation to other pieces and they go nowhere until they can be connected to other pieces. Students may identify the pieces, but not get the big picture. Thematic approaches start by making connections, and they provide experiences that are broad and rich enough in detail to enable students to connect their learning with real life.

In real life, what is learned in one situation will apply to other situations, and knowledge gained in a particular discipline is relevant to other disciplines. It often makes more sense to see relationships among different aspects of the real world than to regard them as discrete entities, even though it may be convenient to treat them separately at times. A simple example is that isolating the sounds of letters is an artificial notion which gives an unrealistic message to students. Letter–sound relationships are important for reading, but they are learned more effectively when they are looked at in the context of known words and in continuous text (Clay, 1991). Similarly, many forms of graphs are useful in depicting information, but they should be learned as students have a need to display data.

To take a more complex example, a logbook is a kind of journal that systematically records required observations. It would be possible, but rather pointless, to teach students what a logbook was without putting them in the position of needing to use one. They could be taught the differences between the self-selected thoughts and observations of a journal or diary and the structured, consistent observations of a logbook. They could even undergo

THE POET ▶
PONDERS

THE TADPOLE'S DREAM

When I hatched in the water
I looked just like a fist,
So I stayed in my pond
But I felt a strange wish.

Someday . . . Someway . . .
I will live on the land.
I'm not quite sure how
But I'm sure that I can.
My body will change,
Someday soon it will start,
I can feel it inside me
Deep Deep in my heart.

So I never gave up
And one spring day I found
I'd grown arms and long legs
So I hopped on the ground.

And now I eat flies,
I sit in the sun
With big blinky eyes
In a world full of fun.

But I always remember
The first bullfrog-rule:
When a kid comes to catch
you,
Jump back in the pool.

simulated experiences where they pretended to be a ship's captain, for example. But if the genre of logbooks is to make practical sense to students it should be learned, supported by whatever specific teaching is necessary, in the context of a real need—an instance of how logbooks are actually used in our culture.

An illustration of this is given in the sample planning unit on "Chickens Aren't the Only Ones" later in this chapter. Observations of chicks in the classroom should be recorded in systematic ways, and students would readily learn how logbooks work because compiling them would have a real purpose, providing an opportunity to compare the data gathered by the students with that displayed in resource books, and opening up explorations of ways to depict the records of observations. This indicates something of the advantage that thematic approaches have in associating interesting information across the curriculum and in providing a means to learn both subject matter and language skills.

DIFFERENT STYLES OF THEMATIC UNITS

The word *theme* has several related meanings, at least three of which are significant in understanding the idea of thematic units. A theme can be a repeated visual or auditory effect in art and music, an element that is common to several parts of a painting, or a piece of music around which other elements are arranged. Themes are also organizing or orienting principles that shape ideas or discourses in a culture. And this meaning of theme can be extended to denote the topic of discourse—what we talk or write about. In the past, the term *theme* was used to name a topic assigned by the teacher for students to write about, but this usage is not what we mean when we discuss thematic units. Our focus is on those meanings that help teachers and students to bring together a variety of experiences around a common organizing principle.

Thematic units always make connections among experiences, but their scope varies greatly. At one extreme, a thematic unit might simply be a single class session that ties together students' experiences with two different books, such as a traditional and a contemporary version of a fairy tale. At the other extreme, a thematic unit might provide a vast range of options that centered around an organizing idea such as "Change," which could keep a class occupied gainfully for a whole year.

Thematic units can be whole-class activities where the teacher leads activities that all the students undertake together, or in which more than one class—even a whole school—participates. Units can be conducted as group activities, which are later combined so that the rest of the class learns from the group that has done each study. Another way of developing thematic units is to initiate individual projects with related topics (Ward, 1988) so the class builds up a great deal of information that can be shared. This approach benefits from teacher modeling. For example, the teacher could model how to do a biographical mini-project about a notable inventor, gathering information with the students, identifying the key elements of a report, and demonstrating ways of presenting the information. Students could then independently construct projects on other famous inventors following the model project closely or not, depending on their own stage of development in such work. As will be obvious from these few examples, there is no one right way to conduct thematic units.

SOURCES FOR PLANNING THEMATIC UNITS

WHERE DO IDEAS FOR UNITS COME FROM?

▶ Curriculum requirements. The starting point for a plan may be skills or content the teacher is required to teach by the education authority. The teacher may begin by identifying a skill that must be taught and practiced and then seek to find content that provides opportunities to work on the skill. Alternatively, it may be coverage of the content that is required and the teacher may then focus on identifying the language abilities which will be taught and practiced within the unit.

▶ The interests of the teacher or students that may emerge from other learning for individuals, a group, or the class. Often an interesting aspect of some other study may trigger a fascination in the teacher or one or more of the students that leads to a thematic study for the class or to a group or individual project.

▶ The stimulus of a direct experience. A particular experience, individual or shared, planned by the teacher or occurring incidentally, may trigger a

These hamsters ▶ came to the class during a theme study of animals. They remained as the class pets.

desire to continue study of related topics. Excursions often provide an organizing focus for a thematic unit.

▶ The stimulus of a book or other vicarious experience. Perhaps the teacher reads a book to the class and the story, or the information, or some idea in it arouses such interest that the class or one or more individuals extend their engagement with the ideas into a thematic unit.

▶ Seeing a unit that another teacher has found to be successful. Thematic units can be versatile, so an effective unit at another grade level or in another school can be adapted to a new situation.

▶ Events of local or national importance. These may provide excellent opportunities to explore ideas across the curriculum. However, it is suggested that teachers avoid overemphasis on thematic units on holidays and festivals. These can be stimulating and interesting, but they often assume an unrealistic importance in the curriculum and take up a great deal of time without contributing much to students' knowledge.

A MODEL OR FRAMEWORK FOR PLANNING THEMATIC UNITS

The most important idea in planning thematic units is the realization that the unit should advance students' knowledge both of subject matter or content and of language and work skills. Each thematic unit undertaken in the classroom automatically fits in some way into a sequence of activities or units. Teachers may plan with an emphasis on the content they want the class to work with, or an emphasis on the skills they want them to develop, but in an integrated or thematic unit both strands will always be involved. If it is the first unit of the school year, then it will set the tone for much of what will happen in the class for some time to come. The initial thematic unit provides an orientation to a productive mode of learning. This is a time to establish work habits, identify the strengths of the class the teacher will build on in later units, and begin identifying areas of student performance that may need specific attention. This attention to ways of working is not confined to the opening unit but will be maintained throughout the year. However, it is only one side of the value of thematic units for learning. The other side is the information that students learn to handle. Notice that this is not just a matter of learning information itself, but becoming adept at gathering, selecting, transforming, recording, and reporting information.

Teachers using thematic approaches have objectives that address the processes of how students learn, and other objectives that address the content of what students learn. Both kinds of outcomes are important and should be planned for, but because thematic units allow students to explore so many ideas in such a variety of ways, it must be expected there will be outcomes that are important and useful but differ from and go beyond those actually intended and planned. This open-endedness of outcomes means planning must be open-ended. Teachers who use thematic units effectively *do* plan carefully, but they know they must add to and adjust their plans as the unit progresses. They will also find that some of the planned worthwhile activities no longer fit within the available time and need to be deleted from the plan.

The children in Lois Botha's class became so excited after reading Jerry Spinelli's *Maniac Magee* that the story spun itself into a thematic unit. Lois used the *Sketch to Stretch* (see Chapter 13) activity to allow children an opportunity to express their ideas about the story. Figure 15.1 shows Josh's comprehension of Chapters 5, 6, 7, and 9.

FIGURE 15.1 ▶

The children then moved into collaborative groups to recreate dramatic scenes from the story. They researched various aspects of the story. They wrote letters to Jerry Spinelli; some asked complex questions about plot development. The unit concluded with a party when Spinelli's responses arrived in their classroom.

When students and teachers become jointly engaged in developing ideas in thematic units, the teachers' expectations of what students can do, or what they are ready to learn, tend to be overtaken by the reality of students' accomplishments.

An information base for learning provides a launching pad that enables learning to take off and travel far beyond what students are likely to achieve when they are not engaged with real ideas but are simply focusing on language skills. But this learning progress is not just learning of content. When students have real purposes for reading, listening, talking, and writing, they develop their language skills to fulfill their need to understand and to communicate. And when they need more information about how to accomplish some task they really want to complete, they are more easily taught the necessary skills in focused learning episodes, or mini-lessons.

As students learn subject matter and language skills to accomplish language tasks, they need to be provided with opportunities to demonstrate their mastery and control. These chances to perform have traditionally been overpowered by the notion of testing, but a more productive view would be to see them as a time to display learning, by pulling together what the students have learned and to transform it or represent it in some way that involves more than just repeating what has been covered in the program.

Several aspects of learning discussed in the preceding paragraphs can be identified as stages in the sequencing of activities within thematic units.

◀ KIDS' CORNER

Name _Jordan Estes_

Age _12_

Interests _Sports, Gymnastics, drawing, Cheerleading, swimming, and fishing with my dad._

What do you like most about school?

Getting to talk and be with my friends.

What's your favorite subject? Why?

In the past I have liked math because it has been so easy but this year its gotten harder so I like atheletics because I like working out and we have fun.

What's your favorite book? Why do you like it?

Anne of Green Gables. I like this book because it is fiction but if you didn't know that you would think it was non-fiction. It is sad, funny, and serious all in one and I enjoyed it.

What advice do you have for teachers?

I think you should spend more time on the things kids don't understand and less on the things kids do understand.

INITIATING ACTIVITIES

The first stage of a unit is made up of initiating activities that provide an introduction connecting to earlier units or experiences but having as its main purpose to orient the students to the new theme or topic. This stage focuses on one or more significant ideas and experiences that will frame the unit of study. It involves the use of one or more stimulus events to open up the study, to give the teacher and students an opportunity to shape the unit, and to negotiate the kinds of activities that will take place within the theme. Teachers vary in their willingness and readiness to allow students to play a major role in developing the curriculum. For many teachers it is more appropriate for them to take the major role in planning themselves and allow limited scope for the students to design or select activities. But there is a growing number of teachers, especially those who work with middle and upper grades, who feel comfortable giving students a considerable say in how they will engage in the study of a topic and in choosing the actual topic to study. Wherever you fit on this continuum of teachers, you should recognize that students learn more effectively when they are able to assume a degree of responsibility for their own learning. The initiating activity should give them an enthusiasm for the thematic topic and a belief that it has many interesting possibilities for learning.

Evaluation of the program and assessment of the students' learning begins at this stage. Teachers should make observations of student attitudes, for example, and in some units at least there will be samples of work that can be gathered for comparison with later efforts. Students should be helped to understand that assessment which demonstrates they do not know something is helpful both to themselves and to the teacher in identifying what needs to be learned during the unit.

ENHANCING ACTIVITIES

The second stage of the unit constitutes the major portion of the study. Planning for this stage involves identifying worthwhile activities that will extend students' knowledge of the content and their control over language functions. This stage may be called the enhancing activities. Most of the learning within the unit will take place in this stage. The enhancing activities fulfill two functions that might be viewed as either parallel or intertwined. The modes of language—listening, speaking, reading, and writing—are the vehicles for most learning to take place. Language-arts teaching has as its purpose to enhance the ability of students to use language for a wide range of purposes in a wide range of situations. But these language abilities are learned most effectively when we use language for real purposes in real situations. Teaching language skills is done in the context of using language to get things done. Teachers can vary the focus of their attention from the message in a written or spoken communication to the form or structure of the language used or to some particular element of the language. This change of focus needs to be made at times when the teacher believes more information about how language is used to fulfill particular tasks will enhance students' performance of those language tasks and improve their ability to apply what they learn to new language settings or to use the same function with other subject matter.

BROD BAGERT

1. Which book of yours has given you the greatest pleasure?

Steel Cables. This is an adult book of love poems written in the voice of committed love. The thoughts and feelings expressed in this book are some of the most important ones in my life—it's about my relationship with my wife, my kids, my parents. I still enjoy reading the poems in this book.

2. Which book has surprised you most in terms of its public reception?

Let Me Be the Boss. This is a book of poems in a child's voice, written for children to perform orally. I guess I was surprised because the reaction of the critics and of the children was so totally different. The critics were cool and said the book was uneven. Children find the poems wildly entertaining.

3. What would you like people to remember about your work?

I want people to discover in my poems their own passion for life—to laugh, to cry, to look up at the sky and hope again.

4. What impact do you hope your work will have on children?

I want my work to help children to love poetry because they have found material in their own voice, something that made words seem more friendly. And through performing these poems, I want them to develop oral eloquence by fostering a generation of people who can express their thoughts out loud.

Children love to read and act out the wildly funny poems of Brod Bagert, who has been compared to Shel Silverstein for his sense of the outrageous in his poetry. His books include ***Chicken Socks, Let Me Be the Boss,*** and ***If Only I Could Fly.*** His adult titles include ***Steel Cables, Bullfrog at Café du Monde,*** and ***Alaska.***

Thus at certain times during the enhancing activities of a thematic unit the teacher's focus is on language skills. Nevertheless, the major importance will be attached to the subject matter, content, or message of the material being studied, and if students are going to enjoy thematic approaches and get the most benefit from them, it must be clear to them that the unit is not just an excuse to teach skills.

Evaluation of the program is essential to ensure this stage is developing children's understanding and skills, because if it is not doing so the program needs to be adjusted. Part of the evaluation process may involve assessment of students' performance, but the emphasis should be on evaluation that is formative rather than summative. Assessing how well the students have learned what has been negotiated and what else they have achieved is an ongoing process and depends on careful observation at all stages of the unit.

SYNTHESIZING ACTIVITIES

The third and final stage of the thematic unit can be called the synthesizing activities. In many ways this is the most significant part of the evaluation

and assessment of the unit, but it should serve more to provide opportunities for students to bring together what they have learned and to display aspects of their learning outcomes. In many instances, this stage should encourage transformation of the material learned so it is clear the student has internalized it and is not just reproducing it. The synthesizing activities constitute more than a test situation and more than a single culminating activity, although both of these may be part of their nature. Where possible, the synthesizing activities should provide students with opportunities to talk, write, and use other forms of display for an audience that goes beyond the teacher and the rest of the class. Parents need to have some involvement in all stages of thematic units, but the synthesizing activities should give them a chance to celebrate learning with their children.

Thematic units do not necessarily proceed as tidily as plans or descriptions imply. A thematic unit may not separate clearly into three stages, but planning within this framework makes it easier for the teacher to visualize progress. The terms used in this framework are those used by the Queensland (Australia) English Syllabus (1994). Other formats for planning units use different terms. For example, Allen, Sampson, and Teale (1989) use the terms *focusing, developing,* and *continuing* to indicate three stages in each activity within a unit. Whether dealing with activities within units, or the whole of a thematic unit, it is important to be responsive to the students' interest in the part of the study taking place and to extend, adjust, or cut off the activity to get maximum benefit from it. Where it is feasible, the students will make decisions for themselves about their progress through a unit. Teachers who want their students to develop independence give them options for decision making within the overall plan of the unit.

SOME PRINCIPLES FOR PLANNING UNITS

DON'T FORCE COVERAGE OF THE CURRICULUM

Teachers planning thematic units should avoid artificially forcing the unit to cover every area of the curriculum. Some units may naturally have a strong science emphasis; others do not. In some cases, it is easy to find useful applications of mathematics activities, but at other times the connection may require more squeezing into shape than is appropriate just to write math problems on the thematic topic, for example. If the math concepts are not being used for genuine math purposes, they should be left out and dealt with separately during the unit. There are many other ways to integrate math as shown in Griffiths and Clyne (1993). Teachers who cannot find good quality poetry that fits the theme would find it better to use none (or to write their own!) in the unit. Good poetry can be used for other purposes alongside rather than within the theme.

Thematic units vary in the emphasis they place on different aspects of the curriculum. One may emphasize social studies/art/health, for example; another may emphasize science/math/music, but all will be undergirded by language.

USE CHILDREN'S LITERATURE AS THE CORNERSTONE OF YOUR UNITS

Thematic units afford teachers a natural opportunity to move children into books. Books may serve as a resource for background information about the theme, or they may constitute the theme.

PROVIDE BALANCE WITHIN OR BETWEEN UNITS

Among the elements that should be balanced in the curriculum are input and self-expression, fact and fiction, imagination and information, simple and complex ideas, historical and contemporary settings, and distant and local issues. Balance does not require an equal amount of each of these. The teacher needs to be sensitive to what has already been covered and to how the students are coping with particular activities, ensuring that the program does not overemphasize input, for example, without giving the students a chance to express their own thoughts, but not expecting them to express opinions without being exposed to ideas that will help them form opinions. Balance is also achieved from one unit to another and not necessarily within a unit. Thus a particular thematic unit may heavily emphasize fictional material, but subsequent units may balance this by a stronger emphasis on factual material.

USE THE PLAN AS A GUIDE ONLY

It is common for thematic unit plans to contain more activities than are required in the program or than can be fitted into the time available, even when it is the teacher's own plan based on firsthand knowledge of the students. Students' abilities are not static over time and their interests also change, so the implementation of the plan must take account of this. The plan should be used as a guide, almost like a menu to choose from. The plan can only be an approximation. If a teacher follows a plan to the last letter of detail, it suggests the plan has been implemented without careful observation of the students' learning and development over the duration of the unit.

IDENTIFY THE CRUCIAL ASPECTS OF THE UNIT

It may be helpful to identify in the planning the key elements among the activities. These may be activities that practice requirements of your education system, such as essential elements or common curriculum elements. Identifying these in advance may help you select which aspects of the plan must be retained as it is adapted. Other aspects of the plan may be optional, activities that are worthwhile but may be replaced by others which emerge from students' interests, additional information, or from resources the students bring from home.

DO WHAT COMES NATURALLY

There is no one right way to plan and implement a thematic unit. Teachers think and work differently, so their units take different shapes. But individual teachers also take different pathways to planning their own units depending on such factors as the initiating idea, their familiarity with the

CLASSROOM VIGNETTE

Dan Darigan (1994) constructed a theme for intermediate grade students on "Secrets." He started by sharing a sampling of poems from Charlotte Huck's *Secret Places* and then discussed with the children the many dimensions of "Secrets." Using Literature Circles (see Chapter 14), children read the following picture books:

The Changing Maze

Amelia's Road

FIGURE 15.2 ▷

Secrets of the Past

Pyramid
Build a pyramid from your own handmade clay stones.
Digging Up Dinosaurs
Construct your own animal skeleton.
Tales Mummies Tell
Mummies Made in Egypt
Write a TV news report on an archeological finding.
Into the Mummy's Tomb
Pharaohs and Pyramids
Dinosaur Mysteries
Ancient Egypt
Hieroglyphs: The Writing of Ancient Egypt
Create your own hieroglyphic alphabet--send a note to a friend.
Number the Stars
Stepping on the Cracks
Use a Venn diagram to compare the secrets of these two World War II novels.
The Magnificent Mummy Maker

Secrets of the Future

The Giver
Write the important "history" you would pass on to future generations.
The Green Book
Write about something you would want to take and something you want to hide on a similar trip.
The White Mountain Trilogy
Make a time capsule for the year 2200.

Ghostly Secrets

Something Upstairs
A Ghost in the House
The Magic Circle
The Riddle of Penncroft Farm
Wait Until Helen Comes
A Ghost in the Third Row
The Revenge of the Wizard's Ghost
Construct a comparison chart for these "Ghost" books.
The Dark Thirty
Write your own tale set during the "Dark Thirty"

Number Secrets

Ann's Mysterious Multiplying Jar
Collect 1,000,000 of something, like tabs from soda cans.
Anne's Hat Tricks
Write simple logic problems.
Make a class book.
I Hate Math Book
Aha, Gotcha!

Fantastic Secrets

Knee Knock Rise
The Witches
Redwall
Others See Us
Just So Stories
Write your own pourquoi tale.
Take a trip to the zoo and write about "real" secrets you have learned about.
Forgotten Door
Present a Story Theatre based on this book.

Secrets Sorrows

On My Honor
As Joel, record a diary entry that talks about Tony's death.
A Taste of Blackberries
Use a Venn diagram to compare the above two books.
Blow Me A Kiss Miss Lilly
Name Upstairs, Name Downstairs
Beyond the Ridge
Badger's Parting Gifts
Through Grandpa's Eyes
Construct a comparison chart for these picture books concerning death.
Tracker
Risk 'a' Roses

Secrets Mysteries

The Man Who Was Poe
The Westing Game
The House of Dies Drear
Graven Images
Construct a comparison chart for these mysteries.
The Egypt Game
Write a story from the point of view of the professor when he hears of a new game "The Gypsies"
The Way to Sattin Shore
Make a diorama if Sattin Shore.
Make a "Mystery" game with game board.

Continued

The Orphan Boy

The Mysteries of Harris Burdick

The Wednesday Surprise

The Voice of the Great Bell

After pondering the "secrets" these books contain, children branched out to read many other books with "secrets." Figure 15.2 details the choices available to the class.

FIGURE 15.2 ▶

   (cont.)

Scientific Secrets

The Way Things Work
Have a mini-science fair showing how things really work.
The Book of Science
Build and demonstrate something from this book.
Secret Clocks
On a zoo trip, record differing sleeping habits of animals in a journal.
Secret Life of Cosmetics
Secrets of a Wildlife Watcher
Sketch a series of animals, their homes, or footprints you have observed.
What's the Difference: A Guide to Some Familiar Animal Look-Alikes
Strange Creatures

Secrets Places

Dream Spinner
Tom's Midnight Garden
The Root Cellar Stonewords
Invent and make a model of your own time machine.
the Secret Garden
The Bridge to Terabithia
write about an imaginary place you would like to travel to.
The Lion, The Witch and the Wardrobe

Secrets of the Heart

What Hearts?
Baby
Jacob Have I Loved
Collect data surveying your classmates' feelings about their siblings.
Holding Me Here
Hold on to Love
Read a "Love" poem -- try writing one.
Shiloh
Write a story about a pet you have loved.
Rescue, Josh McQuire

Secrets

Natural Secrets

Secret Language of Snow
Secrets of the Venus Fly Trap
Start your own terrarium.
The Lore and Legend of Flowers
Design a "time travel guide" for the historical significance of the rose.
Interview a horticulturalist about roses or your favorite flower.
A River Ran Wild

Secrets of Success

Calamity Jane: Her Life and Her Legend
Eleanor Roosevelt
Franklin Roosevelt
Malcolm X
Lincoln: A Photo Biography
Write a biography of a famous person.
Deborah Sampson: Secret Soldier
Frank Thompson: Her Civil War Story

Secrets of Life

Where did I come from?
Growing Up
Ask a Doctor, Nurse, or Mid-Wife to come into the class for a presentation.
Mountain of Tibet
Write your own folk tale about how life carries on.
Tuck Everything
Water of Life
Compare the two waters: their curses and blessings.

Secrets Foods

Bread, Bread, Bread
The Bread Book: All About Bread and How to Make it
Make It
Grow your own wheat, grind it, and make your own bread.
Make bread from a frozen, store-bought product.
Have a baker come to your class.
Strega Noma
Pasta Factory
Make pasta and sauce from scratch.
Write invitations inviting family, friends or other teachers.
Sam's Sandwich
Make a pop-up "Sam" book with secret surprises.
What Food Is This?
The Amazing Potato
Write the history of your favorite food.

Children become ▶
"authors" during
thematic unit
research.

topic and resources, and the students' knowledge and perceived learning needs. All of these factors interplay with the personality and creativity of the teacher. Plans should appeal to the students and the teacher. If a topic does not seem worth spending a good deal of quality time with, it would be better to plan a few quick activities to teach the main points or to provide resources for a different approach. Thematic units should be joyful and interesting experiences.

VARY THE TIME ALLOCATION FOR WORKING ON THEMATIC UNITS

As we already indicated, the length of thematic units should vary. It is also advisable to vary the amount of time allocated within the timetable on different days within the conduct of a particular unit. Because this kind of work brings so many aspects of language and learning together, it benefits from having blocks of time rather than single short sessions in the daily program. Because school situations vary so much, it is not possible to recommend a particular way of working, except to note that sometimes the amount of time allowed is too great and makes difficulties for students who do not prioritize their own use of time well, and sometimes it is too short to allow students' interests to develop fully. A balance must be provided, and if possible, allowance made for some students to continue on individual studies while others have switched to working with the teacher. Some units start from a single event like the reading of a book and gradually develop as students' interests are extended. In other cases, a whole day might be devoted to a high-impact set of experiences that launch the unit with a bang.

LIMITING THE UNIT

Some thematic units can seem so rich in worthwhile activities that they could continue for a whole year.

CLASSROOM VIGNETTE

Melbourne grade 6 teacher Judy Menotti stimulated her class's interest in varied aspects of their environment and how it affected their lives. Students began a range of individual and group explorations of the relationship of people to their environments. These studies kept branching and extending throughout the curriculum for a whole year's program. The students identified and defined many needs and problems and undertook research on issues, wrote letters, listened to guest speakers they had invited, went on field trips, and reported in depth in a variety of ways to each other on their own studies. They developed very sophisticated skills in planning their activities, in coordinating their work with others, and in communication. The classroom was always filled with interesting displays mounted by the students themselves, and the students passed on much of what they were learning to students in other classes.

Extended thematic studies have exciting possibilities, but put a very heavy demand on the teacher's ability to monitor and support such a complexity of learning. Most teachers employing a thematic approach to teaching and learning would find it more effective and more convenient to run a range of themes in a school year.

Teachers need to be careful observers of children's learning behaviors, the outcomes of their work, the level of engagement with tasks within the theme and the quality of interaction within groups, to ensure that what are intended as worthwhile activities keep being worthwhile. Some types of units can keep students happy and busy, yet not really contribute significantly to their learning. Students may become very successful at giving teachers what they want, but not be learning new things. Thematic units are opportunities to expand students' worlds, their knowledge and skills, and to affect their attitudes in positive ways, but teachers need to guard against letting themes drag on too long. The level of interaction and challenge and the quality of outcomes must be considered in deciding how long to continue, but even when these are all satisfactory, it may be better to curtail a study so new challenges and new ideas are faced. In the sample unit "Chickens Aren't the Only Ones" in this chapter, it would be easy to extend the study onto dinosaurs, which would certainly be popular with many students, but to do so would distract attention from the main issues of the unit. Thematic units that capture the students' interest and enthusiasm can provide the stimulus for further "at home work," which can continue for some students on their own initiative after the unit at school has moved on to another theme.

THEMATIC UNIT TEACHING AS ACTION RESEARCH

Action research is taking place when a researcher:

1. identifies a problem or issue to investigate,
2. plans an action that may overcome the problem,
3. puts the plan into effect,
4. observes the effects of the action,
5. modifies the action plan to improve it based on what is observed about its effects, and
6. continues the cycle.

Action research is ideally suited to teachers as researchers in their own classrooms. In an important sense, all teachers should be action researchers all the time because effective teaching requires a sense of direction, good planning, monitoring of learning and of how the planned activities are working out in practice, and an ability to improve teaching and learning by studying the effects of activities on students' learning. Teaching needs to be accompanied by sensitive observation—to be evaluative—so it determines the value to students' learning of the activities and tasks undertaken. Teachers who see themselves as action researchers bring an open-minded attitude to their use of thematic units that will be productive in improving both planning and monitoring of learning.

"Experiences for ▶
Literacy" offers
teachers a useful
starting point.

Experiences for Literacy

Teacher's
Guide

Pets
Real and Not So Real

Roach Van Allen

Michael R. Sampson

William H. Teale

DLM
Teaching
Resources

Commercially produced thematic units may provide a useful starting point for some teachers, particularly those who are not experienced in planning to integrate different activities across the curriculum. But whether the unit is prepared by the teacher who uses it or by someone else, there is a danger of teachers developing expectations of how a thematic unit should proceed and how the students should progress with it. These expectations may appear to be set in concrete with all aspects of scope, sequence, and implementation following already established pathways. Some teachers might implement the same thematic units in the same way year after year, especially if they were enjoyed by the previous class. Almost inevitably, this would lead to students' learning outcomes being limited. On the other hand, those who teach evaluatively, who observe students carefully (who "kid watch," Goodman, 1985), and who reflect on students' responses, contributions to discussions, control of written and spoken genres, and their level of interest, will adjust activities and expectations accordingly. The same thematic topic implemented in successive years by such a teacher would most likely vary considerably in development and outcomes because of the nature of the students themselves. In addition, a learning teacher is likely to have new ideas and new resources to try whether the unit is the same or different.

THEMATIC UNITS AND PARENT PARTICIPATION

Parent participation in students' learning programs can be a significant factor, not just in the success of the learning, but also in the relationship of home and school. Support from home can provide useful resources of information and experience. When teachers use project work as an important part of their program, especially when the projects are individual and carried out at home as well as at school, there are real difficulties in establishing just what should be the role of parents in supporting their children's learning (Ward, 1988). Thematic units can use parental support in a variety of ways if teachers help parents to understand what they are trying to do and why they would value parent participation.

This requires more than just keeping parents informed about what the thematic unit topics will be. Most parents have experienced the following scenario, or one much like it.

"Hi, dear. How was school today?"

"Okay."

"What did you do today?" (Or, "What did you learn today?")

"Oh, not much."

End of conversation. The child and parent may not share anything else about what is happening at school because neither has any real enthusiasm for it, and neither has any deeper knowledge of how to share their concerns or interests. Teachers need to find ways of building the interest of students and parents for what is happening in the program. Thematic units make it more possible for parents to be partners in their children's learning.

Cherry Ward, K-1 teacher in Townsville, Australia, seeks to build strong communication links with parents of her class. She uses frequent letters and notes in their homework folders to keep them informed about what is happening in the program and makes copies of her planning, including a list of the major resources she will use, available to parents so they can support their children's learning at home and, where appropriate, send additional resources to school. At times parents have particular expertise they can share with the class. At the end of many thematic units, Cherry and her class hold a celebration concert. On this early evening occasion, the class or individual books written during the unit are officially launched. The children perform songs and instrumental music from their program, display artwork, and read pieces of their informational writing to the parents. The announcements are jointly written in the class and are all made by the children. One of the features of the celebrations is that they give all the children opportunities, rather than being confined to a few of the more advanced students. Although attendance at ordinary school meetings is not high, these occasions draw great crowds of supportive parents, relatives, and friends.

One of Cherry's thematic units focused on wheat. It included a trip to a bakery, but it also involved a talk from a parent who had grown up on a wheat farm and a demonstration of cooking chappatis by a mother who grew up in India. The celebration concluded with a bread party where parents brought a great variety of types of bread they had made or bought. There was considerable interest in the children's work but also a lot of communication among parents that added to the enthusiasm for what their children were achieving.

THE TEACHER'S ROLE IN THEMATIC UNITS

Although there are other aspects that could be discussed, three roles for the teacher in thematic units are outlined here.

CHOOSING LANGUAGE ACTIVITIES TO EXPLOIT THE CONTENT

Especially during what we have termed the enhancing activities of a unit, the teacher combines attention to developing students' knowledge with activities that develop particular language abilities. Semantic webs open up vocabulary development; cloze passages constructed on the unit theme by the teacher focus attention on specific aspects of language that can be talked about in a postcloze discussion and extend comprehension; note taking and reconstruction of texts develop the ability to select and retain information. These and many other activities are examples of how the teacher can use what the students are learning about to enhance their language skills. Most of the language activities within a unit should be chosen for their relevance to real-life learning. For example, in a unit on spiders, teaching the genres of report writing and description is going to be more productive than activities that list the menu for a spider's lunch or the spider's invitation to a party sent to a fly. That is not to say that such activities would not provide pleasure and variety for students, but it would make more impact on those students who transfer knowledge less readily if they learned to write menus in the course of preparing a meal, and invitations when inviting the principal and their parents to a display of their work.

MONITORING AND SUPPORTING STUDENTS' LEARNING

One of the major purposes for using a thematic approach is that it makes independent learning more possible. Teachers need to be realistic in catering to the range of abilities within the class and in considering what their students are capable of doing. If the teacher's expectations are too low, the students will be restricted in their learning outcomes because they do not get the chance to think for themselves. If expectations are too high, the students may not obtain all the benefit they should from the unit. Teachers need to monitor carefully the work of individual students, keeping anecdotal records, checklists, and samples of work for portfolios to ensure they are providing the optimal amount of support. Students who have difficulty completing work may need closer supervision than others. One danger to guard against is the self-fulfilling prophecy that limits students' growth in independence because they already appear to lack independence.

USING FOCUSED LEARNING EPISODES, OR MINI-LESSONS

As the teacher monitors the learning experiences of students, particular learning needs will emerge. Sometimes these will be for a solitary student, but very often it will be clear the class, or at least a significant proportion of the students, would benefit from specific teaching of a skill. These teaching sessions focus on the particular need and give the students a chance to practice the new learning. An example would be teaching students different text structures or graphic displays for showing comparisons and contrasts. Or the

◀ DeeAnne Barker conducts a mini-lesson.

teacher might find that although students know how to represent comparisons, some of them need to be taught how to take notes in a way that ensures all of the criteria for comparison can be discussed. For example, if you are comparing frogs and toads, you cannot proceed from having information about the habitat of the frog and the feeding habits of the toad: You need matching details about each of them. A mini-lesson on such a topic could be fitted easily and effectively into the ongoing work of the class.

PLANNING A UNIT: A GENERAL SEQUENCE

Planning a thematic unit can begin in several different ways. The teacher can begin with an idea for one or more worthwhile activities, with an idea of the content to be explored, with a particular book or other experience as a starting point, or with a particular language function or ability that the students need to develop. Planning will not follow an invariable sequence, but the following sections first describe a general planning procedure and then show how that can be applied to a particular thematic unit.

The first stage of planning can be simply a listing of books, experiences, and worthwhile activities that come to mind immediately. With experience, teachers build up a repertoire of activities and ways of using resources. It is usually easier to plan the possible activities in separate subject areas. Although this conflicts in some ways with the idea of integrating across the curriculum, it provides a framework for recording the brainstorming process, directs and stimulates thinking, and ensures that all areas of the curriculum will be considered, even though some may not be included in the final plan. The teacher seeks to make connections among the different areas, and there will be overlapping of activities. For example, an activity may be listed as part of the science curriculum but involve brainstorming, listing, and classifying and be seen also as promoting oral language and thinking skills.

The beginning stage of a plan, perhaps with the exception of some of the books listed, is likely to be open enough to suit several different grade levels. This has a side effect of being very beneficial to team planning in situations where teachers can work together. The initiating experiences may be shared but lead to different enhancing activities. (Of course, the early stages of the planning will not necessarily identify what is actually used as the initiating activity of the unit.) Teachers working in a team could brainstorm possible resources and activities together and then start to sort them into levels of application for different groupings of students. For example, a grade 1 teacher and a grade 5 teacher could go through this stage together and then refine the plans for their own classes, but they might still benefit from teaming for at least some of the implementation of the plan. Because of the wide range of abilities evident in any class, whether it is multiage or a single grade, the planned experiences and the difficulty level of the tasks must be kept broad. This breadth is also needed to cater to the differences in students' strengths and interests that vary from one curriculum area to another. In general, older students will start a thematic unit with more background knowledge than will younger ones, but their progress will not necessarily follow the same pathways.

OVERVIEW PLAN for Younger Children

Resources

Chickens Aren't the Only Ones - Heller
The Chick and the Duckling - Ginsburg
Good Morning, Chick - Ginsburg
The Ugly Duckling - Mayer / Locker
Childcraft - Animals
Mysteries and Marvels of Bird Life
Mysteries and Marvels of Animal World - Gaaman
The Happy Egg - Krauss
Are You My Mother? - Eastman
Pancakes and Painted Eggs - Chapman / Niland
Five Little Chickens - an old jingle
in Sounds of Numbers - Martin
Brown Bear, Brown Bear, What do you see?
- Martin
Polar Bear, Polar Bear, What do you hear?
- Martin
Mysteries and Marvels of Ocean Life- Morris
What's Inside? - Carolick

Chickens Aren't the Only Ones

WRITING
* Innovation on "Good Morning, Chick" - class or personal recount(s) e.g. We (I) did — ; like this, etc.
* Innovation on "Five Little Chickens" e.g. "Three Fat Lizards."
* Innovation - class / group / individual on "Brown Bear..." using oviparous creatures.
* Recipe writing - ways to cook eggs. Compile class recipe book.
* Log writing - noting changes in creatures in classroom.
* Letters - arranging for, thanking for, animals for classroom observation.
* Report writing and description - joint (teacher and children), pairs or individual.

MATHEMATICS
Number: * Gathering and comparing numbers of eggs laid, from species to species, or kind to kind. Specific instances or generalised.
* Graphical representation - survey favorite ways to eat eggs, e.g., boiled, poached, fried, not at all ...
* Oral or written word problems using numbers found in research. Solving own and others' problems.
Measurement: * Relative measurements of eggs - length, circumference, weight. Measured with standard and non-standard measures.
* Time - compare incubation and hatching durations.
- time to boil an egg.
Space: * Study shapes of eggs, e.g., spherical, elipsoid.
Make out of play dough.

POETRY
* Baby Chick -
Aileen Fisher

ART
* Mural paint and collage of "The Ugly Duckling"
* Illustrations - crayon and paint for enlarged text of "The Chick and the Duckling", "The Happy Egg" and "Five Little Chickens". Make into class books for shared reading.
* Painting on hollow eggs. Dot designs. Hang as class mobile. Examine painted egg designs from various cultures.
* Crushed egg - shell mosaic designs. Shells dyed, then crushed and glued on small cards. Individual.

READING
* Teacher - readings of available fiction books.
* Teacher - readings of extracts from informational books; modelling of use of reference books, e.g., table of contents, index.
* Research reading for information.
* Text reconstruction e.g. sentence strips of passages from "The Happy Egg" and "The Chick and the Duckling."
* Sentence - halves cards - texts of familiar books.
* Picture / text matching and sequencing of "The Chick and the Duckling" episodes.
* Story theatre of "Are You My Mother?"
* Reading and following recipes using eggs.

SPEAKING AND LISTENING
* Brainstorming and classifying oviparous creatures - small group activity.

SCIENCE
* List, research, list and classify oviparous creatures. (word cards or picture cards or both).
* Observation / caring for / researching needs of oviparous creatures in classroom.

MUSIC / MOVEMENT
* Listening - "Ballet of the Unhatched Chicks." Moussongsty.
* Acting out chicks hatching from eggs to above music.
* Acting out different oviparous creatures hatching. Discuss differences in movements. e.g., compare chicks and tadpoles.
* Singing "There Once was an Ugly Duckling".

An alternative way of starting the planning process is to ask the students to brainstorm possibilities or for the teacher and students to do this together. Many teachers using thematic approaches report they were surprised at how effective it was to incorporate student input into their planning at different stages in the process (see also Farnsworth, 1990, and other chapters in Atwell, 1990), and many thematic units have been initiated by the students' own interests and ideas. The teacher, of course, must always consider whether the ideas that students come up with have enough potential learning opportunities and available resources to be worthy of extended study.

The teacher then researches the topic, gathers resources, and considers possible visiting experts, excursions, and artifacts to bring into the classroom. As the plan takes shape, the teacher modifies the initial outline, adding or deleting planned worthwhile activities after obtaining further information and ideas from the resources consulted. The modifying process will take into account the relevance of different curriculum needs and perceptions about the students' learning needs. Figure 15.3 (see page 429) shows an outline plan for a unit for the primary grades on egg laying or oviparous creatures that originated from Ruth Heller's book, *Chickens Aren't the Only Ones*.

The planning outline is then operationalized by sequencing the activities from the initiating activities through the enhancing activities to the synthesizing activities, and by the teacher considering what language and other skills will be emphasized as the class engages in learning content or subject matter.

The plan is put into effect, but optimally it will remain flexible and adaptable throughout the unit. A thematic unit should always be a learning experience and not simply a matter of working through a prepared set of activities.

SUMMARY

Thematic approaches to learning add interest to the program for both the teacher and the students, but they also facilitate learning by making connections easier. Teachers can plan integrated activities that give scope for a wide range of explorations of ideas, learning of interesting content, and development of language and other skills. When students participate in the planning process they are more likely to understand and appreciate what they are learning. Thematic approaches can be more difficult to implement for the teacher because of the adaptability required, but the advantages in interest and learning gains will repay the effort.

PATHWAYS TO THEMATIC UNITS

The student:

▶ connects information from many different sources.

▶ recognizes the relationships among different ideas.

▶ experiences a variety of working styles.

► uses language for real purposes in many curriculum areas.

► develops independence and interdependence in undertaking studies.

► demonstrates learning in a wide variety of ways.

The teacher:

► realizes the advantages of teaching language and other skills while students are engaged in learning content matter.

► becomes more adaptable in planning activities that cater to students' needs and interests and modifying plans as units progress.

► makes realistic connections among different areas of the curriculum.

► involves colleagues and parents in building a community of learners.

16 PATHWAYS TO CONTENT INTEGRATION

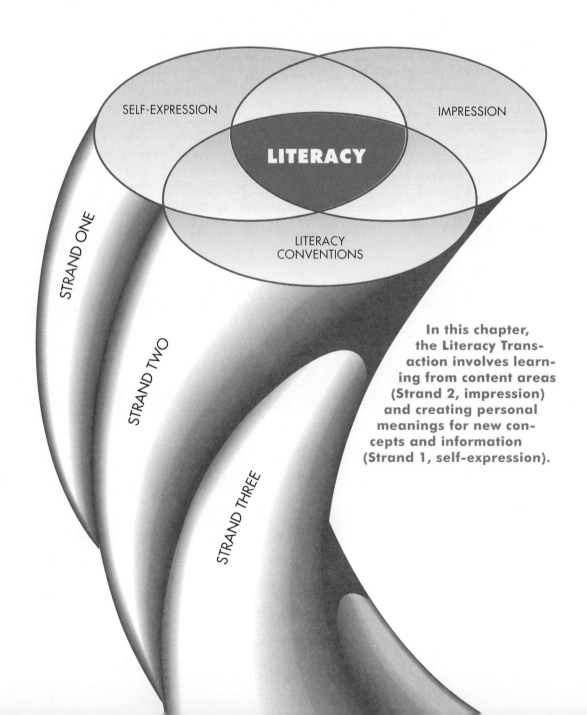

SELF-EXPRESSION

IMPRESSION

LITERACY

LITERACY CONVENTIONS

STRAND ONE

STRAND TWO

STRAND THREE

In this chapter, the Literacy Trans-action involves learn-ing from content areas (Strand 2, impression) and creating personal meanings for new con-cepts and information (Strand 1, self-expression).

PATHWAYS TO PONDER

. . . .

▶ **WHY DO READERS HAVE PROBLEMS COMPREHENDING EXPOSITORY TEXT?**

▶ **WHAT ARE THE VARIOUS TEXT STRUCTURES AND HOW DO THEY IMPACT COMPREHENSION?**

▶ **HOW DOES LITERACY IN THE TOTAL CURRICULUM INVOLVE MORE THAN READING AND WRITING?**

▶ **HOW CAN BASIC RESEARCH SKILLS BE DEVELOPED IN THE CONTENT AREAS?**

▶ **HOW ARE ART AND LITERACY RELATED?**

▶ **HOW IS MATHEMATICS LANGUAGE?**

▶ **WHAT IS THE RELATIONSHIP BETWEEN MUSIC AND LITERACY?**

▶ **HOW CAN LITERATURE MAKE SOCIAL STUDIES MORE ATTRACTIVE TO STUDENTS?**

▶ **HOW CAN TEACHERS INTEGRATE SCIENCE AND LITERACY?**

When do children develop language-arts and literacy skills? During the language-arts period? Yes, to a certain extent. But children actually develop language-arts skills throughout the curriculum—in science, in math, in social studies, and through art and music activities. In this chapter we examine how literacy learning has no respect for subjects in school. We look at the power children's literature has for content learning. We conclude that literacy learning and content learning should go hand in hand, and we show you ways to integrate your curriculum.

USING CHILDREN'S LITERATURE IN CONTENT AREA INSTRUCTION

Why do good readers often become poor readers when asked to read their social studies or science books? It's because that material, which is called expository text, is written in a different style than the narrative text the students encounter in children's books.

This problem often occurs about the time of the "fourth-grade slump" (Chall, Jacobs, & Baldwin, 1990) when students are confronted with the responsibility of gleaning much of their academic information from content textbooks. This is a frustrating situation for both students and teachers. Why doesn't the skill in reading children's literature transfer to reading content material?

The reasons for problems in reading expository text are numerous. In many primary classrooms, basal readers are used as the major source of reading materials (Anderson, Hiebert, Scott, & Wilkinson, 1985). Most of the selections in these basals are stories, poems, and plays (Flood & Lapp, 1990); therefore, many children lack extended exposure to informational text. In addition, some students may lack essential background knowledge necessary to glean critical information from technical vocabulary, graphs, charts, and labeled illustrations. In many content classrooms, teachers attempt to overcome students' lack of expertise with informational text by orally presenting the content material (Armbruster et al., 1991; Goodlad, 1984; Ratekin, Simpson, Alvermann, & Dishner, 1985). However, this does not solve the problem, for even if children are exposed to the necessary information, they have not had the opportunity to become proficient readers of content texts.

In order to achieve success in school, students must acquire the skills necessary to comprehend expository text, for content texts are used in 75% to 90% of American classrooms (Tyson & Woodward, 1989). Even more importantly, if students are to become productive individuals in our society they must be able to glean information from numerous informational texts such as travel guides, magazine articles, instruction manuals, newspapers, and business forms and memos.

Let's consider the basic difference between the structure of narrative and expository text. Narrative text tells a story and whether it is a mystery, adventure, romance, or comedy, the story contains the key components of characters, setting, a problem, a series of events that occur to solve the problem, the climax, and the resolution. Proficient readers know these important items of "story grammar" contain the crucial information in the story. As a result of being familiar with the text structure, it is easier for students to activate their schema and monitor their comprehension. Successful readers are able to interact with the text at an affective level and become part of the story. The story "plays in the mind" and understanding occurs. In contrast, expository text does not possess this familiar text structure. There is no "story" and students often are unable to interact with the text in a way that activates their schema. An expository text might include descriptive text, a sequence of events or instructions, a cause and effect passage, a comparison and contrast session, or a problem and solution section (Meyer, 1975; Piccolo, 1987). In addition, no attempt is made to "tell a story." As a result, students who are successful readers of "stories" may find it difficult to interact with expository text and find themselves merely "calling the words" in order to finish the assignment. Consequently, students are often unsure what is important and try to remember everything. They often find themselves overwhelmed by the amount of material, fail to understand it, and as a result remember little if any of the key concepts. One 10-year-old boy summed it up this way: "The social studies book doesn't give you a lot of detail. You don't imagine yourself there because they're not doing it as if it were a person" (Levstik, 1989). For this child, nothing "played in the mind" when he read the social studies text.

Research has shown that familiarity with various text structures aids students in comprehending expository materials (Englert & Hiebert, 1983; Horowitz, 1985; Slater, 1985). Fortunately, there are many children's books that "tell stories," yet contain text or concepts which expose children to the various expository text structures. We now explore children's books that contain these structures and present instructional applications that aid in "bridging the gap" between narrative and expository text.

DESCRIPTIVE TEXT

Books containing descriptive text require students to answer one or more of the following questions:

What is it?

What is its purpose?

What does it look like?

What is it used for?

Many children's books provide opportunities for children to focus on these questions. For instance, Eric Carle's *A House for Hermit Crab* exposes children to this descriptive format by introducing them to various sea animals by describing their actions. In *The Magic School Bus Inside the Earth*, the students categorize their rock samples by writing descriptions of them. Joanna Cole continues this format in *The Magic School Bus Lost in the Solar System* when the characters make a chart with descriptions of the various planets. Alexandra Day gives a humorous twist to descriptive language in her *Frank and Ernest* books, in which the two main characters (an elephant and a bear) have jobs in which they fill in for people in various occupations who must be absent from their work for diverse reasons. In the first book, *Frank and Ernest,* they run a diner for a week and must become familiar with the terminology used to order meals. Students are exposed to descriptive phrases when Ernest requests "Eve with a lid and moo juice" to represent a "piece of apple pie and a glass of milk" or "paint a bow-wow red, and I need a nervous pudding" to signal the customer has ordered a "hot dog with ketchup" and "a serving of Jell-O." *Frank and Ernest Play Ball* finds the two main characters managing a baseball team and once again attempting to become familiar with the specialized descriptive language such as "meal ticket," "bullpen," and "fly hawk."

Many alphabet books utilize descriptive language. James Rice writes vivid descriptions for Texas places, things, and people in the *Texas Alphabet*. May Elting and Michael Folsom describe why a certain letter of the alphabet represents an unexpected item in the unique alphabet book, *Q Is for Duck—An Alphabet Guessing Game.*

INSTRUCTIONAL APPLICATIONS

These books can be utilized to assist children in recognizing descriptive text and identifying what information is important. For instance, in *A House for Hermit Crab,* children have the opportunity to verbalize physical descriptions of the animals by describing the art. Students may use the format of *The Magic School Bus Inside the Earth* and *The Magic School Bus Lost in the Solar System* to categorize and describe items they are studying. The *Frank and Ernest* books provide a humorous way to describe items, and students might follow that format and plan a balanced meal using their own descriptive language.

◄ **THE POET PONDERS**

OPEN UP

Some things are pretty tricky.
Did you ever wonder why
The sun gets big and orange
At the bottom of the sky?

What grows hair on Daddy's
*   face?*
Who puts black in tar?
Where do locusts come from?
How heavy is a star?

Well don't let questions scare you
Cuz you don't have far to look,
The whole world is your crystal ball
When you open up a book.

Alphabet books provide a framework for students to identify and write descriptively about a subject they are studying such as the "Dinosaur Alphabet" or the "Solar System Alphabet." Additional activities that cause students to focus on the descriptive attributes include writing a personality sketch or wanted poster of a historical or generic (such as a polluter or an environmentalist) character. Writing or dramatizing an advertisement for a factual place, procedure, or thing requires students to utilize highly descriptive language. Students become proficient in descriptive language when they have the opportunity to take a content concept and expand it with descriptive words and phrases that "paint a picture in the mind." For example, descriptive words and phrases could be added to the word *dinosaur* until a specific dinosaur is identifiable by the stated characteristics. Children become aware of the power of descriptive language when they write or verbalize a description of a content concept (place, thing, person, or procedure) in order for another student to draw it. The strength of the description is assessed by the artist's rendering. Often, revision and collaboration result.

SEQUENTIAL TEXT

Sequential passages in text require students to ask the following questions:

How do you do this?

What are the steps in this?

What happened first, second, third . . .

What do I do first?

Books such as Charles Oz's *How a Crayon Is Made* and *How Does Soda Get into the Bottle?* and Aliki's *How a Book Is Made* expose children to the series of steps in making a product. Joanna Cole takes children on sequential tours of the solar system and the water cycle in *The Magic School Bus Lost in the Solar System* and *The Magic School Bus at the Waterworks*. In Paul Fleischman's *Time Train*, children take a trip back through time to visit the dinosaurs. Biographies and autobiographies expose children to the sequence of significant events in a person's life and often aid children in realizing what it was like to live through a specific time period. Jean Fritz brings historical characters alive by weaving their unique human characteristics into her intriguing presentation of biographical information in books such as *And Then What Happened, Paul Revere?*, *Why Don't You Get a Horse, Sam Adams?*, *Where Was Patrick Henry on the 29th of May?*, *What's the Big Idea, Ben Franklin?*, *Will You Sign Here, John Hancock?*, *The Great Little Madison*, and *Traitor: The Case of Benedict Arnold*. Robert Burleigh's *In Flight: The Journey of Charles Lindbergh* shows readers the sequence of events leading to an important historical event in a person's life. *Bill Peet: An Autobiography* exposes children to the concept that someone can tell about his or her own life through both text and drawings. As children are exposed to the sequence of events in the lives of real people, they are confronted with what Jean Fritz (1981) refers to as "the very stuff of life."

INSTRUCTIONAL APPLICATIONS

Students have the opportunity to sequence information by constructing flow charts of the information presented in the children's books. Familiar sequences of events can be charted first, such as two third graders did in "How to Get Ready to Play Football" and "How to Catch a Girl." Children can then move to charting new material, such as "How to Plant Beans" (see pages 439, 440, and 441).

Comic strips are also an excellent format for illustrating the sequence of events of a procedure or an event. *The Magic School Bus at the Waterworks* contains a wall story of the sequence of the characters' trip through the water cycle. Any sequenced information can be put in this format. The children must select the important items, illustrate them, and write a short description. They then attach the information to the wall or bulletin board in sequential order. In lieu of this, students could construct a flip chart of the information. In order to provide opportunities for discussion and revision, give the children the opportunity to practice the sequence by each child holding one of the written descriptions and illustration and placing themselves in the correct order.

Any of these formats can also be used if students are presenting biographical or autobiographical information. If children are attempting to identify the important steps in a procedure, they could write a help wanted ad for someone to do the procedure. The ad must contain the ordered "steps" the person would be responsible for.

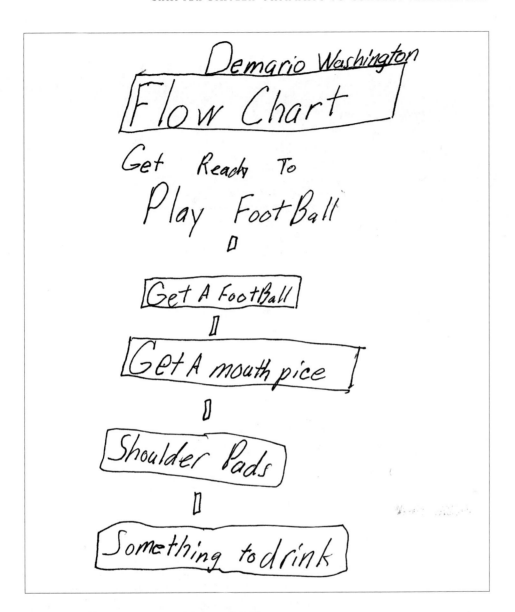

COMPARISON AND CONTRAST TEXT

Text that has the structure of comparison and contrast focuses on these issues:

How were these things or ideas alike? To what extent?

How were these things or ideas different? To what extent?

How were these things or ideas the same? To what extent?

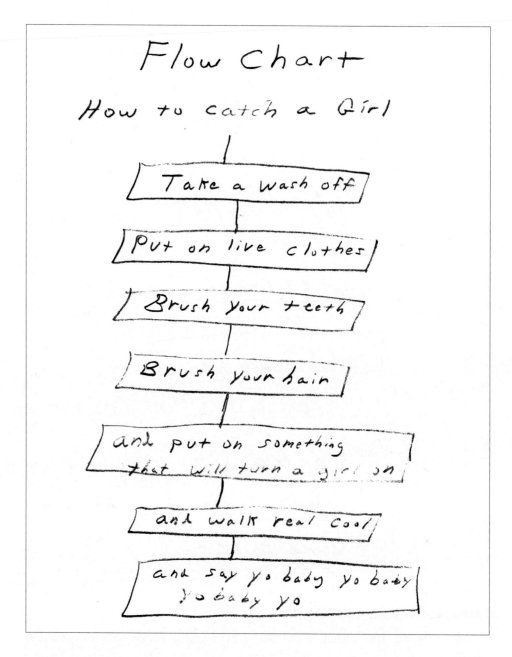

Karen Ackerman's *The Tin Heart* is the story of two friends at the beginning of the Civil War. Their fathers' differing viewpoints on the issues become a dividing point, because one family lives on the Ohio side of the Ohio River and the other lives on the Kentucky side. Children have the opportunity to compare and contrast changes caused by the passage of time when they read *In Two Worlds: A Yup'ik Eskimo Family* by Aylett Jenness and Alice Rivers because a picture of both present and past village life is presented. Patricia Lauber contrasts old beliefs about dinosaurs with updated information in *The News*

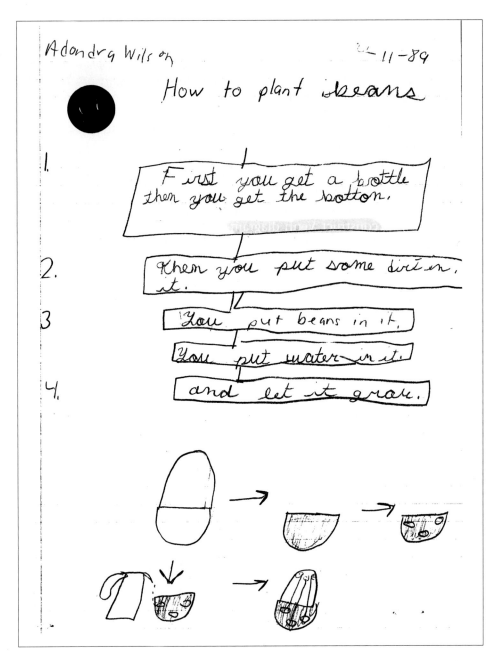

About Dinosaurs. As children are exposed to the commonly held beliefs about the validity of the existence of the brontosaurus, they are given the update that the brontosaurus was an incorrect classification resulting from the erroneous joining of the head and body of two different dinosaurs. Eric Carle weaves a story portraying the results of a chameleon comparing and contrasting his qualities with those of other animals and assuming some of their characteristics in *The Mixed-up Chameleon.* In Paul Goble's *Death of the Iron Horse,*

the viewpoints and perceptions of Native Americans are portrayed and contrasted with those who were instigating the westward expansion of the railroad. While the traditional European viewpoint of Christopher Columbus's "discovery" of America is portrayed in Joan Anderson's *Christopher Columbus: From Vision to Voyage* and Peter Sis's *Follow the Dream: The Story of Christopher Columbus,* students are exposed to the reaction and concern of a young Native American boy in *Encounter* by Jane Yolen. Figure 16.1 shows the contrasting views of Christopher Columbus and a Native American child as portrayed in *Christopher Columbus: From Vision to Voyage* and *Encounter.*

INSTRUCTIONAL APPLICATIONS

As students are exposed to the varied viewpoints and ideas in the trade books, they can construct Venn diagrams depicting the views that are alike and different. Figure 16.2 demonstrates the differing views of the two fathers in *Tin Heart.* Exploration and research of the issues could result in a panel discussion comparing objects, ideas, or viewpoints. During this process, children become aware that different sources often present conflicting information. Therefore, copyright dates, credentials of the author, and reliability of the publication must be examined. Children can utilize the information to write editorials depicting the differing views or to write interviews depicting the contrasting opinions—for instance, editorials or interviews could be writ-

FIGURE 16.1 ▶

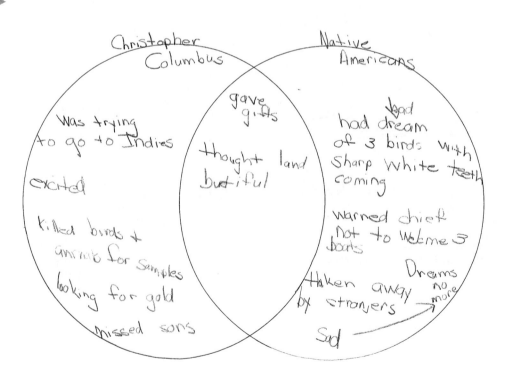

ten and conducted depicting Christopher Columbus's and a Native American's views of Columbus's exploration.

CAUSE/EFFECT TEXT

In order to glean important information from cause/effect text, students must determine:

Why did this happen?

What action(s) instigated this (these) event(s)?

What caused this?

When a little boy falls asleep and dreams he is on a train ride, animals explain why they must board the train in order to escape extinction in *Hey! Get Off Our Train* by John Burningham. In *The Great Kapok Tree*, Lynne Cherry details how a logger in the Amazon Rain Forest is made aware of the effect of his actions on the various animals and people who live there. Remy Charlip uses the delightful pattern of *Fortunately, Unfortunately,* to trace the logical effect of each action as a young boy attempts to reach his destination of a birthday party in New York City.

INSTRUCTIONAL APPLICATIONS

When children incorporate the pattern in *Fortunately, Unfortunately,* they can trace the cause/effect relationship of many content concepts. Elisa, a fifth grader, wrote about the Pilgrims:

Fortunately, the Pilgrims wanted to be free to have their own church. Unfortunately, they couldn't do that in England. Fortunately, the Pilgrims had a ship called the Mayflower. Unfortunately, the ship was very small. Fortunately, they still decided to leave England in September 1620 to come to America. Unfortunately, they did not arrive in America until November 1620. Fortunately, they started Plymouth Colony along Cape Cod Bay. Unfortunately, it was winter and many people died. Fortunately, the Indians showed them how to survive. And, fortunately, some lived so they could have Thanksgiving and fortunately they invited the Indians, and fortunately, they had a big dinner, and fortunately, we still do!!!

The cause/effect relationship can also be explored as children write newspaper stories or editorials depicting the cause of a problem and its effect.

PROBLEM/SOLUTION TEXT

Text that depicts problems and solutions concentrates on the following issues:

THE POET ▶
PONDERS

BEAUTY AND THE BEAST

There was a dark castle,
And a courageous girl,
And a prince trapped
In the body of a beast,
And a wilting rose to scent the air
Of an untouched wedding feast.

As I read these fairy tales
I begin to understand,
They speak a truth as lasting
As the sky...
And the sea...
And the land.

What problem occurred and how will it be solved?

Can we prevent this problem from occurring again?

Was this problem perceived the same way by everyone?

Problems and solutions are examined in *A River Ran Wild* as Lynne Cherry chronicles the pollution and reclamation of the Nashua River. Ruth Heller depicts the problems that animals face in trying to protect themselves in the wild and the solutions provided by protective coloration in her books *How to Hide a Butterfly and Other Insects, How to Hide an Octopus and Other Sea Creatures, How to Hide a Polar Bear and Other Mammals, How to Hide a Crocodile and Other Reptiles,* and *How to Hide a Whip-poor-will and Other Birds.* The life threatening problem caused by the Alaskan oil spill is examined by Gloria Rand as she chronicles the rescue and treatment of animals in *Prince William.*

INSTRUCTIONAL APPLICATIONS

Children can examine the problems portrayed in these texts, brainstorm alternative solutions for the problems, and do research to determine if any of

---

THE POET ▶
PONDERS

HISTORY HELP

He made us learn the names,
He made us memorize each date.
He said,

"History repeats itself.
Learn now before it's too late."

So I'm gonna learn my history,
Even though the past is done,
But I wish I could find some simple way
To help make history fun.

their suggestions have been implemented. Panel discussions can also be conducted concerning problems and various solutions. The "cubing" strategy (Vaughan & Estes, 1986) may be adapted to extend thought and research concerning problems and solutions. Cover a cube of foam rubber or a cubical box with contact paper. Using self-stick removable notes, put the following descriptors on the various sides:

1. Describe the problem.
2. Describe the solution.
3. Associate or compare this problem/solution to another situation.
4. Argue for the solution given in the text.
5. Argue against the solution given in the text.
6. Think of an alternative solution.

Students may work in pairs or groups as they "roll" the cube and follow the instruction that comes up.

BECOMING INDEPENDENT LEARNERS

Texts have many structures and convey information in many different formats (Meyer, 1975; Piccolo, 1987). Vygotsky (1978) refers to the importance of "scaffolding" children to the next level of learning. Fortunately, teachers can aid children as they attempt to "read to learn," for research has shown that familiarity with diverse text structures increases children's proficiency in gleaning information from expository text (Englert & Hiebert, 1984; Horowitz, 1985a, 1985b; Slater, 1985). Instructional environments that include quality and quantity exposures to varied text patterns through children's literature provide children with the "scaffold" of the familiar format of a children's book as an introduction to an unfamiliar organizational pattern. When we increase children's ability to comprehend expository text, we are helping them move onto the pathway of becoming independent lifelong learners.

DEVELOPING RESEARCH SKILLS

One technique of teaching literacy in the content areas is to confront students with questions they may not understand—not because answers don't exist, but because they have not found them for themselves. Children are helped to understand that problems are not solved once and for all, but that one problem leads to another. They discover that solving problems is the great adventure of learning.

Literacy in the content areas of the curriculum is enhanced and extended through six essential strategies and techniques:

▶ Promoting a searching attitude
▶ Developing research skills
▶ Using a variety of resources
▶ Using a table of contents and index

▶ Using alphabetical arrangement

▶ Using library reference skills

PROMOTING A SEARCHING ATTITUDE

Children who search for answers to their questions may not always find those answers, but if they continue to seek, they demonstrate an attitude toward solving problems that is far more valuable than finding answers every time. They learn to use a scientific method of thinking that leads to individual, independent searching.

The self-confidence and assurance necessary to launch into the unknown, into creative thinking and creative production, come from repeated opportunities to search for answers to one's own questions. This means that teachers in a meaning-centered curriculum place no emphasis and little value on students' ability to fill in blanks of prepared worksheets. Children may use some such aids as models in preparing their own work to be used with their peers in learning centers, but the *process* is regarded as a more valuable learning experience than the *product*. To be able to ask questions that reflect the intended meaning of an author may be as valuable a skill as the ability to answer questions that already have the major ideas identified.

Students practice numerous oral, writing, and reading skills as they search for answers. In addition, they can gather data from personal interviews, telephone conversations, and observations. They can study pictures, listen to recordings, use computers, and test possibilities and alternatives.

THE POET ▶
PONDERS

MADAM CURIE'S BIOGRAPHY

I wondered:
What she was like at school?
Was she well-behaved or bad?
Was she always happy,
Or was she sometimes sad?

Then, when I read her biography,
I thought...how strange,
She seems just like me,
And I felt a voice from deep inside,
Could it be?
Oh could it really be?

Lee Davis teaches a fifth-grade class that usually has several students who are branded "nonreaders." During the early weeks of school he diminishes the emphasis on reading printed matter and helps every student develop interest around which future reading can be planned. He invites a series of "experts" to visit his class to serve as resource persons for interviews.

Each student is encouraged to formulate questions. Techniques for carrying on interviews are discussed, guides are developed, and students who have special interest in the visitor's area of expertise are invited to lead the interviews. All students can participate, however. Among the people he invites are an automobile mechanic, an architect, a cook, a pilot, and a gardener.

After the series of visiting experts, Lee lets each student choose to become expert in some field. The student prepares for an interview by the class members. Searching begins. Students use all kinds of resources to prepare. Poor readers find resources they can use. Many of them find that they have interests about which they know more than anyone else in the class. Their interest in reading in their specialty mounts as their time for the interview approaches. Vocabularies are extended as students search for words to fit into categories that have been agreed on.

Edna Brown suggests broad topics for word lists that students can extend as they read. She begins with a topic such as "Homes Around the World." Children add to the list any word they find that tells the kinds of homes people live in. She uses other topics, too. Some of these topics are "Imaginary Characters," "Roots That Are Used for Food," "Kinds of Weather," "Machines That Have Levers," and "Waste That Pollutes."

Reference books are useful when students search for answers to questions. They should be supplemented with picture sets, filmstrips, and books of information that have an index and a table of contents.

Terry Scribner has a bulletin board where she posts questions that have come up in class discussions. "Do all insects have six legs?" is an example. Children search for scientific information, find pictures, and make displays in answer to each question. Terry feels it is much more important to stimulate a positive attitude toward searching than for her to furnish the answers.

DEVELOPING RESEARCH SKILLS

Persons and objects in their environment help preschool children find answers to their questions. At school they have additional sources to provide the information needed to satisfy curiosity and widen their scope of thinking.

The oral interchange of young students with classmates, teachers, and other adults is a prime resource for young children. It continues to contribute as they learn to use books and other material that involve reading symbols. In addition, most classrooms have a wealth of nonbook material—toys, plants,

◀ Local surroundings provide many opportunities for basic research.

animals, machines, maps, pictures, microscopes, charts, study prints, films, and recordings. At home, most students have access to books, television, computers, and radio. Some schools provide study trips for groups of students to find out firsthand about things they study and discuss. All these can be used to build abilities in using resources and to stimulate interest in listening, speaking, and learning how to write and read.

SEARCHING FOR INFORMATION

To give students only one source that contains a satisfying answer is to limit the development of their thinking powers. The goal in a meaning-based curriculum is to give them a variety of resources and let them search out the answers that satisfy them and solve their problems.

Even before children learn to read much of printed material, they can be introduced to the idea of searching in many places to find answers. Picture books, picture encyclopedias, and CD-ROM provide information on many topics. When children think they have located information in a book they cannot read, the teacher can read to them to verify its usefulness.

As reading ability increases, students are encouraged to seek their own answers in reading material. In so doing, they soon discover that different books have different purposes. Some are fiction and are for pleasure reading only. Some are full of facts. Some give most of their information through pictures. Some have an alphabetic arrangement. Some mix fact and fiction.

Older students usually rely on reading as a way to find most of their information. They have to know how to locate pertinent information and develop abilities through using a table of contents and index, skimming, and using topical headings and other aids for finding information. Such older students find encyclopedias are the richest source of specific information and that

CLASSROOM VIGNETTE

In the first week of school, Lois Lyons begins to take dictation from students in first grade. She displays the stories and reads from them when she is ready to introduce new skills. A bulletin board has several captions on sheets of paper, with room to list words from the stories. The captions may include first-time words, words that begin alike, rhyming words, sentences with commas, first words in quotations, first words in sentences, and sentences with question marks. In their own stories, students discover characteristics that they need to recognize in the language of others.

Experimenting with common materials helps young students find answers to questions and ask new ones. Here are some common questions that students can research through observation:

What colors of paint are mixed to form other colors?

What effect have light and darkness on the growth of plants?

What materials produce electricity when a balloon is rubbed against them?

What kinds of paper absorb water?

What causes evaporation?

Children can record their discoveries by writing simple statements. Some may be able to find information in simple illustrated books on the subject. Others may reinforce their information by viewing a filmstrip on the topic. A class diary can be kept on observations when changes occur fairly rapidly.

Continued

dictionaries contain definitions which may give them clues for further research. As they work, they find need for abilities in reading charts, maps, and other materials that consist primarily of symbols to be interpreted.

History, geography, and science are examples of subject areas that require students to locate information from numerous sources. Need exists for the development of locational skills. The procedure for teaching content subjects should require the pupil to use the index, the table of contents, topic headings and subheadings, and all the important parts of books. Students develop the ability to identify unknown words, find their pronunciations in the dictionary, and select appropriate meanings for words in terms of use in context. They use alphabetically arranged material easily, such as dictionaries and encyclopedias and other reference material. Researchers must also learn to skim to locate needed information. They come to know that no one book, film, collection of objects, or field trip will have all the answers they are seeking. When they learn to use the laboratory of varied resources provided them, they come to enjoy thinking out problems that are important to them. Such skills do not need to be developed in an artificial reading situation. They should come naturally as children search for information.

Teachers of young children initiate research techniques naturally as they provide resources that have lead questions, resource cards, and demonstrations. Some easy ones to provide include the following:

1. A magnifying glass and rocks, leaves, flowers, or wood with different grains. Children discover differences with close examination.

2. Animal life in an aquarium or terrarium. Children talk about their observations, write or dictate some of them, and extend their information by using books placed in the vicinity.

3. Simple balances for comparing weights. Children guess weights by size and then put items on a balance to check their predictions. They seek answers to why some small things weigh more than other larger ones.

4. Simple measuring devices. Children make approximations and then verify them with accurate measurements.

5. Maps of areas where students live or have traveled. Trips—real and imaginary—can be charted. Children learn to read the grids on maps and other reference techniques for locating places.

Broad experiences of trying things out, of getting into unknown situations, of being curious about how things work, and of wanting to know what it means can launch students into research that requires reading and writing. While they are waiting to read and write well enough for mature research activities, they need repeated successes in finding satisfactory solutions to simple personal questions. By using multiple resources that require minimum skills in reading, they can participate in research during the period when print reading yields no real information.

USING A TABLE OF CONTENTS AND INDEX

Teachers of content subjects are usually supplied with textbooks that have a table of contents and index. These are of minimal use in teaching locational skills when one book is used day after day as the text. Science and social studies books can be useful, however, in teaching students how to use tables of contents and indexes in other books. Students very quickly learn that researchers do not begin at the first page of a book and read every page to the end in order to find needed information. Rather, they go as directly as possible to the information they need by using resources that most publishers provide in books.

USING ALPHABETICAL ARRANGEMENT

Understanding alphabetical arrangements is an important reading skill for carrying out research. It is a skill that can be introduced early in school programs with assurances that normal activities will require its use over and over.

Some experiences that offer opportunities for teaching alphabetic arrangement are discussed here.

Patricia Patterson uses textbook sets to teach locational skills. A group of students with identical books race to find answers to questions. They select a question from a stack of cards that Patricia prepared. She reads the question that is answered somewhere in the book the children are using. The winner—the one who finds the answer first—tells the class what key word or idea in the question was used in conjunction with the index or table of contents to find the answers to the question.

When the class first starts having these races, all the questions have key words that are in the index. As students learn to use this clue, questions are formulated that do not contain a word in the index of the book they are reading. They have to think of synonyms in order to locate information.

After students learn to find answers to questions by using an index, Patricia inserts cards in the stack that have topics from the table of contents printed on them. When they see or hear one of the topics, students skim the table of contents to locate that topic and then turn to it in the book.

These activities assure students some degree of skill in using other books to find information efficiently and rapidly.

Some books have locational aids, and some do not. In many ways the titles and physical appearance of the books give clues before the books are opened.

Conrad Collins has many books in the classroom, so each time a topic is being studied in depth, he puts an assortment of books on a table and plays a game with the students. He asks them to pick, on the basis of physical appearance and title only, a book they think will contain something on a topic he names. He may take a topic such as "Weather" and work from that to various subtopics.

Students learn rapidly that most books of information have a table of contents and an index where they can verify their prediction. Storybooks may have a table of contents but no index. Books for pleasure reading seldom have either. If needed information is in the book, the reader has to search for it with no locational aids.

Conrad never relies on one source of information on a topic that is studied in depth, so he feels he must help students know how to recognize and use many sources.

1. Use picture dictionaries for browsing and for building an awareness of why and how one word follows another in alphabetical arrangement.

2. Make word books that grow from the use of the initial letter to second- and third-letter arrangements. The words can be ones the children collect and write or they can be words cut from magazines.

3. Keep word files with dividers for each letter of the alphabet.

4. Read and examine a telephone directory to find names of families represented in the classroom.

5. List in dictionary order words that have been collected on the Word Wall in the classroom.

ERIC CARLE

1. Which book of yours has given you the greatest pleasure?

Do You Want to Be My Friend? Friendship is very important to me, and I know it's important to little children—adults often forget just how important it is. I still remember my early friendships and that influenced me in writing the book.

2. Which book has surprised you most in terms of its public reception?

The Very Hungry Caterpillar. I am still surprised at its popularity after all these years. For a long time people asked me why it was so popular and I couldn't answer them. I have decided after 25 years that it has been so well received because it is a book of hope—the ugly duckling growing up. The insignificant little worm can grow up and unfold his wings and fly off.

3. What would you like people to remember about your work?

My contribution has been that I have reached the very young before they can even read. Mothers with 6-month-old and 1-year-old children have come up to me and said their children cannot go to bed at night without hearing *The Very Hungry Caterpillar* again.

4. What impact do you hope your work will have on children?

I want to introduce very young children to literature—what my German publisher calls "the absolute beginners."

Working with torn and painted paper, die-cut pages, and even sound effects, Eric Carle provides books which appeal to beginning readers and give them the sense that reading is a happy surprise, a thing always to enjoy. His works include *The Very Hungry Caterpillar, The Very Busy Spider, The Very Quiet Cricket, Brown Bear, Brown Bear, What Do You See?, House for Hermit Crab, Mixed-Up Chameleon, Draw Me a Star,* and *Grouchy Ladybug.*

6. List books on a topic by alphabetical arrangement of the authors and titles.

7. Use encyclopedias to illustrate a major reference source that has alphabetical order. Notice key words for topics and the use of last names of people. Look for cross references that send the researcher to other volumes.

8. Play games that require students to alphabetize words in order to win.

Dictionaries are a special kind of alphabetically arranged book for researchers and have several useful features:

1. Pronunciation keys to aid with new words found during research.

2. Sources of words that might be useful in research (found in some dictionaries).

3. Multiple definitions so researchers have a chance to find a meaning that fits the context of their reading material. Students doing research may find words they recognize at sight but do not understand in a particular setting because the words carry new meanings that need to be looked up in a dictionary.

From the beginning of research activities in primary grades, a collection of dictionaries should be available. Some should be simple enough for good readers to use independently. Others might be difficult to read, but they will probably be the ones the children need when they study topics of interest to them. If they can find in the dictionary words that are new to them in reading material, they can usually find someone to help them with dictionary pronunciation and definitions.

USING LIBRARY REFERENCE SKILLS

If we want children to become researchers, they need access to a library and assistance in developing library reference skills. They must have opportunities to become secure amid a mass of materials that have nothing to do with the topics being studied.

One way to establish a secure feeling is to teach the use of a *library card catalog.* With some knowledge of alphabetical order, arrangement, key words, and names of authors and titles, a student can find books, films, picture sets, records, kits of material, and magazines on topics of interest. Everything is coded and arranged in an order so that once the code is understood, materials can be located with a minimum of help from librarians. Most card catalogs are now accessible by computer.

Skimming is a reading skill that must accompany efficient use of library reference materials. No researcher has time to read everything carefully. Key ideas must be selected and located in materials by skimming to the point at which the needed information is found. Then careful reading for detail may take place.

In a learning center environment recommended for a meaning-centered curriculum, students who have easy access to a library for reference reading are not limited to one source for reading. They are challenged to get involved in the excitement of learning from resources like those used by adult researchers, such as CD-ROM. Programs deny students a feeling of security, adequacy, and achievement when all children read the same book and supply the same answer. Students should question, observe, predict, verify, and validate as they search out solutions to problems in various sources.

ART AND LITERACY

As we've mentioned throughout this text, children need opportunities on a daily basis for self-expression. Art affords such opportunities.

Many art skills are learned naturally as young people progress through developmental levels of expression with art media. Because art is not totally intuitive, direct instruction and modeling of processes and techniques are important. Skills, as well as freedom of expression, are necessary if art is to contribute to language growth. The attributes of creativity are essential in both forms of communication, language arts and visual arts. In school settings, concepts of both language and art must be translated into performance. Speaking, writing, and reading can be natural extensions of the visual arts.

ART ACTIVITIES FOR LANGUAGE GROWTH

Self-expression in art increases awareness of the elements of composition—line, depth, color, texture, form. As children have experience in using many media, they use these elements in various combinations. The natural conversation accompanying these experiences requires the use of words of the form-classes—nouns, verbs, adjectives, and adverbs. The classifications of descriptive words used most frequently in literary selections are those that are used most often in talking about art—color, size, shape, texture, feelings, contrasts, and comparisons. Talking about the creative process and the finished artwork builds and extends children's language base.

Young children draw, paint, and sculpt forms representing their visual images of real and imaginary subjects. Usually they do not plan the arrangement of forms but place them in the pictures or mold them in accordance with immediate importance. This lack of planning does not detract from the value of their self-expression. To deny children the exploratory phase of art would be like denying speech until they can speak with poetic expressions.

Older students may be aware of creating a design, having a center of interest, developing rhythm in the work through repetition of form and color, and applying all the elements of composition with a selected medium. This development takes place gradually and should always be accompanied with freedom of expression through experimentation.

Teachers who provide time and space for visual portrayal of experiences are guided by fundamental concepts which help them select activities that contribute to language growth. These fundamental concepts include the following:

1. **To express themselves in art, students need to be encouraged to invent, to improvise, and to fabricate.** Art offers students a chance to arrange common materials such as boxes, buttons, paper rolls, and other objects in pleasing and uncommon ways. Tissue-paper overlay with its color and transparency creates not only many hues and values from the variety of colors and shapes of paper torn for the overlay effect, but also a magical effect. *Finger painting* provides opportunities to use fingers, hands, and parts of the arm to apply and distribute paint on a glazed piece of paper.

2. **To communicate effectively, students must be able to see many possible solutions to a problem and choose one to develop.** *Colored chalk* can be used on wet paper to create a color wonderland. Students respond to its ease of application and immediate representation of something bold and bright—a dragon, a field of flowers, a design of flames, the spirit of a circus. Chalk on newspapers yields instant designs suggested by the arrangement of print.

DeAnna Tarrant — Name

13 — Age

Basketball, Church (Youth) — Interests

What do you like most about school?

I like the social part of school. I am a regular people person! And ever since kindergarden I have made new friends and lost some to.

What's your favorite subject? Why?

My favorite subject is History. I love to learn about what happened in Texas and the United States before I was born. I also like History because many of my deceased relatives were not able to tell me about the depression or war.

What's your favorite book? Why do you like it?

My favorite Book is a wrinkle in Time. I love this book because it is mysterious and it has a good message.

What advice do you have for teachers?

I think teachers should make an effort to get to know their students. I don't know many of my teachers as a friend. I think if I did I would find it much easier to learn from them.

Sand casting with a variety of tools for making impressions in wet sand and with a variety of objects for embedding before pouring plaster offers a chance for expressiveness in a simple but unique way for each student.

Limited palette painting with crayons, watercolors, or tempera interprets a subject in one dominant color and mixes of that color to achieve depth and form. It is a way of varying interpretations of a subject rather than reporting photographic details. Variation can be achieved by cutting colored photographs from magazines, choosing portions of the same basic color, cutting shapes, and arranging them into a design.

3. **To arrange parts into a design with unity is an ability students develop for realistic and abstract representation.** *Collage* is a process of forming artistic compositions by placing items such as cloth, buttons, seed, braid, string, and cardboard in an arrangement and gluing them down. Dabs of color and some related lines are usually added to unify the design. Collage techniques can be observed in the work of famous artists such as Braque and Picasso. Collage is a way of doing something unusual with the usual.

   Paper-and-paste projects, especially those dealing with abstract designs, provide practice in arranging for unity, variety, contrast, line, rhythm, and form. Students practice arranging and rearranging the cut or torn forms before they paste them together to form the finished work.

   Traditions of other cultures, such as the Mexican piñata and Japanese origami, might encourage students to experiment with paper creations of their own.

   With freedom and encouragement, students naturally apply themselves to the pleasing experiences of tearing, cutting, pasting, building, and shaping constructions.

4. **Artists must be able to bring sharply differing elements into harmony through design and color.** *Texture painting* with sand, cornmeal, crushed eggshells, and other textured materials can be used to change all or part of the surface of a painting. Students who use textured materials are redefining their use and thinking in new directions about materials for self-expression.

   Carving is a subtractive process, the opposite of modeling. As students experiment with cutting, scratching, and gouging with simple tools, they produce works with contrasts in light and shadow, in bright and dull, in smooth and rough.

5. **Students need to be able to translate a word or words into a visual representation.** *Tempera painting* is a form of communication that most young students can deal with before they can write for themselves. Later the pictures become illustrations for the written word rather than the story itself. Easels and supplies for tempera painting should be available in every literacy-oriented classroom. Freedom of expression with tempera paint is as significant as the illustration of a word or a story.

   As students observe their world in order to paint the things in it, they are able to see variety. A tree is not always green; clouds are not always white; the sky is not always blue.

   Crayon is usually the first medium for art that students use. It should be encouraged for expressing of ideas and for illustrating.

   Clay modeling is a process of working from lumps, slabs, or coils to create three-dimensional objects. Clay can be kneaded, rolled, stretched, cut, joined, pinched, and pulled. Some of the products are fired in a kiln. Much clay work is a series of new beginnings; students decide one thing after another as they create objects with clay.

6. **To enjoy art, one does not depend on oral statements but on feelings generated by the total effect of the process and product.** *Paper sculpture* is the shaping of paper by rolling, folding, pleating, or wadding to achieve structural designs. Paper can be fringed, curled, and punctured for decorative effects. For a dispensable art form, paper sculpture has no set rules but has many new beginnings as one procedure leads to another.

   Paper lamination is a process of applying strips of paper dipped in wet paste to a framework such as newspaper coils, chicken wire, boxes, bottles, and balloons. The student must monitor the changing form to determine the need to build up areas as the form becomes an animal, a totem pole, or a mask.

   Drop-dry-draw is a process of dropping thick or dry tempera on very wet paper. The paint "explodes" and runs together. After it dries, the artist decides what is there—real or imaginary—and outlines it with a marker.

   Doodling drawn with crayons and pencils can be filled in with color and a few features to represent feelings such as love, happiness, and fear, to create imaginary creatures, or to make pleasing designs.

7. **To represent what an artist sees or imagines when handling natural materials requires minimum adjustments.** *Natural objects* provide opportunities to apply the maxim "art is in the eye of the beholder." Children see the shapes of animals, machines, and people in rocks, branches, driftwood, seedpods, shells, and clouds. Some natural materials need a little carving, scratching, or painting to bring out features and to highlight areas for a center of interest. The similarities observed require acute visual perception.

   Collections of look-alike objects foster the use of figurative language in the classroom—similes, metaphors, and personification.

8. **To exaggerate an idea is permitted and promoted in art activities.** *Mosaics* are surface pictures made by inlaying in patterns small pieces of colored glass, stone, seed, cardboard, or other material. Whatever its subjects—animals, birds, people, a landscape, insects—a mosaic should have a strong center of interest around which the remainder of the design is built.

   Murals usually exaggerate a few major objects or ideas by making them big and bold. Supporting ideas are small and subdued in comparison with the major ones. Murals can be drawn with tempera, chalk, or crayons. Attached paper sculpture can give depth to major ideas, and cut paper can add boldness to areas of emphasis. A mural is, in effect, an outline of an idea for an essay or other language production.

9. **All people share the desire to create and decorate.** *Stitchery* is a process of combining materials and placing decorative stitches on them. It involves tactile experiences of choosing materials of various textures, types, and sizes, and then manipulating them. It is a way of making pictures that is used all over the world.

   Weaving consists of threading strips of material such as yarn, string, cloth, or paper (the weft) over and under, back and forth through strips of material laid out in parallel rows and held firmly at both ends (the warp). The weaver develops an artistic design by utilizing the elements of color, value, texture, and pattern. The processes employed by students will help them appreciate the skill and artistry of weavers of all periods and regions.

10. **Artists learn how to show motion with static materials.** *Puppets* of all kinds—paper bag, sock, finger, laminated, stick—can transport a student to a land of fantasy and make-believe. Materials are chosen and arranged so motion is possible in the use of puppets in language activities. The personality and voice of a puppet can be transmitted by the feelings and voice of a child. Puppets help the manipulator try out new ways of saying things.

Mobiles hang in space and seem to float in the air if their creators have related each part to the whole in such a way that there is balance of the space-line-form concepts. Unity of design permits mobiles to be ever changing as they move. They are just like a well-written story or poem that is ever changing for its readers.

MATH AND LITERACY

RESPONDING TO NUMERALS AND NUMBERS

Numerals are everywhere in the environment of students. Most children have some experience in reading them before entering school programs. They can turn the television dial to a channel they want. They read numbers on houses and streets. They read prices in newspapers and catalogs. They watch the numerals whirl around at gas stations as the pumps record the number of gallons and the amount to be paid. Most of them play games that use numerals in some way. There is no way an active, involved human being can escape the experience of reading numerals.

NUMERALS AND NUMBERS IN NEWSPAPERS

Children can identify numerals they know in advertisements, and they can read the numbers that tell team standings in the sports pages.

CLASSROOM VIGNETTE

Rita Brown collects enough grocery advertisements for each child to have one page. She names a numeral, and students point to the place where they see it. From there she advances to saying the price of something, and students try to find that number on the advertisement. They find the numbers in both large and small print. With the help of the teacher they read numbers along with the names of products.

She also provides a blank book for students to use to paste in numbers they can read. When a book is filled, it is placed in the Book Center and used for practice reading.

NUMERALS IN THE ENVIRONMENT

Numerals are found in so many places that most students are unaware the numbers they read automatically are important. Many of their activities depend on some use of numbers.

NUMBERS IN STORIES AND POEMS

From the earliest nursery rhymes a child hears and says, the concept of number is required for understanding. "Hickory, Dickory, Dock," "Baa, Baa, Black Sheep," "One, Two, Buckle My Shoe," and "Rub-a-Dub-Dub" are examples. Most stories and poems require some understanding of numbers and words that stand for numbers, and the ability to read them is assumed.

NUMBERS EVERYWHERE

Walking in a neighborhood, taking trips to shopping centers, reading newspapers, and viewing films accentuate the variety of ways that numbers are used to make life meaningful. To be independent in everyday life, people must be able to read numbers, and students in school need to gain the assurance they can read number signals accurately.

GEOMETRIC SHAPES SURROUND US

Geometric shapes are found everywhere. However, often children are given opportunities to identify the various shapes only on a worksheet or in their math book. Children can enhance their understanding of geometric shapes by finding them in their environment.

RESPONDING TO GRAPHIC AIDS

Maps, graphs, charts, signs, and diagrams are in the reading environment of students at home and at school. They usually appear in a combination of symbols that includes lines, shapes, dots, colors, numerals, and words. To be able to read them meaningfully as a life experience may be essential for many students. To be able to read them in school experiences may provide

CLASSROOM VIGNETTE

   Ann Breedlove chooses stories appropriate for reading numbers and number words. Children read silently and list all the number words and numbers in a story. For oral reading of the same story, students are asked to skip the words on the lists they have made. They find that many stories lose their meaning when number concepts are omitted.

   Juana Garza makes a set of cards with numbers on them for the Writing/Publishing Center. Some are very small numbers, and some are very large. Children draw one, two, or more of the cards and write stories that involve the numbers. They produce scientific stories to include the smallest ones, and often use space travel or astronomy as topics that require the largest numbers.
   She also uses sets of cards for storytelling. The cards are placed in a paper bag. She draws a card and begins a story that uses the number written on the card. Then one student after another draws from the bag in turn and includes the numbers drawn in a continuation of the story. An attempt is sometimes made to keep the story realistic; at other times the story is nonsense.

   Marcella Valdez uses children's literature to help her students develop concepts about numerals. Her children love the excitement of *Bicycle Race,* a Donald Crews counting book that is bursting with suspense, excitement, and motion. The children chant out the numbers that appear on the riders as the contestants near the finish line.
   Marcella's students also enjoy the adventure of another counting book, *If You Take a Pencil,* by Fulvio Testa. The book allows the children to voyage to lands far and near as they count such things as nine "billowing sails" and twelve "treasure chests." Such books expose the students to the language and concepts of mathematics without their having to endure "lessons" in math.

basic meanings in curriculum areas such as social studies, science, and mathematics.

The meanings inherent in graphic aids can be developed best when they are used to record and represent real experiences.

Children can make maps of walking trips and field trips.

Those who travel during the school year or during the summer months can be encouraged to collect maps of their travels and bring them to class to share. Children can bring letters postmarked at different places and locate the points of origin on a large map.

Traffic signs that have shape, color, and symbols as a part of the message are available in most communities. Children are usually interested in these and can make miniatures for use in their play in the classroom and on the playground. Some school grounds can be developed with roadways that include the major traffic signs students will encounter.

CLASSROOM VIGNETTE

Mike Hooper encourages students in his sixth-grade class to build a control panel for at least one machine each year. They choose a jet, a submarine, a spaceship, or some other machine that has a control panel with dials and gauges. They usually begin by studying an automobile dashboard. They see that most panels require the reading of numbers. From there they begin to build a control panel that will register necessary information for their vehicle. During the process they come in contact with meanings represented by numerals in modern transportation systems and in scientific studies.

Jim Hicks uses films to focus on reading numerals. Children watch for numbers as they view films. They either call them out or write them down as they see them flash on the screen on highway signs, license numbers, prices of things, street numbers, house numbers, and other common places.

Reading numbers for meaning and for the purposes intended is not automatic. Most students need opportunities to try out their skills, check for accuracy, and try again to make meaningful responses to numbers they see in and out of school.

Sue Ward gives her students many opportunities to talk about the numbers they see in their environment and how they are used. She brings in real-world materials such as advertisements, road maps with mileage charts, catalogs, newspapers, cookbooks, and magazines, and students use these materials to write story problems (see Figure 16.3). Children discuss the decision-making processes involved in formulating the problem, and how it is solved. The writing of the story problems and the resulting talk about the process enhance the

Continued

Graphs showing growth of plants and height and weight of students can be part of an ongoing learning environment. The making and reading of these graphs can serve as the basic instruction in how to read other graphs.

Many instructions on how to put things together include diagrams. Children might be willing to bring models to school, such as home appliance manuals, that have diagrams as a major part of the instruction for assembly. School engineers and custodians usually have diagrams showing how machinery works. Parents who work with diagrams may be willing to show students how they read them in their work.

Charts of books read and classroom duties can be initiated in kindergarten through the use of color and shape codes. As students learn to read printed symbols, words can be added to the organizational charts.

Reading that does not depend on motions left to right and top to bottom and on alphabetical symbols is so important, it needs to be dealt with directly. Experiences in this type of reading build a base for more complex reading of graphic aids as students study technical content. Graphic aids provide ways of communicating specific information and relations that can be expressed

children's understanding of the structure of story problems and their proficiency in reading and solving story problems.

FIGURE 16.3 ▶ **TOM THUMB: A MATH STORY PROBLEM**

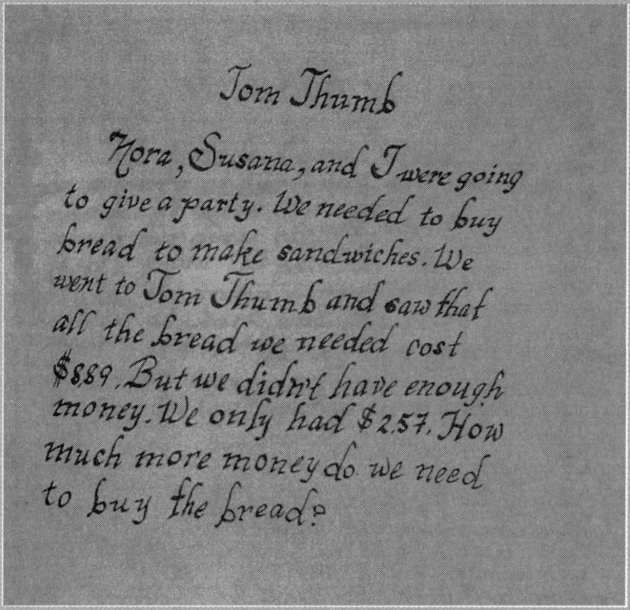

> Tom Thumb
>
> Nora, Susana, and I were going to give a party. We needed to buy bread to make sandwiches. We went to Tom Thumb and saw that all the bread we needed cost $8.89. But we didn't have enough money. We only had $2.57. How much more money do we need to buy the bread?

effectively without words or with a minimum of words for maximum information.

Many children's books present mathematical concepts in a familiar and meaningful context. Books such as Eric Carle's *The Grouchy Ladybug* expose children to the concept of time through the memorable travels and adventures of the cranky ladybug; his *The Very Hungry Caterpillar* exposes children to counting as the caterpillar tries to appease his ravenous appetite. Alexander in Judith Viorst's *Alexander, Who Used to Be Rich Last Sunday* exposes children to the concept of how quickly money can disappear if you do not count it and remain aware of the balance, and Jose Aruego and Ariane Dewey's *Five Little Ducks* presents a delightful retelling of a familiar chant as baby ducks leave their mother (subtraction) and return (addition).

MUSIC AND LITERACY

Rhythmic responses are basic to every person's communication. As nonverbal forms, they are as significant in many cases as the verbal forms of response that may or may not accompany them.

Janet Anderson believes her fifth-grade students demonstrate their understanding of mathematical concepts when they are able to make real-world applications of the information. After working with geometric shapes, Janet invited her students to write about places where they had seen the shapes in their environment. When Jonathan turned in the following book about a summer trip, Janet knew he was comfortable with the concept of geometric shapes.

Continued

The printed word can suggest only basic body responses, but most literary works draw on our background of self-expression through rhythmic experiences. Movement is so basic to life that every sentence spoken or printed has a verb in it or one implied. To assume that because children move freely, they understand and engage in a wide variety of rhythmic responses is to assume what is not true for many of them.

Many children in our schools are shy and inhibited about expressing themselves with their hands, feet, fingers, toes, and body. They have been made to feel that to be still and quiet is a virtue of highest priority for success in school. These shy children, along with all the others, are expected to enter into reconstructing the meanings of cold print not reflective of familiar language or ideas, and to call it reading.

These procedures and behavioral objectives are applied to children without the slightest inventory of their level of self-confidence in expressing personal meanings in sounds of music and in sounds of language. Some schools thrust what they call *self-selection reading programs* on children who have never had an opportunity in school to learn how to self-select a simple body rhythm. Students who lack the self-confidence and self-concept needed to make personal responses to music are often the same ones who cannot remember words, cannot reply to questions of meaning, and cannot decide which book to read when given a choice.

LANGUAGE DEVELOPMENT THROUGH RHYTHMIC RESPONSE

The language of movement, which is essential for speaking, writing, and reading in sentences, can be fostered and refined through rhythmic responses.

The words of movement and their meaning can be learned in other ways, but efficient instruction links the actual movements to the words. These words of movements, when experienced and verbalized, can be used for writing and will be recognized in reading to an extent not possible without meaningful interpretation. Here are some ways in which children develop language through rhythmic response:

moving to rhythmic music

pantomiming with body movements while listening to music

responding to films without words

responding by writing

MOVING TO RHYTHMIC MUSIC

Through instructions and demonstrations, children acquire a repertoire of responses from which they can select some that could become personalized at later times.

SOCIAL STUDIES AND LITERACY

Social studies has the unfortunate reputation as being the least popular subject among elementary school students. That's probably because social

CLASSROOM VIGNETTE

Mary Miller, a second-grade teacher, involves her children in rhythms for the following body movements when they are appropriate to a story or song:

clapping of hands	slapping of abdomen
clicking of tongue	swinging of arms
rocking of body	jumping
marching	running
skipping	galloping
hopping	swimming

Teachers can participate by actually helping students move to the rhythm of music rather than by just moving while music is playing. The teacher can show the students how to clap the accents and be a partner while another student claps, marches, or tiptoes. Then the students can improvise, experiment, vary, and create. They can build rapport with the teacher and with other students in these easy nonthreatening activities that will build the self-esteem they can rely on should they face later challenges in language-recognition skills.

studies, particularly history, is presented often as a long, long series of names, dates, and events (Beesley, 1994). When social studies is reduced to such trivia, its heart and soul—culture—is left out.

Where textbooks have failed in the inclusion of culture, children's books have succeeded. Children have available more books than ever before that focus on their world and its history. In addition to excellent historical fiction, students can now read outstanding biographies written in a style that lures them in. Jean Fritz and Tomie dePaola illuminate the revolutionary war period with *Shh! We're Writing the Constitution;* Fritz makes James Madison human and understandable to children in *The Great Little Madison.*

Civil War history comes alive in *The Boy's War* by Jim Murphy. Likewise, young readers can encounter the horrors of the holocaust in Lois Lowry's *Number the Stars* and Jane Yolen's *The Devil's Arithmetic.*

Geography is featured with a look at the land and her people in *Yonder* by Peter Johnston. This book also does an excellent job of picturing the cycle of life. Farm life is featured in Nancy Price Graff's *The Strength of the Hills: A Portrait of a Family Farm.* This outstanding book is an in-depth examination of a family farm in Vermont; it provides children with outstanding pictures and text of farm life.

Hundreds of books are now available that look at ethnic life; Bill Martin Jr tells the penetrating story of a young Korean American in *Yo Grocer* (in press). We discuss many more ethnic titles in Chapter 17.

Thus, as you can see, social studies is best presented in the school curriculum through children's books. Textbooks serve best as reference books—children's books do a better job of telling the stories of the people and their homes.

SCIENCE AND LITERACY

Science should be students' favorite subject. And it would be, if the teaching of science was turned upside down. Instead of memorizing the scientific names of parts of the human body or the chemical properties of a specific substance, children need to be freed to explore the world of science from the perspective of their own interests. Instead of reading about science in textbooks, students need to experience science at a hands-on level.

FUN SCIENCE BOOKS

Trees by Harry Behn, illustrated by James Endicott.

Flash, Crash, Rumble, and Roll by Franklyn Branley, illustrated by Barbara & Ed Emberly.

The Very Quiet Cricket by Eric Carle.

The Magic School Bus at the Waterworks by Joanna Cole, illustrated by Bruce Degan.

CLASSROOM VIGNETTE

Gary Bowman, a middle school science teacher in California, believes literacy learning and scientific learning are best learned together. Students in his class are always challenged to apply what they are studying; they must approach all learning with the idea that I must understand this because I have to present this information to someone else. Gary capped a study of the digestive system with a competition—students were asked to write and illustrate a poem that would express some aspect of what they had learned. Three of his students from Round Valley Middle School wrote *Ode to a Broccoli,* which we've reproduced here (Figure 16.4).

Another method Gary uses to give children a forum to share what they've learned is through class newspapers. His Science Fair issue by third graders is printed on page 65; the Special Oceanography issue of his middle school's Scientific Journal is printed on page 66.

There is one constant in all of Gary Bowman's teaching—he always begins a unit of study with a rich stack of children's books that capture the students' interest and desire to learn. A list of some of the "Fun Science Books" he uses begins on page 467.

FIGURE 16.4 ▶   **ODE TO A BROCCOLI**

ODE TO A BROCCOLI
by Corey Fugman, Evan Gatfield, and Jason Pickett, Round Valley Middle School, 1991

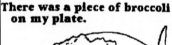

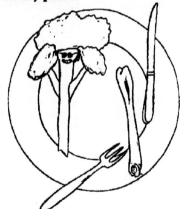

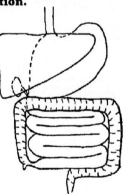

Continued

FIGURE 16.4 ▷
(cont.)

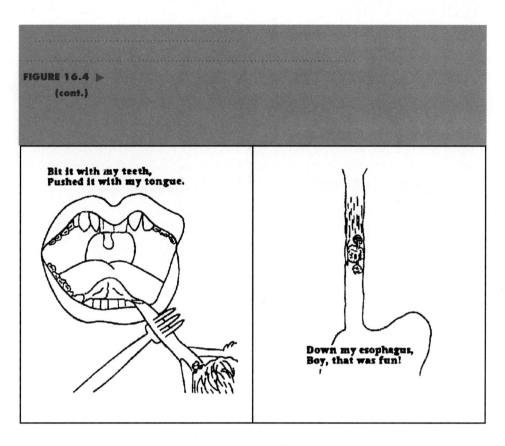

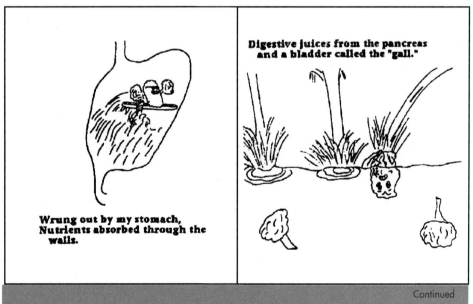

Continued

FIGURE 16.4 ▷
    (cont)

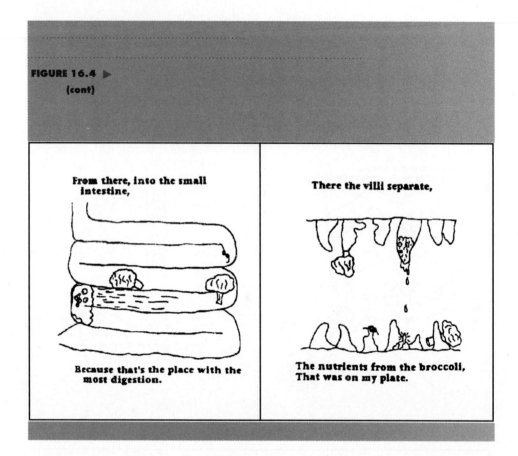

From there, into the small intestine,

Because that's the place with the most digestion.

There the villi separate,

The nutrients from the broccoli, That was on my plate.

The Magic School Bus Inside the Earth by Joanna Cole, illustrated by Bruce Degan.

The Magic School Bus Inside the Human Body by Joanna Cole, illustrated by Bruce Degan.

The Magic School Bus Lost in the Solar System by Joanna Cole, illustrated by Bruce Degan.

The Magic School Bus on the Ocean Floor by Joanna Cole, illustrated by Bruce Degan.

Bartholomew and the Oobleck by Dr. Seuss.

McElligot's Pool by Dr. Seuss.

Feathers for Lunch by Lois Ehlert.

Is Your Mama a Llama? by Deborah Guarino, illustrated by Steven Kellogg.

Plants That Never Bloom by Ruth Heller.

How to Hide an Octopus and Other Creatures by Ruth Heller.

How to Hide a Butterfly and Other Insects by Ruth Heller.

How to Hide a Polar Bear and Other Mammals by Ruth Heller.

How to Hide a Crocodile and Other Reptiles by Ruth Heller.

How to Hide a Whip-poor-will and Other Birds by Ruth Heller.

Aardvarks, Disembark by Ann Jonas.

Color Dance by Ann Jonas.

Listen to the Rain by Bill Martin Jr/John Archambault, illustrated by James Endicott.

The Bird Alphabet Book by Jerry Pallotta, illustrated by Edgar Stewart.

The Flower Alphabet Book by Jerry Pallotta, illustrated by Leslie Evans.

The Frog Alphabet Book by Jerry Pallotta, illustrated by Ralph Masiello.

The Icky Bug Alphabet Book by Jerry Pallotta, illustrated by Ralph Masiello.

The Underwater Alphabet Book by Jerry Pallotta, illustrated by Ralph Masiello.

The Sun, the Wind and the Rain Alphabet Book by Jerry Pallotta, illustrated by Ted Rand.

Water's Way by Lisa Westberg Peters, illustrated by Ted Rand.

Baby Beluga by Raffi, illustrated by Ashley Wolgg.

Hurricane by David Wiesner.

SUMMARY

We began this chapter with a comprehensive look at how children's books can be used across the curriculum. Strategies for interacting with expository text were examined through many classroom vignettes. Art and music were highlighted as threads that cut across the curriculum. Mathematics was considered in a holistic manner as we looked at ways for children to connect their worlds with the world of mathematics. Social studies was examined from a cultural perspective. We concluded with a look at Gary Bowman's California classroom and its emphasis on hands-on science.

PATHWAYS TO LITERACY ACROSS THE CURRICULUM

The student:

▶ can use a variety of resources in the classroom and find answers to questions.

▶ is aware of numerous resources outside the classroom and can use them.

▶ uses tables of contents and indexes of books as guides to finding information.

▶ searches through reference books to find out if the books contain material relevant to the problem.

▶ uses dictionaries.

CLASSROOM VIGNETTER

   Deanne Barker believes that writing anchors her second graders' understanding of information. During a study of dinosaurs, she shared Margaret Wise Brown's *The Important Book* and provided materials for her students to research and determine what they considered the most important items about the various dinosaurs. Here are some of the responses from the children as they used the format from *The Important Book* to portray their knowledge.

Continued

▶ develops skill in using alphabetical arrangements.

▶ skims to locate specific information that needs detailed study and analysis.

▶ summarizes information and ideas.

▶ keeps records of sources used to collect information.

▶ uses a variety of art materials to express ideas.

Note that while some of the pages give factual information such as weight or number of teeth, others demonstrate children's personal understanding of the information such as "The most important thing about a brontosaurus is he could give another dinosaur a ride," or "The most important thing about a stegosaurus is that you couldn't hug his tail!" The child is using personal language to demonstrate the understanding that the brontosaurus was the largest dinosaur and that the stegosaurus had spikes on his tail.

▶ enjoys artistic products of others.

▶ appreciates and uses the art of other cultures.

▶ reports on visits to galleries, art shows, and art museums.

▶ can tell stories about some of his or her own paintings.

▶ uses descriptive categories of words in talking and writing about art—color, shape, size, texture, feelings, contrast, comparison.

- ▶ uses names of things in talking about art.
- ▶ uses art to illustrate his or her own books.
- ▶ uses art to display poems in the classroom.
- ▶ uses abstract art for self-expression.
- ▶ creates imaginary characters and creatures.
- ▶ responds in meaningful ways to numerals and numbers in the environment.
- ▶ grows to understand the language and concepts of mathematics.
- ▶ responds to graphic aids in the environment in ways that help solve problems.
- ▶ responds to music listening by writing thoughts, interpretations, and feelings.
- ▶ increases vocabulary of verbs as a response to rhythms.
- ▶ composes simple rhythms to accompany poetry.
- ▶ responds rhythmically to words of movement.
- ▶ pantomimes meanings of common words.
- ▶ substitutes words to fit basic rhythms of chants and games.
- ▶ selects movements for hands, head, feet, and body while listening.
- ▶ knows and responds rhythmically to games and chants that repeat language patterns.
- ▶ reads the biographies of great people.
- ▶ looks at the world through the eyes of other people.
- ▶ takes a more personal look at history by reading historical fiction.

17 PATHWAYS TO INCLUSION OF ALL LEARNERS

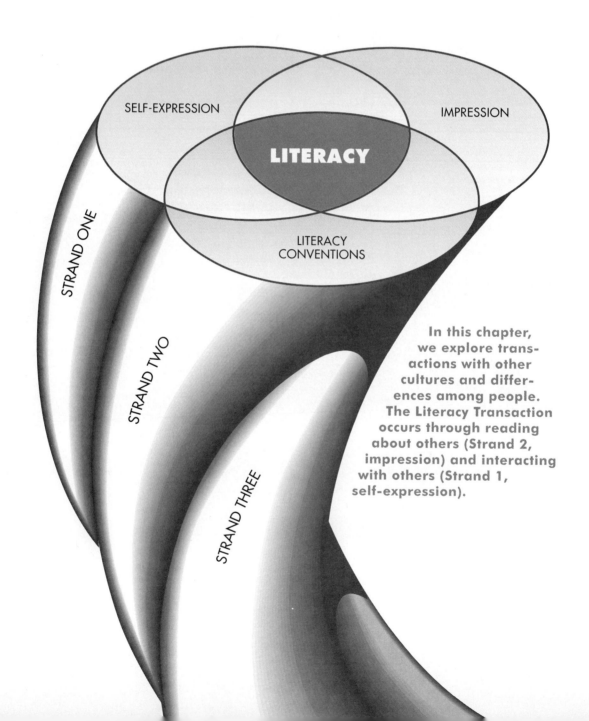

SELF-EXPRESSION

IMPRESSION

LITERACY

STRAND ONE

STRAND TWO

STRAND THREE

LITERACY
CONVENTIONS

In this chapter, we explore transactions with other cultures and differences among people. The Literacy Transaction occurs through reading about others (Strand 2, impression) and interacting with others (Strand 1, self-expression).

CHAPTER OUTLINE

PATHWAYS TO PONDER

▶ WHAT WAS WRONG WITH THE MELTING POT THEORY OF AMERICA?

▶ WHY IS IT IMPORTANT FOR TEACHERS TO ACCEPT AND HONOR THE CULTURE OF THEIR CHILDREN?

▶ WHAT TYPES OF LITERACY TRANSACTIONS HOLD THE GREATEST VALUE FOR BILINGUAL STUDENTS?

▶ WHAT IS THE VALUE OF ETHNIC LITERATURE IN THE CLASSROOM?

▶ WHAT DOES "INCLUSION" MEAN TO SCHOOL PROGRAMS?

▶ HOW ARE MAINTENANCE PROGRAMS CONGRUENT WITH THE MEANING-CENTERED PHILOSOPHY?

* Sheryl Santos of Arizona State University and Isela Montez of the Greenville, Texas, school district contributed to this chapter.

CULTURALLY AND LINGUISTICALLY DIVERSE LEARNERS

Our nation was once thought of as a melting pot, a place where the masses of the world could come together and blend into a new people. Immigrants were to put away their pasts and "melt" together as they became "Americans." But the romanticism of the melting pot theory died hard in reality. People cannot divorce the past, for the past contains their essence as human beings. Culture cannot be left behind or dismissed—when culture is denied, the person is denied. Even with the best efforts of many, however, "Americans" never became one nation with one culture. Instead, we are one nation with many people, one nation with many cultures, one nation with many strengths. Instead of a melting pot, modern-day America is a beautiful tapestry. And that's good news for children like Hunda, the Korean American child in the story excerpted here.

> I speak American words always when I speak to my father. If he hear me speak in words of my heart, he tell me, "In English! In English!" He does not know American words hurt in my mouth like sharp sticks.
>
> At school when I try first to speak America, everyone laugh ha ha hee hee, and my face hurt with shame and tears in my eyes. I do not speak at school now. I am silent like a busy ant.
>
> "You are now America!" my father tell me. He is lifting baskets of corn and radishes that my uncles take for carry down the outside steps into the room under Yo Grocer. "I learn with all my might to speak English," he tell me,
>
> "I want to better build Yo Grocer. America words belong you to America."
>
> "My uncles not speak America, Father," I say with politeness.
>
> "They are too old to learn America," my father say without politeness. "You, Hunda, are young! You learn to speak America with all your might and Yo Grocer will be with a big sign of bright lights with bigger better room and many more customers coming to buy each day what is fresh for eating."
>
> "Yes, Father," I say. I make a swallow to take the hurt out of my mouth and out of my ears.
>
> Bill Martin Jr

Meaning-centered curricula value the differences that children bring to the classroom. Many children have failed in school because of the old melting pot theory. Their language and culture were rejected as new language and new ways were imposed on them. They were considered deficient, and many failed because their self-esteem was destroyed and because the techniques used to teach a second language of "standard English" were so different from the way they had learned their first language.

Another group of people who have been excluded from the mainstream of American education are the physically and emotionally handicapped. Fortunately, all children are now being invited into our classrooms. With this move, American classrooms are now beginning to look like the American population, with all races and types of people included.

LANGUAGES AND CULTURES IN THE UNITED STATES

Presently, the largest numbers of linguistically different learners represent various Spanish-speaking national origins. Others are Asian or dialect-speaking Americans.

Language differences are not unique to first-generation Americans. Physical and cultural isolation from middle-class America have perpetuated ethnic dialects and fostered different learning styles, cultural values, behavioral traits, and other differences. Without meaningful opportunities for frequent interracial, intercultural socialization, the process of *acculturation*—internalizing cultural aspects from other groups—is lost.

Americans now number 248,709,873, according to the 1990 census. The largest minority group is the African Americans (29,986,060), who constitute 12.1% of the population. The fastest growing minority group in America is Hispanic. Nine percent of the total population, some 22,354,059 Hispanics, reported themselves. However, with the large number of undocumented persons, the actual count is assumed to be much higher. Native Americans accounted for 0.8% (1,878,285) of the population; the Asian population has grown to 7,273,662 people (2.9%).

Who are the Hispanics? *Hispanic* is an umbrella concept encompassing persons of U.S.-born, immigrant, or refugee status from any Spanish-speaking ancestry, nation, or territory, regardless of race. Although the major unifying thread is their Spanish-speaking ancestry, we must also realize the majority of Hispanics in this country also have Indian and/or African origins. Therefore, persons of Indian and Spanish backgrounds are termed *mestizo;* those of African and Spanish heritage, *mulatto;* and persons of African and Indian ancestries are *zambo.*

Teachers, therefore, should not assume Hispanics are a homogeneous ethnic group. Many cultural, linguistic, political, and economic differences exist among Hispanics. Many Spanish-surnamed students do not even speak Spanish and are actually more assimilated into the American culture than that of their national origin. Sensitivity on the part of the teacher is required to make appropriate curricular decisions.

Like Hispanics, Indochinese students are also culturally and linguistically heterogeneous. The term *Indochina* was coined by the French colonists in their attempts to rule the nations of Laos, Cambodia, and Vietnam. Presently, wars and political turmoil have led many Indochinese to seek refuge in the.United States. Many of the refugees from Indochina are ethnic minorities who were persecuted when the communists took over the region. These groups include many Chinese ethnics, Hmongs, and other nationals of the three countries.

As teachers, we should be careful to be aware of the child's nationality as well as other pertinent information concerning educational background, culture, and family life. It is very common to find refugee students who have never experienced formal schooling in their native land. Providing appropriate educational services for students with no native language literacy skills is no ordinary challenge.

Furthermore, students who come to America escaping the horrors of war, intolerance, deprivation, and the deaths of their loved ones oftentimes have

Jonathan Sampson _____ Name

_12_ _____ Age

Sports, Reading, Viedo games Interests

What do you like most about school?

I LIKE LEARNING AND BEING ABLE TO BE WITH MY FRIENDS. I ALSO LIKE THE CLASSES WITH INTERESTING TEACHERS.

What's your favorite subject? Why?

I LIKE READING AND SCIENCE BECAUSE I HAVE GOOD TEACHERS AND THEY HELP YOU LEARN.

What's your favorite book? Why do you like it?

MY FAVORITE BOOK WOULD HAVE TO BE A SERIES OF BOOKS. THE HARDY BOYS IS WELL WRITEN AND I ENJOY THE MYSTRY.

What advice do you have for teachers?

TEACHERS NEED TO BE MORE EXCITING AND TRY TO APPEAL TO THE STUDENTS MORE OFTEN.

emotional and psychological wounds in addition to their cognitive needs. On the other hand, some are Indochinese students enrolled in public schools who have had exceptional educational backgrounds in their country of origin and have persevered to reach new heights of academic success.

DIALECTS AND LITERACY LEARNING

Remember the melting pot theory that we opened the chapter with? Remember our stance that we should view children as a tapestry rather than a

melting pot? Nowhere is this need more paramount than when we consider the dialects and language patterns of the children in our classrooms.

First, let's define dialect. Dialects are the variety of linguistic speech patterns found in a language population. Dialects vary in terms of pronunciation, grammar, and vocabulary. Dialects may involve both regional varieties, such as the dialect spoken in Maine, and social variety, such as African American vernacular English (Gollnick & Chinn, 1990).

African American vernacular English is spoken primarily by African Americans in lower socioeconomic neighborhoods. Again, teachers should not assume this dialect is common to all lower socioeconomic African Americans, or that it is somehow substandard or defective. It should be thought of as different—not deficient.

African American vernacular is characterized by a consistent phonological system and grammatical structure different from standard English. Unfortunately, it does not enjoy the prestige of standard English. Once again, what we term *standard* simply means the variety of language in the United States heard on TV, including national newscasts, used in educational settings and business and national publications; it is generally used by educated speakers and writers, regardless of race.

Everyone speaks some sort of dialect. We really can't say that regional speech from one section of the country is more standard or acceptable than from another region. Certainly you can "hear" the difference from region to region—you may be able to identify a speaker from the Far West, New England, the Midwest, or the South. But who's to say which region's speech is superior? The truth lies in the purposes for language—to communicate. Thus language that communicates is effective language.

**THE POET ▶
PONDERS**

OUR COUNTRY'S QUILT

*We had very little to keep us warm
Against the coming winter storm,
Just a pile of old discarded rags
Tattered torn and stuffed in bags,*

*There was gabardine,
Some faded silk,
Beaded buckskin and a cotton
   shawl,
Calico and old wool pants,
And a lace mantilla from a formal
   ball.
There was lots more cloth from
   which to choose
But each piece was too small to use.*

*So we gathered what we had,
While remaining very calm,
And we cut each patch in a special
   shape
To reveal its special charm,
Then we snipped and sewed and
   stitched,
And we all danced arm in arm,
To celebrate this country-quilt . . .
Our colorful and varied quilt . . .
This one-of-a-kind American quilt
We've made to keep us warm.*

Copyright Brod Bagert 1993
All Rights Reserved

This does not mean we as teachers are content for children's language to remain stationary. However, in a meaning-centered program, our goal is *not* to eradicate children's home-rooted language. Rather, our goal is to add to the language they bring to the classroom. Our goal is for children to have choice and flexibility in the ways they express themselves through language.

Understanding, speaking, reading, and writing standard English enhance children's likelihood for success. Dependent on one's ability to manipulate standard English are tasks such as scoring well on standardized tests, making a good impression on a job interview, speaking publicly to a multicultural audience, filling out government documents, traveling to other countries, and so on.

LEGAL REQUIREMENTS FOR EQUAL EDUCATIONAL OPPORTUNITIES

Local education agencies are legally bound to provide equal educational opportunities for every student. With respect to linguistically different students, the Supreme Court's decision in *Lau* v. *Nichols* (1974)—six years after the passage of the Bilingual Education Act—set a precedent ensuring that the educational rights of language minorities were met. Interestingly, this litigation was brought to the courts on behalf of 1,800 Chinese-speaking students in San Francisco, a reminder that American schools enroll students representing almost all worldwide language communities, ethnicities, national origins, and social classes.

Although many of these students are foreign born, countless numbers of U.S.-born citizens have divergent dialects and cultural values. The American problem of racial, ethnic, and class separatism continues to hamper our idealistic view of education as a great equalizer. Implanted in the minds and hearts of American educators is the belief that one can reach one's chosen life goals if given the opportunity of a good education. In part, the fulfillment of this ideal will depend on the quality of instruction and services offered in public schools across the nation.

Perhaps the most crucial of all subjects for the academic and personal success of the culturally and linguistically diverse learner is the language arts. Without the ability to control the standard English so valued by the educational, business, and political establishments, many students will continue to fail. They will drop out of school at alarming rates and be relegated to the lowest socioeconomic levels of society. The inability to bridge language and cultural gaps causes our nation a great loss in human potential, human resources, and undiscovered talent and genius.

INCLUSION OF ALL LEARNERS

As we near the 21st century, we find American schools that are more diverse than at any time in our history. Our children are more diverse in ethnic makeup, more diverse in levels of achievement, and more diverse in physical abilities. Just as the civil rights movement of the 1960s led to integrated schools that reflected the ethnic makeup of the United States, the Individuals with Disabilities Education Act (IDEA) is leading to classrooms that reflect the inclusion of all learners—the blind, the deaf, and other handicapped individuals.

This means that children are no longer separated because of their differences. It also means our children will see a school environment that is like the environment out of school—all types of people will be there. Consider the story of Duane, a child with muscular dystrophy, as seen through the eyes of his classmate Rena (Figure 17.1).

What is inclusion and what does it mean to the classroom? First, inclusion means different things to different people. Hollis and Galegos (1993) state,

> It may refer to (1) eliminating all categorical special education programs and personnel, (2) returning all students to their home campuses, (3) integrating all students with disabilities in the regular education program to the maximum extent possible, or (4) eliminating all special education classrooms and educating all students with disabilities in the same classrooms as their age-appropriate, nondisabled peers. (p. 1)

While the battle rages concerning which of these alternatives will be selected, classroom teachers will undoubtedly be working with increased numbers of disabled students. Instruction for disabled children must be meaning centered and relevant. Disabled children can accomplish great things when they have teachers and classmates who believe in them.

BILINGUAL EDUCATION PROGRAMS AND LITERACY LEARNING

The realization of the importance of acquiring English has been a two-edged sword for language minorities. There has been a proliferation of bilingual

FIGURE 17.1 ▶

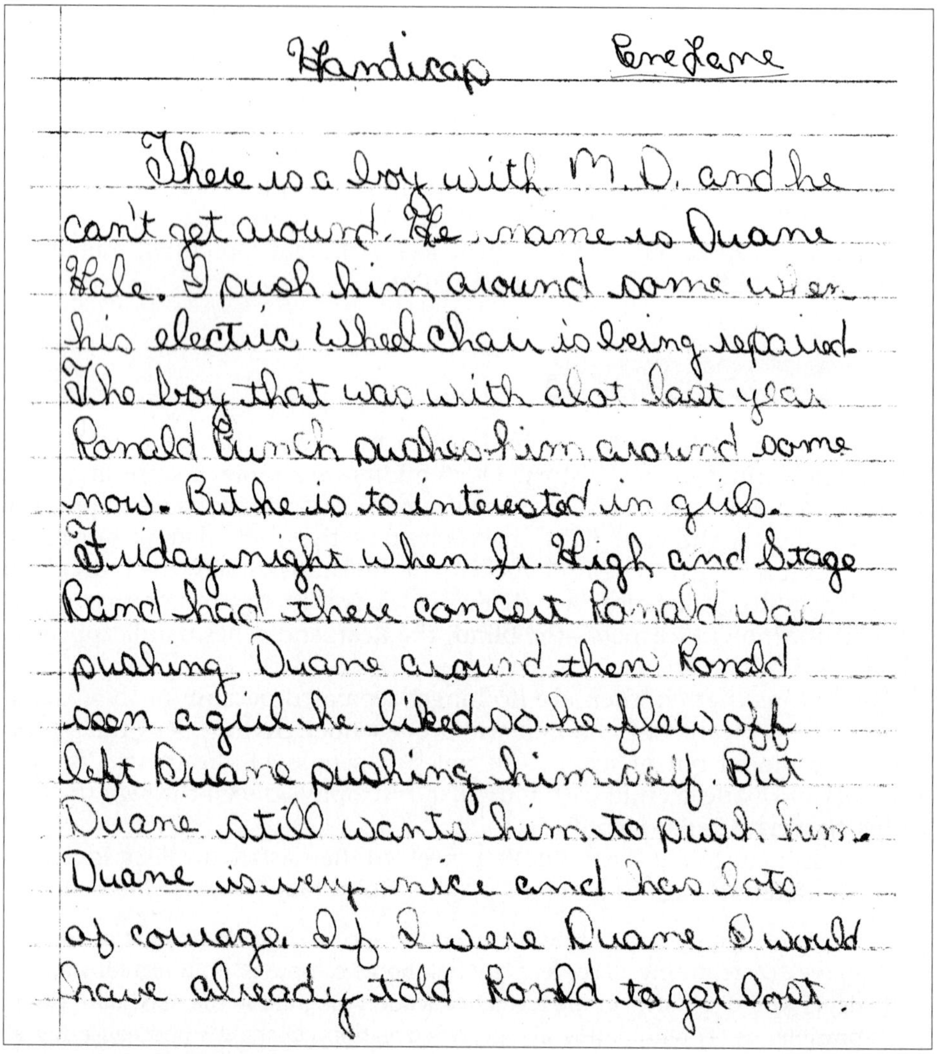

Handicap   Lorelame

There is a boy with M.D. and he can't get around. He name is Duane Hale. I push him around some when his electric wheel chair is being repaired. The boy that was with alot last year Ronald Bunch pushes him around some now. But he is to interested in girls. Friday night when Jr. High and Stage Band had there concert Ronald was pushing Duane around then Ronald saw a girl he liked so he flew off left Duane pushing himself. But Duane still wants him to push him. Duane is very nice and has lots of courage. If I were Duane I would have already told Ronald to get lost.

education and English-as-a-Second-Language (ESL) programs as federal and state agencies provide funding sources and technical assistance. The rush to move students as quickly as possible from bilingual education into all-English programs, however, has sometimes undermined the quality of the educational experience.

Unfortunately, the acquisition of English has supplanted not only the learning of other content areas but also the acquisition of literacy itself. Research clearly suggests that students who possess literacy skills in their native language are more successful in academic endeavors and are even more capable of achieving success in English than those who do not have native-language literacy. Despite this, the national trend is for less native-language instruction, not more.

The debate has centered on two opposing philosophies or types of programs. *Transitional programs* have as their goal that bilingual students should be quickly moved to the point where they can receive instruction in English from the standard school curriculum. *Maintenance programs,* however, value the child's first language as experiences are being gained in a second language. Goals of maintenance programs are for the first language to be maintained and for students to receive instruction in a language they comprehend, not a foreign tongue. The teacher's goal should be to produce students who are fluent in two languages. However, in working toward that goal, teachers should take steps to ensure that students are not pushed exclusively into a second language until they are fluent in their first tongue.

To this effect, Cummins (1981) has warned educators not to confuse a person's ability to communicate orally in "everyday language" with competence in the academic or "formal" language needed for school success. He terms these two types of language skills basic interpersonal communication skills (BICS) and cognitive academic language proficiency (CALP). Teachers should take heed not to assume that because limited-English-proficient (LEP) students seem to do fine in face-to-face social situations, they possess the needed skills to achieve content mastery through higher level cognitive tasks.

Current funding patterns show an increase in programs and services that do not emphasize either native-language development or literacy. As quality bilingual education programs decline, and as more language minorities enter the mainstream without adequate native language fluency and literacy, language-arts teachers will be further challenged to implement creative and appropriate strategies for their linguistically diverse students.

Fortunately, students do quite well in literacy learning with programs that feature the kinds of practices discussed throughout this book. More money is not the answer to language minority needs—better programs are. Meaning-centered curricula are based on the latest research, which indicates that children are capable of learning in both languages at the same time so long as experiences are meaningful and relevant. When teachers provide students opportunities to express themselves in creative ways, both languages grow and confidence increases.

The stakes are tremendous. Literacy, achieved in any language, is more than just an advantage for students: Reading and writing are requisite skills and the media of communication for academic subjects. For example, how many children fail social studies because they cannot read the textbook? Failing a math examination because of word problems is also a common result of inadequate literacy skills.

What can the teacher do to promote literacy in the classroom? Following are some helpful practices:

▶ Provide native-language versions of texts when available as an aid to transferring literacy skills and guiding comprehension in conceptually difficult subject areas.

▶ Collaborate with LEP students and devote individual time and attention to them to be certain they understand what is expected as well as the purpose or goal of each particular reading assignment.

▶ Develop specific lessons designed to help students strengthen reading strategies, such as scanning, skimming, searching for facts, inferring information, and drawing conclusions.

▶ Devote time to the development of trust and rapport with LEP students and their families. This entails permitting students the luxury of being wrong and allowing them time to ask questions and think aloud.

▶ Provide a resource library of bilingual trade books, picture books, taped stories, and native-language literature. This will help develop a positive attitude toward reading in general as well as an acceptance of the home language as a "language of literacy."

▶ Call on parents for assistance and input. LEP parents can help build a resource library. They can also serve as surrogate teachers at home by reading to and with their children. The more students read in their native language, the better they will eventually read in English (Brown & Santos, 1986).

HELPING CHILDREN ACQUIRE ENGLISH

Thanks to breakthroughs in second-language acquisition theory, practitioners are now realizing the importance and relevance of the relation between research and practice. Classroom teachers, responsible for the progress of all students, and prepared with some basic principles and tenets of second-language acquisition theory, will be more confident and successful serving students for whom English is not the home language. We begin by briefly addressing what Stephen Krashen (1982) terms the *learning/acquisition distinction* to see how this concept affects the climate and activity within the classroom setting.

Traditionally, the focal point of foreign-language instruction has been on the grammar or formal structure of a given language. This information, passed on to students by a series of rules, drills, repetitions, and patterned dialogues, is often taught through the medium of the native language instead of the target language itself.

This method could be likened to teaching a child to ride a bicycle by having him or her memorize a set of how-to rules without ever getting up on the bike. Using the grammar method, language competence is measured by written examinations in which students merely demonstrate their knowledge of the rules, isolated vocabulary meanings, and other specifics—a process commonly called "language learning." In most cases, such methods are counterproductive and deadening. (Many current programs offer more realistic and exciting ways to learn a foreign language.)

On the other hand, current research has supported the notion that second languages are really not learned at all: They are acquired in much the same way that children acquire their native tongue, in a subconscious process that, given the right environment and condition, should flourish somewhat effortlessly and naturally. Therefore, as we strive to promote acquisition, we should become increasingly aware of the criteria or set of conditions that facilitate

◀ **A Native American honors his heritage by sharing his tribe's history with a fourth grader.**

optimum language acquisition. The major responsibility of teachers is to ensure that their classroom methods, strategies, and behaviors are consistent with what we have come to realize are basic cornerstones of second-language acquisition.

As teachers strive to develop and implement curricular strategies and materials, we should ask ourselves several questions about classroom activities (Krashen, 1982, p. 125):

1. Will the students be getting adequate, understandable exposure to the target language?
2. Are the students relaxed and anxiety free?
3. Is the curriculum relevant and meaningful to the students?
4. Has the curriculum broken free of overreliance on a grammar-based scope and sequence?

Teaching behaviors that create an environment rich in the target language at a level slightly at or beyond the actual abilities of the students have proven to be the best way to approximate native-language acquisition conditions. The creative language-arts teacher should be able to simulate an environment rich in the target language by using household items, clothing, pictures of people engaging in everyday activities, and other visual representations of daily life. Store catalogs, magazines, and other low-cost sources make consumable curricular materials students can relate to. An excellent detailed analysis of this environment may be found in Krashen and Terrell's (1983) book *The Natural Approach*.

Another strategy that permits a relaxed environment as well as comfortable exposure to the target language is the use of culturally relevant songs. As music is introduced into the curriculum, students begin to feel an air of excitement, expectancy, and unity.

Music offers other advantages: Language skills that go beyond the aural/oral abilities include the development of reading and writing. For students with little or no interpersonal contact with native speakers, music provides them with an authentic cultural experience they can internalize and that will serve to make them feel a part of the new culture and its people. In addition, in a classroom with students who are linguistically mixed, the use of culturally based music promotes the non-English languages introduced through bilingual versions of selected songs, enhances the self-concept of LEP students, and provides a vehicle for cross-cultural relationships.

UNDERSTANDING CULTURES THROUGH BOOKS

We live in a golden age of children's books. As children of the 1960s and 1970s became the parents of the 1990s, they brought to parenting a strong sense of the importance of reading. And with their interest in reading came higher incomes with greater buying power. This created an extraordinary marketplace for children's book sales, and publishers jumped into this market niche with more that 5,000 new children's book titles per year. And the quality of these books has been at an all-time high. World class artists love to paint for children, and their works have made the modern children's books mini art galleries. Eric Carle, Trina Schart Hyman, Ted Rand, Steven Kellogg, Tomie dePaolo, and Donald Crews are just a few of the great artists we refer to. But an even greater development has been the advent of writers who write featuring the cultural groups of the United States and the world. This inclusion of all races and cultures provides a sense of belonging to minority children, and benefits all readers because these books give us all a greater knowledge of the cultures of the world. Ten years ago, not many examples of good multicultural literature existed. Today, multitudes of books in many genres exist (Darigan, 1994). Here's Dan Darigan's list of great multicultural books by genre:

AFRICAN AMERICAN

Ader, D.A. (1993). *A picture book of Rosa Parks*. New York: Holiday.

Aardema, V. (1975). *Why mosquitos buzz in people's ears*. New York: Dial.

Aardema, V. (1981). *Bringing the rain to Kapiti Plain*. New York: Dial.

Aardema, V. (1983). *The Vingananee and the Tree Toad: A Liberian tale*. New York: Puffin.

Aardema, V. (1984). *Oh, Kojo! how could you!* New York: Dial.

Aardema, V. (1991). *Traveling to Tondo: A tale of the Nkundo of Zaire*. New York: Knopf.

Adoff, A. (1968). *I am the darker brother: An anthology of modern poems by Black Americans.* New York: Collier.

Adoff, A. (1970). *Malcolm X.* New York: HarperCollins.

Adoff, A. (1973). *Black is brown is tan.* New York: Harper.

Aliki. (1965). *A weed is a flower: The life of George Washington Carver.* New York: Simon & Schuster.

Anderson, J. (1986). *Juma and the magic jinn.* New York: Lothrop.

Angelou, M. (1993). *Life doesn't frighten me.* New York: Stewart, Tabori & Chang.

Archer, J. (1993). *They had a dream: The civil rights struggle from Frederick Douglass to Marcus Garvey to Martin Luther King and Malcolm X.* New York: Viking.

Bang, M. (1976). *Wiley and the Hairy Man.* New York: Macmillan.

Belton, S. (1993). *From Miss Ida's porch.* New York: Four Winds.

Bowden, J.C. (1979). *Why the tides ebb and flow.* Boston: Houghton Mifflin.

Boyd, C.D. (1948). *Circle of gold.* New York: Scholastic.

Boyd, C.D. (1986). *Forever friends.* New York: Macmillan.

Boyd, C.D. (1987). *Charlie Pippin.* New York: Macmillan.

Brenner, B. (1978). *Wagon wheels.* New York: Harper.

Bryan, A. (1991). *All night, all day: A child's first book of African-American spirituals.* New York: Atheneum.

Bryan, A. (1992). *Sing to the sun.* New York: HarperCollins.

Cameron, A. (1968). *More stories Julian tells.* New York: Knopf.

Cameron, A. (1981). *The stories Julian tells.* New York: Pantheon.

Clifton, L. (1978). *The boy who didn't believe in spring.* New York: Dutton.

Clifton, L. (1979). *The lucky stone.* New York: Dell.

Crews, D. (1991). *Bigmama's.* New York: Greenwillow.

Cox, C. (1993). *The forgotten heroes: The story of the buffalo soldiers.* New York: Scholastic.

Denenberg, B. (1991). *Nelson Mandela: No easy walk to freedom.* New York: Scholastic.

Dragonwagon, C. (1990). *Home place.* New York: Macmillan.

Ellis, V.F. (1990). *Afro-Bets first book about Africa.* Orange, NJ: Just Us Books.

Feelings, M. (1974). *Jambo means hello: Swahili alphabet book.* New York: Dial.

Feelings, T. (1981). *Daydreamers.* New York: Dial.

Feelings, T. (1993). *Soul looks back in wonder.* New York: Dial.

Ferris, J. (1989). *Arctic explorer: The story of Matthew Henson.* Minneapolis: Carolrhoda.

Flournoy, V. (1985). *Patchwork quilt.* New York: Dial.

French, F. (1991). *Anancy and Mr. Dry-Bone.* Boston: Little, Brown.

Greenfield, E. (1974). *Sister.* New York: Harper.

Greenfield, E. (1978). *Honey, I love and other love poems.* New York: Harper.

Greenfield, E. (1981). *Daydreamers.* New York: Dial.

Greenfield, E. (1993). *William and the good old days.* New York: Harper-Collins.

Grifalconi, A. (1986). *The village of round and square houses.* Boston: Little, Brown.

Hale, S.J. (1990). *Mary had a little lamb.* New York: Scholastic.

Haley, G.E. (1970). *A story a story: An African tale.* New York: Macmillan.

Hamilton, V. (1967). *Zeely.* New York: Macmillan.

Hamilton, V. (1968). *The House of Dies Drear.* New York: Macmillan.

Hamilton, V. (1971). *The Planet of Junior Brown.* New York: Macmillan.

Hamilton, V. (1985). *The people could fly: American Black folktales.* New York: Knopf.

Hamilton, V. (1988). *In the beginning.* San Diego: Harcourt.

Hamilton, V. (1990). *Cousins.* New York: Philomel.

Hamilton, V. (1993). *Plain city.* New York: Scholastic.

Hansen, J. (1980). *The gift-giver.* New York: Clarion.

Hansen, J. (1986). *Yellow Bird and me.* New York: Clarion.

Hansen, J. (1994). *The captive.* New York: Scholastic.

Haskins, J. (1989). *Count your way through Africa.* Minneapolis: Carolrhoda.

Hartman, W. (1993). *All the magic in the world.* New York: Dutton.

Havill, J. (1985). *Jamaica's find.* Boston: Houghton Mifflin.

Hill, E.S. (1991). *Evan's corner.* New York: Viking.

Hooks, W.H. (1990). *The ballad of Belle Dorcas.* New York: Knopf.

Hoffman, M. (1991). *Amazing Grace.* New York: Dial.

Hopkinson, D. (1992). *Sweet Clara and the freedom quilt.* New York: Knopf.

Howard, E.F. (1991). *Aunt Flossie's hats (and crab cakes later).* New York: Clarion.

Hoyt-Goldsmith, D. (1993). *Celebrating Kwanzaa.* New York: Holiday.

Hudson, W. (1993). *Pass it on: African-American poetry for children.* New York: Scholastic.

Hughes, L. (1993). *The dream keeper and other poems.* New York: Knopf.

Isadora, R. (1979). *Ben's trumpet.* New York: Greenwillow.

Johnson, A. (1990). *When I am old with you.* New York: Watts/Orchard.

Johnson, A. (1993). *Toning the sweep.* New York: Orchard.

Jones, R. (1991). *Matthew and Tilly.* New York: Dutton.

Keats, E.J. (1962). *The snowy day.* New York: Viking.

Keats, E.J. (1964). *Whistle for Willie.* New York: Viking.

Kimmel, E.A. (1988). *Anansi and the moss-covered rock.* New York: Holiday House.

Lawrence, J. (1993). *The great migration: An American story.* New York: HarperCollins.

Lester, J. (1985). *The Knee-High man and other tales.* New York: Dial.

Lewin, H. (1983). *Jafta.* Minneapolis: Carolrhoda.

Lewin, H. (1983). *Jafta and the wedding.* Minneapolis: Carolrhoda.

Lewin, H. (1983). *Jafta's father.* Minneapolis: Carolrhoda.

Lewin, H. (1983). *Jafta's mother.* Minneapolis: Carolrhoda.

Lyons, M. E. (1990). *Sorrow's kitchen: The life and folklore of Zora Neale Hurston.* New York: Scribners.

Lyons, M.E. (1993). *Starting home: The story of Horace Pippin, painter.* New York: Scribners.

Marzollo, J. (1993). *Happy Birthday, Martin Luther King.* New York: Scholastic.

Mathis, S.B. (1971). *Sidewalk story.* New York: Viking.

Mathis, S.B. (1975). *The hundred penny box.* New York: Viking.

McCurdy, M. (1993). *Escape from slavery: The boyhood of Frederick Douglass in his own words.* New York: Knopf.

McDermott, G. (1972). *Anansi the spider.* New York: Henry Holt.

McKissack, P.C. (1988). *Mirandy and brother wind.* New York: Random House.

McKissack, P.C. (1989). *Nettie Jo's friends.* New York: Knopf.

McKissack, P.C. (1992). *The Dark Thirty: Southern tales of the supernatural.* New York: Knopf.

McKissack, P.C., & McKissack, F. (1992). *Sojourner Truth: Ain't I a woman?* New York: Scholastic.

Mendez, P. (1989). *The black snowman.* New York: Scholastic.

Mitchell, M.K. (1993). *Uncle Jed's barbershop.* New York: Simon.

Mitchell, R.P. (1993). *Hue Boy.* New York: Dial.

Moss, M. (1990). *Regina's big mistake.* Boston: Houghton Mifflin.

Moss, T. (1993). *I want to be.* New York: Dial.

Musgrove, M. (1976). *Ashanti to Zulu: African traditions.* New York: Dial.

Myers, W.D. (1988) *Scorpions.* New York: Harper.

Myers, W.D. (1992). *The righteous revenge of Artemis Bonner.* New York: HarperCollins.

Myers, W.D. (1993). *Malcolm X: By any means necessary.* New York: Scholastic.

Myers, W.D. (1993). *Brown angels: An album of pictures and verse.* New York: HarperCollins.

Parks, R., & Haskins, J. (1992). *Rosa Parks: My story.* New York: Dial.

Patrick, D.L. (1993). *The car washing street.* New York: Tamborine.

Paulsen, G. (1993). *Nightjohn.* New York: Delacorte.

Pinkney, A.D. (1993). *Alvin Ailey.* New York: Hyperion.

Pinkney, A.D. (1993). *Seven days for Kwanzaa.* New York: Dial.

Polacco, P. (1992). *Chicken Sunday.* New York: Philomel.

Price, L. (1990). *Aida.* New York: Harcourt.

Ringgold, F. (1991). *Tar Beach.* New York: Crown.

Ringgold, F. (1992). *Aunt Harriet's Underground Railroad in the sky.* New York: Crown.

Ringgold, F. (1993). *Dinner at Aunt Connie's house.* New York: Hyperion.

Rodriguez, A. (1993). *Aunt Martha and the golden coin.* New York: Clarkson Potter.

Rollins, C.H. (1993). *Christmas gif'.* New York: Morrow.

San Souci, R.D. (1989). *The talking eggs.* New York: Dial.

San Souci, R.D. (1992). *Sukey and the mermaid.* New York: Four Winds.

Schroeder, A. (1989). *Ragtime Tumpie.* Boston: Little, Brown.

Smalls-Hector, I. (1992). *Jonathan and his Mommy.* Boston: Little, Brown.

Steptoe, J. (1986). *Stevie.* New York: Harper.

Steptoe, J. (1987). *Mufaro's beautiful daughters.* New York: Lothrop.

Taylor, M. (1975). *Song of the trees.* New York: Dial.

Taylor, M. (1976). *Roll of thunder, hear my cry.* New York: Dial.

Taylor, M. (1981). *Let the circle be unbroken.* New York: Dial.

Taylor, M. (1987). *The friendship.* New York: Dial.

Taylor, M. (1987). *The gold Cadillac.* New York: Dial.

Taylor, M. (1990). *Mississippi bridge.* New York: Dial.

Taylor, M. (1990). *The road to Memphis.* New York: Dial.

Thomas, J.C. (1993). *Brown honey in broomwheat tea.* New York: HarperCollins.

Towle, W. (1993). *The real McCoy: The life of an African-American inventor.* New York: Scholastic.

Turner, A. (1987). *Nettie's trip South.* New York: Macmillan.

Udry, J.M. (1966). *What Mary Jo shared.* New York: Scholastic.

Walter, M.P. (1985). *Ty's one man band.* New York: Scholastic.

Walter, M.P. (1989). *Have a happy. . . .* New York: Lothrop.

Ward, L. (1978). *I am eyes, Ni Macho.* New York: Morrow.

Warner, L.S. (1993). *From slave to abolitionist: The life of William Wells Brown.* New York: Dial.

Williams, A.W. (1992). *Working Cotton.* New York: Harcourt.

Williams, V.B. (1982). *A chair for my mother.* New York: Greenwillow.

Williams, V.B. (1983). *Something special for me.* New York: Greenwillow.

Williams, V.B. (1986). *Cherries and cherry pits.* New York: Greenwillow.

Williams, V.B. (1990). *More, more, more, said the baby.* New York: Greenwillow.

Winter, J. (1988). *Follow the drinking gourd.* New York: Knopf.

◀ Children's books offer a window into many cultures.

NATIVE AMERICAN

Achimoona. (1985). Fifth House, 20 36th St. East, Saskatoon, Saskatchewan, Canada S7K 2S8.

Adler, D.A. (1993). *A picture book of Sitting Bull.* New York: Holiday.

Ahenakew, F. (1988). *How the birch tree got its stripes.* Saskatoon: Fifth House.

Ahenakew, F. (1988). *How the mouse got brown teeth.* Saskatoon: Fifth House.

Ancona, G. (1993). *Powwow.* San Diego: Harcourt Brace.

Baker, O. (1981). *Where the buffaloes begin.* New York: Viking.

Beatty, P. (1990). *Wait for me, watch for me, Eula Bee.* New York: Morrow.

Begay, S. (1992). *Ma'ii and Cousin Horned Toad.* New York: Scholastic.

Benton-Banai, E. (1979). *The Mishomis Book: The voice of the Ojibway.* Indian Country Communications, Rt. 2 Box 2900-A, Hayward, WI 54843.

Bierhorst, J. (1990). *The sacred path.* New York: Morrow.

Bierhorst, J. (1990). *Spirit child: A story of the nativity.* New York: Morrow.

Bierhorst, J. (1993). *The woman who fell from the sky.* New York: Morrow.

Brescia, B. (1981). *A'una.* Daybreak Star, P.O. Box 99100, Seattle, WA 98199.

Bruchac, J. (1993). *The first strawberries.* New York: Dial.

Caduto, M.J., & Bruchac, J. (1988). *Keepers of the Earth: Native American stories and environmental activities for children.* Golden, CO: Fulcrum.

Cameron, A. (1985). *How raven freed the moon.* Madeira Park, British Columbia: Harbour.

Cameron, A. (1987). *Raven returns the water.* Madeira Park, British Columbia: Harbour.

Clark, A.N. (1941). *In my mother's house.* New York: Viking.

Cohen, C.L. (1988). *The mud pony: A traditional Skidi Pawnee tale.* New York: Scholastic.

Cohlene, T. (1990). *Clamshell boy: A Makah legend.* Hahwah, NJ: Watermill Press.

Cohlene, T. (1990). *Dancing drum: A Cherokee legend.* Hahwah, NJ: Watermill Press.

Cohlene, T. (1990). *Little firefly: An Algonquian legend.* Hahwah, NJ: Watermill Press.

Cohlene, T. (1990). *Quillworker: A Cheyenne legend.* Hahwah, NJ: Watermill Press.

Cohlene, T. (1990). *Turquoise boy: A Navajo legend.* Hahwah, NJ: Watermill Press.

Culleton, B. (1984). *April raintree.* Pemmican Publications, 412 McGregor St., Winnipeg, Manitoba, Canada R2W 4X5.

Culleton, B. (1985). *Spirit of the white bison.* Manitoba: Pemmican.

Dameron, J. (1984). *Sequoyah and the talking leaves.* Cross Cultural Education Center, P.O. Box 66, Park Hill, OK 74451.

dePaola, T. (1983). *The legend of the Bluebonnet: An old tale of Texas.* New York: Putnam.

dePaola, T. (1988). *The legend of the Indian paintbrush.* New York: Putnam.

Esbensen, B.J. (1989). *Ladder to the sky.* Boston: Little, Brown.

Goble, P. (1978). *The girl who loved wild horses.* New York: Macmillan.

Goble, P. (1980). *The gift of the sacred dog.* New York: Macmillan.

Goble, P. (1988). *Her seven brothers.* New York: Bradbury.

Goble, P. (1989). *Beyond the ridge.* New York: Bradbury.

Goble, P. (1993). *The lost children.* New York: Bradbury.

Gregory, K. (1990). *The legend of Jimmy Spoon.* New York: Harcourt.

Highwater, J. (1981). *Moonsong lullaby.* New York: Morrow.

Hill, K. (1990). *Toughboy and Sister.* New York: McElderry Books.

Hoyt-Goldsmith, D. (1991). *Pueblo storyteller.* New York: Holiday.

Hoyt-Goldsmith, D. (1993). *Cherokee summer.* New York: Holiday.

Hudson, J. (1984). *Sweetgrass.* New York: Philomel.

Jacobs, S.K. (1993). *The boy who loved morning.* Boston: Little, Brown.

James, B. (1990). *The dream stair.* New York: HarperCollins.

Jeffers, S. (1991). *Brother Eagle, Sister Sky.* New York: Dial.

King, J.C. (1987). *Arctic hunters: Indians and Inuit of northern Canada.* Vancouver: Douglas & McIntyre.

Keeshig-Tobias, L. (1991). *Bird Talk.* Sister Vision Press, P.O. Box 217, Station E, Toronto, Ontario, Canada K0L 2H0.

Kleitsch, C. (1985). *Dancing Feathers.* Annick Press, 15 Patricia St., Willowdale, Ontario, Canada M2M 1H9.

Loewen, I. (1986). *My mom is so unusual.* Winnipeg: Pemmican.

Martin, B., & Archambault, J. (1987). *Knots on a counting rope.* New York: Holt.

Martin, R. (1992). *The rough-faced girl.* New York: Putnam.

Martin, R. (1993). *The boy who lived with the seals.* New York: Putnam.

McDermott, G. (1993). *Raven: A trickster tale from the Pacific Northwest.* San Diego: Harcourt Brace.

McLain, G. (1990). *The Indian way: Learning to communicate with Mother Earth.* John Muir, P.O. Box 613, Santa Fe, NM 87504.

Miles, M. (1971). *Annie and the Old One.* Boston: Little, Brown.

Munsch, R., & Kusugak, M. (1988). *A promise is a promise.* Toronto: Annick Press.

New Mexico People and Energy Collective. (1981). New Seed Press, P.O. Box 3016, Stanford, CA 94305.

Nowman, H. (1987). *Who-Paddled-Backward-With-Trout.* Boston: Little, Brown.

Oritz, S. (1988). *The People shall continue.* San Francisco: Children's Book Press.

Petersen, P. (1993). *Inunguak: The little Greenlander.* New York: Lothrop.

Reynolds, J. (1993). *Frozen land: Vanishing cultures.* San Diego: Harcourt Brace.

Root, P. (1993). *Coyote and the magic words.* New York: Lothrop.

Roth, S.L. (1990). *The story of light.* New York: Morrow.

San Souci, R. (1978). *The legend of Scarface: A Blackfeet Indian tale.* New York: Doubleday.

San Souci, R. (1981). *Song of Sedna.* New York: Doubleday.

Sewell, M. (1990). *People of the breaking day.* New York: Atheneum.

Shetterly, S.H. (1991). *Raven's light: A myth from the People of the Northwest Coast.* New York: Atheneum.

Sloat, T. (1993). *The hungry giant of the Tundra.* New York: Dutton.

Sneve, V.D.H. (1993). *The Navajos: A first Americans book.* New York: Holiday.

Sneve, V.D.H. (1993). *The Sioux: A first Americans book.* New York: Holiday.

Sneve, V.D.H. (1994). *The Seminoles: A first Americans book.* New York: Holiday.

Speerstra, K. (1980). *The Earthshapers.* Naturegraph, Box 1075, Happy Camp, CA 96309.

Steltzer, U. (1981). *Building an igloo.* Toronto: Meadow Mouse.

Steptoe, J. (1984). *The story of Jumping Mouse.* New York: Morrow.

Stevens, J. (1993). *Coyote steals the blanket: A Ute tale.* New York: Holiday.

Strete, C.K. (1990). *Big Thunder Magic.* New York: Greenwillow.

Ude, W. (1993). *Maybe I will do something: Seven coyote tales.* Boston: Houghton.

Te Ata. (1989). *Baby rattlesnake.* San Francisco: Children's Book Press.

Wheeler, B. (1984). *I can't have Bannock but the beaver has a dam.* Winnipeg: Pemmican.

Wheeler, B. (1986). *Where did you get your moccasins?* Winnipeg: Pemmican.

Weisman, J. (1993). *The storyteller.* New York: Rizzoli.

Wood, N. (1993). *Spirit walker.* New York: Doubleday.

Yellow Robe, Rosebud. (1979). *Tonweya and the eagles, and other Lakota tales.* New York: Dell.

Yolen, J. (1990). *Sky dogs.* San Diego: Harcourt.

Young, E. (1993). *Moon Mother.* New York: HarperCollins.

Zola, M., & Dereume, A. (1983). *Nobody.* Winnipeg: Pemmican.

HISPANIC

Aardema, V. (1991). *Borreguita and the Coyote: A tale from Ayutla, Mexico.* New York: Knopf.

Ada, A.F. (1991). *The gold coin.* New York: Atheneum.

Ada, A.F. (1993). *The rooster who went to his uncle's wedding.* New York: Putnam.

Adams, F. (1986). *El Salvador: Beauty among the ashes.* New York: Dillon.

Anacona, G. (1982). *Bananas: From Manolo to Margie.* New York: Clarion.

Anacona, G. (1993). *Pablo remembers: The Fiesta of the Day of the Dead.* New York: Lothrop.

Argueta, M. (1990). *Magic dogs of the volcanoes/Los Perros magicos de los volcanes.* San Francisco: Children's Book Press.

Ashabranner, B. (1986). *Children of the Maya: A Guatemalan Indian odyssey.* New York: Putnam.

Bachelis, F.M. (1990). *El Salvador.* New York: Children's Press.

Baden, R. (1990). *And Sunday makes seven.* New York: Albert Whitman.

Bierhorst, J. (1986). *The monkey's haircut and other stories told by the Maya.* New York: Morrow.

Bierhorst, J. (1990). *Mythology of Mexico and Central America.* New York: Morrow.

Brusca, M.C. (1991). *On the Pampas.* New York: Holt.

Cameron, A. (1988). *The most beautiful place in the world.* New York: Knopf.

Carlson, L.M., & Ventura, C.L. (1990). *Where angels glide at dawn: New stories from Latin America.* New York: Lippincott.

Carlstrom, N.W. (1990). *Light: Stories of a small kindness.* Boston: Little, Brown.

Casteneda, O. (1991). *Among the volcanoes.* New York: Dutton.

Cheney, G.A. (1991). *El Salvador: Country in crisis.* New York: Watts.

Cromie, W.J. (1970). *Steven and the green turtle.* New York: Harper.

Cummins, R. (1990). *Children of the world: Costa Rica.* New York: Gareth Stevens.

de Sauza, J. *Brother Anansi and the cattle rancher.* San Francisco: Children's Book Press.

Delacre, L. (1990). *Arroz con leche: Popular songs and rhymes from Latin America.* New York: Scholastic.

Delacre, L. (1993). *Vejigante masquerader.* New York: Scholastic.

Dorros, A. (1991). *Abuela.* New York: Dutton.

Dorros, A. (1991). *Tonight is carnaval.* New York: Dutton.

Ehlert, R. (1992). *Moon rope/Un lazo a la luna*. San Diego: Harcourt.

Finger, C. (1924). *Tales from the silver land*. New York: Doubleday.

Ets, M.H., & Labastida, A. (1959). *Nine days to Christmas: A story of Mexico*. New York: Viking.

Garza, C.L. (1990). *Family pictures/Cuadros de familia*. San Francisco: Children's Book Press.

Gollub, M. (1993). *The twenty-five Mixtec cats*. New York: Tamborine.

Griego, M.C., Bucks, B.L., Gilbert, S.S., & Kimball, L.H. (1981). *Tortillatas para Mama: And other nursery rhymes*. New York: Holt.

Howlett, B. (1993). *I'm new here*. Boston: Houghton.

Jacobson, P., & Kristensen, P. (1986). *A family in Central America*. New York: Watts.

Jenness, A., & Kroeber, L. (1975). *A life of their own: An Indian family in Latin America*. New York: Harper.

Kimmel, E. (1993). *The witch's face: A Mexican tale*. New York: Holiday.

Lattimore, D.N. (1989). *Why there is no arguing in heaven: A Mayan myth*. New York: HarperCollins.

Lewis, T.P. (1971). *Hill of Fire*. New York: Harper & Row.

Lye, K. (1988). *Take a trip to Nicaragua*. New York: Watts.

McKissack, P. (1985). *The Maya*. New York: Children's Press.

Meyer, C. (1985). *The mystery of the ancient Maya*. New York: Macmillan.

Mikaelsen, B. (1993). *Sparrow Hawk Red*. New York: Hyperion.

Miller, C., & Berry, L. (1991). *Jungle rescue*. New York: Atheneum.

Moeri. (1989). *The forty-third war*. Boston: Houghton.

Morrison, M. (1989). *Central America*. New York: Silver Burdett.

Odijk, P. (1990). *The Mayas*. New York: Silver Burdett.

Peduzzi, K. (1991). *Oscar Arias*. New York: Gareth Stevens.

Perl, L. (1983). *Pinatas and paper flowers: Holidays of the Americas in English and Spanish*. New York: Clarion.

Pomerantz, C. (1990). *The Tamarindo puppy and other poems*. New York: Greenwillow.

Pomerantz, C. (1982). *If I had a paka: Poems in eleven languages*. New York: Greenwillow.

Rohmer, H. (1989). *Uncle Nacho's hat*. San Francisco: Children's Book Press.

Sanders, R. (1990). *El Salvador*. New York: Chelsea House.

Soto, G. (1990). *Baseball in April, and other stories*. New York: Harcourt.

Soto, G. (1992). *The skirt*. New York: Delacorte.

Soto, G. (1993). *Too many tamales*. New York: Putnam.

Soto, G. (1994). *Crazy weekend*. New York: Scholastic.

Wisniewski, D. (1991). *Rain player*. New York: Clarion.

ASIAN AMERICAN

JAPANESE

Bang, M. (1985). *The paper crane*. New York: Greenwillow.

Blumberg, R. (1987). *Commander Perry in the land of the Shogun*. New York: Lothrop.

Coerr, E. (1977). *Sadako and the thousand paper cranes*. New York: Dell.

Coerr, E. (1993). *Mieko and the fifth treasure*. New York: Putnam.

Coerr, E. (1993). *Sadako*. New York: Putnam.

Friedman, I.R. (1984). *How my parents learned to eat*. Boston: Houghton.

Hamanaka, S. (1990). *The journey*. New York: Watts/Orchard.

Han, O. S. (1993). *Sir Whong and the golden pig*. New York: Dial.

Havill, J. (1993). *Sato and the elephants*. New York: Lothrop.

Maruki, T. (1980). *Hiroshima, No Pika*. New York: Lothrop.

Paterson, K. (1990). *The tale of the Mandarin ducks*. New York: Lodestar.

Pattison, D. (1991). *The river dragon*. New York: Lothrop.

Sakai, K. (1990). *Sachiko means happiness*. San Francisco: Children's Book Press.

Say, A. (1990). *El Chino*. Boston: Houghton Mifflin.

Say, A. (1991). *Tree of cranes*. Boston: Houghton Mifflin.

Say, A. (1993). *Grandfather's journey*. Boston: Houghton.

Shute, L. (1986). *Momotaro, the peach boy*. New York: Lothrop.

Snyder, D. (1988). *The boy of the three year nap*. Boston: Houghton.

Uchida, Y. (1993). *The bracelet*. New York: Philomel.

Watkins, Y.K. (1992). *Tales from the bamboo grove*. New York: Bradbury.

Wisniewski, D. (1989). *The warrior and the wise man*. New York: Lothrop.

Yagawa, S. (1979). *The crane wife*. New York: Morrow.

KOREAN

Chang, M., & Chang, R. (1990). *In the eye of the war*. New York: Macmillan/Margaret K. McElderry.

Choi, S.N. (1991). *Year of impossible goodbyes*. Boston: Houghton.

Choi, S.N. (1993). *Halmoni and the picnic*. Boston: Houghton.

Climo, S. (1993). *The Korean Cinderella*. New York: HarperCollins.

Han, O.S. (1993). *Sir Whong and the golden pig.* New York: Dial.

Kwan, H.H. (1993). *The moles of Mireuk: A Korean tale.* Boston: Houghton.

McMahon, P. (1993). *Chi-Hoon: A Korean girl.* Honesdale, PA: Boyds Mills.

O'Brien, A.S. (1993). *The Princess and the beggar: A Korean folktale.* New York: Scholastic.

Rhee, N. (1993). *Magic spring.* New York: Putnam.

CHINESE

Ginsburg, M. (1988). *The Chinese mirror.* San Diego: Harcourt.

Haugaard, E.C. (1991). *The boy and the Samurai.* Boston: Houghton Mifflin.

Hearn, L. (1989). *The voice of the great bell.* Boston: Little, Brown.

Lee, J.M. (1982). *Legend of the Milky Way.* New York: Holt.

Lewis, E.F. (1932). *Young Fu of the Upper Yangtze.* New York: Dell.

Lobel, A. (1982). *Ming Lo moves the mountain.* New York: Greenwillow.

Louie, A. (1982). *Yeh-Shen: A Cinderella story from China.* New York: Philomel.

Mahy, M. (1990). *The seven Chinese brothers.* New York: Scholastic.

Paterson, K. (1976). *The master puppeteer.* New York: Crowell.

Porte, B.A. (1993). *"Leave that cricket be, Alan Lee."* New York: Greenwillow.

Rappaport, D. (1991). *The journey of Meng.* New York: Dial.

Waters, K., & Slovenz-Low, M. (1990). *Lion dancer: Ernie Wan's Chinese New Year.* New York: Scholastic.

Yee, P. (1990). *Tales from Gold Mountain.* New York: Macmillan.

Yep, L. (1975). *Dragonwings.* New York: Harper.

Yep, L. (1989). *The rainbow people.* New York: HarperCollins.

Yep, L. (1991). *Tongues of jade.* New York: HarperCollins.

Yep, L. (1993). *American dragons: Twenty-five Asian American voices.* New York: HarperCollins.

Yep, L. (1993). *Dragon's gate.* New York: HarperCollins.

Yep, L. (1993). *The shell woman and the king.* New York: Dial.

Yolen, J. (1988). *The Emperor and the kite.* New York: Philomel.

Young, E. (1989). *Lon Po Po: A Red-Riding Hood story from China.* New York: Putnam.

Zhensun, Z., & Low, A. (1991). *A young painter: The life and paintings of Wang Yani—China's extraordinary young artist.* New York: Scholastic.

SOUTHEAST ASIAN

Crew, L. (1989). *Children of the river.* New York: Delacorte.

Ho, M. (1990). *Rice without rain.* New York: Lothrop.

Ho, M. (1991). *The clay marbles.* New York: Farrar.

Hong, L.T. (1991). *How the ox star fell from heaven.* Chicago: Albert Whitman.

Garland, S. (1993). *The lotus seed.* San Diego: Harcourt.

Garland, S. (1993). *Why ducks sleep on one leg.* New York: Scholastic.

Kidd, D. (1993). *Onion tears.* New York: Beech Tree.

Lee, J.M. (1991). *Silent Lotus.* New York: Farrar.

Surat, M.M. (1983). *Angel Child, Dragon Child.* New York: Scholastic.

Uchida, Y. (1971). *Journey to Topaz.* New York: Scribners.

Vuong, L.D. (1982). *The brocaded slipper and other Vietnamese tales.* New York: Lippincott.

Vuong, L.D. (1993). *The golden carp and other tales from Vietnam.* New York: Lothrop.

Vuong, L.D. (1993). *Sky legends of Vietnam.* New York: HarperCollins.

Wartski, M. C. (1987). *A boat to nowhere.* New York: Signet.

Whelan, G. (1992). *Goodbye, Vietnam.* New York: Knopf.

JEWISH AMERICAN

Abells, C.B. (1983). *The children we remember.* New York: Greenwillow.

Adler, D.A. (1982). *A picture book of Hanukkah.* New York: Holiday.

Adler, D.A. (1989). *We remember the Holocaust.* New York: Holt.

Golden, B.D. (1988). *A Hanukkah tale: Just enough is plenty.* New York: Penguin.

Jaffe, N. (1993). *The uninvited guest and other Jewish holiday tales.* New York: Scholastic.

Jaffe, N., & Zeitlin, S. (1993). *While standing on one foot: Puzzle stories and wisdom tales from the Jewish tradition.* New York: Henry Holt.

Kimmel, E.A. (1987). *The Chanukkah tree.* New York: Holiday.

Kimmel, E.A. (1988). *The Chanukkah guest.* New York: Holiday.

Kimmel, E.A. (1989). *Hershel and the Hanukkah goblins.* New York: Holiday.

Kimmel, E.A. (1992). *The spotted pony: A collection of Hanukkah stories.* New York: Holiday.

Kimmel, E.A. (1993). *Asher and the capmakers: A Hanukkah story.* New York: Holiday.

Kuskin, K. (1993). *A great miracle happened there: A Chanukah story.* New York: HarperCollins.

Lasky, K. (1981). *The night journey.* New York: Puffin.

Lowry, L. (1989). *Number the stars.* Boston: Houghton Mifflin.

Matas, C. (1993). *Daniel's story.* New York: Scholastic.

Oberman, S. (1994). *The always prayer shawl.* Honesdale, PA: Boyds Mills.

Orlev, U. (1990). *The man from the other side.* Boston: Houghton Mifflin.

Polacco, P. (1988). *The keeping quilt.* New York: Simon & Schuster.

Rogasky, B. (1988). *Smoke and ashes: The story of the Holocaust.* New York: Holiday.

Schwartz, H., & Rush, B. (1992). *The Sabbath lion.* New York: Harper-Collins.

Strom, Y. (1991). *A tree still stands: Jewish youth in Eastern Europe today.* New York: Philomel.

Toll, N.S. (1993). *Behind the secret window: A memoir of a hidden childhood during World War Two.* New York: Dial.

Treseder, T.W. (1990). *Hear O Israel: A story of the Warsaw ghetto.* New York: Atheneum.

van der Rol, R., & Verhoeven, R. (1993). *Anne Frank: Beyond the diary.* New York: Viking.

Vos, I. (1991). *Hide and seek.* Boston: Houghton Mifflin.

Yolen, J. (1988). *The Devil's arithmetic.* New York: Viking.

CARIBBEAN

Berry, J. (1992). *Ajeemah and his son.* New York: HarperCollins.

Buffett, J., & Buffett, S.J. (1988). *The Jolly Mon.* New York: Harcourt.

Crespo, G. (1993). *How the sea began: A Taino myth.* New York: Clarion.

Dorris, M. (1992). *Morning Girl.* New York: Hyperion.

Humphrey, M. (1987). *The river that gave gifts.* San Francisco: Children's Book Press.

Joseph, L. (1990). *Coconut kind of day: Island poems.* New York: Lothrop.

Joseph, L. (1991). *A wave in her pocket: Stories from Trinidad.* New York: Clarion.

Joseph, L. (1992). *An island Christmas.* New York: Clarion.

Wilson, B.K. (1978). *The turtle and the island: A folktale from Papua New Guinea.* New York: Lippincott.

Yolen, J. (1992). *Encounter.* San Diego: Harcourt.

MIDDLE EASTERN

Aamundsen, N.R. (1990). *Two short and one long.* New York: Houghton Mifflin.

Ashabrammer, B. (1990). *An ancient heritage: The Arab-American minority.* New York: HarperCollins.

Climo, S. (1989). *The Egyptian Cinderella.* New York: HarperCollins.

Heide, F.P., & Gilliland, J.H. (1990). *The day of Ahmed's secret.* New York: Lothrop.

Pitkanen, M.A. (1991). *The children of Egypt.* Minneapolis: Carolrhoda.

RUSSIAN

Afanasyev, A.N. (1990). *The fool and the fish.* New York: Dial.

Dolphin, L. (1991). *Georgia to Georgia: Making friends in the U.S.S.R.* New York: Tamborine.

Kismaric, C. (1988). *The rumor of Pavel and Paali.* New York: Harper.

Mikolaycak, C. (1984). *Babushka.* New York: Holiday.

Ransome, A. (1968). *The fool of the world and the flying ship.* New York: Farrar.

AFRICAN AND SOUTH AFRICAN

Gordon, S. (1990). *The middle of somewhere: A story of South Africa.* New York: Watts/Orchard.

Grifalconi, A. (1992). *Flyaway girl.* Boston: Little, Brown.

Isadora, R. (1992). *At the crossroads.* New York: Greenwillow.

Knutson, B. (1993). *Sungura and Leopard: A Swahili trickster tale.* Boston: Little, Brown.

Maddern, E. (1993). *The fire children: A West African creation tale.* New York: Dial.

Margolies, B. (1990). *Rehema's journey: A visit in Tanzania.* New York: Scholastic.

McDermott, G. (1992). *Zomo the rabbit: A trickster tale from West Africa.* San Diego: Harcourt Brace Jovanovich.

Mollel, T.M. (1990). *The orphan boy.* New York: Clarion.

Mollel, T.M. (1992). *A promise to the sun.* Boston: Little, Brown.

Mollel, T.M. (1993). *The king and the tortoise.* New York: Clarion.

Onyefulu, I. (1993). *A is for Africa.* New York: Dutton.

Stanley, D., & Vennema, P. (1988). *Shaka: King of the Zulus*. New York: Morrow.

Stock, C. (1993). *Where are you going Manyoni?* New York: Morrow.

Walker, B.K. (1990). *The dancing palm tree and other Nigerian folktales*. Lubbock, TX: Texas Tech University Press.

Wisniewski, D. (1992). *Sundiata: Lion king of Mali*. New York: Clarion.

SELECTED TITLES ACROSS AND ABOUT OTHER CULTURES

Baer, E. (1990). *This is the way we go to school: A book about children around the world*. New York: Scholastic.

Dorros, A. (1992). *This is my house*. New York: Scholastic.

Gerstein, M. (1987). *Mountains of Tibet*. New York: Harper.

Latimer, J. (1991). *The Irish piper*. New York: Scribners.

Maddern, E. (1993). *Rainbow bird: An aboriginal folktale from northern Australia*. Boston: Little, Brown.

Maestro, B., & Maestro, G. (1991). *The discovery of the Americas*. New York: Lothrop.

Meeks, A.R. (1993). *Enora and the black crane*. New York: Scholastic.

Morris, A. (1990). *Loving*. New York: Morrow.

Morris, A. (1990). *On the go*. New York: Morrow.

Rattigan, J.K. (1993). *Dumpling soup*. Boston: Little, Brown.

Sage, J. (1991). *The little band*. New York: Macmillan/Margaret K. McElderry.

Serfozo, M. (1990). *Rain talk*. New York: Macmillan/Margaret K. McElderry.

Shannon, G. (1991). *More stories to solve: Fifteen folktales from around the world*. New York: Greenwillow.

Stanley, F. (1991). *Last princess: The story of Princess Kaiulani of Hawaii*. New York: Four Winds.

Te Kanawa, K. (1989). *Land of the long white cloud*. New York: Arcade.

Topooco, E. (1993). *Waira's first journey*. New York: Lothrop.

Wisniewski, D. (1990). *Elfwyn's saga*. New York: Lothrop.

Unfortunately, some are quick to criticize multicultural literature. Such critics pick out an element of a book and harshly proclaim it misrepresents the cultural group. Many times these criticisms are unfounded or inaccurate. The danger such censorship represents is that a good book may not be read, or worse, talented authors will shy away from writing books that feature certain cultural groups. Thus we should read books from a positive perspective—not with an eye toward criticism.

Two-time Newbery Award winner Katherine Paterson says, "My books will never be politically correct—that is, they will always run the risk of offending someone" (Paterson, 1994). As long as we have authors with this attitude, our children will have multicultural literature to read.

THE MULTICULTURAL SCHOOL

Ralph Sanders, principal of an Intermediate School in Greenville, Texas, seeks to promote an environment in his school that celebrates the diversity of the United States. Teachers have formed a multicultural awareness committee that is proactive in promoting knowledge about cultures. The committee meets every two weeks. In order to give you a picture of the committee's activities, we've reproduced a copy of the minutes from a meeting on the following page (Figure 17.2).

CLASSROOM VIGNETTE

The committee offers new teachers to the building these tips about cultural understandings:

1. Be aware of different cultures and sensitive to their beliefs.

2. Remember that all kids, regardless of color, have the same needs—to be loved; to be valued; to be respected.

3. Children from different cultures may react differently to discipline. For example, Anglo children may look the teacher in the eye as a sign of respect; African American children may avoid eye contact as a sign of respect.

4. Don't emphasize color. Don't identify a child by color by saying things like "that black child" or "that Chinese girl."

5. Respect children's names. Learn to pronounce them; don't shorten or "Americanize" children's names.

6. Be accepting of children's dialects.

7. Celebrate the holidays of the cultural groups in your room.

8. Assign new children a "buddy." An English-speaking buddy can help orient new LEP students in school situations (e.g., lunchroom, playground, music, recess).

Children who speak little or no English, perhaps more than any others in school, are at the mercy of their teachers and classmates. The teacher's sensitivity, respect, attitude, and common sense can make the difference between a classroom climate permitting students to thrive and develop or one in which students languish and retreat into their own private shells. For students to

FIGURE 17.2 ▶

Multicultural Awareness Committee

Minutes of meeting–Sept. 14

Aida Collin called the meeting to order. First thing on the agenda was Mexican Independence Day–September 16th. Leanne Trammell said that 5 ESL students will do a short reading in English and Spanish about Mexican Independence Day on Thursday, Sept. 16th during morning announcements. Also, Linda Muhl will supply 2 sentences dealing with Mexico's Independence to all 6th grade English teachers to be used for their oral language activity on Sept. 16th. Pat Brock will do the same for the 5th grade classes. Mrs. Deaton and Mrs. Gulley will be teaching a song in Spanish to all music classes this week. A discussion followed on how we could coordinate the entire school into a similar celebration project for next year. It was suggested that planning should be done in May so that we could have better school-wide participation.

Next item on the agenda was the Jewish New Year. It begins Sept. 15th at sundown. Since there was not enough time to fully plan for this event, the only thing that we will do this year is to have one of Mrs. Collin's students mention the event during morning announcements. *[Today at sundown, the Jewish people begin Rosh Hashana, the Jewish New Year. Each Jew makes his or her own peace with the observance of Yom Kippur (the Day of Atonement) on Sept. 25. On the Jewish calendar it is the year 5,754. The next time you go to the library find out what is the name of the calendar we use and where it did come from.]* Discussion followed about the possibility of other dates and special holidays that could be mentioned and studied during the year. Further discussions on this topic will be held next meeting.

Next on the agenda was the reading activity suggested by Norma Johnson to the reading teachers encouraging students to read biographies of people from different cultures. Students could also design bookmarks about certain authors from the various ethnic groups. Aida Collin will prepare a list of books and authors and give this list to the team leaders.

The last item on the agenda was the Drug-Free Kites. It was suggested that we could ask the students to use words from different languages when they design their kites. Leanne Trammell will ask her ESL students to write some phrases down in their own native languages and furnish those to the rest of the student body. Also, Linda Muhl will contact the Foreign Exchange Program Coordinator and ask if the foreign exchange students at the High School can provide us with phrases such as "Say No To Drugs" in their native languages. It was also suggested that we could have the High School Foreign Language classes help us too.

Before adjourning the meeting, it was approved that the meetings of the Multicultural Awareness Committee will be scheduled for the last Tuesday of every month. Next meeting will be September 28th.

acquire English, the affective domain must be addressed as vigorously as the cognitive domain.

SUMMARY

This chapter highlighted the importance of holistic instruction and its relation to the language and literacy acquisition of students from divergent multicultural backgrounds. Bilingual children need instruction that is holistic and authentic. In this chapter and throughout this book we have shared specific strategies sensitive to the special needs of second-language learners. Such instruction does not focus on bits and pieces or parts of language; parts are examined only within the whole and not in isolation.

Language is learned based on function, purpose, and need. Bilingual children need the same meaning-based instruction with which all students are best served. Whereas many students who speak English as a first language can "fill in" missing information that the standard curriculum requires from their experience base, some ESL students sometimes cannot do so, and they fail.

ESL children, therefore, are not always on equal footing. Children who are successful with ambiguous school tasks succeed because of the language base gained from home, where their parents operated as a primary interpretive language community. Minority children, however, often lack this base; consequently, it's vital that we provide them with literacy tasks that are authentic and meaningful.

PATHWAYS TO MULTICULTURAL UNDERSTANDINGS

The student:

▶ has many opportunities for the use of second language in a nonthreatening atmosphere.

▶ has opportunities to explore and value his or her own culture.

▶ has opportunities to share his or her own culture with others.

▶ learns about the culture of others.

▶ experiences communication through many media, including art, music, and drama.

The teacher:

▶ learns about the varied cultures of the children in the classroom.

▶ demonstrates multicultural acceptance.

▶ knows laws that affect instruction of bilingual children.

▶ receives all children into the classroom with an expectation that they'll learn.

▶ encourages self-expression of students through varied media.

▶ believes that children with handicapping conditions can be successful in the classroom.

▶ understands and applies basic principles of language development during instruction.

AFTERWORD: WHERE PATHWAYS CONVERGE

We began this text with a hope for the literacy future of children. We close with great confidence in the abilities of children to build a literacy storehouse for themselves that will sustain them for their lifetime voyage with books. These are the truths we've arrived at:

Teachers who love the language of literature demonstrate that love through the choices they make in their reading *with* students BUT they reflect the feeling that the best books are yet to be written.

They share art objects and art prints that are meaningful and that, to them, demonstrate the great art of the past BUT they imply in their interaction with students that the greatest paintings are yet to be painted.

They share the inventions of great scientists with enthusiasm and appreciation BUT they remind students that the greatest inventions for the benefit of humankind are yet to be made in the future.

Teachers bring students in contact with the great masters of classical and modern music BUT they remind children that the greatest music will be composed in the future.

Reading in the content fields of the school curriculum is important, and teachers use it as a base for understanding places and people and a few of the reasons they act as they do BUT the teacher who is responsive to students and their potential remains convinced that

▶ the greatest explorations are in the future;
▶ the greatest governments are yet to be formed;
▶ the greatest structures are yet to be built;
▶ the most important ideas for the benefit of humanity are ahead of us.

AND, perhaps, by some chance, some of those who will bring it all about are in our schools today.

Can we offer these potential leaders less than an opportunity to respond in personal ways to writing that

▶ generates productive thinking?
▶ allows freedom of expression?
▶ stimulates individuality and pride?
▶ values ingenuity?
▶ satisfies curiosity?

There are many ways for literacy programs to instill in students the complex skills and knowledge that permit literacy to be a significant part of children's lives. However, we suggest there are three major ideas for teachers toward this end. These ideas, our Literacy Transaction Model, were discussed in Chapter 1. When implemented, the model assures a measure of success for each student.

▶ **IDEA 1:** *Self-expression.* The natural language a student uses for communication is a basic ingredient in reading and writing. It must remain used and useful throughout the period when refined skills are being developed.

▶ **IDEA 2:** *Impression.* Growing language is being influenced from many sources and by many people. Each student deserves to try out new forms of communication under the influence of successful practitioners. These influences culminate in personal responses that seek ever-higher levels of quality, fluency, and flexibility in communication.

▶ **IDEA 3:** *Conventions.* Reading and writing development are influenced by the literacy children find in their environments. Children develop as writers when they compare and contrast their writing with the works of others.

We close this book with an appeal for teachers to structure language-arts programs in a creative manner and to provide students with opportunities and activities that will enable them to reach their potentials as fluent language users.

When instruction becomes
   destructive to the joy of
   learning—
that instruction should be abolished
   or modified
in such a manner
as to lead potential learners
to experience
the power
the beauty
and the magic of their language.

from: MARKINGS, Dag Hammarskjold

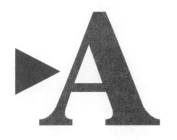

CALDECOTT MEDAL WINNERS

1994: *Grandfather's Journey,* Allen Say (Houghton Mifflin)
1993: *Mirette on the High Wire,* Emily Arnold McCully (Putnam)
1992: *Tuesday,* David Wiesner (Houghton Mifflin)
1991: *Black and White,* David Macaulay (Houghton Mifflin)
1990: *Lon Po Po,* Ed Young (Putnam)
1989: *Song and Dance Man,* Karen Ackerman (Knopf)
1988: *Owl Moon,* Jane Yolen (Philomel)
1987: *Hey! Al,* Arthur Yorinks (Farrar, Straus & Giroux)
1986: *The Polar Express,* Chris Van Allsburg (Houghton Mifflin)
1985: *Saint George and the Dragon,* T.S. Hyman (Little, Brown)
1984: *The Glorious Flight,* Alice and Martin Provensens (Viking)
1983: *Shadow, Blaise, Cendrars,* Translated & illustrated by Marcia Brown (Scribners)
1982: *Jumanji,* Chris Van Allsburg (Houghton)
1981: *Fables,* Arnold Lobel (Harper)
1980: *Ox-Cart Man,* Donald Hall, Pictures by Barbara Cooney (Viking)
1979: *The Girl Who Loved Wild Horses,* Paul Goble (Bradbury)
1978: *Noah's Ark,* Peter Spier (Doubleday)
1977: *Ashanti to Zulu,* Margaret Musgrove, Pictures by Leo and Diane Dillon (Dial)
1976: *Why Mosquitoes Buzz in People's Ears,* Retold by Verna Aardema, Pictures by Leo and Diane Dillon (Dial)
1975: *Arrow to the Sun,* Gerald McDermott (Viking)
1974: *Duffy and the Devil,* Retold by Harve Zemach, Pictures by Margot Zemach (Farrar)
1973: *The Funny Little Woman,* Lafcadio Hearn, Retold by Arlene Mosel, Illustrated by Blair Lent (Dutton)
1972: *One Fine Day,* Nonny Horgrogian (Macmillan)
1971: *A Story a Story,* Gail E. Haley (Atheneum)
1970: *Sylvester and the Magic Pebble,* William Steig (Windmill)
1969: *The Fool of the World and the Flying Ship,* Retold by Arthur Ransome, Illustrated by Uri Schulevitz (Farrar)
1968: *Drummer Hoff,* Adapted by Barbara Emberly, Illustrated by Ed Emberly (Prentice-Hall)
1967: *Sam, Bangs & Moonshine,* Evaline Ness (Holt)
1966: *Always Room for One More,* Sorche Nic Leodhas, Illustrated by Nonny Horgrogian (Holt)
1965: *May I Bring a Friend?,* Beatrice Schenk de Regniers, Illustrated by Betti Montresor (Atheneum)
1964: *Where the Wild Things Are,* Maurice Sendak (Harper)
1963: *The Snowy Day,* Ezra Jack Keats (Viking)
1962: *Once a Mouse,* Marcia Brown (Scribners)
1961: *Baboushka and the Three Kings,* Ruth Robbins, Illustrated by Nicolas Sidjakov (Parnassus)
1960: *Nine Days to Christmas,* Marie Hall Ets and Aurora Labastida (Viking)
1959: *Chanticleer and the Fox,* Barbara Cooney (Crowell)
1958: *Time of Wonder,* Robert McCloskey (Viking)
1957: *A Tree Is Nice,* Janice Udry, Illustrated by Marc Simont (Harper)

1956: *Frog Went A-Courtin'*, Retold by John Langstaff, Illustrated by Feodor Rojankovsky (Harcourt)

1955: *Cinderella*, Illustrated and Retold from Perrault by Marcia Brown (Scribners)

1954: *Madeline's Rescue*, Ludwig Bemelmans (Viking)

1953: *The Biggest Bear*, Lynd Ward (Houghton)

1952: *Finders Keepers*, Will Lipkind, Illustrated by Nicolas Mordvinoff (Harcourt)

1951: *The Egg Tree*, Katherine Milhous (Scribners)

1950: *Song of the Swallows*, Leo Politi (Scribners)

1949: *The Big Snow*, Berta and Elmer Hader (Macmillan)

1948: *White Snow, Bright Snow*, Alvin Tresselt, Illustrated by Roger Duvoisin (Lothrop)

1947: *The Little Island*, Golden MacDonald, Illustrated by Leonard Weisgard (Doubleday)

1946: *The Rooster Crows*, Maude and Miska Petersham (Macmillan)

1945: *Prayer for a Child*, Rachel Field, Illustrated by Elizabeth Orton Jones (Macmillan)

1944: *Many Moons*, James Thurber, Illustrated by Louis Slobodkin (Harcourt)

1943: *The Little House*, Virginia Lee Burton (Houghton)

1942: *Make Way for Ducklings*, Robert McCloskey (Viking)

1941: *They Were Strong and Good*, Robert Lawson (Viking)

1940: *Abraham Lincoln*, Ingri and Edgar Parin d'Aulaire (Doubleday)

1939: *Mei Li*, Thomas Handforth (Doubleday)

1938: *Animals of the Bible*, Dorothy P. Lathrop (Lippincott)

B NEWBERY AWARD WINNERS

1994: *The Giver*, Lois Lowry (Houghton Miffilin)

1993: *Missing May*, Cynthia Rylant (Franklin Watts)

1992: *Shiloh*, Phyllis Reynolds Naylor (MacMillan)

1991: *Maniac Magee*, Jerry Spinelli (Little, Brown)

1990: *Number the Stars*, Lois Lowry (Houghton Mifflin)

1989: *Joyful Noise: Poems for Two Voices*, Paul Fleischman (Harper & Row)

1988: *Lincoln: A Photobiography*, Russell Freedman (Houghton Mifflin)

1987: *The Whipping Boy*, Sid Fleischman (Greenwillow)

1986: *Sarah, Plain and Tall*, Patricia MacLachlan (Harper)

1985: *The Hero and the Crown*, Robia McKinley (Greenwillow)

1984: *Dear Mr. Henshaw*, Beverly Cleary (Morrow)

1983: *Dicey's Song*, Cynthia Voigt (Atheneum)

1982: *A Visit to William Blake's Inn: Poems for Innocent and Experienced Travelers*, Nancy Willard (Harcourt)

1981: *Jacob Have I Loved*, Katherine Paterson (Crowell)

1980: *A Gathering of Days*, Joan W. Blos (Scribners)

1979: *The Westing Game*, Ellen Raskin (Dutton)

1978: *Bridge to Terabithia*, Katherine Paterson (Crowell)

1977: *Roll of Thunder, Hear My Cry*, Mildred D. Taylor (Dial)

1976: *The Grey King*, Susan Cooper (Atheneum)

1975: *M. C. Higgins, the Great*, Virginia Hamilton (Macmillan)

1974: *The Slave Dancer*, Paula Fox (Bradbury)

1973: *Julie of the Wolves*, Jean Craighead George (Harper)

1972: *Mrs. Frisby and the Rats of NIMH*, Robert C. O'Brien (Atheneum)

1971: *Summer of the Swans*, Betsy Byars (Viking)

1970: *Sounder*, William H. Armstrong (Harper)

1969: *The High King*, Lloyd Alexander (Holt)

1968: *From the Mixed-Up Files of Mrs. Basil E. Frankweiler*, E. L. Konigsburg (Atheneum)

1967: *Up a Road Slowly*, Irene Hunt (Follett)

1966: *I, Juan de Pareja*, Elizabeth Borton de Trevino (Farrar)

1965: *Shadow of a Bull*, Maia Wojciechowska (Atheneum)

1964: *It's Like This, Cat*, Emily Neville (Harper)

1963: *A Wrinkle in Time*, Madeleine L'Engle (Farrar)

1962: *The Bronze Bow*, Elizabeth George Speare (Houghton)

1961: *Island of the Blue Dolphins*, Spock O'Dell (Houghton)

1960: *Onion John*, Joseph Krumgold (Crowell)

1959: *The Witch of Blackbird Pond*, Elizabeth George Speare (Houghton)

1958: *Rifles for Watie*, Harold Keith (Crowell)

1957: *Miracles on Maple Hill*, Virginia Sorensen (Harcourt)

1956: *Carry on, Mr. Bowditch*, Jean Lee Latham (Houghton)

1955: *The Wheel of the School*, Meindert DeJong (Harper)

1954: *. . . And Now Miguel*, Joseph Krumgold (Crowell)

1953: *Secret of the Andes*, Ann Xolan Clark (Viking)

1952: *Ginger Pye*, Eleanor Estes (Harcourt)

1951: *Amos Fortune, Free Man*, Elizabeth Yates (Dutton)

1950: *Door in the Wall*, Marguerite de Angeli (Doubleday)

1949: *King of the Wind*, Marguerite Henry (Rand McNally)

1948: *Twenty-One Balloons*, William Bene du Bois (Viking)

1947: *Miss Hickory*, Carolyn Sherwin Bailey (Viking)
1946: *Strawberry Girl*, Lois Lenski (Lippincott)
1945: *Rabbitt Hill*, Robert Lawson (Viking)
1944: *Johnny Tremain*, Esther Forbes (Houghton Mifflin)
1943: *Adam of the Road*, Elizabeth Janet Gray (Viking)
1942: *The Matchlock Gun*, Walter D. Edmonds (Dodd, Mead)
1941: *Call It Courage*, Armstrong Sperry (Macmillan)
1940: *Daniel Boone*, James Daugherty (Viking)
1939: *Thimble Summer*, Elizabeth Enright (Farrar and Rinehart)
1938: *The White Stag*, Kate Seredy (Viking)
1937: *Roller Skates*, Ruth Sawyer (Viking)
1936: *Caddie Woodland*, Carol Ryrie Brink (Macmillan)
1935: *Dobry*, Monica Shannon (Viking)
1934: *Invincible Louise*, Cornelia Meigs (Little, Brown)
1933: *Young Fu of the Upper Yangtze*, Elizabeth Foreman Lewis (Macmillan)
1932: *Waterless Mountain*, Laura Adams Armer (David McKay)
1931: *The Cat Who Went to Heaven*, Elizabeth Coatsworth (Macmillan)
1930: *Hitty: Her First Hundred Years*, Rachel Field (Macmillan)
1929: *The Trumpeter of Kradow*, Eric P. Kelly (Macmillan)
1928: *Gayneck: The Story of a Pigeon*, Dhan Gopal Mukerji (Dutton)
1927: *Smoky, the Cowhorse*, Will James (Scribners)
1926: *Shen of the Sea*, Arthur Bowie Chrisman (Dutton)
1925: *Tales from Silver Lands*, Charles J. Finger (Doubleday)
1924: *The Dark Frigate*, Charles Boardman Hawes (Little, Brown)
1923: *The Voyages of Dr. Doolittle*, Hugh Lofting (Lippincott)
1922: *The Story of Mankind*, Hendrik Willern Van Loon (Liveright)

C CORETTA SCOTT KING AWARDS

1994
Author: Angela Johnson, *Toning the Sweep,* Orchard/Jackson.
Illustrator: Tom Feelings, *Soul Looks Back in Wonder,* Dial.

1993
Author: Patricia C. McKissack, *The Dark-Thirty: Southern Tales of the Supernatural,* Knopf.
Illustrator: Katherine Atkins Wilson, *The Origin of Life on Earth: An African Myth* retold by David A. Anderson/SANKOFA, Sight Productions.

1992
Author: Walter Dean Myers, *Now Is Your Time!: The African American Struggle for Freedom,* HarperCollins.
Illustrator: Faith Ringgold, *Tar Beach,* Crown.

1991
Author: Mildred D. Taylor, *The Road to Memphis,* Dial.
Illustrator: Leo and Diane Dillon, *Aïda* told by Leontyne Price, Gulliver/Harcourt Brace.

1990
Author: Patricia and Frederick McKissack, *A Long Hard Journey: The Story of the Pullman Porter,* Walker.
Illustrator: Jan Spivey Gilchrist, *Nathanial Talking* by Eloise Greenfield, Black Butterfly.

1989
Author: Walter Dean Myers, *Fallen Angels,* Scholastic.
Illustrator: Jerry Pinkney, *Mirandy and Brother Wind* by Patricia McKissack, Knopf.

1988
Author: Mildred D. Taylor, *The Friendship,* Dial.
Illustrator: John Steptoe, *Mufaro's Beautiful Daughters: An African Tale,* Lothrop.

1987
Author: Mildred Pitts Walter, *Justin and the Best Biscuits in the World,* Lothrop.
Illustrator: Jerry Pinkney, *Half a Moon and One Whole Star* by Crescent Dragonwagon, Macmillan.

1986
Author: Virginia Hamilton, *The People Could Fly: American Black Folktales,* Knopf.
Illustrator: Jerry Pinkney, *The Patchwork Quilt* by Valerie Flournoy, Dial.

1985
Author: Walter Dean Myers, *Motown and Didi,* Viking.
Illustrator: no award.

1984
Author: Lucille Clifton, *Everett Anderson's Good-Bye,* Holt.
Illustrator: Pat Cummings, *My Mama Needs Me* by Mildred Pitts Walter, Lothrop.

1983
Author: Virginia Hamilton, *Sweet Whispers, Brother Rush,* Philomel.
Illustrator: Peter Mugabane, *Black Child,* Knopf.

1982
Author: Mildred D. Taylor, *Let the Circle Be Unbroken,* Dial.
Illustrator: John Steptoe, *Mother Crocodile: An Uncle Amadou Tale from Senegal* adapted by Rosa Guy, Delacorte.

1981
Author: Sidney Poitier, *This Life,* Knopf.
Illustrator: Ashley Bryan, *Beat the Story-Drum, Pum-Pum,* Atheneum.

1980
Author: Walter Dean Myers, *The Young Landlords,* Viking.
Illustrator: Carole Bayard, *Cornrows* by Camille Yarbrough, Coward.

1979
Author: Ossie Davis, *Escape to Freedom,* Viking.
Illustrator: Tom Feelings, *Something on My Mind* by Nikki Grimes, Dial.

1978
Author: Eloise Greenfield, *Africa Dream,* Day/HarperCollins.
Illustrator: Carole Bayard, *Africa Dream* by Eloise Greenfield, Day/HarperCollins.

1977
Author: James Haskins, *The Story of Stevie Wonder,* Lothrop.
Illustrator: no award.

1976
Author: Pearl Bailey, *Duey's Tale,* Harcourt Brace.
Illustrator: no award.

1975
Author: Dorothy Robinson, *The Legend of Africana,* Johnson.
Illustrator: Herbert Temple, *The Legend of Africana* by Dorothy Robinson, Johnson.

1974
Author: Sharon Bell Mathis, *Ray Charles,* HarperCollins.
Illustrator: George Ford, *Ray Charles* by Sharon Bell Mathis, HarperCollins.

1973
Jackie Robinson (as told to Alfred Duckett), *I Never Had It Made,* Putnam.

1972
Elston C. Fax, *17 Black Artists,* Dodd.

1971
Charlemae Rollins, *Black Troubador: Langston Hughes,* Rand McNally.

1970
Lillie Patterson, *Martin Luther King, Jr.: Man of Peace,* Garrard.

D

READER'S THEATER SCRIPTS

A BUG'S PICNIC

by Rick Kilcup

Characters: narrator, bugs . . . as many as you want . . ., and humans.

Props: Picnic stuff! Like a basket, paper plates, blanket, etc. Will need a spray can labeled "People Repellant." Might even have some sandwiches.

Costumes: Not really necessary but if the bugs had headband bug masks it would really look great!

NARRATOR: It's summer and the weather's just right for picnics! How'd you like to come along on one? Well, let's go . . . but I've got to warn you that this isn't your everyday ordinary picnic!
(Bugs enter, crawling, hopping, flying, etc. They are looking around for something and carry picnic basket.)

Bug 1: This looks like a good spot for a picnic!

Bug 2: Yup, it sure does!

Bug 3: Let's just hope that THEY don't find us!

All BUGS: You can say that again! (They settle down, unpack the picnic basket, spread out the table cloth, and get ready to eat.)

BUG 4: Sandwiches anyone? We've got nectar on rye and aphid on whole wheat!

ALL BUGS: Sounds great, let's pig out! (Sandwiches get passed out.)

BUG 5: This is the life!

BUG 6: Yup and THEY haven't found us yet!

BUG 7: They'd better not! Nothing can spoil a picnic faster than THEY can! (Others nod in agreement, ad lib.)

HUMAN 1: We were right, there was a picnic going on here!

HUMAN 2: Yup, we can smell a good picnic a mile away!

HUMAN 3: Just look at those goodies!! Let's go mess up their picnic and have a feast!

OTHER HUMANS: Great idea! (They sneak over and begin pestering and gobbling the food!)

Bug 8: Eeeek! THEY'RE here!

BUG 9: Oh no, humans! Shoo! Go away you pests! (All bugs begin swatting at humans who dodge out of way and continue to pester and eat, the bugs can ad lib yucky comments.)

BUG 10: (Reaches into picnic basket and pulls out can of spray.) I'll put an end to these pesky critters! (Sprays.) Take that you bothersome humans!

ALL HUMANS: Oh no! Not That! We'd better split! (They run off, coughing.)

BUG 11: (Bugs settle back to eat in peace, #11 holds up can for audience to see.) People Repellent, never leave home without it!

THE END!

POOR OLD LADY

....

Traditional

1: Poor old lady, she swallowed a fly,
I don't know why she swallowed a fly.

2: Poor old lady, I think she'll die.

3: Poor old lady, she swallowed a spider.
It squirmed and wriggled and turned inside her.

1: She swallowed the spider to catch the fly.
I don't know why she swallowed a fly.

2: Poor old lady, I think she'll die.

4: Poor old lady, she swallowed a bird.
How absurd! She swallowed a bird.

3: She swallowed the bird to catch the spider.

1: She swallowed the spider to catch the fly,
I don't know why she swallowed a fly.

2: Poor old lady, I think she'll die.

5: Poor old lady, she swallowed a cat.
Think of that! She swallowed a cat.

4: She swallowed the cat to catch the bird.

3: She swallowed the bird to catch the spider.

1: She swallowed the spider to catch the fly,
I don't know why she swallowed the fly.

2: Poor old lady, I think she'll die.

6: Poor old lady, she swallowed a dog.
She went the whole hog when she swallowed the dog.

5: She swallowed the dog to catch the cat.

4: She swallowed the cat to catch the bird.

3: She swallowed the bird to catch the spider,

1: She swallowed the spider to catch the fly,
I don't know why she swallowed the fly.

2: Poor old lady, I think she'll die.

7: Poor old lady, she swallowed a cow.
I don't know how she swallowed the cow.

6: She swallowed the cow to catch the dog,

5: She swallowed the dog to catch the cat,

4: She swallowed the cat to catch the bird,

3: She swallowed the bird to catch the spider,

1: She swallowed the spider to catch the fly.
I don't know why she swallowed a fly.

2: Poor old lady, I think she'll die.

8: Poor old lady, she swallowed a horse.

All: She died, of course.

RIP VAN WINKLE
READER'S THEATRE ADAPTATION

David Canzoneri

Narrator: In a small Dutch community in the Catskill mountains, a crowd gathered at the Union Hotel beneath a brand new flag made up of stars and stripes. They were discussing the new government led by General George Washington when an old man with a long grizzled beard, worn-out clothes and a rusty worm-eaten musket wandered into the meeting. A crowd gathered around the man, stroking their chins and laughing at his worn-out clothes.

Crowdmember 1: "On which side did you vote, old timer?"

Rip: "What?"

Crowdmember 2: "Are you a federal?"

Crowdmember 3: "Or are you a Federalist?"

Rip: "I don't even know what that means!"

Narrator: "A wise old man elbowed his way through the crowd, planted his hands on his hips and eyed Rip sideways."

Old Man: "He wants to know if you believe that power should rest with the people or with the government. I want to know what brings you to the election with a gun on your shoulder. Are you trying to start a riot?"

Rip: "Alas! Sir! I am a poor, quiet man, a native of the place, and a loyal subject of the king, God bless him!"

Crowdmember 1: "The king? I thought we got rid of all those filthy redcoats!"

Crowdmember 2: "He must have missed the ship when we chased those redcoats back home!"

Crowdmember 3: "Maybe he's a spy. Maybe they're planning to attack again!"

Crowdmember 1: "Grab him!"

Crowdmember 2: "Away with him!"

Narrator: "The crowd advanced angrily toward Rip, who held up his hands pleadingly."

Rip: "Please! Please! I mean no harm! I merely come in search of my neighbors who used to keep about the tavern."

Narrator: "The wise old man held up his hand, halting the crowd. Then he turned to Rip and demanded . . ."

Old Man: "Well, who are they? Name them."

Rip: "Nicholas Vedder, for one. Where is Nicholas Vedder?"

Crowdmember 1: "Nicholas Vedder? Why, he is dead and gone these eighteen years! There was a wooden tombstone in the churchyard that used to tell about him, but that's rotten and gone, too."

Rip (puzzled): "What's become of Brom Dutcher?"

Crowdmember 2: "Oh, he went off to the army in the beginning of the war; some say he was killed at the storming of Stony Point—others say he was drowned in a squall at the foot of Anthony's Nose. I don't know—he never came back again."

Rip (even more puzzled): "Where's Van Bummel, the schoolmaster?"

Crowdmember 3: "He went off to the wars too, was a great militia general, and is now in Congress."

Rip (utterly despairing): "War? Congress? Eighteen years! What has happened? What has happened to my dear, dear friends? What has happened to my town? What has happened to Rip Van Winkle?"

Crowdmember 1: "Rip Van Winkle? Oh yes, I remember him. He was a simple, good natured man, a kind neighbor and . . ."

Crowdmember 2: ". . . a henpecked husband. A real shrew of a wife he had at home!"

Crowdmember 1: "Yes, but her temper produced his meekness of spirit. Some even say a nagging wife is a blessing in disguise."

Crowdmember 2: "If that's the case then he was thrice blessed!"

Judith: "Rip Van Winkle was my father, sir. But, it's twenty years since he went away from home with his gun, and never has been heard of since—his dog Wolf came home without him, but whether he shot himself or was carried away by the Indians, nobody can tell. I was then but a little girl."

Rip: "Judith. This grown up woman, you are Judith?"

Judith: "Yes, sir, but how do you know me?"

Rip: "I am your father! Young Rip Van Winkle once—old Rip Van Winkle now! Does nobody know poor Rip Van Winkle?"

Judith (in disbelief): "Father! This is you?"

Old Man: "Sure enough! It is Rip Van Winkle. It is himself! Welcome home again, old neighbor."

Rip: "Judith, you said Wolf came home, where is he, the little rascal!"

Judith (sadly): "Dear Father, remember that was twenty years ago. He is long since gone."

Rip: "Oh, yes. I haven't yet realized it. Twenty years! And all my friends gone! Where is your mother?"

Judith: Oh, she too died a short time later; she broke a blood vessel in a fit of passion at a New England peddler."

Rip (sighs): "A drop of comfort, at least, in that!"

Old Man: "Where have you been these twenty long years?"

Rip: "It seems but yesterday. I had gone squirrel hunting with Wolf, rest his soul, and we unconsciously scrambled to one of the highest parts of the Kaatskills. Panting and fatigued, I threw myself on a green knoll overlooking the lordly Hudson river. As evening approached and I began to descend, I heard a voice calling . . ."

Narrator: "Rip Van Winkle, Rip Van Winkle."

Rip: "Through a clearing came a short, square-built old fellow dressed in the antique Dutch fashion. He was bent under the weight of a keg and I hurried to offer him neighborly assistance."

Old Man: "That was indeed the Rip Van Winkle I knew: ready to attend anybody's business but his own. He always found tending his own farm and family matters next to impossible."

Rip: "The stranger led me through a ravine and into a hallow where his strange companions were playing at ninepins. Whenever they rolled the balls, a sound like rumbling peals of thunder echoed along the mountains. The men looked like the figures in the old Flemish painting hanging in the parlor of Dominie Van Shaik, the village parson. I suppose Dominie is . . ."

Crowdmember 1: "Yes, long gone, too."

Judith: "Please continue, if you can, Father."

Rip (takes a deep breath): "Well, the men beckoned me to serve the ale. As I passed the flagons around I felt compelled to sample the liquor. Being a naturally thirsty soul, I was soon tempted to repeat the draft. After several tastes, however, my eyes began to swim, my head reeled, and I fell into a deep sleep, waking only this morning. My musket is no longer blue steel, but rust and wormwood. My dog, my friends and my wife are all gone. My house is in shambles. And I have become an old man. At first, I thought the ale was playing tricks on me, but you have convinced me that everything really has changed by twenty years!"

Crowdmember 1: "You really expect us to believe this story?"

Crowdmember 2: "The only part I believe is the sampling of the ale!"

Crowdmember 3: "He's as crazy as he looks."

Narrator: "The crowd laughed and jeered at Rip. Then, a small bespectacled man pushed his way through the crowd and held up his hand for silence. Almost immediately the crowd fell silent. The man adjusted his jacket, cleared his throat and began to speak."

Peter: "You have no reason to disbelieve this man. I, Peter Vanderdonk, ancestor of the great historian, can assure you that his story is most certainly true. The Kaatskills have always been visited with strange happenings. It is well known that Henry Hudson, the first discoverer of the river and surrounding country, keeps a vigil there every twenty years. With his crew of the Half Moon, they keep a guardian eye over the river and the great city called by his name. My own father once saw them playing ninepins in the hollow and I myself heard the sound of the balls like peals of distant thunder one summer afternoon. I say Welcome home, Rip Van Winkle. It is good to have you back."

Old man: "Whatever the learned Vanderdonk says is fine by me."

Crowdmember 1: "Me, too. Let's welcome our old neighbor back."

Narrator: "The crowd gathered around Rip, patting him on the back and shaking his hand. With such an affirmation coming from the famous and respected Peter Vanderdonk, Rip was quickly welcomed back into the village. Having reached the age where he could be idle without criticism, he became a regular fixture and was reverenced as a patriarch of the village, telling his story to every stranger who would give him an audience. To this day, the villagers never hear a thunderstorm without thinking that Henry Hudson and his crew are at a game of ninepins. And it is a common wish of all henpecked husbands to have a taste of Rip Van Winkle's ale to escape the tirades of the shrew. As for Rip, he never tells the tale without tugging thoughtfully at his beard and saying . . ."

Rip: "Hmm. Maybe now I should change my name to Rip van Wrinkle!"

END

OLD BIKE AND NEW BIKE

Bill Martin Jr

Old Bike: Don't wobble, You've got to keep your balance.

New Bike: I'm trying! I'm trying!

Old Bike: You're less than a day old and already you've got a wobbly front wheel.

New Bike: It wasn't my fault. That stupid dog stood right there and refused to move. I hit him. Ker-plunk!

Old Bike: Oh, that was funny!

New Bike: No, it wasn't funny! I was doing my best and what happens! I get sprocket shock and a wobbly wheel. That may be funny to you but not to me.

Old Bike: Calm down, little one, calm down. We all went through it. Use your training wheels!

New Bike: Training wheels? So you know what everybody would say?

Old Bike: What about the new bike next door? He uses training wheels.

New Bike: He's a sissy!

Old Bike: Then take your knocks and forget it.

New Bike: *(after a pause)* Say, Old Bike, did you hear that kid holler when I dumped last night? *(he chuckles)* He thought he was killed. The sight of a little blood and he powed out of his mind!

Old Bike: Donald is going to take a lot of spills until you get the hang of balancing.

New Bike: He thinks he's so smart! He thinks he has to learn to ride. He can't figure out that it's us bikes that do the learning.

Old Bike: I don't like to bear bad news, but looks who's coming!

New bike: Oh, no! It's Donald's little sister!

Old Bike: Yes, you're going to get a workout. With Donald and his little sister both riding you before you get your balance—you'll be bent and twisted forever.

New Bike: Why don't you take her for a ride? Give me a break.

Old Bike: I'm willing but she likes you. Face up to it! I've had my day. Everybody likes a new bike. She wouldn't ride me.

New Bike: Well, here goes. Wish me luck!

Old Bike: Well, c'est la guerre!

KNOTS ON A COUNTING ROPE

Bill Martin Jr

Boy: "Grandfather, tell me the story again. Tell me who I am."

Grandfather: "I have told you many times, Boy."

Boy: "But tell me again, Grandfather. Tell me about my name."

Grandfather: "You know your name, Boy. You know the story by heart."

Boy: "But it sounds better when you tell it. Please tell it over and over, Grandfather. I like to hear you say my name."

Grandfather: "Then listen carefully, Boy. This may be the last time for telling the story. The counting rope is almost filled with knots."

Boy: "This cannot be the last time, Grandfather. Promise that this will not be the last time."

Grandfather: "I cannot promise you anything, Boy. I love you. I love you very much. That is better than a promise."

Boy: "And I love you, Grandfather. Tell me the story again. Please."

Grandfather: "Once there was a boy child. . . ."

Boy: "I was the boy child, wasn't I, Grandfather?"

Grandfather: "Yes, you were the boy child in the story."

Boy: "And I was very strong, wasn't I, Grandfather?"

Grandfather: "No, you were not strong, Boy. You were very little and very sick. We thought you were going to die."

Boy: "But *you* knew that I wouldn't die, Grandfather. Tell me that part again."

Grandfather: "One day when you were very sick and your breath was too weak for crying, two great blue horses came galloping by. Suddenly they turned and looked at you. You reached up your arms to them."

Boy: "And that is when you named me!"

Grandfather: "Yes, we named you Boy Strength-of-Blue-Horses. It is a strong name."

Boy: "Did I need a strong name, Grandfather?"

Grandfather: "All children need strong names to grow strong."

Boy: "And what did you say, Grandfather?"

Grandfather: "I said, 'See how the horses speak to him. They are his brothers from beyond the dark mountain. This boy child will not die. The blue horses have given him strength to live.' "

Boy: "Did I grow strong, Grandfather?"

Grandfather: "Yes, Boy, you grew strong and you are becoming stronger every day. Some day you will be strong enough to cross over beyond the dark mountains."

Boy: "How strong must I be, Grandfather? Tell me that part again."

Grandfather: "You must be so strong, Boy, that you will not speak with anger even when your heart is filled with anger."

Boy: "And that is not all, Grandfather. Tell me the next part."

Grandfather: "You must be so strong, Boy, that you want to know what other people are thinking even when you are listening to your own thoughts."

Boy: "Now tell me the last part, Grandfather."

Grandfather: "You must be so strong, Boy, that you will stop to think of what happened yesterday and what will happen tomorrow in knowing what you want to do today."

Boy: "Is it hard to be strong like you, Grandfather?"

Grandfather: "Strong people are not born strong, Boy. They become strong by thinking they are strong. They dream of themselves as being strong enough to cross over the dark mountains."

Boy: "Will I ever be strong enough to cross over the dark mountains, Grandfather?"

Grandfather: "You already have crossed over some of the dark mountains, Boy. The mountains have no beginning and no ending. They are all around us. We only know that we are crossing them when we want to be weak but choose to be strong."

Boy: "Maybe I will not be strong enough, Grandfather, to cross over all of the dark mountains."

Grandfather: "Oh, yes, you will be, Boy Strength-of-Blue-Horses."

Boy: "Then you must keep telling me the story, Grandfather. You must never stop telling me the story."

Grandfather: "But I will stop telling the story, Boy, when I have tied the last knot on the counting rope. Now that I have told the story again, I tie another knot, just as I did before. When the rope is filled with knots, you will start telling the story to yourself. That is the way you know you are strong. That is the way you become strong."

REFERENCES

Afflerbach, P., Norton, J. L., & Johnston, P. (1989). *The composition of the report card: Making the grade in the language arts.* Paper presented at the National Reading Conference, Austin, TX.

Allen, R. V. (1985). Let students have their say. In *Forty-ninth Yearbook, Claremont Reading Conference.* Claremont, CA: Claremont Graduate School Center for Developmental Studies.

Allen, R.V., Sampson, M.R., & Teale, W. (1989). *Experiences for literacy.* Worthington, OH: SRA.

Altwerger, B., & Flores, B. (1994). Theme cycles: Creating communities of learners. *Primary Voices K–6, 2*(1), 2–6.

Alvermann, D.E., & Moore, D.W. (1991). Secondary school reading. In P.D. Pearson, R.Barr, M.L. Kamil, & P. Mosenthal (Eds.), *Handbook of reading research* (Vol. 2). New York: Longman.

Anderson, R. A., & Pearson, P. D. (1984). A schema-theoretic view of basis processes in reading comprehension. In P. D. Pearson (Ed.), *Handbook of reading research* (pp. 255–292). New York: Longman.

Anderson, R. C., Hiebert, E. H., Scott, J. A., & Wilkinson, I. A. G. (1985). *Becoming a nation of readers. The report of the Commission on Reading.* Urbana: University of Illinois, Center for the Study of Reading.

Armbruster, B. B., Anderson, T. H., Armstrong, J. O., Wise, M. A., Janisch, C., & Meyer, L. A. (1991). Reading and questioning in content area lessons. *Journal of Reading Behavior, 23,* 35–59.

Aronson, E. (1978). *The jigsaw classroom.* Beverly Hills, CA: Sage.

Atwell, N. (1987). *In the middle.* Portsmouth, NH: Heinemann.

Atwell, N. (1990). *Coming to know: Writing to learn in the intermediate grades.* Portsmouth, NH: Heinemann.

Baghban, M. J. M. (1984). *Our daughter learns to read and write: A case study from birth to three.* Newark, DE: International Reading Association.

Baskwill, J., & Whitman, P. (1988). *Evaluation: Whole language, whole child.* Toronto: Scholastic Tab.

Beers, C., & Beers, J. (1981). Three assumptions about learning to spell. *Language Arts, 58,* 573–580.

Beesley, S. (1994). *The social studies connection.* Paper presented at the conference of the International Institute of Literacy Learning, Memphis, TN.

Bettelheim, B., & Zelan, K. (1982). *On learning to read.* New York: Knopf.

Bird, L. B. (1989). The art of teaching: Evaluation and revision. In K. S. Goodman, Y. M. Goodman, & W. J. Hood (Eds.), *The whole language evaluation book.* Portsmouth, NH: Heinemann.

Bissex, G. L. (1980). *GNYS AT WRK: A child learns to write and read.* Cambridge, MA: Harvard University Press.

Bissex, G. L. (1981). Growing writers in classrooms. *Language Arts, 58,* 785–791.

Bissex, G. L. (1982, November). Writing conferences: Alternative to the red pencil. *Learning,* pp. 74–77.

Bissex, G. L. (1985). Watching young writers. In A. Jaggar & M. Smith-Burke (Eds.), *Observing the language learner.* Urbana, IL: National Council of Teachers of English.

Bloomfield, L. (1933). *Language.* New York: Holt, Rinehart and Winston.

Bond, G. L., & Dykstra, R. (1967). The cooperative research program in first-grade reading instruction. *Reading Research Quarterly, 2,* 10–41.

Boomer, G. (1984). Literacy, power, and the community. *Language Arts, 61,* 575–584.

Bortnick, R., & Lopardo, G. S. (1976). The cloze procedure: A multi-purpose classroom tool. *Reading Improvement, 13,* 113–117.

Bracken, D. K. (1972). The teacher's function in developing listening skills. In H. A. Klein (Ed.), *Quest for competency in teaching reading.* Newark, DE: International Reading Association.

Brandt, R. (1988). On assessment in the arts: A conversation with Howard Gardner. *Educational Leadership, 45*(4), 30–34.

Bransford, J. D., & McCarrell, N. S. (1974). A sketch of a cognitive approach to comprehension: Some thoughts about understanding what it means to comprehend. In W.B. Wiemer & D.S. Palermo (Eds.), *Cognition and the symbolic processes.* Hillsdale, NJ: Erlbaum.

Bridge, C. (1979). Predictable materials for beginning readers. *Language Arts, 56,* 503–507.

Bridge, C. (1986). Predictable books for beginning readers and writers. In M. Sampson (Ed.), *The pursuit of literacy: Early reading and writing.* Dubuque, IA: Kendall/Hunt.

Britton, J. N., Burgess, T., Martin, N., McLeod, A., & Rosen, H. (1975). *The development of writing abilities (11–18).* London: Macmillan Education Ltd.

Brown, D. L., & Santos, S. L. (1986). Promoting literacy in the classroom: From theory to practice. In Rudy Rodriguez (Ed.), *Teaching reading to minority language students* (pp. 1–6). Rosslyn, VA: National Clearinghouse for Bilingual Education.

Calfee, R. C., & Perfumo, P. (1993). Student portfolios: Opportunities for a revolution in assessment. *Journal of Reading, 36*(7), 532–537.

Calkins, L. M. (1979). Andrea learns to make writing hard. *Language Arts, 56,* 569–576.

Calkins, L. M. (1980). Children learn the writer's craft. *Language Arts, 57,* 207–213.

Calkins, L. M. (1981). When children want to punctuate: Basic skills belong in context. In R. D. Walshe (Ed.), *Children want to write. . . .* Rosebury NSW, Australia: Primary English Teaching Association.

Calkins, L. M. (1983). *Lessons from a child: On the teaching and learning of writing.* Portsmouth, NH: Heinemann.

Calkins, L. M. (1986). *The art of teaching writing.* Portsmouth, NH: Heinemann.

Calkins, L. M. (1991). *Living between the lines.* Portsmouth, NH: Heinemann.

Calkins, L.M., & Harwayne, S. (1987). *The writing workshop: A world of difference.* Portsmouth, NH: Heinemann.

Cambourne, B., & Turbill, J. (1988). *Coping with chaos.* Portsmouth, NH: Heinemann.

Canady, R. J. (1977). *Consistency of teachers' methods of teaching reading to specific learning theories.* Unpublished doctoral dissertation, University of Arizona, Tucson.

Cardenas, J. A. (1986). The role of the native language in bilingual education. *Phi Delta Kappan,* pp. 359–363.

Carlton, L., & Moore R. H. (1971). *Reading, self-directive dramatization and self-concept.* Columbus, OH: Merrill, 1971.

Chall, J., Jacobs, E., & Baldwin, L. (1990). *The reading crisis: Why poor children fall behind.* Cambridge, MA: Harvard University Press.

Chomsky, C. (1969). *The acquisition of syntax in children 5 to 10.* Cambridge, MA: MIT Press.

Chomsky, C. (1971). Write first, read later. *Childhood Education, 47,* 296–299.

Chomsky, C. (1980). Stages in language development and reading exposure: Thoughts and language. In M. Wolf, M. McQuillan, & E. Radwin (Eds.), *Harvard Educational Review, 14,* 201–229.

Chomsky, N. (1965). *Aspects of a theory of syntax.* Cambridge, MA: MIT Press.

Clark, R.P. (1989). *Free to write.* Portsmouth, NH: Heinemann.

Clay, M. (1975). *What did I write?* Auckland, New Zealand: Heinemann.

Clay, M.M. (1991). *Becoming literate: The construction of inner control.* Auckland, New Zealand: Heinemann Educational.

Clem, C., & Feathers, K. (1986). I lic spiders: What one child teaches us about constant learning. *Language Arts, 63,* 143–147.

Clemmons, J., Laase, L., Cooper, D., Areglado, N., & Dill, M. (1993). *Portfolios in the classroom: A teacher's sourcebook.* New York: Scholastic.

Costa, A. L. (1989). "Re-assessing assessment." *Educational Leadership, 46*(9), 35–57.

Cox, V. E. (1971). *Reciprocal oracy/literacy recognition skills in the language production of language experience approach students.* Unpublished doctoral dissertation, University of Arizona, Tucson.

Cramer, R. L. (1978). *Writing, reading, and language growth: An introduction to language arts.* Columbus, OH: Merrill.

Crapsey, A. (1914). *Verse.* Rochester, NY: Manas Press.

Cullinan, B. (1990). *Literature and the child.* San Diego: Harcourt Brace Jovanovich.

Cummins, J. (1981). Four misconceptions about language proficiency in bilingual education. *NABE Journal, 5,* 31–46.

Cunningham, P. M., Moore, S. A., Cunningham, J. W., & Moore, D. W. (1983). *Reading in elementary classrooms.* New York: Longman.

Dale, P. (1976). *Language development* (2nd ed.). New York: Houghton Mifflin.

Dalton, J., & Boyd, J. (1992). *I teach: A guide to inspiring classroom leadership.* Melbourne: Eleanor Curtain.

Daniels, H., & Zemelman, S. (1985). *A writing project: Training teachers of composition from kindergarten through college.* Portsmouth, NH: Heinemann.

Darigan, D. (1994). Multicultural literature. In M. Sampson & T. Thomason (Eds.), *Reading, writing, and literacy learning* (3rd ed.). Dallas, TX: International Institute of Literacy Learning.

Davey, B. (1983). Think aloud: Modeling the cognitive processes of reading comprehension. *Journal of Reading, 17*(1), 44–47.

DeFina, A. (1992). *Portfolio assessment: Getting started.* New York: Scholastic.

DeFord, D. E. (1981). Literacy: Reading, writing and other essentials. *Language Arts, 58,* 652–658.

DeFord, D. E. (1985). Validating the construct of theoretical orientation in reading instruction. *Reading Research Quarterly, 20,* 351–357.

DeFord, D.E. (1986). Children write to read and read to write. In D. Tovey & J. Kerber (Eds.), *Roles in literacy learning: A new perspective.* Newark, DE: International Reading Association.

Dewey, J., & Bentley, A. F. (1949). *Knowing and the known.* Boston: Beacon Press.

Doake, D. (1988). *Reading begins at birth.* Toronto: Scholastic Tab.

Dobbyns, L., & Crawford-Mason, C. (1991). *Quality or else.* New York: Houghton Mifflin.

Donaldson, M. (1978). *Children's minds.* Glasgow, Scotland: Fontana/Collins.

Douglass, M. (1986). Writing and reading across the curriculum. *Forty-ninth Yearbook, Claremont Reading Conference,* Claremont, CA: Claremont Graduate School Center for Developmental Studies.

Dudley-Marling, C. (1985). Microcomputers, reading, and writing: Alternatives to drill and practice. *The Reading Teacher, 38,* 388–391.

Durkin, D. (1972). *Phonics, linguistics and reading.* New York: Teachers College Press.

Durkin, D. (1978–1979). What classroom observations reveal about reading comprehension instruction. *Reading Research Quarterly, 14,* 481–533.

Durkin, D. (1981). What is the value of the new interest in reading comprehension? *Language Arts, 58,* 23–43.

Durkin, D. (1983). *Teaching them to read* (4th ed.). Boston: Allyn & Bacon.

Dyson, A. (1987). The value of "time-off task": Young children's spontaneous talk and deliberate text. *Harvard Educational Review, 57,* 396–420.

Eanet, M. (1978). An investigation of the REAP reading/study procedure: Its rationale and efficacy. In P. D. Pearson & J. Hanson (Eds.), *Reading: Discipline inquiry in process and practice.* Urbana, IL: National Council of Teachers of English.

Eanet, M. G., & Manzo, A. V. (1976). REAP—A strategy for improving reading/writing/study skills. *Journal of Reading, 19,* 647–652.

Eisner, E. (1990). "Winning race not a valid goal, ASCD Told." *ASCD Update, 32*(4), 1–3.

Englert, C., & Hiebert, E. (1983). Children's developing awareness of text structures in expository materials. *Journal of Educational Psychology, 76,* 65–74.

Erickson, F. (1989). Literacy risks for students, parents, and teachers. In J. B. Allen & J. M. Mason (Eds.), *Risk makers, risk takers, risk breakers: Reducing the risks for young literacy learners.* Portsmouth, NH: Heinemann.

Farnsworth, L. (1990). In the schema of things. In N. Atwell (Ed.), *Coming to know: Writing to learn in the intermediate grades.* Portsmouth, NH: Heinemann.

Farr, R., & Carey, R. F. (1986). *Reading: What can be measured?* (2nd ed.). Newark, DE: International Reading Association.

Farr, R., & Tone, B. (1994). *Portfolio and performance assessment: Helping students evaluate their progress as readers and writers.* Fort Worth, TX: Harcourt Brace.

Farris, P.J. (1993). *Language arts: A process approach.* Madison, WI: Brown & Benchmark.

Ferreiro, E., & Teberosky, A. (1982). *Literacy before schooling.* Portsmouth, NH: Heinemann.

Fisher, G. (1983). Lemonade for sale. *Electronic Learning, 2,* 78–82.

Flood, J., & Lapp, D. (1990). Types of writing included in basal reading programs, kindergarten through second grade: An investigation of changes from 1983 to 1989. In J. Zutell & S. McCormick (Eds.), *Theory and research: Analyses from multiple paradigms. Thirty-ninth yearbook of the National Reading Conference.* Chicago, IL: National Reading Conference.

Fox, S. E., & Allen, V. G. (1983). *The language arts: An integrated approach.* New York: Holt, Rinehart and Winston.

Fritz, J. (1981). The very truth. In B. Hearne & M. Kaye (Eds.), *Celebrating children's books.* New York: Lothrop, Lee & Shepard.

Fuhler, C. (1994). Response journals: Just one more time with feeling. *The Journal of Reading, 37,* 400–405.

Fulwiler, T. (1987). *The journal book.* Portsmouth, NH: Boynton/Cook.

Furth, H. G. (1970). *Piaget for teachers.* Englewood Cliffs, NJ: Prentice-Hall.

Galda, L., Cullinan, B.E., & Strickland, D.S. (1993). *Language, literacy and the child.* Fort Worth, TX: Harcourt Brace.

Gambrell, L. (1986). Reading in the primary grades: How often, how long? In M. Sampson (Ed.), *The pursuit of literacy: Early reading and writing.* Dubuque, IA: Kendall/Hunt.

Gardner, H. (1991). *The unschooled mind: How children think and how schools should teach.* New York: Basic Books.

Gentry, J.R. (1984). Developmental aspects of learning to spell. *Academic Therapy, 20*(1), 11–19.

Giacobbe, M.E. (1991). The politics of process. In N. Atwell (Ed.), *Workshop 3.* Portsmouth, NH: Heinemann.

Glasser, W. (1992). *The quality school: Managing students without coercion.* New York: HarperCollins.

Gollnick, D.M., & Chinn, P.C. (1990). *Multicultural education in a pluralistic society.* New York: Merrill.

Goodlad, J. (1984). *A place called school.* New York: McGraw-Hill.

Goodlad, J. I. (1983). A study of schooling: Some findings and hypotheses. *Phi Delta Kappan,* pp. 465–470.

Goodman, K. S. (1976). *What's universal about the reading process.* Paper presented at the First Japan International Reading Conference, Tokyo.

Goodman, K. S. (1985). Reading: A psycholinguistic guessing game. In M. R. Sampson, J. H. White, K. M. Feathers, & I. L. Rorie (Eds.), *Literacy and language instruction* (pp. 14–22). Lexington, MA: Ginn Press.

Goodman, K. S., & Goodman, Y. A. (1978). *Reading of American children whose language is a stable rural dialect of English or a language other than English.* Final Report, Project NIE-C-00-3-0087. Washington, DC: HEW, National Institute of Education.

Goodman, K. S., Goodman, Y. S., & Hood, W. J. (1989). *The whole language evaluation book.* Portsmouth, NH: Heinemann.

Goodman, K. S., Smith, E. B., Meredith, R., & Goodman, Y. (1988). *Language and thinking in school: A whole language curriculum.* Katonah, NY: Richard C. Owen.

Goodman, Y. (1980). The roots of literacy. In M. P. Douglass (Ed.), *Forty-fourth yearbook, Claremont Reading Conference,* Claremont, CA: Claremont Graduate School.

Goodman, Y. (1985). Kidwatching: Observing children in the classroom. In A. Jaggar & M. T. Smith-Burke (Eds.), *Observing the language learner.* Newark, DE: International Reading Association.

Goodman, Y., & Burke, C. L. (1980). *Reading strategies: Focus on comprehension.* New York: Holt, Rinehart and Winston.

Goodman, Y. A., & Burke, C. L. (1972). *Reading miscue inventory: Procedure for diagnosis and evaluation.* New York: Macmillan.

Goodman, Y. M. (1989). Evaluation of students: Evaluation of teachers. In K. S. Goodman, Y. M. Goodman, & W. J. Hood (Eds.), *The whole language evaluation book.* Portsmouth, NH: Heinemann.

Gordon, C. J., & Pearson, P. D. (1983). *The effects of instruction in metacomprehension and inferencing in children's comprehension abilities* (Tech. Rep. No. 277). Urbana, IL: University of Illinois, Center for the Study of Reading.

Graves, D. (1978). *Balance the basics: Let them write.* New York: Ford Foundation.

Graves, D., & Sunstein, B. (Eds.). (1992). *Portfolio portraits.* Portsmouth, NH: Heinemann.

Graves, D. H. (1975). An examination of the writing processes of seven-year-old children. *Research in the Teaching of English, 9,* 227–241. Urbana, IL: National Council of Teachers of English.

Graves, D. H. (1979). What children show us about revision. *Language Arts, 56,* 312–319.

Graves, D. H. (1981). Patterns of child control of the writing process. In R. D. Walshe (Ed.), *Donald Graves in Australia "Children want to write . . ."* Portsmouth, NH: Heinemann.

Graves, D. H. (1983). *Writing: Teachers and children at work.* Portsmouth, NH: Heinemann.

Graves, D. H. (1986). *The Mast Way Project.* Paper presented during the New Hampshire Writing Project seminar, Durham, NH.

Graves, D. H. (1989a). *Experiment with fiction.* Portsmouth, NH: Heinemann.

Graves, D. H. (1989b). *Experiment with nonfiction.* Portsmouth, NH: Heinemann.

Graves, D. H., & Hansen, J. (1983). The author's chair. *Language Arts, 60,* 176–183.

Graves, D. H., & Stuart, V. (1985). *Write from the start: Tapping your child's natural writing ability.* New York: New American Library.

Griffiths, R., & Clyne, M. (1993). Real books and real mathematics. In M. Stephens, A. Waywood, D. Clarke, & J. Izard (Eds.), *Communicating mathematics: Perspectives from classroom practice and current research.* Melbourne: Australian Council for Educational Research.

Hall, S. E. (1985). OAD mahr gos one writing with young children. *Language Arts, 62,* 262–265.

Hall, S. E., & Hall, C. (1984). It takes a lot of letters to spell ERZ. *Language Arts, 61,* 822–827.

Halliday, M. A. K. (1973). *Explorations in the functions of language.* London: Edward Arnold.

Halliday, M. A. K. (1980). *Text and context: Aspects of language in social–semiotic perspective.* Sophia Linguistica VI. Tokyo: Sophia University Press.

Hansen, J. (1987). *When writers read.* Portsmouth, NH: Heinemann.

Hansen, J. (1989). Anna evaluates herself. In J. B. Allen & J. M. Mason (Eds.), *Risk makers, risk takers, risk breakers: Reducing the risks for young literacy learners.* Portsmouth, NH: Heinemann.

Hansen, J. (1992). Literacy portfolios emerge. *The Reading Teacher, 45* (8), 604–707.

Hansen, J., Newkirk T., & Graves, D. (1985). *Breaking ground: Teachers relate reading and writing in the elementary school.* Portsmouth, NH: Heinemann.

Harp, B. (Ed.). (1991). *Assessment and evaluation in whole language programs.* Norwood, MA: Christopher Gordon.

Harste, J. (1993). Inquiry-based instruction. *Primary Voices K–6.* Premier issue, pp. 2–5.

Harste, J., Short, K., & Burke, C. (1988). *Creating classrooms for authors.* Portsmouth, NH: Heinemann.

Harste, J. C., Burke, C. L., & Woodward, V. A. (1982). Children's language and world: Initial encounters with print. In J. A. Langer & M. T. Smith-Burke (Eds.), *Reader meets author: Bridging the gap* (pp. 105–131). Newark, DE: International Reading Association.

Harste, J. C., Burke, C. L., & Woodward, V. A. (1983). *The young child as writer-reader, and informant.* Final Report, NIE Grant 80-0121. Bloomington: Indiana University Press.

Harste, J. C., & Carey, R. F. (1979). Comprehension as setting. In J. C. Harste & R. F. Carey (Eds.), *Monograph in language and reading studies: New perspectives on comprehension* (pp. 4–22). Bloomington: Indiana University School of Education.

Harste, J. C., Woodward, V. A., & Burke, C. L. (1984a). Examining our assumptions: A transactional view of literacy and learning. *Research in the Teaching of English, 18,* 84–108. Urbana, IL: National Council of Teachers of English.

Harste, J. C., Woodward, V. A., & Burke, C. L. (1984b). *Language stories and literacy lessons.* Portsmouth, NH: Heinemann.

Head, M.H., & Readence, J. E. (1986). Anticipation guides: Meaning through prediction. In E. K. Dishner, T. W. Bean, J. E. Readence, & D. W. Moore (Eds.), *Reading in the content areas* (2nd ed.) (pp. 229–234). Dubuque, IA: Kendall/Hunt.

Heald-Taylor, G. (1989). *The administrator's guide to whole language.* Katonah, NY: Richard C. Owen.

Heath, S. B. (1983a). *Ways with words: Ethnography of communication, communities, and classrooms.* Cambridge, England: Cambridge University Press.

Heath, S. B. (1983b). *Ways with words: Language, life and work in communities and classrooms.* Cambridge, England: Cambridge University Press.

Heilman, A. W., Blair, T. R., & Rupley, W. H. (1990). *Principles and practices of teaching reading* (7th ed.). Columbus, OH: Merrill.

Heimlich, J. E., & Pittelman, S. D. (1986). *Semantic mapping: Classroom applications.* Newark, DE: International Reading Association.

Henderson, E.H. (1985). *Teaching spelling*. Boston: Houghton Mifflin.

Henderson, E. H. (1986). Understanding children's knowledge of written language. In D. B. Yaden, Jr., & S. Templeton (Eds.), *Metalinguistic awareness and beginning literacy: Conceptualizing what it means to read and write* (pp. 65–77). Portsmouth, NH: Heinemann.

Henderson, E. H., & Beers, J. W. (1980). *Development and cognitive aspects of learning to spell: A reflection of word knowledge*. Newark, DE: International Reading Association.

Hiebert, E. H., Valencia, S. W., & Afflerbach, P. P. (1994). Definitions and perspectives. In S. W. Valencia, E. H. Hiebert, & P. P. Afflerbach (Eds.), *Authentic reading assessment: Practices and possibilities* (pp. 6–21). Newark, DE: Internationaal Reading Association.

Hittleman, D. R. (1988). *Developmental reading, K–8: Teaching from a whole-language perspective* (3rd ed.). Columbus, OH: Merrill.

Holdaway, D. (1979). *The foundations of literacy*. Portsmouth, NH: Heinemann.

Holdaway, D. (1986). The structure of natural learning as a basis for literacy instruction. In M. R. Sampson (Ed.), *The pursuit of literacy*. Dubuque, IA: Kendall/Hunt.

Hollis, J., & Gallegos, E. (1993). Inclusion: What is the extent of a school district's duty to accommodate students with disabilities in the regular classroom? *Texas School Administrator's Legal Digest, 9*(9), 1–8.

Horowitz, R. (1985). Text patterns: Part 2. *Journal of Reading, 28*, 534–541.

Hotchkiss, P. (1990). Cooperative learning models: Improving student achievement using small groups. In M. A. Gunter, T. H. Estes, & J. H. Schwab (Eds.), *Instruction: A models approach* (pp. 167–184). Boston: Allyn & Bacon.

Hubbard, R. (1985). Drawing parallels: Real writing, real reading. In J. Hansen, T. Newkirk, & D. Graves (Eds.), *Breaking ground: Teachers relate reading and writing in the elementary school*. Portsmouth, NH: Heinemann.

Huck, C. (1993). *Children's literature in the elementary school* (5th ed.). Fort Worth, TX: Harcourt Brace Jovanovich.

Idol-Maestas, L., & Croll, V.J. (1985). *The effects of training in story mapping procedures on the reading comprehension of poor readers* (Tech. Rep. No. 352). Urbana: University of Illinois, Center for the Study of Reading.

Jaggar, A., & Smith-Burke, T. (Ed.). (1985). *Observing the language learner*. Newark, DE: International Reading Association.

Johnson, D. W., Johnson, R. T., & Bartlett, J. K. (1990). *Cooperative learning lesson structures*. Edina, MN: Interaction.

Johnson, D.W., Johnson, R.T., & Holubec, E.J. (1993). *Circles of learning: Cooperation in the classroom*. Edina, MN: Interaction.

Johnston, P. (1992). *Constructive evaluation of literate activity*. White Plains, NY: Longman.

Kagan, S. (1990). *Cooperative learning resources for teachers.* San Juan Capistrano, CA: Resources for Teachers.

Kamil, C., & Randazzo, M. (1985). Social interacting and invented spelling. *Language Arts, 62,* 124–133.

Kamler, B. (1984). Ponch writes again: A child at play. *Australian Journal of Reading, 7,* 61–70.

Kasten, W. (1989). *Celebrating the writing of children.* Paper presented at the International Institute of Literacy Learning Conference, Boston, MA.

Kasten, W. (1993). The meaning-centered classroom. In M. Sampson & T. Thomason (Eds.), *Reading, writing and literacy learning* (2nd ed.). Dallas, TX: International Institute of Literacy Learning.

Kasten, W. (1994). Literature circles for the teaching of literature-based reading. In L.G. McKay (Ed.), *Flexible grouping in the elementary grades.* Boston: Allyn & Bacon.

Kasten, W.C., & Clark, B.K. (1993). *The multi-age classroom: A family of learners.* Katonah, NY: Richard C. Owen.

Krashen, S. D. (1982). *Principles and practice in second language acquisition.* New York: Pergamon.

Krashen, S. D., & Terrell, T. D. (1983). *The natural approach: Language acquisition in the classroom.* New York: Pergamon/Alemany.

Labov, W. (1982). *The study of nonstandard English.* Urbana, IL: National Council of Teachers of English.

Larrick, N. (1991). *Let's do a poem: Introducing children to poetry.* New York: Delacorte Press.

Lee, D. M., & Allen, R. V. (1963). *Learning to read through experience.* New York: Appleton-Century-Crofts.

Lee, P. H. (1965). *Korean literature: Topics and themes.* Tucson: University of Arizona Press.

Lefevre, C. A. (1970). *Linguistics, English, and the language arts.* Boston: Allyn & Bacon.

Levstik, L. S. (1989). Coming to terms with history: Historical narrativity and the young reader. *Theory into Practice, 29,* 114-119.

Lindfors, J. W. (1987). *Children's language and learning* (2nd ed.). Englewood Cliffs, NJ: Prentice Hall.

Lindgren, H. C. (1986). *Educational psychology in the classroom.* New York: John Wales & Sons.

Lundsteen, S.W. (1976). *Language arts: A problem-solving approach.* New York: Harper & Row.

Lundsteen, S. W. (1989). *Language arts: A problem-solving approach.* New York: Harper & Row.

Lundsteen, S.W. (1990). Learning to listen and learning to read. In S. Hynds & D.L. Rubin (Eds.), *Perspectives on talk and learning.* Urbana, IL: National Council of Teachers of English.

Manzo, A. V. (1969). The ReQuest procedure. *Journal of Reading, 13,* 123–126.

Martin, B. (1990). *Reading for pleasure, reading for life.* Paper presented at the annual conference of the International Reading Association, Atlanta, GA.

Martin, B., & Sampson, M.R. (1994). *Touching tomorrow with language.* Paper presented at the annual conference of the International Reading Association. Toronto, Canada.

Marzano, R. J., & A. L. Costa. (1988). Question: Do standardized tests measure general cognitive skills? Answer: No. *Educational Leadership 45*(8), 66–71.

May, F. B. (1994). *Reading as communication.* Columbus, OH: Merrill.

McCombs, B.L. (1991). Motivation and lifelong learning. *Educational Psychologist, 26*(2), 117–128.

McDanial, T. R. (1984). A primer on motivation: Principles old and new. *Phi Delta Kappan, 66*(2), 119–121.

McGee, L. E., & Richgels, D. J. (1990). *Literacy's beginnings: Supporting young readers and writers.* Boston: Allyn & Bacon.

McInnes, J. (1986). Children's quest for literacy. In Tovey & Kerber (Eds.), *Roles in literacy learning: A new perspective.* Newark, DE: International Reading Association.

Messick, S. (1989). *Validity in educational measurement.* (Linn, R. Ed.)

Meyer, B. J. F. (1975). *The organization of prose and its effects on memory.* Amsterdam: North-Holland.

Moffett, J. (1981). *Active voice.* Portsmouth, NH: Heinemann.

Moffett, J., & Wagner, B. J. (1983). *Student-centered language arts and reading, K–13: A handbook for teachers* (3rd ed.). Boston: Houghton Mifflin.

Monson, D. L. (1985). *Adventuring with books: A booklist for pre-K–grade 6.* Urbana, IL: National Council of Teachers of English.

Moore, D., Readerve, J., & Rickelman R. (1982). *Prereading activities for content area reading and learning.* Newark, DE: International Reading Association.

Morrow, L. M. (1992). *Literacy development in the early years: Helping children read and write* (2nd ed.). Boston: Allyn & Bacon.

Morrow, L. M., & Smith, J. K. (1990). *Assessment for instruction in early literacy.* Englewood Cliffs, NJ: Prentice Hall.

Murphy, S., & Smith, M.A. (1991). *Writing portfolios: A bridge from teaching to assessment.* Markham, Ontario: Pippin.

Murray, D. (1982). Write research to be read. *Language Arts, 59,* 760–768.

Murray, D. (1984). *Write to learn.* New York: Holt, Rinehart and Winston.

Murray, D. (1989). *Expecting the unexpected.* Portsmouth, NH: Heinemann.

Murray, D. (1990). *Read to write.* Fort Worth, TX: Harcourt Brace Jovanovich.

Nason, J. (1983). *An investigation of the transition from oral language to written language of selected elementary students.* Unpublished doctoral dissertation, East Texas State University, Commerce, TX.

Newman, J. (1984). *The craft of children's writing.* New York: Scholastic.

Newman, J. (1985). *Whole language: Theory into use.* Portsmouth, NH: Heinemann.

Newman, J. (1990). *Finding their own way: Teachers exploring their assumptions.* Portsmouth, NH: Heinemann.

Ogle, D.M. (1989). The know, want to know, learn strategy. In K. D. Muth (Ed.), *Children's comprehension of text* (pp. 205–223). Newark, DE: International Reading Association.

Page, W. D., & Pinnell, G. S. (1979). *Teaching reading comprehension.* Urbana, IL: National Council of Teachers of English.

Palinscar, A. S., & Brown, A. (1986). Interactive teaching to promote independent learning from text. *The Reading Teacher, 39,* 771–777.

Paterson, K. (1994). Cultural politics from a writer's point of view. *The New Advocate, 7,* 85–91.

Pearson, P. D. (1985). Changing the face of reading comprehension instruction. *The Reading Teacher, 38,* 724–738.

Pearson, P. D., & Johnson, D. D. (1985). *Teaching reading comprehension.* New York: Holt, Rinehart and Winston.

Pearson, P. D., & Johnson, D. D. (in press). *Teaching reading comprehension.* Fort Worth, TX: Holt, Rinehart and Winston.

Petre, R. M. (1969). *Quantity, quality and variety of pupil responses during an open-communication structured group Directed Reading–Thinking Activity and a closed-communication structured group Directed Reading–Thinking Activity.* Unpublished doctoral dissertation, University of Delaware.

Pflaum, S. W. (1986). *The development of language and literacy in young children* (3rd ed.). Columbus, OH: Merrill.

Phinney, M. (1989). *Reading with the troubled reader.* Portsmouth, NH: Heinemann.

Piaget, J. (1959). *The language and thought of the child* (rev. ed.). New York: Humanities Press.

Piccolo, J. (1987). Expository text structure: Teaching and learning strategies. *The Reading Teacher, 40,* 838–847.

Pils, L. J. (1991). Soon anofe you tout me: Evaluation in a first-grade whole language classroom. *The Reading Teacher, 45,* 46–50.

Raine, I. L. (1994). *Spelling is a developmental process.* Paper presented at the Center for Professional Development and Technology Conference, Commerce, TX.

Rankin, E. F. (1977). Sequence strategies for teaching reading comprehension with the cloze procedure. In P. D. Pearson & J. Hanson (Eds.), *Reading theory, research, and practice. Twenty-sixth yearbook of the National Reading Conference.* Washington, DC: National Reading Conference.

Ratekin, N., Simpson, M., Alvermann, D., & Dishner, E. (1985). Why teachers resist content reading instruction. *Journal of Reading, 28,* 432–437.

Read, C. (1980). What children know about language: Three examples. *Language Arts, 57,* 144–148.

Rhodes, L. K. (1979, May). *Visible language acquisition: A case study.* Paper presented at Twenty-fourth Annual Reading Association Convention, Atlanta, GA.

Rhodes, L. K. (1981). I can read! Predictable books as resources for reading and writing instruction. *Reading Teacher, 34,* 511–518. Newark, DE: International Reading Association.

Rief, L. (1990). Finding the value in evaluation; Self-assessment in a middle school classroom. *Educational Leadership, 47,* 24–29.

Rosenblatt, L. M. (1978). *The reader, the text, the poem.* Carbondale, IL: Southern Illinois University.

Rosenblatt, L. M. (1983). The reading transaction: What for? In R. P. Parker & F. A. Davis (Eds.), *Developing literacy: Young children's use of language* (pp. 118–136). Newark, DE: International Reading Association.

Rosenblatt, M. (1993). *Reading as transaction.* Paper presented at the Federation of Northeast Texas Universities, Denton, TX.

Roser, N., & Frith, M. (1983). *Children's choices: Teaching with books children like.* Newark, DE: International Reading Association.

Routman, R. (1988). *Transitions.* Portsmouth, NH: Heinemann.

Rumelhart, D. E. (1980). Schemata: The building blocks of cognition. In R. Spiro, B. Bruce, & W. Brewer (Eds.), *Theoretical issues in reading comprehension.* Hillsdale, NJ: Erlbaum.

Rumelhart, D. E. (1984). Understanding understanding. In J. Flood (Ed.), *Understanding reading comprehension* (pp. 1–20). Newark, DE: International Reading Association.

Sampson, M. B., Sampson, M. R., & Linek, W. (1994). Circle of questions: Engaging students in interaction with text. *Reading Teacher, 47,* 543–545.

Sampson, M. R. (Ed.). (1986). *The pursuit of literacy: Early reading and writing.* Dubuque, IA: Kendall/Hunt.

Sampson, M. R. (1982). A comparison of the complexity of children's dictation and instructional reading materials. In J. A. Niles & L. A. Harris (Eds.), *New inquiries in reading research and instruction. Thirty-first yearbook of the National Reading Conference* (pp. 177–179). Washington, DC: National Reading Conference.

Sampson, M. R., Allen, R. V., & Sampson, M. B. (1991). *Pathways to literacy: A meaning-centered perspective.* Fort Worth, TX : Holt, Rinehart and Winston.

Sampson, M. R., & Briggs, L. D. (1983). A new technique for cloze scoring: A semantically consistent method. *Clearing House, 57,* 177–179.

Sampson, M. R., Briggs, L. D., & Coker, D. R. (1984). Assessing the listening comprehension of children. *Reading Improvement, 21,* 59–63.

Sampson, M. R., Briggs, L. D., & Sampson, M. B. (1986). Language, children and text: Match or mismatch? In M. Sampson (Ed.), *The pursuit of literacy: Early reading and writing.* Dubuque, IA: Kendall/Hunt.

Sampson, M. R., & Sampson, M. B. (1980). Components of a language experience approach: Catalyst for change. *Journal of the National School Development Council, 9,* 10–14.

Sampson, M. R., & White, J. A. (1983). *The effect of student-authored, patterned language, and basal reader materials on the performance of beginning readers.* Final Report. Grant # 1501-9309. Commerce, TX: Graduate School, East Texas State University.

Sampson, M. R., Valmont, W. J., & Allen, R. V. (1982). The effects of instructional cloze on the comprehension, vocabulary, and divergent production of third-grade students. *Reading Research Quarterly, 17,* 389–399.

Schickedanz, J., & Sullivan, M. (1984). Mom, what does U-F-F- spell? *Language Arts, 61,* 7–17.

Seaborg, M.B. (1994). The parent connection. In M. Sampson & T. Thomason (Eds.), *Reading, writing and literacy learning.* Commerce, TX: International Institute of Literacy Learning.

Searfoss, L. W., & Readence, J. E. (1985). *Helping children learn to read.* Englewood Cliffs, NJ: Prentice-Hall.

Sharan, D., & Hertz-Lazarowitz, R. (1980). A group investigation method of cooperative learning in the classroom. In D. Sharan, P. Hare, C. D. Webb, & R. Hertz-Lazarowitz (Eds.), *Cooperation in education* (pp. 14–46). Provo, UT: Brigham Young University Press.

Sharan, Y., & Sharan, S. (1990). Group investigation expands cooperative learning. *Educational Leadership, 47*(4), 17–21.

Sherk, J. K. (1973). *A word count of spoken English of culturally disadvantaged preschool and elementary pupils.* Kansas City, MO: College of Education, University of Missouri at Kansas City.

Short, E., & Ryan, E. (1984). Metacognitive differences between skilled and less skilled readers: Remediating deficits through story grammar and attributional training. *Journal of Educational Psychology, 76,* 225–235.

Singer, H., & Donlan, D. (1983). Active comprehension: Problem-solving schema with question generation for comprehension of complex short stories. *Reading Research Quarterly, 17,* 166–185.

Skinner, B. F. (1957). *Verbal behavior.* Boston: Appleton-Century-Crofts.

Slater, W. (1985). Teaching expository text structure with structural organizers. *Journal of Reading, 28,* 712–718.

Slavin, M. L. (1983). *Cooperative learning.* White Plains, NY: Longman.

Slavin, R. E. (1987). Cooperative learning and the cooperative school. *Educational Leadership, 45,* 7–13.

Smith, E. B., Goodman, K. S., & Meredith, R. (1976). *Language and thinking in school* (2nd ed.). New York: Holt, Rinehart and Winston.

Smith, E. B., Goodman, K. S., & Meredith, R. (1987). *Language and thinking in school* (3rd ed.). New York: Holt, Rinehart and Winston.

Smith, F. (1973). *Psycholinguistics and reading.* New York: Holt, Rinehart and Winston.

Smith, F. (1982). *Writing and the writer.* New York: Holt, Rinehart and Winston.

Smith, F. (1983). *Essays into literacy.* Portsmouth, NH: Heinemann.

Smith, F. (1985). Demonstrations, engagements, and sensitivity: A revised approach to language learning. In M. R. Sampson, J. H. White, K. M. Feathers, & I. L. Rorie (Eds.), *Literacy and language instruction.* Lexington, MA: Ginn Press.

Smith, F. (1993). *Whose language? What power?* New York: Teachers College Press.

Spencer, P. L. (1957). Reading is creative living. In *Twenty-second Yearbook, Claremont College Reading Conference.* Claremont, CA: Claremont College Press.

Spencer, P. L. (1970). *Reading reading.* Claremont, CA: Claremont College Press.

Stauffer, R. G. (1969). *Directing reading maturity as a cognitive process.* New York: Harper & Row.

Stauffer, R. G. (1976). *Teaching reading as a thinking process.* New York: Harper & Row.

Stauffer, R. G. (1980). *The language-experience approach to the teaching of reading* (2nd ed.). New York: Harper & Row.

Stetson, E., Seda, M., & Newman, C. (1988). *Spelling instruction: What research supports as effective.* Paper presented at the 78th Annual Conference of the National Council of Teachers of English, Boston, MA.

Stewart, R.A., & O'Brien, D.G. (1989). Resistance to content-area reading: A focus on preservice teachers. *Journal of Reading, 32,* 396–401.

Sulzby, E., Teale, W.H., & Kamberelis, G. (1989). Emergent writing in the classroom: Home and school connections. In D. S. Strickland & L. M. Morrow (Eds.), *Emergent literacy: Young children learn to read and write.* Newark, DE: International Reading Association.

Taylor, D. (1983). *Family literacy: Young children learning to read and write.* Portsmouth, NH: Heinemann.

Taylor, D. (1986). *Family literacy.* Portsmouth, NH: Heinemann.

Taylor, W. L. (1953). Cloze procedure: A new tool for measuring readability. *Journalism Quarterly, 30,* 415–433.

Teale, W. H. (1982). Toward a theory of how children learn to read and write naturally. *Language Arts, 59,* 555–570. Urbana, IL: National Council of Teachers of English.

Teale, W. H. (1986a). The beginnings of reading and writing: Written language development during the preschool and kindergarten years. In M. Sampson (Ed.), *The pursuit of literacy.* Dubuque, IA: Kendall/Hunt.

Teale, W. H. (1986b). Home background and young children's literacy development. In W. H. Teale and E. Sulzby (Eds.), *Emergent literacy: Writing and reading.* Norwood, NJ: Ablex.

Temple, C. A., Nathan, R. G., & Burris, N. A. (1982). *The beginnings of writing.* Boston: Allyn & Bacon.

Texas Education Agency. (1989). *TEAMS instructional strategies guide.* Austin, TX: Texas Education Agency.

Thomason, T. (1990). *Editing vs. coaching: A whole language approach to the teaching of writing.* Paper presented at the conference of the International Institute of Literacy Learning, Los Angeles.

Thomason, T. (1993). *More than a writing teacher.* Texas: Bridge Press.

Thomason T. (1994). *The writing conference.* Paper presented at the conference of the International Institute of Literacy Learning, Boston, MA.

Tierney, R., Carter, M., & Desai, L. (1991). *Portfolio assessment in the reading-writing classroom.* Norwood, MA: Christopher-Gordon.

Tierney, R. J., Readence, J. E., & Dishner, E. R. (1990). *Reading strategies and practices: A compendium.* Boston, MA: Allyn & Bacon.

Toffler, A. (1980). *The third wave.* New York: Bantam.

Trelease, J. (1989). *The new read-aloud handbook* (3rd ed.). New York: Penguin Books.

Tuinman, J. J. (1979). Reading is recognition—When reading is not reasoning. In J. C. Harste & R. F. Carey (Eds.), *New perspectives on comprehension* (pp. 38–48). Bloomington: Indiana University School of Education.

Tyson, H., & Woodward, A. (1989). Why students aren't learning very much from textbooks. *Educational Leadership, 47,* 14–17.

Unia, S. (1985). From sunny days to green onions: On journal writing. In J. Newman (Ed.), *Whole language: Theory in use.* Portsmouth, NH: Heinemann.

Vacca, R.T., & Vacca, J.A. (1993). *Content area reading* (4th ed.). New York: HarperCollins.

Valencia, S. (1990). A portfolio approach to classroom reading assessment: The why, whats, and hows. *Reading Teacher, 43,* 338–340.

Valencia, S., McGinley, W., & Pearson, P.D. (1990). Assessing reading and writing. In G. Duffy (Ed.), *Reading in the middle school* (2nd ed.) (pp. 124–153). Newark, DE: International Reading Association.

Valencia, S., & Pearson, P. D. (1987). Reading assessment: Time for a change. *The Reading Teacher, 40,* 726–732.

Valencia, S.W., Hiebert, E. H., & Afflerbach, P. P. (Eds.). (1994). *Authentic reading assessment: Practices and possibilities.* Newark, DE: International Reading Association.

Van Metre, P. (1972). *Syntactic characteristics of selected bilingual children.* Unpublished doctoral dissertation, University of Arizona, Tucson.

Vaughan, J., & Estes, T. (1986). *Reading and reasoning beyond the primary grades.* Newton, MA: Allyn & Bacon.

Vaughan, J. L. (1981). *A self-monitoring approach to reading and thinking.* Paper presented at the 71st Annual Convention of the National Council of Teachers of English, Boston, MA.

Vaughan, J. L. (1982). Instructional strategies and adolescents' reading: Research revelations. In A. Berger & H. A. Robinson (Eds.), *Secondary school reading: What research reveals for classroom practice.* Urbana, IL: National Council of Teachers of English.

Vygotsky, L. S. (1962). *Thought and language.* Cambridge, MA: The MIT Press.

Vygotsky, L. S. (1978). *Mind in society.* Cambridge, MA: Harvard University Press.

Ward, G. (1988). *I've got a project on!* Australia: PETA. Distributed in the United States by Heinemann Educational Books, Portsmouth, NH.

Ward, G. (1993). Will the real shared book experience please stand up? In M. Sampson & T. Thomason (Eds.), *Reading, writing, and literacy learning* (2nd ed.). Dallas, TX: International Institute of Literacy Learning.

Wardhaugh, R. (1971). Theories of language acquisition in relation to beginning reading instruction. In F. B. Davis (Ed.), *The literature of research in reading, with emphasis on models.* New Brunswick, NJ: Graduate School of Education, Rutgers University.

Watson, D. (1989). *Whole language: Inquiring voices.* New York: Scholastic.

Weber, R. M. (1970). First graders' use of grammatical context in reading. In H. Levin & J. P. Williams (Eds.), *Basic studies in reading.* New York: Basic Books.

Wells, G. (1986). *The meaning makers.* Portsmouth, NH: Heinemann.

Wickwire, M. (1990). Why teachers must be writers. In J. Newman (Ed.), *Finding our own way: Teachers exploring their assumptions.* Portsmouth, NH: Heinemann.

Wiggins, G. (1993). Assessment: Authenticity, context, and validity. *Phi Delta Kappan, 75*(3), 200–214.

Wilkinson, A. M. (1971). *The foundations of language.* London: Oxford University Press.

Wolf, D. Bixby, J., Glenn, J., III, & Gardner, H. (1991). To use their minds well: Investigating new forms of student assessment. In G. Grant (Ed.), *Review of research in education* (Vol. 17). Washington, DC: American Educational Research Association.

Wuertenberg, J. (1986). *Conferencing with young authors.* Paper presented at the Annual Bill Martin Jr Literacy Conference, East Texas State University, Commerce, TX.

Wuertenberg, J. (1990). *Writing is for celebration.* Paper presented at meeting of the International Institute of Literacy Learning, Seattle, WA.

Wurman, R.S. (1990). *Information anxiety.* London: Pan Books.

Yaden, D. (1983). *Children's developing concept of story.* Paper presented at the National Reading Conference, Dallas, TX.

Yellin, D., & Blake, M. E. (1994). *Integrating language arts: A holistic approach.* New York: HarperCollins.

Zaharias, J. A. (1983). Microcomputers in the language arts classroom: Promises and pitfalls. *Language Arts, 60,* 990–995.

CHILDREN'S BOOKS REFERENCED

Ackerman, K. (1990). *The tin heart.* New York: Atheneum.

Ahlberg, J., & Allan, A. (1978). *Each peach pear plum.* New York: Viking.

Alexander, L. (1991). *The remarkable journey of Prince Jen.* New York: Dutton.

Alexander, L. (1992). *The fortune-tellers.* Illustrated by Trina Schart Hyman. New York: Dutton.

Aliki. (1986). *How a book is made.* New York: Harper & Row.

Allard, H. (1977). *Miss Nelson is missing!* Boston: Houghton.

Allen, C. (1986). *Circus horses.* Allen, TX: DLM Teaching Resources.

Anderson, J. (1991). *Christopher Columbus: From vision to voyage.* New York: Dial.

Anno, M. (1981). *Anno's journey.* New York: Philomel.

Atwater, R., & Atwater, F. (1987). *Mr. Popper's penguins.* Boston: Little, Brown.

Avi. (1992). *Nothing but the truth.* New York: Farrar.

Babbitt, N. (1975). *Tuck everlasting.* New York: Orchard.

Banks, L.R. (1982). *The Indian in the cupboard.* New York: Doubleday.

Baylor, B., & Parnell, P. (1978). *The other way to listen.* New York: Scribners.

Baylor, B., & Parnell, P. (1980). *If you are a hunter of fossils.* New York: Scribners.

Behn, H. (1949). *Trees.* New York: Henry Holt.

Blumberg, R. (1985). *Commodore Perry in the land of the Shogun.* New York: Lothrop, Lee & Shepard.

Blumberg, R. (1989). *The great American gold rush.* New York: Lothrop, Lee & Shepard.

Branley, F. (1985). *Flash, crash, rumble, and roll.* New York: HarperCollins.

Brett, J. (1989). *The mitten.* New York: Putnam.

Briggs, R. (1978). *The snowman.* New York: Random.

Brinkloe, J. (1985). *Fireflies.* New York: Macmillan.

Brittain, B. (1983). *The wish-giver: A tale of coven tree.* New York: Harper.

Brooks, P. S. (1983). *Goodnight moon.* New York: Lippincott.

Brooks, P. S. (1983). *Queen Eleanor.* New York: Lippincott.

Brown, M. (1961). *Once upon a mouse.* New York: Scribners.

Brown, M. W. (1947). *Goodnight moon.* New York: Harper & Row.

Bunting, E. (1991). *Fly away home.* New York: Clarion.

Burleigh, R. (1991). *Flight: The journey of Charles Lindbergh.* New York: Philomel.

Burningham, J. (1989). *Hey! Get off our train.* New York: Crown.

Byars, B. (1977). *The pinballs.* New York: Harper.

Carle, E. (1975). *The mixed-up chameleon.* Saxonville, MA: Picture Book Studio.

Carle, E. (1984). *The very busy spider.* New York: Philomel.

Carle, E. (1986). *The grouchy ladybug.* New York: HarperCollins.

Carle, E. (1987). *A house for hermit crab.* Saxonville, MA: Picture Book Studio.

Carle, E. (1987). *The very hungry caterpillar.* New York: Philomel.

Carle, E. (1990). *The very quiet cricket.* New York: Putnam & Grosset.

Charlip, R. (1987). *Fortunately, unfortunately.* New York: Macmillan.

Chase, R. (1943). *The Jack tales.* Boston: Houghton.

Chaucer, G. (1982). *Chanticleer & the fox.* Illustrated by Barabara Cooney. New York: Harper.

Cherry, L. (1990). *The great kapok tree—A tale of the Amazon Rain Forest.* New York: Harcourt Brace Jovanovich.

Cherry, L. (1991). *A river ran wild.* San Diego: Harcourt.

Chorao, K. (1984). *The baby's bedtime book.* New York: Dutton.

Cleary, B. (1984). *Dear Mr. Henshaw.* New York: Morrow.

Cole, J. (1984). *An insect body.* New York: Morrow.

Cole, J. (1986). *The magic school bus at the waterworks.* New York: Scholastic.

Cole, J. (1986). *The magic school bus lost in the solar system.* New York: Scholastic.

Cole, J. (1987). *The magic school bus inside the earth.* New York: Scholastic.

Cole, J. (1990). *The magic school bus inside the human body.* New York: Scholastic.

Cole, J. (1992). *The magic school bus on the ocean floor.* New York: Scholastic.

Crews, D. (1978). *Freight train.* New York: Greenwillow.

Dahl, R. (1986). *The fantastic Mr. Fox.* New York: Knopf.

Dahl, R. (1988). *Matilda.* New York: Viking.

Day, A. (1988). *Frank and Ernest.* New York: Scholastic.

Day, A. (1990). *Frank and Ernest play ball.* New York: Scholastic.

de Regniers, B. (1988). *Sing a song of popcorn.* New York: Scholastic.

dePaola, T. (1975). *Strega Nona.* Englewood Cliffs, NJ: Prentice-Hall.

dePaola, T. (1985). *Tomie dePaola's Mother Goose.* New York: Putnam.

Douglass, B. (1984). *Good as new.* New York: Lothrop, Lee & Shepard.

Ehlert, L. *Feathers for lunch.* New York: Harcourt.

Ehrlich, A. (1989). *Rapunzel.* New York: Dial.

Elting, M., & Folson, M. (1980). *Q is for duck—An alphabet guessing game.* New York: Clarion.

Evert, G. (1993). *John Brown: One man against slavery.* New York: Rizzoli.

Fitzhugh, L. (1964). *Harriet the spy.* New York: Dell.

Fleischman, P. (1991). *Time train.* New York: HarperCollins.

Fleischman, S. (1982). *McBroom and the big wind.* Boston: Atlantic/Little, Brown.

Fox, M. (1985). *Wilfrid Gordon McDonald Partridge.* Brooklyn: Kane Miller.

Freedman, R. (1985). *Cowboys of the wild west.* New York: Clarion.|

Freedman, R. (1988). *Lincoln: A photobiography.* New York: Clarion.

Fritz, J. (1973). *And then what happened, Paul Revere?* New York: Coward, McCann & Geogegan.

Fritz, J. (1974). *Why don't you get a horse, Sam Adams?* New York: Scholastic.

Fritz, J. (1975). *Where was Patrick Henry on the 29th of May?* New York: Putnam.

Fritz, J. (1980). *Where do you think you're going, Christopher Columbus?* New York: Putnam.

Fritz, J. (1982). *George Washington's breakfast.* New York: Putnam.

Fritz, J. (1982). *What's the big idea, Ben Franklin?* New York: Putnam.

Fritz, J. (1987). *Will you sign here, John Hancock?* New York: Scholastic.

Fritz, J. (1989). *The great little Madison.* New York: Scholastic.

Fritz, J. (1991). *Traitor: The case of Benedict Arnold.* New York: Penguin.

Gannett, R. S. (1987). *My father's dragon.* New York: Knopf.

Giblin, J. C. (1985). *The truth about Santa Claus.* New York: Crowell.

Goble, P. (1987). *Death of the iron horse.* New York: Bradbury Press.

Goode, D. (1988). *Cinderella.* New York: Knopf.

Grimm Brothers. (1972). *Snow-White and the seven dwarfs.* Illustrated by Nancy Ekholm Burkert. New York: Farrar.

Grimm Brothers. (1975). *Thorn Rose.* Scarsdale, NY: Bradbury Press.

Guarino, D. (1989). *Is your mama a llama?* New York: Scholastic.

Heller, R. (1981). *Chickens aren't the only ones.* New York: Grosset & Dunlap.

Heller, R. (1984). *Plants that never bloom.* New York: Grosset & Dunlap.

Heller, R. (1985). *How to hide a butterfly and other insects.* New York: Grosset & Dunlap.

Heller, R. (1985). *How to hide a polar bear and other mammals.* New York: Grosset & Dunlap.

Heller, R. (1986). *How to hide a crocodile.* New York: Grosset & Dunlap.

Heller, R. (1986). *How to hide a whip-poor-will and other birds.* New York: Grosset & Dunlap.

Heller, R. (1986). *How to hide an octopus and other sea creatures.* New York: Grosset & Dunlap.

Henkes, K. (1991). *Chrysanthemum.* New York: Greenwillow.

Hudson, W. (1992). *Pass it on: African American poetry for children.* New York: Scholastic.

Hughes, S. (1982). *Alfie's feet.* New York: Lothrop, Lee & Shepard.

Hunt, I. (1964). *Across five Aprils.* New York: Follett.

Hutton, W. (1979). *The sleeping beauty.* New York: Atheneum.

Hyman, T. S. (1982). *Little Red Riding Hood.* New York: Holiday.

Isadora, R. (1991). *At the crossroads.* New York: Greenwillow.

Jacques, B. (1987). *Redwall.* New York: Philomel.

Jenness, A., & Rivers, A. (1989). *In two worlds: A Yup'ik Eskimo family.* Boston: Houghton Mifflin.

Jonas, A. (1983). *Round trip.* New York: Greenwillow.

Jonas, A. (1990). *Aardvarks, disembark!* New York: Greenwillow.

Kalan, R. (1981). *Jump, frog, jump.* New York: Greenwillow.

Kellogg, S. (1984). *A rose for Pinkerton*. New York: Dial.

Kennedy, X. J., & Kennedy, D. M. (1992). *Talking like the rain: A first book of poems*. Boston: Little, Brown.

L'Engle, M. (1962). *A wrinkle in time*. New York: Farrar, Strauss & Giroux.

Lasky, K. (1983). *Beyond the divide*. New York: Macmillan.

Lasky, K. (1983). *Sugaring time*. New York: Macmillan.

Lauber, P. (1989). *The news about dinosaurs*. New York: Bradbury.

Lewis, C. S. (1961). *The lion, the witch and the wardrobe*. New York: Macmillan.

Livingston, M. C. (1979). *O sliver of liver*. New York: Atheneum.

Lobel, A. (1970). *Frog and toad are friends*. New York: Harper.

Lobel, A. (1980). *Fables*. New York: Harper & Row.

Longfellow, H. W. (1983). *Hiawatha*. Illustrated by Susan Jeffers. New York: Dial.

Lord, B. B (1984). *In the year of the boar and Jackie Robinson*. New York: Harper.

Louie, A. (1988). *Yeh Shen: A Cinderella story from China*. Illustrated by Ed Young. New York: Philomel.

Macaulay, D. (1988). *The way things work*. Boston: Houghton.

MacLachlan, P. (1985). *Sarah, plain and tall*. New York: Harper & Row.

Martin, B. (1970). *My days are made of butterflies*. New York: Holt, Rinehart and Winston.

Martin, B. (1983). *Brown Bear, Brown Bear, what do you see?* New York: Henry Holt.

Martin, B. (1993). *Old devil wind*. New York: Harcourt Brace Jovanovich.

Martin, B., & Archambault, J. (1985). *Here are my hands*. New York: Henry Holt.

Martin, B., & Archambault, J. (1986). *White Dynamite & Curly Kid*. New York: Henry Holt.

Martin, B., & Archambault, J. (1987). *Knots on a counting rope*. New York: Henry Holt.

Martin, B., & Archambault, J. (1987). *Listen to the rain*. Allen, TX: DLM Teaching Resources.

Martin, B., & Archambault, J. (1988). *Up and down on the merry-go-round*. New York: Henry Holt.

Martin, B., & Archambault, J. (1989). *Chicka chicka boom boom*. New York: Simon & Schuster.

Martin, R. (1989). *Will's mammoth*. New York: Putnam.

Martin, R. (1992). *The rough-face girl*. New York: Putnam.

Mayer, M. (1984). *The sleeping beauty*. New York: Macmillan.

McCloskey, R. (1943). *Homer Price*. New York: Viking.

McPhail, D. (1982). *Pig pig rides*. New York: Dutton.

Meddaugh, S. (1992). *Martha speaks*. Boston: Houghton.

Mollel, T. (1991). *The orphan boy*. New York: Clarion.

Murphy, J. (1993). *Across America on an emigrant train*. New York: Clarion.

Naylor, P. R. (1992). *Shiloh*. New York: Atheneum.

Newman, J. M. (1989). *Finding our way: Teachers exploring their assumptions*. Toronto: Irwin.

Norton, M. (1995). *The borrowers*. San Diego: Harcourt.

Numeroff, L. (1987). *If you give a mouse a cookie*. New York: Macmillan.

O'Dell, S. (1960). *Island of the blue dolphins*. Boston: Houghton.

Ormerod, J. (1982). *Moonlight*. New York: Lothrop.

Osborne, M. P. (1991). *American tall tales*. New York: Knopf.

Oz, Charles. (1988). *How a crayon is made*. New York: Simon & Schuster.

Oz, Charles. (1988). *How does soda get into the bottle?* New York: Simon & Schuster.

Pallota, J. (1986). *The icky bug alphabet book*. Watertown, MA: Charlesbridge.

Pallota, J. (1988). *The flower alphabet book*. Watertown, MA: Charlesbridge.

Pallota, J. (1989). *The yucky reptile alphabet book*. Watertown, MA: Charlesbridge.

Pallota, J. (1991). *The furry alphabet book*. Watertown, MA: Charlesbridge.

Pallota, J. (1991). *The underwater alphabet book*. Watertown, MA: Charlesbridge.

Pallota, J. (1992). *The victory garden alphabet book*. Watertown, MA: Charlesbridge.

Parker, N. W., & Wright, J. R. (1987). *Bugs*. New York: Greenwillow.

Paterson, K. (1978). *The bridge to Terabithia*. New York: Crowell.

Paulsen, G. (1987). *Hatchet*. New York: Bradbury Press.

Peet, B. (1959). *Hubert's hair-raising adventure*. Boston: Houghton.

Peet, B. (1989). *Bill Peet: An autobiography*. Boston: Houghton.

Perrault, C. (1988). *Cinderella*. Illustrated by Diane Goode. New York: Knopf.

Perrault, C. (1991). *Puss in Boots*. Illustrated by Fred Marcellino. New York: Farrar.

Peters, L. (1991). *Water's way*. New York: Arcade.

Pinkwater, D. M. (1976). *Lizard music*. New York: Dodd, Mead.

Polacco, P. (1988). *The keeping quilt*. New York: Simon & Schuster.

Potter, B. (1902). *The tale of Peter Rabbit*. New York: Penguin.

Prelutsky, J. (1983). *Random House book of poetry for children*. New York: Random.

Raffi. (1983). *Baby beluga*. New York: Crown.

Raffi. (1989). *Five little ducks*. New York: Crown.

Rand, G. (1992). *Prince William*. New York: Henry Holt.

Rawls, W. (1961). *Where the red fern grows*. New York: Doubleday.

Rylant, C. (1991). *An angel for Solomon Singer*. New York: Orchard.

San Souci, R. D. (1989). *The talking eggs*. New York: Dial.

Scieszka, J. (1993). *The stinky cheese man and other fairly stupid tales*. New York: Viking.

Sendak, M. (1963). *Where the wild things are*. New York: Harper & Row.

Seuss, Dr. (Theodore S. Geisel). (1947). *McElligot's pool*. New York: Random.

Seuss, Dr. (Theodore S. Geisel). (1957). *The cat in the hat*. New York: Random.

Seuss, Dr. (Theodore S. Geisel). (1977). *Bartholomew and the Oobleck*. New York: Random.

Shaw, C. (1947). *It looked like spilt milk*. New York: Harper & Row.

Silverstein, S. (1974). *Where the sidewalk ends: Poems and drawings*. New York: Harper.

Simon, S. (1991). *Neptune*. New York: Morrow.

Sis, P. (1991). *Follow the dream: The story of Christopher Columbus*. New York: Knopf.

Spinelli, J. (1991). *Maniac Magee*. Boston: Little, Brown.

Steig, W. (1970). *Sylvester and the magic pebble*. New York: Simon & Schuster.

Steptoe, J. (1987). *Mufaro's beautiful daughters*. New York: Lothrop.

Stevenson, R. L. (1978). *Treasure Island*. New York: Putnam.

Stevenson, R. L. (1981). *A child's garden of verses*. New York: Macmillan.

Surat, M. (1983). *Angel child, dragon child*. New York: Scholastic.

Taylor, M. (1977). *Roll of thunder, hear my cry*. New York: Dial.

Taylor, M. (1990). *Mississippi bridge*. New York: Dial.

Turkle, B. (1976). *Deep in the forest*. New York: Dutton.

Van Allsburg, C. (1982). *Jumanji*. Boston: Houghton.

Van Allsburg, C. (1984). *The mysteries of Harris Burdick*. Boston: Houghton.

Viorst, J. (1972). *Alexander and the terrible, horrible, no good, very bad day*. New York: Macmillan.

Viorst, J. (1978). *Alexander, who used to be rich last Sunday*. New York: Macmillan.

Waber, B. (1972). *Ira sleeps over*. Boston: Houghton.

Watson, W. (1989). *Wendy Watson's Mother Goose*. New York: Morrow.

Wiesner, D. (1990). *Hurricane*. New York: Houghton.

Wells, R. (1989). *Max's chocolate chicken*. New York: Dutton.

White, E. B. (1952). *Charlotte's web*. New York: Harper.

Wiesner, D. (1992). *Tuesday*. New York: Clarion.

Winthrop, E. (1985). *The castle in the attic*. New York: Holiday.

Wood, A. (1984). *The napping house*. San Diego: Harcourt.

Worth, V. (1974). *More small poems*. New York: Farrar, Straus & Giroux.

Yashima, T. (1955). *Crow Boy*. New York: Viking.

Yolen, J. (1987). *Owl moon*. New York: Viking.

Yolen, J. (1990). *Devil's arithmetic*. New York: Viking Penguin.

Young, E. (1990). *Lon Po Po: A Red Riding Hood story from China*. New York: Philomel.

Zelinsky, P. O. (1987). *Rumpelstiltskin*. New York: Dutton.

Zim, H. (1976). *The big cats*. New York: Morrow.

LITERARY ACKNOWLEDGMENTS

26 From: Comprehension as Setting. In J. C. Harste & R. F. Carey (Eds.), New Perspectives on Comprehension, 1979.

34 Reprinted with special permission of Cowles Syndicate, Incorporated.

65 Used with permission from The International Institute of Literacy Learning.

68 Reprinted with permission of the National Council of Teachers of English.

88 Reprinted with permission from Macmillan.

160 Used with permission from The International Institute of Literacy Learning.

176 Photo and text used by permission of Henry Holt and Company, Inc.

277 Used with permission from Creative Growth with Handwriting, 2nd ed. Copyright 1979, Zaner Bloser, Inc., Columbus, Ohio.

280 Used with permission of Scott, Foresman, and Company.

282 Used with permission of the publisher, Zaner Bloser, Inc., Columbus, Ohio. Taken from Handwriting: The Way to Self Expression. Copyright 1991.

292 Reprinted with special permission of Cowles Syndicate, Incorporated.

296 Used with permission of DLM, Incorporated. From Experiences for Literacy by R. V. Allen, M. Sampson, and B. Teale.

330 Reprinted with special permission of Cowles Syndicate, Incorporated.

334 Reprinted with permission of William Morrow & Company.

338 Reprinted with permission of Jerome Harste and the International Reading Association.

346 Reprinted with special permission of Cowles Syndicate, Incorporated.

469 Reprinted with permission of The International Institute of Literacy Learning.

PHOTO ACKNOWLEDGMENTS

7 Michael Hagan	225 Michael Hagan	399 David Walvoord
12 Michael Hagan	244 Michael Hagan	401 David Walvoord
81 Michael Hagan	267 David Walvoord	449 Wayne Dennis
99 David Walvoord	298 Michael Hagan	487 Wayne Dennis
110 Jason Barnes	301 Michael Hagan	
203 Michael Hagan	319 Michael Hagan	All other photos by
210 David Walvoord	340 Michael Hagan	Michael and Mary
212 Joan Hagan	353 Michael Hagan	Beth Sampson.
215 Wayne Dennis	396 Michael Hagan	

NAME INDEX

Gerstein, M., 504
Giacobbe, M. E., 207
Gilbert, S. S., 498
Gilliland, J. H., 503
Ginsberg, M., 397
Ginsburg, M., 500
Glasser, W., 304, 305, 306, 308, 311
Glenn, J., III, 306
Goble, P., 441–442, 495
Golden, B. D., 501
Gollnick, D. M., 481
Gollub, M., 498
Goodall, J., 158–159
Goode, D., 392
Goodlad, J., 375, 435
Goodman, K. S., 265, 271, 281, 333, 334, 335, 337, 339, 340
Goodman, Y., 25, 265, 271, 297, 308, 333, 334, 335, 339, 341, 347, 425
Gordon, C. J., 365
Gordon, S., 503
Gore, J., 139
Graff, P., 467
Graves, D., 130, 131, 210, 274–276, 294, 306, 307, 308
Greenfield, D., 490
Gregory, K., 495
Griego, M. C., 498
Grifalconi, A., 490, 503
Griffiths, R., 418
Grimm Brothers, 390
Guarino, D., 471
Guccini, G., 41

Hagan, J., 193
Hale, S. J., 490
Haley, G. E., 490
Halliday, M., 18
Hamanaka, S., 499
Hamilton, V., 490
Hammarskjold, D., 512
Han, O. S., 499, 500
Hansen, J., 131, 304, 307, 308, 490
Hargrove, T., 42
Harp, B., 306

Harste, J., 8, 25, 26, 28, 29, 245, 246, 309, 331, 344, 345, 371, 378, 379
Hart, K., 136–137
Hartman, W., 490
Harwayne, S., 206–207
Haskins, J., 490, 492
Haugaard, E. C., 500
Havill, J., 490, 499
Head, M. H., 369
Heald-Taylor, G., 302
Hearn, L., 500
Heath, S. B., 27, 29
Heather, G., 166
Heide, F. P., 503
Heimlich, J. E., 363
Heller, R., 251, 269, 430, 445, 471
Henderson, E. H., 245, 247, 258
Henkes, K., 391
Hernandez, M., 40
Hertz-Lazarowitz, R., 55
Hicks, J., 462
Hiebert, E., 291, 308, 435, 446
Highwater, J., 495
Hill, E. S., 490
Hill, K., 495
Hittleman, D. R., 363
Ho, M., 501
Hoffman, M., 490
Holdaway, D., 25, 33–34, 339, 354
Hollis, J., 483
Holubec, E. J., 53, 54
Hong, L. T., 501
Hooks, W. H., 490
Hooper, M., 462
Hopkins, L. B., 270
Hopkinson, D., 490
Horowitz, R., 435, 446
Houston, G., 393
Howard, E. F., 490
Howard, L., 120
Howlett, B., 498
Hoyt-Goldsmith, D., 490, 495
Hubbard, R., 214
Huck, C., 402, 420–421
Hudson, J., 495
Hudson, W., 389, 490
Hughes, L., 490

SUBJECT INDEX

in preschool years, 24
second-language acquisition, 486–488
theories of, 5–8
Language-acquisition device (LAD), 7
Language Arts, 401
Language-arts program. *See also* Oral language;
  Reading; Spelling; Writing
  classroom vignettes on, 47, 49–50, 57, 62
  components and practices of successful programs,
    50–53
  cooperative learning in, 53–58
  daily schedule, 48
  heterogeneous or homogeneous grouping in,
    58–59
  linguistic principles in, 18–20, 264
  model of language environment and literacy, 324
  multiage classrooms, 59–60
  NCTE guidelines on, 67, 68
  parents and, 60–67
  physical arrangement for, 49–50
  pillars of, 67, 69–71
  process classroom, 46, 47–53
  program planning in, 60, 61
  teacher's interactions with students in, 53–59
Language processing, sociopsycholinguistic view of,
  345
Language setting, 344–345
Languages, in U.S., 479–480
Lau v. *Nichols,* 482
Learners. *See* Culturally and linguistically diverse
  learners; Students
Learning/acquisition distinction, 486–487
Learning centers, guidelines on, 60
Legal requirements, for equal educational
  opportunities, 482–483
LEP (limited-English-proficient) students, 485
Letter stage, of spelling, 249, 250
Letter writing, 136, 166
Letters of alphabet, relations between sounds and,
  255–256
Letters to parents, 62–63, 236, 426
Library card catalog, 454
Library reference skills, 454
Limerick, 196
Limited attention space, and listening, 83
Limited-English-proficient (LEP) students, 485
Linguistics
  cues from, for spelling instruction, 255–257
  factors influencing spelling, 258–260
  guidelines for refining communication, 284–285
  morphological factors in, 259
  phonological factors, 258
  principles of, 18–20, 264
  sociopsycholinguistic view of language
    processing, 345
  syntactical factors in, 259–260
Link, for reading comprehension, 361–362
Listening
  activities enhancing listening abilities, 91–93
  classroom vignettes on, 79, 88–89, 91
  creative listening, 81
  critical listening, 80
  developing listening abilities, 85–87, 94
  Directed Listening and Thinking Activity, 357–358
  discriminative listening, 80
  emotional factors and, 82–83
  to exchange ideas and form judgments, 94
  factors affecting, 81–83
  importance of, 78

for information, 80, 94
intelligence and, 83
kinds of, 78, 80–81
for main ideas, 80
music and, 87, 93
oral reading and, 92
to organize ideas, 80
physical environment affecting, 82
physical factors of students and, 83
poor language development and, 83
preformed opinions and, 83
psychological environment affecting, 82
reading aloud and, 87–90
reading instruction and, 87
for relaxation and enjoyment, 81, 94–95
simple listening, 78, 80
storytelling and, 90–91
to student-written materials, 93
for varied points of view, 80
Literacy. *See* Oral language; Reading; Reading
  comprehension; Spelling; Writing; Writing
  classroom
Literacy beginnings
  classroom vignettes on, 27, 39–42
  competence areas for, 32–33
  doing and, 33–34
  experiences as foundations of, 34–43
  primary versus secondary reading in, 35, 37
  reading, 24–28
  responding to natural environment, 37–38
  responding to sensory impressions, 38–43
  in school settings, 31–34
  sharing and, 33
  sight and, 38–39
  smell and, 40, 41
  sound and, 40
  taste and, 41, 42
  touch and, 42, 43
  writing, 28–31
Literacy development. *See* Language-arts program;
  Reading; Writing
Literacy Transaction Model
  acquisition in, 15
  conventions strand in, 13, 320, 323, 512
  diagrams of, 9, 15
  implementation of, 14–18
  impression strand in, 9, 12–13, 320, 322, 511
  linguistic diversity and, 18–20, 264
  overview of, 9–10
  perception in, 16
  prediction in, 16
  production in, 16–18
  self-expression strand in, 9, 10–12, 319–320, 322,
    511
Literature Circles, 395–398

Main ideas, listening for, 80
Maintenance programs, 485
Manuscript writing, 277, 278, 280
Mapping
  conceptual mapping, 363–365
  story maps, 365, 366–367
Maps, 460–463
Marathon writing activity, 57
Markers, in Writing Area, 219
Mathematics
  geometric shapes, 460, 464
  graphic aids, 460–463
  number diary, 460